D0031236

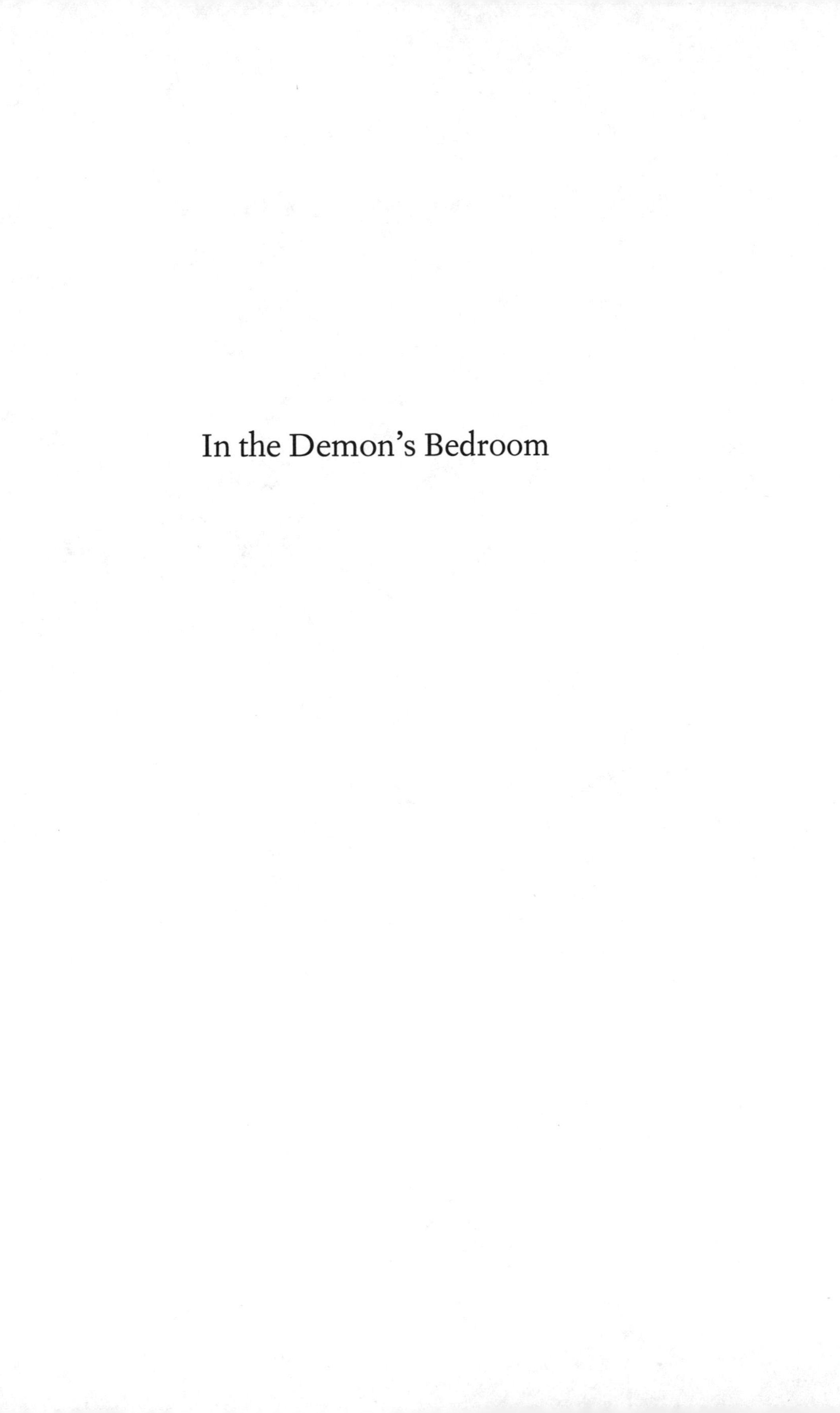

In the Demon's Bedroom

In the Demon's Bedroom

Yiddish Literature and the Early Modern

Jeremy Dauber

Yale
UNIVERSITY PRESS
NEW HAVEN AND LONDON

Published with assistance from the Atran Foundation Fund and the Institute for Israel and Jewish Studies, Columbia University, and from the foundation established in memory of Philip Hamilton McMillan of the Class of 1894, Yale College.

Yale University Press books may be purchased in quantity for educational, business, or promotional use. For information, please e-mail sales.press@yale.edu (U.S. office) or sales@yaleup.co.uk (U.K. office).

Set in Fournier type by IDS Infotech Ltd., Chandigarh, India
Printed in the United States of America.

Library of Congress Cataloging-in-Publication Data

Dauber, Jeremy Asher.
In the demon's bedroom : Yiddish literature and the early modern / Jeremy Dauber.
p. cm.
Includes bibliographical references and index.
ISBN 978-0-300-14175-7 (cloth : alk. paper) 1. Yiddish literature—History and criticism. I. Title.
PJ5120.5.D38 2010
839'.109—dc22

2010019274

A catalogue record for this book is available from the British Library.

This paper meets the requirements of ANSI/NISO Z39.48–1992 (Permanence of Paper).

10 9 8 7 6 5 4 3 2 1

For Miri

How can my Muse want subject to invent
While thou dost breathe, that pour'st into my verse
Thine own sweet argument?

For it was taught in a Baraisa: Rabbi Eliezer says: the dead that Ezekiel resurrected stood on their feet, uttered song, and then died. What song did they utter? "God puts to death with justice and brings to life with mercy." Rabbi Yehoshua says that they uttered the following song: "God puts to death and brings to life, He brings down to the grave and raises up." Rabbi Yehuda says: It is true, it was a parable. Rabbi Nechemia said to Rabbi Yehuda: If it is true, then why do you say a parable? If a parable, why do you say it was true? Rather say: in truth it was a parable.

—*BT Sanhedrin 92b*

Contents

Acknowledgments ix

1. The Study of Early Modern Yiddish Literature: A Theoretical Introduction 1

2. "Are Ye Fantastical, Or That Indeed Which Outwardly Ye Show?": A Comparative Case Study 50

3. The *Seyfer Mesholim:* The World of Fable 87

4. Thinking with *Shedim:* What Can We Learn from the *Mayse fun Vorms?* 140

5. The Allegorical Spirit: Dybbuk Tales and Their Hidden Lessons 172

6. The "Tale of Briyo and Zimro": What Makes a Yiddish Romance? 213

Coda. Looking Back: Concluding Considerations 255

Notes 265

Bibliography 357

Index 387

Acknowledgments

Authors of academic monographs are, in their own way, highly fortunate: much of their audience is also engaged in the writing of books. The author can therefore know that his or her readers are acutely aware of the particularly interdependent nature of the process—and just how much we owe to those we thank.

Parts of this book were written as a Harry Starr Fellow at Harvard University; my thanks to the Center of Jewish Studies there, and to the conveners of that year's fellowship, Ruth Wisse and Avi Matalon, for their generosity and hospitality. My gratitude also to the audiences and faculties of the University of California at Berkeley, Indiana University-Bloomington, the University of Maryland, and Princeton University for allowing me to present works in progress at various seminars and conferences, and for the valuable response and feedback I received there.

Sections of chapters 4 and 5 have appeared, in earlier iterations, in *Jewish Studies Quarterly* and the edited volume *Jewish Literature and History: An Interdisciplinary Conversation*. My thanks to the editors and readers of those volumes, particularly Andrea Schatz, Sheila Jelen, and Eliyana Adler, for their hard work and excellent suggestions.

David Form and Agniezka Legutko-Olowka helped to provide research assistance for this book; my thanks to them, and I owe a particular debt of gratitude to Sarah Ponichtera, whose indefatigable efforts can be seen on every page of this book. My thanks also to the staff of Columbia University's Interlibrary Loan for their hard work tracking down stray articles and rare books.

Alyssa Quint read most of this book in draft; her painstaking attention and excellent advice has been frequently heeded and constantly appreciated.

My colleagues at Columbia University, and particularly the Department of Germanic Languages, have been constantly supportive; Mark Anderson, Andreas Huyssen, Dorothea von Mücke, and Harro Muller have been warm and welcoming to a junior faculty member in his first job, and now, alongside new colleague Elisheva Carlebach, to a newly-tenured faculty member learning a new set of ropes. I am deeply grateful to Peg Quisenberry and Bill Dellinger, for their willingness to help out with advice and support of the general, logistical, and even existential kind. And a very special thanks goes to Michael Stanislawski, for more than I can say.

Outside Morningside Heights, my thanks to Ruth Wisse, David Roskies, Seth Wolitz, Joel Berkowitz, Jean Baumgarten, and Jerold Frakes. All of them have been unstinting with their experience, knowledge, wisdom, and advice; I look forward to continuing the conversations and learning more from them. At Yale University Press, my thanks go to Jonathan Brent for championing this book, and to Sarah Miller, Alison MacKeen, Christina Tucker, and Ann-Marie Imbornoni, who shepherded it on its way to publication. Thanks also to Deborah Bruce-Hostler for her careful copyediting, and to Nancy Zibman for the index.

My parents, Cheryl and Eddie Dauber, and my brothers and sister-in-law, Noah, Andrew, and Sara, have been hearing about this book for some time now; I'm thankful and appreciative that they still ask about it—and for so much else.

And finally, simply, and deeply—this book is for Miri.

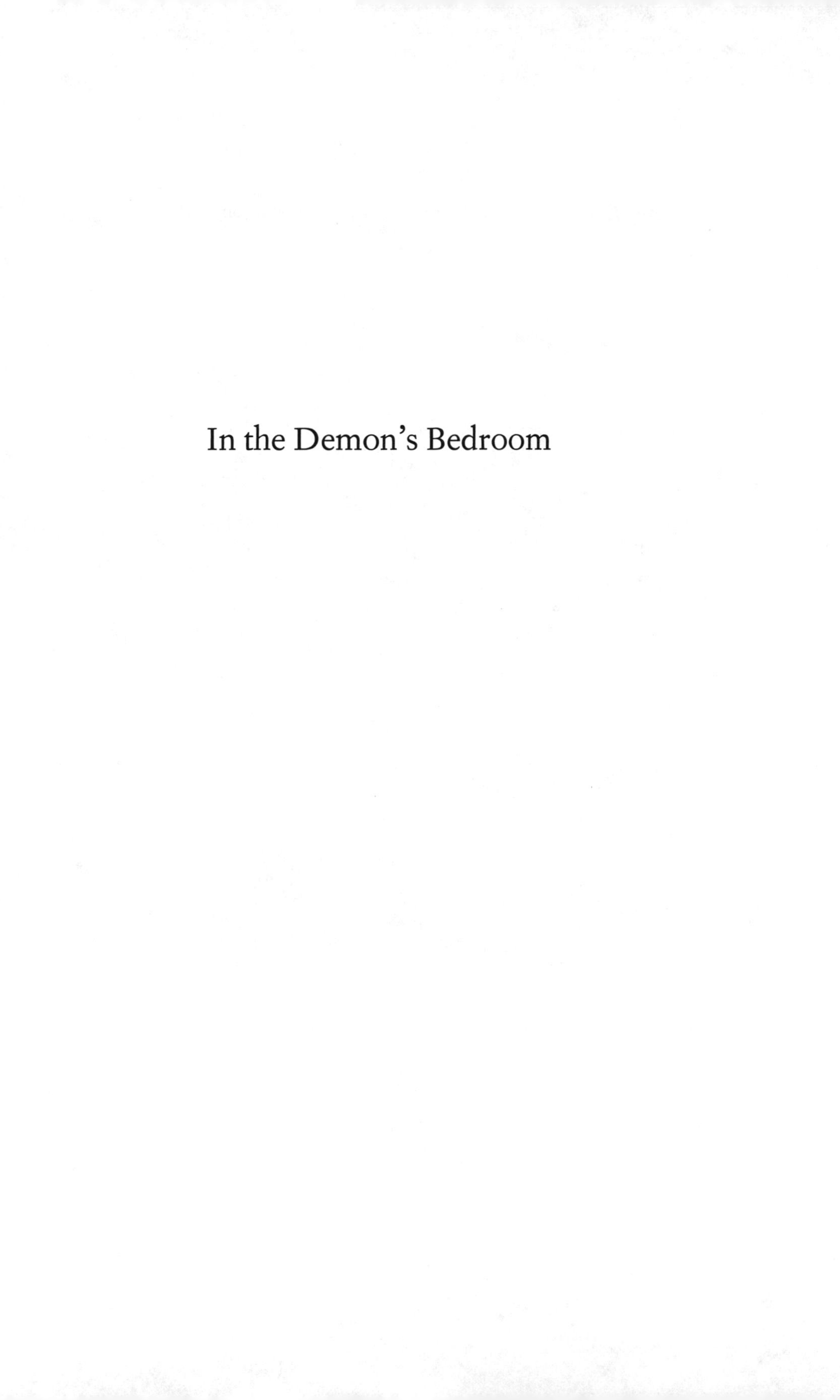

In the Demon's Bedroom

1. The Study of Early Modern Yiddish Literature

A Theoretical Introduction

Why Yiddish literature? Why early modern Yiddish literature? And why demons?

First, let us take the general importance of discussing works of popular and populist Jewish literature for granted, even if this hasn't always been possible. Earlier generations of scholars, often burdened with the ideological baggage of the "language wars" between Hebrew and Yiddish, may have debated whether vernacular literature was an appropriate subject of scholarly study, but such battles are long over. Widely read and generally accessible texts merit academic interest quite as much as those that were available solely to scholarly elites. And while the Yiddish literature of the early modern period—especially that of the sixteenth and seventeenth century—has been less frequently discussed than its later counterpart, I hope to show here that it represents a particularly valuable corpus of literature in this regard.

To stress this is not merely to advocate a teleological approach, arguing, as some have done, that the study of these early modern works is vital in large part because of their major impact on modern Jewish literature.[1] This assertion of influence is of course undeniable; the period under discussion—and particularly the eight decades from 1540 to 1620—saw the publication of numerous works that would remain staples of Jewish reading, popular and otherwise, until and even after the arrival of modernity fundamentally changed Jewish reading habits along with every other aspect of Jewish culture. Examples abound: the *Tsene-rene* (published in 1616) introduced centuries of Yiddish readers to the commentaries surrounding the weekly Torah portion, and to the world of Jewish legend and lore that stemmed from them; and the credulity-stretching chivalric adventures of the protagonist of the *Bovo-bukh* (published in 1541) eventually became a byword, as a skeptical listener might tell a raconteur that his stories were tall tales in the manner of the *Bovo-bukh*—or, as they might put it, *bobe mayses*. And specific texts were not the period's only legacy to later readers. The era this book discusses also saw the rapid and substantive development—and in some cases the emergence—of literary subgenres or tropes that would inspire later Jewish writers in a variety of languages. It was during this period, for example, that tales of dybbuks first flourished—tales whose stylistic and structural echoes would be heard in the works of writers as varied as S. An-sky and Paddy Chayevsky—and, also, that the centuries-old theme of the union of man and demon was revitalized, a theme that would find its most powerful (and lubricious) exponent in Isaac Bashevis Singer.

Viewing and discussing the works in this teleological light, however, reduces them to objects of merely antiquarian interest, ignoring the extent to which they so captivated contemporary readers' imaginations. First and foremost, then, these works should be read, enjoyed, discussed, and studied because they possess precisely that most elusive of attributes: literary and aesthetic quality. The collections, stories, and books discussed here—as I hope will become apparent in the course of this investigation—richly repay closer observation, and in doing so display their authors' care and craft in composition. Some scholarly work has of course already been done on this period, discussed in greater detail later in the chapter; but many of these great works remain criminally understudied and underanalyzed, particularly with respect to their status *as* significant literary works. Introducing readers of Jewish and non-Jewish literature alike to these exciting and provocative early modern texts might be sufficient to recommend this study on its own.

It may be, though, that the relative inattention paid to these texts is an artifact of previous generations of scholars' tendency (a tendency, it should be said, now entirely in decline) to dismiss these texts' literary features along with their more general dismissal of the texts' readers; that is to say, the books and stories were read to be as literarily simple (and as accordingly uninteresting) as their readers themselves were often assumed to be. Though I do not intend to engage in syllogism here—as the chapter will show, complex considerations of audience differentiation must be taken into account—it may be hoped that nuanced readings that allow for the complexities of these works might in turn allow us to reconceive the complex capacities for nuance and reading on the part of their audiences, capacities which, as we will see, are not themselves necessarily dependent on conventional markers of audience sophistication such as textual education or linguistic knowledge.

Though early modern Jewish literature offers ample opportunities to investigate unexamined works and their rarely examined readers, limitations of space and time have narrowed this book's focus to one essential group: narrative works, in the broadest possible sense of that term, that modern audiences might consider, in varying ways, to feature supernatural, fantastic, or simply incredible elements. Focusing on this aspect of the works, an aspect we might consider as a mode—an approach to text that crosses genre lines—rather than as a specific genre, allows us to investigate questions of belief and skepticism, perception and literary judgment, and audience differentiation, which may in turn allow us to ask some grand questions: How might contemporary audiences have read these texts? What might their reading practices say about their sophistication as readers—and, by extension, as thinkers? And can this more nuanced sense of sophistication allow us to speculate on the sense of fiction, or literature, they might have had? I hope, in other words, that these textual analyses will redefine—or at least refine—some of the regnant paradigms in the study of early modern Jewish culture by bringing these particular texts (and, by extension other, similar texts), their audiences, and those audiences' capacities to greater critical attention.

Not only does such a line of investigation allow a more specific examination of the audience as readers in a particular capacity; it also offers a framework with which to approach two broader questions at issue in this book and in the study of the period more generally. The first question is: how does the study of these texts allow us to think about Jewish literature in a comparative context? Many of the supernatural entities under discussion—and the concomitant questions they raise about belief and skepticism—have counterparts in contemporary non-Jewish spheres.[2] One detailed comparative case study that makes significant reference to coterritorial Christian traditions concerning witchcraft, possession, and demonology will allow us to see how methodological approaches implemented in that more developed field are useful in the field of early modern Jewish cultural studies, and how variances in cultural positioning affect the specific development of literary works, particularly in a "minor" culture and literature.

The reference to minor literatures, a classic term in literary theory, brings us to the second broader question: how might the particularities of early modern Yiddish texts, readers, and writers allow for the refinement of broader literary theoretical approaches raised by the texts? Though texts concerning demons, dybbuks, talking animals, and mysterious chivalric doings—all subjects of the following chapters—naturally raise questions about belief, skepticism, and knowledge, they also touch on a host of other theoretical areas: gender, orality, reading reception, and studies in allusion and allegory, among others. Much of the remainder of this introduction will try to show how a range of particular theoretical approaches can enrich and fruitfully illuminate the study of early modern Yiddish literature. If we follow the hermeneutic circle's constant oscillation between theory and textual evidence,[3] the particularities of this body of texts may even allow us to complicate—and refine—some of these theoretical approaches' traditionally articulated assumptions and understandings.

Not all the approaches discussed here will be treated at equal length, nor will the subsequent specific textual analyses rely on them all. These are also ideal types, in interpretive terms, and particular texts are often best understood by conflating different theories' lessons. I believe, however, that many of them are helpful to the study of early modern Yiddish literature (though the list above, and the discussion below, is hardly exhaustive). My hope is that these brief outlines may spark greater scholarly engagement with early modern Yiddish texts, both in their own right and as a means to develop comparative and theoretical work in the period more generally.[4]

At its heart, though, this is primarily a work of literary analysis. Accordingly, the theoretical considerations, comparative methodologies, and incorporation of current historical research, while intended to suggest how close examination of the works themselves can provide possibilities for exploring the questions raised above, are consciously treated within the framework of individual studies intended first and foremost to provide insight into these rich and remarkable texts.

Early Modern Yiddish Literature and Its Scholarship: A (Very) Brief Overview

The conventional necessity to outline Yiddish literary history before the modern period or to investigate the history of its scholarship in great detail has, in recent years, been elegantly and masterfully abrogated. The former task was accomplished by Jean Baumgarten in his 1993 *Introduction à la littérature yiddish ancienne*;[5] that work's recent publication in an expanded and revised English-language translation by Jerold Frakes obviates the need for any substantive overview.[6] Baumgarten's work covers a vastly wider range of material both temporally and generically, treating substantial amounts of nonnarrative material, and thus necessarily spends less time on literary analyses of particular texts and their broader ramifications—a luxury available here precisely because of Baumgarten's achievement.

Frakes himself takes care of the latter lacuna. Aside from his indefatigable work on the Baumgarten translation, his monograph *The Politics of Interpretation* provides a magisterial overview of the scholarship on premodern Yiddish through most of the last century,[7] and his *Early Yiddish Texts*,[8] a mammoth masterpiece whose carefully selected, scrupulously rendered Yiddish-language texts are accompanied by superb headnotes and exhaustive bibliographic data, will remain the standard in this area. As a result, my discussion here will remain limited, focused primarily on points that are relevant to our specific topic. For those less familiar with the milieu, however, a brief orientation and introduction are probably desirable.[9]

While often associated with a certain ideological tendentiousness, the observation that early modern Yiddish texts potentially reached a much wider readership than those composed in other languages, both Hebrew and the coterritorial vernacular, is unquestionably accurate.[10] It was characteristic practice of the communities that composed the Jewish diaspora to create local "Jewish vernaculars" that combined, in various proportions, grammatical and lexical aspects of the coterritorial language with the sacred Hebrew language, thus avoiding the necessity of Hebrew's profanation and maintaining the cultural insularity of linguistic independence. Though many of these vernaculars have existed throughout Jewish history—scholars have identified dozens—Yiddish, the vernacular of Ashkenazic Jewry, is one of, if not the, most widespread and robust. Yiddish began in the Rhine Valley region around the beginning of the eleventh century, a "fusion language," to use Max Weinreich's formulation, combining Middle High German, proto-Romance language, and the mixture of Hebrew and Aramaic used in canonical and sacred Jewish texts. As its speakers spread throughout Europe over the next seven centuries to locations including the Italian peninsula, the Low Countries, and territories eastward in what would become Germany and central and eastern Europe, pushed by historical depredations such as local expulsions and persecution and lured by increasing and diverse economic opportunity and security, the language shifted and developed variously to reflect local conditions. It became the lingua franca of most of European Jewry, with the exception of Sephardic communities in Spain and Portugal, spoken by all strata of Ashkenazic society. As we will see in more detail below, Yiddish *readership*—a term I will take to include its authors, its audience, and how they in turn wrote and read Yiddish—is a good deal more complicated.

The earliest written trace of Yiddish is a rhymed couplet written inside a larger Hebrew letter in a holiday prayer book from the late thirteenth century; the sentence, wishing good fortune upon the individual who carries the (quite heavy) prayer book to synagogue, reminds its later readers of one aspect of contemporary and subsequent Yiddish texts: their role in emphasizing and supporting traditional Jewish culture and accentuating their own subordinate status relative to linguistic and other hierarchies (the Yiddish, after all, is in this case practically a literal footnote to the Hebrew). However, the first major collection of Yiddish texts that remains extant—the Cambridge Codex of 1382—illuminates another aspect of Yiddish's reflection of Jewish society.[11] In juxtaposing poems on biblical figures with long, essentially unchanged versions of Germanic knights' tales, Yiddish becomes revealed in its role as a mediator between coterritorial culture and a Jewish community often linguistically incapable of textual encounters with non-Jewish neighbors—even if historians have shown that such cultural porosity was more common than previously supposed, in social and economic terms. These twin roles of Yiddish literature—subordinate and subversive, internal and other, adaptive and creative—underscore its excitement to readers and its value to scholars.

Unlike Frakes' and Baumgarten's broader surveys, this book concentrates solely on texts from the sixteenth and seventeenth centuries and only briefly mentions thematically relevant materials composed slightly earlier and later. As mentioned earlier, it is that period—particularly between 1540 and 1620—that saw the composition of many of the vernacular works that eventually played a central role in Ashkenazic life. This was a period of historical ferment for the Yiddish-speaking and Yiddish-reading community, as was the early modern period more generally. As the aftereffects from the Spanish Expulsion rumbled across all of Jewish Europe and the Mediterranean, they were matched by internal migrations by Ashkenazic Jews across the Alps into Italy and throughout the German lands, allowing for cultural and intellectual encounters among various Jewish constituencies. These encounters occurred during—and were deeply affected by—the Renaissance and Reformation, where European intellectual currents of classicism, mysticism, and scientism permeated the Jewish community, by encounters as narrow as Christian Hebraists and kabbalists learning language and text from local rabbinic experts and Jewish writers and scholars working for Christian printers, and as broad as the circulation of folkloristic tropes and master narratives ranging from fable literature to Arthurian saga. Such circulation was aided immeasurably by the rise of print culture. Discussed in more detail below, the rise of printing allowed the spread of knowledge, framed as it was in the Yiddish vernacular, to occur far more easily—the first Yiddish book was published in the early 1530s. This in turn spurred not only the democratization of knowledge but concomitant elite fears about loss of social and moral control. One particular example, the spread of (relatively) popular mystical knowledge through Yiddish ethical treatises and later translations of canonical kabbalistic texts, arguably helped to encourage the groundswell of support behind the false "mystical messiah" Sabbatai Zevi in the second half of the seventeenth century and his successor Jacob Frank in the eighteenth—movements that threatened to tear apart the Jewish community and have, in many ways, been viewed as a rupture and gateway to modernity. These trends were revealed and battles were fought through a dizzying variety of Yiddish genres: liturgy, epic, conduct book, historical poem, fable, medical text, and many more besides. I can deal with only a small subsection of them here. Still, the texts studied here can, in their own way, provide a useful introduction to some of the major issues in early modern Yiddish literature, early modern Jewish society, and indeed early modern studies.

Any attempt to periodize premodern Yiddish literature—even via the inductive method of focusing on specific texts composed at a specific time—must take previous efforts at Yiddish literary and linguistic periodization into account. Most of these efforts have to some extent subordinated the former to the latter, most famously in Max Weinreich's division between Old Yiddish (1250–1500), Middle Yiddish (1500–1750), and Modern Yiddish (1750–).[12] The nuances of the debate are less relevant to our purposes; it should merely be noted that attention to undoubted (and undoubtedly subtle) linguistic divisions may privilege linguistic discontinuities at the expense of literary continuities, in generic, ideological, or aesthetic terms. Similarly, a reader-centered model may itself reveal several continuities revolving around the literary survival of linguistically archaic materials, perhaps most notably in works related to biblical translation. Such discontinuities have been characterized not only in linguistic time but in linguistic space: the undoubted differentiation between Western and Eastern Yiddish has similarly inflected the periodization debate, but the linguistic analysis can obscure (though it can also illuminate) how literary texts transcend such divisions.[13] For our purposes, then, questions of strict periodization will be largely avoided:[14] the texts discussed will be studied as products of their particular times and places of composition, read within a system of discourse affecting those contemporaneous, local communities. Some analysis (most notably of the she-demon tales) is precisely contingent on the local moment of interpretation, that is, its comprehension is contingent on recovering interpretive dynamics present between readers and writers at "time zero," before an enshrined interpretive tradition develops over generations, a tradition that potentially obscures as much as enlightens.

A brief overview of the history of Yiddish scholarship on this premodern Yiddish literature—schematic in nature and boasting notable exceptions—may also be worthwhile.[15] Though scholarship on Yiddish certainly existed in the premodern period, much of it was confined to a study of the language alone and did not concern itself with the literature written in that language, and so lies largely beyond our interest here. This research was conducted by non-Jews as well as Jews;[16] perhaps the comparatively lesser scholarly attention given to Yiddish language and literature by contemporary Jews stemmed from its undeniably lower place in the Jewish multilingual hierarchy.[17]

Modernity's arrival, and with it the arrival of modern Jewish scholarship—beginning with the *Wissenschaft des Judentums* and ranging to the Soviet critics of the first decades of the twentieth century, its centers expanding from western Europe to include eastern and central Europe—is, as Frakes has noted, inherently entangled with a variety of complex ideological positions concerning Jewish acculturation, Marxist doctrine, or nationalist sentiment, to name just three factors.[18] This period, however, saw the undeniable rise of substantive *literary* criticism of premodern Yiddish literature, along with the foundational bibliographic work essential to all future scholars.[19]

With eastern European Jewry's destruction came the annihilation of its cultural institutions, its textual repositories in large part (the survival of much of YIVO's holdings notwithstanding),[20] and of course its scholarly community. Stalinist repression slowed the work of those who had survived in the Soviet Union to a standstill. The first decades of the postwar period accordingly saw limited scholarship on Yiddish, and particularly premodern Yiddish literature.

Germany was an early locale for the expansion (or reexpansion) of interest in premodern Yiddish literature. Such interest can be easily traced to Western Yiddish and medieval German's similar linguistic features and the indisputable cultural interchange between old Yiddish and medieval German literature, to say nothing of the complex relationship of Germans to Jewish culture more broadly in the postwar period.[21] Early scholarship focused prominently on the earliest periods of Yiddish literature,[22] on comparable and comparative materials,[23] and on linguistic and philological considerations.[24] More recent work by major German scholars of premodern Yiddish has widened its focus both temporally and generically[25]—though this is hardly to suggest that the field has left behind its earlier concerns,[26] nor to minimize the debt that everyone working in the field owes to the critical or facsimile editions of specific works produced there, and to the often exhaustive apparatus and introductory essays accompanying those editions.[27]

Complementing the German scholars in their project of increasing the accessibility of premodern Yiddish texts was Chone Shmeruk, whose microfiche collection of Yiddish books proved (and proves) invaluable for a later generation of Yiddish scholars.[28] Shmeruk and other Israeli scholars (most notably Chava Turniansky and Sara Zfatman) have done yeoman's work in producing detailed bibliographies of Yiddish narrative prose,[29] Yiddish printed works in early modern Italy and Poland,[30] and careful studies on the various and varying editions of seminal Yiddish works as they move through time and space, to name just a few accomplishments.[31] Given these interests, Israeli scholars are unsurprisingly interested in internal thematic, literary, and textual transmigrations in Jewish (and specifically Yiddish) literature,[32] though their work is hardly limited to the solely Jewish sphere, as we will see in several of our specific studies. While the German and Israeli approaches are foundational and highly instructive, this study can and should be seen as building upon their work rather than constituting either a linguistic study[33] or a textual-bibliographic endeavor.

Our geographically oriented survey of contemporary premodern Yiddish scholarship could hardly omit France's Jean Baumgarten, whose book-length survey is only the complement to (or perhaps the apotheosis of) his influential and exhaustive articles and books.[34] Perhaps most notable for this study among Baumgarten's manifold contributions is his careful attention not only to the corpus of premodern Yiddish literature as a whole but to that corpus' *generic* divisions—an insight valuable to our theoretical structure and literary analysis.[35]

In English-language work (meaning largely American work, since few non-Americans are producing English-language research), with a few notable early exceptions,[36] the study of premodern Yiddish *literature* (as opposed to language) has yet to develop substantially. Recently, Glikl of Hameln's memoirs have attracted increasing attention by scholars interested in studying Jewish social life, women's lives, and life writing;[37] most of these scholars would not characterize their main research interests as Yiddish literature, however, pre- or early modern or otherwise; and (Frakes notably excepted) few of the scholars in the increasingly flourishing field of Yiddish studies in America currently focus on pre-nineteenth-century (at times even pre-*late* nineteenth-century) Yiddish literature. This simply means there is more work to do, building on and developing the extant international scholarship.

Belief, Skepticism, and Audience

Given this book's primary purpose as an exploration of a number of literary texts, rather than a full-fledged study in intellectual history or an exhaustive analysis of an entire field, it must limit itself to gesturing at possibilities; mindful of the limitations thus imposed,[38] these approaches, which read the texts with an eye to potential fissures, complexity, skepticism, and anxiety, rather than simple acceptance, blind piety, and implicit assumption of stupidity, will nonetheless suggest the possibility of a rich and complex interpretive and literary life of audiences less generally discussed in medieval and early modern Jewish studies. Returning to a, perhaps the, prevalent characteristic of the texts under discussion—the presence of what we would now call "fantastic" or "supernatural" elements—allows us to more fully demonstrate this complexity, and provides a basis for aspects of all the following case studies, Jewish and comparative alike, and helps us to develop more refined theoretical models in areas outside the immediate epistemological ones. Such demonstration may consist of several theoretical observations.

1. A belief existed within Jewish society that certain fantastic creatures (defined by modern standards) could exist and certain fantastic actions could take place, or could have at one time.[39]
2. Such beliefs were, at least in global terms, not necessarily differentiated between elites and nonelites; disbelief was not a requirement for membership in the elite, nor was it directly associated with that constituency.[40]
3. Such beliefs, while widespread, were neither universal nor unqualified; lack of belief (what we will term skepticism), in its various modes, definitions, and degrees, coexisted with belief; the degree of skepticism associated with certain claims may be correlated with certain audience subgroups (which may not necessarily be located along the elite-nonelite axis).[41]
4. Skepticism as a concept with respect to the fantastic can be divided into two ideal types: a universal skepticism about the *general* existence of a particular supernatural phenomenon (denying the existence of witches and diabolic pacts), and particular skepticism about a specific claim within a generalized structure of belief (denying that the lady down the street is a witch, but believing witches exist).[42]
5. The early modern period, as we will see through our comparative case study that allows us to borrow from a far more researched field, is perceived by scholars and by contemporaries as a period of increasing, though by no means total, skepticism.[43]
6. Many discussions of this increasing skepticism in the Jewish context, and some about the more general phenomenon, focus on the first type of skepticism.
7. The less discussed second level of skepticism is predicated on individual (or subgroup) evaluation of a presented "fantastic" truth-claim or set of truth-claims, evaluation which itself is contingent on a series of external factors.[44]
8. The second type of skepticism (and perhaps even the first) may be delimited, localized, and even contain internal logical inconsistencies. The most notable instantiation of these limitations lies along the temporal scale: skepticism about the current existence of prophets is not determinative about belief in biblical accounts of prophecy.[45]
9. Such presented claims may be oral, textual, or societal in nature;

evaluation must accordingly have been predicated, in isolation of the general belief in the universalized version of that truth-claim, on the presenter's general reliability in conjunction with the specific context.[46] Two illustrative examples: an early modern Jewish woman who believes in demons' existence may not believe her small child's teary claim that a demon is hiding under his bed, particularly if she knows he has heard a scary tale about demons earlier that day; alternatively, a businessman might view his debtor's claim that a mutual business partner, possessed by a dybbuk, threw all the money the debtor owed the businessman into the river, necessitating more time for repayment, with skepticism.[47] The combination of far more likely alternatives and the tellers' structural or situational unreliability may allow "historicized common sense" to prevail in such cases. Put another way, the "reader's" lived, experienced reality generates their evaluation of particular truth-claims—a lived reality structured and viewed through their own epistemological and ontological categories, of course, whose modern interpretation via textual trace demands another application of the hermeneutic circle.[48]

10. Focusing more directly on textual claims, the only kind discussed directly in this book, the concomitant "textual skepticism" can occur on both the first and second levels. Instantiation of the first level seems clear: those expressing universal skepticism about witchcraft would obviously treat any text purporting to provide a true account of witchcraft skeptically. This with the potential caveat (embodied in point 8) that even such ostensibly universalized skepticism may be stratified across temporal or sacral lines, where canonized holy texts or ancient texts may be given a "pass," either logically (through delineating firm contours and boundaries to belief and disbelief, incorporating them specifically and concretely into one's weltanschauung), or illogically (simply refusing to articulate or consider one's own contradictory beliefs).[49]
11. Textual skepticism of the second sort can flow from the textualized analogues of the examples given in point 9; a more detailed focus on textual forms of unreliability might revolve around profit motives (publishers considering texts' veracity as providing an added degree of commercial appeal) or polemic value (a true story might pack greater moral appeal),[50] though both claims deserve—and will receive, in

subsequent chapters—a certain degree of elaboration. Readers' awareness of such possibilities—and authors' awareness of that awareness—results in authorial textual formulae insisting on the texts' veracity as they betray anxiety about the texts' reception as veracious, as we will see in our discussion of the dybbuk tale.[51]

12. These formulae are recognizable to the contemporary reader (and, by extension, to the modern critic through an act of historical imaginative reconstruction) by means of a seemingly paradoxical but situationally natural competence in reading certain textual phrases as precisely implying their semantic opposite. This may be facetiously termed the "Law and Order" rule: as numerous fans of the long-running television drama know, occasionally—though by no means always—the show opens with a title card reading: "The following story is fictional and does not depict any actual person or event." Reading this prefatory statement, a cultural outsider equally distant to twenty-first-century American culture as are we to early modern Jewish society might accept this statement at face value and suggest that these programs, either as metonymic for all others' practice, or holding only here, but in contradistinction to others' practice, are entirely fictional creations. But we, the show's cultural contemporaries or near-contemporaries, know that both logical readings are precisely incorrect and that the exact opposite is the case: famous for its "ripped from the headlines" ethos of transforming yesterday's tabloid news into today's scripted programming, "Law and Order" employs this warning only before episodes whose characters' or cases' *similarity* to actual events is so recognizable to its contemporary audience that without this fig-leaf assertion of fictionality they would rightly risk legal action. The introductory text therefore provides readers clues to authorial intent (that the work be read as fictional) and the anxiety subverting that intent which demonstrates its precise opposite. Full comprehension of this dynamic requires reading the text in precisely the opposite of its literal sense—a reading strategy so clear to individuals familiar with the cultural context that no particular elite knowledge is needed, but possibly elusive to even elite "readers" alien to that context. Explicit statements about intent, narratorial or otherwise, along with other internal evidence, must therefore be closely and skeptically examined from the position (as much as possible) of a contemporary reader.[52]

Our emphasis in the second part of this section on "textual skepticism," while understandable given the textualized circumstances of our reception of these works, requires still further development to account for the complexities of the expanded notion of "reading" in the period. Such development, in the next section, allows us to bring another theoretical discourse to bear on these texts and helps us better comprehend the circumstances of their reception more generally, before entering into consideration of theoretical issues concerning the texts themselves.

Orality, Literacy, and Audience

The works discussed in this book, though all first appearing after the invention of the printing press, were nonetheless composed during the period of transition from oral to print culture;[53] even the latest-dated works circulate within a society whose practices of textual and information dissemination are predicated on oral delivery and circulation in a way very different from modern reading practices. As such, the theoretical work on the relationships between orality, literacy, and oral and written cultures has particularly valuable application to early modern Yiddish literature.[54] Our discussion will limit its focus to two main areas: how the contemporary awareness of the continuum between oral and written literary cultures affected the composition of these texts by their authors, and, following that, how those conditions may have affected readers' circulation, comprehension, and reception of the texts.[55]

First, the authors. Much of the theoretical discussion of authorial activity in this regard revolves around the maintenance of particular epithets, formulae, and mnemonic devices in poetic-epic forms that seem to serve primarily to evoke traces of those or generically similar texts' original oral performances.[56] Analogous formulae appear and have been examined in numerous early modern Yiddish texts, perhaps most notably in "biblical epics" like the *Shmuel-bukh* and the *Melokhim-bukh*, which derive from earlier Yiddish forms and are clearly modeled in part on non-Jewish oral epics. Indeed, these formulae are among the evidence marshaled by scholars in support of their now-debunked theory for the existence of Jewish troubadours or *shpilmener*, illustrating how textual features may, if improperly interpreted, yield historically inaccurate while textually and logically reasonable conclusions.[57] The lack of *shpilmener*, however, hardly implies an absence of oral performance broadly defined; such broad definition can include the popular and influential itinerant preachers (*maggidim*), the wedding jester (*badkhen*), or even less formal group readings or performances, which allowed writers to calibrate the continued importance and practice of oral performance and the linguistic and "literary" habits associated with it—in similar fashion to Parry, Lord, and Foley's researches—and to transfer them into texts designed for written circulation (if, at times, oral delivery).[58] By similar, I do not mean identical; a culture lacking strong bardic performative traditions may have deaccentuated the mnemonic devices so vital in true oral contexts.[59] However, such a transitional model incorporating oral expansion and circulation of written material may nonetheless privilege certain explanations that seem part of oral discourse—moral formulae, concluding phrases in folk phraseology, narratorial flourishes—for listeners' pleasure, readers' evocation of previous oral discourse, and even, at times, mnemonic aid.[60] To develop this further, we must turn to the readers.

As evidence for the precise nature of nonelite reading patterns is fugitive[61]—given the apparent lack of large sociological interest to contemporary writers—our discussion must remain conjectural. Nonetheless, it can arguably be asserted that even in texts addressed to those with only vernacular literacy and informational knowledge that stems solely from vernacular contexts, a concomitant authorial realization exists that such literacy operates along a continuum and such knowledge is expandable through extratextual circumstances.

This expansion is capable along several different axes: examples include the *maggidim*, mentioned above, who may have employed Yiddish books and, in "reading" them to an audience probably composed of members scattered along the literacy continuum, may have expanded orally upon the text during performance to assist comprehension; certainly the *firzogerin*, the woman's synagogal prayer leader who amplified, explained, and led the *tkhines* and other prayers, illustrates the complex interaction of written text, oral dissemination, and variably literate audience.[62] Perhaps a more generally overlooked home for this learning process, however, is the home itself; particular household members participate in a constellation of textual reading aloud, oral "reading" or recitation, and oral commentary and amplification, with mother, father, and even children in the course of education all variously and potentially participating in the different aspects of the process.[63]

This final aspect of oral commentary and explication in an informal context—in contradistinction to the much-discussed and undeniably important models of oral explanation and pedagogy as conducted in contemporary educational institutions such as *kheders* and the yeshivas, which are, in general terms, part of the elite pedagogical process and as such beyond our purview here—may be an overlooked and underappreciated means of explaining how some of the gaps previously mentioned are filled. That is, it is the precisely *oral* performance of these texts that provides the opportunities for these textual gaps to be explored, discussed, and filled by additional information absent within the text itself.[64] This transferred information obviously does not originate within the household itself, necessitating our conceptualization of a broader network for the transmission of this external information (though not limited to that information) at least partially and perhaps even largely oral, with various means of transmission, including:

1. Elite to elite transmission. As briefly mentioned above, oral expansion and commentary on textual narrative and knowledge gaps arrive primarily (though hardly solely) within the standard educational process, as an ancillary if integral component to text-oriented learning. Such orally delivered material itself presumably is often, though not always—particularly in more elite educational settings and moments—transmitted along with a textual marker indicating the written source of that information, which both allows for future retrieval and implicitly reasserts the elite hierarchy of written text over oral material (and, by extension, elite over vernacular language).[65]
2. Elite to nonelite transmission. Cases in this category, such as the public lecture by a *maggid* or a household explication by a learned father, have also been discussed earlier; it should be noted that, as a corollary to point 1, elite knowledge may also have an oral source, either from within an educational context or past circumstances unrelated to education (see point 6 below). Such information exchange, in an ideal model, takes place at "time zero" (a perfect model of information flow, where all information the recipient receives about the text comes from this interaction with a fully knowledgeable transmitter); in practice, the model can be more complicated, as we will see in point 4.
3. Elite to potential elite transmission. A primarily theoretical construct, treating (male) children yet to enter the textually centered educational

process, where oral information may be associated with hierarchized and textualized markers.

4. Nonelite to nonelite transmission. While the information necessary to comprehend and fill the various textual gaps must at some point come from a knowledgeable source, that transmission need not proceed directly within a household from elites (either full-grown or in school) to nonelites, termed "time zero" above. In reality, certain books, after their first appearance and circulation within a society, will develop a vertical oral tradition of explication around certain gaps, built on, but now external to, the explanatory flow originally necessary for comprehension. A mother may orally transmit to her daughter, for example, the precise information necessary to understand a particular passage in the *Tsene-rene*, information she may have received from *her* mother (or at time zero). Such information may be only a small portion of the transmitted oral knowledge, of course; it is, arguably, the most immediately and directly recoverable as necessary information (given the books' acknowledged circulation and importance). Obviously, the power and vitality of such traditions are contingent on the passage of time since publication and circulation, and on the book's centrality to local and global Jewish reading society.[66]
5. Nonelite to future nonelite transmission. Essentially identical to point 4, but included for the sake of logical consistency.
6. Nonelite to potential elite transmission. Another arguably underaccentuated approach, this corollary to the "slumming elites" approach advanced below notes that all potential elites (that is, future male scholars) receive a great deal of early information from an oral, domestic tradition, along with pathways to comprehension and conceptualization of certain narrative, ideological, and even literary approaches to Jewish text, history, and culture, which, due to their primacy, are hard to efface. Such a condition—similar in some ways to the memory-based alterations and "fallacies" famously anatomized by S. Y. Abramovitch in his memoirs[67]—is particularly relevant to a time when texts were in comparatively limited circulation. Profound early memories, then, themselves conditioned through oral, potentially nonelite structures, may well have yielded important effects on these elites—especially important for our purposes in their later authorial capacities. The general absence of discussion of such effects by their

> authors may be connected to either their perceived unimportance given the social hierarchies of value, or even a conscious rejection of this educational model because of those hierarchies.

Arguing from absence—even an absence almost definitional when it comes to orality—is always perilous; still, at least in theoretical terms, the approach may deserve attention, perhaps allowing future studies of writers raised in this and similar traditional settings to attend to vernacular and orally recognized sources in their discussions of elite writers as well as the elite textual ones.

Readers, Reading, and Audience: Some Theoretical Approaches

What happens, though, when we move to written texts?

Any examination of early modern Yiddish literature attempting to transcend New Criticism-esque study of the text per se must grapple with questions of how these texts emerge from—and therefore reflect in a critically informative manner—a complex dynamic between author and reading community.[68] Approaching the question of readership entails an acknowledgment of our task's conjectural nature[69] and the complicated extension of the definition of "reading," a topic to be returned to below; it must also acknowledge the extant scholarly tradition on the question, aided by the authors' (or editors,' or publishers') propensity to explicitly include addressees in their prefaces, title pages, and colophons.[70] The frequent invocation of women and young girls as the addressees, added to other evidence such as the application of the name *vayber-taytch* to the lettering of Yiddish books and the grammatically female construction of the addressee in the *Tsene-rene*, arguably the most popular premodern Yiddish book, led to an early critical propensity to gender premodern Yiddish readership.[71] Perhaps such scholarly assessments were shaped by personal experience with a fundamentally continuous—yet centuries-removed—tradition, where circumstances may have changed without seeming to; complementarily, the scholars' own selection biases, arguably a combination of elite backgrounds and culturally ingrained sexism among other factors, may have played roles in their construction of the past.[72]

More recent work by scholars like Chava Weissler and Jean Baumgarten, conversely, has focused on the broader range of addressed readers, arguably encapsulated in the striking phrase appearing in the introduction to the 1602 *Brantshpigl*, "women and men who are like women," to remind of the texts' own expansion of the audience to transcend gender, and instead to locate the relevant constituent distinctions and demarcations along educational lines.[73] Yiddish texts were aimed at all those literate in Yiddish but incapable of reading or fully comprehending Hebrew texts (in practice, few readers were seemingly capable of reading non-Hebrew lettering).[74]

If the textual evidence suggests the largely uneducated audience of Yiddish readers as a primary audience for the works, the corollary question concerns the definition of "uneducated." For our current purposes—though this will be modified later in the chapter—the addressees are sufficiently educated to be functionally literate[75] in a Yiddish which may at times include archaisms or (due to varying contingent geographic circumstances of composition) foreign or nonlocal words.[76] Such abilities already portray this audience as far more "educated" than many of their coterritorial counterparts.[77] In this context, the readership is "uneducated" in terms of formal, substantive canonical and textual knowledge, as contemporaneously defined:[78] they are a reading community whose access to classical Hebrew and Aramaic Jewish texts is highly limited.

The complexities inherent in describing that limitation, however, are apparent in a further introductory comment of the *Brantshpigl*'s: "For our holy books are written in Hebrew; sometimes they include *pilpul* from the *Gemore*, which many people cannot understand."[79] This emphasis on *partial* comprehension—understanding aspects of the canonical material, but failing to apprehend others—may first increase our sense of the textual abilities of some components of the Yiddish reading audience. More, though, it allows us to briefly shift our focus to the authorial task of creating material for audiences with certain levels of knowledge and education, but knowledge and education not always linked to textual apprehension or access. Might there be a way—absent the ability to speak to these readers, or the writers who compose knowing their weaknesses *and* their strengths, of recovering the particular competencies and levels of comprehension possessed by the readers and relied upon by the author?

Allusion

One clear method of articulating the knowledge levels and interpretive competencies of an audience who may lack access to a set of texts about the information within them is a deep investigation of the authorial employment of allusions to those texts. I have elsewhere written at some length about the usage of allusion in Hebrew and Yiddish literature, particularly maskilic literature, and its relevance to literary theory.[80] Many of the same lessons apply here, and need not be repeated; one element mentioned there but not discussed in detail should be emphasized, however, given the differences in audience between the eras discussed.

That element centers on allusion's identity as not precisely information, but rather as a marker aiming at a specific storehouse of information, of which the particular graphological and textual expression yielding that information—and its precise recognition in that form by its readers—is only one part. For example, a writer of a new text might render Genesis 6:9's characterization of Noah, "he was a righteous man in his generation," in either the original Hebrew *ish tamim haya bedorotav*, or the Yiddish *A gerekhter, erlakher* (sic) *man in zayn doyr*,[81] the new text in which the resulting rendering could appear could be either essentially Hebrew or Yiddish. Five different potential combinations result, each generating subtly different information for the student of these texts, and of Jewish allusion more generally:

1. The original biblical quote appears in a Hebrew text. Given the intended reading audiences' presumed level of education (Hebrew texts being almost always aimed at elites), recognition and comprehension of such a basic biblical text would have been taken for granted.[82] Shared understanding of allusive capacity might empower readers to employ—and readers to look for—thematic puns, linguistic similarities, and other such literary features.
2. The allusion appears in different Hebrew words in a Hebrew text. Such behavior, while a theoretical possibility, seems intertwined with the processes of "normalization" of the Hebrew language associated with the postmaskilic period and therefore beyond the scope of our discussion here.
3. The Yiddish allusion appears in a Hebrew language text. Another largely theoretical possibility, it seems, with the exception of glosses (suggesting in this case a beginners' text) or perhaps an instance of reported speech.
4. The Hebrew quote appears in a Yiddish text. This type of allusion—along with corollary information about the existence or nonexistence of

accompanying Yiddish explanation, or the extent to which its constituent words belong to the Hebrew-Aramaic component of the Yiddish lexicon—are instrumental in helping us to pinpoint the Yiddish-speaking audience's educational level.[83]

5. The Yiddish quote appears in a Yiddish text. Such an allusion's linguistic qualities can tell us little about its addressees' educational level (presuming the allusion to be written in the same linguistic register as the remainder of the text); information must be derived from other aspects of the text and the allusion.

I have avoided in each discussion the allusion's ostensible purpose, presumably to activate the reader's recollection of the constellation of stories and interpretations surrounding Noah in general and his (objective or comparative) righteousness in particular,[84] such reminders empowering and encouraging readers to seek thematic and narrative connections with the newer work. This division of the allusion's operation is intended to accentuate the fact that *such allusions do not depend on the recognition of textual markers; rather, paratextual or narrative tropes may suffice*, ones close enough to the original text to preserve semiotic meaning, but whose linguistic flexibility may allow for real gaps in textual and linguistic education. While generally understood within studies of allusion concerning a single language (and perhaps even clearer in the subfield of parody, where allusions often transcend—or eschew—the mere linguistic),[85] the observation may bear repeating in a book where most allusion must "survive" the rigors of translation and alteration of the most basic linguistic and lexical tenets.

Some of the texts discussed in this volume feature examples of the fourth combination mentioned above, where the Hebrew element is maintained, allowing detailed case by case analysis of audience linguistic comprehension and interpretive ability; such approaches will be accordingly utilized within the book. But in numerous early modern Yiddish texts—some of which are the basis for our study here—the texts' allusive quality is quite high absent the concomitant, arguably expected, proportion of allusive or retextualized Hebraisms (in contrast to words part of the general Yiddish lexicon). Refocusing on allusion's informational, rather than linguistic component, necessitates the shift in critical attention to other questions: what is the minimal informational necessity for activating an allusive reference? What absent information is necessary to understanding the narrative (and allusive) context? How do our various lenses of textual interpretation define the resulting gap's size and shape? While the last question recalls how these attempts at historical recovery are contingent on a necessarily subjective reconstruction of contemporary cultural patterns of meaning (a return once more to the hermeneutic circle), external information about how the text "works," logic, and internal textual clues may provide real assistance in answering at least the first two questions.

This new focus on allusion's information content then begs the corollary question of these allusions'—and their supporting information's—knowledge and circulation among elite and nonelite audiences alike. Conventional and generally unavoidable modern scholarly patterns of citing allusive or alluded-to material from its appearances in elite textual sources such as the Babylonian Talmud or Genesis Rabbah must be judiciously balanced with the resulting propensity to perpetuate conceptualizations of patterns of information distribution—among all knowledge classes—not necessarily grounded in reality. These allusions, which need not be grounded in textual specificity, need not even be grounded directly in text: the informational content necessary to decoding the allusion in the text the individual now encounters may have come from nonelite vernacular texts (such as the *Tsene-rene*), and even from nontextual sources as disparate as itinerant preachers, local storytellers, family members, or primary educators, among other means of transmission.[86] Such questions are generally conceived of as studies in popular knowledge, with some justification, but the implied focus may lead to overlooking another important constituency for these informational networks: an audience I have termed "slumming elites."[87]

By "slumming elites," I mean only to suggest that *simply because a given audience can read texts or acquire information in a certain language or at a certain level of textual complexity within a language does not mean they will necessarily do so, when the possibility exists of acquiring that text's information in more easily available linguistic or epistemological formats.*[88] An analogous modern case might be those with knowledge of a particular foreign language who nonetheless prefer reading novels written in that language in English translation. Several explanations can be offered for such behavior; all, in one way or another, stem from literacy's—even "elite" literacy's—nature as a continuum, rather than blanket apprehension of a language's[89] every aspect. Some elites, then, may have inherent conceptual or educational difficulties understanding particular texts' subtleties; or understanding may be possible given sufficient time and energy, but either those are lacking, or such effort would rob them of the pleasure they would derive from encountering that texts' content in a more (or most) familiar language;[90] or—a more likely possibility then than now—a particular text's availability was greater in the nonelite format than in its elite version for reasons relating to expense of books, vicissitudes of printing, or other similar factors. These and many other possibilities may complement the expansive claims for a broader audience of "every person, whether a scholar, an ordinary Jew, a master of the house or a woman" in one text, to say nothing of the sophistication and creativity of literature written solely in that vernacular.[91]

Such considerations about elite audiences for ostensibly nonelite texts inevitably affect our considerations about audience capacity for those texts, and particularly for the comprehension of certain levels of allusive material. However, allusion is perhaps the literary feature of these texts where educational differentiation matters *most*; and even there its pattern has often been changed to "service" potentially broader groups (while remaining informative to us about what these groups knew). This differentiation, however, recedes in discussions of other literary competencies conventionally *connected* with educational achievement, but which in fact do not *necessarily or inherently* flow from it. In further discussion of these readers and their capacities, this point about dissociation—and those competencies—will be more fully delineated.

How do we define literary sophistication, or even competency, by a particular reading group or in general? Perhaps the easiest way, as treated above, is to connect it to the (essential) mastery of an educational tradition that allows familiarity with and access to a specific textual canon, along with its accompanying language(s); despite that metric's importance—especially to the work of attempting to recover historical literary dynamics through the lens of allusion—it may not be the only such metric. The following section will address a few others in outline, most of which will reappear in some form in the book's case studies.

Literary Modes (I): Parody

The parodic mode[92] and the concomitant competencies demanded of its reading community are perhaps the ones most clearly connected to a general (though, as we will see, not necessarily specific) discussion about allusion;[93] that is, for readers to fully understand a text's authorially determined parodic function, one must recognize the parodied text and "the incongruity between the parodied text and the parody"; such recognition allows for its parodic version's comprehension and full enjoyment.[94] The reader's role in such a process—and thus the determination of his or her competency—can be expanded, particularly given our use of the mode to cover a broad range of theoretically related but distinct subgenres such as burlesque, pastiche, irony, satire, and metafiction.[95]

Varying audiences may fail to recognize a given text as parodic, if its narrative seems internally coherent.(as are many) and is pleasurable (as are some).[96] (Such considerations may affect our analysis of the "Tale of Briyo and Zimro," for example, a text that may or may not have been read parodically by its entire audience.) Such perspective may lead to further questions about parody's specific mechanics and its relevance to our investigation: are there particular signals that identify a text as parodic? How do those signals operate within the broader contexts of early modern Yiddish literature, and how does that contextualization assist us in creating a picture of the audience and its capacities?[97] The parodic mode's possible extension from specific texts to genres, authorial styles, or conventions, an extension that may actually take the conceptual form of concentric circles (that is, a specific parodied text also generally parodies that text's author's style and the genre in which the author is writing), means that readers' recognition of parodic material may operate on broader levels without specific awareness of the text or even direct encounter with the genre (little boys seem to know a great deal about Westerns, even if they've never seen them).[98]

This reader-oriented view of parody may modify—and have consequences for—our analysis of the truth-claims (factual or historical) made in these parodic texts and their "truthfulness"; not, of course, primarily in terms of a positivistic reconstruction of actual occurrences hidden within a parodic text but rather as another guidepost in the author-reader relationship. We may tentatively suggest two ideal types of parodic discourse, ends of a continuum, in this vein, differentiating them by the position they take to the parodied text. (The "text" here can be either a literary document or a lived historical experience, the latter point of more interest to us at the present moment). A "verisimilar" parody's literary power may stem from its marked similarity to the parodied text (or an ostensibly first-seeming faithful textual representation of the event) and its ability to gradually enlighten its audience as to its parodic nature.[99] While analysis of the epistemic processes behind this awareness's development is beyond our scope here, one can certainly imagine how differing rates resulting from authorial plotting can complexly interact with either the failure of their design or audiences' perspicacity (penetrating the parodic frame earlier than expected) or cluelessness (failing to recognize the author's signals).[100] In the latter case, a parodic text purporting to be historical or nonfiction mistaken for a "straight" text may be highly instructive for our investigation into audience historical consciousness, a topic analogous—though not identical—to the questions surrounding readers' belief and skepticism in the supernatural.[101]

Conversely, "caricatured" parody might consist of parodic pictures which, while maintaining the identity of a recognizably parodied text, are so extreme as to present no reasonable questions of verisimilitude or their parodic status.[102] These types—and the continuum between them—are essentially differentiated by differing degrees (and definitions of) the catalysis of the parodic consciousness; that is, what precisely—and how much of "it"—is necessary to catalyze said consciousness. The answer is contingent on historically reconstructed criteria of "verisimilitude" and "caricature"—criteria that can be at least partially recovered by inductive examination of texts and, once more employing the hermeneutic circle, permit speculation as to contemporary cultural mentalities, particularly (though not solely) how the claims of fact (if we can define which, within a parodic text, are aimed and received as such) mattered to readers; if they were taken as true; and how those claims interact with a skeptical sphere catalyzed by parodic consciousness either stemming from uneasy subversion (in verisimilitude's case) or textual dismissal (in the case of caricature).[103] This is, of course, not our sole concern or even, in our larger context, necessarily the primary one; but its relationship to audience competencies to separate out various types of information, and its analogousness to the questions of "truth" or "reality" related to our discussion of the supernatural, make it an important topic of discussion.

Literary Modes (II): Moral Polemic

As I have written elsewhere with respect to literature of the Jewish Enlightenment, generally polemic in mode, polemics are definitionally intended for their audience to apprehend them, or they fail in their intended purpose of swaying group opinion.[104] We may also generally presume contemporary writers were better positioned to evaluate their audiences' capacities and abilities than we are, forced to reach back across the centuries.[105] Though not an entirely unproblematic assumption—an untalented writer, for example, may have misunderstood his[106] readership's capacities, or chooses for various, perhaps ideological, reasons to speak beyond (or below) his audience's capacities—such problems are insufficient to eliminate the polemic's analytic value in this regard for our purposes.

Some of our case studies, most clearly the discussion of the *Seyfer Mesholim* (Book of Fables) in chapter 3, will allow us to investigate audience competency in apprehending particular narrative polemics'[107] moral lessons—necessarily a question of interpretive skill. In some cases, where the author clearly and explicitly articulates the desired moral teaching he derives from the narrative (often, though not always, in an epimythic ending, as in the *Seyfer Mesholim*), interpretive questions revolve around the audience's ability to render the lesson pleasingly congruent with narrative text, or vice versa; though the text provides guidance through the moral's inclusion, guidance is not identical to total narrative explication.[108] Basic questions of textual comprehension aside (whose difficulties would presumably be either linguistic or allusive, thus treated above), analysis might focus on comprehension of narrative elements extrusive for such polemical purposes, and what competencies—practical interpretation of symbols, narrative gaps, and the like—are required to provide the moral the extra power derived from its illustrative supporting narrative.[109]

A focus on readers' integrative skills is only one type of analysis, predicated on a model of continuity; one may, however, focus on narrative texts with moral valence where either no explicit moral statement is given, or alternatively posit texts where audiences are invited to (or, despite authorial desire, do) attend to the *rupture* between expressed moral and the "apparent" narrative lessons of the text.[110] Such cases may stem from authorial infelicity, or, more complexly, a narrative multivocality suggesting (purposefully or no)[111] a more complicated moral atmosphere requiring more nuanced moral speculation.[112] Our discussion of the *Seyfer Mesholim* and a seventeenth-century dybbuk tale will use these cognitive ruptures as the basis for much of their respective chapters' interpretive work.

Attention to discontinuity, rupture, and nuance allows deeper speculation as to both authorial agenda and readerly competency. If readers are able to problematize these polemics by virtue of recognizing their narrative or moral nuance, what are the signals that allow them to do so, and how extrusive must they be? Are they predicated on outside information (either the consequences of allusive material in the text, or the contradiction between textual claims and external lived or textual experience), or are they inherent in the text itself (for example, failures in narrative logic or mismatches between text and moral, though to some extent ways of reading and structuring information always have some external basis).[113] Must such problematization result from some form of textual "failure," or might the existence of certain estranging or defamiliarizing elements be sufficient—and what criteria in turn are used to determine what is strange or unfamiliar? Must they be linked to classical textual knowledge or educational achievement? How is the solution suggested, internally or externally, and how do the above considerations relate to that? All these questions will emerge to some extent in the subsequent chapters' various case studies.

Literary Modes (III): Allegory

A full examination of the allegorical mode[114] and its application to early modern Yiddish literature is far beyond our abilities here; however, given its explicit and implicit relevance to at least two of our case studies—the fable collection in chapter 3 and the tale of spirit possession in chapter 6—we will engage in some limited discussion of its theoretical aspects and practical applications, focusing on two particular elements. First, the allegory may be conceptualized along a continuum of extrusiveness; that is, texts on the one hand like the medieval *Everyman*, whose allegorical nature is loudly self-proclaimed,[115] overpowering the straightforward narrative by directing readerly attention to the work's "true" or "deeper" meaning; on the other, works like our dybbuk tale, where the narrative operates sufficiently cleanly on a superficial level to disguise (to readers of varying levels of textual competency or sophistication) its allegorical nature. One might conceptualize these points on the continuum in terms of the twin traditions of allegorical composition and allegorical interpretation; the more or less pronounced use of symbols (or more or less pronounced symbols) may be a key to locating a given text along this continuum.[116]

The questions we apply to works in this mode are somewhat similarly structured to the previous two: even in the most extrusive cases, what are the skills employed by readers in exercising allegorical understanding? How do they reflect shared communal knowledge (relied upon by the author in crafting his work) and literary "tools," and how are they dependent on (or independent of) educational differentiation? In less extrusive cases, how *little* is necessary to catalyze an audience's allegorical response, mindful of that audience's differentiated nature and reading competence, assuming the catalyzing signals to be certain textual markers, narrative gaps, or literary cruxes?[117] How does audience failure to grasp a text's allegorical dimensions reflect authorial failure? In many of our cases, like the dybbuk text in chapter 5, this last is a necessarily theoretical question, as we have little or no contemporary reception history for these works. Our inability to provide concrete answers is connected to the *inherent* indeterminacy of interpretation of much though not all writing in the allegorical mode;[118] this "failure," while less inherent to functioning of the mode than in the polemic, can nonetheless be a major factor if the allegorical dimensions are key to didactic, polemic, or moral efficacy.

A particular type of readerly failure to ascertain authorial allegorical intent may interact significantly with a historicized approach to allegorical consciousness, a feature itself relevant to our study of the dynamics of reading. Though we might assert that modern assignation of a text to the allegorical mode vitiates any sense we might have of it as historically "real" in its details (while presumably gesturing at the author's sense of a more abstract truth), the late medieval and early modern approach rather insisted on the possibility of simultaneous historical truth and allegorical import, even seeing its allegorical value as *confirmation* of its historical truth.[119] In other words, literary strategy that generates skepticism for us may achieve precisely the opposite effect within this historical reading community, reminding us once more to predicate our judgments about belief and skepticism on historically meaningful sensibilities, not current ones. This said, historical distance can also be overemphasized, and certain shared tenets of logic and transhistorical "common sense" may be judiciously applied to, for example, posit the extrusive allegorical nature of an *Everyman* and connect that to a sense of the audience's judgment about his (and its) historical reality.[120] An entity like the dybbuk, with its judicious straddling of the worlds of belief and skepticism, as well as life and death, provides an intriguing case study in this regard.

Conclusory Mode: Narratology

These various "activist" modes of authorial discourse—allusion, parody, polemic, allegory—all revolve at heart around the issues of authority raised most explicitly in legal texts. Such questions, whose treatment here has been focused around the writer-reader interaction, are inevitably related to the twin discourses of reader-response theory and narratology. Essential to this elaboration is the reminder that texts do not operate in a vacuum; their narrative, logical, and epistemic gaps, generally so "obvious" they are overlooked by the casual reader (whose casualness derives from either native familiarity with the text's cultural and epistemic milieu or from such learned reconstruction that native equivalence has been acquired), offer stark evidence about the nature of societally basic knowledge that is "taken for granted."[121] A full theoretical discussion is not necessary here, and individual chapters will focus on practical aspects of these questions.[122] Our discussion has only meant to attend to the notion that the reader's attention to the narrative's constructed nature is potentially conceptualized along many axes (aside from the ones above, these include attention to narratorial unreliability, to textual multivocality, to complex narratological frame, to ironic tone, to strategies of inclusion and exclusion of material, and many other features), and that all mandate, or at least enable the display of, readerly competence or perhaps even sophistication in comprehension—which hardly accords with these audiences' traditional portrait.[123] Though we must take care in distinguishing interpretively between our present conceptualization of these narratological complexities, contemporary authorial conceptualizations (to the extent they are differentiated, differentiable, and/or recoverable), and the various audiences' potential comprehension (and mis- or incomprehension) of the complexities, such complications are marginal when compared to the potential benefit in understanding the texts and their readers.

Genre Theory

Our discussion of various textual modes as a starting point to developing a picture of readerly competency, and of belief and skepticism associated with contextualized forms of reception, leads naturally to a discussion of a particular form of textual reception: the relation of genre consciousness and the theoretical discourse surrounding it to our understanding of readerly identity and development.[124] This is particularly important for our succeeding case studies, since the texts under discussion in the remaining five chapters have been taxonomized, classified, and interpreted along generic lines—approaches that simultaneously illuminate and obscure, as we will see.

Without delving too deeply into the massive amount of scholarship on the topic, some basic points are worth rehearsing: first, literature is divisible into various genres;[125] second, genres possess formal standards and conventions generally agreed upon by a particular society's authors and readers;[126] third, these standards and conventions tolerate a certain degree of flexibility, allowing their own parody, deconstruction, or inversion without violating the epistemic pact between author and reader;[127] and fourth, the first three points may be relied upon in attempts to reconstruct contemporary intellectual relations between readers and writers—particularly with regard to literary competency and belief and skepticism. Debates rage over particular genres' specific content, boundaries, and definitions (given the latter's propensity to change within specific historicized contexts),[128] and individual works' generic membership,[129] but the first three points are generally agreed upon. The fourth point, however, can be further developed with reference to our subject, though specific analysis will be left to the individual case studies.

As alluded to above, contemporary readerly *awareness* of these first three points—and internalization of them within their own reading processes—is itself indicative of readerly competency; to recognize a work's genre identification (by internalizing its use of generic conventions), and using that identification and the work's specific employment of generic convention to decode the text, solving narrative and/or thematic gaps or cruxes, itself displays externally derived abilities.[130] (A continuum of readerly sophistication can be inductively demonstrated by the extent to which audiences can cognize and employ generic variations, or works that straddle or internalize various genres.)[131]

As such, readerly reception of a text may be highly influenced by the generically related operations readers perform on it—not only conceptually, but attitudinally and epistemologically. That is, internalized knowledge and manipulation of generic conventions allow not only straightforward narrative understanding, but provide clues to the reader about how to approach that text's claims—both moral claims and truth-claims.[132] To take the former first: contemporary texts, which are often imbued with strong polemic or didactic components, have their polysemic potential shrunk to a more circumscribed universe of meanings closer to the authorially intended "goal" in large part through universally accepted generic understandings that shape readerly understandings of a text's meaning and intent.[133] Such reduction is accomplished by allying hegemonic positions with comfortable obedience to generic convention, and, as we will see, is attempted differently according to whether the genre is fable, chivalric romance, or folk tale.[134]

Authorial desire (particularly in moral genres) to delimit possible meanings notwithstanding, multivocality and subversiveness flourish within generically delineated material even as those generic constraints may attempt to act to reinforce hegemony, and many of our specific studies will allow for the readerly possibility of "reading against the generic grain" and the resulting consequences for our conceptualization of readers' abilities.[135] Fables may resist their morals; narrative cruxes or uncertainties may complicate a "typical" tale of spirit possession; and investigating those complications may suggest certain equivalently complex readerships. Still, the general picture of interaction between reader and text as one of accommodation to generic norms, rather than rebellion or subversion, may once more alert us to the necessity of careful historicization of readerly relations; contemporary audiences may have been more drawn to works closely hewing to genre expectations and conventions than we are today, with our interest, shaped by modernism and postmodernism, in disruptions, fissures, and inversions.[136] This is hardly to suggest audiences were uninterested in "unconventional" works—particularly when those unconventional works had conventions in their own right, such as parody. Nor does it mean readers were unaware of these disruptions, or that said awareness lacked meaning. I simply suggest the possibility of their greater pleasure in works following precise genre outlines, though of course modern readers of romance novels, or television watchers of forensic serials, might disagree that the joys of slavishly following convention have abated one bit.

Unquestionably, though, to turn to our second point, our historical positioning vis-à-vis contemporary readers results in significant differences when we consider the perspective of the ontological status—the truth-claim—of a text whose contours conform quickly to generic convention. A more generalized form of the observation about the allegorical mode above, the observation is simply that after a literary revolution identifying classic marks of "real accounts" as close attention to individual, unique, and disparate details, we tend to view stories whose details closely match what we recognize to be standard literary conventions of a particular genre with greater skepticism. Reading a story, for example, about a strapping, lantern-jawed young man who married a beautiful blonde young woman after rescuing her from the railroad tracks to which she had been tied by a mustachioed man with a toothy grin, it seems clear that the various conventional details inserted into this brief narrative distance us, rather than the reverse, from accepting the story's veracity.

This recognition focuses our attention particularly on genre's effect on the more complex case of secondary skepticism: our narrative has no indications of alerting our primary skeptical instincts (people do get married, after all, and rope, railroad tracks, and mustaches all exist); the perception simply arises in these concepts' and objects' particular instantiation in this story. By contrast, in the early modern conceptual framework, a broader sensitivity to and belief in the universe's patterned, harmonious, and ordered arrangement resulted in the opposite conclusion drawn from the identical (and identically recognized) evidence. Such recognition reminds us that our definition of "historicized common sense" must be constantly reassessed to illuminate (and even foreground) the epistemic disjunctures between that period and our own. Still, patterns of belief and skepticism in the early modern period are related to primary, not just secondary, skepticism, as certain genres and subgenres (such as witchcraft narratives) and even the "patterned model" itself are coming under attack. Nelson writes, for example, that in the early modern period, "[n]arratives written in verse"—as are Shakespeare and Marlowe's plays and the spirit possession tale—"seemed more likely to be fictional than those written in prose because of the artificiality of the medium and because poetry was traditionally the father of lies."[137]

Simultaneously, of course, skepticism can be leveled and qualified by sophisticated genre identification and definition itself, particularly when the epistemic truth-claims adduced within society are themselves in a liminal state—a liminality that can be associated, and played out through, the clash of genres. To take one brief example discussed in more detail later in the book, folklore and fable literature can each be seen as specific genres, each therefore making certain potentially contradictory claims clarified in the reader's mental schema through processes of generic assignation and association of epistemic status to genres or subgenres. Talking animals, for example, are presumably understood as fictional personifications of human attributes in fable literature, and thus claims asserted within those texts are discounted (primary skepticism, *generically* determined); in contrast, a contemporary vernacular explication of biblical accounts of Balaam's ass adduces a different kind of truth-claim cognized by the readers (involving questions of primary belief, *generically* determined), which in turn might lead to an account of a contemporary wonder-working rabbi's speech with animals (no primary generic skepticism, as rabbinic accounts are not *inherently* believed or disbelieved, and contextually contingent secondary skepticism). Such considerations, if heavy going in the abstract, can be useful and more usefully illustrated with reference to specific texts, as we will see.

Genre and Cultural Porosity

The centrality of genre consciousness to the reconstruction of the dynamics of early modern Yiddish reading begs the corollary question of those genres' origin and construction. Though this book's attention is primarily focused on specific texts as instantiations of genres present in readers' contemporary consciousness,[138] rather than examining those genres' historical origins and vertical tradition, one specific way of perceiving those origins illuminates another theoretical approach useful to our previous—and subsequent—discussions of early modern Yiddish literature.

Previous scholarship, as mentioned earlier, has focused on the influence of internal and external literary traditions on early modern Yiddish genres;[139] while the reconstruction of contemporary relationships between Jews and non-Jews is best left to historians,[140] the ever-increasing accentuation of the porosity of borders between Jewish and non-Jewish social, intellectual, and cultural life certainly reinforces the critical emphasis on generic similarities, rather than discontinuities.[141] Given the complexities of the actual dynamics of cultural porosity on the level of particular texts and their particular readers, some theoretical refinement might be useful in light of our interest in genre, reading, and knowledge.

Though our texts' authors are often anonymous—and even when their identity is known, their actual biographies and educational status are usually unclear—they are generally understood to be better educated than much of their audience.[142] This comparative advantage is particularly apparent with respect to materials and genres demonstrating cultural porosity, since it often (though not always) implies knowledge of the languages in which these works and genres appear. Their creative choice, then, predicated on personal intellectual ability and/or ideological, polemic, aesthetic, commercial, or practical reasons, could be either to directly model their literary works on external texts (or conventions of external genres), or to ignore them (either through ignorance of them or cultural ethnocentrism) and rather rely for models and influence on vertical genre definitions and instantiations from within "internal Jewish tradition," mindful (even if the author is not) that such earlier traditions may themselves derive from external sources, or are some mixture of internal and external elements. These decisions will come into play, for example, in the investigation of chivalric romances written in a Jewish key like the "Tale of Briyo and Zimro," where, it may be argued, questions of literary incorporation, adaptation, and rejection of "foreign" genres are in fact a major theme of the work itself.

As the writers operate with respect to their readers' knowledge, attention to the readerly perspective provides additional insight into the pervasiveness of textualized awareness of this porosity and its relation to traditionally examined patterns of specifically *educational* contact. Such perspective can be conceptualized in two different ways, viewing the texts in terms of their function as coherent entertainment or as thematically meaningful narratives.

Our analysis might begin by suggesting that our previous connection of readerly pleasure and adherence to understood generic norms notwithstanding, it may be the case that a generically identifiable (in the abstract), culturally derivative text can yield genuine entertainment without actually being recognized, generically or in terms of cultural context. Readers who encounter their first detective novel, for example, need know nothing of the traditions and conventions of "locked room" mysteries to take intellectual pleasure in attempting to determine how the murder was accomplished without obvious means of ingress or egress. If the only thing readers require is comprehension of the basic operations of narrative,[143] with the narrative supplying any other information necessary for its own decoding—because of its author's awareness of the reading community's lack of information about the genre qua genre—the author's "cultural gatekeeper" function vis-à-vis an unknowing audience is a viable critical model.

Given, however, the texts' general propensity—reflecting apparent authorial choice—not to provide that necessary information in its entirety, the critic may justifiably interrogate the audience's source for that narratively necessary information, while discounting narrative gaps bridgeable by logic and general knowledge (in our example, we could take for granted that readers understand that people want to discover a murderer's identity, or that people with motives for murdering the victim should be suspected more than people who lack them). But with genres prominently featuring specific types of knowledge that are not logically derivable, and particular texts reliant on, but not mentioning, that knowledge (for example, that vampires fear the sun, or that evil spirits will be banished with the dawn), we may reasonably assign audience knowledge, if not to generic convention, to other sources that may include oral commentary, earlier Jewish texts, or non-Jewish written or oral cultural transmission, allowing investigation into the circulation of particular data.

This "narrative coherence" approach has been addressed in other contexts, but questions of cultural porosity can also be investigated through the presence of thematically meaningful tropes whose lack of recognition and interpretation by the audience would not hinder basic narrative comprehension or pleasure in reading but which are familiar to those themselves knowledgeable of particular aspects of external texts or genres. This is related to allusion, of course, but here the intertextuality is not with a particular text but a genre (though the readers' and writers' knowledge of the genre can of course be focused through a specific text). Such questions are once more inextricably connected to questions of audience stratification, and, though generally seen in terms of models of *textual* transmission and influence, can of course be viewed in light of our previous discussion of the relations between oral and written cultures. The free oral circulation of legends from both the non-Jewish world more generally and the Jewish world more particularly, for example, has been localized in print collections that identify certain broad thematic or narrative topoi with local traditions, conditions, and locations.[144] Such processes of transmission allow us once more to refine our model of contemporary notions of belief and skepticism, as authenticity is generically and epistemically gained (and perhaps on rare occasion lost) through the transformation from oral non-Jewish legend to written Jewish text.

Ideology, Politics, and Social History

The above discussion of cultural porosity and literary transmission and transformation alludes only briefly to those dynamics' ideological and political dimensions, a perspective that can be fruitfully applied to our examination of the production and dissemination of premodern Yiddish literature more generally. Frakes' exhaustive and brilliant investigation of the role ideology plays in premodern Yiddish studies—which includes a careful definition and review of theoretical treatments of ideology—will undoubtedly remain the standard work on the scholarship around the language and literature, reminding us to constantly interrogate the subjectivity of critical positions (including our own).[145] A few observations here may complement his work with respect to ideology's operation as an authorial strategy in early modern Yiddish literature more directly, and its relation to political questions more broadly defined.

Such discussion must differentiate itself from the discussion of polemic above by noting that first, many studies of ideology in literature focus on a specific text's participation in a given system of power relations and its effort, through expressing a hegemonic or counterhegemonic position, to uphold or subvert that particular system. Attention to the text's agenda in that specific systemic or social light differs from merely recognizing its operation in the polemic mode, investigating its rhetorical power and success without historicizing it. Second, and more important for our purposes, while a polemic requires comprehension by its audience to succeed as a literary work, an ideological text need not predicate the operations on readerly acknowledgment of its ideological agenda; such an agenda can by contrast be masked for strategic or aesthetic reasons (it may offend authorial sensibilities to be that blatant, or a text may simply, while expressing by its nature a given ideological position, not be a pressing element of the authorial agenda). In looking at every Yiddish case study within this book, we will see how the texts operate, in various manners, to perpetuate or subvert these systems of power relations—not always in the manner that the reader might expect, or that generic convention would generally imply.

Just as a polemic text can be creatively and subversively misinterpreted by readers, however, a text whose ideological structure is hidden or muted can certainly be "opened" to reveal its implicit positions via commentary, oral or otherwise, within a community of discourse. Such a history of the discursive relations around texts, with respect to the revelation of their ideological structures and indeed their reinterpretation, especially as texts are revised and rewritten in later generations, presents a valuable direction for study;[146] this book, by contrast, focuses more on the text as it is at "time zero," with its first implied reading community, attending in part to the writers' manner of ideological articulation and what its relative obscurity or clarity might suggest.[147]

Despite occasional efforts at conflation, ideology and politics are not identical; this is particularly important in our study, as much of early modern

Yiddish literary production, generally speaking, revolves around ideologically fraught positions regarding readers: their reading choices, the connection of those choices to moral (mis)behavior, the dangers and possibilities of the autonomy gained by providing vernacular information, and so forth. These ideological questions, like all ideological questions, are historicized, related to the rise of printing, the flourishing of Italian humanism and Christian Hebraism, and the spread of popular Lurianic mysticism, to name just a few influential contemporary factors.

Beyond this, however, certain texts, *almost always implicitly*, address political questions in the more narrowly defined sense, concerning Jewish conduct as a communal and/or corporate body in relationship to other political bodies, like kingdoms, churches, and principates. For example, chivalric or romance texts concerning leadership and leaders can be viewed as explorations of broader Jewish political concerns, as we will see in our discussion of "The Tale of Briyo and Zimro"; individual *mayses* about, for example, rabbis' relations with Roman emperors in the *Mayse-bukh* are also easily interpretable in these terms. Such ideas were largely not actionable for most of the texts' readers; but practical powerlessness hardly implies lack of interest or concern. Still, a broader range of texts can easily be viewed in light of internal Jewish politics, particularly the critique or exploration of the nexus of contemporary political-social-economic power structures, sometimes implicitly, sometimes explicitly. As our case studies ranging from Shakespeare to she-demons will show, "supernatural" literature is often notably suited for such explorations behind the veil of allegory, thus allowing us to investigate readerly competency in unveiling the particular critique behind the general story.

The texts' investigation of contemporary social and political practices, if in hidden or metamorphosed form, in turn suggests their potential utility as historical sources above and beyond that accentuated in this chapter, and in the book, as aids in recovering (and reevaluating) a sense of the Yiddish reading audience's intellectual capacities and literary competencies, general legal mores and questions, and degrees of cultural porosity. The invaluable scholarship on contemporary historiographical consciousness, both elite and vernacular, by scholars such as Yosef Yerushalmi and Michael Stanislawski,[148] the attention paid by Chava Turniansky to specifically historically oriented early modern Yiddish texts such as commemorative songs,[149] and the work by Stanislawski, Moseley, Davis, and others on histories of individual lives,[150] that is, autobiography or egodocument, mean that this study need not focus on this question's application to early modern Yiddish texts or genres that explicitly gesture at "historical" processes. Perhaps, however, less methodological attention as to how texts *not* "advertising" themselves as in any way historical may nonetheless have a certain utility for social historians. While necessary to approach these narrative and supernatural texts skeptically, given that *all* texts must be so viewed, the subject at least warrants brief treatment.

The texts, at the highest level of abstraction, may serve as informative social documents with respect to ideologies and polemic mentalities, illuminating at least the author's sense of contemporary crises, problems, and solutions both realistic and unrealistic. To the extent that such efforts are intended for comprehension, they are contingent on readerly recognition of these problems as somehow grounded in real (and therefore potentially recoverable) historical conditions. Recognition—and the concomitant attempts to recover the historical realia that recognition provides—should be tempered by the awareness that reform-minded individuals consciously or unconsciously present an overly problematized picture of historical reality to demonstrate the necessity to adopt their own solutions; additionally, this may take the form of caricatured, satirized, or parodic discourse generating distance from mimetic, historically "accurate" accounts—though the precise relation between these forms of discourse might be harder to determine than one might like to assume.

Such attempts, which bear much in common with the efforts of new historicist and cultural materialist critics, are valuable, providing highly nuanced, compelling, and substantive readings of texts, marshaling contemporary intellectual, religious, and political debates, notions, or controversies to illustrate how a given literary text comments on contemporary issues and is in turn shaped by them. A further discussion might focus on more concrete, mimetic details present within texts belonging to narrative literary genres and ask how these details of everyday life, and, even further, the quotidian details only half-present beneath a cloud of narrative implication might help us to reconstruct the lived life of early modern Jewry, given these texts' "fictional" status either to contemporary or current readers.

It should be clear by now that the relevant methodological heuristic adduced here to address the question will adopt a reader-response approach, modified and complemented by an application of genre theory. More concretely put: contingent on the particular genre, the epistemic bargain between writer and reader to provide either greater textual verisimilitude (in genres where said verisimilitude is desirable for either polemic or commercial effect) or to provide more meaningful and substantive entertainment (even if verisimilitude by generic definition is not an option), results in the desirable—if not strictly necessary—minimization of the dissonance produced by the inclusion of narratively irrelevant historically inappropriate details that contradict the story's norms and milieu, allowing remaining details to gain import and value for social historians.

Narrative irrelevancy is a central aspect of this model, mindful of its generic inflection and the individual text's own narrative aims within that genre: that is, readers and writers alike may understand a particular genre to narratively disregard certain kinds of details from the perspective of creating dissonance by changing them from contemporary contextualized expectation. The details of mechanisms of transport in Jane Austen's novels, for example, are generally irrelevant to the development of her narrative; accordingly, her desire to render those details in fully describing a character's travel but to avoid making them obtrusive suggests those details will be sufficiently correct to allow contemporary readers, knowing those details' truth or falsehood, to enjoy them in their narrative place without feelings of dissonance and providing us with intriguing micro-data. Examples of this sort of information will be touched upon throughout the book.

One final feature of these texts that affects this model should be discussed: the prevalent appearance and the seeming early modern readerly tolerance of anachronism. Such tolerance, often taken as a sign of contemporary audiences' lack of awareness of historical periodization and change, or their simple unconcern, must be modified by insisting on that tolerance as a matter of degree—since certain literary texts predicated on their function as quasi-historical representation, such as the Purim play, derived some of their precise and specific comic power from audience awareness of the slippage of anachronistic jokes and references into the mouths of the traditional biblical characters—and the recognition of those jokes as anachronistic. Such knowledge is accentuated by the generic knowledge that provides permission for anachronism to be recognized and enjoyed; other contexts, which are less playful by nature, may indeed rely on comparatively greater historical ignorance, but again, this may be a matter of degree. In the classic example of literary anachronism—the clock in *Julius Caesar*—one may ask whether the same apparent unconcern for anachronism might have emerged if Caesar was seen operating a printing press. This question of how audiences tolerate massive anachronism—and what this may say about their own historical consciousness—will be addressed in our discussion of the pseudo-chivalric tale of Briyo and Zimro.

Gendering Early Modern Yiddish Literature

If the theoretical discourses of readership and genre and their possibilities for the study of early modern Yiddish literature—and the life that literature illuminates—are to this point relatively unexplored, other discourses whose utility has been more generally recognized should not go unnoted. Much recent scholarship in the field has related to the study of gender, often explicitly or implicitly viewing the corpus of texts as space for women's voices (or those voices' problematized representation by men) to be heard or explored.[151] This work's generally nuanced and sophisticated nature[152] does not imply that complementary questions cannot be posed to expand on those approaches further.

For example, any study of women as producers of old Yiddish literature is necessarily (at least based on extant material) predicated on highly sparse data, since very few contemporary texts can be definitively said to be composed by women. The fairly significant exceptions—Glikl of Hameln's *Memoirs* and some *tkhines*, or penitential prayers—have been studied fairly extensively, at least comparatively speaking, and will therefore not be treated here in detail (though the *Memoirs* will be discussed in a coda). Still, even this small corpus may offer a significant, if previously unexplored, contribution to theoreticians of gender studies, particularly with regard to exploration of women's "separate writing" (or *écriture féminine*). Extant models of such composition, conventionally constructed as an oppositional structure within a hegemonic social and economic discourse, have been largely figured by Irigaray, Jardine, and others through the lens of Christian women's historical role in preindustrial western European society.[153] The resulting model may not fully account for Jewish women's historical positioning, which featured comparatively greater economic and social power. Such comparatively greater practical empowerment may express itself in voice and writing less differentiated from hegemonic positions; simultaneously, our discussion of the stratification of Jewish textual discourse around education *inflected* by gender, rather than gender itself—"men who are like women"—suggests a continuum of vernacular discourse along the axes of allusivity and educational stratification that may minimize the *kind* of differentiation between texts.

This is not, however, to deny that works designed entirely for women, if not by women, like the *tkhines* literature, possess linguistic and literary characteristics particularly applicable to the *feminine* (as opposed to the disempowered or uneducated) voice; the invocation of the matriarchs and the use of certain grammatical structures are examples.[154] Still, women's broad participation in the consumption of early modern Yiddish literature may demand a reexamination of questions of a particularistic "women's voice" as one of numerous options available to contemporary women; such examination will become particularly relevant in our discussion of dybbuk literature.

Questions of gender, however, are hardly limited to questions of women; and the recent emergence of the discourse of masculinity studies—separate from the propensity to unconsciously identify masculine culture and hegemonic culture more generally—may have its use in approaching early modern Yiddish literature, and vice versa.[155] Much of this work requires revision to account for the vicissitudes of Jewish history in particular: for example, a construction of medieval masculinity that relies heavily on the challenges to gender identity predicated on the transition to a celibate clergy, or the role of "the self-denying husband modeled on Joseph," the husband of Mary, for later-in-life husbands based on changes in medieval Italian inheritance law, is hardly directly applicable to the Jewish sphere.[156] And even much of the limited intersection of the two fields so far has essentially been dedicated to the definition of Jewish masculinity against, and in contrast to, the heroic, chivalric, physicalized constructions of masculinity in the non-Jewish realm, establishing an alternative ideal based on intellectual achievement and reifying the chasm between the two cultures' self-conceptions and ostensible hierarchies of value.[157] Such reification implicitly insists on the establishment of a single (sexual) masculinist hierarchy for Jews (and arguably for non-Jews as well), an insistence possibly complicated by Jewish vernacular literature, particularly chivalric literature. It may even be possible to conceptualize, as we will see in our discussion, competing or alternative hierarchies of value, which, inflected strongly though not solely through the lens of gender, indicate the complex composition of the Jewish audience and their ambitions, influences, and desires.

New (or renewed) emphasis on the dimensions of Jewish masculinity may yield dividends for the study of the Jewish body more generally. Though the last fifteen years have seen increasingly valuable work reflecting what Barbara Kirshenblatt-Gimblett has termed "the corporeal turn" in Jewish studies,[158] the late medieval and early modern period, with its often-noted fascination with the body and its earthiness, offers a particularly rich seam of material to be sifted through employing this theoretical lens. Yiddish literature—through its vernacular legal codifications that create and control a specifically populist-oriented discourse around bodies, dealing with topics ranging from menstrual purity laws to proper slaughtering techniques; through its scatological Purim plays, which reflect contemporary attention to corporeal grotesqueries, standing in stark juxtaposition to the body's symbolic role as representative of divine image; and even through the supernatural narratives, which challenge the view of the body as a coherent and impermeable entity, particularly, though not solely, via the mechanism of dybbuk possession—allows for a dazzling and complex repository of popular means of conceptualization of this most basic of all things, which in turn allows for engaging with the complexities of the culture that creates such a varied repository.

Final Approaches: Identity, Geography, Textuality

Questions of body necessarily lead to questions of mind; and questions of mind lead ineluctably to questions of self. Any conception of authorship—certainly the strong notion of authorship in the form of a knowing, self-conscious author inherent in many of this chapter's theoretical discussions—relies on a concordant conception of the self, and as such the development of the author's role is integrally connected to the particular notions of selfhood developing in the early modern period. These notions of individuality, in authorial and personal terms, can be seen most prominently in autobiographical discourse. Even if the autobiography, as currently defined, is not a genre extant in the period according to some, egodocument or life-writing was inarguably present; it will not be our focus here, but is mentioned simply to note that many of the questions adduced in the field with respect to autobiography's utility as a historical source are simply specialized forms of the most general questions asked about any authors—how they know who they are (and how that identity is influenced and, to some degree or another shaped, by the fields of contemporary historical, social, and cultural trends), and how they choose—employing their own talents, individual knowledge and expertise, stylistic habits and decisions, processes controlled by the circumstances of publication, and other similar factors—to structure and put that knowledge to use in their writing. Though these various areas of influence cannot all be dealt with here—some will be taken up in individual studies—three particular areas of significant and often underappreciated theoretical economy are worth some abstract examination.

Perhaps the primary analytic lens, at least in breadth if not necessarily in importance, is the adoption of a regionalist or geographic approach to the literary corpus. I mean here not the current increasingly fashionable theoretical discipline of calculating the effect of the natural or geographic features of the area in which a text is composed on its nature or appeal,[159] though certain texts or writers may lend themselves strongly to such an approach. Instead, "regionalism" as applied to early modern Yiddish literature might focus on the opposing dynamics of the particularities flowing from the individual nature of specific centers of Yiddish writing and publishing and their effect on authorial desires and demands, and balance this against the universalizing (and thus region- and particularity-effacing) tendencies that some of those publishers adopted. As much of the extant scholarship on Yiddish literature emphasizes or taxonomizes its work along geographic axes, the development of complementary critical and literary discourses focusing on those centers' styles and approaches is certainly of interest.

Such a place-centered (perhaps, more precisely, publisher-centered) approach yields the related question of the effect of the *actual* printing, publishing, and production process on the literary texts, their meanings, and their receptions.[160] Several subordinate questions and direction for research necessarily emerge: we have already addressed the utility of investigating a particular work's textual history, tracing its progress from manuscript to print to subsequent reprint(s), using textual changes, locations of republication, sales figures, and financial information, among other data, to provide information ranging from the practicalities of early modern Yiddish literary culture to the ideological agendas and epistemological suppositions of authors, publishers, and audience.[161] In practice, much of this work is rendered impossible (or at least indeterminate) by history's vicissitudes, since many links in the textual chain are no longer extant; some of the work that *can* be done by modern scholars is beyond the scope of a work of literary criticism and lies more properly in the realm of literary history.[162] Again, the studies here, relying on a historicized and contextualized writer and reader and the literary and epistemological pact between them, will focus on "time zero," as far as it can be reconstructed; that is, the text's original date of publishing and/or composition and the original reading community or communities to which it is addressed.

Temporarily putting aside subsequent textual changes (post time zero), though, still permits plenty of textual manipulation to work with. Even the *editiones principes* of works like the *Seyfer Mesholim* were predicated on earlier printed or manuscript texts, meaning that editors' or anthologists' textual transformations are vital to any understanding of textual operation, with all of the variously adduced epistemological implications, as we will see in chapter 3. Such changes may result from the new citer-anthologist's changed historical circumstances, which find their analogue in a new calculation of the different audience's ability to render the old text ideologically palatable or epistemologically intelligible. Other theoretical possibilities for textual manipulation of course also exist, deriving less from authorial purposes than publishers' commercial necessities (it may be financially necessary, for example, to trim a certain number of pages), or the vicissitudes of the process more generally (human error, such as typographical or printing error).[163] Generally speaking for our purposes, the strong and long-standing interpretive and informational continuities within the Ashkenazic tradition mean the resulting changes affect various weightings of interpretive strategies and particular repositories of knowledge within the differentiated strata of the local target community, and may even mark changing ideological trends among communities or subcommunities, though such suppositions must be treated delicately.

A final approach related to the extratextual process of book production is the role of illustrations and other visual art in the communicative field of early modern Yiddish literature. Varying deconstructive approaches that accentuate the graphological and imagistic significance (and signification) of lettering may have something more to offer the study of early modern Yiddish literature, and vice versa, than in many other periods, given the wide variety—and clear hierarchization—of the texts' numerous typefaces and font sizes, and how they reflect printers' practical and (conscious or subconscious) ideological decisions about rendering Hebrew, Yiddish, or other vernacular languages.[164] Such decisions, presumably clearly "decodable" by the audience, remind us of some early printed texts' components and provide us with another literary competency for analysis.

A significant scholarly discourse is devoted to examining the role of visual arts in late medieval and early modern society more generally and, increasingly, in the Jewish world in particular, focusing on images' role in simultaneously transmitting and canonizing certain narratives and interpretive conventions.[165] With printing's advent, the increasing flood of handbills, woodcuts, and book illustrations reflected the greater audience—and greater effect—such visuals could garner. As such, visual texts that accompany early modern Yiddish printed materials can be similarly investigated both as carriers of semiotic information in their own right, possibly "opening up" the text for audiences lower on the literacy continuum, with conventions and repositories of relied upon knowledge decodable, and as interactive complements (and complications) to the textual materials they accompany. In our discussion of the *Seyfer Mesholim*, understanding its illustrations becomes a key to understanding its readership.

Attention to the illustrations' potentially complicating nature stresses not only the possible dissonance of the individual artistic choices with either authorial intent or a standard, historically contextualized, readerly interpretation of the text, but also the possible intervention of other entities and agendas—most notably publishers employing previously published images for financial reasons, some of which may well have been recognizable to members of the audience.[166] First, these aesthetically divergent images create powerful interpretive suggestions on the part of the viewer retroactively applied to the written text. Who, for example, raised on cinematic and televisual Frankensteins, can read Mary Shelley's novel without dissonance upon encountering her monster's volubility and intelligence—a dissonance Shelley never intended and her original readers would assuredly not have felt?

Further, the images' potential recognition by the audience may create an epistemological dissonance relevant to our previous considerations of textual belief and skepticism: does their reemployment generate a certain skepticism about the claims of the text the image bids to represent, either due to the dissonance itself or because such recycling seems unscrupulous on the publisher's part (particularly if the latter has claimed the illustrations to be new)? How do historical, narrative, logistical, or representational inaccuracies (or dissonances with the information provided in the text) catalyze audience consideration of the inaccuracies' consequences—if indeed they do—and does that recognition matter? Such questions will become apparent in our investigation of the interplay between text, image, and caption in the *Seyfer Mesholim*.

Finally, editors' or publishers' changes and alterations in later editions of a text are not limited to content or illustration, but to language changes as well, given the increasing geographical diversity of Yiddish speakers during the period. The fine extant scholarship on this aspect of early modern Yiddish literature and historical linguistics—an aspect undiscussed in our efforts to understand the texts at time zero—has focused on the host of methods knowledgeable and canny authors and publishers have used to deal with these trends, including notably the addition of glossaries explaining local vernacular words, not only "difficult" *loshn-koydesh* words, and their clear efforts to minimize or eliminate local idioms or grammatical singularities to render their texts maximally intelligible to the widest number of Yiddish speakers. This said, while this is hardly a linguistic study, careful attention to the individual texts' language will also be stressed here, as individual authorial choice of these building blocks of text and theme are integral to understanding the works, their authors' styles and, arguably, their agendas. The close study of these texts' Yiddish and the information they generate about the contemporary language as a whole, its inflection in various more finely delineated moments, regions, and (a generally less discussed aspect of this topic) audiences, and its relationship in these textual forms to demotic speech has been admirably undertaken by various scholars, most notably Erika Timm, and could not be repeated here even were it desirable to do so.

Conclusion, and Plan of the Work

No survey of this sort could possibly be exhaustive, and this one is certainly not; this outline is offered with the anticipation that others will both complement and expand upon the various theoretical discussions briefly adumbrated here. My hope has only been to suggest these approaches' utility to the study of early modern Yiddish literature more generally, to illustrate how some of them may be challenged, or at the very least supplemented, by the complex circumstances of early modern Yiddish literature and finally, to foreshadow and provide a theoretical substructure for a number of discussions—particularly concerning allusion, reader reception, the role of convention and genre, and belief and skepticism—that will appear in many of the case studies. Though the theoretical discussions present these approaches as ideal types, in practice, as the following chapters will show, such ideal types are rarely best employed singly, instead requiring a synthetic approach to make the most sense of a given text.

And the texts under discussion in the next five chapters and coda present a set of intriguing and complex challenges. After an excursus into comparative study in chapter 2, discussed more fully below, chapter 3 focuses on the Yiddish fable tradition, and specifically the animal fables of the 1697 *Seyfer Mesholim*, a revised version of a sixteenth-century fable collection, the *Ku-bukh*. An analysis of the *Seyfer Mesholim* allows us to see how a strong editorial hand can reshape literary texts for ideological purposes. More important, however, are those purposes themselves; the chapter as a whole focuses on the ideology of the fables and the morals themselves, suggesting that the work as a whole provides a complex attempt to accommodate pietistic structures of virtue rewarded and vice punished to the demands of a skeptical, knowing audience. Beyond that, the chapter accentuates the conservative socioeconomic message of the collection—its counseling of subordination to the regnant social hierarchy—and its attempt to domesticate class resistance and resentment through the fabulistic medium. Such a discussion takes place through the lens of examination of the audience's understanding of conventions of fable, particularly its reduction of human complexity to an animal's essential nature, and expands to discuss how the book's various conventional features—its narratorial presence, its prefaces and invocations, and even its woodcuts—reflect on the capacities and contours of its intended audience.

The fourth chapter moves from fable to folktale, and from talking animals to a more classically supernatural sphere: the demonic world. With the folkloric submotif of the marriage of men and she-demons in early modern Yiddish literature, our analysis continues our discussion of genre, asking how attention to audience knowledge of generic conventions might deepen our reading of these works and, in turn, suggesting that deep reading of such genre works could enhance our understanding of the audience. The little previous scholarship done on these folktales, reading them back through later eighteenth- and nineteenth-century moralistic works involving demon sexuality and concupiscence, reads these works primarily as moralistic tales about the dangers of sexual immorality. Instead, close attention to the sixteenth- and seventeenth-century works on their own terms illustrates that these tales of demon marriage are not so much about sex as they are about class; and, with the application of judicious historical contextualization, the chapter shows how the anxieties these horror stories represent are economic, not erotic. Using this approach, the chapter will then branch out to discuss the implications for the audience's understanding of symbolic structures and readers' abilities to solve narrative puzzles.

The fifth chapter moves from symbolism to allegory and from folktale to chapbook. The seventeenth century saw the rise of the circulation of small pamphlets and books purporting to relate unique, marvelous, true, and wondrous events: among these, spurred by the new interest in the soul, its immortality, and its migrations coming from the Safedian spiritual and kabbalistic revival, is a spate of tales about spirit possession by dybbuks, and their exorcism at the hands of rabbis. Focusing primarily on the most involved, nuanced, and lengthy of these extant tales—"The Tale of the Evil Spirit in Koretz During the Time of War"—the chapter discusses ways in which the comparative framework of European Christian supernatural experience, especially demonic pacts, possession, and its attendant phenomenon, witchcraft, provides important lessons for thinking about the phenomenon of dybbuk possession in Jewish life. Literary renditions of dybbuks, which were almost without exception male human spirits possessing women, must be seen as part of an account of the domestication of Jewish women who, like their non-Jewish counterparts, were attempting to break out of prescribed social roles; work on gender and witchcraft, for example, is particularly valuable here.

Of equal importance, the chapter's close reading of the story as a deep reflection on the philosophical questions of theodicy following disaster allows for investigation of the work's uneasy fluctuation between seemingly historic or authenticating details and a reversion to epic and archetypal structures. This, in turn, allows an investigation of the role of recognition and interpretation of allegorical structures by the popular reading public, an investigation based again, as in the previous chapter, on the existence of narrative puzzles and odd features to the story whose solutions are predicated largely on the ascription by the author (and by the interpreter) of complex literary consciousness to the community.

The final chapter draws on the significant discussion of sexuality in the stories of demon marriage and of dybbuk possession, even if the accounts of the latter works that the previous chapters provide attempt to shift the regnant focus to other crucial and less observed aspects of the text. Such study of gender and sexuality, which focuses primarily on the feminine, may suggest in turn the value of focusing once more on questions of masculinity; this provides an intriguing lens through which to view a sixteenth-century Yiddish chivalric tale, the "Tale of Briyo and Zimro." Recourse to the current field of masculinity studies, particularly studies of medieval masculinity, helps us to understand the images of Jewish knights in this adaptation of the chivalric genre, and may help lead us to a reevaluation of long-held positions about idealized characteristics of Jewish manhood as rabbinic manhood in the period under discussion.

Beyond this, however, close reading of the work allows us a specific lens into viewing the intended audience's perspective on parody and history: the work, though perhaps viewed as "pseudo-chivalric" by some today, is not advertised as such, and close analysis allows us to investigate dissemination and reception of readers' consciousness, parodic or otherwise, which is itself predicated on audience understanding of literary convention from non-Jewish material and conceptualization of the grand schemas of Jewish history and political behavior. Taken in sum, we begin to glimpse just how rich the field is—and through our analysis of these texts, and the texts, genres, and conventions that they rest upon, hope to bring more attention to this brilliant and absorbing period of Jewish literary efflorescence.

The merits of such an approach may be amply illustrated with recourse to a comparative case study, employing two (significantly more) canonical texts. Doing so allows the illustration of a methodological process with reference to works possessing a more fully developed scholarly discourse. This provides a series of practical explorations into the supernatural and its reception in the early modern period; the results will illuminate our subsequent investigations, indicating the continuities and ruptures between the study of early modern literature in general and early modern Yiddish literature in particular—and suggesting the value of the study of both in tandem and the utility of one to another. Finally, this approach illustrates how two texts, precisely contemporaneous with our works, written for what was clearly at least in large part a nonelite audience, bear complex and subtle messages that necessitate analysis and understanding, and, in insisting that much of such works' impact derives from the processes of analysis and understanding undergone by contemporary readers, reminds us of how precisely nuanced and thoughtful vernacular and popular culture can be. And so, we enter into the first of our demons' chambers: the Elizabethan stage.

2. "Are Ye Fantastical, Or That Indeed Which Outwardly Ye Show?"

A Comparative Case Study

We begin with a somewhat unlikely question: what made Edward Alleyn retire?

Though critics of Jewish literature may be unfamiliar with Alleyn's name, it is well known to scholars of early modern literature and drama: Alleyn, the leading tragic actor of the late sixteenth-century English stage, may have been the first to assay the role of Doctor Faustus in Christopher Marlowe's eponymous play.[1] The details of his performances, however, are of less concern to us than their cessation.

As is well known, Marlowe's *Doctor Faustus* tells the story of the scholar whose arrangements with diabolic forces lead, inevitably, to his damnation.[2] This is not the place for a detailed analysis of the play's many complexities, which has been profitably undertaken elsewhere.[3] Though we will return to the play itself later in the chapter, our interests for now lie solely in the belief—generally shared by contemporary audiences and actors alike—in the supernatural forces summoned by Faustus in Marlowe's play, and the way that such belief uneasily interacted with the representation of those forces in an aestheticized and fictional context.[4]

Apparently, even simply watching the play was quite an experience for the audiences, who were "work[ed] up into hysteria" seeing it.[5] Their fright seems to have come primarily from "the diabolical apparatus used in the productions [, which] caused great excitement and terror. Shag-haired devils with squibs in their mouths ran roaring over the stage; drummers made thunder in the tiring-house; technicians made artificial lightning in the heavens."[6]

It may be more than understandable, then, that when, according to one contemporary account, "the actors suddenly found one devil more on the stage than there should have been" during a performance, it so unnerved the actors that they stopped the show; this diabolic appearance was also traditionally given as the reason for Alleyn's retirement.[7] Less than four decades later, in 1633, the Puritan William Prynne wrote of the "visible apparition of the devil on the stage at the Belsavage Playhouse, in Queen Elizabeth's days (to the great amazement both of the actors and spectators) whiles they were there prophanely playing the History of Faustus, the truth of which I have heard from many now alive, who well remember it, there being some distracted with that fearful sight."[8]

Though Prynne's Puritanism—and thus, presumably, his antitheatrical bias—could well allow us to attribute ideologically polemical tendencies to his ascription of maleficent doings around the secular (and thus sinful) theater,[9] for now our interest is drawn to his unquestioned acceptance of the devil's appearance on the stage, an acceptance that emulates the earlier audiences of the Alleyn stories. Also of interest for our purposes is that in these stories contemporary audiences are presented with a complex conflation of the true thing with its false representation; that is to say, there are both real and fake devils on the stage, and this phenomenon is entirely acceptable to the audiences both of *Doctor Faustus* and the stories about it.

Such acceptance is not, in itself, surprising; Elizabethan audiences certainly believed in what we would now refer to as "supernatural" forces, though significantly, as we will see, their cognition and categorization of these forces would have been substantially different from our own.[10] Elizabethan audiences were also clearly able to recognize that representations of these supernatural forces may well be "fictional," even as they acknowledged that those forces, through their mastery of illusion and their powers over humans' perceptions, are themselves capable of playing with their own representations and others' perceptions of those representations—a point we will return to that will become increasingly important in our analysis. Further, Prynne's statement as well as the earlier accounts all agree on one point: that some process exists that enables one to distinguish between a true "supernatural" encounter and a "fictional" one, between the "visible apparition of the devil" and an actor playing Mephistopheles. And it is here that we begin to inquire into one of this book's subjects: what are the criteria employed in this process of differentiation? And how does the development (or, perhaps more precisely, the articulation) of these criteria help us to understand literature more generally and popular Jewish literature in particular?

To begin answering these questions, several points should be made that allow us to begin elucidating, in a practical manner, the methodological approaches employed throughout the book. The first and most important of these points is the accentuation of skepticism, rather than belief, in understanding epistemic approaches employed by popular audiences to cultural works placed before them. Doing so does not by any means intend to gainsay the level of popular belief in the "supernatural" subjects under discussion, be they devils, ghosts, demons, or dybbuks. Recent studies of the early modern period in this regard have come quite rightly to portray the balance between belief and skepticism as a field of negotiation, rather than a simple binary construct.[11] Accordingly, discussions of popular belief cannot be constructed in the abstract, and must be conducted with reference to specific cultural contexts and the clues these contexts give.

To return, then, to the Elizabethan theater, we can begin to more subtly articulate this community's particular balance between belief and skepticism by listing the two different contemporary perceptual understandings apparent from the Alleyn and Prynne stories; a more complex taxonomy of perception, cognition, and belief will develop from a second "historical" example and the chapter's subsequent readings of *Doctor Faustus* and *Macbeth:*

1. That the observers are witness to an actual manifestation of the supernatural event that purports to be taking place; that, in other words, they truly do see the devil, and all know and agree this to be the case;
2. That they know themselves to be witness to a clearly and universally accepted fictional representation of the supernatural event that purports to be taking place; that, in other words, they see a figure they know to be an actor put on the greasepaint and then assert his identity as Mephistopheles or an attendant demon.

In the Alleyn and Prynne stories, we have a mixture of both these events. That is, audience and actors alike are aware that they are in the presence of the second type of perception until something alerts them that they are in the presence of the first. (Who "they" are differs in each story; we will see how that difference is significant.) The Prynne account is less helpful here in identifying what that "something" is; though it may be that the phrase "visible apparition" refers to the appearance of the "true" diabolic figure on stage, perhaps becoming apparent at a specific moment,[12] we have little detail other than that it was sufficiently impressive to render the actors and spectators alike "distracted."

Compare this, however, to the Alleyn story, which is far more instructive for our purposes. Again, in the Prynne story, the proof of the demonic appearance, whatever precisely it may have been, was sufficiently impressive in itself that it struck the viewing actors and spectators as self-evidently miraculous. (This said, one might investigate the criteria to prove this level of "self-evidence" as well, since the latter is by definition a subjective term.) In the Alleyn account, by contrast, all of the actors believed themselves to be in the devil's presence, but their belief seems to have stemmed from the *indirect investigative results of their contextual surroundings*. Direct perception, in other words, was insufficient to make their determination; instead, their realization came from the analytic combination of their knowledge of the number of fake devils supposed to be on stage, and their perception of the number of figures actually on stage. This is, significantly, why the Alleyn story focuses on actors and not audience, *contra* Prynne: the nature of this process makes it logically impossible for audiences to make such a determination, ignorant as they would have been of the number of actors supposed to be presently on stage. As such, our understanding of the historical process of negotiating the balance between belief and skepticism is predicated on our understanding of the complex "reading" and judgment of the situation by those within it.

A brief example from contemporary historical context should clarify this point, while reminding us of this investigation's relevance to Jewish questions. Readers are undoubtedly familiar with the broad outlines of the Christian legend of the Wandering Jew, that figure cursed by Jesus to tarry and to testify to the Crucifixion's truth and Jesus' divinity until his return to claim his kingdom. Scholarship has shown that despite the legend's long history, it was the age of printing that allowed for its broad circulation and greater entrance into the (Christian) collective, mass, nonelite consciousness, mostly through chapbooks published and disseminated in the Germanic lands. These chapbooks spread not only the legend's general outlines, but subtropes attached to it; for our purposes, the most important of these is the notion that the Wandering Jew would bring bad luck to a community in which he tarries.[13]

Once this knowledge circulated, a new phenomenon arose: communal ledgers and record books note the arrival of individuals claiming to be the

Wandering Jew and offering to quickly leave the community—thus preventing misfortune's arrival—if they were paid to do so.[14] Certainly, such behavior would be unsurprising to Christian audiences with a stereotypical view of Jews as mercenary, and, presumably, of this archetypal Jew as archetypally so. However, the communal authorities were well aware of the mercenary capacities of not only Jewish immortals, but those of many other individuals of less unique provenance (as some scholars have noted, the period was an age, if not uniquely tainted by fraud, certainly tarred with its dark brush).[15] They therefore asked a question, which we might phrase: given our belief in the Wandering Jew's existence, what signs and marks can we employ—what criteria can we articulate—to prove this man is who he claims to be, rather than a regular individual attempting to blackmail (or, more precisely, *fraudulently* blackmail) our community? The details of the process are unimportant here; what is relevant to our concerns is the emphasis on a skeptical approach within a structure of belief, borne out by an investigative process.

Such processes rely on certain epistemic assumptions whose nature and relative weight differ within the multiple and overlapping systems present within a culture. The best current scholarship on contemporary demonology, particularly on witchcraft and possession, focuses on such processes, often illustrating how different cultural positionings and surroundings allow for different outcomes based on relative weighings of different truth-claims within an investigation that, by definition, weighs between skepticism and belief in the particular case, if not the general.

However, since this book is not primarily a work of history, but rather literary studies, I would like to suggest a further analytic frame: that the dynamics of *contextual* skepticism discussed in these historical examples can be applied equally to *textual* skepticism; that similar structures of doubt and belief are in play when it comes to looking at *texts* regarding "supernatural" events as well—even, and at times especially, when such texts make truth-claims on their audiences. It is this employment of investigative and logical processes in examining matters of belief that this book seeks to emulate. How do texts suggest, within themselves, complicated questions about fictiveness and skepticism when it comes to such "supernatural" matters? How do those questions then relate to the belief structures and literary capacities of the (potentially differentiated or stratified) audience? And finally, does this approach yield deeper readings of some of the canonical, though understudied, Jewish literary texts of the period?

Beginning to answer these questions necessitates a return to our theoretical schema of popular perceptions of the "supernatural," where we will add some complexities, and a close analysis of two literary texts from the Elizabethan and Jacobean theater—texts written, it bears noting once more, at precisely the same time as the Jewish works discussed throughout the book, and appealing to audiences with at least as little, if not significantly less, education (however one might define that word) as most of the contemporary Jewish audience for those works.

Another Look

In positioning the audience (now using that term in its most general sense) vis-à-vis entities or events with ostensible claims to the supernatural, the two ends of the spectrum have already been established: (1) that viewers are witness to an actual manifestation of the event, and know and agree this to be the case, or (2) that they universally agree on what is an objectively fictional representation of a purported supernatural event. Other possibilities remain to be considered, however, which can be divided into two further categories, modifying or supplementing the above.

The first category obtains only in the case of mass direct experience with the event (as in the stories mentioned above, that take place in a theater); the second, moving from experience towards literary representation of that experience, occurs at one remove, either from the level of the group to the individual, or in a medium that achieves the *effect* of individual transmission even if read and accepted in group form—that is, an authored literary text. (This form may include, for example, an oratorical recitation in a group setting, where a single individual is telling the story, or even the case of a group reading a manuscript or chapbook together. Such cases feature a solitary authorial voice, and the entire audience, despite actual physical multiplicity, perceives the texts as individual consumers—a lonely crowd, so to speak.) Among the possibilities of experience and perception:

1. They are witness to an actual manifestation of the event, and know and agree this to be the case.

1a. Adopting a modern, secular, entirely naturalist perspective, we assert that though all believe themselves to be witness to an actual supernatural event, and it is universally accepted within the contemporary social context that they did so witness, they did not in fact do so, since we ourselves know that such an event could not possibly have taken place. Instead, the phenomenon must be explained as some form of mass hysteria, hypnosis, or psychosis. For our purpose—to understand the contemporary period's intellectual, cultural, and literary dynamics—this is not a particularly fruitful approach to consider, as such "pure skepticism" is practically unheard of at the time, and so will be largely ignored through the book. It has, however, been included here for the sake of logical completeness.

1b. We might also, for completeness' sake, add a corollary, following the taxonomic differentiation within Elizabethan culture between "wonders" (something within the bounds of the natural order as it was then defined, a more expansive conception than today's) and "marvels" (something that was not): Adopting a modern, secular, entirely naturalist perspective, we assert that though all believe themselves to be witness to an actual *natural* event, and it is universally accepted within the contemporary social context that they did so witness, they did not in fact do so, since modern conceptions of the boundaries of the *natural* exclude the event from that category, and so such an event could not possibly have occurred.[16]

2. They universally agree on what is an objectively fictional representation of a purported supernatural event.

3. They believe themselves to be witness to an event clearly purporting to be either a true supernatural event, or a representation of a supernatural event, but are actually uncertain of or mistaken as to its nature. Uncertainty may arise from a variety of causes:

3a. "Supernatural" interference. It may be the case that a "real" supernatural event is taking place, as contemporary society would have judged were they to have (from their perspective) full understanding of the situation; however, given the situation's vicissitudes, the event occurring is not the one the audience believes to be taking place, or, at least, the audience is unsure of its metaphysical provenance. Given contemporary emphasis on the devil's particular power to illude and to mask perception—that, in the formulation of one contemporary thinker, "both internal visions and external apparitions may be nothing but demonic attempts to taint the human process of understanding ... the devil ... may lead the *intellectus agens* to mistake the nature of a given external message, either visual, auditory, or totally intellectual"[17]—such a possibility figures prominently in literary treatments of questions of the supernatural, as we will see below. Importantly, such perceptual confusions are or at least can be, according to contemporary understanding, apparent to more than a single individual, and so we can speak of the "audience" within this taxonomical possibility, at least for simplicity's sake, as an undifferentiated whole, though stratification may take place here as well, contingent on metaphysical capabilities (see, ceteris paribus, categories 4a and 4b below).

3b. Special effects. Given the stratification of experience, education, aesthetic sophistication, and intelligence within any broadly defined audience, it may be that some subgroups of the audience for a given supernatural effect believe this supernatural effect to be occurring, while other individuals with more privileged information (for example, actors or audience members with a better view of the stage, or readers privy to the particular circumstances of a book's authorship) know better. The location of the boundaries between subgroups' identification as believers or skeptics is, of course, contextually (and at times generically) determined: when the audience in question is attending a theatrical performance, for example, general contextual assumptions lean towards skepticism. Even here, though, as the Alleyn and Prynne narratives remind us, there is the possibility of belief. But also, it must be said, of doubt; not everyone in those audiences may have shared our chroniclers' and their subjects' perspective of the affair.[18]

4. A final category necessary for inclusion is that of "natural" perceptions, by which I mean features pertaining to a particular individual that cause them to perceive certain supernatural events as occurring, whether those events are, by the society's predictive rules, actually existent or not. Individuals displaying such "natural" perceptions may include:

4a. Those who are, by virtue of their particular, individual gifts of natural magic, more "attuned" to actually occurring supernatural phenomena than are others. Such gifts were believed to be either heritable[19] or earned, the latter by virtue of one's spiritual refinement or, conversely, one's engagement with diabolic forces. They may also be "augmented" by other means not inherently connected to the person, such as through interaction with the supernatural entities themselves, or by possession and use of certain items with magical properties.[20] Such attunements can be problematic: the information gleaned of supernatural entities or phenomena by the individual so attuned may well be incorrect, either maliciously or simply because of "transmission problems."

4b. Those who perceive something they believe to be supernatural that does not, in actuality, exist, due to some internal factor that causes aberrant, erratic perception. These internal factors, from the contemporary cultural and historical perspective, may stem from a combination of physiological and psychological factors. Such an explanation differs from that advanced in 1a, even though it too provides what might be called a "rational" or "naturalist" explanation; the former relies on a scientist perspective denying the *possibility* of perceiving such supernatural factors; here, rather, the individuals (or those individuals' observers, or readers of these individuals when they appear as characters in texts) are indeed under certain circumstances *able* to perceive supernatural phenomena, but are not actually doing so in this case.

These last three cases, at the very least, allow potential discrepancies between individual and group perspectives concerning the same field of perception: that is to say, the group insists they see nothing (or something), to be contradicted by the individual, either "correctly" or "incorrectly." Our next task, then, is to ask what sorts of processes, criteria, and proofs can be marshaled to determine the difference between 3a, 3b, 4a, and 4b, and to ask if such knowledge is ever possible or recoverable from the perspective of an outside "reader" of the situation, both from inside the "reading" community of the historical individual and looking back from our modern position.

Perhaps the possibilities of stratification afforded by these last three cases, which move from a generally monolithic group identity to a more individual, flexible dynamic, in turn afford us other possibilities that allow us to explore how these issues function not in historical, lived settings (mediated as they necessarily are through their textual accounts), but through works that were, more conventionally if complexly, coded as literary; examining the latter may help us to understand the former. That is, fascinating continuities (and discontinuities) exist between a historical approach to such questions whose evidence is now only available to us in textual form (and thus is somewhat open to literary-critical approaches in its interpretation) and a historicized approach to material consciously created, disseminated, and responded to as literary. An examination of *Doctor Faustus* and *Macbeth* will help illuminate these issues and provide concrete examples.

Macbeth

Macbeth is conventionally dated to 1606, possibly late in the year. The arguments for the precise dating are largely not relevant here,[21] but a historical perspective on the period of its creation, particularly regarding attitudes towards the supernatural, is vital. *Macbeth* is, after all, Shakespeare's most supernaturally sated play, particularly (and unusually so) with regard to the figure of the witch.[22] Although the "weird sisters" appear in one of the play's main sources, Holinshed's *Chronicles*,[23] Shakespeare's highly original treatment of the witches in *Macbeth* is an unusual one by contemporary standards. As some critics have noted, the play excludes discussion of the aspects of witchcraft that were the typical basis of most treatments of the subject,[24] allowing Shakespeare to focus on the raging contemporary debates over belief, skepticism, and witchcraft—particularly since his royal patron, James I, was a major figure in the debate. Indeed, most critics characterize James, whose own early *Daemonologie* was published in 1597 (probably written around 1593), and Reginald Scot, who wrote the *Discoverie of Witchcraft* in 1584, as the towering representatives of the positions of belief and skepticism, respectively, in the witchcraft debate—a debate conducted in the shadow of the 1590s' increase in English and Scottish witchcraft prosecutions, a phenomenon that would certainly also have influenced Shakespeare and his audience.[25]

The first shot across the bow is by Scot,[26] who ringingly affirms that "whatsoever is reported or conceived of such witchcrafts I dare avow to be false and fabulous."[27] Much has been made of Scot's arguments that the antipathy to witches can in large part be traced to a general repugnance for women who are "old, lame, blear-eyed, foul, and full of wrinkles, poor, sullen, superstitious, and papists, or such as know no religion," and that simple correlation between these women's presence—and their occasional displays of hostility to others—and bad events subsequently befalling their neighbors, is at times taken as proof of witchcraft or *maleficia*. Such error can be seen as a classic example of the employment of flawed logic in an inherently logically reasonable process, though Scot challenges people's basic assumption of witchcraft's existence, not only their logic. (It should be said that he does acknowledge the existence of an obstacle to clear navigation of the process: the recursively complicating interference of the accused woman herself who, understanding the general tendency to engage in this logically flawed identification, may consciously or unconsciously abet it by confessing or through similar perpetuating activities.)[28]

This last notwithstanding, Scot traces what he sees as general errors in fact and logic to a broad intellectual failure among the populace, stemming largely from its participation in a toxic religious, literary, and cultural discourse:

> The common people have been so assotted [made into a fool] and bewitched, with whatsoever poets have feigned of witchcraft, either in earnest or jest, or else in derision; and with whatsoever loud liars and cozeners for their pleasures herein have invented, and with whatsoever tales they have heard from old doting women, or from their mothers' maids, and with whatsoever the grandfool their ghostly [spiritual] father or any other morrow-mass priest had informed them; and finally with whatsoever they have swallowed up through tract of time, or through their own timorous nature or ignorant conceipt, concerning these matters of hags and witches; as they have so settled their opinion and credit thereupon, that they think it heresy to doubt in any part of the matter.[29]

Scot's emphasis on the role of convention and cultural and literary norms in creating popular epistemic structures bears keeping in mind for our larger project; what should be likewise noted, though, is that his perspective on the "supernatural," defined in its broadest manner, is significantly less unidimensional, and hardly thoroughly skeptical: his book's opening observation, that "the fables of witchcraft have taken so fast hold and deep root in the heart of man that few or none can nowadays with patience endure the hand and correction of God,"[30] directly connects his skeptical need to debunk witchcraft with his pious belief in an interventionist, providential God. As he writes later, "we fly from trusting in God to trusting in witches," and scholars have noted his acceptance of natural magic, and his "flat proclamation of belief in the veracity of some Scriptural accounts as opposed to others ... his brand of skepticism, then, cannot be said to be that of a modern rationalist."[31]

In the pamphlet *News From Scotland* (1592), conversely, the author similarly cites the Divine presence to prove *his* point: that God has actively intervened to have "lately overthrown and hindered the intentions and wicked dealings of a great number of ungodly creatures, no better than devils, who, suffering themselves to be allured and enticed by the Devil whom they served and to whom they were privately sworn, entered into the detestable art of witchcraft." The pamphleteer presents James I as a holy "child and servant of God," who is able to investigate these cases of witchcraft directly;[32] James himself, in turn, writes his *Daemonologie* in response to Scot and other skeptics in order, in his words, "to resolve the doubting hearts of many."[33] Certainly his 1604 "Act Against Conjuration, Witchcraft, and Dealing with Evil and Wicked Spirits," rendering the making of a diabolic pact a capital crime,[34] suggests a strongly held belief in these entities that seems to transcend a simple strategic articulation of politically convenient opinion.[35] This said, James' precise definition of witchcraft's contours is subtler than a simple portrait of a believer might suggest; in *Daemonologie*, he emphasizes the devil's capacity to confuse and illude witches and magi, and his insistence that "witches' flights are no more than diabolical illusion [while considering] the Sabbat an indisputable fact" reminds us of the possibility of false belief within the true, even as Scot posited true belief despite the false.[36]

The witchcraft argument, then, as several critics have observed, allowed Shakespeare—and, in turn, allows us—to use these specific questions and tropes to address the swirling and nebulous status of belief and skepticism in that society more generally. If as early as the mid-eighteenth century Samuel Johnson could write that Shakespeare "only turned the system that was then universally admitted to his advantage, and was far from overburdening the credulity of his audience," and that the "reality of witchcraft or enchantment—which, though not strictly the same, are confounded in this play—has in all ages and countries been credited by the common people, and in most by the learned themselves,"[37] these anthropological investigations may be slightly at odds with his subsequent catty (though not incorrect) observations about social behavior. Of James' arrival in London as king, and James' interest and belief in witches being generally known, Johnson writes: "Thus the doctrine of witchcraft was very powerfully inculcated, and as the greatest part of mankind have no other reason for their opinions than that they are in fashion, it cannot be doubted but that this persuasion made a rapid progress, since vanity and credulity cooperated in its favor."[38]

Lacking Johnson's incomparable style, one might only observe that given the nature of the topic, and the fact that, as Carroll puts it, "a belief in witchcraft requires, or rests upon, an underlying cultural *structure* of belief in magical power—either Christian and/or folk or popular,"[39] actually making such deep-seated epistemic changes (whether from skepticism to belief, or vice versa, or even shifting along the continuum between the two) may not have been as complete or as easy as adopting new fashions at court. The subject of witchcraft was prominent, *and* it was controversial, as Carroll notes; and in the end "[i]t is impossible to specify what Shakespeare's audience in 1605–06 'believed' about witchcraft."[40] Forced to proceed in the absence of definite specification, one may instead follow Stephen Orgel's dictum that this "is a culture in which the supernatural and witchcraft, even for skeptics, are as much part of reality as religious truth is. Like the ghost in *Hamlet*, the reality of the witches in *Macbeth* is not in question; the question, as in *Hamlet*, is why they are present and how far to believe them."[41] To expand and specify Orgel's point with reference to our general questions, then, we may pose one of the more famous questions about the supernatural—witches and ghosts alike—in *Macbeth*, one asked by spectators, readers, and critics alike: what does Macbeth see, how and why does he see it, and how does he understand his seeing of it?

Strange Sights

Seeing and believing are hardly identical in *Macbeth*, of course; as critics have noted, illusion is "not merely a utility, but a central preoccupation" of the play, an observation accentuated by the fact that two-thirds of the play, written for daylight production, has action set in darkness.[42] Nonetheless, Brooke argues that in much of the play's vast critical tradition, "the obvious problems of sensational credulity—witchcraft, ghosts, apparitions—are not discussed, or are assigned to projections of Macbeth's fevered brain, or to the atmospherics of Evil, or—worse—to the supposed credulity of Jacobean audiences."[43]

Any serious discussion of illusion or "sensational credulity"—and thus of belief, skepticism, and the supernatural—must be structured around the five important "strange" sights[44] Macbeth sees during the play, one in each act; in order of appearance, they are the three witches themselves, the floating dagger, Banquo's ghost, the visions shown him by the witches, and

Birnam Wood's arrival in Dunsinane.[45] In a play constantly concerned with various and varied questions of perception and interpretation, Shakespeare brilliantly lays out the gamut of Elizabethan perceptual strategies regarding things that lie on the border between the real and the unreal.[46] The play is not *only* about supernatural perception, of course; for example, much of *Macbeth*'s delicate balance revolves around the contrast between the illusions and "the naturalism invested in the Macbeths' relationship ... [resulting in] a sharp dichotomy between realism and supernatural phenomena."[47] A full interpretation of the play, however, is not at issue here, and we will focus only on the latter aspect.[48]

Immediately after the first exchange between Macbeth, Banquo, and the witches, the witches "vanish," according to the stage directions (1.3.78).[49] Banquo and Macbeth marvel:

> BANQUO. The earth hath bubbles, as the water has,
> And these are of them. Whither are they vanished?
>
> MACBETH. Into the air; and what seemed corporal melted,
> As breath into the wind. Would they had stayed!
>
> BANQUO. Were such things here as we do speak about?
> Or have we eaten on the insane root
> That takes the reason prisoner? (1.3.79–85)

Banquo has already expressed doubts about the witches' essence and, indeed, existence earlier in the scene, asking them: "I' the name of truth, / Are ye fantastical [by which he means "existing only in the imagination"][50] or that indeed / Which outwardly ye show?" (1.3.52–54). This subsequent exchange, though, is central to our purposes, as it illustrates the nuanced process of skepticism and investigation discussed above. Banquo first briefly attempts to posit a "natural" explanation for the figures' sudden disappearance (the "bubbles" of line 79);[51] then, further struck by their message (and, perhaps, by how closely that message mirrors the pair's internal desires), wonders if indeed these now problematized appearances result not from nature, nor actual supernatural manifestation, but rather from an organic or physiological process resulting in hallucinations that *model* actual supernatural phenomena, a movement from 1b to 4b on our list above.[52] By the scene's end, though, Banquo has resolved his doubts about the facticity of the witches' existence:

MACBETH. Your children shall be kings.

BANQUO. You shall be king.

MACBETH. And Thane of Cawdor too. Went it not so?

BANQUO. To the selfsame tune and words. (1.3.86–88)

Banquo replaces his doubts about the witches' existence with an entirely different concern. When Ross, several lines later, informs Macbeth that he has been declared Thane of Cawdor, Banquo asks, amazedly, "What, can the devil speak true?" (1.3.107), and later, in an aside to Macbeth, Banquo warns:

> But 'tis strange;
> And oftentimes to win us to our harm
> The instruments of darkness tell us truths,
> Win us with honest trifles, to betray's
> In deepest consequence. (1.3.124–127)

Banquo has shifted the grounds of his concerns from the *actuality* of his (their) supernatural experience to its *nature;* that is, he has now moved from 4b to 3a on our list. What is the cognitive basis for his shift? It seems unlikely that it stems solely or even primarily from Ross' news about the thaneship. First, given Banquo's skeptical bent (which models our own, as modern and imagined contemporary readers), it would be illogical for him to assume that simply because he dreamed of Macbeth's thaneship and it then came to pass that the former must be a true encounter, not mere dreamed coincidence. More importantly, if more subjectively, Banquo's response to Ross suggests he receives Ross' news not as the necessary proof of the truth of their encounter, but rather as more data for his second speculations about the encountered beings' nature. Finally, and most definitively, Banquo's tone of assent to Macbeth's assertions, which themselves assume the witches' existence (1.3.86–88), suggests the shift has already occurred. What, then, accounts for his acceptance—and for his concerns?

Perhaps the clearest answer is simply in Banquo and Macbeth's joint realization of their identical perception of the event in all its details (as Banquo puts it, "the selfsame tune and words").[53] Logic—that is to say, Elizabethan logic as much as our own—dictates that even were both individuals to suffer physiologically induced hallucinations, those hallucinations would not be identical; thus, the object perceived must be something outside themselves. That this answer is noted though not emphasized in the text simultaneously shows its importance as proof and its powerful economy. This said, the perceived thing's precise essence, rather than its existence—to say nothing of its purpose—is still a matter of interpretation, and Macbeth and Banquo may have differing perspectives on the question of the maleficence of these creatures and their claims' trustworthiness.[54] James expressed Banquo's concern powerfully (if perhaps slightly less poetically) in his *Daemonologie:* "For that old and crafty serpent being a spirit, he easily spies our affections, and so conforms himself thereto to deceive us to our wrack."[55] Of course, Banquo's argument would be impossible—to himself, to Macbeth, and to the audience trying to make dramatic and literary sense of their questions and their choices—without shared epistemic ground concerning matters demonological, and the process of navigating it.

For now, though, the relevant point is that both Banquo and Prynne, when inveighing against *Doctor Faustus*, employ identical grounds for proof of perception, that is, the communally identical nature of that perception. Compare this to the next act's strange sight, arguably Macbeth's most famous soliloquy:

> Is this a dagger I see before me,
> The handle toward my hand? Come, let me clutch thee.
> I have thee not, and yet I see thee still.
> Art thou not, fatal vision, sensible
> To feeling as to sight? Or art thou but
> A dagger of the mind, a false creation,
> Proceeding from the heat-oppressed brain?
> I see thee yet, in form as palpable
> As this which I now draw.
> Thou marshal'st me the way that I was going,
> And such an instrument I was to use.
> Mine eyes are made the fools o' th' other senses
> Or else worth all the rest. I see thee still,
> And, on thy blade and dudgeon, gouts of blood,
> Which was not so before. There's no such thing.
> It is the bloody business which informs
> Thus to mine eyes. (2.1.34–50)

This first part of Macbeth's soliloquy focuses entirely on the empirical reality of his perception, employing skeptical and investigative approaches similar to that of the first episode. Here, Macbeth reaches conclusions precisely opposite to those of the previous encounter; ending with the flat assertion that "there's no such thing," he dismisses the perception as "a dagger of the mind, a false creation," resulting from a combination of physiological and psychological causes (his "heat-oppressed brain," that is, the pathological overpresence of heat, then seen as a fluid substance that, as a property of the humors, weighed on the brain, resulting in passion and fever,[56] as well as his natural sense of guilt about his imminent act of regicide, "the bloody business which informs"). Macbeth, capable of careful self-diagnosis, is therefore positioned not only as a character but as a spectator to his own drama.

But despite his understanding of the "natural" factors that might cause his errant perception, Macbeth also considers and undertakes other proofs and investigations. He first attempts to touch the dagger, and finds it to be insubstantial: "I have thee not, and yet I see thee still." For Macbeth, though, such proof is hardly definitive: spirits could possess the quality of insubstantiality, after all, and it should be noted that neither Macbeth nor Banquo even bothers to attempt applying a "touch test" to the witches in Act I. As has been seen, being with Banquo affords the possibility of proof through joint identical visual apprehension; here, however, Macbeth encounters the phenomenon alone, rendering such proof unavailable. Indeed, with Macbeth's comments, "Mine eyes are made the fools o' th' other senses / Or else worth all the rest," he temporarily entertains the possibility that his visual perceptions may still be—may particularly be—*more* acute and correct than all his other senses' evidence, able to perceive things beyond the reach of natural sensible apprehension.[57] Macbeth, in short, is asking whether he himself belongs to category 4a or 4b, as the overly attuned or the erratically perceiving individual.

This expansive possibility is itself weighed and rejected by the analysis of other, new evidence: the perceived object's transformation from an unbloodied dagger to a bloodied one while remaining present in Macbeth's frame of sight. To Macbeth, this transformation seemingly interprets and confirms his previous observation that the dagger is leading him towards Malcolm's bed-chamber, suggesting to him that it has emerged from his psychologically fraught imagination, not some external source. Such proofs, clearly, are hardly authoritative: even given contemporary perspectives on optics and visual illusions,[58] we (and Macbeth) should remain somewhat in doubt. But Macbeth has one additional piece of evidence available to him for analysis of which the audience is not yet aware; and a second crucial piece of evidence exists, *not* (necessarily) weighed by Macbeth, but taken into account by Shakespeare and by spectators past and present—evidence that may assist us in moving our methodological speculations forward.

Identifying these pieces requires turning to the third strange sight: the appearance of Banquo's ghost. Notably for our purposes, Macbeth initiates the process of recognition of the supernatural entity in the same indirect fashion and "investigative" process illustrated in the Alleyn story about *Doctor Faustus*; it is his inability to find his seat because all the chairs are, to his sight, occupied that leads to his further moment of closer looking, his full recognition of the figure occupying the "place reserved," and to his potentially self-incriminating comments: "Thou canst not say I did it. Never shake / Thy gory locks at me" (3.4.50–51). Lady Macbeth tries to explain away her husband's seemingly odd behavior to their assembled guests, saying:

> Sit, worthy friends. My lord is often thus,
> And hath been from his youth. Pray you, keep seat.
> The fit is momentary; upon a thought
> He will again be well. (3.4.53–56)

Lady Macbeth's highly instructive comments remind us firstly, the lessons of Act I notwithstanding, that joint audiences do not joint perceptions *necessarily* make: no one on stage besides Macbeth can see Banquo's ghost. Secondly, though, and more importantly, they raise a previously unknown predisposition of Macbeth's to psychological instability, and particularly to fits. One might argue that Lady Macbeth is simply inventing this malady on the spot to cover up her husband's potentially fatal admission—it would hardly be her first lie in the play—but Macbeth's comments later in the scene suggest otherwise: "Do not muse at me, my most worthy friends; / I have a strange infirmity, which is nothing / To those that know me" (3.4.88–90). The comment's most likely construction is that Macbeth is suggesting that people exist who are aware of—and unconcerned by—his preexistent illness; Macbeth would hardly be likely to implicate other people (though admittedly they remain an unspecified "those") were the facts in this matter unconfirmable.

If Macbeth *is* so afflicted, we certainly understand why his hypotheses about the dagger are skeptically and naturalistically weighed towards the presumption of hallucination unless proven otherwise. And indeed, Lady Macbeth's characterization of the current event accordingly—and logically—refers to and concurs with Macbeth's characterization of the previous event as such, when she refers to the ghost as "the very painting of your fear / This is the air-drawn dagger which you said / Led you to Duncan" (3.4.61–62). The last line of Lady Macbeth's speech, "When all's done / You look upon a stool" (3.4.68), clearly indicates she does not see the ghost, nor, from their (lack of) reaction, do any of the other banquet guests. Judging from one of our main criteria shared by Macbeth, the confirmation of one's perceptions by others, and Macbeth's sense of his own perceptual deficiencies, Macbeth should be predisposed to side with Lady Macbeth here, not his own perceptions, which have by his own lights been misleading in the past. Why, then, does Macbeth insist so stubbornly that he has in fact seen the ghost—and possibly even that Lady Macbeth must have seen it as well and is lying in her denials? (This is a possible, perhaps likely, construction of Macbeth's statement that "You make me strange / Even to the disposition that I owe / When now I think you can behold such sights / And keep the natural ruby of your cheeks / When mine is blanched with fear" [3.4.113–116]).

Numerous answers can be suggested, some predicated on the changing nature of Macbeth's psychological state, some on the different epistemic status of spirits compared to that of visions in Elizabethan society. Another answer is possible, though, one that elides the differences between Macbeth and *Macbeth*, and begins to move us from within the text to the questions of text themselves—questions that will occupy, not only the rest of our analysis of *Macbeth*, but our transition to *Doctor Faustus* and discussion of topics related to the book as a whole. The answer itself is not textual, but contextual and extratextual; that is, it relates to the interaction between the lived world of the production of the play and the action of the play itself. The play's stage directions make clear that an actual, physical actor played the Ghost of Banquo, an actor who entered and exited at various times during the scene, occupied Macbeth's chair, and so on.[59] No such stage directions exist with regard to the dagger, and it seems likely, particularly given the real (though not insurmountable) obstacles to presenting a floating, moving dagger that suddenly spurted clots of blood from its blade and handle on the contemporary stage, that Shakespeare's audiences did not, in fact, see a dagger.[60]

Such considerations, which operate *solely* on the level of the play's production as a fictional, aesthetic spectacle, should in no way apply to the character Macbeth, who "sees" the dagger in the same way he "sees" Banquo. For audiences, however, a significant difference exists between their perceptions of these two phenomena—a difference that may substantially influence their judgment of the phenomena's differing "realness."[61] I would suggest that, in some liminal way, this difference refracts back into Macbeth's world, providing him a degree of certitude he has previously lacked. That is, judgments concerning the existential status of Banquo's ghost, ostensibly internal epistemic processes for Macbeth, are somehow shaped not only by the textually provided contextual factors indicating the boundaries of possible perception—and here, the confluence of those factors renders determination of the ghost's existential reality impossible for Macbeth—but also by the *extratextual* perceptions of the audience, in this case predicated on apprehension (that is to say, generic) convention. Such pressures generate the audience's realization that the reality of the actor playing Banquo influences, if not generates, a kind of reality within the play itself; as we will see throughout the book, a similar combination of internal and external processes may help yield richer and more determinative readings.

Ultimately, however, the status of Banquo's ghost remains inevitably undecided, and indeed undecidable: and it is unsurprising that this central perceptual conundrum (central in both the thematic and spatial senses; it occurs near the play's midpoint) is then divided in the final two acts to indicate how determining the "truth" of these strange sights is always, ultimately, a matter of interpretation analogous to textual interpretation, again allowing us to perceive Banquo's ghost as a kind of text that may therefore be interpreted using extratextual materials and knowledge.

Recall that during Macbeth's second visit to the witches, he asks the answer to a question, and the witches offer him the choice of receiving it from either themselves or their masters. Macbeth's reply, "Let me see 'em" (4.1.77),[62] privileges the ocular perception he has both valorized and questioned in earlier encounters. As with the witches, who are their catalyst if not their actual source, no doubt seems present about the apparitions' existence (in the sense of definition 4b), though the connection of perceptual illusion to any sort of diabolical forces, like the witches' presumed "masters" (4.1.77), makes clear definition of their particular identity inherently difficult (in the sense of definition 3a). Macbeth's questioning has accordingly shifted from the grounds of their existence to understanding their message—an understanding related to the trustworthiness of their nature and naturally and thematically continuous given the connected "indeterminacy of the visual meaning of each of these three apparitions," the armed head, the bloody child, and the child crowned with a tree in his hand, with "the equivocation of the prophecies they deliver."[63] The particularities of interpreting the images are unnecessary to our discussion; what matters is that their indeterminacy allows for and demands an open field of interpretation.

Such indeterminacy—delimited at first within the witches' very bodies themselves,[64] but now expanding substantially through the play's world—is the focus of the last two acts' strange sights, as the ground of Shakespeare's discussion shifts from perception to conception. This shifting occurs in two distinct manners. The first and clearest is how the prophetic texts themselves are ambiguously structured between two distinct meanings.[65] Famously, the prophecies that "none of woman born shall harm Macbeth" (4.1.94–95) and that "Macbeth shall never vanquished be until / Great Birnam Wood to high Dunsinane Hill / shall come against him" (4.1.107–109) are both interpreted doubly in the play; first, of course, by Macbeth as reassurance of his eternal power and safety, taking these as impossibilities (his response to the second prophecy is the flat "That will never be" [4.1.109]), and subsequently by all the characters—and the universe of the play itself—to refer, respectively, to Macduff's status as a child birthed by caesarean section and Malcolm's strategy that "let every soldier hew him down a bough / and bear 't before him" (5.4.4–5). This type of "oracular ambiguity," often expressed by a supernatural power and leading to a hubristic leader or nation's destruction, is a well-known literary convention.[66]

More interesting for our purposes, though, is the second shift: the replacement of ostensibly supernatural "readings" of the prophecy with naturalistic explanations appealing to the skeptical mindset—and yet doing so in order to confirm the supernatural voice's truth. That is, the epic register, mythic language, and provenance of the prophecies—or, to phrase this in language relevant to our book more generally, the epistemic, generic, and stylistic truth-claims—seem to demand an accordingly supernatural response. This is certainly Macbeth's understanding and expectation; his reaction to the second prophecy—"Who can impress the forest, bid the tree / Unfix his earthbound root? Sweet bodements, good! / Rebellious dead, rise never till the wood / of Birnam rise ..." (4.1.110–113)—illustrates his interpretive process as conceiving the claims solely in supernatural terms, reversing the natural order both in vegetative terms (the trees' animation) and human ones (the raising of the dead). But naturalistic interpretations of the prophetic language also exist—the ones actually appearing in the play. And it thus emerges that the final act's "strange sight"—5.6's stage directions, "Enter Malcolm, Siward, Macduff, and their army, with boughs"—ends up exploiting the ambiguity of the word "strange" itself. Odd and rarely seen such a sight may be, but certainly explicable naturalistically.[67]

Such a message, then, where the supernatural ultimately privileges the explanations of the natural, once more allows us to illustrate how central these questions of perception are to an audience uneasily balanced between belief and skepticism, and how *Macbeth* marshals increasing perceptual skepticism in the interest of belief in a universal supernatural order. It is hardly insignificant that just as skepticism about witchcraft was often cast, even by skeptics within a pious belief structure, as we have seen, in a similar process God makes "a surprising number of appearances" in *Macbeth*—fifteen, to be exact—and that Shakespeare thus employs the supernatural as a means of casting the "providential order" the play suggests into relief. As Miola writes, "Coleridge noted long ago that the witches 'strike the key-note' of the play, but there is an insistent, if quiet, divine counterpoint,"[68] even as Macbeth, as the play goes on, becomes increasingly identified with the devil.[69]

Doctor Faustus

Macbeth's diabolism—indeed much of *Macbeth*'s perceptually and cognitively oriented treatment of its supernatural elements—owes a large debt to *Doctor Faustus*, a play that, to quote one of its critics, "dramatizes ocular experience to a unique degree ... We are continually made conscious of the eye, of what it beholds, likes, and dislikes; how it reacts and affects the mind; how it is attracted, fascinated, repelled, manipulated, and misused."[70] The play's general outline is well known: Faustus' desire for transcendent knowledge, his arrangement with the devil, his eventual damnation. Scholars have noted the political scores settled and philosophical debts paid in Faustus' figure, opinions, and fate; such materials, discussed elsewhere in great detail, will hardly be touched upon here.[71] Less attended to, however—and of concern here—are Marlowe's uses of perception to address belief, skepticism, and the blurred lines between fiction, theatricality, and reality, a strategy that finds its much subtler successor in *Macbeth*.[72]

Such a discussion might begin by categorizing Faustus' sights and experiences and the varying types of supernatural or magical events more generally, along with their apperception by both *Faustus*' characters and its audience. To this end, I will not necessarily proceed in order of the dramatic action, but follow more closely the categories established above.[73]

The first type, then, are the supernatural sights recognized by characters as clearly existent entities and by the audience as clearly fictional representations of existent plausible supernatural figures. Given that the play's action centers on the invocation of the devil and the making of a diabolic pact, and that such action was considered eminently possible within contemporary "structures of belief," appearances of entities involved in this process are apprehensible and should theoretically be able to be introduced to the audience without much trouble. The simplest, most paradigmatic appearance of and response to a supernatural figure, then, is of Lucifer (or Lucifer/Beelzebub)[74] in 2.3.713ff, where Faustus' response is one of simple terror: "O, who art thou that lookst so terrible?" (2.3.716). Here, Faustus' response is conventional: it mirrors the simplest type of audience understanding of conventional demonic form (terrifying-looking) and viewers' perceptual strategies (that what they see and what Faustus sees is essentially identical and corresponds to "reality"—that is, this is what the demon looks like, and what you see is what you get).

This paradigmatic model of appearance and perception, though, is almost entirely dissimilar to other examples articulated throughout the play. Early in *Faustus*, before conjuring Mephastophilis, Faustus summons a devil; his response upon its appearance, however, is not terror but comic dismissiveness: "I charge thee to return and change thy shape / Thou art too ugly to attend on me. Go, and return an old Franciscan friar / That holy shape becomes a devil best" (1.3.266–269). Besides the marked shift in tone, to be discussed later, Faustus' comments reveal his (and his audiences') shared recognition of the devil's capacity to change its shape at will, thus simultaneously delineating and disseminating more nuanced (but still generally understood) conventions about the "pliant" demonic form, to use Faustus' own subsequent (if ultimately ironic) characterization. Such a comment also illuminates conventional understandings of perceptual strategies towards the supernatural, that the pliant demonic form has the capacity to illude characters'—and the audiences'—eyes alike, but in a way universally accepted as a normal part of the supernatural order.

Such strategies are articulated—and complicated—for characters and audience alike in Faustus' contract with Mephastophilis. The relevant terms (or "promises"), for the moment, are the fourth and the fifth ones: that

Mephastophilis "shall be in [Faustus'] chamber or house invisible," and "that he shall appear to the said John Faustus at all times in what form or shape soever he may please." In including these "promises," Marlowe has, in his adaptation of the contemporary understanding of the devil's relationship with those who compact with him, created the opportunity for sophisticated theatrical enterprise. The first promise allows for the comedy of invisibility and for the dramatic tension of ironic positioning, and the second affords the foregrounding for the role of disguise, masking, costuming—the very essence of theatricality, as we will see.[75]

More importantly, this contractual form, with its expression, is *itself* how the audience understands the nature of the relationship and its fictional and theatrical representation, generally and with specific reference to perception. In other words, a mutually recursive relationship exists between the historical, contextual, and extratextual understanding the spectators bring to their viewing (their individually and communally prior knowledge concerning demonic pacts, which allows them to judge this presentation's plausibility), and the information about the pact garnered from the stage action itself, which illustrates how those facts will be (literally) played out in this specific setting. In our subsequent examination of Jewish literature throughout the book, we must (at least theoretically) attempt to maintain a distance between these differing perspectives before once more conflating them in textual analysis, which, in our case, is often the source of most of the information we possess.

The contract's terms begin to be illustrated immediately after the pact is made; Mephastophilis agrees to fetch Faust "a wife in the devil's name" (2.1.593), and returns "with a devil dressed like a woman, with fireworks" (2.1.594–595), a figure who allows us to address the perceptual complexities attendant on the contract. Most simply, all spectators, at whatever remove, may understand this as a fulfillment of the pact, which contains the promise that "Mephastophilis shall do for him and bring him whatsoever." Since, however, Mephastophilis' true power lies in the world of spirits and perception, rather than the world of actuality,[76] as we will see, he seems unable to bring a real human being, despite his later protestations to the contrary. Mephastophilis must instead settle for summoning a lesser devil, and causing it, through his mastery of others' perception, to *look* like a wife; we may similarly presume his promise to "cull thee out the fairest courtesans, / And bring them ev'ry morning to thy bed" (2.1.601–602) would yield spirit-courtesans, rather than the genuine article.

Such limitations will be addressed subsequently; here, our focus is on the summoned devil-wife's appearance both to Faustus and spectators alike. Faustus must understand the "wife" to be a devil in disguise, along with the audience, or his response to Mephastophilis' question "how dost thou like thy wife?"—"A plague on her for a hot whore!" (2.1.596–597), punning on a double sense of "hot" as "sexually aroused" and "fiery"—is largely nonsensical.[77] But no direct indication is given in Mephastophilis' *language* (or anyone else's) that this being is a devil. This potential dissonance raises questions about Faustus' and the audience's sight—or, more precisely, their interpretive operations in processing that sight.

One possible explanation might rely on audiences' sufficiently deep immersion in a particular set of cultural mores that they know that any wife the devil brings for Faustus must by definition be something else. Given, however, the clear semiological uncertainty existent within communally understood and agreed-upon cultural mores, as we saw in discussing *Macbeth*, relying on such straightforwardness seems dubious. Another, more likely option stems from the figure's actual on-stage appearance: that some aspect of this devil's particular appearance—metatextually and theatrically—announces its "true" diabolic nature beneath its external womanlike appearance, that is, it is in disguise and can be recognized to be so even as it is supposed to successfully deceive.[78] And an additional level of complexity is of course added by the adoption of all women's (and "women's") roles by men on the Elizabethan stage.

This simultaneous conflation of recognition and disguise is of course basic theatrical convention, which reiterates (in a slightly different fashion) our lesson learned from *Macbeth:* that knowledge can be gleaned from an *audience's* positioning, which helps the characters' understanding (to say nothing of our own), and that conventional codes—here, of the theater—that reassign Faustus to the mode not of character, but of spectator[79] (part of a larger dynamic of actor-director-spectator in the play), allow him to make these judgments as his audience does.[80]

Such a case, however, suggests a certainty—even if contextually inspired—the play wishes to complicate. As mentioned briefly earlier, Mephastophilis' trafficking in illusion in large part stems from his limited abilities to affect the world of reality, limitations well known and generally articulated within contemporary demonological discourse, particularly with reference to the conjuration of humans. Understandably, then, Faustus, using his Mephastophilis-given powers, is unable to conjure the actual shades of Alexander and his mistress when asked to do so by the emperor Charles V, instead offering that "such spirits as can lively resemble Alexander and his paramour shall appear before your Grace."[81] Illusion's power, though, should hardly be minimized: the spirits' arrival proves that methods of typical sense perception are insufficient to distinguish between spirits and "real people," as the emperor's amazed response—"Sure these are no spirits, but the true substantial bodies of those two deceased princes" (4.1.1106–1107)—clearly indicates.

Such inherent inability to distinguish between illuded and actual sense-perception contributes to and exacerbates Faustus' own increasing psychological instability, so similar to Macbeth's, and the audience's growing uncertainty about many of the represented entities' ontological status. As noted above, a term of the diabolic pact is Mephastophilis' ability to exist unseen near Faustus and others; the accordingly accentuated unseen and/or barely perceived world, played early in the text for comedy, creates a mounting paranoiac and horrific mood as the play progresses. By the final act, Faustus, like Macbeth with his dagger, seems to perceive something that is unseen not only by other characters, but the audience as well—accentuating our sense of Faustus' increasing psychological derangement brought on by his own sense of guilt and horror at his approaching damnation.

Faustus' escalating aberrant behavior resembles Macbeth's in another way: externalized observers (here, the scholars rather than Lady Macbeth) attribute Faustus' current state at least partially in error to an illness that combines psychological and physiological factors ("Belike he is grown into some sickness by being over-solitary. / If it be so, we'll have physicians to cure him," 5.2.1394–1396). Faustus, alluding to their medicalized diagnosis of a "surfeit" (presumably of certain humors), recasts it in moral terms: "A surfeit of deadly sin that hath damned both body and soul" (5.2.1398–1399). The scholars' diagnosis clearly strikes a horrifically ironic note: Faustus' "sight" seems to be of an approaching figure ("Comes he not? Comes he not?" 5.2.1391–1392), making their diagnosis of "over-solitariness" precisely wrong. However, acknowledging the seemingly regnant mode of irony here rather than simple diagnostic accuracy (that Faustus' vision *is* a pathological symptom) demands the concomitant assumption that the figure Faustus sees—and that the audience does not—is present. Such an approach suggests that our *interpretive* judgments about Faustus' derangement and the "facts" of the drama are, like in our previous cases, predicated on contextual information, but that employing these interpretive processes leads ineluctably to precisely the inverse conclusion: that a figure's absence, not its presence—reliance on conventionally and logically understood theatrical magic, rather than "objectively" perceived reality—yields certain conclusions about the truth of Faustus' perceptions, rather than our own.

Such heuristic duplicity, rather than uniformity, pervades Marlowe's text in a way absent in *Macbeth*, as Marlowe, the theatricalist par excellence, delights in continuously reformulating his audience's rules of perception in his theatrical game. This delight seems a specific and considered joy in play, rather than simple logical inconsistency. Compare, in this vein, the good and evil angels who battle for Faustus' soul; Faustus' reaction to their second appearance, and to their claims, is notable:

> GOOD ANGEL. Faustus, repent: yet God will pity thee.
>
> EVIL ANGEL. Thou art a spirit: God cannot pity thee.
>
> FAUSTUS. Who buzzeth in my ears I am a spirit?
> Be I a devil, yet God may pity me;
> Ay, God will pity me if I repent.
>
> EVIL ANGEL. Ay, but Faustus never shall repent. (2.3.641–646)

Unlike the previously discussed unseen figure, both good and evil angels are played by actors; they have dialogue and clearly demarcated entrances and exits. One might suppose this form of "dramatically constituted identity," then, to place them on the identical perceptual and cognitive register to Mephastophilis and *Macbeth*'s witches. Conversely, perhaps supported by the observation that these spirits, unlike Mephastophilis, are not summoned through conjuration, numerous critics suggest that Marlowe is echoing the well-known Renaissance tradition of *psychomachia*. That is, he intends these particular spirits to be—and to be understood by the audiences familiar with the convention as—not similar, ontologically present spirits, but rather externalized, physicalized (or perhaps better "spiritualized") projections of Faustus' own riven personality, embodying his depressing presentiment of his foreordained damnation against the optimistic possibility of repentance.[82]

The angels' third appearance (2.3.706–710) certainly supports this approach; there, their chiming response to his question, "Is't not too late?" notwithstanding, Faustus barely reacts to them. He does not engage with them while they are on stage at all; the only potential evidence of his recognition of their presence occurs after their exit. Even that response, though—the line "Ah, Christ my saviour, seek to save distressed Faustus' soul!" (2.3.711–712)—can easily be understood as an expression of psychological torment, of which the spirits (whether attended to by Faustus or not) have simply been another projection; it is easy, then, to ascribe these presences—visible on stage though they may be—to the "simple" working of his imagination, reordering the rules but still rendering them defined, with clear borders.

However, Faustus' markedly different reaction to them compared to the other supernatural types he has perceived—Mephastophilis on the one hand, the approaching entity on the other—may give us pause. The odd formulation Faustus uses to question the angels' identity—"Who buzzeth in my ears I am a spirit?"—not only suggests his difficulties in perceptual and ontological identification, but locates those difficulties in a particular condition specific to Faustus' character: his inability to identify—to properly conceive and taxonomize—himself. The evil angel's charge that he seemingly guiltily repeats—that he is a spirit—clearly evokes the terms of his pact with Mephastophilis, whose first and primary claim is "that Faustus may be a spirit in form and substance." The most straightforward understanding of this unusual formulation is that Faustus, by signing the devil's pact, has transformed, ultimately, into no more than a damned soul, and is therefore reduced to his (damned) spirit, under the devil's control as other spirits are.

Perhaps it is this spirit transformation that allows Faustus to perform his own magic, since he is now more properly a member of that magical world than the "regular" one. Indeed, Lucifer tells Faustus that now he will be able to "turn thyself into what shape thou wilt" (2.3.803), an ability that has previously seemed the province of demons and spirits. As such, we might suggest a variant version of—and solution to—the *psychomachia* problem: it is Faustus' own blurred state of being between body and spirit that allows him to conjure his own psyche as present "real" spirits, sharing his ontological level, much as he conjures Alexander.[83]

A similar conceptualization is evident in Faustus' comic encounter with the pope and the friars; the scene's comic nature does not detract from its thematic congruence.[84] Mephastophilis tells Faustus that "do what thou wilt: thou shalt not be discerned" (3.1.876–877), and indeed the scene's comedy stems largely from Faustus' invisibility. Invisibility to the other characters, that is; he is visible to the audience, who has no doubt about Faustus' reality. However, Mephastophilis' claim that Faustus will not be "discerned," meaning perceived, seems untrue: the pope hears Faustus' voice from the beginning, and the cardinal and then the friars seem able to perceive the existence of some actual force that continues to snatch the pope's dish and cup. "Seem," because the recognition and perceptual processes are unclear. The friars are at first unable to hear Faustus' mocking "Fall to, and the devil choke you and you spare." When the pope asks who's there, the friar responds with the seemingly paradoxical "Here's nobody, if it like your Holiness" (3.1.881, 883). Given our analysis, this is less paradox than a move along a perceptual and ontological continuum: Marlowe's apparently intended pun, substituting "no body" for "nobody," accentuates Faustus' move towards spirit, a dynamic apotheosized with the cardinal of Lorraine's precise identification of Faustus as such ("My Lord, it may be some ghost newly crept out of Purgatory, come to beg a pardon of your Holiness" [3.1.895]).

Characterizing Faustus in terms of liminality between body and spirit, natural and supernatural, "believed" and "disbelieved" entity powerfully explains why much of Faustus' exercise of his magical or spirit powers involves the summoning of figures who uneasily (even by Elizabethan standards) straddle the categories of history and myth.[85] Further, Faustus manipulates these figures to produce aestheticized versions of history and myth, adding an additional level of complication of simple assignation of reality and "fiction" to the figures—and, by extension, to himself as well. Faustus brags, "Have I not made blind Homer sing to me / Of Alexander's love and Oenon's death? / And hath not he that built the walls of Thebes / With ravishing sound of his melodious harp / Made music with my Mephastophilis?" (2.3.665–669); his move from the world of body to that of spirit is matched, via his weaving himself into the mythic and fiction-making process, with a move from the sphere of "reality" to "fiction."

The resulting confusion about Faustus' ontological status—on his part, and to some extent on ours—culminates in Faustus' conjuration of Helen to the scholars, and some ostensible inconsistencies about her presentation, conception, and perception.[86] Helen should presumably be considered by Faustus and the audience alike as identical to Alexander and his paramour, in metaphysical terms; that is, Faustus is actually conjuring a demon that resembles her, not Helen herself. Here, though, Faustus does not repeat his previous caveats to the emperor, instead simply stating that "you shall behold that peerless dame of Greece, no otherways for pomp and majesty than when

Sir Paris crossed the seas with her" (5.1.1286–1288). Arguably, Faustus simply misrepresents his abilities to impress his scholarly audience, but his later conversation about Helen with Mephastophilis makes little if any reference to the spirit theory he advances earlier; his statement requesting "That I may have unto my paramour / That heavenly Helen which I saw of late" (5.1.1350–1351) gives no indication that Faustus regards this new "paramour" as similar in nature to the demonic "wife" Mephastophilis has previously provided him, which should logically be the case. However, Faustus' increasingly precarious mental state—which can be characterized, as discussed, by a blurring of the lines between history, myth, and reality, echoing the wavering between body and spirit—may allow us to view Helen in her classic role as temptress, here the final temptation where demonic spirit is (blasphemously) misunderstood as historic-mythic flesh—a category error of perception with theological ramifications.

Faustus expresses such confusion in his most famous speech: "Was this the face that launched a thousand ships / And burnt the topless towers of Ilium? / Sweet Helen, make me immortal with a kiss. / Her lips suck forth my soul: see where it flies!" (5.1.1357–1360). Faustus' "was this" can now be clearly read not only as an admiring exclamation, but as a genuine question regarding the identity of the perceived and signified of that perception, a question that could only be asked by a man so in the throes of sickness and damnation that he has lost sense of clear epistemic lines and ontological divisions: was this indeed Helen, or someone (or something) else? Faustus' own remaining suspicions about the answer—and Marlowe's means of revealing the rightness of those suspicions to the audience—might be seen in Faustus' entreaty for Helen to immortalize him with a kiss. Perhaps Faustus simply intends to impute something succubus-like or vampiric to the entity kissing him, suggesting she/it possesses genuine supernatural means of conferring immortality, at best a sign of an inchoate awareness that this is something other than the mortal Helen.

But a stronger reading is afforded by Marlowe's characterization of Faustus' mental state and particularly the emphasis of his desires for imbrication in eternal myth and epic. By kissing Helen, Faustus becomes the lover of the mythic, and therefore immortal, beloved: he himself thus enters the sphere of myth (or at least of history) and so achieves metaphorical, if not "actual" supernatural, immortality. Faustus' next lines bear out this reading nicely: "I will be Paris, and for love of thee / Instead of Troy shall Werternberg be sacked; / And I will combat with weak Menelaus, / And wear thy colors on my plumed crest; / Yea, I will wound Achilles in the heel / And then return to Helen for a kiss" (5.1.1364–1369). Faustus' linguistic register shifts between a sense of reality, differentiating between actual and metaphorical epistemic levels, and his personalization and instantiation within the mythic structure. Ultimately, *Faustus* shows, in its eponymous character, movement away from the physical, a tropism expressed along two continua: either towards fictionalization (classically and mythically), or "fictionalization," that is, towards identity with supernatural beings who, though *potentially* perceived as real in the Elizabethan world, must be treated with some skepticism, given the difficulty of perceiving their presence.

One may accordingly read Faustus' final attempted negotiation—"I'll burn my books" (5.2.1507)—as not only embracing a standard means of proving one's abandonment of magic, following Roger Bacon's classic example,[87] but as Faustus' specific attempt to liberate himself from becoming—and desiring to become—an actual part of those selfsame books. But he has gone too far toward self-imprisonment in the spheres of myth and history, and burning his books would now mean destroying himself, a creature of literature; the resulting logical impossibility reminds us that logic is, of course, the devil's trap. And so the move away from physicality—from realness—continues: by play's end, when Faustus calls on his birth stars to "draw up Faustus like a foggy mist," 5.2.1476, and begs his body to "turn to air," 5.2.1500,[88] the devils who arrive to drag him off accordingly have a more real aspect than the spirit-Faustus—so much so that they soon appear full and breathing (so to speak) on Alleyn and Prynne's stage.

Which leads us to our next twist in Marlowe's game with his audience and his readers, since Faustus' struggle with his increasing fictionalization occurs within a play peculiarly attuned, as often noted, to the self-reflexive and metatheatrical. The play emphasizes these distinctions between the supernatural events depicted therein and their self-conscious performance from its first moments, with the chorus' announcement that "we must perform / The form of Faustus' fortunes, good or bad" (Prologue, 8–9), and with many of Mephastophilis' temptations taking theatrical form.

In the devil's dance (2.1.525ff), for example, Mephastophilis says in an aside, "I'll fetch him somewhat to delight his mind"; then, according to the stage directions, "Enter [Mephastophilis] with Devils, giving crowns and rich apparel to Faustus, and dance, and then depart." Faustus' response to the event—"Speak, Mephastophilis: what means this show?" (2.1.527)—positions him analogously to the audience in searching for interpretive models to process the sight; Mephastophilis' reply, "Nothing, Faustus, but to delight thy mind withal / And to show thee what magic can perform" (2.1.528–529), suggests the necessity for Faustus and readers alike to connect the devil's actual metaphysical capability with the delights of the theatrical spectacle, as seen in a different context earlier in the chapter.[89]

The play's prime performer, however, is of course Faustus, who engages in the "true" magical acts discussed above, as well as theatrical legerdemain.[90] Legerdemain was commonly discussed at the time in conscious contradistinction to magic. As P. G. Maxwell-Stuart writes: "The magician may set out to deceive other people by the use of techniques he or she knows do not work, or which appear to work only because of the operator's skill in prestidigitation and the arts of illusion—a type of magic the medieval and early modern world recognized and called *praestigia* (trickery)—or the magician himself is deceived by the higher power or intelligence to whom he directs his invocations, supplications, and demands."[91] Remembering this allows us to refine our sense of Marlowe's portrayal of Faustus as a creator of fiction, and by extension as a fictional character himself, one who moves from the world of actuality toward the world of spirit, from the magic tricks to tricking magic (where, like Macbeth, the trick is on him).

Several examples of legerdemain appear in *Doctor Faustus;* we will remain with Faustus himself as the subject of discussion, as these continue to illuminate the epistemic relations between author, character, text, and audience when it comes to the supernatural. Faustus convinces a horse-courser to buy a horse made of straw from him, asking only that the man not ride it in water. The latter does so, the horse melts, and the courser angrily approaches Faustus for a refund. Though none of these miraculous events occur on stage, we see something even more remarkable: when the horse-courser finds Faustus, who is with Mephastophilis, certain disaster is averted when the horse-courser somehow "manages" to pull Faustus' leg off his body; he runs off, terrified, never to be seen again. The scene's comedy, of course, relies on the horse-courser's belief that he actually maimed Faustus, and the equally obvious audience knowledge that the actor playing Faustus did not actually have his leg removed (to be reattached a moment later) on a nightly basis. But what is Faustus the character thinking? And how should the audience interpret these thoughts?

Is Faustus engaging in theatrical legerdemain, as Robin and Rafe have clearly done earlier when they taunt a vintner by passing a goblet back and forth through sleight of hand?[92] If so, then his first response, "O, my leg, my leg! Help, Mephastophilis! Call the officers! My leg, my leg!" (4.1.1209–1210), is simply an example of his love of performance and his subsequent comment, after the horse-courser's departure ("What, is he gone? Farewell he! Faustus has his leg again and the Horse-Courser, I take it, a bottle of hay for his labor," 4.1.1217–1218), is mockingly ironic. But another interpretation exists, prefigured once more by Robin's scene: Robin introduces his own legerdemain with the promise to "gull [the vintner] supernaturally" (3.2.991). Since he has no intent to do anything supernatural but merely to *pretend* to do so, such language seemingly supports Faustus' thesis that borders between the supernatural and the natural can be clearly delineated—so much so that they are absolutely falsifiable; something can be defined as one type of act (or entity) claiming one when the other is objectively the case—as good a definition of legerdemain as any other. After Robin gulls the vintner naturally, something odd happens that gives the lie to his (and our) first interpretation: his gibberish recitation seems to summon Mephastophilis, who "sets squibs at their backs" (3.2.1011)—an apparently unexpected turn of events, as Robin seems surprised and alarmed at Mephastophilis' appearance.[93]

The events uncannily foreshadow the accounts surrounding *Doctor Faustus*' closing, suggesting, perhaps, their apocryphal nature; they certainly blur the lines between natural, explicable human legerdemain and supernatural demonic activity. Such slippage, read back into the horse-courser story, may suggest that both Faustus and the audience believe Mephastophilis has transcended legerdemain to actually carry out Faustus' claim about his leg—Faustus' first response may be taken as genuine alarm and his second as relief. Thematically, such an interpretation accentuates Faustus' increasing spiritual dis-integration and transformation into a spirit figure; the body, turning into a soul, is losing coherency. The scene, however, is left ambiguous, and, it seems, intentionally so.

In the historical sphere, to judge (at least positivistically) whether certain events actually happened and how they happened—Is this a real figure? What happened to Faustus' leg?—often necessitates either ambiguous unanswerability or stark either/or choices, truth or falsehood. But operating solely within the literary (or dramatic sphere), ambiguity can be embraced and expanded into allegory and metaphor; either/or choices about Faustus, his essence, his actions, can become both/and. Marlowe's love of this form of literary ambiguity, and its centrality to understanding his work's willed blurriness and to our study of early modern literature more generally, are exemplified in the pageant of the Seven Deadly Sins, metaphors (or perhaps more precisely metaphysical concepts) paraded before Faustus as a "pastime," in Lucifer's words (2.3.730).

The Seven Deadly Sins, as speaking roles, are clearly played by actors; Lucifer intriguingly suggests they will appear to Faustus in their "proper shapes" (2.3.731). Presumably the actors carried props and wore costumes suggesting those shapes, possibly aided in that effort by visual conventions suggested in their speeches, such as Covetousness' "leathern [money] bag" (2.3.749). This said, what truly constitutes "proper" shaping (in constructing representations of entities apprehensible by the audience) is not only or even primarily the deployment of visual symbols; no stage directions of such symbols appear in the text (though possibly those symbols were so well known that costumers needed no such directions). Rather, and diametrically opposite to a scheme of full and simple physical representation, the sins are "created" and shaped through the textual composition of lines that are paradoxical or otherwise impossible to represent physically, a strategy that casts doubt on the ability to physically represent these allegorical beings, even as they physically appear on stage. Envy's speech may be the clearest in this respect:

> I am Envy, begotten of a chimney-sweeper and an oyster-wife. I cannot read, and therefore wish all books were burnt. I am lean with seeing others eat. O, that there would come a famine through all the world, that all might die, and I live alone! Then thou shouldst see how fat I would be ... (2.3.762–765).

The audience must first embrace the paradoxical notion that a metaphysical concept is born of naturalistic physiological processes; second, the reversal of biological fact, that Envy's starvation is linked to others eating; and, finally, a paradox in Envy's structure of proof—to prove its assertions requires seeing Envy fat, but such a sight is by definition impossible, since according to Envy all potential observers will have already died of famine. Even here, then, in the most seemingly clear-cut case of categorizing a non-natural being, Marlowe's studied attempt to blur category lines is apparent; using performance, paradox, and an investigation into the mechanics of allegory, he questions our understanding of these conceptualizations in their ostensibly perfect abstraction.[94]

Our discussion of *Faustus* can end in this paradoxical light by taking up its famous description of hell. Early in the play, Mephastophilis, that ostensibly physical creature, both metaphorizes and naturalizes his ostensibly physical residence, saying that it "hath no limits, nor is circumscribed / in one self place, for where we are is hell, / And where hell is, there must we ever be" (2.1.566–568). But when Faustus, skeptical at this early stage and perhaps even encouraged by Mephastophilis' comments, goes further, saying, "Come, I think hell's a fable," Mephastophilis replies, "Ay, think so, till experience change your mind" (2.1.573–574). Another dynamic, nuanced mixture of supernatural truth and skeptical, investigative judgment processes: Faustus, even conversing with the devil himself, denies his place of residence, and Mephastophilis' own denial—his proof of a proposition that for his audience was a matter of belief—is predicated on experiential discovery that in its own way is almost scientific in nature.[95] This complex conjunction is notably articulated in a fashion so as to rigorously skirt—but just as rigorously to avoid—logical contradiction, at least dramatically speaking, and insoluble paradox. Faustus' simple and willful negativity is foolish and even paradoxical; but, of course, to illuminate his folly in its guise of wisdom—and to display it *as* illogical and paradoxical—may be seen as the play's purpose. One may imagine *Faustus*' audiences, possibly having heard the Alleyn story, heeding Mephastophilis and not Faustus, realizing that theater, like all literary texts (even if more obviously so) is built on some form of deception, and that sometimes deception is the most important sign of truth. The deceiving, theatrical devil's appearance—to Faustus and to Alleyn, in fictional form and historical "reality"—indicates metaphysical veracity and honesty, just as this playful, questioning, skeptical play can be seen as strictly, forcefully moral—or, perhaps, the other way around.[96]

Concluding Considerations

It is not my intent to argue for direct influence between Marlowe and Shakespeare (and their respective audiences) and the contemporary Jewish texts and readers discussed throughout the book, though, as we will see in subsequent chapters, non-Jewish influences in matters regarding the supernatural—images, tropes, patterns of thought—on this Jewish literature are highly significant.[97] Above and beyond specific information about contemporary demonology, which will be useful in our chapters on demon tales and spirit possessions, our discussion of *Macbeth* and *Doctor Faustus* has been offered with hope to elucidate several valuable methodological points, drawn from our theoretical discussion and honed in a richly developed scholarly field, guiding the conceptualization of subsequent analyses in less well-traveled areas.

The first and most important is the necessity of crediting the texts, their authors, and their readers with the deep logic and rigorous conceptual and epistemic structures our analytic abilities can serve to illuminate. Previous critics of *Macbeth* and *Doctor Faustus*, even recently, have attempted to dismiss certain (ostensibly) confusing or contradictory aspects of the works with comments like "Shakespeare was not so logically scrupulous"[98] or that "it is a mistake to look for complete consistency of characterization in Renaissance drama."[99] It seems at least equally plausible to assert that the texts and authors carefully obeyed their own logic(s), and our task is to attempt to explore or recover their intent as best we are able. This chapter's discussion of *Macbeth* and *Doctor Faustus* illustrated how analysis of canonical literary texts may reveal authorial assumptions about—and negotiation of—their audience's (and audiences') various abilities to comprehend complex questions of belief, skepticism, epistemology, and narratology, particularly with regard to—and by using the test case of—what would now be termed the works' "supernatural" elements. Such questions were certainly posed abstractly in elite circles; Shakespeare and Marlowe, however, insert them into the frame of common discourse, thus providing us the possibility to speculate on such complex questions of reception and discourse in a more popular setting—not to mention illuminating authorial literary strategies more generally. These processes may be employed to investigate another set of authors, texts, and readers precisely contemporaneous to the Globe's groundlings—the writers and readers of early modern Yiddish literature.

Such efforts, secondly, will occur both within and without the analyzed texts. In this chapter, we have seen Faustus and Macbeth live and die by stories and those stories' interpretations: interpretations they themselves also shape, as makers who are made in part by their readers' or spectators' lived understanding, which guides and privileges (though never ultimately determines) certain interpretive approaches, along with other extratextual factors such as literary conventions more generally.

Framing the discussion this way, it should be stressed, is not intended as a postmodern move; nor is it to locate a deconstructive impulse at play in these two works (though it is certainly possible to apply such readings), but rather to suggest something more historically grounded and recoverable in the system of interpretive relations between writers and readers more generally: a consciousness at play that conflates text and life in suggesting that lived lives (and certainly the textual recapitulation of those lives available to a broader readership) can be subsumed within generalized literary structures, such as but not limited to allegory and metaphor. Put another way, the texts—particularly those incorporating the supernatural that are recognized as epistemically or ontologically complex—illuminate the working out by writers and readers of how something can be (and can be recognized as) simultaneously true and false, both illusion and reality. Perception—and through that, perspective in the broadest sense of how we interpret the data before us—will be the key to that working-out process, by characters, readers, and writers alike. It can already be seen, from the examples adumbrated in this chapter, how these matters operate differently (if analogously) for different texts, as they lie on different points on a contextually and historically expressed local axis of historiographical versus belletristic consciousness. Our discussion of the role of theatricality in these cases is only the most apparent example of how generic context matters deeply in identifying and determining the grounds of discourse, and how a consensus exists between creator and audience as to in precisely which categories, generic and otherwise, the text belongs. All binaries under discussion represent the end point ideal types; as we have seen, genres deal in ranges, and most texts stand in an in-between mode. The Yiddish works discussed here, for example, almost never explicitly proclaim their fictiveness—quite the opposite. But if the Prynne story (a classic "historical" account) and *Doctor Faustus* (a clearly belletristic text) show how these "clearer" texts initiate meaningful discussions about contemporary readers' and writers' mentalities, their complex negotiations between belief and skepticism in literary and conceptual terms, and the manner of their participation in—and constitution of—the literary community, analysis of our less canonical, more complex cases may assist not only students of Jewish literature, but those delving deeper into these approaches in the study of the early modern more generally. We now turn to those Yiddish texts, then, and begin with an example with the clearest links to non-Jewish literature, one whose epistemic questions seem (at first glance, at least) most simply drawn: from the world of fable.

3. The *Seyfer Mesholim*

The World of Fable

So think I none so simple would say Aesop lied in the tales of his beasts; for who thinks that Aesop writ it for actually true were well worthy to have his name chronicled among the beasts he writeth of.
—Sir Philip Sidney, *An Apology for Poetry*

He does not mean that the fabulous is wholly untrue, or that the fictitious is necessarily false; fact, not truth, is the opposite of fiction. He means that, although the fable may deviate from actual truth, it may still be true in its own way.
—Harry Levin

Our theoretical discussion asserted a central—if hardly unique—role of generic constitution and its conventional identification (by readers and writers alike) as an analytic tool for the study of early modern Yiddish literature, and our second chapter demonstrated the necessity of understanding a set of supernatural texts from a comparative context through their generic—in that case, theatrical—lens. Such investigation into the "epistemological pact" formed—particularly, in this study, around topics related to the supernatural defined in its broadest sense—allows for fine-grained examination of states of communal belief and skepticism, as well as writerly constructions and contemporary understandings of readers' intellectual and ideological constitution more generally. The next four chapters accordingly entertain individual studies of narrative texts from varying, if at times related, genres and subgenres—the fable, the Yiddish chivalric tale, the folktale (specifically the "marriage of a she-demon" motif), and the "true account" of supernatural events (specifically the dybbuk tale). This chapter's analysis, featuring a genre whose epistemological status—particularly when it comes to the "supernatural" question—is prima facie clear to writers and readers alike, provides an ideal test case for illuminating the complexity of readerly understandings, expectations, and mental operations within such clearly delineated generic space; processes themselves illuminated through that reader's construction, observation, and manipulation by a strong writerly presence. Analysis of the latter allows some discussion of how a strong editorial hand's manipulation of earlier texts is a literary, epistemological, and ideological maneuver.

The Seyfer Mesholim: *The* Ku-bukh *Redux*

R. Moses b. Eliezer Wallich's *Seyfer Mesholim* (Book of Fables), containing thirty-four fables along with introductory and concluding materials, was first published in 1697 by Johannes Wust in Frankfurt am Main.[1] "First published," though, is inexact; as Eli Katz has noted, the *Seyfer Mesholim* is essentially a "reissue," with minor but significant changes, of an earlier 1595 fable collection published in Verona called the *Ku-bukh* (Cow Book).[2] The *Ku-bukh* itself, lost for centuries, was only recently rediscovered in the 1980s;[3] such lack of posterity should not be taken as a reflection of its contemporary popularity, though, which was sufficient for the *Mayse-bukh*'s anthologist to attack it by name in his preface for its secularity.[4] Perhaps it was such undeniable commercial appeal that led Moshe Wallich to republish it a century later; perhaps also mindful of its critical reception, he did so as a pious text, complete with the rabbinical approbation absent in the work's first version. Examining how the essentially identical text can be presented—and, theoretically, serve for readers—in these precisely opposite ways allows us to focus on the book's ideology, its manipulation, and its reception by anthologizers and intended readers alike.

Scholars have investigated the differences between the *Ku-bukh* and its reissue by Wallich as the *Seyfer Mesholim* in detail. The differences consist largely, though not entirely, of Wallich's reorganization of the stories' sequence, his deletion of a single story from the original, and substantial changes in title pages, colophons, prefaces, and epilogues.[5] More specifically, Wallich seems also to have eliminated archaicisms, provincialisms, Italianisms, sexually allusive or vulgar material, and references to specific characters or religious practices both Jewish and Christian.[6] These efforts have been explained as an attempt at modernization and universalization, presumably to maximize audience appeal.[7]

Wallich's own sense of what most appealed to his audience, though, may be seen most clearly in his own direct attempts at such appeal: on his book's title page.[8] There, Wallich boasts of his own compilation of the following text, and its derivation from various older, more authoritative sources. His overstatement of his editorial claims notwithstanding,[9] the nature of his cited sources is of particular interest here. Wallich correctly identifies two sources of the book's fables: Isaac ibn Sahula's mid-thirteenth-century *Meshal Ha-kadmoni* (Ancient Parable)[10] and Berachiah Ha-nakdan's late twelfth- or early thirteenth-century *Mishlei Shualim* (Fox Fables);[11] however, he fails to mention a third source, Ulrich Boner's fourteenth-century Middle High German fable collection *Der Edelstein*.[12] It may be, as some critics have suggested, that Wallich's exclusion of Boner's collection stems from ignorance, an ignorance extended by the critics to Wallich's knowledge of the work's sources more generally.[13]

Given the first two books' ubiquity in the Jewish community, Wallich's own elite upbringing, suggesting formal Jewish education and familiarity with Jewish literature more generally (as his work in the production of this book is itself evident testimony),[14] and his self-evident interest in fabular literature, unfamiliarity with those first, Jewish texts would be unlikely, though certainly possible. It seems similarly unlikely that someone devoted to the production and dissemination of fables in Germany at precisely the moment of a "contemporary upsurge in the popularity of anecdotal literature in Germany and elsewhere in Europe," which yielded several German fable collections such as *Schimpf un Ernst*, *Esopus*, and *Edelstein*,[15] given even normal patterns of cultural porosity, would have been unfamiliar with these fables of non-Jewish origin at least in broad outline, and perhaps even from their particular source. This said, Jewish access to non-Jewish materials in non-Hebrew alphabets was significantly more limited. Whether this posed an obstacle to Wallich specifically seems to remain unknown, but his audience would certainly have been less familiar with the material—and it could have been more subject to elite objection (thus dimming its commercial prospects). Another possible explanation therefore emerges: Wallich's explicit citation of the two Hebrew sources on the title page—and *only* those sources—suggests not only his own real recognition of those sources, but his acknowledgment of those names' power as high-status Hebrew texts, and perhaps even their specific recognition (through popular quotation, general conversation, or other such modes of transmission) in a community whose desires for comprehension may have outmatched their capabilities.

Similar strategic considerations are evident in Wallich's actual language on the title page, *dos ikh hob melaket geven oys dem loshn hakoydesh oys dem seyfer moshel hakadmonim un seyfer mishlei shaulim* [sic] ("which I have compiled out of the holy tongue out of the book *Meshal Ha-kadmoni* and the book *Mishlei Shualim*"). The maintenance of the titles in original untranslated form assists our understanding of the intended audiences' capabilities, and possibly suggests these words' inclusion as contemporary *loshn-koydesh* components of the Yiddish lexicon. It is possible, however, that any Hebrew title, regardless of its actual comprehension by its audience, would have seemed valuable by virtue of its phonological (and orthographical) semiological power and impressiveness. This may particularly be the case given the misprints in the titles.[16]

The language also indicates an effort, while subscribing to traditional hierarchies of value by "proving" the book's merit in citing its Hebrew provenance, to simultaneously minimize any differentiation between the fables' Hebrew and Yiddish forms predicated on linguistic difference. Such consideration might also conceptualize Wallich's failure to mention his third, non-Jewish source as his desire to present the book as a model Jewish moralistic work, "unsullied" by non-Jewish sources that commonly aroused traditionalist ire.[17] Alternatively, one could argue that Wallich's exclusion does stem from his ignorance of the non-Jewish source despite his awareness of the first two; such a reading supports an even greater traditionalist mindset on Wallich's part, and thus, perhaps, a more traditionalist approach to the book. This dynamic of reconceptualizing the work as a pious text will be important in our discussion of the book's complex ideology, how it is shaped by its form and intended audience, and how the rabbinic approbation and Wallich's newly composed material, among other features, appeal to that audience.

Finally, the title page reminds us of the extent to which the purchase and consumption of literature operate in a public space. "Come ... inspect this handsome book," Wallich writes. "You won't flee from it. And do buy it. When you read what is in it your heart will rejoice" (1a.29). Granted a bit of metaphorical license for the rhyme scheme and generic conventions, the text may still provide some insight into the process of contemporary book buying: significant inspection before purchase and reading. Assuming the message is not merely conventional, we might suggest that such inspection may have continued for a fairly extended period, since the author marshals arguments for purchase well into the second page of a three-page introduction (see 2b.32–33).

Returning to R. Joseph Samuel of Cracow's rabbinic approbation, it turns out to be, as Katz puts it, "noticeably reluctant"; he writes that "while [Wallich] did not consult me, before starting, as to whether he should print this book, nevertheless now that the book has been completed it should not occur to anyone to reprint it and thereby to cause damage to the aforementioned R' Moshe" (1b.7).[18] Nonetheless, the rabbi notes that "every fable and metaphor will in the end bring one to greater fear of the Lord" (1b.3), the reason previous authorities (*harishonim*) had not prevented their publication. Though R. Joseph Samuel's comments about fabular literature as an older—and potentially morally useful—genre are correct, our discussion of the fables in *Seyfer Mesholim* will help us understand why presenting precisely this text as pietistic was so urgent and so difficult. Before an exploration of the fables' specific themes and ideologies, though, some general discussion may prove helpful to understand the audience to whom those messages were addressed. Doing so will enable us to begin our specific series of investigations into the reading dynamic of contemporary Yiddish audiences more generally, analyzing the role of their understanding of genre convention, and their epistemological approaches to the supernatural or "nonrealistic." Having accomplished that, we can create a clearer picture of how that more articulated audience approached the work.

Reading the Fable

Who read the *Seyfer Mesholim*, and how did they read it? As Leo Fuks notes, Jewish familiarity with the fable stems from the biblical period, and the genre is well enshrined in Talmudic sources; by 1697, as mentioned above, readers could have encountered the *Seyfer Mesholim*'s two most prominent Jewish sources in the vernacular, to say nothing of the likely oral and manuscript circulation of fables. This panoply of possibilities suggests a likely general familiarity with the genre and its conventions.[19]

Such expansiveness is borne out by examining the text: the author directly addresses "husbands, women, and maidens" (*manen, vayber, un yungfroyen*, 1a.29) on the title page to come inspect the book; in his introduction's[20] conventional, formulaic opening, he addresses "all women and pious folk" (*ale di vayber un frumen layber*, 2a.1), and his later suggestion to use the book "to teach the children that God will grant you" (3a.41) expands his potential audience even further, to say nothing of his pleas in the book's invocation for God to "let this book please all, young as well as old," and even to succeed in foreign lands where he is unknown (3b.7–8). Such breadth of address seems to quiet any assertions limiting the audience of this or similar works to women (though it should be noted that in the book's final lines, the narrator, amidst a series of rhetorical figures, includes a conventional reference that he has "written this book for the women with his own hands," 58a.202–203).

This said, aspects of the introductory material complicate our understanding either of the work's universal appeal or its universal audience. Examples include the traditionalist Hebraic abbreviation appearing at the bottom of the first page,[21] the Hebraic nomenclatural acrostic emerging within the introduction (2a–b);[22] the usage, on the introductory page, of a biblical paraphrase of Psalm 122:7 to provide the date;[23] and, perhaps most importantly, the composition of the rabbinic approbation, or *haskome*, *entirely* in Hebrew (1b). The complications of such features, however, are not predictive in terms of constituting readership knowledge and functions; in these cases, as in the case of the titles, failure to understand the *haskome* or these other Hebraic features by the assumed and asserted broad readership does not render them functionally useless. Quite the opposite. If the approbation is similar in nature to a seal, then its simple presence—even and especially its uncomprehended presence—illustrates its function as a feature of a holy book in its apprehension by the audience abstractly and functionally without concomitant textual comprehension. In this sense, the *haskome* powerfully performs its pietistic task to justify the fable collection and fables more generally.

To suggest the potential incomprehensibility of the *haskome* hardly implies the unintelligibility of all Hebrew, or Hebraisms (and, by extension, the concepts or ideas they sometimes imply) to the audience; a more precise investigation of such elements within the fables themselves, where their comprehension seems necessary for narrative comprehension, offers a first nuanced approach into defining that audience, rather than being forced to dismiss (at least potentially) the elements as inherently uninformative for our concerns. An exhaustive list of these terms is unnecessary and perhaps undesirable, but some general points about their appearance and employment may be helpful.

Aside from the traditionalist flavor provided by certain Hebraist formulae (such as *salik*; see 5a.105 and 10a.78), Hebraisms are used by the author to create tone and more fully articulate character. Many of the early fables, for example, contain almost no Hebraisms whatsoever; by contrast, later tales, featuring a traditional Jewish *melamed* (fable 26) and a hypocrite whose seeming piety is reflected in playing at traditional Jewish observance (fable 29), have dozens. Such differentiation of language and, indeed, theme also relates to the stories' differing provenance; as Frakes points out, material taken from ibn Sahula's *Meshal Ha-kadmoni*, where "Jewish cultural practice is often the direct focus of the fable," undergoes less drastic editorial reshaping.[24]

Even a brief examination of the words' usage in their current context illustrates their frequent employment as playful and intriguing rhymes to meet the needs of the constant rhyme scheme; one particularly amusing example is the usage of *takhes/kadakhes* (backside/ague) in 15b.110. (Such rhymes do not always consist of two Hebraic components; the Hebrew phrase *baruch haba adoni*, 45a.294, for example, is summoned to rhyme with "macaroni"!) However, some of the words or phrases cited without explanation, like *zolel vesovei* and *mevulvol [in] moyekh* (49b.120 and 50b.280), certainly challenge any minimalist conceptualization of the Hebrew linguistic component's capaciousness, and may allow us a glimpse into the audience's comprehension of and familiarity with the contemporary Jewish legal, textual, and metaphysical conceptual canon.

Take, for example, the unexplicated usage of the phrase *lo tilbash kilayim* in 31a.66–67; though also cited as a rhyme for *mitzrayim*, the text here is predicated on the comprehension of a concept not directly located within the Hebraic component of the Yiddish lexicon. An instructive example outlining the level of Jewish knowledge more broadly comes from the epimyth to the fable of the false guardian (23b.105–106); speaking of "faithless women" (a topic we will return to below), the moralist writes: "Even Adam earned death on account of his wife, that evil toad. And Samson had his eyes put out." Given the use of Adam and Samson without fully referring to the entire story—Delilah, necessary to understanding Samson's relevance here, is not even mentioned—we can speculate that the moralist assumed general knowledge of these biblical stories by readers, as well as the possibility of their application. Again, these serve as examples to help determine the limits, rather than to provide the particular limits themselves.[25] The point is not (yet) to argue for particularly expansive capacities in this regard, merely to provide, as a starting point, *proof* of specific conceptual knowledge.[26]

Such knowledge is demonstrated even more fully when it is joined to proof of the audience's ability to recognize its ironic function, and thus to begin to address their literary sophistication. Hebraisms are occasionally employed not for their smooth congruence with character, but precisely for their comically jarring nature. In the fable of the dog and the cow, for example, the dog's attempts to seduce the cow provide an opportunity for the author to employ marriage-related Hebraisms—the dog's self-description as a *meyukhes* (35b.98), his insistence on providing a *ketuve* (36a.105), and the cow's worries about relatives by marriage (*mekhutonim*, 36a.134). Such examples clearly and necessarily invoke the incongruity between the fable's universal nature (and its conventional understanding as such), and the intrusion of the Jewish presence into this sphere, an intrusion apotheosized by the metonymic employment of Hebraisms. A more conceptual and comprehensive example—one that displays audience familiarity with a Hebrew allusion—follows: bragging about his distinguished lineage, the dog claims he is "descended from the pious and quiet dogs, who refrained from barking in Egypt, the night when Israel left Egypt land. And in return God gave them a good reward. He commanded that they be given all the *treyf* [nonkosher] meat, as is still done according to the law" (36b.147–152). Though the text is narratively coherent on its own, understanding the reason behind the dog's claim relies on knowing Exodus 11:7 ("But not a dog shall growl at any of the Israelites—not at people, not at animals—so that you may know that the Lord makes a distinction between Egypt and Israel") and Exodus 22:31 ("you shall not eat any meat that is mangled by beasts in the field; you shall throw it to the dogs"). A second story, the fable of the fox and the raven, is even more comically dependent on Jewish motifs: the fox's physical behavior is described in Jewish terms (he stands on his hind legs and looks at the stars as if he were about to recite the blessing over the new moon, *mekadesh levone*, 5b.50–54), and the excuse he gives for getting the raven to sing is that tomorrow is *Rosh hashone* and he wants to hear the raven's cantorial *nigunim*! Such "Judaization," then—a common phenomenon in contemporary Yiddish literature and its scholarly treatment—can be placed within our broader discussion.

If Judaization was, as many critics have argued, a response to commercial considerations (concerns that audiences would reject it as alien or that it would transgress rabbinic standards),[27] then the Hebraization here can be seen as a continuation of the Judaizing, pietistic strategies we have seen Wallich adopt by other means. But further than that, we may argue that Wallich's general neutralization of religious elements, both Jewish and Christian, which Katz correctly asserts, is not in fact an attempt to explicitly avoid Judaization; the number of remaining Hebraisms and the significance of their application render such a hypothesis contingent on Wallich's editorial, anthological, or stylistic failure. Rather, Wallich's employment and maintenance of Hebraisms can be seen as a careful attunement on his part to his audience's comprehension of and desire for the fable's generic conventions, while simultaneously realizing and playing on the audience's ability to process Jewish elements as explicit comments on, and playfulness with, those conventions.

A brief discussion of some other features of this literary text potentially coded as conventional—aspects ancillary to the particular generic form, but essential to this text—will allow us to refine our sense of its audience's readerly capabilities. Such refinement is important to our construction of readerly sophistication sufficient to decide the subtle ideological complexities at hand in Wallich's work—since though the text itself seems superficially unsophisticated, a look at its features reveals nuance requiring epistemological sophistication in its navigation. This sophistication allows us to reflect on our broader themes of belief and skepticism about a "supernatural" text predicated on generic form in a genre superficially easy to dismiss as fantastic—and therefore the one in which the rules may be hardest to discover. The three conventions discussed will be, respectively, the rhyme scheme, the narrator's role, and the place of the book's images.

Reading the Conventions: Rhyme, Narration, Visuality

As we briefly noted previously, the *Seyfer Mesholim*, like the *Ku-bukh*, is a rhymed text, generally aa/bb/cc,[28] which may illustrate the fable literature's liminal state between oral delivery and written text.[29] The author significantly boasts in his invocation that the book is "well written, illustrated, and prepared, *just as one person speaks to another*" (3b.6–7, emphasis mine). Such claims of mimesis and representativeness—claims clearly intended as a selling point by the author—are obviously complicated by the rhymed nature of both narration and characters' dialogue. Granting that early modern Jews (a) did not in fact regularly speak in rhyme; (b) could differentiate between their own speech and that represented in the text; and (c) could cognize such difference as semiotically significant,[30] such a claim seems highly odd. One could argue the simply conventional nature of the claim itself, or that (c) is incorrect, or—and in my mind most likely—that the interaction between lived experience and the rhymed claims of the text recapitulates the readers' sense of the tension between artifice and naturalness that is the essence of the fable; but any of these outcomes suggests something about the writer and his readers, and the last once more expands our sense of readers' critical, suspicious approach to claims made by author and text.

Such a hermeneutic of suspicion—or, more precisely, suggesting readerly capability to employ critical judgment about claim and convention to distinguish between reality and fiction—allows the extension of such close critical readership to other aspects of the rhymed text, allowing for the weighing of textual claims against their sense of authorial necessity determined by convention and theme. Readers may well have understood how this interplay of conventional and thematic factors can yield "deformations" of the "facts" of the narrative—which in turn helps to produce an image of a potentially more knowing and skeptical reader. Such readerly awareness can be extended to incorporate another convention of the text, and of much of contemporary Yiddish literature: the active and intrusive writer-narrator.

Recent scholarship on early modern Yiddish literature, influenced by the last several decades' revolutions in narratology, has stressed the conventional nature of narratorial comments rather than attempt to read them for nuggets of authorial biography. Such shifts are particularly justified when, as per our discussion, some of the introductory material's "facts" about the author-narrator are clearly included for the rhyme's sake; any attempt to read the author's introductory line *bei veter un vind / nokh vayb oder kind / toyber oder blind / nokh gezang nokh fayfn* (2a.7, "in weather and wind, neither wife nor child, the deaf nor the blind, nor singing nor piping [disturbed the author as he was writing]") as providing genuine historical information about his family status or writing process is *prima facie* ridiculous. Most relevant here, though, is the possible recognition of such phrases as conventional tropes by *contemporary audiences*, a recognition arguably heavily assisted by the "factual deformations" occasioned by the rhyme, which alert readers to their conventional nature. This recognition of convention—which leads to a skeptical approach concerning these "biographical facts"—may be extended to those conventional poses in the introduction and invocation aimed to appeal to skeptical buyers, in which the author presents himself as a dedicated worker, a sufferer for his art, and a pious servant of God, as attested to in the invocation.[31] Such conventional poses—which may generate suspicion as much as belief—create a dynamic that operates through the reader's encounter with the entire text.

Certain conventional narratorial statements address this skepticism and suspicion. The narrator's first intrusion at the first fable's very beginning, an insistence that the fox and the stork are good friends "such as one finds even today" (*az men nokh hayt des tags gefint men*, 4a.2–3), invokes experiential proof to attest to his story's essential truth. Given the narrative's focus on a talking fox and a stork, this is admittedly a difficult task, but his emphasis here on truth and proof is a hallmark of the explicit narratorial intrusion throughout the book. For example, the narrator asserts his stories' unchallenged provenance, claiming the second fable's action occurs "as I have *truly* read" (*far eyn gantze varhayt ikh dos lez*, 5a.2–3),[32] and tells us in the third fable (6b.24–25) that he "wants to tell the truth without deception" (*di vorheyt vil ikh redn / zikher ohn ale lign*); in that fable's moral, he even explicitly requests the reader to "believe me" and swears in God's name![33] Other examples of the narrator's insistence on his own veracity, such as "I tell you truly" (*far vor zog ikh aykh dos*, 10b.16–17) and "I tell you this without lying" (*ikh zog aykh dos on gelugn*, 17a.33–34), abound. Clearly, deception is on the narrator's mind: his constant emphases on truth-telling, conventional or no, reflect his concern that the stories' truth will not be accepted.

Such concern at first seems paradoxical if we are to assume the communally shared knowledge of the "untruth" of the narrative's superficial action; this only resolves when we accept that readerly sophistication is such that awareness of the genre's truth lies in the precise rejection of its narrative to focus on the narrative's interpretation—which leads to a strong authorial-narratorial-moralistic role[34] and the constant struggle of readerly skepticism against that interpretation.

Indeed some of the narrator's truth-assertions, even within their conventional forms, create doubt even as they conventionally seek to dispel it: one example is the phrase "Very well, be that as it may" (*nun vol on zay dem vi dem zay*, 14b.3–4).[35] The narrator assists in this "rejection" of the superficial reading of these stories, which could theoretically focus on the acceptance of their supernatural nature, by constantly alerting readers to the book's constructed nature and his role in constructing it. To give just a few examples, he guides readers through the text by insisting he will "present another fable in the same manner" (8a., caption), or by informing the reader what "one learns about a crow" (10b.1); by (ostensibly and perhaps conventionally) insisting on his editorial intelligence and his aesthetically accomplished presentation of both narrative and moralistic materials: "[there are] many more things than I have mentioned here," 30a.56; and even at times ending with a pious wish for his listeners' well-being ("May we yet fare better still, today and forever"; 42a.477–479). Such statements illustrate the narrator's self-presentation as not merely the fables' presenter but their interpreter, alerting us—and the readers—to his recognition (and concomitant anxiety) that such interpretation is personalized and thus, at least theoretically, subjective and subject to separation from the facts of the narrative.

Given our continuing development of readerly capability, we can understand why this is so, and can therefore also understand the resulting necessity and desire to develop an authoritative (or authoritarian) voice—which, at the same time, shows concern that that voice will remain unheeded. Statements like "This fable, I want to let you know, is for many a person . . ." (16a.137), or "From this I have drawn an analogy and brought this fable" (17a.48–49, see also 18a.91) are cases in point. Similar attempts to serve as a particular and personalized instantiation of the moral voice ("Therefore I admonish everyone," 16a.141) or to accentuate the text's moral message ("That, in truth, is why I told you this," 23b.107) present his wisdom as a double-edged sword, displaying doubt, not certainty. Take, for example, the *muser-haskel* to the fable of the greedy innkeeper (31); there, the narrator, addressing the reader, writes, "I need not speak longer of this. You have understood everything that I have brought out in this fable" (51b.348–350). The narrator's continued address, though—an additional eleven lines reiterating the fable's lesson—proves the narrator's doubts in his assertion, unsurprising given the ease of recognition, by author and reader alike, of the exceedingly tenuous connection between the moralist's lengthy interpretation and the fable's actual details.

This narratorial wavering between certainty and doubt is occasionally expressed in the author's contrapuntal distanciation from the presented text, in contrast to the main mode of narratorial activism. One fable opens, for example, with the strangely alienating phrase "It appears according to the story" (21b.1); at times he depersonalizes himself in favor of the more neutral book ("This book tells [*batayt*]," 22b.1); or he occasionally positions himself analogously to the audience vis-à-vis his material ("as the fable has told us," 27a.65). Some of these distancing effects operate by displacing the stories to the mythic level: "they tell that across the sea" (26b.1) and "this fable has been told for a long time" (27a.61). Such anxiety, then—proven to us (and accentuated) by the very efforts to alleviate it—is generated by authorial recognition of readerly capability, a dynamic modeled over the course of the chapter. That anxiety emerges from authorial knowledge of the readers' potential difficulties in accepting authorial ideology, given how the fable's structure is predicated on interpretations of narratives that are subjective, and whose subjectivity encourages alternative readings, and of the complex interpretive demands of the narratives themselves. A discussion of a final textual convention will deepen our understanding of this epistemological dynamic even further.

Among the *Seyfer Mesholim*'s more striking features are the numerous woodcuts illustrating its various fables, making it one of the most heavily illustrated early modern Yiddish texts;[36] no set proportion of woodcuts to text seemingly exists, though longer fables unsurprisingly have a larger number of illustrations. This feature was apparently an important selling point: the author brags on the introductory page not only that the work appears *in der gutn taytshn shprakh* ("in good Yiddish"), but *mit kuper shtik dernokh* ("with copper materials [engravings] as well") (1a.5–6), misrepresenting (or mistaking) the woodcuts for engravings.[37] In his introduction he identifies the visuals as characteristic of the book: "But charming and fine I made this book of mine with the pictures in it. Deer, wolves, foxes, and apes, / Lions and bears with each fable. Whether they be many or few, the moral below strikes the target" (2a.9–10). Such juxtaposition of the images to the moral suggests they also play a role—and a consciously conceived one—in textual interpretation. Guiding that interpretive process—and our analysis of it—is that the woodcuts are captioned; since each fable begins with an illustrative, captioned woodcut, we may, remembering Wayne Booth's comments on the "rhetoric of titles" and their role in signaling authorial intrusion,[38] discuss the interaction of image, caption, and story in developing our sense of readerly sophistication, skepticism, and the resulting relationship with the author.

The moral valence of this complicated relationship is usefully articulated at the introduction's end, in the writer's boast about the book's material aspects: "Clean white paper, the letters like sapphires; beautifully decorated, like biting into an apple" (3a.40). This description, which certainly applies at least in part to the illustrations, combines a curiously questionable sensuality (at least morally speaking) with an image resonant of the primal act of sinful consumption. Such a complexly mixed presentation of the work's production and consumption as involving licit and illicit pleasure is central to illuminating the paradoxes and contradictions between writers and readers (and understood as such) in this literature straddling the sacred and the secular.

But these illustrations' ambiguous location between moral and immoral status—their expansion of the temptation to succumb to the sensual pleasures of visual enjoyment,[39] rather than as accentuations of the texts' moral messages—is paralleled by their capacity to serve as either distractions from the narrative or powerful hermeneutic shortcuts. At the end of his introduction, the author writes: "I don't want to write any more now, but to spend my time resting. Now don't delay; I will soon begin again. For the time will come when the mute will speak. That means the illustrations (*figurn*) that are within. Each will speak and interpret (*bataytn*) a fine fable (*bayshpil*)[40]" (3a.47–50). Such an autogenerative, self-reflexive interpretive process—locating the interpretive power squarely within the image itself, rather than placing the obligation on the audience to make meaning of that image—begs the question of these images' interpretive power within this reading world, and how it might be generated and employed by the writer for receptive unanimity on his audience's part.

The introduction invests the images with messianic and miraculous resonances, unsurprising given one of art's roles in late medieval and early modern society, as a genuine aide-mémoire.[41] This assistance may have functioned in two distinct ways; first, as a specific reminder to individuals wishing to memorize the texts for purposes of oral recitation, at a time of continued societal transition between orality and literacy. Such possibility seems somewhat remote, if only because of the great gaps between the information provided by the visuals and the specific details of the particular stories as rendered in the text (though they might be useful in recalling the stories' general outlines). The more intriguing possibility—more clearly suggested in the introduction—would be as a didactic and interpretive aid for general readers.[42]

This possibility depends on recognized communal consensus of the equivalence of image and meaning, a topic previously explored by students of medieval church art and Bible illustration. A manifesto for this perspective can be seen in the statement of the Seventh Church Council of Nicaea in 787: "The execution of pictures is not an invention of the painter, but a recognized proclamation of the laws and traditions of the overall Church. The ancient fathers caused them to be executed on the walls of the churches: it is their thought and tradition that we see, not that of the painter. To the painter belongs the art, but the arrangement belongs to the Church fathers."[43] Such communal equivalence—and its utility for us—could be complicated and expanded to the extent that we conceptualize the book's audience not as an undifferentiated mass of intelligent readers, but rather a stratified set of subgroups of varying literacy levels, for some of whom, on the less literate levels of the continuum, the pictures and captions might have provided far more meaningful emphasis on the relative weighting of a story's aspects, weighting perhaps even further accentuated by others—preachers, parents, even more educated children—explaining the moral with reference to the visuals.[44]

For simplicity's sake, our main focus here will be limited to one (presumably large) subgroup of the reading audience: that group which can apprehend text, visuals, and captions, whose habit is to read books "in order," that is, they read the story from beginning to end by moving their eyes down the page, taking in, in their order of appearance on the page, text, caption, and visual. These assumptions about readers' habits—not unreasonable ones, but of course by no means definitive—allow for full exploration of the complicated questions of reading reception generated by the interaction between text, caption, and image—as well as further insight regarding our readers' sophistication and potentially skeptical frame of mind.

Our analysis begins by examining the curious first and second images of the first fable of the fox and the stork, each of which actually contains two foxes and two storks (4a, 4b). The second caption, however—"Here the stork has invited the fox to his house and gives him food in a tall cruse"—teaches us that the two duos' collocation within the same image actually refers to different events occurring at different times within the same story. This artistic choice, then, seems an attempt to solve the problem of reflecting dynamic action in a static medium;[45] another solution, illustrated in the second fable's first visual (5a), is to represent a dynamic action in the caption and present the static image as a "snapshot" of a certain part of that action.

The image's caption reads that a "raven took a piece of cheese and flew up on a tree; and the fox quickly approached," while the visual merely renders the raven perched on the tree, cheese in beak, and the fox, having finished his approach, simply sitting at the tree's base. Such reading of these images in temporally dislocative terms shows not only the existence of arguably different strategies of visual interpretation than our own, but that such interpretive strategies can be at least partially recovered by tracking their aberrance from the textually represented fact of the caption, which allows us to begin to see how readerly interpretation judges and sifts the truth-claims of authorially given, captioned, fact.

This interpretive role is accentuated by the editorial strategy of including a slightly altered version of an earlier woodcut in the same fable, not only to comment on its first appearance, but to indicate narrative change.[46] However, the editor also recycles his woodcuts in a different fashion, employing the identical woodcut in different stories addressing the same general themes: the illustration for the fable of curing the sick lion (15; 17a) is the same one used for the fable of the old lion (11; 14a), and the one used for fable 12, the donkey held in partnership (15b), is the final visual of the story of the father, son, and donkey (20a). Such economy of images, it should be noted, definitionally gives the lie to the author's boast in his introduction that images suggest one specific interpretation.

The resulting awareness of multiple interpretations of the same image—potentially liberating for the reader, certainly anxiety-provoking for the author who attempts, in a moralistic text, to present a single normative interpretation—is naturally delineated and bounded most explicitly by the caption, which in our reading model is always encountered immediately preceding or at least essentially simultaneous to readers' scanning of the image, necessitating reflection on its role in establishing meaning.[47] Such interpretive activity is accomplished in even what seem to be the most innocuous of texts. In the fable of the father, the son, and the donkey (16), for example, the caption ostensibly describes precisely the image's action: "Here are a man and his son riding on a donkey; and two men are standing not far off" (18a). Read more closely, however, the description identifies which of the depicted individuals occupies the primary position within the narrative, preparing the reader for the textual encounter to follow.

Captions certainly serve to clarify interpretive possibilities when the visual, either by virtue of the limited mimetic possibility due to technological limitations or by simple aesthetic representative convention, is largely unhelpful in explicating particular narrative details: the twentieth fable features a prostitute, but the reader would have difficulty recognizing the woodcut's richly dressed lady as such without the caption's identification (23b). Similarly, the caption can call attention to details necessary or desirable for interpretive purposes that the woodcut—again either due to the artist's aesthetic choice or technical limitations—can easily lose; for example, in the first visual of the fable of the donkey and the lapdog (23), the lapdog in question is extremely difficult to see; if not for the caption, the woodcut's role in explicating the fable might remain incomprehensible. Admittedly, such explication can occasionally sacrifice more than it adds; in the case of the fable of the false guardian (29), which will be discussed in more detail later, a Jew, unable to carry his purse on a holiday, entrusts it to a false guardian. The holiday's identity—Sukkot—is not revealed in the story until 38b.111–112; readers of the visuals and captions, however, would have become aware of it earlier on the page, reading the caption: "Here is the old man in his holiday dress, palm frond and citron in hand," and seeing an item in the woodcut now (after reading the caption) clearly identified as such. Perhaps the necessity to clarify the image also necessarily sacrifices a certain narrative suspense.[48]

The captions, far from merely serving exegetical functions, occasionally provide interpretively desirable, necessary, or meaningful information found nowhere else in the text; for example, the caption states that the father, son, and donkey ride over "Veronese moors" (19a), of which there is no other clear narrative or visual evidence. Beyond that—and vital to our sense of this convention's importance to the reader-writer interaction—the caption writer, besides providing factual information, can also levy moral judgment. On 43a, for example, the visual presents two adulterous lovers lying together, a fact known from earlier in the text; the caption adds, "Here are both of them lying together; God give them trouble and sorrow." This interjection's necessity may have been catalyzed and shaped by demands of the rhyme scheme here (rhyming *beyd* with *leyd*); nonetheless, the particular form the choice takes stresses the freedom and perhaps importance to make such moral pronouncements in this venue as well as their artificial nature. In much the same way, the caption writer's judgmental explanation in the fable of the greedy innkeeper—"how badly the innkeeper cheated him!" (49a)—can be connected with the rhyme *rayt/bashayt*. Convention's strong—and potentially dissonance-generating—role becomes even more apparent when the moralistically judgmental comment is never borne out by the narrative text. In another caption in the same fable, the innkeeper's wife—who is never, at least directly, implicated in his fraud—is referred to as "an evil toad" (51a); such puzzling ascription is partially explicated in our recognition of the necessity for a rhyme with the caption's first half, describing the innkeeper's death (*beyz kroyt* to rhyme with *iz toyt*).

The failure of such attempts at "fixing" interpretations is not simply seen by the subtle appearance of formalistically influenced judgmental asides; broader aberrations between text, caption, and image in the most seemingly basic ways strengthen the sentiment. A case in point is the visuals' placement—and the information they depict—with reference to the story. The first fable's second image, for example, whose caption was mentioned above, seems placed at a thematically appropriate division between the narrative's two main sections: the caption reiterates the narrative moment where the fox has just accepted the stork's invitation to his house. The image, however, depicts the fox and the stork walking together, apparently to the stork's house (the object that appears on the woodcut's other side)—contradicting the narrative, which tells the reader that the stork has been at its house all day preparing the meal, and the fox arrives alone! Perhaps this reading of this particular visual is subject to interpretation; but other examples provide more explicit contradictions. Towards the end of the second fable, of the fox, the raven, and the cheese, the caption reads: "Here is the fox quickly running away with the cheese into a beautiful green forest (6a)." The woodcut, however, depicts the fox sitting on its haunches, absolutely motionless. Captions state that "a dove devours" what a farmer has sown, while the visual clearly depicts two doves (16a); that a woman is "sitting" when she clearly stands in a doorway (43b); and that a rider has his horn "at his side" when the woodcut presents it at his lips (54a). A caption at the beginning of the fifth fable reads "Here is a raven eating a carcass. And the eagle flies up to him" (7b), belied by the eagle's portrayal as perched on a tree. Even if one argues that questions of economy or supply pressed previously extant woodcuts into service that failed to match the *narrative*, it seems unlikely that the writer of the *caption* was unfamiliar with the images before him. All this begs the question of whether such discrepancies between caption, image, and narrative are meaningfully cognized ones for this audience and, if so, whether they encourage a skeptical affect towards the work—and its message—as a whole.

Some of this possible skeptical orientation can be articulated along previously established lines: for example, the caption describing a donkey "on its side" (*af zayt*) when the image depicts it hanging by its legs (15b) results from employing the word *zayt* to rhyme with the word for the workmen (*arbeits-layt*) who carry the donkey, once more reminding us of the rhyme scheme's operation in deforming readerly expectations and asserting artificiality that beggars belief—not only in the text, but in its author's standing.

True, not all dissonances are entirely ungrounded; one contradictory caption, which states that a cow is "freed from the rope" when it is explicitly depicted roped to a tree (36a), is influenced in its reading by the cow's liberation in the narrative immediately preceding the captioned visual. In such cases, we may suggest that the visuals can function as a recapitulation of the action, providing a pleasing opportunity for the reader to compare his or her mental image against the artist's own version. (The image of the woman hanging her husband on 23b, for example, might be seen as an image of particularly salacious interest.) Similarly, seemingly "irrelevant" visual details (that is, which do not seem placed for decoding or interpretation) can certainly be taken to be created for the artist's and reader's visual pleasure. But such general statements about visual pleasure should not explain away the interpretive (and thus authority-based) difficulties the woodcuts cause.

Other aspects of the visuals afford space to challenge the unproblematized equivalence between image and authorized representation. One might question the conventional nature—and how dissonant the convention would have been—of the varying proportionality of the represented images. In the fable of the country mouse and the city mouse, for example, one mouse appears to be approximately five times the other's size, for no stated or apparent reason (12a); in another fable, two men are depicted walking, one approximately three times the other's size (39a).[49] And a particular focus on the human images might raise the question of the woodcuts' ability (or lack of same) to represent emotion, comparing the clear depiction of grief on the widow's face as she mourns over her husband's grave (22b) to the peasant's impassive, uninformative features (30a), necessitating a caption that informs us "his labors have become irksome."[50]

Interpretation of these tales within a specifically Jewish, not universally literary, context becomes relevant here as well. The narrative and textual aspects of the question will be treated in more detail below; suffice it to say here that one caption's identification of a pictured murdered individual as a Jew (27a) raises several important questions. How does one visually identify a Jew? Is the seeming necessity for the caption to assert the murdered man's Jewishness testament to difficulties of visually differentiating contemporary Jews from non-Jews?[51] Is the discarded hat on the ground a key to the man's Jewish identity, or merely an irrelevant detail? The apparent desire to insist occasionally on the image's Jewishness sometimes generates narrative problems; in the fable of the false guardian, the woodcut on 40b has the illustrated figure still holding the palm frond celebrating Sukkot, though by this point in the narrative (see 41a.315) the holiday has been over for a month. One might ask if such logical inconsistencies apparent within the juxtaposition of text and narrative and introduced for the seemingly ideological purpose of further "Judaization" of the text would also generate skepticism.

Our investigation of the woodcuts' interpretive possibilities may be finally illuminated by a brief discussion of the book's sexually charged images (the conjunction of gender, misogyny, vulgarity, and sexuality will be addressed more fully later in the chapter). On 43a, an adulterous couple appears together in bed, one atop the other; the phallic sword to the couple's left, pointing directly at them, is too rampant to be anything but a visual pun. The adulteress' hairstyle in these woodcuts (here, 43a, and 44b), which makes her appear as if she is sporting horns, may be another example of a visual pun, though it may also be a standard contemporary hairstyle. Technically, of course, it is the deceived husband who wears the cuckold's horns; and in the story's last woodcut, he does so; the horns are directly referred to in the caption and narrative, and the woman's headdress may accordingly be an echoing visual motif.[52] The artist's decision to place actual horns on the husband's head, however, is a unique case where the visual expresses the text's metaphorical construction as mimetically real. This may appear a nice distinction in a work where talking foxes are artistically presented as ontologically real, but crucially, for our purposes, the two are extremely different: *the latter simply reflects the visualized analogue of the conventional rules of the fable as understood by the reader, and the former seems to break those rules*—a phenomenon that activates once more, and perhaps profoundly, our sense of the reader's potential sophistication at interpreting authorial, artistic play, and allows us to investigate an audience's sense of generic rules through (among other stratagems) their occasional aberration. What precisely these "rules of reality" might be is the next section's subject.

"Rules of Reality" within the Conventional Fable

What sorts of "facts" do the visuals—and the stories, and the book as a whole—teach us? Certainly any information about the reading public's social history and circumstances gleaned from the work must be treated very skeptically by scholars. True, the details of the ban threatened against those reprinting the work without permission reveal contemporarily meaningful ways individuals might attempt to circumvent it: "it should occur to no one to reprint it; neither the whole book, nor half, nor part of it; with or without illustrations; neither Jews nor others" (1b.12–14). The extrusive details scattered throughout the book without comment about material goods, clothes, places, and the like are valuable precisely because they are unremarked: their unquestioned acceptance by the reader (or more precisely the reader's presumed unquestioned acceptance on the writer's part) may suggest these items' circulation within social discourse.[53] Such circulation, however, implies plausibility rather than actuality, particularly if the "social facts" in question are narratively meaningful. For example, the author's statement on the Florentine custom of lion hunting (9b.51), important as it is for the continued narrative action of the fable of the shepherd and the lion's paw, must be taken with a grain of salt.[54]

Historically (if not literarily) meaningful details are employed in the moralist's service as well as the storyteller's, potentially even more informatively. Fable 25, about a faithful watchdog who refuses a piece of bread offered by a thief wishing to enter his master's house, is, as narrative, fairly uninteresting. Its moral, however, as long if not longer than the story itself, contains many extremely specific details about a servant's appropriate behavior towards his master, which obviously refer to "real world" situations and are as such relevant to social historians as well as students of contemporary mores (30a.40–53). The moralist's offer of a reward (*lon*) for proper service seems expressed not only in material, but theological terms. Two similar lists with similar moral valences appear elsewhere in the book. The first is located in the *melamed*'s long monologue to an (inattentive) peasant, containing a series of requirements, obligations, and practices seemingly part of his regular, or at least optimal, job description (31a–b.95–125); the second, in the fable of the adulterous wife, takes the form of a very long sermon about wifely duties delivered by a pious cuckold to his wife. Both might allow us to reconstruct, at least partially, values praised at this particular time (44a–b.132–230).[55]

But generally speaking, the fable seems by its very nature a nonrealistic genre in which such details, which elsewhere might be employed for authenticating purposes, seem to fulfill a more playful or perhaps subversive purpose.[56] The fable was, as discussed, a genre of real interest to contemporary Jews and non-Jews alike,[57] but one whose earlier Jewish instantiations incorporated skepticism about morality and illustrative narrative's capacity to dictate morality as a valuable part of the literary process. As Katz puts it, the *Meshal Ha-kadmoni* treats "religio-philosophical themes" such as reason, repentance, and fear of God through "the rhetorical device of an interrogator who questions the validity of each of the concepts, supporting his skepticism with illustrative tales, and a respondent (the author) who defends them with similar (presumably more persuasive) illustrations."[58] While such visible skeptical opposition to the authoritative discourse—perhaps easier to allow in a Hebrew source aimed at a small elite—is not apparent in the *Seyfer Mesholim*, we have seen and continue to see how textual features here allow for skepticism's emergence, culminating in our discussion of the book's complex and problematized ideology. Such skepticism, however, is definitionally operative in a context aware of the existence of certain rules and conventions;[59] part of our work to investigate this text and Jewish reading knowledge more generally is to attempt to articulate those rules' operation by discovering moments where the rules seem to be in tension or actually broken. The horns' appearance in the woodcut mentioned above is one example; discussion of several others helps illustrate the boundaries of Yiddish readers' reading knowledge, skepticism, and genre sensitivity.

The fable's betrayed husband angrily and regretfully describes his growing horns, hair, and beard at length (48a.559–562). The message seems clear: due to his inability to act like a true man—both sexually and morally speaking, as his inattentiveness to his surroundings is excoriated by the moralist—the man is turning himself into an animal. The text accordingly provides an archetypal statement of the stories' ontological slippage between humans and animals. Such slippage, which here occurs in narrative "reality," but is elsewhere expressed by the figurative animalistic descriptions and imagery in general usage,[60] is of course powerfully reversed in the genre of the animal fable by the ascription of human characteristics to animals—an assumption that seems so straightforwardly nonrealistic that it would pass undocumented. Close examination of the ways in which this ascription operates, however, reveals complexities that allow investigation of genre sophistication and problematization.

Some of the animals' human characteristics are simply behavioral, accepted without comment: on 7b.49, an ape sorrows like a human over his favorite son's death; a lion with a thorn in his paw can rationally consider what would benefit him and be useful for his recovery; and his "nature" (9a.18) prompts him to approach a peasant. Such human behavior, however, has limits, though those limits are not always clearly defined. One example is when the humanized animal kingdom interacts with the human kingdom. In the ninth fable, a rooster and a hen act like humans, talking of buying and selling corn—until they go to stay with a human farmer and once again act like animals (11a.1–22); conversely, in the fable of the belling of the cat (14), the cat and the mice all seemingly coexist with humans, and yet they are not only capable of intelligent discussion and interaction among themselves, but behave like humans in more interactive ways, such as when the mice buy a bell (cf. 16b.28).

The convention rapidly becomes even more complicated. In some of the fables featuring humans, the animals are simply animals, mute and unintelligent (such as the twelfth fable's donkey, who is simply the three sons' inherited property). Conversely, in the fable of the ass and the lapdog (23), the human's lapdog is simply an animal with no evidence of any intellectual or other anthropomorphic characteristics—befitting its narrative role as a passive object of envy—but the ass that envies it philosophizes at length about fortune's cruelty. Their mutual owner is incapable of understanding the donkey when, attempting to emulate the lapdog, it jumps onto his lap; similarly, in the fable of the faithful watchdog (25), the thief seems incapable of understanding the dog's speech to him. Before attempting to establish this mutual incomprehensibility of human and animal in the tales, though, we should remember that in an earlier fable, the lion can speak to the shepherd. The differentiation between stories and even within them—the constant unmaking and remaking of the apparent rules of reality—seems at times a playful, comic attempt on the author's part. The narrator's comment about the injured lion—"He couldn't take a step; it would have helped if he had a horse to ride" (9a.14–15)—can only be predicated on authorial recognition of readerly ability to recognize the incongruity, and the slippage, between the fable's narrative and metanarrative levels, an ability predicated on audience knowledge of, and sophisticated ability to manipulate, genre conventions.

Such sophisticated consciousness of this and other sorts of slippage between various ontological weltanschauungen engenders another reaction by readers and characters alike, one seen earlier in the book: wonder. Whether it is the spectators who observe the seemingly "nonrealistic" act of the lion kissing the shepherd (where "no greater wonder had ever been seen," 10a.82–83); or, conversely, when the mouse, in the fable of the mouse and the weasel, sees the mousetrap for the first time and perceives it as a "wonder" (34a.65), which would only be the case for an anthropomorphized mouse; or the odd (though perfectly naturally explicable) sight of two men carrying their donkey, described as a wondrous event (*vunderlikhn zakhn*, 19b.78); or a peasant's bizarre behavior, interpreted by observers as "wondrous" and therefore sensible (cf. 27b.237–238)—all are encounters between the boundaries of levels of convention, or narrative law.

However, such apparently playful narrative slippage hardly precludes questions rising from the narrative's simple logic itself. According to the narrative of the fable of the fox, the raven, and the cheese, for example, the raven speaks before singing (5b.42); wouldn't that make him drop the cheese in his beak? A lion previously unable to walk can now run (9a.21); and a flayed wolf remains alive (18a.77–78). Other problems are logistical: in the fable of the false guardian (29), the narrative is less than clear about the use of money on the holiday, and the seeming inattention to the ensuing narrative difficulties may inform us about audiences' relative interest in specific narrative details.[61] It may be, however, that many seemingly erroneous details in this and other stories are actually attempts at humor, such as the falsely pious individual's recitation of penitential prayers on a holiday where they are omitted (38b.113). Such comedy is in turn predicated on audience understanding that this behavior's particular incongruity lies in its liturgical incorrectness, not simply its pretence at sanctimony, allowing us in passing to comment on the audience's lived knowledge of ritual.

More importantly for understanding of the text's "reality," though, the individual's narratively odd behavior now becomes explicable in a naturalistic, psychological context, allowing us to investigate whether and how our psychologized sense of the construction of reality is relevant here. Though the author takes pains to render narrative acts more plausible in several cases,[62] one particular story—the fable of the murdered Jew and the partridge—is particularly relevant. In a fable read in a book of animal fables, the narrative of a Jewish merchant treacherously murdered who, with his dying breath, claims an observing partridge will avenge him, clearly suggests an eventual supernatural and miraculous comeuppance for the murderer.

That is, the reader expects supernatural—or, within the book's provenance, generically natural—intervention by the partridge to reveal the crime. As the story unfolds, though, the murderer's discovery results from his own action: his need to giggle, mock, and make fun, apparently stemming from a psychological compulsion after he sees the aforementioned partridge caught and roasted.[63] The lord asks for an explanation of his laughter; his psychological need for confession renders his moment of ultimate freedom the scene of his downfall.

Perhaps it is ironic that at the moment of the Jew's murder it is the murderer who adopts the mantle of "reality," of throwing off the conventions of the animal fable genre: when the Jew says, "Do you see that partridge sitting on the tree? It will tell [the lord] of this," the murderer replies, "I pay no heed to partridge or grouse ... For they cannot talk or speak, no matter who wants to reveal it" (27b.51–60). But it is precisely the murderer's correctness in his claim, and his misinterpretation (proven retroactively) of the Jew's claim of the partridge's "talking" as supernatural, that lead to his downfall and apotheosize the error only made by the most basic fable reader: to mistake its power by substituting its "reality" for reality. His skepticism, after all, is still predicated on a modicum of belief; otherwise why such relief when the bird is roasted?

Such error—with compulsion that mirrors the confusion of ontological status but resolves by narrative's end to a more naturalistic mode, using the supernatural to do so—not only echoes our experience in *Macbeth* and *Faustus*, but touches on the very basis of the fable genre: the idea of the essential persona, the unchangeable ontological state of human beings (or the unchangeable overriding characteristic that defines them), which allows them to be symbolized by animals. Such an interest in essence—particularly through its inverse, the possibility (and fear of possibility) of human change—has become the subject of increasing study by scholars of the medieval and the early modern.[64] This will be returned to presently; suffice it to say for now that the centrality of unchanging human essence leads many of the fables that feature human characters to revolve around the exposure of hypocrisy and deceit to reveal a person's "real self." The fable of the greedy innkeeper (31),[65] whose kindness and generosity is revealed as deception when the bill comes due, is a case in point. His lodger's natural if paradoxical combination of weary recognition of this general sort of behavior (49b.115–125) and tragic surprise at "truly recognizing" it in the particular case of his host

(49b.147–149) reminds readers of their own perceptual shifts between idealism and cynicism about the human condition.

The same tale, though, offers an opportunity to see how these questions play out on the continuum of supernatural belief and skepticism, with the appearance of the vials containing the elixirs of life and death. These elixirs—which figure prominently in the innkeeper's comeuppance (cf. 50a.190)—are less important as particular wondrous entities (as per 50b.224) than in their instrumental role in illuminating the (narrative) universe's ability to reify things to their essential status: the righteous live and the wicked die. Such reification, however, is once more accomplished through such an implausible narrative action that it must be explained by psychological compulsion: the innkeeper, who has extorted these elixirs of death and life from his patrons, decides to test them by drinking the death elixir and having his wife revive him with the life elixir. Such stunningly stupid behavior by a man previously portrayed as the apotheosis of cunning—so stupid it threatens to undermine the tale itself—generates concomitant narratorial-authorial anxiety, and two dozen lines are accordingly dedicated (51a.310–326) to an attempted explanation about his incorrect reasoning and expectations. The attempt, again, can be methodologically significant: it indicates a problematic element, contextually defined, by virtue of its catalysis of authorial action which itself is predicated on the author's assumption of his reading audience's capability to cognize it as such.

A thematic solution might exist to the narrative's problem, perhaps accentuating the innkeeper's eternally acquisitive nature, his need to take everything, including the poison, into himself, but a more likely answer is based on a particular psychologized model of human behavior, particularly compulsive behavior, defining the latter as a drive towards reversion to the essence, which is in turn an externalized reflection of moral fate. The innkeeper takes the death elixir, in other words, because he *must* die, as the servant laughs because he *must* be punished, since evildoers *must* be. Such a characterization, while hardly "realistic" by our definition, can be logically seen as such on its own terms; such essential characterization and its relation to action—and the attempts to explain the action to avoid skepticism—can be useful in our examination of defining a particular group, which in turn will further refine our understanding of the audience as readers and as individuals.

Readership, Essence, and Gender

Our previous discussions have shown women to be a significant part of the audience for early modern Yiddish literature in general, and this work in particular, a significant deviation in the fable genre's general reception historically.[66] Given its masculine and masculinist origins, it may be unsurprising to find that numerous aspects of the *Seyfer Mesholim* reflect what Katz has called "the author's pervasive misogyny," its intended audience notwithstanding;[67] the work thus reflects not only the misogyny present within Jewish late medieval and early modern life more generally,[68] but also a particular literary and generic tradition. A brief examination of the most egregious stories in this regard allows us to investigate the portrayal of women and its relation to our questions of genre, "reality," essence, and readership.

The *Seyfer Mesholim*'s discussion of women occurs primarily in three fables, the only ones where female (human) characters are clearly the protagonists—the fable of the widow and the young guard (19), the fable of the flayed donkey (20), and the fable of the adulterous wife (30). In the first, a seemingly sober account of a bereaved, apparently pious widow almost immediately turns into a denunciation of women's essentially sexual and lustful nature, suggesting that their inconsolable grief simply derives from their current lack of sexual satisfaction and that with the arrival of another source, they will immediately abandon their virtuous state for its diametrical opposite.[69] Here, the grieving widow's consolation comes in the form of a young man sent to watch over a thief's hanged body; his first desire to satiate physical urges, a longing for food and drink (22b.39), is transformed as the two converse in a quasi-philosophical discourse in which his support of living joyously and unmindful of grief is connected immediately to the taking of a new sexual partner (23a.53–60).[70]

Bad as the young man's behavior may be, his is clearly merely a catalytic role; once the widow has made love to him, she willingly assists her partner—who has gotten into trouble, as the thief's body he was charged to watch has disappeared—by exhuming her husband and hanging him on the gallows in the thief's place. Adding insult to injury, she not only does so happily, but "curse[s] and revile[s]" her old husband in the process, wishing him "sorrow and pain" (23a.93–94). The moralist addresses the story particularly to "faithless women whose behinds are always itching" (23b.101), but the narrative's insistence on women's capacity to shift radically from piety to faithlessness, and even, subversively, its revelry in the exercise of women's deceptive ingenuity, allow us to speculate that the author's charges may be broader, possibly illuminating his view of women's essential nature—that piety only masks true ugliness. Efforts to characterize women's nature as essentially deceptive or morally vacillating are therefore unsurprisingly summed up in an animal comparison: a woman can be compared to a bee, since she "speak[s] words sweet as honey while behind his back she stabbed and stung" (46a.364–367).

Such characterization is accentuated in the next fable; its protagonist's identity as a prostitute means no necessity exists to erect a scaffolding of virtuous disguise around the essential feminine characteristic (authorially speaking) of sexual promiscuity. Given this freedom, the author moves on to feature another unvirtuous, "essential" feminine aspect: vanity. The prostitute is anxious to hear others' opinions of her "day and night" (24a.40); upon discovering their uniformly negative character, she broods about how to make people "stop talking about her and forget about her" (24a.41–42). Repentance or increased virtuous actions never occur to her; instead, the narrator has her resort to a display of "conventional" feminine ingenuity through morally opprobrious theft and violence. Stealing a donkey, she flays it and drives it to the marketplace, beating it to ensure its arrival: when the townspeople see it, "[t]hey had so much to say about the donkey that they couldn't talk about them both" (24a–b.73–75). True, the story's end implicates the morally distractible audience, not only the woman,[71] and its moral—in an attempt to express socially recognizable realities along with ideal behavioral norms, as discussed in detail later—focuses on reputation's transitory nature, rather than sin's permanence, but one can hardly conceive of this as a positive feminine portrait.

Such assumed essential characteristics are, in their own way, also social "facts" internalized into the text, and coexist uneasily with their various interpretations by author and readers alike. The resulting dynamic process—an interpretive process—is neatly adumbrated in the final fable focusing on a woman, the fable of the adulterous wife. As in the previous two fables, the adulterous woman's cunning is employed to improve her situation (logistically, not morally). Here, her deception is achieved not only through her clever lies to her husband, but also through specifically gendered behaviors such as cooking food and the excellent performance of other conventional housewifely duties. The double-edged nature of her performance of these tasks in the wrong spirit—to engage in activities that fulfill her gendered role while simultaneously fulfilling her essentially deceptive role—can be seen in the pun about her housework, which renders the house "clean/pure" (*reyn*, 43a.77). Obviously, one of these readings is highly ironic.

As the narrative situation worsens, she commits greater crimes (again, theft; she robs her husband of all his savings when she leaves with her lover). Here, however, the accusation against the woman is complicated in the assignation of external, contingent causes. Her adulterous activities (if not, perhaps, desires), it is suggested, are activated by the combination of two separate, external factors: her overly pious husband's inattentiveness to her, in the bedroom in particular (thus failing to satisfy her essential sexual appetite) and in the home more generally (thus not assuaging her vanity, which needs satiating).[72] Such a construction explains the moralist's ostensibly puzzling, disproportionately long attack on the husband, compared to the wife, in the epimyth: she, after all, can do no better, but he has the capacity for responsibility and improvement. Narratively, the illustrated improvement occurs at the story's end, where the husband, in an aria of regret, recognizes his erroneous actions and accepts both his fate and his horns (as we have seen, not entirely metaphorically).

This insistence on a lived, "worldly" approach on the moralist's part, which deemphasizes piety and time spent in the synagogue or house of study in favor of careful attention to his household and the world around him, is portrayed as an *interpretive* as well as behavioral shift: the husband's foolishness is located in his incapacity to assess the correct "significance" (see 47a.458) of the facts he perceives. Upon his return to find an empty house and missing money, he quickly concludes his wife must be taking her jewelry and his savings to "lend to poor brides. In this I see again her boundless piety" (47a.472–473). (In fact, he is so unmanned by folly and by fact that he seems to become the woman, setting the table for her and waiting for her return from her apparent dancing!) Giving others the benefit of the doubt is generally praised in a conventional moral text. Here, however, mindful of skepticism—about moral behavior and the author's interpretive authority—the narrative addresses these tensions by throwing the conflict between an idealistic vision of the world as it should be and the skeptic's (or cynic's) version of the world as it is into stark and sharp relief.[73]

Indeed, this character's interpretive crisis—matched by that of his author—mirrors the reader's critical process. The author's almost parenthetical aside (thus vital for our purposes)—"Surely one needn't sympathize with one who wants to be too saintly, as this man was" (48a.581–582)—suggests his concern that readers will precisely so sympathize, particularly given that the man's pious behavior accords quite well with the model behavior valorized in other works. The narrator's assertion of such behavior as folly—in narrative *and* moral terms—jars the reader out of conventional categories, both of moralistic literature more generally and of the fable's desire to establish simple essential equivalences (villainous woman, pious man). In doing so, he reminds us of the nuances of the fabulist genre, which occupies a *liminal* state between essential ideal and experiential reality; he also, however, acknowledges readers' abilities to read texts against the desired grain, based on their own conventional codes and "subversive" desires.[74]

Such desires to read and interpret differently are now particularly unsurprising, given authorial positioning of some significant portion of the intended audience as deceivers, whores, and adulteresses. To expand the fable's audience from its elite, classically erudite male body of readers to a more universal one certainly allows for commercial success, and, perhaps more importantly, morally aids a group perceived as essentially problematic. Simultaneously, such expansion guarantees awareness that the latter group by its very nature—both as female readers with experience of and complex affect to misogyny, and as (from the author's perspective) an essentially deceptive, rebellious gender—may *naturally* "misread" narrative elements, or, perhaps more precisely, read them differently. The author accomplishes this in two ways: by propounding a particular ideology, and by establishing an authorial and authoritative interpretive schema by virtue of an explicit and strong narrator to attempt to persuade readers of that ideology. The remainder of the chapter will address these two aspects.

The Fable and Its Moral(s): Between Ideology and Story

One of the *Ku-bukh*'s earliest bibliographic mentions—by Shabbatai Bass in 1680—explicitly yokes the fables to their surrounding moral framework: "and after each fable its moral is brought out, in rhyme in the Yiddish language."[75] Bass' conjunction of the two parts of the text is echoed by the *Seyfer Mesholim*'s title page, where Wallich reminds and perhaps even instructs his audience how to read his work: "In each case the explanation teaches how people (*laytn*) should conduct themselves" (1a.7–8). The desired conduct is more explicitly detailed in the work's preface, adapted by Wallich from the *Ku-bukh*'s: "Young, rich, and poor; to each [the work] shows how he should flee from evil counsel so deep" (2a.11). Though we will return to the audience's economically stratified nature, since economic questions are at the book's moral and ideological heart, our first focus must be on the work's introductory development of a larger moral, psychological, and cognitive framework of human action and decision making that can be tested and exemplified in the author's fables and their morals.

Such a framework depends on the rejection of others' deeply seductive "evil counsel." It acknowledges the role of depression—or "very gloomy things"—in creating a mental condition easily susceptible to moral error, and is mindful of the power of certain mental states—particularly covetousness and arrogance—to lead to inattention to divine decrees and desires, particularly a lack of Torah study and thus total moral failure, which one pridefully "thinks ... will be forgiven him without any reproach" (2b.17). Such attitudes are particularly powerful and prevalent, as the introduction accentuates, if they result from wealth: the statement the author attributes to the morally problematic individual, *ikh raykh unt frum bin* ("I am rich and pious"), can be interpreted as an attack on the identification (not an uncommon one in any age) of the accumulation of wealth with the attainment of moral virtue (2b.15).

Like other contemporary works, the introduction locates (im)moral behavior within an eschatological framework of divine reward and punishment in the world to come, as well as emphasizing morality's role in hastening the messianic redemption. Notably, these considerations are again rendered in economically linked language, though here in precisely the opposite manner than before: the author writes that when one is snatched from the world "like a fish from the river," the "un-rich/impure soul" (*di neshome nit raykh*) will be "washed with soaps and lye" (2b.16). Conventional economic structures—as opposed to moral ones—are irrelevant in a world which itself privileges essential nature, truly defined, as the book will attempt to show, in moral terms above all: neither gold nor currency is "good" there, the author writes, presumably in the word's commercial and moral senses. Rather, the man will be beaten about the head, punished with snakes, and his flesh and bones will be withered in a "hot fire."

Despite theoretical awareness of the wicked's fate, the author notes that individuals rarely translate this knowledge into practice, showing the shrewd if cynical insight into human capacity for self-delusion and behavior more generally that will permeate the work: rather, the individual, simply believing the rules are inapplicable to him, "goes to his rest with good hope" (2b.24). The author notes similarly in his invocation: "We allow ourselves to be led astray by evil temptations. But we should perceive that they lead us into the depth of hell (*in der tifn heln*), and we should note how they bring about our fall. Yet we do not obey our virtuous inclinations (*yetser tov*), and for that we will suffer great torment when we arrive at the last judgment. That is where one finally realizes what one has come to" (3b.13–17). The work's contrast between its warnings' emphasis on physicality and its careful anatomization of the abstractions and ethereality of the soul and of psychological calculation may serve in this case as a conceptually metonymic version of the fabulistic structure generally speaking, where the practical must always illuminate the abstract.

Such emphases in the introduction are not merely—or even primarily—intended to provide a subtle thematic correlation of the book's operative medium to its thematic message, particularly given how such juxtapositions can easily be read as conventional statements. More straightforwardly, the author's juxtaposition of the book's commercial success with the Jews' ultimately desired goal—he implicitly connects his book's purchase, dissemination, and reading with the messianic redemption (1a.13)—reflects his ingenuity at yoking the moral issues he raised concerning wealth to his own commercial interests. As we have seen, he argues that wealth provides a psychological hindrance to moral elevation, and should be disregarded (asserting "neither great nor small should mind being humble as sheep," 2b.28). Further, he suggests that people—especially his problematized female audience—should rid themselves of some of their luxurious assets (particularly their clothing, which potentially expresses not only wealth, but immodesty and arguably sexual license) and engage in economically and morally unimpeachable hard, prosaic work. Both strategies will, however, necessarily result in capital accumulation, which, problematically, creates the wealth that leads to moral corruption, so the money must be spent.

Luckily, the author just happens to have on hand the ideologically approved solution to the ethical conundrum he has created: the purchase of a specific moral commodity, that is, this book:

"Every girl, even if it grieves her, should sell part of her clothing / And do anything she can to earn money, whether baking bread or force-feeding geese, / And earn even more by spinning with the spindle, or if she's shut in, by plucking geese. / Velvet and silk do not adorn like this book that I'm writing ... Don't miss it at any price, if you like it. You won't be cheated if you buy something like this ... Keep the money together that you have accumulated, and don't buy anything else, but come running / To get my book" (2b–3a.29–34).

The text's concern about *any* accumulation emphasizes what might be referred to as the book's "paranoid style"; though wealth is specifically demonized, all classes—the book's *universal* readership—are subject to these economic processes' morally deteriorating effects, which can be reversed through employing those same economic processes to purchase the book in question.

Audience members reading and debating the book's purchase and dissemination may well have noticed the potential hypocrisy of this sales pitch masquerading as moral guidance (to say nothing of the skepticism engendered by the author's assurances of the buyer's *not* being cheated). Such authorial motives notwithstanding, correlation between spreading moral virtue and his own commercial success—even success derived through pious denunciations of wealth, the result of such success—may be sincerely meant, if logically paradoxical. This contradictory desire for and implicit valuation of commercial success and the awareness and denunciation of its corrosive effects mirror general communal desires for both piety and luxury; the resulting debate about wealth's morally ambiguous value and its association with this worldly and ultimate reward will be a focus of this chapter and the next.

A final example taken from the introductory material illustrates the point, and leads to a discussion of the fable literature itself. As mentioned, the introduction refers to death by describing the soul as snatched "like a fish from the river"—an image notable for its animalistic nature in a book of animal fables as well as its emphasis on the suddenness of encounters with mortality. In the first version in the *Ku-bukh*, the quick death clearly refers only to the wicked individual, not the righteous man. Wallich, however, shifts the order of the original texts' lines to place the phrase "Too quickly and swiftly comes one's end; before he turns around he is extinguished" (2b.21) *between* descriptions of the good and the wicked man, thus potentially applying it to both types of individual. Admittedly, such transposition was done at least in part to facilitate the acrostic spelling of Wallich's name and location, and so one may still read the text (though less intelligibly) to refer to the wicked man. One may also suggest, though, such a shift reflects Wallich's wish to acknowledge the moral ambiguities articulated in his text, his aims, and his conventions, which he anxiously suspects are read and understood by his sophisticated audience—ambiguities apotheosized here in the fact that early death, as is well-known, comes not only to the wicked, and texts attempting to reflect, order, and speak truth to human nature and existence must grapple with this.

Taken further, we can say that such a gap between lived experience and schematic moral framework is anagogically recapitulated not only as the gap between the stories and their morals, to be reflected on by the ideologically minded author, the carefully attentive and skeptical reader, and the later critic; but it is also the gap essential to the general understanding of the fabulistic genre itself, which relies on the awareness of the gap between realism and fantasy (and its bridgeability), between "reality" and the fiction that reflects (while distorting in animal form) the essence of that reality. Seeing how all these elements—ideological, epistemological, economic—fit together necessitates a close look at the fables, their morals, and their structure.

Katz has described Wallich's reordering of the *Ku-bukh*'s first five fables as "apparently pointless" and "puzzling" in light of his "deliberate approach."[76] From our perspective, however, emphasizing Wallich's efforts to create a moralistic text which itself acknowledges moral ambiguity, and the fable's implication, structurally and generically, in this effort, his movement of the fable of the fox and the stork to the primary place is perfectly sensible. Perhaps more than any other fable, it expresses the ambiguities of morality and of the genre by definition, providing a conceptual overview of the work to come. In closely analyzing the first few fables, we may begin to articulate the outline of Wallich's thinking and its textual presentation; a brief discussion of many of the other fables will assist discussion of these specific ideas and other topics relevant to our investigation.

As may be recalled, the fable of the fox and the stork[77] concerns a tricky fox who serves food to his friend the stork in a manner rendering it impossible for the latter to eat, due to his long beak; after weathering the fox's mockery, the stork has his revenge by inviting him to a banquet where the food is placed in a long, narrow vessel, putting it out of the fox's reach. The stork gets the last word, and the fox is repaid for his trickery "in equal measure" (5a.96–97).[78] The epimyth, or *muser-haskel*, states its lesson clearly: "Anyone who wants to trick or fool his friends or companions is surely not pious or virtuous and will soon be repaid in equal measure" (5a.102–104). The move from the fable's active form (where the stork does the repaying) to the *muser-haskel*'s passive one (where the repaying agency is left undefined) reflects the uneasy fit of the narrative's moral lesson and normative ideological practice as the moralist would have it: airy simplicities about an "eye for an eye" notwithstanding, moral revenge is God's business, not for the would-be righteous. Additionally, the moral ignores the active deceit of the stork's behavior—narratively unproblematic but problematic in a moral lesson, catalyzing reader awareness of the gap between story and teaching.

Such distancing from the narrative consciously detracts (and distracts) from the lessons learned from the narrative's delightful play itself, with its mocking, comedic content and tone. The tension between narrative joy and epimythic dryness may well be inherent to the genre's form, but it is particularly notable here, as it is our first notice of the psychologically—and thus readerly—motivating forces of mockery, shame, and honor that serve as an almost alternative ideological construct, deriving far more from surrounding non-Jewish culture than internal Jewish traditions and demonstrating generic and readerly cultural porosity.[79] Such psychological centrality is concretized in the fox's primary, catalyzing role as someone who mocks (*shpotn*, 4a.29, see also 4b.74) the stork.

More, his role here—as a sly deliverer of sarcastic and witty remarks (4a.25–35) and a cosmopolitan, discriminating oenophile (4b.55)—is that assigned to him in fabular literature more generally. It is unsurprising, then, that in this now first-placed fable, not only is the archetypal European (and, due to *Mishlei Shualim*, the archetypal Jewish) fable animal featured, but featured in a story explicitly and narratively dependent upon his conventionally defined "essential" characteristics. It is precisely their physical features and their assigned roles as representative creatures of fable that enable the tricks catalyzing the fable's action (were it not for the fox's snout and the stork's beak, the dinners would have been safely—and unentertainingly—eaten).

Simultaneously, the reader is reminded that the "essentiality" of the essential characteristic necessary for the operation and interpretation of the fable is itself conventional and socially constructed. After all, whatever the objectively sly nature of a fox is, that slyness is hardly recognized in reality through its use of sarcasm or its oenophilia, nor is its essential wisdom illuminated through its attention to detail and capacious memory except in the nonrealistic, fabular world—where it is perfectly natural (4a.24). Similarly, the fox's proverbial propensity to mischief is clearly recognized as a playfully artificial development within the readers' conventional schema of characterological assignations. Other seemingly jarring details playfully but significantly remind the readers—through their violation of the "rules of reality"—of the narrative's essentially artificial nature: the fox and stork's unremarked eating and ownership of other animals (such as a milk cow; see 4b.61–62), or the logistics of the pair's handshake (where the fox grabs the stork by the wing, 4a.15–16).

This book's exploration of the fables' essentialist aspect develops as the book continues: the second story, of the fox and the raven (5a–6a), relies once again on the fox's explicit identification with wisdom and cleverness as well as the raven's association with its proverbial propensity to thieve (in this case, cheese, 5a.1). The fox's wisdom here, transcending that displayed in the first tale, is his ability not only to recognize another fabulistic animal's essential physical attributes but its conventionally assigned characterological attributes. Here, he plays on the bird's proverbial vanity, and uses the raven's known love of shiny objects to couch his clever appeal more seductively (5b.21–22, 27–29).

Indeed, the raven's behavior—predicated again on its vanity, here its false belief in its voice's beauty—is precisely illustrative of folly through the narrative's reliance (and the raven's moral obligation to rely) on knowledge external to the narrative about its conventional proverbial "essential feature": its naturally harsh, rasping voice. The *muser haskel*'s statement that "a man who does not know himself is surely a fool" (6a.77) is predicated on the fable's luxury of establishing such knowledge as firm and essential, not subjective. "[C]onsider well who you are and observe yourself in the mirror," the moralist counsels (6a.79–80), but a highly subjective observer's close look does not necessarily yield subjective truth. Put another way, such narratives—and the concomitant advice drawn from them by the moralist—beg the question: is the fable a mirror, reflecting humans with essential characteristics and natures similar to those of the represented animals, which are therefore unchangeable and inescapable, or are human essences changeable—presumably a necessary assumption for a didactic moral text to function?

Such potentially destabilizing concerns are thematically reflected (the unintentional pun excused) in the third fable; Wallich's intentional reordering of it from its original location in the *Ku-bukh* suggests an awareness of structural and metageneric concerns apparently less important to the first version's author. First, the fable of the dog's reflection—where a dog, holding a piece of meat in his mouth, drops it upon seeing his reflection in a stream because of his greedy desire to get the meat held by the "other dog"—now directly provides an elegant variation of the identical motif advanced in the previous fable (greedy animal with food in its mouth loses it by opening its mouth and dropping it), perhaps reason enough for the changed position. But the particular catalyst for that motif's iteration—the dog's view of its own reflection and misidentification—allows for not only an organic link between the third *story* and the second *moral* (since the trope of mirroring and reflection appeared only in the latter fable's epimyth), but also allows Wallich to suggest a tentative answer to the question posed about essence above which that moral generated. The narrative clearly shows how it *is* possible for these essential creatures to mistake their own identity (and, by extension, their essence), to look into a mirror and misunderstand themselves. Such deception, which according to the narrative stems from the dog's "foolish sense[s]" (*zayn nereshter zin*, 6b.10), is reminiscent of the discourse of illusion and sense-deceiving in the early modern period more generally discussed with reference to Shakespeare and Marlowe in the previous chapter. And so the fable collection, through a process of subtle reorientation, establishes its continued relevance as it expands and redefines the limits that earlier instantiations of the genre (that is, the earlier stories) have created—in much the same manner as we have seen the "rules of reality" be unmade and remade.

Such increasing complexity and ambiguity are paralleled in the work's rapidly complicating moral structures. In both the first and second fables, the character who takes revenge goes unpunished: and the second fable's *muser-haskel*, which focuses on the vainglorious and self-deceiving, does not mention this. Within the narrative itself, the raven's behavior and his understanding of it raises explicitly moral questions. He attributes his success in stealing the cheese to God's assistance (*er meynt got hot in glaykh berutn*, 5b.8–9), and though the moralist attempts to prove such thought a sign of the raven's self-deception, the narrative's end and the fox's triumph hardly convince us of the association of fortune and virtue. If anything, the story ends with the gleeful and almost gratuitous addition of insult to injury: not only does the fox gain the cheese at the raven's expense, but mocks the raven for his loss. The use of the word *shpot/geshpet* (5b.71–72) is indicative here; the associated mockery, trickery, and language of gaming (see *shpil*, 5b.48), remind us of Marlowe's tricks and games, and of the vital moral, epistemic, and even ontological role of not only deception, but self-deception, in the early modern perspective. This role's centrality can be further contextualized by examining the third fable's moral.

As previously noted, the second and third fables are structurally and narratively similar, but the characters' differing motivations (the raven's vanity and the dog's greed) allow for differing moral accounts that focus separately on intent and action, as well as the introduction of an additional level of ambiguity. After warning against greed, the third *muser-haskel* reads: "For everyone should be satisfied with what God has decreed for him (*beshert*) and not increase his possessions with unjust gain. And he should live cheerfully all his life with the possessions that God has given him. For it's all a matter of luck and fortune" (*mazel un brokhe*, 6b.31–34). We will return in greater detail to the moralist's particularly economic turn in his definition of contentment. For now, it is enough to note that the moralist, using the fable form to uncover essential truths obscured by deception and trickery, by others' flaws and by one's own, here champions a kind of class-based essentialism undergirded by knowledge and understanding of one's place in the financial order, a place theologically guaranteed and upheld (it is God who gives possessions).

The moralist's next sentence, however, accentuates the skeptical response, which yields a seemingly paradoxical conclusion: such essentialism, resulting in ostensibly unchangeable states, is subject to the ebbs and flows, the transformations and reversals, of Fortune, which is simultaneously an integral part of the world's essential nature but acts to uproot essentiality: like the river that washes away the dog's meat, Fortune proves the nonuniformity and instability present within unchanging nature, and thus the possibility of undermining every authoritative, primary textual message. Accordingly, the next fable discusses Fortune in its most meaningful instantiation: it takes as its topic nothing less than children's life and death, addressing the seeming capriciousness that characterized that phenomenon in the early modern period.

In the fourth fable, of the favored and despised monkey children, an ape with two sons, suddenly beset by a ferocious lion, literally attempts to throw his less favored son to the lions to save himself and his beloved child; his chosen stratagem, though—putting the hated monkey on his back so he can throw him off at any time—fails when the latter hangs on tightly, and the beloved son is eaten instead.[80] The moralist could have explicitly interpreted the narrative as another example of trickery gone wrong—as deceptiveness' ultimate failure, building on the theme's primacy in the earlier stories. Instead, he writes: "This fable surely applies to many a foolish man who acts in this manner. He cannot know which one will flourish and which will die; which will survive to be the heir after his death. Therefore he should love all his children: the girls as well as the boys, those who are grown and those still young" (7b.52–55).

The moral accentuates Fortune's wild powers, for good and ill. The ostensible moral failing displayed—favoritism—is apparently not *inherently* morally problematic; rather, its failure lies solely in its indeterminacy. The universe is unclear (at least to our limited perceptual capabilities) because of Fortune's chaotic and disordering effects (here personified as the wild, chaotic lion). Such indeterminacy may be retroactively clarified, revealing how Fortune has acted to truly yield ultimate "essential nature," but it highly complicates any attempt at the kind of knowledge-based action advanced earlier—again generating readerly skepticism. In its own way, Fortune is therefore also a kind of subjective trickery and deceit, insofar as it obscures (but only to us) the universe's working order.

In fact, careful attention to and recognition of this chaotic force, whose violence, primacy, and real-world presence pose significant challenge to abstract theological moralism and may even overpower the ostensible idealized moral order, are crucial. The fifth fable serves Wallich as exemplary in this regard; he may have relocated it here from its original position in the *Ku-bukh* for this reason. In the fable of the raven and the eagle, a poor raven discovers a carcass and, singing for joy, alerts the eagle; the latter's fury at not being propitiated with part of the carcass leads him to take the entire thing for himself. The fable can clearly be read, particularly in light of the last epimyth just seen by readers, as a call for submission to feudalistic, chivalric, or analogous political and monarchical hierarchy, a hierarchy generated by Fortune but invested with moral valence. The eagle's angry comments—"For you wanted to keep the carcass to yourself and didn't summon me. What way is that to treat your lord? (*azoy tustu daynem hern*) ... You know that I am the king" (8a.29–33)—might imply his snatching the carcass from the raven is an appropriate punishment for the latter's violation of this hierarchical order.

The explicitly stated moral, however, questions not only submission to this worldly order, but to a higher one as well: "This fable surely informs you concerning one who finds something (*fint eyn funt*) and cannot keep silent about it. His own lips bring about his downfall" (8a.39–41). The moralist's comments fly in the face of the biblical mandate to return lost property,[81] to say nothing of the apparent injunction to defraud the regnant government of its proper share. Perhaps the moralist yields to a vision of Fortune—in the guise of the sudden, lucky find—as regeneration of a new set of essential states, which in turn redetermine the application and construction of rules. Such accommodation to reality—albeit in abstracted framework—may help to alleviate readerly skepticism while simultaneously complicating moral message (and the place of moral literature).

This multivocality—the deconstructive tension of chaotic challenge to order acknowledged and purportedly recreated and reconstituted in the ideal model—is outlined in the first few fables' interplay between fable and story, essence and antiessence, and accentuated by their careful reordering; in the remainder of the book, this is developed at great length and with great nuance. A structure of recapitulation and variation already appears in the sixth and next fable, which diverges markedly from its predecessors in featuring human protagonists.[82] Playfully addressing the genre's tendency to compare humans to animals, those comparisons here are not effaced so much as made metaphor: the lady, mocking the chivalric swain who talentlessly and discordantly serenades her, compares him to an animal—in this case, an ass (8b.32–39)—explicitly and at length, an obviously generically self-reflexive observation providing another opportunity to speculate on the question of humanity's essentially animalistic nature. The story's seeming moral, presented here in the narrative, rather than the epimyth, is that the man "never undertook to sing again for he learned *that it did not become him*" (*dos es iz im nit voyl an zam*, 8b.52), a reminder of the dangers of attempting to escape your essential nature, which, as in other stories, will lead to "mockery (*eyn shpot*) in everyone's eyes" (8a.46).

A similar fable, of the raven and its borrowed plumage (fable 21), suggests the inevitable failure of attempts to escape one's essence: though the raven, who denudes itself of its own feathers and cloaks itself in those of others, enjoys temporary success, his eventual discovery leads to the feathers' removal by their rightful owners, leaving him with none at all and exposure to great shame (*shand*; 25a.62). The raven's desire to change his physical essence, expressed in physical form, can change neither his image nor his moral status, as his later actions (thieving and deception) prove. However, the moralist's original application of the tale, a lesson of arguably moral essence, to one "who doesn't want to know himself" (25a.66), gives way to an excoriation of those attempting to change their economic, not moral, states: "so it is good advice that one to whom God has provided no wealth ought not to make a show with other people's goods, and should not covet more" (25a.71–73).

Such insistence on subordination to the current socioeconomic hierarchy—an insistence that flows from the acceptance of economically essentialist states—continues in the next story. In the fable of the ass in the lion's skin (fable 22), the ass's foolishness stems from his identification of superficial appearance with true essence: he "was full of joy at having found this fine garment. He primed himself for wondrous deeds. He thought he was the equal of a lion" (25b.21–24). The "wondrous deeds," characterologically and essentially leonine, are cast here into a socioeconomic and bourgeois context, not the expected chivalric and epic one: the ass's brave quest is no more (and no less) than rebellion against his master the miller, who loads him down with sacks and beats him (see 25b.28–31). However, modern readers' expectations of authorial sympathies generated from the portrait of the ass as downtrodden workingman—particularly given the broad and ostensibly economically differentiated audience of the vernacular—are frustrated first by the ass's essential (and conventional) identification as the apotheosis of foolishness; second, by the story's general narrative-moral thrust, which parallels this attempt at economic change with the problematized attempt to change essence articulated earlier in the book, establishing readerly conventions of approved and disapproved behavior; and third, and perhaps most intriguingly, the story's great emphasis on, and sympathy for, the miller's perspective.

The reader learns (26a.50–54) that while the miller had indeed cruelly beaten the donkey and fed it little, his loss of the donkey results, as both he and the narrator inform us with great pathos, in his and his children's impoverishment. Beyond our sympathies, our identification with and admiration for the miller stems also from our analogized positioning to him, particularly in his wise ability to look beyond false essence to see true essence. He is capable (cf. 26a.65) of recognizing his donkey by its ears, the ineradicable aspect of its true essence, after first using a cognitive, interpretive process: "He looked at it from this side and that, and finally it seemed to him that it was he. For in size it was the same as the donkey he had lost" (26a.63–67). The narrative's development—first establishing identification with the ass, problematizing that identification through readerly knowledge and understanding of the work's conventional and ideological structures, and then providing an oppositional identification—not only provides ideological signposts for readers' accommodation to contemporary socioeconomic hierarchies, but also acknowledges, by the very efforts it takes to do so, its readers' subversive or revolutionary desires requiring domestication.[83]

The following fable, of the donkey and the lapdog, similarly employs the donkey to symbolize someone attempting to escape his own essential (socioeconomic) status, but more explicitly incorporates the element of Fortune. The donkey envies the lapdog, whose job, due only to Fortune's vicissitudes, is merely to entertain his lord and live in luxury, as compared to his own lot, full of backbreaking labor and beatings. The donkey's attempt to switch jobs involves his pleasing the lord (extremely unsuccessfully) through song; the author may see his harsh, braying voice as analogous to the fruitless, annoying complaints of those challenging contemporary socioeconomic hierarchies. The donkey's fate in the narrative—to be beaten bloody by his lord, who interprets the donkey's efforts to climb into his master's lap as violent ones—simply and purely expresses the entire structure of class war in brief. The hierarchies are justified within a moral context: the moralist counsels acceptance of God's gifts, manifold or lacking, suggesting that one "should eat his bread in good spirit and not try to equal the lord and the rich man. And one should be satisfied with little as well as with much. If God wishes it thus, he should refresh himself with it and not strive against it" (27a.66–69).

Such a message of subordination and acceptance is difficult to accept, activating readers' skepticism on ideological grounds in a manner parallel to their skepticism on epistemic or narrative grounds in manners discussed elsewhere in the chapter. Accordingly, the author creates several "safety valves" to help his message's bitterness. The first and most powerful, as we have seen, is his allowance and acknowledgment of the possibility for change in essential (read: socioeconomic) status. Such change, however, by definition cannot come from individuals' volitional actions, emerging, instead, from Fortune's quasi-miraculous operation in the world.

Fable 26, the fable of the peasant and the scribe, is illustrative. The story itself is straightforward enough, narratively speaking: a foolish peasant loads his donkey with stones on one side and silk on the other to "balance" the two sides; he meets a scribe (*melamed*) who attempts to convince him of the error of his ways. The story's end, however, diverges significantly from our expectations: we would imagine the wise scholar will be vindicated and the fool will suffer, but precisely the opposite occurs. It is precisely because the peasant ignores the scholar's advice to discard the stones that, upon his arrival at a town where whetstones are in high demand due to local edict,[84] he can sell his stones extremely profitably.

The story can be read as tongue in cheek, and internal evidence of a comic tone undoubtedly exists.[85] The story's rejection of the *melamed*'s approach may be a vilification of his desire to change his own economic state; it is, in fact, his disparagement of his own job—his own essence—that leads to the peasant's rejecting his advice. But the story's attack against one person's change of economic state is mirrored by its acceptance of—and playful exultation in—the other's: one can indeed gain a fortune, it tells us, but only through Fortune. Indeed, the moralist suggests in an epimyth that challenges conventional views of "moral guidance" that "one should seek advice from someone for whom the stars are favorable and in a period when things are going fortunately for him. And one should place oneself in the company of such people. Then he will easily enjoy a large measure of Fortune and God will give him happiness and prosperity" (28a.298–301). Even God is seemingly implicated in—if not subordinate to—Fortune's force.

Fortune's operation in human affairs, though, is not often presented as revolutionary, but generally as enforcing a conservative order. Such presentation is apparent in the fable of the false guardian (29), where a merchant, taken in by an old man's religious hypocrisy, entrusts him with his purse over the holiday: upon his return to claim it, the keeper denies any knowledge of the article, plunging the merchant into poverty. He is saved by the fortunate arrival of a second, clever merchant, who outsmarts the old man and restores the first merchant's fortunes—in both senses of that word.

The story, which features numerous themes relevant to our discussion,[86] prominently features Fortune: the second merchant, who explicitly says that "God sent me to be his good fortune (*mazel*, 42a.460)," is instrumental in instantiating the worldview the narrator expresses earlier: that "it is the case that all things must come to an end (*oys gang*, 39b.208–209)." Though this may simply mean that things will work out for the best, it more likely suggests that they will return to their essential states, those dictated by God and Fortune originally, and that the universe will intervene so as to assure that return. The story can in fact be seen as structured between characters' warring interpretations of *mazel*, as the first merchant believes *mazel* has brought him to the old man (38b.120), and the old man—when no one else is around, so it is not part of his falsely pious show—seems genuinely thankful to God for sending him the merchant (38b–39a.133, 140–145).

Though the old man's impulse in so thinking is now comprehensible—after all, if Fortune is blessed by God, why can't he view a credulous merchant's fortunate arrival as God's blessing?—he has incorrectly construed the situation; Fortune has actually arrived to lead to his unmasking and downfall, to the resolution and appearance of his true state. Such a story, by reinforcing the essentiality of economic states through Fortune's intervention—the rich merchant, despite temporary setbacks, ultimately remains rich—reminds the reader that though Fortune's wheel keeps turning, it may well turn back to where it began.

Given the rareness of Fortune's transformative changes—and the recognition of such within the text—a second safety valve is necessitated: acknowledgment of the naturalness and justification of audience envy and anger deriving from recognition of the unfairness of such essential difference (particularly in an economic context). In the fable of the dog and the cow (28), a dog, angry with his lot in life compared to the cow's, becomes homicidally angry and attempts to kill the cow—a significant exacerbation of the similar dynamic illustrated with the donkey and the lapdog discussed above. This fable, though, dissipates these tensions not only by playing them out in a vicarious, fictional setting to achieve readerly catharsis—true of all the fables—but by developing and accentuating the notion of the great chain of being, particularly stressing the difficulties and obligations of all life's stations that go unrecognized by those within other stations. The farmer, representing the God's eye (and moralist's) perspective, explains in an argument to his wife and thus to the story's readers both animals' respective importance, and the specific functional variance directing their different treatments.[87]

Still, the fable argues that individuals' failure to comprehend their—and everyone's—appropriate place in an overarching system leads to systemic, even metaphysical destruction, through the inevitable creation of evil, seen here as morality's inversion, as the latter is defined as proper acceptance of essential function. The dog, in its ontologically problematic frustration, swears by the thieves whose function it is to drive away (35b.68–70), and his evil plan to murder the cow manifests itself in persuading the latter to act inessentially, like a dog, or at least to marry one. (Such (attempted) miscegenation seems to refer not to relationships between Jews and non-Jews, but rather to changes in domestic and financial station.) In the cow's foolish acceptance of that offer, and her subsequent death by drowning at the dog's hands—as she lies on her back, he pushes her underwater as they attempt to cross a river—the fabulist illustrates the clear inability to cross a liminal line of essence (symbolized in that dangerous physical barrier), and the personal and moral destruction resulting from not only the attempt, but from envy's role in catalyzing that attempt: it not only destroys one, but takes others along. The author relies on the reader's identification with the morally problematic emotions the situation engenders, and then manipulates the narrative to firmly reject those emotions' necessary corollaries.

In the seventh fable, the lion is brought low by a thorn in his paw, which is then removed by a shepherd; even seeming divergences from the identity of animal and essence employ a temporary device (here, the lion's weakness) for narrative development (the plot depends on the eventual restoration of the lion's ferocious identity).[88] Still, such violent transitions of essence—from potency to impotency to potency once more—not only illustrate our previous points about "true" essence but may also assist in explaining the fable's seemingly puzzling moral structures, or, perhaps more precisely, articulate how a pietistic reading community asserts moral structures to explain narrative elements rendered confusing by those very same structures previously imposed upon the narrative in the first place. The shepherd transforms from a figure of virtue to one of vice, stealing everything he can: caught, imprisoned, and sentenced to be thrown to the (identical, now captured) lion, he is spared when the lion, recalling his duty to repay the shepherd for his previous good turn, kisses him instead of eating him. In response to the wondering audience's question of "how it happened that the lion didn't harm him. *Had he deserved such a reward from God—or from folk*" (*oyb er fun got hot far dint eyn zelkhn lon / oder um di layt*, 10a.85–86, emphasis mine), the shepherd explains his previous action, and the people decide to let not only the lion, but the shepherd, go free.

Both actions are bizarre, narratively speaking: releasing a dangerous lion and a shepherd, who, his act of kindness to the lion notwithstanding, is facing punishment for an entirely different set of crimes! The former behavior may become understandable given the story's moral emphasis not only on loyalty (the epimyth reads, "happy is he that has a loyal heart and steadfastly remembers the good done him," 10b.109–110), but also the crowd's recognition, as a result of these loyal actions, of the lion's essentially noble (and thus presumably nondangerous) behavior. Less obvious, though, is the crowd's expansion of the idea of essential continuous, moral behavior to the shepherd; despite his later actions, he has been revealed as "essentially" good and can therefore be freed, much as a lion lamed by a thorn in his paw does not alter his essentially powerful state. As such, a narrative crux is solved by a further refinement—or perhaps a remaking—of the rules about essence.

The next fable, which also powerfully foregrounds the moral issue of repayment, allows us to consider this and other moral structures in the work. The fable also features the king of beasts; it is the well-known fable of the sick and dying lion, first appearing in Yiddish literature as early as the Cambridge Codex of 1382.[89] Although the fable shares the previous one's structure of asserted potency–represented impotency–final recovery, the sick lion's recovery here is presented as only a sop (if an ideologically meaningful one) to structural necessity. Rather, the story, in an obvious political allegory, emphasizes the sick lion's servants' failure to meet their moral and chivalric obligations, and the lion's recognition of the subordination of idealism to realpolitik. Still, the fable's text at least partially resolves the struggle in idealism's favor, even if tinged with a nod to psychological reality: the lion's recuperation results from his desire to avenge himself upon his servants. Such a lesson coexists uneasily with the story's epimyth—if not the part that in "misfortune (*unglik*) no one can be counted on, neither old friends nor new, neither young nor old" (14b.51–52), then certainly the subsequent call to trust only in God's friendship, unless the latter is defined as another acknowledgment of the regnant order.[90]

Such political considerations are, perhaps unsurprisingly in a fable collection written for early modern Jewry, more generally and expansively treated in reference to questions posed to and about power's victims, rather than its possessors.[91] Even here, though, the moralist's interests reassert themselves: another apparently political fable, of belling the cat (14), seems dedicated to lamenting the price of political inaction when brave representation—despite a unanimity of decision—is lacking. The fable's use of the word *kahal* (16b.21) is noteworthy in this context, and the fable's political application is expressed explicitly in the *muser-haskel*: "From this I have drawn an analogy and have brought this fable that applies to a community (*gemein*) which sits down together with intelligence and good sense" (17a.48–49).[92] The *muser-haskel*, however, first applies the story to those who jointly take counsel to "defeat

Satan and escape him" (17a.45), not a political enemy, an odd change given the story's allegorical clarity. Theologization is hardly an uncommon gesture for the moralist, however; nor is his eventual application of the fable's apparently political lessons to class strife, and the difficulty if not impossibility of overcoming said strife due to its essential nature—"Even if they undertake to do various things, the rich and the poor will not be able to smooth out their differences" (17a.51–52), like mice and cats.[93]

This is not to say that no alternative structures of value or action are suggested. In the ninth fable of the fox and the chicks, for example, we see the moralist's value of, and admiration for, the use of wit, words, and wisdom to avoid physical threat, even when it involves lying for self-preservation's sake (12a.81–82);[94] these values of *klugheyt* and *zinen*, wisdom and sense, expanded in the thirteenth fable of the clever doves (16a.20), reveal wit not merely to be a reactive device for escaping emergency, but as an ability to undertake long-range planning and action to prevent future threats (here, the doves eat the hemp seeds the farmer plants, so they cannot be later caught with the net he will weave from the ropes he will braid from the hemp).

The treatment of wit and its valuation for self-preservation, even when it necessitates temporarily immoral action, combine with the ethos of repayment of evil intent to create a more nuanced political allegory in the fifteenth fable, another story of the ill lion. Here, the narrative takes a turn reminiscent of the book of Esther: the evil advisor (here, the wolf) attempts to solve the ailing authority figure's problems by planning his hated rival's death (here, of the fox); the rival's secret knowledge undermines the plan, however, and the advisor's own suggestion convicts him. (In the fable, the wolf's plan to send the fox to find a cure for the lion results in the fox's statement that the "foreign authorities'" suggested cure is a wolfskin garment.) The moralist finds it necessary to state explicitly that self-defense is not nor has it ever been forbidden, though simultaneously stating that "one should not contemplate doing evil against another" (18a.97–99), once more illuminating the tensions between ideal moral behavior and political, realistic necessity. Those tensions are recapitulated in the fable's presentation of the fox as the story's hero, balancing his essential reputation as the wit necessary to the narrative's motion with his conventional role as an amoral (if not strictly evil) figure. He can be compared in this vein to the entirely evil wolf, the moralist's "evil spider full of malice and poison," the comparand to the evil thinking person (18a.85–90, quote 88).

The wolf's fate is to be mocked, as he must now run around skinless, which not only parallels Haman's (penultimate) fate in the book of Esther, but is thematically congruent with the categories of honor, shame and mockery mentioned briefly as major motivating forces in the book.[95] These considerations also catalyze much of the action in the fable of the father, the son, and the donkey (16); there, a father and son, worrying about others' opinions and mockery (*shpot*),[96] continually change their mode of travel with their donkey, reaching such heights of frenzy that they themselves will carry the donkey on a pole! The pair's ultimate reaction, however, and their means of transcending one of those motivating forces, make explicit what is only subtly apparent in the previous story upon noticing the connection to Esther: the irrelevance of the external worldly order's blandishments compared to an individual sense of eternal, divine will. The father says, at the story's end, "What is one to do so that people don't always mock and scorn? Therefore I will turn only to God and care no more about the mockery of people. I will do only what seems right to me" (19b.88–92). If we can view the previous story's salvation through wit and the other political allegories as preaching restoration of a political order according with Divine desires for the world's proper conduct, such comments illuminate the attempt by fables and morals alike to domesticate even witty and subversive tales into conservative settings.

This does not mean the fabulist practices an unblinking conservatism and is unmindful of the possibility of a problematically corrupt political order. In the fable of the wolf as judge (18), our essential identification of the wolf as evil develops when we read of his appointment by the lion to serve as de facto ruler. The tale again reminds us of the book's complex attempts to negotiate the argument between a skeptical or realistic sense of a world governed by contingent, shifting falsehood, and a moralist vision of an ideal world order presided over by a meaningful and interventionist God. Certainly, the *muser-haskel* suggests falsehood's omnipresence, expressed in flights of allegorically rhetorical fancy: "Falsehood has set her foot in this world and erected her tent and fortified her ground. Truth has closed her lips, for falsehood has covered the earth. Justice has completely fled" (22a.68–70). But even in the midst of such affirmation of "realistic" perspective, the writer's specific recourse to allegory reminds his readers of such constructions' essentially superficial and artificial nature, "superficial" used here in the more technical sense of covering over the actual, essential truth: such narrative representations of the world, while perhaps mimetically accurate, are not ultimately so. Fable comes to represent truth, which comes to serve merely as illusion: this is these stories' constant revolution.

This perspective is most clearly—and particularistically—evident in another political allegory, the fable of the murdered Jew and the partridge. As mentioned earlier, the fable concerns a lord who guarantees a Jew safe passage, sending along his servant to ensure his guarantee, but the servant murders the Jew instead. Relevant here is simply that the servant's most heinous crime may not be viewed as the murder, or the plunder of the body, but rather the direct betrayal of the servant's oath of allegiance to his lord, who directly requested he protect the Jew.[97] Such value structures can certainly be viewed as reflecting chivalric ideology; however, given the express reference to a Jewish character here, this can also be easily interpreted as an allegorical representation of the Jewish perspective towards the varying political relationships of Jews, non-Jews, and God. The non-Jew is simply present to guard—or to punish—Jews for their actions and, as in the prophetic perspective, his destructive role is eventually punished within the long *durée* of historical (here, narrative) time; that destruction accordingly reveals him as definitionally villainous. The notably internal nature of the collapse—that it comes most from the servant himself—now affords another explanation: it is, unsurprisingly, something else essential within him—here, his role as God's and history's pawn—that is inescapable and informative.

Conclusions

The *Seyfer Mesholim*'s final *muser-haskel* and colophon clearly show that the collection's penultimate fable, of the diligent and lazy servants, was intended as its final one.[98] The reader, however, encounters the text as follows: fable 33 (of the lazy and diligent servants); the moralist's first interpretation of fable 33; fable 34 (of the horse and the donkey); the moralist's interpretation of fable 34; and the moralist's *second* interpretation of fable 33, which organically flows into a general epilogue to the entire work. A focus on the texts as they were (and are) experienced will allow us to make some suggestions about the *Seyfer Mesholim*'s concluding strategies—and some concluding statements about the work as a whole.

The fable of the lazy and the diligent servants borrows a common motif from parabolic discourse;[99] images of servants and masters to characterize the Jews' relationship to God are also widespread.[100] Such intertextuality prepares allusively aware subgroups of the reading community for another allegorical reading, arguably like that of the murdered Jew advanced above, that transcends the potentially universalist interpretive approach to these fables generally adopted within the work (and this chapter), instead locating it within a familiarly Jewish discursive context. The fable itself, focusing on a king's order to his two servants to prepare a dance-hall for his daughter's wedding and their respective efforts both in that regard and in maintaining the suit of clothes he has provided each of them, offers, as its first moral suggests, a fairly straightforward encomium to diligence and industry, in contrast to sloth and slovenliness (cf. 55b–56a.253–275). Such an explanation, however, regards the text merely as a moral exemplum, not a full-fledged fable: a close reading of the narrative, considering its nuances and details, frustrates any simple, reductionist moral application, allowing us once more to see a space opened for readerly skepticism and authorial nuance in an attempt to address that skepticism. Perhaps this is why this epimyth features another statement by the moralist potentially read as betraying his anxiety: "This fable is surely not lacking in much that is useful and good in the world, as I can well demonstrate" (55b.253–254).

Examples of the narrative cruxes include the introduction, immediately after the narrative's statement that no one exists whom the king can trust, of the faithful retainers in whom he trusts completely (53a.15–17); the odd emphasis not merely on the servants' appropriately industrious accomplishment of their preparatory work, but also on their maintenance of their suits, and other hygienic standards; the general request's very nature, and its clear representation as a test within the narrative; and mockery's central role in the text, where the lazy servant is roundly mocked, not simply at the tale's end, but in its middle as well. While these difficulties are potentially ignored or solved independently by the reader, they are nonetheless accentuated by the surprising juxtaposition of the story to the collection's final fable, a jarring reversion from a "realistic" depiction of court maneuvers to another tale of talking animals.

The final fable of the horse and the donkey, in which the latter mocks the former for his fall from his former exalted state and his current obligation to pull the plow, is less a plotted narrative and thus a full-fledged fable than an opportunity for theological, historical, and thematic closure. The donkey's gleeful summation reads: "In spite of everything, you must pull the wagon in great sorrow and suffering, while God has helped me. I have been relieved of all my sorrow. And surely a great commandment has been laid upon you: that you never again mock me as you used to. God has given you your just reward" (56a–56b.24–30). His words, spoken in revenge for his shame and maltreatment, combined with the specific (and highly rare) reference to God in an animal fable, suggest a second consecutive, conclusory progression from the universal to the Jewish, allowing us to read the fable as a specifically Jewish allegory focusing on the consolatory nature (from a traditional perspective) of the historicized end state.

The consolation, which is predicated on the other's humiliation—shame notably generated by deprivation of fine clothing, here the horse's velvet cloth, silver bridle, and silken cloths and ornaments (see 56a.15–22), illustrates thematic continuities between the two final stories. If the moral to fable 34 focuses familiarly on the story's economic aspects, again invoking Fortune's sudden shifts that yield drastic poverty or wealth, the much less common phrasing of its end—"And he should acknowledge Almighty God who has bestowed it upon him. In this way he will derive happiness from his money and property, and will surely be transported to the hereafter" (56b.40–42)—conceptualizes the general moral lesson in specifically Jewish terms. Such particularistic reading in turn allows the specification of the previous fable's lesson, legitimating the address of the fable of the servants' political and economic ramifications within an explicitly Jewish framework, overlaying a second reading onto the first.

That interpretive shift, visually accentuated by a border on 56b, is evident in the moralist's intent to "interpret the fable in another fashion and with a different sense which fits it very well and which points nicely to the hereafter, which is pleasing to every person" (56b.2–7). That interpretive schema views the king's order to clean his house while keeping one's own clothes clean as a test to "cleanse [one's] heart of all sin" (56b.33), and the brief term of preparation provided is the "time that God gives every person for the course of his life" (56b.30–31). Such a reading explains many other narrative features: the cavalier who arrives to summon them before the king, the king's final judgment of the servants, the diligent servant's reward and the lazy servant's punishment: all find their analogues—treated in depth by the moralist—in a classical Jewish treatment of good and bad action and concomitant reward and punishment.

However, these behavioral models coexist uncomfortably with the generic requirements of the fable. The king's test, definitionally predicated on free will to choose the right behavior, is uneasily juxtaposed with the ethical determinism necessarily created by the fable's essentializing nature. The story's *moral* interpretation, that is, depends on seeing the lazy servant's problematic behavior as a willed act equivalent to one who, in the moralist's words, has "spent his time openly and in full view pursuing uncleanness wherever he could find it, lying with other women. And even if it became known, he didn't care, but went on eagerly pursuing his own pleasure" (57a.67–74). The narrative and generically meaningful reading, though, stresses essence, as we have seen: the lazy man acts this way because of who he naturally is, the reason his behavior rates mockery, not rancor, by others. It is thus hardly surprising that, asked by others about his subpar performance of his duties, he replies: "there is no reason for me to be embarrassed since I am fulfilling my duty to my lord in all faithfulness" (53b.118–120). Hardly a moral rebel, the lazy servant simply fulfills his essential nature; and the resultant shortcomings hardly seem comparable to moral offense.

The moralist's conflation of these different moral stances—a sleight of hand he attempts to disguise with long descriptions (57a.110–58a.200) of paradise's joys, hell's torments, and God's power—is his attempt to impose interpretive unanimity on narrative complexity. So viewed, his statements of hermeneutic anxiety in the epilogue ("Toward this goal [of people's achieving the hereafter] I will direct my interpretation," 56b.10; "I will tell you the meaning of that," 57b.144; "Therefore I warn everyone seriously," 57b.158–159), can be seen, in a dynamic we have seen in many aspects of the work, ideological, thematic, and formal, as a final attempt to impose interpretive control over the narrative and a final illustration to the readers of the possibility of such control's absence—a last opportunity for the skeptic to get his innings in. Such a reading also neatly complements—and possibly explains—the "final" story's subject of seemingly identical servants who "read" their master's commandment differently, and may therefore be trusted (or not); why that fable's interpretations are divided by a second fable that simultaneously clarifies and complicates the interpretive hermeneutic through an accentuation of particularistic Jewish interpretation and a reaffirmation of Jewish faith against an implied skepticism; and how agreements made by master and servant—God and his Jewish people, in the moralist's interpretation—can be viewed as models for the epistemological pact, which generates a range of interpretations, many possible, some privileged differently by different groups.

This type of blurring between reality and fiction is the fable's very province, and so it is unsurprising that the writer infiltrates himself into the story at the epilogue's end: "And I too would gladly be like the good and diligent fellow, that things may go as well with me" (58a.200–202). Reminding ourselves that the good and diligent fellow's reward is to sit at the feudal king's right hand, we can see how, even for the moralist, fable and interpretation—his own interpretation—have become one; how even storytellers are seduced by their stories, as their own interpretive efforts explain away complications and in the many explanations activate readerly skepticism and perhaps generate alternative, creative interpretation. As the next chapter will show, such readerly interpretive structures can only become more complex—and more illustrative of readerly sophistication—as the reader's sense of questions of belief and skepticism become more subtly activated.

We also begin to see, through our analyses of the fables' concerns, not only the model of the epistemological pact, and methodologies for its explication, but aspects of its content. Using the specific features of the particular genre—here, the fables' natural inclination towards conservatism of essential nature—the elite composers extend its lessons to apply to theological, socioeconomic, and sexual conservatism, and subtly craft their message to incorporate potential critiques, the most powerful of which come from the world's experienced complexities themselves. In doing so, they use the universal message of the fable—the inchoate sense that their purpose is to describe the way the world is—and shift it to encompass their idea of what the world should be. No plan is, however, perfect, and stories and interpretations create their own resistances. But the topics of concern we have seen addressed in the *Seyfer Mesholim*—the tensions between rich and poor; the challenges to the notion of theological order in an increasingly skeptical world; the place of women in that changing world and the threat their empowered natures might pose to the established order—are all very much topics we will take up in chapters to come.

4. Thinking with *Shedim*

What Can We Learn from the Mayse fun Vorms*?*

The seventh reader interrupts you: "Do you believe that every story must have a beginning and an end? In ancient times a story could end only in two ways: having passed all the tests, the hero and the heroine married, or else they died. The ultimate meaning to which all stories refer has two faces: the continuity of life, the inevitability of death."

—Italo Calvino, *If on a Winter's Night a Traveler*

How does our understanding of a particular genre of Yiddish text—an approach which, though of course not solely literary, is generally conceptualized in literary terms—help us to think historically about ways of understanding the early modern Jewish community? This interest in a genre-based approach is twofold. First, it is to suggest how narrative texts written in the vernacular, and in a particular genre in that vernacular, allow for a nuanced view of social norms and transgressions that complement and complicate our understandings of early modern Jewish society, a view whose nuance comes in part from the change in social positioning occasioned by a switch to the vernacular. Second, it is to suggest how literary readings of a narrative text—readings that pay attention to ambiguities, unresolved contradictions, extrusive symbols, and the like, and rely on these details to suggest interpretive possibilities—yield what we may call "epistemological evidence"; that is to say, they explore the capacities of the audience to serve as textual interpreters, which may then lead us to revise our traditional conceptualization of the literary sophistication of the audience and dissociate it from questions of linguistic and textual knowledge, the traditional markers of cognitive differentiation in scholarly historical approaches to the early modern Jewish community.

The genre this chapter focuses on may be referred to as the supernatural horror story, and the specific subvariation of that genre is the trope of the marriage of a man and a she-demon. The conceptualization of the "supernatural" in the early modern period has been discussed, in various ways, in previous chapters; in beginning here, it should be noted that the study of supernatural fiction, and specifically supernatural horror, even during this period, often concerns the establishment and transgression of social mores, codes, and boundaries. Borders are designed to be crossed and not to be crossed—to establish boundaries that by their establishment beg to be broken. As a result, the study of supernatural fiction in a particular society may be particularly suited to examining that society's notions of limits and boundaries, not only of socially sanctioned or transgressive behavior but also, for lack of a better term, of socially constructed reality. This case may be strengthened because, in almost any traditional construction of the supernatural—certainly in the Jewish literature of the early modern period—the same creatures who can be relied upon to break through certain moral and physical boundaries are themselves explicitly rule-bound. The borderless have borders of their own, and to examine where those higher borders, so to speak, lie, may be extremely telling.

This analysis relies on the symbolic dimensions of these supernatural figures: the fact that they stand in for something beyond themselves within society, and that it is up to the readers to determine precisely what that something is. Those determinations are often, therefore, a matter of interpretation, since the stories themselves may not give an explicit interpretation or *muser-haskel* type ending, as we have seen in the previous chapter—and even if they do, as we have also seen, such an ending only privileges, but fails to exclude, other interpretations. In this sense, then, we might say that the levels of meaning or interpretation given to a text are, in these tales about borders, themselves borderlines: to read a story in one particular way—to see it as exemplifying something—encloses it, and blocks off other possibilities. Attempts to recover the historical communal dynamics of interpretation are themselves historically valuable, of course, and highly illuminating.

Recent trends in the scholarship of what we would refer to as supernatural activity in the early modern era in a Christian or wider European context may be helpful here, particularly insofar as they demonstrate a shift in their attention to the literary aspects of accounts and discussions of demonology in the early modern period. Stuart Clark, in *Thinking with Demons*, writes:

"the historian, like an ethnographer of language, can concentrate quite precisely on the properties conferred on witchcraft by representational conventions, on the resources and repertoires of linguistic behaviour that enabled witches to mean something to those who wrote about them ..."[1] Similarly, Walter Stephens, in his book on the centrality of the issue of demonic copulation to the crisis of belief in the early modern period, invites us to call attention not only to the literary structures and details of the texts of witchcraft theorists as essential clues to the author's complex intents, but also to the fact that what witchcraft theorists "claimed to worry about is not usually what their reasoning shows them to be worrying about,"[2] and that a studied attention to the seeming fissures of logic in the text given an ostensible interpretive lens based on varied extrusive factors may require a different interpretive lens rather than a dismissal of a text as problematic or confusing. In that vein, in this chapter, which focuses largely on one well-known supernatural tale from the sixteenth century, we suggest a reading that complements, rather than follows, the traditional critical understanding of the story; doing so may allow us to speculate more broadly on social and epistemological norms of the period.

The *Mayse fun Vorms* is one of the most important versions of the "marriage of a man and a she-demon" trope in modern literature; it remains extant in a manuscript from Trinity College, Cambridge, and has been reprinted by Sara Zfatman in modern transcription. No colophon exists; the work is certainly written in northern Italy after 1514 and within the first half of the sixteenth century, probably the 1520s, presumably originating in folkloric (and probably oral) material from a slightly earlier source, and is therefore one of the earliest cases of Yiddish narrative we have.[3] The subgenre has appeared in many later Yiddish versions (sometimes where the relationship takes place without benefit of actual matrimony, for example), in places as varied as the eighteenth-century moralistic work *Seyfer Kav ha-yoshor*, I. L. Peretz's "Monish," that manifesto of modern Yiddish literature, and, transmuted, in several works of Isaac Bashevis Singer. In these latter tales, the sexual aspects of the relationship have been unquestionably foregrounded, perhaps borrowing from the European tradition of the succubus, or from internal traditions connecting demonic activity with concupiscence. Such a connection is made explicit by the *muser-haskel* that appears at the end of the *Kav ha-yoshor*'s she-demon tale, sometimes referred to as the "Tale of Poznan":

"One can find a clear proof from this story about one who gets involved with the followers of Lilith or Makhles, the mothers of the demons: such a man is uprooted together with his family, and they all perish. Every man should therefore be warned against improper fornication, for sometimes a she-demon appears in the guise of a harlot[4] and mates with a man, causing him and his family to perish. Each man must therefore take care to mate only with his wife and not waste his seed. And if, willingly or not, he does waste his seed, he should immediately do penance, and then it will be well with him. Selah." (117)[5]

The monster, here, is not particularly far from the metaphor. The author himself gives us significant direction in how to first approach the story: clearly, she-demons are presented here as primarily figures of sexual seduction, who both literally exist and also serve as tropes to represent the desire for unsanctioned sexual behavior. This explicitly refers to the patronization of prostitutes, as well as, apparently, masturbation.[6] Comments of critics such as those by Neugroschel, that "the underlying distress may partly derive from anxiety about Jews who leave the fold to marry Christians,"[7] may be based on hints in the text, but may also be an eisegetical maneuver given modern concerns about intermarriage:[8] the text makes no mention of intermarriage in its final warnings, seeming to view the relationship with the she-demon, even in a long-term fashion that leads to children, as a sunken, aberrant, and perverse reliance on sexual pleasure within the Jewish fold.

However, critics such as Neugroschel may have read the undeniably sexual aspects of these stories backwards when they seek to apply them wholeheartedly to earlier eras and texts; the earlier "Tale of Worms," though it shares some formal characteristics with the Poznan text, is significantly longer and far more literarily complex. While the Poznan tale, at its end, explicitly calls attention to the sexual aspects of the she-demon tale, I hope to demonstrate in this chapter how the Worms text uses the formal and structural frameworks of the she-demon tale to make a series of more complicated critiques and examinations of contemporary Jewish economic and moral practices, and, in the end, reflect on the very nature of this literature itself. As such, this analysis will hardly focus on the sexual critique that is so obviously present in the tale in the *Kav ha-yoshor*, though, as we will see, issues of gender remain highly important, though not solely so. In a short coda, we will return to the Poznan tale and see how certain conventions and tropes remain present, even as their configuration and presentation yield extremely different thematic results.

Of Men and (She-)Demons: A Brief History

Though a history of Jewish demonology through the ages is far beyond our scope here, it is fair to trace the development from a very minor presence in the canonized Hebrew Bible to a significantly richer and more developed canon of demonological works in the apocalyptic writings of the second century BCE to the first century CE, in which "evil spirits work ... to thwart and undo God's plan for the world." As early as the book of Jubilees and the Testament of the Twelve Prophets, the demonic forces take the form of seducers; as early as 1 Enoch, deriving scriptural strength from Genesis 6, the role of the demon as sexual seducer and miscegenator comes forth.[9] An important trope originating in this period is the role of the strong feminine demonic force, a sign of unrestrained, pagan, female sexuality, often, though not always, explicitly connected with otherness in the non-Jewish sense.[10] The Talmud mentions demons a great deal,[11] often rendering them as spirits that will haunt ruined places and will engage in acts of possession resulting in mood change. Such images, of course, are strongly reminiscent of the portraits of demons in the New Testament; though Jewish and Christian demonologies would substantially diverge, certain common tropes and ideas would also develop.

Perhaps the most important common idea—certainly the most important for our purposes—is the notion of sexual congress between humans and demons. Such a concept is predicated on the possibility for demons to take on corporeal form, whether human or other kinds of beings, a corporealization that marks a change, within the early medieval Jewish sphere, from the general Talmudic conceptualization of demons as bodiless and largely imperceptible.[12] The idea of fauns mating with women was well known from the time of Augustine; these fauns were identified as demons by the seventh-century encyclopedist Isidore of Seville.[13] Many of the Christian stories that develop in the medieval era, however, involve human women mating with male demons (incubi), as opposed to human men with female demons (succubi).[14]

Much of the discussion revolving around the former—particularly in the late medieval and early modern era—was intimately connected to questions of witchcraft, since witchcraft was contingent on the establishment of a demoniac pact that often involved sexual congress with the male devil (or the Devil). As a result, the question of demonic copulation became intimately linked with the questions about female sexuality, sexual pleasure, empowerment, and societal place that are well known to be at the center of analyses of the witchcraft phenomenon, occurring during a time characterized by one of its foremost scholars as an explosive period in misogyny.[15] The stories are also—though we will not discuss this at length here—relevant to the broader discussion of belief and skepticism about the supernatural world; for now, suffice it to say that the rise and fall of the emphasis on the demonic pact and the witch cult can be tied to anxieties about the weakness of belief in revealed religion more generally.[16] As Walter Stephens has cogently and compellingly argued, the emphasis on demonic copulation in the Renaissance and early modern period stems from anxiety concerning the epistemological and ontological status of these supernatural creatures, rather than firm belief in them.[17]

It may not be surprising, then, that some of the central questions concerning succubi in the Christian world surrounded their role in rendering a man impotent, which was perceived to have consequences for the gendered balance of power within society writ large, not merely within the family.[18] Such traditions, expressed as early as Aquinas,[19] seem far less common within Jewish tradition. Indeed, as we will see, the Jewish emphasis on sexual relationships between men and she-demons appears almost always in narratives of (at least technical) potency and fecundity. It is fair to say, though, that they are equally animated by a fear of strong women's sexuality, within and without the context of marriage and motherhood. Perhaps the most prominent early example of a Jewish she-demon that seduces men is Lilith, traditionally known as Adam's first wife. Myths of Lilith appear in the tenth-century Alphabet of Ben Sira, which describes her divorce from Adam as a result of her desire to be the dominant sexual partner. Subsequently, she becomes a succubus, and the nocturnal emissions produced by the men she seduces, or from the results of their masturbation, become demons.[20] Lilith's additional function as a child-killer and even a child-eater, an antimother and anti-Eve, is reminiscent of the most extreme oppositional perspective between pleasure and procreation, mother and anti-mother.[21]

The Christian focus, which revolves around the mode of reversal and inversion, is itself deeply resonant of the Christian demonological position, which has the tendency to view the demonic world as a dark mirror of the human world, an "anti-world in which normal polarities were reversed" and where "all things echoed the primal disobedience [the Fall] by reversing their normal roles and relationships."[22] It may even be the case that such rhetoric of inversion, when it is used in Jewish contexts, is a Jewish internalization of the Christian perspective of Jews as diabolical or demoniac, a "natural" outgrowth of the equivalence on their part of the devil with temptation and the wrong path.[23] Still, it may not be surprising in this vein that normative Jewish tropes of demonologization, particularly concerning the sexual relationship between men and demons, move away from rhetoric of inversion and towards one of mimesis.[24]

Perhaps the best example of the "road taken"—one in which demon society reflects, in its own way, surprising similarities to contemporary Jewish society—is the highly influential tenth-century "Tale of the Jerusalemite," which features a visit by a man to the land of the demons and a marriage between that man and a she-demon. Though the tale itself has certain non-Jewish antecedents, Joseph Dan rightly concludes that the author transforms them so fundamentally it can, in many respects, be considered a practically original, Jewish work.[25] A discussion of the tale is beyond our scope here; suffice it to say that the story's protagonist, when he stumbles upon the land of the demons after a shipwreck and a magical flight atop a bird called the Kikufa, is struck a number of times—as is, seemingly, the story's narrator—by the resemblance of the demons' behavior to that of traditional Jews: they study Torah, they pray, they have synagogues, they judge according to Jewish law.[26] The primary difference, it seems, is that they are much more easily driven to homicide towards those who break laws and oaths: unfortunately for our protagonist, this includes the oath he has made to his demon mate.[27]

Importantly for our purposes, then, not only does the story—which was translated and adapted into Yiddish in the early modern period on a number of occasions[28]—focus on similarities rather than discontinuities, but its lessons, its usage of the demon world and demon marriage to focus on the deleterious consequences of breaking oaths and commitments rather than on the erotic aspects of the marriage, point the way forward to looking at demonic marriage as something other than about the marriage itself. The stated moral of the original tale—"Accordingly, a son should always obey his father's commands and must never break an oath"—may be illustrative, though of course not proof positive, of this approach. Equally important, however, is the reminder that such norms of reading, such interpretive lenses, may change over time and for different reasons. By the time a version of the tale appears in Prague in 1660, for example, the moralist's ending has changed to an erotic one, focusing around the wife in question; this is, in Zfatman's words, "a 'surprising' ending that has no organic or logical connection to the development of the story."[29]

The end of the seventeenth century is, already, an extremely different time period from the early sixteenth, the latest possible date for the composition of the *Mayse fun Vorms*; the earlier period, right around what one critic has referred to as the "golden age of the demoniac"[30] and another as a "period of new fascination with and fear of the devil,"[31] is worth considering on its own terms. In that vein, it should be noted that the tale—which, though continuing the theme of demon marriage, has no direct narrative connection to the "Tale of the Jerusalemite," some critical comment notwithstanding[32]—does not have a clear moral; whether by intent or accident, we, as the readers may have been, are left to try to interpret the employment of these tropes on our own. Given what we have seen to be the complex and semiotically ambiguous nature of the she-demon trope, we may have to turn to the internal evidence of the tale for our guidance.

The Mayse fun Vorms

A summary of the *Mayse fun Vorms* may be in order before proceeding. The tale, which has antecedents in medieval Christian narrative (particularly the work of William of Malmesbury), apocryphal and midrashic material (likely the book of Tobit and the Midrash Tanchuma), and German folk narrative,[33] concerns the young son of a wealthy rabbi and his wife. The boy, on the holiday of Lag Ba'omer, goes to the Jubilee Gardens in Worms to play hide and seek with his friends. Ultimately, he is appointed "it," and, in looking for his friend Anshel behind the various trees in the garden, comes to a hollow tree where he sees a hand sticking out. He tells Anshel (for this is whom he believes it to be) to come out; when the hand does not move, the boy takes a golden ring from his own finger and places it on the hand, saying that he betroths Anshel. The hand then vanishes, which alarms the boy no end—his parents have given him that ring, and it's expensive. When he returns to his friends, he encounters Anshel, who denies being in the tree. They return home; his father promises him another ring, more expensive than the first; everyone forgets the matter.

The boy becomes a man, and is betrothed to the daughter of a wealthy man; on his wedding night, he and his bride go to the bedchamber, where he immediately falls asleep. In the middle of the night, a figure, richly dressed, comes to the wakeful bride, and tells her that this is her husband, not the bride's. The bride tells her to go away, that the groom is hers; the figure strangles the bride. When the groom awakes, he finds her dead. Three years later, the same thing happens, this time with the daughter of a distant relative. Another ten years or so pass, and the parents are beginning to worry that their son will remain unmarried, and that their fortune will be dissipated: they hit upon the idea of marrying their son to a girl from the local poorhouse, who, with lack of dowry, will have sufficiently few matrimonial choices to be desperate. The girl agrees to do this, on the condition that if she dies, the groom's parents will take care of her mother until her death.

The wedding takes place, under subdued circumstances; once more the she-demoness approaches, and issues her challenge: the poor girl is deferent, insisting that the demoness take her groom. As a result, the she-demoness spares the bride, on the condition that one hour a day the groom will disappear and that the bride should never attempt to discern where he goes. This agreement holds for some time, but, our narrator says, the natural curiosity of women gets ahold of the bride, who one day follows her husband into his bedroom, where he has disappeared. She looks under the bed and sees a stone, which rolls away; there she discovers a hole and a ladder; she climbs down the ladder, traverses a wood, and then finds the demon's house, and, eventually, the demon's bedroom, where the two are sleeping arm in arm. The bride discovers that the demon's long golden hair is lying on the floor; she places it on a stool, thus consigning the demon to death, since she touched her "shame," and when that happens, the demon has to die. The demoness dies, the husband returns to his wife, and they hold a joyous celebration to replace the subdued one of the past.

A somewhat odd and complicated tale, with some knotty and confusing details. As suggested earlier, a first analysis might follow later writers' adoption of the genre focus on the story's sexual aspects, reading the she-demon as the fulfillment of either adulterous sexual desires or the locus of the seductions and dangers of intermarriage. Scholars such as Tamar Alexander have taken this approach. (One might focus, in this reading, not only on the erotic fantasia of having multiple sexual partners or of polygamy more generally but of having sex in the middle of the day.)[34] If we recall our conceptualization of the traditional horror tale as a series of markers of social borderlines and punishment for transgression of those lines, then we can see how this reading might emerge clearly and suggest the story is read as an exemplum for the imposition of traditionalist erotic behavior.

Some features of such a reading might focus first on the studied attempts of the tale to inculcate a sense of Apollonian idyllic reality before the eruption of Dionysian demonic chaos into its midst—a structure common to most horror stories. Such attempts revolve around the establishment of harmonic union between mythic and contemporary, *then* and *now*. While the text takes great pains to point out that "the German town still known today as Worms" still contains a thriving "Jewish community," it accentuates the tale's location in a mythic past: the story takes place "years ago," in a community that "goes back to the generations of Jesse" (118).[35] Such idyllic sensibility is expressed further by the perfect harmony between familiarity and distance, structure and play, in the discussion of the catalyzing event that allows the young boy to betroth his demon wife, which revolves around one of the Jewish calendar's most minor holidays: Lag Ba'omer. The narrator writes that "now when the holiday of Lag-Baomer rolls around, the students like to have a good time" (118), and where they seek that good time is of special interest to us: "The town of Worms has a public park called Havel Park, and people who have been here must know where it is" (118).

While the inclusion of such a sentence allows us room to speculate fruitfully on the linkage between historical recollection and literary reimagination—the narrator creates a feeling of authenticity by inviting the readership to call upon their own experiences of travel to the place[36]—it also allows us to explore a second aspect of the tale as horror story: the way that harmony gives way to liminality, and the tale continuously presents borderlines and borderlands, which are, of course, easily transgressed.[37] The choice of Lag Ba'omer, then, is precise, as a holiday that is arguably the most suitable to symbolize this liminal state. Perched precariously as a joyous break in the middle of a period of mourning, it seems to derive its celebratory state from the tradition that it is a date on which sadness does not occur.[38] Similarly, it is ironically reversed as a holiday that celebrates the continuation of Torah study—but always celebrates it in a way that seems antithetical to the practice of Torah study as it was lived in Europe, by going out into nature.[39] A similar liminal state seems to obtain in the description of where the yeshiva boys go to play. Havel Park is clearly a specific park space, which is wooded, but contains a tree line that seems to mark the boundaries of the park; parks in general occupy the line between nature and artifice. This idea that simple harmony gives way to a multitude of secret, liminal meanings may be concretized by the fact that the game the yeshiva boys play is hide and seek.

If we are in a moment of liminality, in terms of both time and space, then the standard reading of the text can clearly point to a transgression of those liminal boundaries by the rabbi's son, which then, ineluctably, leads to all that follows: the unnamed rabbi's son hunts for Anshel "behind all the trees," and then goes further, to another tree that seems to be beyond that. One might note that the simple presentation of the supernatural manifestation (a hand sticking out of a tree, which the boy believes to belong to Anshel) with the delayed recognition of the identity of that manifestation (when he finds out that he was mistaken) generates a kind of suspenseful or horrific effect, which begins to set the unsettling tone that will be amplified later in the story. The transgressiveness of the outcome, though, seems clear: a wrongful erotic act, symbolized by an impossible marriage between human and demon, that leads to horrific punishment in the embodied form of the avenging demoness.[40] This terrible figure, then, in a manner similar to that of many monsters, becomes curiously and paradoxically conservative: upholding Jewish law at the same time as she zealously breaks it.[41]

Such a reading, however, seems to ignore numerous aspects of the story that range from mildly odd to truly puzzling. To check just a few of them off briefly, they include:

1. The sexual behavior ostensibly punished in the conventional reading of the story would be that of the husband's wrongful erotic desires; and yet the man in this text is presented as anything but sexual. A presexual child when he betroths the she-demon (and, in fact, he believes it to be his friend—and so a homoerotic element is introduced into the mix)[42], he remains entirely passive through the entire experience, which is played out, largely, while he is so deeply asleep as to seem essentially narcoleptic. His passivity in his erotic behavior extends to the matchmaking, which is done entirely through his parents.[43]
2. The behavior of the final, surviving wife complicates any notion of sexual virtue ascribed to her as well. That is to say, if this horror story is to reestablish sexual norms through the survival and triumph of the sexually virtuous (which is a staple of horror fiction that lasts through the slasher movies of today), then the wife's behavior—her agreement to share her husband with the she-demon, and ultimately her victory through a pose of submission, lifting the demon's hair to

the stool and leaving the two asleep together—hardly seems to be the act of a woman dedicated to championing the norms of sexual monogamy. In fact, the ones who do—the first two wives, who tell the she-demon that the husband is theirs—are the ones who are punished for doing so; the she-demon, hearing this, flies into a rage and strangles them.

One might make the assumption that she is punishing the wives for their adulterous behavior. This, however, first presumes that a marriage between a she-demon and a man was considered legally binding within the social and narrative conventions of the time; second, that intent does not matter (since the wives, of course, did not have adulterous intent); and third and most importantly, that it is the wives that should be punished, given that the transgressive act from a structural perspective—though, it should be said, not from a tortious perspective—is the husband's, not the wife's.

3. Further, the third wife triumphs, at least at the beginning, by virtue of lying: in her first encounter with the she-demon, she claims that she knows nothing of the deaths of the previous two wives, which is demonstrably, according to the story, not the case: she has just heard from the son's mother, a few lines earlier, that "You've probably heard what's happened to our son twice" (121).[44] Such deception may be understandable when faced with a homicidal supernatural creature, but complicates our ability to view her as a paragon of virtue. Why is the story structured in this particular way?
4. The she-demon claims that she has to die if someone touches her, and specifically her shame. Without becoming too indelicate, several questions emerge: (a) she has touched humans before, including the earlier wives she has strangled; (b) her husband, presumably, has touched her "shame," whatever that may mean,[45] and (c) the wife has only, according to the story, touched her hair.

Following Stephens' dictum, we may find that it is not the story that is insufficient, or the logic of its teller, but rather the interpretive lens often used to approach it, and if we can find a different one to employ that is—to use another favored term of Stephens' (borrowed from Umberto Eco)—more economical, we may be more satisfied with this as a complementary, not to say alternative, approach. It seems that the story is far less a horror story about sex than it is about class; and that it complexly (but remarkably) acknowledges the horrific realities of class inequity during the period and satisfies its nonelite audience's desire for voyeuristic revenge upon those who most explicitly commodify, while ultimately staying within the conservative norms of society—providing a kind of wish-fulfillment fantasy within those norms. It critiques the system while upholding systemic structures.

Chanita Goodblatt, another critic who has given attention to this text, has rightly and brilliantly focused on the tale's complexities, but her readings use these complexities to move away from a particular polemic interpretation and instead generate a sense of ironic subversion within the tale, an approach that seems to primarily stem from her contention that the third problem—the wife's immoral behavior—provides an insuperable obstacle to what I'll refer to as a "conservative" reading of the story for sophisticated readers who are capable of working through the tale's complexities.[46] And Zfatman, the tale's closest reader, comes to the decision—as a result of some of these factors—that the story has no moral component at all, and is simply literary.[47] Perhaps a close look at some moments of the text—and a crucial allusion used within the text—may allow us to develop an interpretation that overcomes this obstacle, and thus show how this text may function as a polemical vehicle of moral reinforcement—though in a far more sophisticated manner than what we generally think of as a typical moral text. We may then ask what this says about the audience that is potentially encouraged to read the work in such a fashion.

It nearly goes without saying that while there was eros in marriage, the institution of marriage in sixteenth-century European Jewish society was much more of a transaction than it is today.[48] It seems that all of the nonnormative sexual markers mentioned above, while they may possibly be taken to indicate signs of the aberrant nature of this nonnormative sexual union, may also direct the reader to look away from the construction of this marriage (and thus this tale) as solely a reader for sexual mores,[49] and instead to focus on another aspect of this betrothal: not the erotic union that will eventually result, but the loss of the golden ring—which is indeed what concerns the child, as it is a ring given to him by his parents. Similarly, the false betrothal itself, part of a general discussion abounding within the legal literature of betrothal under false or mistaken pretenses, must in that light be viewed not as part of an erotic discussion but rather as part of a primarily legal and economic discourse (of course, with certain moral ramifications).[50]

Indeed, the son's general passivity can be traced to his role as the receptacle of the parents' problematic socioeconomic mores, which are symbolized by their passing the ring to the son: their main motivating source is the comfortable and undisturbed transition of wealth from one generation to the next.[51] Consider their response even to the loss of the ring: the rabbi, upon hearing the story of the loss of the ring, merely says: " 'Go and bring my son home and tell him not to worry. I'm going to give him a lovelier one' " (119).[52] The ring, or wealth more broadly, has first become the perceived sum and substance of the child's relationship with his parents. More importantly, this interchange seems to show how money becomes a superficial solution to emotional problems while the deeper moral dynamic within is avoided: as a pedagogical or parental move, the notion that there are to be no consequences for the loss of a valuable object must be troublesome. Here, though, the rabbi and his wife merely encourage the notion that, in the face of infinite supply (as we believe, given how wealthy they are reported to be), any item that can in theory be replaced is valueless; its loss is immaterial. Such an attitude explains how "the ring was forgotten" (119).[53]

Troublingly, the same attitude—towards replacement and forgetfulness—will soon be shifted from commodities such as rings to the commodities within Jewish society that the rings represent—that is, wives. The moral consequences will be far more dire, and yet the parents' attitude will remain the same until, in marital terms, the rabbi and his wife are faced with the possibility of a bankruptcy of the flesh, a dearth of heirs. After arranging the various marriages, taking care to find brides with appropriately large dowries, and after the first two wives' deaths, "the rabbi said: 'Dear wife, what should we do? We have an only son and great wealth, and if he stays unmarried, all memory of us will be wiped from the earth and our wealth will be scattered among strange hands. But what father will allow his daughter to marry our son?' And they shared their anguish and misery with each other" (120).[54]

I would suggest, then, that the son, who betroths with gold and summons up a demon with long golden hair who always appears richly dressed,[55] is in fact simply drawing to himself the embodied result of his family's desires: that the demon is the spirit of gold as commodity, of wealth, and indeed of ownership itself.[56] In this sense, it may be worth reading the episode of the first full appearance of the she-demon: "No sooner did the groom lie down than he fell asleep. The bride, however, lay awake. And as she lay there, she saw someone coming to the bed: a beautiful woman *dressed in gold and silk*. The woman said to the bride: 'You brazen hussy, why have you laid down with my husband, who married me in a tree?'[57] The bride retorted: 'That's not true! He's my husband! I married him today, so get away from here!' Upon hearing this, the woman strangled the bride and left her corpse next to the groom" (119–120).[58] This particular "representational convention," to use Clark's phrase, allows us to see this struggle as not so much over sexual monogamy but over the ownership of the man, that he in fact has become the passive object to be fought over, and that it is the lesser claims of the wife—for whose claim of ownership can surpass the spirit of ownership itself?—that lead to her destruction.[59] The son's passivity—his symbolic representation of the community's unconscious and untroubled acceptance of these errant mores the she-demon apotheosizes—allows him to sleep through the whole thing.

It is only the poor young woman, able to assuage the demon by not contesting her claim of ownership—by submitting to a hierarchy and to an essentialist definition that there are rich and poor, and that she knows her place—who is able to survive. (Consider the medieval advice for "dealing with a demon that unexpectedly confronts one: 'Don't run, but drop to the ground before him; so long as you are prostrate he will not harm you.' ")[60] The story's horror, in other words, is that the poor will remain poor forever.[61] To more fully observe this, we may turn to one of the most horrific moments—certainly a horror that would have resonated among many of the readers of this vernacular text—that comes when the mother of the groom, visiting the poor girl and her mother in the poorhouse, gives her an ogre's choice of die fast by marrying this wife-killer groom or die slowly through poverty, primarily because, lacking a dowry, she will be unable to gain the fiscal support a marriage would provide, as we see from the text.[62] The rich woman's entreaty, which simply states: " 'This is why I've come here: you've probably heard, as a result of great sins,[63] what's happened to our son twice! So if it's at all possible, I'd like your daughter to marry our son. Who knows? Perhaps she'll be rewarded for her piety and will survive. Then your and your daughter's poverty will be ended' " (121).

While the poor woman and her daughter have taken care to preserve the appropriate niceties of hospitality, complete with a courteous welcome, an invitation to sit, and the reference to the rich rabbi's wife as "dear rebbetsin," the rich woman's reply is notably brusque, lacking any salutation or thanks for the hospitality they have shown. Monstrously, she realizes that her money provides an almost insuperable coercive power. Far more disgraceful, though, is the suggestion that a potential death sentence should be welcomed as the opportunity to "end" the poverty that seems not to have been the fault of the poor in the first place.[64]

But shifting the tenor of the encounter from horror to tragedy is the way that these misshapen mores of the rich rabbi and his wife—allegorically standing in for the power structures of the contemporary Jewish community—have malformed the cognitive processes of both their son and the community around them, even the poor girl and her mother, who articulate the ethos of subservience, of accommodation, that will in fact save her from the she-demon later on. It is, at least at first glance, hard to explain the following exchange between the poor woman and her daughter as anything but an internalization of the warped socioeconomic norms of the richer classes:

"The poor rebbetsin then spoke to her daughter: 'Dear daughter, you've heard what the wealthy rebbetsin has said. Do you want to do this—I won't force you, but I can't supply a dowry. So if you don't accept this offer, you'll remain an old maid.' Her daughter replied: 'Dear mother, we're poor, that's true, and *a poor person is like a dead man*. I'll do it so long as the marriage contract stipulates that if I die, the rabbi will provide for you in his home for the rest of your days. If he agrees, then I'll risk my life and marry his son.'" (121)

While we may note the essentialist phrasing of the poor girl's reply—a poor person is like a dead man, and so she has little to fear, already having suffered the punishment visited by the she-demon on her previous analogues—those who are familiar with the world of midrashic story are aware of the phrase's resonance.[65] According to the midrash, it is used by Jacob to avoid death at the hands of Esau's son Eliphaz; when the latter threatens to kill him at his father's mandate, the former instead gives him all his money and says that since a poor person is like a dead man, he may report back to his father that he has "killed him" and therefore accomplished his filial duty, without the stain of a murder on his conscience. Eliphaz agrees and does so.[66]

Such an intertext does many things for our understanding of the story, one being that it allows us to reinterpret the encounter of the she-demon with the first two wives, to read it as an extension of paradigms long extant in the tradition of Jewish literary reception: as an archetypal encounter between Jew and other, most notably expressed in the meeting between Jacob and Esau after their separation for many years.[67] Such a meeting can, of course, be conceptualized in the conventional sense of Jew and non-Jew, providing some credence to interpretations of the tale revolving around intermarriage; but a closer reading of that encounter reminds us that in its original context Esau is viewed simply as an oppositional, primal force, one who has been (at least from his perspective) *defrauded through financial means*. In Genesis, the birthright is primarily an economic arrangement, where the recipient gets property improved in value through a particular blessing.[68] As such, the story of Jacob and Esau can be seen as a newly wealthy Jew who has fallen afoul of a rampaging, primitive force who *wants his money back*.[69]

The dynamics of the actual encounter, and its explication in the midrashic sources that would have been known as "part of the story" to the conventional reading audience, are also noteworthy: when the two meet, Esau seems to have forgotten all of his desire for money, seemingly satisfied with what he has.[70] He expresses his love for Jacob, "throwing himself upon his neck," and both Jacob and Esau weep. The rabbis of the Talmud, suspicious of Esau's motives from a psychological perspective (What happened to the homicidal rage of just a few chapters earlier? Did the decades dim it so?) instead suggest a fanciful narrative here: Esau, anger still intact after all these years, only pretends to forgive Jacob in order to come close to him. When he does so, "he falls on his neck," intending to bite him and tear his throat out. A miracle takes place, and Jacob's neck turns to stone; Esau's teeth crack on the stone. Then "both weep," Esau for his broken teeth, Jacob because of the pain in his neck.[71] This master paradigm, then, may complementarily explain the source of punishment as the neck, and provides, for the textually alert reader, a potential clue for the further development of master paradigms through which to read the story.

The poor girl–Jacob connection is even more structurally interesting, as it allows for some interesting larger analogies between the midrashic story and the situation in which the poor *rebbetsin*'s daughter finds herself, analogies that support this developing interpretation of the tale. In both cases, the righteous figure is being chased by a predator, and relies on good manners and rhetorical tropes, which are stand-ins for moral action, in order to banish the predator. Interestingly, in both cases the predator, though demonized in the distance (Esau; the she-demon), does not pose the immediate threat to the individual, at least at first: instead, the threat is mediated through a morally ambiguous individual (Eliphaz; the rich *rebbetsin*). In this case, then, we see that the poor *rebbetsin*'s daughter is not only aware of the dangers of her own situation but is aware how these dangers play out in a larger context, even a communal one, as the struggle between Jacob and Esau is anagogical for the entire community's struggle.

But this intertext, even more importantly, allows us to see how an instrumental deception is justified in saving oneself from an implacably hostile force through its recalling of an unimpeachably virtuous source. If we are able to suggest that the poor *rebbetsin*'s daughter is a self-conscious user of texts, then, at the very least, we may propose that her citation is double-edged: though Jacob himself seems to be acquiescing to the rabbinic equivalence of poverty and death (putting aside for the time being the problematic chronology of such acquiescence; it was a commonplace in rabbinic exegesis that the patriarchs were well aware of the details of later rabbinic thought), he does so only as a strategic choice, not a normative statement of belief. As such, we may well consider this text as a means of rebellion against the hegemonic structure, a subversion, even as it seems to recapitulate the culture's norms both through content (privileging wealth) and form (pious citation).[72]

In addition, the usage of the intertext by the writer (if not by the character, who presumably has no knowledge of how the story will end) challenges questions of essentialism even as it asserts them; Jacob's poverty is only a momentary lapse between periods of great wealth, and this allows us to deal with the essential contradiction in values at the story's heart, which is its perspective towards wealth. And finally, and perhaps most crucially, the employment of this midrashic intertext provides authorial legitimation for and examination of the complicated relationship between literature and life. Jacob makes an argument to Eliphaz which, though ultimately grounded in the righteous Eliphaz's acceptance of rabbinic norms, is simultaneously about the power of metaphor: if someone is metaphorically dead, then *for all intents and purposes* it is the same as if they actually were. This is an audacious claim by any standard, but is particularly welcome for those in the business of taking folktales whose cognitive claims are uncertain, and convincing others of the point that they make. The actual truth of the matter is less important than whether or not it is metaphorically true, since the two are in any case analogous.

Thus, the poor woman survives because of her acceptance of her impoverished state within the social order, and, it should be added, the concomitant recognition of that submission by the she-demon, analogous to the pleasure that is taken in the recognition of the poor in the socioeconomic hierarchy by the rich. It may be that part of the reason the she-demon is mollified with the poor girl's statements is because they fit in with her dearest hopes and desires: to have her value acknowledged. (I use these terms consciously, of course; value is key to a system of commodified desires.) Once this recognition takes place de jure, it does not necessarily need to be de facto carried out, in much the same way that an animal who has offered up his neck to the alpha animal in a pack is not necessarily killed. The primal, primitive aspect of this imagery is not unintentional in an analysis of a tale connecting wealth with nature (the insertion of gold into a tree). More, the she-demon allows her to have the man for most of the time, because the issue is not sole possession of the desired commodity; it is, rather, the control over the terms of possession. In this case, there is no question that the she-demon is perceived as the controller: she lays down the terms, and, as far as this encounter is concerned, the poor girl simply acquiesces.

It is clear, however, that such acceptance does not, for the readers or for the story, necessarily equate poverty with virtue and wealth with impiety: if it did, it would first fail to explain the ending where, in the words of the story, "And that was how the poor girl *became rich and respected through her great piety and modesty*. That is why everyone should follow her example." It would also fail, of course, to account for the fact that in many works of Jewish literature the assignation of wealth with virtue is not problematized at all.[73] And finally, as a text that seeks satisfaction in its readership, it would fail to take advantage of the popular desire to equate a happy ending with a transformation in the heroine's material circumstances and a presumed desire on the part of the readers who have identified themselves with the heroine—and the horror of her seeming subjugation to and self-definition by her submissive conduct, which I take here as interpretive of economic submission—to hear that there is, indeed, a possibility of class transformation within society.[74] Such possibility is only potentially present in the text by presenting the virtuous and clever girl's submission as a lie—indicated by including an actual lie there, that she does not know about the situation—and justifying the use of lying through a paradigmatic intertext. Evidence for this may be that the entity that most clearly provides the moral approbation equating poverty with virtue is, in fact, the she-demon, who, in recognizing the poor girl's acceptance of the former's bigamous and possessive terms, praises her: "Dear child, you must be rewarded for your piety, for speaking to me so piously" (122).

The transformation that results as the fulfillment of the true—not demonic—possibilities present in the text is achieved in the final section of the story, where the young woman enters into the demon's bedroom, to find her husband in bed with the demon. Her odd behavior there and the demon's equally odd behavior are telling. As we mentioned earlier, the demon claims that if her shame is touched, she has to die. The only part of the demon that the text indicates the poor girl has touched is her hair, and not her "shame," which one would traditionally assume to be the genitalia. Of course, a sexual reading of this story would recall the Talmudic assignation of a woman's nakedness to her hair, and this seems to be a reasonable explanation. However, it seems to me that a complementary perspective may be offered by our economic reading. In a text that grapples with questions of essentialism, both in terms of demonic forces that represent essential and unfiltered qualities and individual humans who define themselves in similar terms, but at times deceptively so, the process of entering into the demonic world—in a fashion remarkably similar to that of a reversed birth—is an encounter with essence itself.[75]

One might add a gendered dimension to this essentialist reading: that the encounter with this world comes only because of the protagonist's embrace of an essentialist characteristic of woman qua woman, as it was defined in this misogynistic age: curiosity. The journey begins by saying "Now women always want to know a lot more than is useful for them," and the woman says to herself, "I'm willing to risk my neck to find out where he goes. I'm going to follow him, even if I have to risk my neck" (122).[76] Such an embrace of gendered essentialism is also evident in the way in which such behavior constitutes a reversal from her previous actions: if we define her allusive, citatory behavior, her clever emulation of Jacob, as classically "male," her willingness to disregard a previously understood and agreed upon "text" (that is, the oral contract she has entered into with the she-demon) in the name of curiosity is a rejection of that maleness, not just an embrace of the feminine, a transformation from a character who seems to have escaped the bonds of gender to one imprisoned by them.

Again, this recreation of the demonic world as an essential state—rather than a deceptive and/or inverted state, as in Christian demonological tropes of the period—follows the path of demonic virtue set by the ur-Jewish demon tale, the tenth-century "Tale of the Jerusalemite." In doing so, it shows us the way in which non-Jewish tropes must be viewed carefully in their Judaized patterns of use, and finds some consolation for Dan's claim of the relationship between the *Mayse fun Vorms* and the "Tale of the Jerusalemite"—a claim which in general, as we have noted, has been correctly refuted by Zfatman.

If this identification with the demonic world as essential world here holds—and the description of the demon's mansion and bedroom, described as "elegant," containing "fine dishes and cutlery," and a "silken bed," seems to continue to suggest the equivalence—then the frame of the Cinderella story comes into play, where we see that the assignation of wealth with selfishness and virtue with poverty is only temporary, and that there is a meaningful resolution that allows the poor girl (and the readers that identify with her) to have their virtue and wealth as well.[77] In touching the demon's golden hair, the poor girl reminds the demon of its "shame": that this symbol of gold has been used in a symbolic way that does not accord with its ultimate essence as the expression of virtue, and has rather been used for its own ends. In this place of essence, the demonic realm, such a contradiction cannot occur—indeed, one might say that the demon has failed to live up to her own standards!—and so reminding the demon of this contradiction necessarily yields its self-destruction. Note, however, that she does this not through a revolutionary action, but through an act of further submission: that this reminding is done through the most conservative of means; in her encounter with her husband's lover, she makes no sign of resistance whatsoever, acting not merely domestically, but as a domestic. We begin, then, to see how this space seems to bring out the tendencies traditionally (and admiringly) ascribed to women in this woman; witness, for one, the transition from her nature as curious to her nature as demure and entirely nontalkative, which is certainly at odds with the previous negative descriptions of womanhood.

We may also see, in this sense, that if this encounter with the demonic world represents the encounter of the poor girl with the rich world, her reactions are significant: she herself makes obeisance to that wealth by lifting the golden hair from off the floor—realizing that the encounter of the golden hair with the floor, analogous to the world of wealth rubbing shoulders with her own poor status, is shameful, and that there must be an elevation involved.[78] However, such elevation must come, in order to be successful, through the adoption and adaptation of a kind of Jewish pietistic response—here linked to the quiet subordination of any potential "maleness" to a feminine domestic order, concretized through the docile acceptance of the status quo without any objection. If the traditional "realist" view of women's loquaciousness follows the rabbinic comment that "nine measures of speech were given to a woman,"[79] then silence is the sign of the traditional ideal. It is, after all, proverbially golden. Can one who is essentially poor become essentially rich? Yes; the story says, such transformation is in fact possible through the means of piety and good deeds, specifically good deeds that indicate the domestication of rebellion to the status quo.[80]

In doing so, we are allowed a moral solution that valorizes wealth as a reward for virtue, and thus allows the reader to hope for wealth without guilt while literally demonizing those societal structures that seem to value it as an end in itself, allowing the poor to serve as instrumentalities to their own ends, and nothing more. At the same time, this tale's sympathies and *crise de cœur* hardly serve as a call to revolutionary arms: one can see this tale as a nuanced means of reification of social norms while insisting on the possibility of progress.[81]

As such, the story's conclusion does not follow its most obvious literary paradigm—the story of Bluebeard's wife, where another overly curious woman defies an authority figure's demand and enters a specific, sexualized space related to the relations between husbands and wives. The punishment for Bluebeard's wife is death. The wife in our story ends up flourishing: she removes her rival and engages in a full satisfaction of her desires for wealth, marriage, and, perhaps most importantly, her essential and gendered curiosity.[82] This seems to be a primary reason why, at the "remarriage" banquet that ends the story, the rabbi's son's repetition of the entire story to the assembled audience is included, though the reading audience knows it. Solutions that incorporate the oral or folk nature of the story and thus allow for a stylistics of repetition may help, but hardly explain why this episode is repeated at this moment, while very little other information is repeated throughout the tale.[83] In this case, the solution seems to be related to the need to show the reward of the woman, and, for that matter, the storyteller: a return to order, a full explanation.

As such, this interpretation of the story allows for a more detailed reading of this important text. Such an interpretive strategy, notably, does not necessarily challenge our understanding of the mores of Ashkenazic culture; rather, it may allow us to negotiate the hierarchies of value between different valued mores and the means and aims to support and achieve them, the ways in which narratives may be used to trace shifting social stresses and boundaries, how texts can serve simultaneously as nuanced challenges to social order while remaining within that order. We may also think about how these choices are, or at least seem to be, shaped and conditioned by their appearance in the vernacular, and allow this text to serve as an early exhibit in the discussions over populist trends and differing ideological sympathies and their relation to language choice.

But it seems that this story, and, indeed, numerous stories like this one, allow for more than just the examination of nuanced structures of morality where values are, at least temporarily, at odds; they also allow us to speculate as to the capacities of the audience to serve as textual interpreters, as mentioned above. This complementary reading is based on an assertion that some of the most extrusive elements—that is to say, the erotic elements of the she-demon tale—are ancillary rather than essential to a fuller understanding of the story, which allows for it to function as a rather nuanced mechanism of expression of populist wish and socially conservative control. Among the questions that stem from this that are important for our purposes: first, how does the calculation of those elements as "extrusive" depend on a knowledge and understanding of the conventions of demonic marriage or copulation—Jewish and non-Jewish alike—more generally, and what does this say about the level of knowledge of this subgenre by the intended vernacular audience? Second, given such understanding (which itself can obviously be differentiated within the large group of "vernacular audience"), how do the departure from convention and the complexities identified above with the story reflect on the audience as sophisticated users of genre and conventional frameworks? Third, even given an understanding of the problems with the story from a genre perspective, how does an understanding of this solution (a solution that is, let's remember, assisted by a particular allusion that demands a certain familiarity with midrashic material, whether that familiarity comes from written or oral sources) navigate between the dangerous shoals of polemical intent and authorial oversophistication? That is to say, if we agree that some of the moral lessons and values mentioned above are in fact designed to resonate with the audience as a nuanced polemic, such design is itself based on an assumption of the audience's capacity to understand the reading of the story that leads to this polemic. One may be able to take, from this perspective of analyzing the story in terms of its "epistemological evidence," a minimalist or a maximalist approach—that either we understand the story in a way the audience was largely unable to, or that the story's complexities were designed by an author with a mind to their being understood.[84]

One must be aware that this is a continuum and not a boundary: to illustrate this I want to discuss one final example, which, it seems to me, is further along the maximalist criterion than the Jacob-Esau-Eliphaz material. The text itself is quite specific about the time periods between the various marriages; "three years" pass between the first and second marriage; and then "some ten years" between the second and the third, and the text tells us that the third marriage is arranged when the son "reached thirty" (120). At first glance, the precise timing of these events seems to be chosen at random, though it admittedly fits well with our psychologized sense of how confidence in the marriage process would have waned, and that the parents would have seen thirty as a time of real reevaluation.

This said, it should not go unnoted that these dates almost precisely correspond to certain differentiated time periods in the famous cycle of life recorded in the name of Yehuda Ben Tema in the Ethics of the Fathers (5:25): "... An eighteen-year-old, for the marriage canopy; a twenty-year-old, for the pursuit (*lirdof*); a thirty-year-old, for the strength."[85] Calculation suggests that the second marriage occurs around the precise time the Ethics of the Fathers characterizes as "for the pursuit"; though traditional understanding of this strange phrase is that twenty is the age for one to "pursue" a living; the Hebrew verb RDF, with its connotation of vengefulness and chase, seems somewhat at odds with this interpretation. Medieval commentators, therefore, suggest an alternative interpretation: at twenty, an individual is liable for the consequences of his own sins: the results "pursue" the individual, and serve as his nemesis.[86] Such a reading, valuable to the summoning of these kinds of punishing, demoniac forces more generally, is particularly valuable in explaining the she-demon's equally homicidal response to the second, nonobjecting wife: by this point, the seeds that the moral corruption of wealth have sown are being reaped, and the she-demon, the whirlwind, will strike regardless of cause. While at first there might have been the necessity for provocation, the second case is about the gathering of momentum, so much so that there is no necessity for direct provocation. One might go further to suggest how the "Age of Strength" is associated with a new potency on behalf of the husband—in his ability, after all, to satisfy two women, both the she-demon and his third wife—but the point seems clear enough, as another example of the more minor narrative crux solved by a more abstruse knowledge of intertextuality (and the more intense desire to apply that knowledge).

The nature of the complexity of the continuum notwithstanding, I would like to suggest that to focus on the polemic aspects of the text, as well as grounding the distinction between groups of readers at least in part in terms of their abilities to grasp intertextual allusions and employ them in a complex interpretive framework, will allow us to view at least some portion of the intended reading audience as remarkably sophisticated readers, regardless of the fact that they need very little if any of the traditional markers of sophistication and elite education in order to approach this story.

As is clear here, in the demon's bedroom, this place of essences as I have described it, is also a place where metaphorical constitution and real constitution (that is, narratively significant constitution) blur and coincide in a way that is not present in other places in the text. Intentionally or no, the writer has created a sphere, a primordial, prebirth location, or, if one prefers, a demon's lair and a heart of darkness, where there is no disruption between signifier and signified, where words and things are significantly more conjoined than in "real" life. If we can say that this encounter is at the story's heart, then we may also be able to say that this place is the heart of all stories—where tales very much coded as fantasy (or, at the very least, as stories with clearly didactic meanings that tend to stretch credulity as to their existence as historically meaningful narratives) can achieve, somehow, a higher level of actuality, since one of the characteristics of the fantastic sphere is consciously to elide these distinctions.

From Economics to Sexuality: The "Tale of Poznan"

Our examination of the *Mayse fun Vorms* has allowed us to see how these tropes are employed through one interpretive lens: examining the same submotif in a story written almost two centuries later will allow us to see how these images and conventions can be employed in similar ways but for very different purposes. As mentioned briefly above, the she-demon tale of Poznan appears in Tzvi Hirsh Kaidanover's *Kav ha-yoshor*,[87] the eighteenth-century moralistic work; unlike its narrative predecessor, the book provides us both general, conventional context (in its role as a book specifically dedicated to moral improvement) and local interpretive direction (in the paragraphs opening and closing the story) that frame the reader's experience in a way that the simply written *Mayse fun Vorms* does not.

The moral, cited above, harmoniously blends with the introductory paragraph, which reads, in Neugroschel's translation:

> One should know that the mother of all the demons is named Makhles. She has whole gangs of she-demons, who appear to people

> in broad daylight. They adorn themselves with all kinds of gems and jewels[88] and are very beautiful. Often they talk a man into being with them and they bear his children, who are thus half-human and half-demon. In the holy Torah, such illegitimate offspring are called *mashkhisim* [destroyers, demons of destruction]. The man who mates with a female demon is punished afterwards, when she kills him, and his entire family dies out, with no enduring posterity.[89] In regard to such matters, I have written down a story about recent events. (115)

The story focuses on the supernatural phenomenon of a haunted house[90]—or, more precisely, a haunted cellar in the house—and immediately sets itself up, narratively, as a mystery, a puzzle to be solved. Whoever entered was "harmed, and no one knew why. Once, a boy entered the cellar in broad daylight. A mere fifteen minutes later they found his corpse by the cellar door, but *they couldn't tell who killed him*" (115, emphasis mine). The mystery, however, is clearly only established to illustrate its ultimate transformation and rationalization to an explicable order, one in which the supernatural and the natural go hand in hand. As we see, the solution becomes (partially) apparent when the house more obviously displays the signs of demoniac (or, more precisely, demidemoniac) infestation: the *mashkhisim* move in and begin to act in poltergeist-like fashion, throwing around the residents' utensils and tossing their food to the floor.[91]

This simply explains the what, and not the why: "everyone was deeply upset that such a lovely house should be so dreadfully ruined in such a holy congregation as that of Poznan" (116). An attempted exorcism fails, because the demidemons claim that they have a right to the house; appealing to a Jewish court, they argue that "the house in question had once been inhabited by a Jewish goldsmith who lived with a she-demon" (116); the relationship, based on consuming erotic attraction—"the goldsmith truly loved our mother, the she-demon, he could not be without her for even an hour" (116)—was discovered by his human wife, who eventually prevailed upon the husband to procure an amulet that would drive away the she-demon. However, on the husband's deathbed, "the she-demon came to him with the children he had fathered and she began to weep because he was leaving her and her offspring. She fell upon him and kissed him and coaxed him to allow her to live somewhere" (117). The goldsmith, apparently moved by her protestations, offers her the cellar. War and turmoil in the area leave no other direct heirs but the demidemons; and so they insist on their claim. The residents claim title proceeding from the goldsmith's deceased human children, and charge "you are half-demons and not part of the people Israel," adding that "the she-demon had forced herself upon the goldsmith and compelled him to live with her" (117). The court decides in favor of the human residents, and the exorcist (*ba'al shem*) then manages to expel the demons, apparently aided by the force of the ruling (and, perhaps in some part, the demidemons' acquiescence).

The framing paragraphs certainly generate an interpretive frame of the transgressive act based on erotic desires. It may not be the case that the particular narrative of the story bears out the moral's contention that "sometimes a she-demon appears in the guise of a harlot and mates with a man, causing him and his family to perish. Each man must therefore take care to mate only with his wife and not waste his seed"—there is no evidence that the goldsmith ever believes the woman he leaves his wife for to be a harlot (or that he engages in masturbation).[92] Of course, there is no evidence in the story that he believes her to be a she-demon, either. The only accentuation the story provides is of the force of his desire for her—an active desire, where he runs to spend time with her, even abandoning his family on the first night of Passover in order to spend time in bed with the she-demon! Conversely, his wife's discovery of the she-demon's bedroom, and the couple's lying together, is predicated on both this abandonment and, tellingly, the comment that "As for his real wife, he lived badly with her. She must have sensed that there was a good reason for *his failure to perform his conjugal duties* (116, emphasis mine)."[93]

The she-demon, too, is presented as an object of sexual desire, as well as a sexual and erotic being: she is presented as a seducer, as a weeper, as an individual who needs to be taken care of by her "husband" and, most tellingly, as a mother.[94] Indeed, aside from her threatening posture as the sexual surrogate and competitor, the she-demon herself is not presented as harmful—only the demidemons are destructive, the results of the individual man's sin, powerful concretizations of the moralistic text's message that even "victimless" sins such as onanism can have deep and enduring consequences, children, as it were. And if their location—in the cellar of the house—is a concretization of the metaphorical equation of the house to both the family and the human body, we can suggest that the key to their behavior is related to the internal factors that lie deeply within the familial constitution, and, more directly, within the lower half of the body, the location of the genitalia.

Similarly, the spread of the poltergeist-like activity from the cellar up into the main rooms of the house can be taken to suggest the idea that the corruption or perversion that begins with the use of sexual urges for nonreligiously approved ends begins to spread from the basement (that is, merely from the sexual realm), to the realm of all physical objects as well that are being used for profaned purposes. In other words, the story gives a metaphorical depiction of an extremely insightful characterization of the psychological process of moral decline: a deep engagement with the physical in one sphere leads to profane engagement in others as well, other rooms of the house, other spheres of physical activity, most importantly eating.

Such an emphasis on concretization reminds us that the frames are not only interpretive in a moral and literary fashion, but an epistemological one as well: the author of the *Kav ha-yoshor*, in order to drive home the moral message of the text, predicates the importance of the moral message on the manifestation of these supernatural phenomena as literal, not metaphorical.[95] The reason that one should not engage in prostitution or masturbation[96] is, at least in part, because of the existence of demons and the possible appearance of demidemons. As such, ideological considerations mandate the appearance of authenticating details: beginning with the narratorial assurance of the first phrase, "one should know," the odd emphasis that these demons "appear to people in broad daylight," the historical references of the story (the reference to "recent events," the dating of the first part of the story to the years 5441–5442, the linkage of the end of the story to the war in Poland between 5408 and 5418), the scientific or empirical construction of the story (an inexplicable phenomenon at a later date investigated, and the reason stemming from earlier events),[97] the rationalization of the fantastic (that is, the calling of the demons to a judicial review), and, perhaps most importantly, the insistence at the story's end that the reasons for engaging in moral behavior are a prophylactic device against an actual supernatural attack; we see here a neat conjunction of the supernatural and the real.

The ultimate exorcism of the demidemons, then, accomplished by a *ba'al shem*, is both the literal account of a wonder-working rabbi (not strictly hagiographical, since we only know his first name, Yoyl) and its moral and metaphorical analogue of the exorcism of desire and the sexual purification of the individual (since the demons, seemingly, represent the regrettable propensity towards profanation on the individual's part). Both trends are illustrative of a major change in Jewish society between the time of the two stories, and perhaps *the* major change within the representation of the supernatural: the increasing spread and popularization of Lurianic kabbalah within central and eastern Europe in the late seventeenth and early eighteenth centuries. Though the dissemination of notions of *tikkun*, in which material actions are redeemed by *kavvana*, would reach its height in the teachings of Hasidism, books like the *Kav ha-yoshor* introduced these teachings in subtle, hidden form to wider audiences.[98] Though it seems unlikely that the message was apprehended by the wide majority of readers, this does not mean it is not a basic principle of the text. Equally important for our purposes is the "demonization of life" within the kabbalistic worldview more generally[99] and the emphasis in kabbalistic thought—popular and otherwise—on sexual matters, particularly masturbation and nocturnal emissions, which the author of the Zohar believed to be "evidence of intercourse with female demons."[100]

This also accords, incidentally, with the strange description of the children of the *mashkhisim* as *khitsonim*, or "dissenters," as Neugroschel puts it. A more literal translation of the word would be "outsiders," or "externals," again reifying notions of the sexual desires or profanations that the demons represent as shells or husks, *kelippot*, on the outside of the pure, *tikkun*-effecting action. This also explains why the demons here are "invisible": as motivations, temptations, perspectives, they are abstract, though with very real consequences for action. The poltergeist model is therefore a highly compelling one for this story: an invisible yet forceful entity. The house itself, the Jewish body and source of action, should be free of all such husks and outside motivations. Sadly, it is not, and once they begin to have an effect, they become stronger and stronger. This expansionist notion may also explain how the moral structure of the story is still highly effective without being limited to a rigorous equivalence of individual sin and directly evident punishment for that sin through the identical mechanism of the sin; it focuses rather—and precisely—on the corrosive effects of individual sin on the broader environment as a whole. This may help to resolve one critic's difficulty that the protagonist's death is not directly correlated to the events of the narrative; he dies in the war that engulfs the environment. However, in a mystical worldview that correlates everything, such dissociation is only seeming, not real.[101]

All this said, we can see that the text itself retains some elements of the original, economic tropes of its generic predecessor from two centuries past. We might put aside, for the moment, the similarities in descriptive imagery—and not make too much of the fact that the demon's bedroom is similarly beautiful with "many candles, gold and silver vessels, and a bed decorated with gold" (116), since to present the she-demon as appropriately seductive, one might imagine that some form of beauty would be desirable. The inclusion of the information that the husband in question was a goldsmith—a telling detail that seems to have little particular purpose within the narrative—may begin to serve as a reminder of the continuity of the resonance of economic matters within the genre. But most prominent, of course, is that the economization of the romance between the she-demon and her husband has been displaced, as a result of the refocusing of that romance as reflective of erotic and sexual issues, to the internal frame of the narrative. By this I mean not the opening and closing paragraphs, which return to the moral, but rather the catalyzing narrative question: who owns the house?

It is not insignificant that the question driving the story is presented as a tale of economic distress—the house is unlivable, the utensils are unusable—and that the argument between the demidemons and the residents is over a commodity, the questions of rightful inheritance.[102] By this time, though, economics has become relegated to the margins of the story: the true narrative puzzle is not who has rightful claim, but why the demidemons are even there to pose a claim in the first place. And those considerations are firmly located within the realm of the ideological agendas of the story, which concern eros.[103] This is not to say that the author of the *Kav ha-yoshor* was unmindful of issues of socioeconomic distress within the community; he writes scathingly at one point how the rich "strut about in their luxurious clothes and offer huge dowries for their children, while the simple folk of the seed of Abraham, Isaac, and Jacob go about in tatters."[104] It is simply the case that, in an ideological worldview that places the opportunity for providing solutions to that distress firmly upon the individual ability to effect real change through moral improvement, particularly though not solely in the sphere of personal purity (in a corporeal and sexual sense), the narrative can be employed for more useful (from the author's perspective) concerns.

This is also not to say that the change is solely, or perhaps even primarily, a function of the passing of two centuries; there is at least one other Yiddish tale of she-demon marriage from this latter period—the tale of the "Queen of Sheba," found in the 1696 collection of Worms-related stories *Mayse Nisim*—which seems to revolve around issues of economy, not sexuality. In the tale, seemingly pressed into service to explain a particularly odd name, "To the Devil's Head," given to a local house, a poor resident of the house is bemoaning his fortune when he is approached by the "Queen of Sheba," with beautiful golden hair. She promises him wealth if he sleeps with her on a daily basis; he does (in a bed located in his store), and she fulfills her promise. She insists he keep their secret, but when his wife becomes curious she follows him to the store, sees the pair lying together, and though she leaves quietly, the damage is done. The she-demon threatens to kill him, but, upon his begging, relents; she promises to disappear, takes all of his newly acquired wealth with her, and he becomes a pauper once more.[105]

A clear moral statement is included at the end of the story, that one should not go astray after money; and even the subtextual moral message, as Zfatman notes, seems to be financial in nature, connected to the dangers of taking charity.[106] Though a full discussion of the narrative itself is beyond our scope here, even a quick perusal of the summary clearly suggests how imbued the work is with anxieties about money and how the she-demon presents herself, and is represented as, wealth (and her ambiguous demonic nature is a clear indication that wealth achieved quickly always has its moral—in this case adulterous—price).

Returning momentarily to the "Tale of Poznan," a final observation may allow the opportunity for some conclusions. Much of the tale, as we have noted above, occurs on the first night of Passover—the husband's abandonment of his wife, his wife's search for him, and discovery of the demon's bedroom. The author's decision to locate these processes on that particular date may relate to the fact that the first night of Passover is *leyl shimurim*, a night of protection, where individuals have particular protection from evil and demonic forces, explaining why the woman is able to leave the demon's bedroom unharmed. But perhaps more important is the specific time within the Passover seder that the husband leaves: "when it was time to eat the afikomen."

That portion of the seder is known as *Tsafun*, which literally means "the hidden" or "the secretive" but could also be translated as "the esoteric." Secrets are, of course, revealed at this time, and we have seen how the *Kav ha-yoshor*'s popularization of previously esoteric kabbalism means that this narrative metaphorically recapitulates a historicized process of knowledge acquisition. But these interpretations' dependence on different kinds of knowledge in the reading audience, and the employment of that knowledge, resonates for our general discussion of readership.

Indeed, much of this chapter's emphasis is on readership—how various stories with distinctive narrative features generate differing foci and ideological concerns within particular generic conventions, and how the possibility of plying generic distinctions and then to deviate from them as ideological frames become necessary—or problematic—for appropriate interpretation of the narrative is the work of a complex and complicated readership. Such an analysis of the operations that the readers may take on, however, must stem, at least in large part, from a recursive process, a hermeneutic circle, that begins with the gaps and cruxes in the text, and only then expands to see how that text can be mediated through the contextual circumstances we know about ideology, social and cultural facts, and audience knowledge.

These analyses reveal how interpretive frameworks focusing on sexuality may be complemented or replaced by those concerned with economy, or vice versa; how the features of folk and fairy tale may be used to preach an economic conservatism that privileges subordination to socioeconomic hierarchy (while allowing for carefully controlled and thus domesticated revolutionary changes of state); and how discourses of unruly, challenging gender—of curious and questing women, of demonic spirit—are shaped and controlled into virtuous and wealthy, if quiescent, wifeliness and motherhood. And finally, how the demon tales, in differing times and ways, insist on controlling skepticism—whether about the demons themselves, in the case of the *Kav ha-yoshor*, or the messages that they represent, in the tale of Worms. Questions of gender, class, belief, and skepticism are all present in their respective ways.

But they are revealed, it seems, through a process that yields surprising reconceptualizations of even what we believe to be the most naïve of audiences. Those audiences, in these readings, are not the passive men but the curious and questing women, the real heroines of the stories. Indeed, if we allow our readers to go all the way into the demon's bedroom, then we may not be surprised if they emerge, in our estimation, transformed into remarkable beings themselves.

5. The Allegorical Spirit

Dybbuk Tales and Their Hidden Lessons

I question not but several of my readers will know the lawyer in the stage-coach the moment they hear his voice ... To prevent, therefore, any such malicious applications, I declare here, once and for all, I describe not men, but manners; not an individual, but a species. Perhaps it will be answered, Are not the characters then taken from life? To which I answer in the affirmative: nay, I believe I might aver that I have writ little more than I have seen.

—Henry Fielding, *Joseph Andrews*, Chapter 1, Book 3.

At the end of the previous chapter, we discussed how a particular historical movement significantly influenced the changing employment of the conventions of a specific genre, thus displaying readerly sophistication and complexity, and how the vicissitudes of that historical change allowed for the differentiation of authors' and readers' approaches to the ontological status of the material. If the first tale, the *Mayse fun Vorms*, was significantly more interested in presenting the slightest dusting of authenticity to allow for the moral message of myth to come through, rather than focusing on significant details, the Lurianic kabbalists' perspective on the faith-demands it needed to make on its readers necessitated a studied reemphasis on metaphysical and ontological reality—in much the same way we saw in some of the materials concerning the witchcraft debates in the second chapter. Such final speculations, which allowed for an emphasis that simultaneously focused on the importance of authenticity in the narrow, historical sense and the presentation of the material as universally, metaphysically, and allegorically true, allow for an expansion of the complicated questions of belief and skepticism, which themselves allow us to investigate the complicated readers who attempt to untangle the writer's presentation of these questions within that narrative.

In discussing those writers and readers, the observations should be reiterated that writers are themselves first and foremost readers, by definition, and, particularly in the age preceding modernism's aestheticist revolutions, they are acutely attuned to and solicitous of their readers' epistemic conventions, writing mindful of the latter's interpretive strategies, possible objections, potential confusions, and the like—concerns that they share as readers with strategies largely overlapping those of their target audiences'.[1] Their works may therefore provide us with historical information entirely different from the historical acts they purport to recount, and whose historicity may be uncertain. That information might consist of a (partial) historical reconstruction of contemporary readers and writers' "intellectual relations," a concept encompassing questions of the identity of the texts' readers, the knowledge they require to understand them, what that "understanding" might mean, and how the texts themselves might offer the information necessary for answering these questions, at least partially.

The next (sub-)genre we will use to approach these various questions is the tale of dybbuk possession, with specific reference to the late seventeenth-century "Tale of the Evil Spirit of Koretz." The dybbuk tale, by definition, is a story of in-betweenness, as S. An-sky notes in his famous play's subtitle.[2] In investigating the various "worlds" the dybbuk story lies between, we may learn even more about the circumstances of and approaches taken by the readers and writers of early modern Yiddish literature.

Dybbuks: Some General Historical Background

A full discussion of the broad forms of spirit possession in Jewish history—and the techniques for exorcising those possessing spirits—is beyond our scope here and has been admirably discussed elsewhere,[3] but Matt Goldish's general definition, that "a spirit possession is a phenomenon in which a person (or those close to a person) believes that an alien spirit, either a ghost of a dead human or a disembodied person of another type, has entered the person and controls or influences some or all of the person's actions or thoughts, while the person's own spirit or soul is partially or fully dormant," seems largely apt.[4] Though spirit possession so broadly defined is certainly present in Jewish history since at least the time of Jesus and perhaps even during the biblical period,[5] and includes entities variously known as the *ibbur*,[6] *gilgul*, *maggid*,[7] or *ruach*, our discussion here focuses solely on early modern Yiddish spirit possession literature, and therefore primarily on the entity now known as the *dybbuk*, a word taken from the Hebrew for "cleaving" or "sticking."[8] Such emphasis stems not only from this book's temporal focus, but from the fact that few true *narratives* of possession exist before the early modern period, though the previous discussions, mostly technical considerations of spirit possession's nature and attempts to "cure" it, are certainly important for the later narrative developments.[9]

Joseph Dan has provided a useful overview of the earlier period, noting that all conceptions of the dybbuk must be connected by definition to Jewish philosophical speculation about the soul and particularly concerning reincarnation—the idea that "souls are constant while bodies are transient."[10] Dan writes that though the idea of the soul as divisible into various components (some of which, if the souls are those of sinners, can join a new soul in another's body, becoming part of it to help those former components, *nitzotzot*, atone for their previous sinful needs) dates back to the late thirteenth century, "only in the sixteenth century, in works like the *Galya Raza* and, most notably, in the Lurianic kabbalah, did it achieve a central position."[11] The kabbalah's subsequent popularization—particularly Lurianic kabbalah—through works such as Naphtali Bacharach's *Emek Hamelekh* (1648) and Isaiah Horowitz's *Shnei Lukhot Habrit* (1649) allowed for these ideas' spread.[12]

The process of dissemination began slowly, generally in communities of mystics in Italy and the land of Israel, complementing the increasing contemporary Christian European interest in demonology, particularly the "proliferation of witchcraft accusations and cases of spirit possession from the mid-sixteenth to the mid-seventeenth centuries"; the latter were also prominent in Islamic contexts.[13] This combination of external influences and internal mystical focus led to an explosion of Jewish accounts of both benevolent and malevolent spirit possession in the sixteenth and seventeenth centuries,[14] particularly (though not solely) in the Mediterranean region.

Safed, at the epicenter of this activity, was increasingly known as a place where kabbalistic adepts like Moses Cordovero, Joseph Karo, Isaac Luria, and Hayyim Vital "sought to achieve a benevolent and desired state of possession ... insofar as they enabled an individual to reach beyond the limitations of the material world to a world construed as constituting a deeper reality."[15] They did so through the practiced and intentional cultivation of states of trance or possession achieved through proper conduct, preparation rites (including *gerushin*, *yikhudim*, and communing with zaddikim's spirits by, among other techniques, stretching out on their graves), and the repetition of words or sentences.[16] The city itself featured prominently in these developments; its Jewish population tripled in size between 1525 and 1555, and the new wave of mostly Iberian European immigrants seemed particularly preoccupied with death—a preoccupation manifested in a new obsession with possession by the dead in the bodies of the Safedian living.[17] R. Moshe Alsheikh described Safed in 1591 as a city that "has forever been a city of interred dead, to which people from throughout the lands of exile came to die ... who from all the cities of the exile, near and far, does not have in [Safed] a father or brother, son or daughter, mother or sister, or some other of their flesh, them or their bones."[18] Isaac Luria "constantly beheld the dead in his midst" there.[19]

Safed's main kabbalists would perhaps unsurprisingly then distinguish themselves in the rapidly expanding world of possession, in theoretical and legal works as well as possession narratives. Joseph Karo himself (1488–1575), the recipient of a famous *maggid*, was the exorcist in "the first known possession narrative in early modern Jewish sources";[20] Cordovero (1522–1570) writes in detail of the real possibility of malevolent possession by an evil *ibbur*—being "impregnated" by the soul of someone while still alive.[21] Isaac Luria (1534–1572)—through his own writing and that of his disciples'—provides a strong theoretical and practical framework for spirit possession; his kabbalistic writings would therefore serve as the source of much of the popular discourse about spirit possession (as well as mystical thought more generally) in the coming centuries.

Luria applies his parallel dualistic structure between good and evil to questions of transmigration: both good and evil *ibburim* exist, some beneficial to their host and others maleficent. Luria's disciple, Hayyim Vital (1542–1620), one of Lurianic kabbalah's main expositors, defines the evil *ibburim* as "those souls of the wicked, who, after their death, do not merit to enter Gehinnom. They enter living people's bodies due to our numerous transgressions, speaking and telling all that happens to them there, as is known, may the Merciful save us ..."[22] His precise distinction between a *ruach ra'ah* (or our *dybbuk*) and a demon (*shed*) is a case in point; the former was defined as the

> spirit of a person, which after his death enters the body of a living person, as is known. First one must recognize their signs: the demon compels the person, and he moves spasmodically with his arms and

> legs, and emits white saliva from his mouth like horse-froth. With a ghost, he feels pain and distress in his heart to the point of collapse. However, the primary distinction is when he speaks, for then he will tell you what he is, particularly if he speaks after having been compelled by you with adjurations and decrees.[23]

Luria also turns his (and his disciples') attention to spirit exorcism, sending his disciple Vital in 1571 to exorcise a spirit from a possessed Safedian woman;[24] in doing so, he develops a new approach to exorcism that expands on his understanding of possession and develops analogues between God, the created universe, and the human soul that "was its mirror and gateway. When individual souls went astray, then, their rectification required the exorcist to engage with this deep structure."[25]

This engagement was based not only on mystical speculation and incantation, but on a highly medicalized examination and treatment, which allows for rational (and skeptical) approaches to perceived phenomena that may or may not be supernatural. Vital, for example, relies on diagnostic tools to differentiate between various medical and spiritual illnesses, including dybbuk and demoniac possession.[26] The general symptoms of dybbuk possession, "suddenly falling down in a dead faint, exuding a strong odor, xenoglossia, seemingly impossible mental or physical feats and subsequent amnesia" are familiar in many sorts of possession;[27] however, xenoglossia, so different from the other symptoms that potentially seem the result of more "natural" phenomena, was considered "a symptom that was irrefutable evidence of possession," as it had been in Christian culture for centuries.[28] The display of concomitant techniques and models of exorcism became part of the standard hagiographical model not only for Luria and his circle, but in possession narratives more generally.[29]

It may not be surprising, then, that the rise of the possession narrative is simultaneous with a great age of Hebrew hagiographies; Safedian possession narratives begin to appear in print during Luria and Vital's period, serving as the literary—and perhaps the life—models for later possession material.[30] Works containing such narratives include Judah Hallewa's 1545 *Zafnat Paaneah* (Decipherer of Mysteries) and Vital's autobiographical *Sefer Hahezyonot* (Book of Visions); the latter mentions Safedian cases from the 1570s and a case from Damascus as late as 1609. Other seventeenth-century works containing sixteenth-century Safedian accounts include Jacob Zemah's *Ronu le-Yaakov* (Rejoice for Jacob) and *Meshivat Nafesh* (Restoration of the Soul), and Joseph Sambari's *Divrei Yosef* (Words of Joseph).[31] Many of these works serve as the basis for later possession tales, which are often passed off by the author as actual contemporary events, rather than the retellings of the older stories they are.[32] This notably occurred as Safedian tales traveled to both eastern and western Europe. Elijah Falcon's *The Great Event in Safed*, published in broadsheet form and written in response to a possession case that began in February 1571, circulated in Europe by the late 1570s, reaching Poland by 1579–1580 at the latest.[33]

Perhaps the most important expansion of Safedian possession accounts in the seventeenth century occurs in works like Joseph Delmedigo's 1628 *Taalumot Khakmah* (Mysteries of Wisdom), Naftali Bacharach's 1648 *Emek Hamelekh* (Valley of the King), and Menasseh ben Israel's 1651 *Nishmat Khayyim* (Soul of Life). The narratives collected in these works, particularly the last, which "deployed the largest collection of dybbuk stories ever assembled in a single work," serve as the basis for much of the later possession literature, and allow us to move "from the history of spirit possession to a history of its representation."[34] Though a full discussion of *Nishmat Khayyim* is beyond our scope here, a few comments will help introduce our broader discussion.

Scholars have argued that *Nishmat Khayyim* was Menasseh's response to a series of controversies in the Amsterdam community over the soul's nature, its survival after bodily death, and the eternality of punishment.[35] The book argues for the preexistence of the soul against contemporary skepticism and perceived heresy, and uses the phenomenon of spirit possession—which by definition requires a separate, bodiless spirit to do the possessing—to prove that preexistence; in Chajes' wonderful phrase, "revealing the existence of the demonic was the surest way to reestablish faith in the existence of the divine." In doing so, *Nishmat Khayyim* participates in a more widespread tradition employing demonological evidence from contemporary non-Jewish and Jewish sources to support its theologically conservative and pious points.[36]

Such use of proof illustrates Menasseh's strategy of eschewing reliance on authoritative tradition and logical demonstration in favor of privileging proof afforded by direct experience or sense perception—even given the presumed difficulty of "experiencing" a ghost or spirit. Menasseh writes repeatedly that the fact that "spirits of men who have died enter the bodies of the living is a complete proof, over which there can be no doubt, for the immortality of the soul." Menasseh "thoroughly demonized magical activity, aligning himself with the most severe early modern demonological theorists and their scholastic predecessors," and even frames some of the Jewish material in terms highly reminiscent of the Christian European witchcraft literature.[37] Indeed, mutual Jewish and Christian agreement on this phenomenon's essential truth allowed it, for Menasseh, to ostensibly transcend theology and enter the world of rationality, or, for that matter, history.[38] As the rest of this chapter will show, such connections between polemic, historicity, and theological anxiety over communal skepticism—and the role of the supernatural in simultaneously exemplifying and alleviating that anxiety—are strongly at play in our possession account as well.

A second question raised by *Nishmat Khayyim* concerns language and audience. Chajes argues that Menasseh's addressees are generally "a non-Hebrew literate readership, Gentiles, as well as present and former conversos," and *Nishmat Khayyim*'s introductory statements do suggest a Gentile audience. The book is written in Hebrew, however, implying Menasseh had in mind "his Christian Hebraist friends, conversos who had acquired a facility in Hebrew literature, and his rabbinic peers."[39] The complex interplay here between desired audience and that audience's linguistic capability reminds the scholar of the multilingual dynamic within Jewish literature generally speaking, particularly—as our discussion of spirit possession moves to a European milieu—Hebrew and Yiddish literature,[40] where the desire for popular appeal and widespread polemic or didactic effect (to say nothing of commercial success) is balanced against the desire for elite authorial status or esoteric concerns, or both.

It is hardly surprising that in materials concerning spirit possession written in Yiddish, the former elements are more prominently at play. A Safedian possession narrative that also appears in Sambari's later *Divrei Yosef* is in the *Mayse-bukh*, a pietistic anthology published in 1602, though the Yiddish version lacks any identifying details of place or time.[41] In the story as it appears in the *Mayse-bukh*, an evil spirit has entered a young man;[42] the spirit, who has drowned at sea, has been punished for his adulterous sins by becoming a dybbuk.[43] The dybbuk, who demonstrates his power to reveal bystanders' and observers' hidden sins (particularly of a sexual nature, notably homosexuality),[44] is eventually exorcised and flies away.

Few details of any sort are included in the tale; this possession story's notably clear didactic function, entertainingly delivered, clearly renders it a neat fit for this narrative anthology dedicated to providing moral and ethical instruction in the vernacular. The story demonstrates the importance of sexual fidelity and propriety, and illustrates the power of Jewish law in general, proven by an unimpeachable source from beyond the grave ("the world of truth," as it was known), a message aimed directly at the broad audience that was giving the rabbis who authored these Yiddish moral works cause for concern. Issues of audience are central to our discussion of the most extensive and important tale of dybbuk possession in early modern Yiddish literature, a tale mentioned only in passing by most of the latest scholarship on Jewish spirit possession.[45] Before we begin that discussion, some final historical details are worth recalling.

A significant wave of positive spirit possessions occurs following the messianic movement of Sabbatai Zevi in 1665–1666;[46] perhaps most notable is an account of an exorcism in Cairo by Hayyim Vital's son Samuel in the summer of 1666, which includes a significant penitential prayer asking for the soul to be allowed entry into Gehenna. Describing the event, Chajes adds that it "bespeaks a theatricality utterly absent from Luria's method";[47] we will have cause to consider the theatrical elements in our text as well, elements that blur the lines once more between historical fact and literary representation. For the purposes of our account, which traffics in the popular circulation of tropes and archetypes rather than the details of kabbalistic theosophy, the latter is all that is necessary. Recalling Sabbateanism also serves as a useful reminder of just how pervasive the spread of Lurianism—or, at least of Lurianic hagiography—was in eastern Europe.[48] Finally, it should be noted that tales of dybbuk possession also occur in eastern European Jewish religious literature after the early modern period, most notably in mystically oriented Hasidic communities in Poland, Russia, Hungary, and Lithuania.[49]

"The Tale of the Spirit of Koretz": First Considerations

Maase shel ruakh bk'k koretz bishaat haraash milkhama ("The Tale of the Spirit of the Holy Community of Koretz During the Chaos of War") is a sixteen-page octavo chapbook, or *mayse-bikhl*; only one copy of the book remains extant, at Oxford's Bodleian Library, and though it is undated and lacks a place of publication, Sara Zfatman-Biller has identified it as stemming from Prague in the 1660s.[50] She has also suggested the work marks a new stage in the development of "a folk-literary tradition that began to crystallize some hundred years earlier":[51] the first time a dybbuk possession tale had been sufficiently developed to merit its own separate *mayse-bikhl*. It is also seemingly one of the first written cases of dybbuk possession originating in an eastern European context, here the area of Volhynia in the Ukraine, as opposed to the Mediterranean.[52] The story is simple enough: Mindl bat Eliye from the community of Kutlaniye is possessed by a dybbuk and develops "various pathological symptoms." After three years of attempting to cure her, her family and supporters turn to mystics, *baalei shem*, for help. Five wonder-working *baalei shem* from various regions of Volhynia and elsewhere attempt to heal her through various magical means; when they fail, the girl is brought to Koretz, where R' Borekh Kat, assisted by a group of *baalei shem* from Lovertov, expels the spirit.[53]

Understanding the work may involve asking how this dybbuk story functions in both its historical and literary contexts, for writers and readers alike. Put another way: is this story true? What does that mean? How does the author present this text as a narrative that would have struck its readers as a faithful recording of an actual historical event? Are elements included that generate readerly dissonance and difficulty in making that determination? If so, what is these elements' purpose, and why would the author include them? Does the inclusion, exclusion, or artful combination of these "authenticating" and "dissonant" elements help us to reconstruct or define the work's reading community and their abilities to make determinations about literary genre, historical context, and epistemological definition of texts? Finally, are current readers' dispositions to view the story as "inauthentic," or certain elements as "dissonant," influenced by current literary trends and approaches, useful in comprehending this text's "operation" in the late seventeenth century?

Any approach to these questions might profitably heed Matt Goldish's warning in his recent anthology of critical works on Jewish spirit possession that "[e]xplicating the history of possession and exorcism ideas is hampered by the problems of relating possession *events* to possession *accounts*" or J. H. Chajes' comments that his approach to Safed possession narrative, similar to that of recent historians, is less concerned with "ascertaining the historicity of the 'facts' involved so much as determining how the accounts of these facts reflect the mentality of their producers."[54] These warnings provide a telling counterpoint to the comments of one of Yiddish literature's greatest critics, Max Weinreich, about our story. Weinreich writes:

> First, it seems that there can be no doubt, that this was an actual event. I do not mean to say that a dybbuk actually inhabited the young woman and that the famous rebbe Borekh Kat exorcised him, but that there was such a sick young woman, who was dragged around for months from one shtetl to the next, from one bal-shem to the next after she had been ill for several years ... this is certain to me. The entire development of the account is so natural, that we are hardly amazed at all, as we get close to the end of the book, that the writer of the book was present for the entire event.[55]

Though our skepticism may be greater than Weinreich's even from the start, a look at the author's undeniably employed strategies of authentication may help us understand Weinreich's assertion of the material's historical basis (his claim of the account's realistic or naturalistic nature notwithstanding, which, as we will see, may be harder to understand; one might also speculate on his assumptions about the author's cognitive process in transferring what he presumably believes the author thinks is true to the written work now appearing before us).[56] These authentication strategies, some discussed by Zfatman-Biller, include first the specific identification of personalities, possibly including known historical personages, within the text.[57] Second, the specificity of places; no less than seven geographic sites are specified here, all of which, with one exception, are located in the southeastern part of Volhynia in the Ukraine, within a few dozen miles of Berditchev, an important means of generating familiarity—and perhaps authenticity—to eastern European Jews.[58] A third authenticating strategy is the narrative's specification of time,[59] with respect to the short period of time passing between the purported occurrence and its report, as well as the constant mention of particular days of the week or holidays, which at least at first seems to ground the narrative more concretely. A fourth strategy is the story's usage of eyewitnesses, thus continuing Menasseh ben Israel's reliance on empirical evidence through direct sensory experience.[60] We may, of course, have reason to be skeptical about all of these strategies in their representation in a literary account.

Perhaps the best way to begin analyzing this skepticism is through a particularly powerful instantiation of the final authenticating strategy: the narrator-eyewitness's insistence on the story's authenticity, which he also relates to the temporal criterion of proof. His opening remarks in the proem make this clear: "This story occurred in our day / Let the world know about it in every way. / And you can be very sure / That such wonders have never happened before" (61).[61] The statement's contradictions—or at least its contradictory implications—are significant. On a literal level, the narrator is simply stating that any reader's possible doubts about the story's authenticity should be assuaged both by his assertion of its actual occurrence and the presumed possibility of proof given the event's location in contemporaneous time.

On second glance, though, these comments—not to mention the employment of some of the strategies mentioned earlier—seem to betray a particular anxiety: that the story would *not* be considered authentic. Why stress, whether implicitly or explicitly, the story's truthfulness if no sense existed that the alternative might be a possibility?[62] Simply claiming such pronouncements to be matters of standard convention is hardly a solution, as it merely abstracts the question to the nature of the authenticity of the conventions or of the genre. This implication gains particular importance given the quote's second section, which may be taken precisely as one such conventional statement: that no such miracles and wonders, at least to this degree, have ever previously occurred. If simply viewed from the perspective of establishing the story's authenticity, this is a somewhat counterproductive statement: though it is certainly possible to argue that a unique event is also true, it flies somewhat in the face of reason; it is more reasonable, of course, to present this as another example of the same presumably accepted and acceptable stories previously heard and read by individuals. Why this emphasis on uniqueness?

The proem's very next line provides the expected answer: "So that every man this tale can buy" (61). Our writer has commercial interests, and selling averageness hardly seems a successful business strategy. Perhaps the explicit linkage of the story's uniqueness and marvelousness to its commercial prospects stirred up readerly anxieties about the previous claim's historicity; this may tell us something about the reading community's ability—or willingness—both to demand truth in their marvelous stories and to dismiss accounts failing to live up to those demands.

Even if the proem failed to generate readerly anxiety, though, numerous other elements might have done so. Zfatman-Biller notes that despite the text's pervasive authenticating strategies, certain features calling attention to its fictiveness should not be overlooked. At least three of the ostensibly authenticating names are standard typological tropes: these exorcists' names are precisely those of the three patriarchs Abraham, Isaac, and Jacob, which tends to strike modern readers—and perhaps also contemporary ones—as accentuating the text's fictive nature.[63] Despite the authenticity of the place-names mentioned in the text, the geographical travel between them is peculiarly schematized in structure: in alternate episodes, the victim travels to her potential saviors and they subsequently travel to her, in contrast to a unidirectional model, where either she would have constantly gone from place to place or they would come to one place. The story's ending, which conventionally would almost always feature either the spirit's expulsion (or lack of same), or a description of the victim's status after the expulsion (healing, worsening, or death), is strangely divergent here, generating readerly dissonance with a "happy end" (the victim's marriage) unique to the genre; Zfatman-Biller suggests this may simply relate to the author's desire to incorporate a general element of folktale, the concluding marriage of the princess.[64] As we will see, other reasons may exist, which place this seemingly contradictory element in a more unified context. Still, enough elements that generate skepticism exist to allow us not only to question the narrator's claims of authenticity, but to place this text "between two worlds" from an authorial perspective, wondering about the *author's* reasons for undercutting his own authenticity and the concomitant interaction with readers. A deeper look at the narrative and some of its unique features may offer some suggestions in this regard, and about the narrative more generally and the world of readers and writers it inhabits.[65]

One of these unique features—a final element at least formally militating against the authenticity of the text as reportorial document—is the entire narrative's appearance in rhyme. Such extensive usage of rhyme is extremely rare among contemporary Yiddish *mayse-bikhlekh*; of the dozens of extant contemporary *mayse-bikhlekh* ranging to the end of the eighteenth century, only three others were rhymed: *Mayse fun ayn kale*, *Mayse fun shloyme hameylekh*, and *Mayse man un vayb*, all of which were apparently published in the same time and place (Amsterdam, around 1700).[66] While Zfatman-Biller (undoubtedly correctly) suggests this feature proves the text's original language of composition is Yiddish,[67] and that it may serve to indicate actual or (more likely) generic continuity with the literature's oral roots in a period not far removed from such material's oral circulation, where rhyme played a substantial role,[68] the work's rhymed nature may also call attention to its nature as an artificial document, a constructed act of tale telling, thus alerting the audience to consider other ways this purportedly authentic event may be transformed (if not invented) to serve authorial purposes.[69]

Such consideration may develop into full-fledged dissonance when its interaction with another textual feature diverging from contemporary conventions of possession narratives—the treatment of the character of Mindl—is noted. The victim's role in spirit possession narratives is generally highly circumscribed; little is usually known about her (or him) other than her anonymous and passive nature, and she rarely speaks directly. Here, in contrast, the story gives us the victim's name, a description of her physical appearance and character, and a long description of her actual symptoms.[70] The most important and unique divergence, however, consists of her own attempts to exorcize the dybbuk, primarily through her prayers, which are cited at length in the narrative.

As we will see, these prayers are fairly sophisticated both in argument and intellectual range, invoking Talmudic methodology, midrashic material, Jewish legal knowledge, and the like. For now, our focus is simply on their appearance, like the rest of the text, in rhyme. Clearly, differences exist in the "representation of reality" in different Western cultures,[71] and so presenting material in rhyme is not definitionally dissonant. Still, the narrator's explicit suggestion that he is citing Mindl's actual language—"So let me tell you, gentlemen," he writes, "About the prayer that the girl recited then. / Although it's much better to see than to hear, *I'll repeat the words of her prayer*" (65, emphasis mine)—seemingly reflects the studied intent to accentuate these particular words' mimetic authenticity. The question begs itself if the audience would be skeptical that Mindl, in the throes of possession, spontaneously composed a complex rhymed Yiddish prayer.[72] On the one hand, genre conventions certainly demonstrated other heretofore unseen abilities manifesting themselves within the victim, including supernatural strength and a quasi-psychic ability to discern hidden truths (particularly sinful acts): why not, then, a previously unmarked creative ability? But given the entire *text*'s rhymed nature, not merely the dialogue's, the reader might rather be credited for considering this a conscious authorial-narratorial aesthetic position, and so any resulting skepticism about Mindl's language and the authorial liberty in its creation may spread to skepticism about all authorial language in the chapbook—and thus the chapbook as a whole.

The passage's implicit complex and apparently contradictory aesthetic intent is also made explicit in the narrator's intriguing statement that "it's much better to see than to hear." The author-narrator clearly intends, as Menasseh did, to privilege sensory experience—particularly eyewitness testimony—as the best form of empirical proof, and thus, as mentioned above, strives to present himself as an actual eyewitness to the events. Simultaneously, however, the narrator occasionally—but notably—reminds us that certain events have occurred that are either beyond his capacity or not his choice to describe. This forces the reader to consider—in a solely textual account—just how strongly this authorial privileging of sight is meant to be taken.

Remembering our previous concerns about rhyme, the author's dictum may be more broadly read as the hierarchization of visual descriptions over citation of dialogue; that is, as implying the greater truthfulness of visual descriptions than dialogic recapitulations. When the narrator describes the dybbuk's interaction with the rabbi of Koretz, for example, he writes: "Next the rabbi and the spirit had a long conversation, / But no writer could supply a full narration" (70). Though this introductory statement seems belied by what follows—indeed, the recorded conversation between the two composes almost a quarter of the entire narrative—there seems a necessity to distance oneself from this more directly fictionalized form of transmission.[73]

Unusual narrative representation of visual scenes and activities—the narrative's main events—may go comparatively unremarked and generate less skepticism, not only because audiences have conventional expectations of certain visual topoi in any spirit possession narrative, but also, and more importantly, no such expectation—indeed, no possibility—exists that visually observed events will be recalled in any particularly precise language. They can therefore indeed be aestheticized, rhymed, and otherwise manipulated for purposes of readerly entertainment, authorial aesthetic satisfaction, or didacticism in a manner the writer finds useful and the reader less (inherently) dissonant.

The same is not true for dialogue. If dialogue is presented as spoken by a purportedly real person, two possible choices result: the first, that these are the individual's actual words, remembered and faithfully recorded; the second, that, *pace* Thucydides, they are authorial reconstructions of what the individual might or would have said given the circumstances, necessarily highly subjective and dependent on authorial ideologies, agendas, and theories of character and mimesis.[74] If the latter is so, a necessary fictionalizing turn exists, as the author knows his created words are, historically speaking, inaccurate and thus arguably inferior to the event's "real truth."[75] However, the author is also aware that given the text's nature as a constructed literary document, his created dialogue can encapsulate his desired themes or adumbrate his character types more neatly. Created dialogue is as such actually *superior* to the "real" historical truth, as it is most powerfully expressed in the presentation of visual (that is to say, nondialogic) events. Perhaps this explains the author's reasons for casting doubt on his own strategy while simultaneously performing it—since no textual evidence exists that he intends his audience to believe these prayers are not Mindl's precise words; quite the contrary. All this may lead us to suspect the author's complex and constant slippage between authenticity and inauthenticity may be somehow related to his desire to transcend simple entertainment, and that an investigation of authorial ideology may be necessary to explain how this author uncomfortably conjoins different ideas and genres.

In her attempts to determine the chapbook's particular genre, Zfatman-Biller articulates its similarities to other older Yiddish hagiographic and moral works. She correctly illustrates its similarities to the hagiography in its foregrounding of an exorcist figure who exercises his remarkable powers; and her argument that the story is not ultimately hagiographic, given its failure to revolve around R' Borekh Kat, as well as the latter's questionable historical authenticity, when tales of this genre generally focus on historically known figures, seems sound.[76] However, her difficulties in connecting our story to the moral genre may deserve elaboration. Zfatman-Biller correctly notes the story's failure to end with a *muser-haskel*, a clear generic indication. It is also true that, generally speaking, the moral concerns of contemporary dybbuk tales revolve around sin and punishment of both the spirit and the victim; the victim's innocence here is in stark contrast to most dybbuk tales, which feature an also (to some extent) sinful victim who often comes to a tragic (usually fatal) end.[77] Zfatman-Biller's real difficulties with connecting this story to the genre of moral literature traditionally defined, preferring instead to stress the text's literary qualities,[78] may in fact mask its important moral lessons precisely about sin and punishment; determining what these lessons are allows us to further investigate the story and possibly illuminate its connections to the questions of belief, skepticism, and writers' and readers' interpretive skills.

The "Tale of the Spirit of Koretz": A Closer Look

As previously discussed, the chapbook's first lines alert the reader to the tale's authenticity and its uniqueness—"This story occurred in our day / let the world know about it in every way. And you can be very sure / that such wonders have never happened before" (61)—and link its marvelous nature to an attempt to ensure its popular economic success: "So that every man this tale can buy" (61). The next line of the proem, however, links this economic behavior directly to moral activity, a strategy we have seen in our discussion of the *Seyfer Mesholim*: the chapbook's purchase and dissemination will result in "the privilege and the right to enter the Holy Land" (62). The story also concludes with a similar moral (if conventional) motif: "So let us enjoy the rabbi's merits and do / Such good deeds and charity too. / We will then enter the Holy Land when / The messiah comes. And to that we say 'Amen'" (80).[79] Finally, late in the narrative, close to the exorcism, the narrator explicitly invokes the divine, saying that "And now, dear brothers, I'll tell you about / The great miracle that the good Lord wrought" (69). All these examples strongly indicate the authorial attempt—as in the experience of readers apprehending this attempt—to position these fantastic events in relation to a religious or theological order. But especially given Zfatman-Biller's cited difficulties, how is this fantastic tale invested with moral valence? How does reading this spirit possession narrative catalyze ethical improvement?

Our brief discussion of the dybbuk tale appearing in the *Mayse-bukh* certainly shows how the genre *can* be used to discuss contemporary moral problems, to see sinners punished either by their wandering as dybbuks[80] or by being publicly identified as sinners by the dybbuk; similar considerations could imaginably apply here. That story, however, its presumed Safedian origins effaced, takes place in a vague nonworld, introduced only by a generalized "once."[81] Our chapbook's "turmoil of war," though, creates a different kind of victim, one painstakingly described (along with her family) as blameless: Mindl is described as a "chaste soul" (65), and even her community is called a "holy community," a common referent in Jewish texts, but in light of these other considerations perhaps invested with new meaning. In addition, while the dybbuk in other tales provides the host body with great strength or supernatural insight, the only gift Mindl receives is pain: "for three years a spirit had been running through / Her body, leaving her no peace / Causing her strange maladies, / With the first year of her agonies, / The pains got worse, the injuries—Sometimes the spirit broke her bones" (62). As time passes, the pains worsen: the text writes that during the second attempt at exorcism, "the spirit was breaking the girl's bones. / Sometimes he bent her back so low / Until her body looked just like a bow"(64).

Not only is such bending backward a highly conventional sign of "hysterical" behavior, allowing us to begin to view our text through the lens of recent scholarly considerations of gender, particularly on manifestations of women's spirituality and their religious rebelliousness through socially unsanctioned means,[82] but such bending, which thrusts the genitals forward and may mimic other erotic movement, also demonstrates a sexual dimension to the action. While much of the spirit possession literature connects possession and repressed desires for sexual liberation due to the strict regulation of open expression of sexuality,[83] the accompaniment of violence here, visited by a male spirit on a female victim,[84] firmly locates our narrative within the territory of sexual assault and rape.[85] The spirit's turning Mindl upside down, thereby revealing her legs and presumably her genitals,[86] seems symptomatic of rape attempts. Even more persuasive may be the telling detail that the dybbuk "descend[ed] into the girl's thigh, there he broke her leg" (65). Thighs are traditionally related to genitalia in the Bible;[87] the breaking of the leg may thus be seen as anagogically similar to the rupture of maidenhead.

In a later attempt at exorcism, noxious gases derived from sulfur and wormwood are burned like incense inside a barrel beneath a shelf on which Mindl sits, presumably entering her body through her vaginal opening (74).[88] Finally, intertextual circumstances may also come into play; Mindl describes the circumstances preceding her attack as "I went out for a breath of air" (65), reminding the traditional and allusively aware reader of the classic biblical example of rape, Dinah, whose ordeal also begins with the word *vatetse*, "and she went out." Similarly, the non-Jewish ruler's suggestion that Mindl be burned for starting the fire that consumes the town of Lubar (69) is not merely an example of harsh *lex talionis*, which must itself be questioned in a tale about law and penalty, but also may remind readers of the tale of Tamar, another innocent figure involved in a sexualized story sentenced by a harsh authority figure for burning.[89] The alarming tendency among some commentators to connect Dinah's own action with her subsequent rape finds its analogue in the suggestion within Jewish demonological literature that even seemingly small or trivial sins (particularly cursing, using phrases like "To Satan with you!") provide opportunities for possession by evil entities. It certainly prefigures arguments made by works like the *Minkhat Eliyahu* and the *Emek Hamelekh* of how women's problematic sexuality—including their ostensibly greater propensity to sexual impurity—leads to greater incidence of possession. We will return to this discussion of gender later in the chapter.[90]

Though the war referred to in the chapbook's title is likely the one that occurred in western Poland between 1655 and 1660,[91] some critics have also suggested our story may allude to the 1648–1649 Chmielnitzki massacres, which powerfully (and famously) wreaked physical and psychological devastation upon the eastern European Jewish community.[92] Direct textual allusion to the Chmielnitzki massacres or no, the explicit connection made between the title's chaos and war and the narrative's avowedly private, domestic nature may sensibly permit a preliminary identification of Mindl, the suffering, assaulted feminine body, with the suffering Jewish communal body, attacked by external marauding elements.[93] It is unsurprising, then, that Mindl's parents assert that "[t]his distress is on the whole congregation" (64).[94] Community, as we will see, becomes a central touchstone for this text, in delineating both the nature of the problem and its ultimate solution.[95]

Our story can thus be read as an entirely different type of moral tale than those characterized by Zfatman-Biller, but one more in line with the nuanced versions we discovered in the *Seyfer Mesholim*: not simply a traditionally straightforward, neatly organized, literary and moral account of the subsequent and necessary punishment of the wages of sin, but a more historically oriented creation, based on lived experience, of the suffering of innocents. Questions of theodicy are indeed explicitly posed within the story; in analyzing it, we see how nuanced a moral stance this text provides in tackling one of the oldest, hardest metaphysical questions. True, such questions appear in many spirit possession accounts—Goldish notes that "the religious dimensions of possession and exorcism are amongst the most highly visible," and Bilu connects "the principle of the transmigration of souls" to the "solution to the question of the 'ill-fated righteous' "[96]—but this text's particularly complex, unconventional features demand similarly detailed treatment of its moral subtleties.

Such subtleties are most powerfully expressed in one of the text's most unconventional features: Mindl's voice, which, as noted above, we hear on several occasions directly and at great length. Mindl's first speech is a simple call to God to relieve her affliction—prayers that go unanswered (64). Mindl's creative development comes only after—and arguably in response to—her increased pain, and individual miracle workers' failure at exorcism. She begins with the Hebrew liturgical words, "Before God the King exalted and Supreme"; then, perhaps echoing a general tendency in Yiddish literature to move from the fixed and canonical to the improvisatory and personal vernacular,[97] she

> begins to shout and scream: / Almighty God, how much longer must I / Suffer this agony, El Shaddai? / Oh, God of Israel divine! Thou art there! / Thou knowest I went out for a breath of air. / Then the evil spirit flouted the law so just, / The Torah given to all of us. / Now since it was the evil spirit's transgression, / Why should I suffer for his violation? /What sins have I committed so terribly, / That I should suffer so horribly? / If thou dost visit the sins of parents on future generations, / Why should I suffer these five years of tribulations? / Thy wrath usually abates, Thy tender mercy is revealed / Why should I be devastated and concealed? / Thou dost inflict Heaven's harsh decree / On the worst sinner, yet even he / In all his fear / Doesn't have to suffer for more than a year. / Thou dost have qualms, / According to the psalm, / Thou showest pity whatever the misdeed may be. So why hast thou turned away from me? / Am I the worst criminal? / Why didst thou make me drink the bitter gall? (65–66)

Mindl's complaint focuses on essential questions of theodicy,[98] for Jews particularly and humanity generally, challenging God's general sense of justice and his covenant with his chosen people; the "all of us" the Torah is presented to, after all, is a national, not universal, first person plural.[99] She issues her challenge, however, in the traditional learned voice: throwing a previous text, God's own words, against himself. Despite the general social familiarity with the cited texts and ideas, including a concept taken from the book of Exodus immediately after the appearance of the Thirteen Attributes of Mercy,[100] the notion of the efficaciousness of saying kaddish on the suffering soul,[101] and a reference to the Psalms,[102] this type of challenge is classically delineated as "male." Befitting a dybbuk story, even as Mindl is quintessentially female, the suffering Jewish people's passive, violated voice, she is also possessed by the male empowered voice, the voice of textual subversion and challenge. Mindl's talents, then, characterized in the narrator's description of her as "speak[ing] words so wise" (66), are particularly apparent in their implicit and explicit efforts to point out her world's moral contradictions, problematically unifying text and experience just as male and female are problematically identified within her. It is a metaphorical and perhaps epistemological, though not actual, type of xenoglossia, that "proof positive" of dybbuk possession.

Such efforts can be more fully appreciated through a closer look at an early allusion in her first prayer, regarding the visitation of the sins of the fathers upon the sons, or, as the Yiddish sensibly has it given Mindl's personal status, parents and children (the Hebrew can, of course, also be metaphorically translated this way). The words' traditionally understood sense was as an efficacious formula to prevent evil Divine decree, a prime reason for their prominent and repeated recitation in the liturgy of the Day of Atonement.[103] Mindl's citation reminds the reader here—in both the case of the dybbuk possession writ small and the catastrophes it represents—that the promise offered by such recitation has fallen savagely, ironically short.

But a closer look at the cited text confuses as much as it explains. Mindl's plaint seems to rely on taking the verse literally: though the immediately preceding Thirteen Attributes express God's mercy and kindness, this divine "attribute"[104] seems just the opposite; it in fact seemingly contradicts straightforward notions of justice in its punishment of innocents for the sins of guilty others.[105] Mindl insists on the verse's simple logic, a seemingly cruel logic psychologically understandable (and even appealing) to genuine sufferers. If God indeed punishes children for their parents' sins (and notably, Mindl's parents are almost entirely effaced from the narrative, mentioned only as wailing, impotent bystanders), and if, as contemporaries must have insisted, much of the blame for the massacres can be traced to internal, not external factors—to communal moral failings—why punish them? Let God fulfill his promise and punish their descendants!

This is not, of course, the text's generally understood meaning, which is rather simply to insist that the currently praying individuals are not held hostage to previous generations' sins. Here, though, Mindl and by extension the Jewish community are well aware by their own suffering that the punishment has arrived, and their intercessory efforts must practically, logically, and theologically proceed from there, a reversal of those efforts' appearance in most traditional stories, where they occur in the context of an evil decree fixed by man or by Heaven but not yet carried out.[106] The inclusion here and accentuation of such a contradictory textual moment, within both the Bible and in its interpretation, lead to an aporia, a revolutionary understanding and appreciation of the essential complications in ever trying to explain God's ways.

Mindl's second challenge is similarly self-contradictory; there, she juxtaposes her own suffering, which according to her prayer has continued for five years, with that of the wicked. Mindl clearly subscribes to the Jewish tradition that the soul suffers for a year after death before its elevation to heaven or consignment to oblivion; she predicates one of her arguments on that assumption. However, if her possessor is an evil person's soul, rather than the Evil Spirit—a point slightly unclear in the narrative, but perhaps generic considerations tilt us toward the former—then her very lived experience contradicts her belief, since the dybbuk is a soul that has managed to live long beyond the twelve-month period.[107] The text's expression of this contradiction yields several corollaries. We may recognize in Mindl's words her doubts about not only God's justice, but basic traditional metaphysical understanding. Such doubt, however, is also the reader's: the five-year course of Mindl's lived experience is not merely "heard" by readers as evidence from the potentially unreliable spoken word, but "seen," in its form as part of the narratively necessary historical universe of events. If so, another dissonant element has been introduced to the story's readers—and consciously accentuated—by the author. Given our understanding of the story's moral overtones, we may understand his reasoning: this dissonance precisely parallels and calls attention to the dissonant theological challenges tormenting the Jewish community and the story's readers.

Such considerations are further developed through Mindl's citation of Psalms 145:9, her own experience contradicting the verse's claim of God's universal pity. Aside from the repeated contradiction of text and experience, the emphasis in this psalm on God's mercy stands in direct contradiction to the earlier-cited Exodus text's emphasis on God's justice. Mindl's textually sophisticated behavior thus also constitutes an attack on the essential Ashkenazic attempt to harmonize all strains and strata of Jewish text, the rabbinic endeavor par excellence; it may therefore be unsurprising that the text notes that this particular dybbuk case perplexed contemporary rabbis (63).

Mindl's ultimate attempt to discuss theodicy, however, comes in her retelling of the Akedah, the sacrifice of Isaac, in her second prayer. The Akedah (Genesis 22:1–19) has always been considered a central source in Jewish tradition for discussion of faith, reward and punishment, and testing.[108] Mindl is clearly aware of not only the biblical text, but the story's midrashic glosses, given her characterization of the Akedah as "caus[ing] the death of Sarah our Mother" (66), a causal relationship discussed by the Midrash, following the Bible's uncommenting juxtaposition of the two events.[109] Obviously, any tale of theodicy leading to an innocent female's suffering (and, here, death) has great resonance for Mindl. Mindl's inclusion of Sarah's death as an integral part of the narrative accentuates the elements of theodicy, feminizing (and thus personalizing) the story so that it ends not with a young man's salvation but a woman's destruction. Mindl's (and thus the author's) artful retelling of the Akedah also continues to emphasize the theme of parents, children, and generations, obliquely reminding us of the issues of justice previously associated with those themes: "And Thou wast to take him although the boy / Could have many, many offspring by and by" (66). Finally—and intriguingly—the Akedah is used in this ostensibly moral tale to assert Jewish moral superiority above all other nations; Mindl says that "It was really Thy goal / To reveal the virtue of Abraham's soul, / So all nations would worship Thy name and see / That Thou are stronger than any other deity" (67). How does Abraham's practically filicidal action affirm Jewish moral superiority?

The answer, taken from traditional valuation of the Akedah, has vital importance for our analysis: this passage provides the first direct intimations that Mindl sees her possession (thus encouraging the reader to see it) as a test. Directly linking her own experience to her understanding of the Akedah, she juxtaposes the two much as the biblical text juxtaposes Sarah's death to the event: "And now with the evil spirit Thou dost test me / So that every sinful person should see / My suffering, so he'll have the courage to repent" (67).

Even this characterization of her experience, though, contains its own contradictions. Mindl's suggestion that her "test" can be seen as an exemplum for the wicked to repent is puzzling, as it is hardly obvious why any evildoer would derive such a lesson from Mindl's personal experiences. Mindl herself, after all, by her own admission (corroborated by her characterization by the narrator), is blameless.[110] Indeed, the Akedah story seemingly suggests that the narrative of temptation, testing, and potential redemption applies to someone other than the (potential) sufferer, and the wicked should therefore repent not because of their sins' consequences for themselves, but to others; the possibility conversely exists that those others, by their own virtuous behavior, may be able to save the wicked.[111]

Perhaps this is the reason Mindl's penultimate prayer shifts to discussing a community of the unrepentant wicked whose redemption is contingent on others' goodwill: the citizens of Sodom. "Great sins were committed by Sodom's men. / But still Thou didst say: 'If I find ten / Righteous men, I'll forgive their sins.' But then / Wilt thou not find here ten righteous men / Who will pray and fast for a desolate girl? / For Thou keepest Israel" (67). Mindl's prayer further develops a restatement or reevaluation of Jewish theology and theodicy in the wake of a disaster, perhaps no less cataclysmic than Sodom's destruction: God allows such events to occur, if not to punish individual sins, then to allow and create the possibility for communal action and cohesion in tragedy's wake. Just as Sodom's imagined ten righteous figures would have been capable through their merit of staving off destruction, here too community action may be able to prevent continued pain and catastrophe.

Pain is the price the community pays to learn that God's forces exist. But the dybbuk's appearance is not only an empirical proof à la Menasseh ben Israel: its existence definitionally creates a test that we discover can only be passed via the constitution and cohesion of a faithful, traditional community.[112] The author therefore significantly locates the first exorcism attempt on Rosh Hashanah (63), the holiday that expresses God's ultimate judgment and stresses Jewish communal identity. (It hardly seems coincidental that the Talmudic discussion of this concept is also a primary Talmudic source for the twelve-month period of Jewish suffering in Gehenna, a topic of obvious relevance here.)[113]

It is precisely this communal turn that is the dybbuk's undoing. The narrative tells that the beadle Yitsik, "versed in exorcism and excommunication" (63),[114] gathers together a minyan as his first act. Not only does this magic quorum[115] fulfill the archetypal need for efficacious action, but it is an essential article of Jewish faith that God's presence rests upon ten men gathered together, the reason why Jews pray communally rather than individually.[116] In a tale revolving around the implicit charge of God's absence, the suggested solution is the direct evocation of his presence.

Indeed, in the exorcism's final phases, the community is activated as never before; even the narrator describes himself as part of the communal unit, "And when we / The Holy Fellowship did see ..." (67). Though their shofar blowing at the girl's bedside and their "imprecations / and the anathemas and the condemnations" (76) have only temporary effect, real progress emerges only when the exorcists finally enter the community's house, the synagogue. "We then went to the maid again / To see what an impact the exorcism had made. / The girl said: 'He's never been this afraid, / Since you started the exorcism—and I / Don't know why. / She didn't realize the entire community / Had proceeded against him courageously" (76).

Such a seemingly conscious and specific antihagiographical emphasis recapitulates the failure of individual manifest action throughout the work. The "miracle worker ... from Przemyl" Avrom has failed earlier, forced to "return to his town" (65); a later attempt by Rabbi Yakov, while slightly more efficacious—it causes the dybbuk "terrible pain"—is ultimately fruitless.[117]

Hardly insignificant, then, is the fact that the only successful exorcist, Borekh Kat, has a name that means "blessed is the group."[118] Borekh's own perspective, which first echoes the community's earlier fatalistic response in its individualizing, dissociating approach—he tells the dybbuk, "We are mere mortals—that is our fate. / We live today, we die tomorrow. / Our sins are punished by disaster and sorrow" (69)[119]—is tempered by his commitment to act communally. He leaves the dybbuk to go to synagogue (70), thus replacing individual philosophical torment with the possible solace of communal life. Such action seems to yield concrete results from the start: the dybbuk concedes his inability to harm this right-thinking individual—"I will never injure you as of today"—and is at least temporarily prevented from injuring the innocent representative of the communal body—"And the spirit did not torment the maid / While the rabbi prayed" (70).

Indeed, though the text attributes the dybbuk's shaking and fear to the traditional means of exorcism, the anathema and the shofar blasts,[120] it is hardly coincidental that the dybbuk's weakness also comes immediately after the children's recitation of "Amen." A new generation has been instructed in the communal, traditionalist response to tragedy; rebellion has been domesticated not just for now, but the future, so what can a rebellious spirit do but submit? Such a turn towards past and future community formation is further symbolized in the choice to begin this final narrative section on "the first day of Passover," the holiday when the family of Jacob, the namesake of the individualist spirit Yakov who is causing Mindl such pain and distress, is transformed through God's miraculous presence into the people of Israel, and a holiday that serves as a reminder of that communal past and a source of instruction for future generations. A neat structural parallelism thus obtains as well: Passover—previously the source of one of Mindl's and the dybbuk's theological challenges, based on the liturgical omission of the great Hallel and the universal suffering at its cause—now becomes an opportunity for communal cohesion and therefore for rejoicing.

An Alternative Voice?: The Dybbuk Responds

If Mindl's comparatively extrusive presence, sophisticated arguments, and ultimate salvation suggest identifying her voice and her story with the text's primary moral message, we would be remiss, in a text so explicitly (and by generic construction, almost definitionally) polyphonic, in failing to devote space to the story's other main voice—that is, the dybbuk's. Though the text seemingly characterizes Mindl's own prayers as possessing a touch of the dybbuk, the possessing spirit speaks in his own, individuated voice, a voice gained only in direct dialogue with his archenemy the exorcist: the dybbuk first speaks only when Borekh Kat enters the room (69). The confrontation between the two takes, in its broadest outlines, the conventional form of a negotiation between spirit and exorcist, where the former "choreographs" terms and aspects of his own ultimate exorcism and gives account of his punishment after death (71–74).[121] Such accounts provided, in Bilu's words, "dramatic and emotionally charged confirmation of metaphysical beliefs concerning the nature of the 'other world'" imbued with "realistic quality,"[122] and satisfied readers' real curiosity about what occurs after death, information that can only be provided by definition in such extremely rare circumstances.[123]

Though the "interview with the spirit" was a generic convention, Yakov's monologue here is significantly longer and more complex than the average account.[124] Perhaps its most interesting feature for our purposes is that, suitably for a story concerned more with suffering's effects than articulating the precise sins that caused it, the dybbuk's pain and suffering are described in detail, but his sins are referred to only in passing. Such emphasis, in contrast to both Mindl, presented as almost entirely innocent, and to the *Mayse-bukh*'s dybbuk, who prominently foregrounds his wickedness in his brief account of his peregrinations, may simply offer the text the opportunity to consider another aspect of theodicy: not the suffering of the innocent, but the disproportionate suffering of the guilty.

And the suffering does seem disproportionate. Though Yakov claims (boasts?) he "broke every law and regulation / listed in Jewish legislation," he adds in the same breath that he did "commit one good deed back then: / I saved a Jew from some highwaymen" (74). Narratively, the good deed allows him entrance to Mindl's "pure body," which in turn allows possibility of elevation; but thematically it also generates readerly sympathy by locating Yakov within a standard archetype in rabbinic literature: the scoundrel whose one good deed generates the possibility of total and ultimate redemption.

Yakov, aware he has sinned, is thus willing, even "elated" (71) to go to hell; such disposition of his fate seems appropriate, definitive, and clear. It is also, by Yakov's account, a far better fate than encountering the punishing fiends who tear the soul out of the body with horns and grab him when he is inexplicably expelled from hell's ordered sphere. These fiends, in their strangely liminal appearances and shifting linguistic identities—some have "bizarre faces, half-dog and half-cow" (71–72), and another demon is described as having "the countenance / Of a turtle—known in the Holy Tongue as a *tsav*, / And what's called a *tsherepakha* by a Slav, / And what we call a *shiltkrut* in our tongue"—provide a further metaphysical, corporealized, analogue to the question of theodicy discussed above. They remind the reader that, as with theodicy, the greatest terror is a metaphysically uncertain, disordered world, and the dybbuk testifies simultaneously to that metaphysical world's existence and its improper functioning—the reason its very existence is fraught with pain, since even by its own supernatural standards it should not be, and must therefore be beaten back into line. This explains how the dybbuk's voice is polyphonically subversive (as an evil spirit, saying things it should not), then hegemonic (as its presence proves the existence of a metaphysical order), and then subversive once more (as it illustrates that order's fault lines, equivalent to the expression of questions of theodicy). Such structure is at least partially analogous to the Lurianic vision of the breakdown of the Godhead; it is therefore the exorcist's role, in true Lurianic fashion, to effect acts of *tikkun* and return the soul—and thus the metaphysical order—to its proper place.

These metaphors are unsurprisingly corporealized in the dybbuk's description of his travails as being constantly swallowed and spat out (72), causing the spirit great pain. These twin processes of destruction and reconstitution—the dybbuk says they "brought me in terrible fear / To millstones and ground up my body and my soul"[125] and adds that "with disaster and destruction that made him whole in reconstruction" (72–73)—are reminiscent of the story of Jonah, also challenging any simple, binaristic identification of the dybbuk as "bad," instead seeing him as another in a line of disproportionate sufferers raising challenges of theodicy and learning through pain. The dybbuk's travail, then, also becomes analogous to not merely Mindl's suffering and release, but the community's as a whole; such representativeness allows us, metaphorically, to see the dybbuk in Jonah's footsteps, even as a strange and unwilling prophet. Further, though, the particular form of the dybbuk's suffering can be seen as symbolizing the destruction of coherent, unified personal identity and its subsequent reassemblage, itself representing the breakdown of a moral and metaphysical order then reconstituted.

This ongoing process is recapitulated in the dybbuk's continued account, in his shift from describing his suffering at the demons' hands to his various subsequent reincarnations. Though this may blur ideal analytic lines between dybbuk and *gilgul* (in our reconstruction, at least; probably less so in contemporary popular imagination),[126] it allows the clear illustration and application of Lurianic *tikkun* in the dybbuk's story. True, the dybbuk's claim that reincarnation, particularly in a loathsome creature's body, is a traditional means of just punishment for traditional sin is apt;[127] but the details and resonances of this specific journey are particularly relevant to his role as symbol, not individual, and how it illuminates the shifting binary structures of internal or external, Jewish or non-Jewish, morally improving or sinfully backsliding, progress or descent, that represent the contemporary Jewish community's liminal and complex state.

Indicative of this respect are the dybbuk's transmigrations into a hog, that clear symbol of non-Jewishness, and then into a heifer, where he "thought I would find atonement now, / For I figured a Jew would slaughter the cow, / And I would have redemption / Through the slaughterer's benediction. / But my evil fate won eventually, / For a Christian slaughtered me" (73). The narrative's particular juxtaposition of the soul's transmigration into a heifer and its explicit mention of atonement remind allusively aware readers of the *para aduma*, the red heifer, whose ashes are characterized as containing properties of moral purification, with its resonances of sin and atonement—an obvious concern in this text.[128] Notably for our investigation, however, the red heifer is also an animal rife with paradox and contradiction, exemplified in the famous rabbinic dictum that its ashes impurify the pure while simultaneously purifying the impure.[129] Such incorporation of oppositional features in a single entity, particularly related to moral progress or descent, clearly allows space for thematic congruence as well as the entrance of the willed entertaining of paradoxes not ultimately destructuring but rather powerfully esoteric—in the same way that the *para aduma* is given as the classic example of the *chok*, the unexplained (and unexplainable) law.

The parallels continue: the fact that this perfect animal without blemish must be entirely destroyed, reduced to ash, to have any positive moral effect on the community must have resonated strongly both within Lurianic thought and an attendant Jewish historiography connecting destruction and violence with eventual and ultimate salvation, again reminding us of how pain generates the moral virtue that saves the community in our story. Indeed, the reincarnated spirit/heifer's fate—its slaughter by a Christian, which, in narrative terms, prevents him from total elevation—itself analogously identifies the dybbuk with the suffering communal Jewish body, devastated by slaughter at Christian hands.

But not only Christians: the narrative provides another mechanism of generating sympathy for Yakov that has both the implicit and explicit effect of demonizing the Jewish exorcists—and community. Yakov, after all, casts his continued possession of Mindl not as an entirely maleficent act, but rather a struggle for survival; escaping from his cocoon means his destruction, not merely by the congregation but by waiting tormenting demons. This uneasy point—and the role in which it casts the community by extension—persists through the narrative, particularly several hours following the Jewish community's first, violent attacks on the dybbuk, which reach such a pitch they cause Mindl to lose consciousness. Admittedly her suffering stems from the dybbuk's torture; still, the actions themselves replicate the possession: a violent invasion of the girl's body with a nonphysical substance (this time, gas). The narrator's response to Mindl's collapse is at the very least somewhat callous: "As if she were dead the girl fainted away / And for over five hours there she lay. / But we paid no heed, she wasn't dead" (75). Perhaps such sentiments cause the dybbuk's complaints, hypocritical as they may be, to possess a certain power: "You Jews shouldn't call / Yourselves compassionate at all. / You are cruel and ferocious in every way. / You can see that the girl has passed away. / None of you feels sorry for the loss" (75). The Jewish community's only response to this charge is: "Silence! We're prepared / To give you even more reason to be scared!"

While moral equivalence hardly exists between the dybbuk's violence and the violent means necessitated for its exorcism, the necessity for and exercise of such violence, in this context imbued with disquietingly masochistic tendencies—Mindl herself begs the community to "Burn me in sulfur, in fire, burn me well" (75)—demand moral and philosophical reckoning, even if they play themselves out within the world of "fantastic" narrative. The dybbuk tale, then, provides not merely the opportunity to explore Jewish powerlessness and victimization in "this world," most clearly expressed through the *possession*; but also the empowerment granted to Jews in the fantastic, magical, literary world, the wish-fulfillment domain of *yene velt*, most clearly expressed through the *exorcism*.

More corollaries of this increasingly complicated audience identification will be treated later: for now, enough to note some final complexities in this regard: the dybbuk's apparent moral nadir—his possession of Mindl—has been revealed through his account to actually be a comparatively better state: other situations will be far worse, and his current position affords him the opportunity to talk to someone able to assist in his ultimate elevation. Such reevaluation has moral and didactic resonance: what seems disproportionate suffering is in fact, viewed differently, a final stage in an admittedly long and painful process of restoration and liberation. As such, messianic and apocalyptic speculation concerning this text may not be entirely unwarranted—if we take the provocative step of suggesting reader identification with the dybbuk.

Gender and the Spirit of Koretz: A Closer (and Comparative) Look

If this story is indeed offering a nuanced moral lesson about the necessity to reestablish communal theological norms in the face of speculation about theodicy (an extension, perhaps, of forms of other theological skepticism or heretical doubt), it must be added that socially construed norms of belief are not the only ones problematized here; norms of behavior are also called into question, particularly ones tied intimately to questions of gender. Investigations of such negotiations may be undertaken by more closely observing a previously mentioned narrative crux, then suggesting a valuable comparative context that allows the possibility to explore Jewish literary treatment of ecumenically pressing social issues.

We briefly noted the highly sexualized presentation of the possession at the beginning of our analysis, and mentioned that Mindl's first prayer briefly refers to a "bitter gall." Though "gall" is an imprecise translation—the original instead suggests a "bitter goblet of wine"—the original text's own need to rhyme, the image of a woman implicated in sexual issues drinking a bitter goblet, and the awareness (by character and reader alike) of the experience's test-like nature implicitly and anagogically place Mindl in the role of the *sotah*, the adulterous woman accused of sexual impropriety. The *sotah*, by virtue of her own potentially immoral behavior, yields a different resonance from the rape victim: a woman under suspicion. Mindl, of course, insists on her innocence, but innocence did not prevent someone from imbibing the bitter draught at the heart of the *sotah* test.[130] However, the attendant pain and degradation, if the woman was innocent, led directly to childbirth and blessed future generations, inversely parallel to those generations Mindl hopes will bear the brunt of God's anger. In this perspective, then, Mindl's slippage from rape victim to tested married woman suggests narratorial slippage and reframing of the readerly analogue from the innocent, almost modernistic subject of theodicy to the traditionalist sorely tested figure, whose ultimate reward is undoubted.[131] The text's marriage ending, puzzling to Zfatman-Biller, thus becomes a thematically satisfactory closure for this text in particular, not just texts in general.[132]

So prepared, our final narrative discovery that Yakov's primary sin (and the only one mentioned in the text) is adultery (73) seems almost inevitable.[133] Fantastic pietistic narratives suggesting otherworldly punishment for sexual sins were not uncommon, as the *Mayse-bukh* story illustrates;[134] the *sotah*'s image, though, allows us to explore broader dimensions of the writer's and readers' conceptual world of gender roles that transcend straightforwardly erotic and sexual associations.

Significantly, the *locus classicus* against teaching women Torah—Rabbi Eliezer's statement that "anyone who teaches his daughter Torah, teaches her lasciviousness"—is found in the Tractate of Sotah (mSotah 3:4), immediately following Ben Azzai's statement that "if [a *sotah*] had merit, her merit would mitigate [the punishment] for her." On this basis, Ben Azzai said, "A man is obligated to teach his daughter Torah, so that if she drinks [the bitter water], she will know—for merit mitigates." Even Ben Azzai's more lenient view uncomfortably juxtaposes women's learning with a problematized view of their sexuality; both views certainly suggest, in Daniel Boyarin's formulation, "the extraordinary threat that the learned woman represented to the *Babylonian* (and later European) rabbinic culture, a power that threatened to upset the whole apple cart of gender relations and social organization and that had to be suppressed, therefore, by extraordinary means."[135] In discussing the famous Beruriah narrative in BT Avoda Zara 18b, Boyarin goes further, claiming "an essential nexus between a woman studying Torah and the breakdown of the structure of monogamy ... a demonstration that there is an intrinsic and necessary connection between a scholarly woman and uncontrolled sexuality."[136] Adultery—the sin the dybbuk is punished for in our text—is of course antimonogamy's essence.

Boyarin similarly suggests the hypothesis—and it is only a hypothesis—that a change took place in Jewish gender ideology in the early Middle Ages that resulted in a much more essentialized notion of women as dangerous and threatening, and that "the exclusion of women from Torah was not intended to keep them in ignorance, nor was it the product of a sense that women were contaminated and contaminating, as some scholars have erroneously interpreted, but was purely and simply a means for the maintenance of a male power structure via the symbolic exclusion of women from the single practice most valued in the culture, the study of Talmud."[137]

In this light, one may view Mindl's textually sophisticated dybbuk as a gendered intellectual revolt,[138] and its defeat—and her domestication to a life of marriage—as the reestablishment and reinforcement of traditional male-dominated social and intellectual power structures. Indeed, the dybbuk's constant, peripatetic motion within Mindl from thigh to brain (see 67, 68, 74, 75) can itself be seen as symptomatic of the connection between sexual problematization and mental rebelliousness. Feminist criticism has, unsurprisingly, addressed these narrative patterns in broader contexts.[139]

Such revolt against social, intellectual, and gendered power structures can be correlated with skeptical claims more broadly construed, and women's possessions certainly figured into more general anxieties concerning popular (and vernacular) heresy, doubt, and skepticism. Bilu suggests a common transgression among victims, creating vulnerability to the punishing social mechanism of possession, was "doubting the validity of episodes from Jewish history," a transgression "usually committed by women,"[140] and, in an account of an exorcism by Hayyim Vital, Chajes has shown how "sexual licentiousness and popular skepticism emerge in this account ... as fundamental threats to communal leadership struggling to establish a community on the basis of pietistic ideals."[141]

An intriguing moment from our story illustrates the complex (though not necessarily textually sophisticated) understanding of gender's operation within Jewish tradition by readers and how this understanding helps provide *narrative* information, not merely ideological positioning. After a series of efficacious prayers, the dybbuk attempts to bargain with the community. He asks them only to let him "spend this night in peace," and he in turn will "go / As soon as the chickens start to crow," a condition almost certainly related to contemporary belief that evil spirits lose much of their power with the cock's crow.[142] The dybbuk fails to keep his word; upon the community's return from morning prayers, they find him still possessing his host. The dybbuk's ingenious excuse for disregarding his promise: "I told them that as soon / As the chickens (*hiner*) crowed, I would be gone. / But, dear rabbi, it's not my fault, you know. / Not a single chicken has started to crow. / Only the rooster has crowed today (*nayert der hon hot gekret un nit di hiner*). / And so I have to stay." (79)

The entire episode's ostensibly extraneous and confusing inclusion can be explained by locating it firmly within a Jewish readerly context. First, the morning service's traditional opening, which blesses the rooster for having the intelligence to crow only at dawn,[143] invokes a type of intelligence that distinguishes only between sharp binary forms, darkness and light. For the rooster's purpose—and indeed for the purpose of fixing morning prayer time—no blurring exists between day and night; rather, a specific boundary moment exists that separates one entity and the other. The dybbuk's challenge, in attacking this moment, is also attacking the strict binaristic construction of the universe definitionally under assault by its very presence. Second, the dybbuk's casuistic reasoning represents a turn to a kind of corrupted Talmudic hermeneutic in contradistinction to Mindl's plaintive and "literalist"[144] invocation of tradition's promises. Granted, the community had accepted the dybbuk's terms; granted, no chickens crowed. Given, however, that female chickens *never* crow and only male roosters do, both sides clearly understood the community's acceptance of the offer's apparent spirit (that the dybbuk would depart at dawn), rather than its letter. The betrayal of that mutual understanding by the dybbuk also shows the danger of the perversion of tradition by the educated. Thirdly, authorial employment of the "rooster or hen" images continues the thematic concern with atonement and redemption, particularly related to the High Holidays, apparent throughout the narrative. In the ceremony of *kapparot* (atonements), performed immediately before Yom Kippur, individuals would wave a rooster or a hen around their heads while reciting the liturgical formula: "This is my exchange, this is my substitute, this is my atonement. This rooster / this hen will go to its death while I will enter and go to a good, long life, and to peace." That is, the rooster has already figured as a symbol of the innocent who suffers to remove others' sins—a trope familiar in our analysis.[145]

Significantly for us, the translation "this rooster / this hen" above does not stem from Hebrew or Yiddish's inability to make such gendered distinctions; on the contrary, as the dybbuk's bargain illustrates. In the *kapparot* liturgy, rather, men sacrifice roosters, and women sacrifice hens, rendering this particular symbol specifically suited to questions of binaristic gendering and the impassable and ineffaceable gulfs between the two. It may be that this aspect of *kapparot* helped give rise to the popular Yiddish folk saying and social warning about gender-appropriateness, "If a hen begins to crow like a rooster, then off to the slaughterer with it," and it is hardly coincidental that the prayer in praise of the rooster for its ability to observe natural binary divisions is the same one enshrining distinctions of gendered identity, where men thank God for not having made them a woman.

We can see, then, how the narrative as a whole raises the specter (literally) of resistance to the ideas exemplified in this traditional phrase, only to have later narrative developments reveal that resistance's moral bankruptcy. Mindl is indeed, as has been said, "a hen that crows like a rooster,"[146] and the coerced nature of her usurpation of nontraditional gender roles notwithstanding—just as (one could argue) the increase in heretical questioning is often catalyzed by external forces such as the Chmielnitzki massacres—the moral bankruptcy of that usurpation is itself revealed in this false promise of chickens and roosters. In several different ways, then, stray narrative details and puzzles provide keys to a crucial thematic structure within the dybbuk story: presenting it as a tale of the temporary dissolution, then strong reassertion, of socially appropriate gender roles.

A very similar constellation of images, ideas, and anxieties appears in one of the most crucial episodes for the study of both gender and popular belief and skepticism in the early modern period more generally: the European "witchcraze" of the sixteenth and seventeenth centuries. Chajes has linked the study of Jewish spirit possession and Christian demonological studies, as we have seen, and has even written of the concomitant contemporary association of powerful assertions of female spirituality, witchcraft, and demoniac possession, as well as the rise of an increasingly "polemical demonology" that relied on stories precisely in response to increasing skepticism, matched by a similar rise in Jewish spirit possession accounts.[147] Witchcraft and its literary treatment were discussed in an explicitly non-Jewish, non-comparative context earlier in the book; this discussion will complement and expand both that discussion and Chajes' approach, with reference to our particular popular, vernacular treatment of the subject.[148]

Certain methodological similarities to our discussion here are immediately apparent. Scholars of witchcraft, for example, also carefully differentiate between the various categories of widely disseminated laws, demonological discourses and elite witchcraft texts, popularly disseminated beliefs, and actual witchcraft prosecutions and "occurrences," if any,[149] and caution in fact against establishing any monolithic categories of witchcraft law and belief, instead favoring a model of a flexible, dynamic interdependent discourse.[150] Eyewitness accounts were as crucial in witchcraft cases as in dybbuk accounts in affirming their "experiential reality."[151] Some new witchcraft scholarship, in a similar fashion to our study, has focused on these accounts' narrative qualities in considering their historical value[152] and in doing so has suggested the trial narratives' polysemous nature, and their (contextually determined) potential to serve, perhaps simultaneously, as socially supportive and subversive.[153] But the similarities enlighten further in considering questions of gender and society.

Various scholars have characterized witchcraft as "a challenge to the patriarchal order," at least conceptually speaking, and have attempted to understand the witchcraft prosecutions primarily (though not solely) through the interpretive lens of gender,[154] given that both theoretically and actually (though not quite as disproportionately as sometimes stated) women were witch hunts' targets.[155] As Rowlands writes, "from the context of beliefs about witchcraft which were potentially gender-neutral, then, emerged accusations of witchcraft which were gender-biased although by no means gender-specific,"[156] a statement, ceteris paribus, certainly applicable to Jewish spirit possession accounts. Nuanced articulations of this gendered approach rely on the general trope, common in witchcraft studies, of the rhetoric of inversion woven into almost every aspect of contemporary Christian demonology, focusing on witches as "predominantly imagined by contemporaries as the evil inverse of the good housewife and mother; as women who poisoned and harmed others rather than nurturing or caring for them."[157] If this rhetoric of inversion is partially if not exactly identical to the binaristic structures underlying dybbuk narratives,[158] the contemporary cognizing and organizing of that type of "knowledge" is certainly relevant to our discussion.[159] But the similarities between the two phenomena's relationship to gender transcend the abstract.

Found in both phenomena, for example, are the assault on particularly vulnerable societal elements, the ceremonies and the attacks' ability to serve as a site for the complex and conflicted juxtaposition of folk religious beliefs and practices and elite structures,[160] the frequent linkage to "unacceptable sexual behavior," itself contingent on a problematic understanding of women's sexualized nature (particularly when strongly asserted),[161] the central figure's service as a societal scapegoat,[162] and the centrality of actual "sadistic sexual torture" in witchcraft narratives, finding its analogue in the lurid representations of the dybbuk's sexualized torture of its victim.[163] As with dybbuk accounts, a witch's defiant statements could simply be seen as proof of her problematic truculence (while simultaneously allowing, in an admittedly problematic fashion, a comparatively unfettered forum for the expression of the normally marginalized female voice),[164] and both contexts boast complicated countermagical rituals, which included "burning some object associated with the suspect, or ... various rituals and prayers."[165] The public nature of both the witchcraft execution and communal exorcism (ostensibly) didactically reinforced social mores.[166] In short, if witch hunts, in Barstow's formulation, combined demonological beliefs and "moral crusades,"[167] such combination powerfully resonates with Jewish spirit possession narratives.

A clear identification exists between women, especially "witchy" women involved in magical practices, and Jews in the popular German imagination, an identification partially related to the Jews' "strange" bodies and the belief that both groups served Satan. This said, Jews were almost never accused of witchcraft, "the standard explanation for this phenomenon [being] that witchcraft was a heresy, and therefore one had to be a Christian to become a witch."[168] Midelfort brings an intriguing case of witchcraft in 1643 in Schwäbisch Hall, where Bavarian troops prove an individual's innocence by bringing in a Jew, Loeb, to undergo a witchcraft test (by virtue of his declared and known innocence). He writes: "It is fascinating to note that a Jew during this time of stress felt confident enough to undergo such a test. In this region at least, it would seem that witches had so seized the popular imagination that Jews, far from being a constant potential scapegoat, could be used to *prove* the validity of the 'Haller Hexenbad.' "[169] Though Jews were not conceptualized as heretics, the inquisitorial processes concerning heresy, the demarcation of deviance, the punishment of banishing heretics and forcing them to wander from town to town, and heresy's challenge to ecclesiastical and even occasionally secular power structures display strong parallels to our story.[170]

Witchcraft, then, was also clearly connected with changing contemporary dynamics of belief and skepticism; a critical tool of scholarship is regionalized study, allowing scholars to spatially and temporally correlate social trends of witchcraft, skepticism, and counter-religious activity.[171] Williams notes how "the panic over the presence of satanic magic among women in certain areas coincided with the post-Reformation crises of religious diversity and dissidence,"[172] and several scholars have remarked on the "increased emphasis on and concern with matters supernatural during the Thirty Years' War."[173] Indeed, Rowlands connects the "experience and memory of war" with a perceptible increase in the "fear of and credulity about witches from the mid-seventeenth century onwards," according nicely with the analogous circumstances surrounding our chapbook's publication (and arguably its author's perspective);[174] by century's end, however, the pendulum had reversed, and crimes that would have previously been considered diabolic pacts—charms, fortune-telling, magical treasure hunting—"were punished merely as superstitions, or in certain cases as fraud."[175] Regionally, the German lands and western Polish provinces, particularly in the Catholic territories,[176] relied particularly strongly on demonology to persecute marginalized groups (particularly heretics and Jews); this allows us to suggest how such varied characteristics might be relevant to the study of the relationship between theological anxiety and contemporary supernatural focus.[177]

Similarly close study of witchcraft prosecutions generally reveals a rational process of skeptical investigation predicated on the understanding of many accusations' potential baselessness (occasionally leading to slander suits filed by some accused); a contemporary writer asserted that witchcraft trials should be conducted "according to the standards of natural reason and equity," which only seems ironic given modern perspective.[178] Even broader skepticism could be applied to particular elements within witchcraft discourse while believing in that general framework, examples of the "secondary skepticism" discussed in the theoretical introduction. As Behringer writes: "Even during the persecutions of 1590, as far as we can observe, court proceedings were never entirely arbitrary. The courts tested denunciations for their plausibility, paying particular attention to the reputation and social relationships of the denouncer. ... It is evident that some of those questioned did not believe in the effectiveness of witchcraft, and others did not even believe in the existence of witches."[179] The witches' sabbat, for example, generated much skepticism even among witchcraft believers; some witchcraft defenders, unable to discover any tangible evidence of the sabbat (or a witch's ability to fly to same), insisted on our previously-discussed tropes of perceptual illusion; that the devil had illuded the individual into *believing* she had attended a sabbat.[180] Briggs cleverly extends such potential skepticism even to those whose precise actions would suggest belief: "we need not suppose that all who resorted to the cunning folk were convinced of their powers; many may well have been adopting a 'belt and braces' approach, willing to try anything in the cause of self-protection, on the basis that it could do no harm."[181] Rowlands sums it up well in writing that "popular concern about witchcraft was thus not uniform; it varied from individual to individual according to their psychological predisposition to anxiety, their personal relationships with alleged witches and the particular context of their own lives."[182] Such individual variations and determinations were also inflected by the rise of printing and increasing literacy, simultaneously empowering greater interpretive autonomy while spreading the possibilities of conventional perspectives.[183]

Major differences of course also exist between the phenomena: the witchcraft accounts pay far more attention to the witches' "backstories" than the dybbuk narratives do to their victims (or even the dybbuks themselves); a strong connection undoubtedly exists between the worsening European economic situation in the 1560s and the witchcraft craze, and no such connection seems equally apparent here; and most importantly, the diabolic connections at the heart of witchcraft narratives are absent in our genre.[184] Finally, though both phenomena may serve to suppress discord and strengthen the regnant social order, some study of witchcraft has specifically focused on how that support particularly benefited state institutions and organs—a phenomenon clearly less relevant in the Jewish context.[185]

Other comparative and comparable elements from the canonical and contested set of supernatural traditions in the non-Jewish sphere also have relevance here, but they must await a fuller study.[186] For now, it is sufficient to recognize that these dybbuk accounts, potentially understood "in terms of social control by the elite and rebellion or a quest for status by the dispossessed,"[187] where spirits serve as "a vehicle for articulating unacceptable, conflict-precipitating desires and demands" at least partially "a reaction to the strict, instinct-suppressing regulations governing all spheres of communal life, based as these were on rigid religious codes and prohibitions," and where exorcism allows for the expunging of "deviant identity" and its replacement by "a positive conformist one,"[188] have at least one powerfully resonant contemporary non-Jewish social analogue, an analogue that may teach us a great deal, both about gendered approaches and methodology more generally.[189]

Concluding Considerations

Though an even fuller reading of this extraordinarily rich and complex text could elucidate its nuanced, subtle moral positioning still further, space permits only a few more points to expand our sense of the story's moral compass, to address some unanswered questions, and to conclude by referring back to earlier questions posed about history, literature, and audience, and suggesting some further directions for study in this light.

As I suggested throughout the chapter, the author's shifting stance between authenticating and nonauthenticating modes of discourse can be variously viewed as his attempts to incorporate the shifting perspectives and demands of history and literature, reality and allegory, moralizing text and popular entertainment—binaries that are not mutually exclusive, but overlapping, complementary, and at times willfully paradoxical. Which begs the question: how is this story intended to be read, with all its complex and contradictory elements, if the audience is *not* aware of its allegorical dimensions, its allusions, and its thematic structures? To be read simply as entertainment would mean not only readerly failure to encompass writerly depths—always a possibility—but, without apprehending the existence of these dimensions, readers might find the story, in its significant divergence from the adherence to convention desirable for pleasure (from an unsophisticated view of readership), confusing and therefore reject it, resulting in polemic, aesthetic, and commercial failure. This seems unlikely, but if we are instead to consider the writer as "successful" in this regard, we must examine the consequent reconceptualization of the story's readership. How does our general historical sense of audience differentiation in Jewish literature apply here? Are we forced to expand either our historical definition of the chapbook's readership, or that historically understood readership's understanding and literary perspicacity, or both?

Complicating the question further is the recognition of the complexity of assignations and identifications in an allegorized approach to the story. We have suggested that the dybbuk can be read to represent external evil, particularly anti-Semitic forces, or more abstractly the generalized metaphysical misery—like the questions of theodicy—these evil forces necessarily generate. But we have also briefly noted these issues' domestication into solely internal Jewish spheres independent of external catalyst, allowing the dybbuk to simply be seen as the voice of Jewish skepticism and heresy more generally. Our reading of the dybbuk's voice may show how defeating the dybbuk is presented as triumph in an internal struggle against skepticism.[190] Such considerations, however, along with the sympathetic qualities occasionally granted the dybbuk, raise the question of audience positioning: are we as readers of a morally improving text invited to consider ourselves as the innocent Mindl or the doubtful, sinful dybbuk, whose name is eventually revealed to be Jacob, that allegorical name for the Jews par excellence? The only realistic answer is, of course, both, raising the complicated question of how audiences are expected, if indeed they are, to participate in an allegorical reading of this story, which itself frustrates simple assignments of allegorand.[191]

Additionally, does readerly consciousness of the story's allegorical operation somehow detract from its apprehension as "historical" narrative? Certainly, historical Jewish reading patterns permit viewing a particular text simultaneously as history and allegory; and perhaps contemporary audiences might be particularly disposed to view those patterns that seem to be particularly literary and precisely inauthentic to modern eyes as proof of the narrative's allegorical—and thus historical—truth. The author's explicit (though retroactively indeterminate) creation of details activating readerly allegorical consciousness, then, may well be an *authenticating* mechanism, not a skepticism-producing one, despite our instincts to the contrary.[192] In further investigating this approach, historiographical research illuminating the medieval and early modern Jewish tendency to conflate particular and recent historical events with classic moments in the Jewish tradition might be fruitfully applied.[193]

Before concluding a chapter on a phenomenon that unifies various forces, two brief directions for further study that unify disparate entities are worth mentioning. First, though we have briefly discussed the work's relation to contemporary Hebrew and Yiddish dybbuk tales, another possible way to analyze this text and the epistemic claims it makes on its readers is to compare it to other Yiddish works the readers were simultaneously encountering in the "literary marketplace," like the *Mayse Briyo ve-Zimro*, the *Mayse Beit Dovid bimei malkhut peras*, *Ayn hipshe mayse fun drey vayberin*, *Mayse fun ludvig un aleksandr*, and others.[194]

Perhaps even more intriguing is expanded speculation about this text as not merely a moral or theological narrative, as discussed above, but a medical text, or, at least, a text in dialogue with contemporary Yiddish medical literature.[195] While the story certainly suggests dybbuk possession's essential connection to metaphysics, particularly in terms of sin, punishment, and their connection to miracles and matters of the soul, the lines between physical and spiritual sickness are quite porous in late medieval and early modern Judaism. Indeed, the particular and routinized process of expulsion at a trained professional's hands bears substantial similarities to the practice of the healer's art,[196] particularly when Yiddish medical texts also contain remedies for afflictions we might call mystical (for example, the evil eye),[197] and even specific remedies for exorcisms and exorcists take on medical resonances and are differentiated from other (modern) "medical" conditions by contemporary observers.[198] At the start of Mindl's illness, the parents are described in the same breath as consulting *makhsheyfes un doktoyrim* (witches and doctors), and the resulting diagnoses are mixed: some say epilepsy, others say other diseases, and Mindl's condition is first treated by doctors for three years before they turn to holy rabbis.

It should go without saying that in this moralistic and theologically conservative text the medical forces are self-evidently insufficient, and indeed such voices, within this narrative's particular ideological and theological frames, are stand-ins for precisely the kind of skeptical approach writ small that the dybbuk's possession disproves. However, the acknowledged existence of these forces—whether providing a space for the acknowledgment of skepticism, or rather socially constituted "reality," affords a multiplicity of options for historically positioned observers and current critics. A modern scholar's analysis of the possibilities facing observers of "possessed" individuals in a non-Jewish context powerfully shows how belief and skepticism are balanced as a result:

> For instance, the following ways to displace possession are on offer: the possessed are physically ill; they are mentally ill, in a thousand ways; they are poisoned; they are in an altered state induced by drugs; they are acting; they are taking a culturally sanctioned opportunity to express 'bad' feelings about the family, the church and sex; they are reducible to a textual sign. All these possibilities, even the last, were available to an educated early modern observer of the contorted and wildly writhing body of a victim of possession. However, most early modern observers had one more possibility in mind: that the person in question was inhabited by a demon, a demon who had moved into the body as one might invade a country or occupy a house . . .[199]

Continuity, not strong disruption, exists between these approaches, much as it does in early modern Judaism between this world and the next—as our story testifies.

A good number of ghosts haunt this text, not only Yakov: an anonymous writer, a set of unnamed readers, swirling forces of history and how they shape literary decisions and vice versa. In the course of analyzing the text's narrative complexities, we have begun to reach some preliminary conclusions, about the readers' more complicated capacities to decode allegory, the usage of supernatural tales to articulate a nuanced moral message about the defeat of metaphysical doubt in a variety of capacities, and the ability of texts to reflect cross-cultural themes of gender anxiety and rising skepticism. Nonetheless, we should remember that just as the exorcism may be the point of the possession story but not the source of its uncanny energy, our solutions and approaches should yield, when all is said and done, to the provocative, blurred questions and worlds the story embodies.

6. The "Tale of Briyo and Zimro"

What Makes a Yiddish Romance?

Any serious discussion of romance has to take into account its curiously proletarian status as a form generally disapproved of, in most ages, by the guardians of taste and learning, except when they use it for their own purposes.
—Northrop Frye

Our previous three chapters have treated literary texts representative of genres, or subgenres, of early modern Yiddish literature that make various epistemic claims on the reader regarding the supernatural, allowing for the display of nuanced articulation of belief and skepticism. The texts also provide different models of literary sophistication on the audience's part—varied skills and attitudes allowing us to reconceptualize that audience's approach to textual materials without requiring substantial revision in our understanding of their levels of textual knowledge and linguistic ability. Comparative approaches to non-Jewish treatments of the supernatural, in the main and in specific or comparable subgenres under discussion, have assisted in developing our conceptual approach and our specific interpretations. Our final chapter, an examination of still another important genre of early modern Yiddish narrative with more complex connections to the fantastic, the historical, and the coterritorial, will develop our various questions and approaches still further.

Chivalric literature and romance—whether borrowed, adapted, Judaized, or plagiarized—has constituted a part of the Yiddish literary tradition for as long as that tradition has existed; the Cambridge Codex of 1382—our source for "the oldest literary documents of Yiddish literature,"[1] contains a chivalric text. As Jean Baumgarten has noted, a close look at the genre's long history provides unparalleled opportunity to investigate the porosity between Jewish and non-Jewish literary traditions and cultural values.[2] Clear literary and textual analysis of individual works, however, provides equally unparalleled opportunity to speculate how audience consciousness of that porosity, among other features, might illuminate particular aspects of their literary abilities. Examining a remarkable story, the *Mayse Briyo ve-Zimro*, will allow us to speculate on the nature and potential reception of a well-known contemporary Yiddish literary genre; beyond that, though, the text will be used to complicate traditional conceptualizations of Jewish masculinity and sexuality, to investigate our questions of belief and skepticism, to focus on processes of cultural transfer, and to raise some questions that may illuminate popular Jewish historiographical conceptions, particularly the truth-claims the story makes about Jewish power, politics, and statist structures.

The History of Romance: The Yiddish Literary Tradition

The Cambridge Codex of 1382 contains, besides an animal fable,[3] poems about Aaron's death, the righteous Joseph, and paradise, and lists of the weekly Torah readings and the stones on the high priest's breastplate, the famed *Dukus Hornt*, an epic romance.[4] Baumgarten points out that the manuscript's organization "clearly indicates ... two distinct types of texts ... those which are rooted in the Jewish literary heritage (biblical and midrashic epic poems), even if they do show some connections to epic forms of the Christian West; and those simple and obviously Judaized adaptations of texts that derive directly from the coterritorial European culture of the Middle Ages (heroic saga and courtly romance)."[5] The manuscript's separation of the two types (and the presentation of the clearly Germanic epic following the midrashic material), indicates clear authorial knowledge of the two differentiated strata.

The first type's development can be traced through the significant production of biblical adaptations and expansions; these epic narrative "retellings" usually maintained certain biblical passages, while expansively incorporating rabbinic material. Notable examples include the biblical epic poems *Shmuel-bukh* (Augsburg 1543) and *Melokhim-bukh* (Augsburg 1544); the former focuses on the prophet Samuel and David and Solomon's monarchies, the latter spans the period from Solomon's rule to the first Temple's destruction and the Babylonian captivity.[6] In terms of form, these texts provide prime evidence of cultural interchange: they incorporate German epic metrical structures and, like many of these epics, were apparently sung aloud (though their particular melodies, which according to the 1544 edition of the *Shmuel-bukh*'s epilogue are "known by the entire people of Israel," may occasionally have had internal, not external, origins).[7] In content, the texts are modeled primarily on the internal Jewish traditions, though they do (particularly the *Shmuel-bukh*)[8] display certain features of medieval courtly romance, such as the use of "titles borrowed from the German feudal lexicon" and the prominence of combat narratives.[9]

These texts can be contrasted to those known more generally (if pejoratively) as *galkhes bikher* or *galkhes seforim*, that is, texts deriving from Christian sources such as German sagas or Italian chivalric romances.[10] Pejoratives notwithstanding, such works compose a long and distinguished part of Yiddish literary tradition, as well as that tradition's study: as early as 1912, Leo Landau published (in German lettering) the *Artus-Hof* (Arthur's Court), a part of the Widwilt-Wigalois cycle.[11] He notes in his introduction that from the early medieval period European Jews "were well acquainted with the romances of chivalry ... [r]omances seem to have been especially popular," citing the case that Judah the Pious (d. 1213 or 1217) prohibited "the binding of sacred (Hebrew) books on which romances were written in the vernacular" and related that " 'a pious man tore off the cover of a Pentateuch on which, in the vernacular, were written frivolous tales, the tournaments of the kings of the nations.' "[12] He also notes that "of all the ancient epic German poems and tales none seem to have enjoyed greater popularity than those belonging to the Arthurian cycle."[13] Soon after the *Artus-Hof*'s Yiddish appearance, it is joined by books like *Ditrikh von Bern* and *Hildebrand*, among many other German *Volkslieder* and *Volksbücher*.[14]

Knowledge or ignorance of any specific text, it should be said, does not preclude a "general sense" of courtly romantic conventions, as Jewish culture in a European context clearly allowed significant and substantive interaction at least at the broadest levels of cultural communication.[15] Generalized knowledge and the concomitant reception of broad conventions, then, may in turn authorize certain effects of real interest to our understanding and analysis of the text. Finally, it is the transmutation of those themes—both authorially in terms of composition and their organic transformation through their experience in the eyes of observers within a differing cultural context—that generates the lessons important for us. This enables us particularly to examine these questions of cultural adaptation precisely *as* questions.

One reaction became immediately apparent. These works, particularly the *Ditrikh*, became quickly implicated in the conflict of interest between the rabbinic scholars, with their emphasis on morally edifying reading material, and the general readership; in fact, our surest confirmation of the works' existence and popularity stems from their excoriation in those edifying works' introductions.[16] Another way we know of some of these no longer extant works is because of their melodies; written and disseminated in the transitional period between oral and print culture, many of these chivalric materials, like "Herzog Ernst," had particular tunes associated with the sung version of their text. These melodies were then dissociated and applied to other works; "Herzog Ernst" and Hildebrand's memory survive in instructions that other texts be sung to their melodies.[17]

Notably, both "internal" and "external" materials refer to these melodies, and those references, in combination with "spoken turns of phrase taken directly from medieval epic literature,"[18] have suggested to some an aural audience, which according to the texts often consisted of women and girls.[19] Baumgarten correctly and importantly distinguishes between "the recitation (whether prosodic or sung) of epic poems by Jewish storytellers for audiences in the Jewish quarter at festivals or collective assemblies" and "simple borrowings of expressions and epic formulae taken from the repertoire of Germanic heroic poetry, which were mechanically transposed by the Yiddish authors."[20] Nonetheless, these various types of evidence, taken less skeptically, yielded the general understanding among earlier Yiddish critics that these materials were recited by "professional men," who "recited their own works as well as those of others," referred to by the critics as the "Jewish troubadour or 'Shpilman.'"[21] Contemporary research has refuted the Jewish *shpilmener*'s existence, in contrast to their unmistakably present non-Jewish traditional analogues; in earlier periods of undoubted oral transmission, however, Jews may have occasionally performed these materials, and these figures' absence hardly means, given contemporary cultural porosity, that it is wrong to say that "the Jews, too, knew 'tournaments,' festivities modeled on those of the knights, the notion of love and 'amour,' wandering scholars, jesters," and so on—knowledge that will figure into our later discussion.[22] Once the epics begin to circulate in printed form, "the reception of the texts was in particular via reading, both individual and collective,"[23] and certain individuals, be they writers, copyists, or schoolmasters, did act in the precise manner that was assigned to the nonexistent *shpilman* by earlier critics: they adapted the non-Jewish literary material to Jewish settings.

The nature of these adaptations varied, depending on the "author" and the text; some individuals were essentially transcribers, while others not only added "idiomatic peculiarities but also [eliminated] passages whose moralizing characters were too specifically Christian. Scenes from the world of chivalry were often omitted if the description was felt to be unacceptable in a Jewish milieu because of the violence of colours or crudeness of language."[24] Other related processes in dealing with Christian religious material included neutralization (removing any reference to a particular religious tradition), Judaization (replacing the Christian religious tradition with analogous referents from the Jewish tradition), or ironization (investing the text resulting from either of those choices, or even maintaining the original material, with an alienating sensibility precisely because of a recognition shared by author and reader of that original material's "problematic" nature).[25]

Fuks feels such "Judaization" often dims the chivalric materials' full aesthetic effect—"we miss in the Yiddish Arthur tales the chivalrous atmosphere, its exaltation, manners, and customs"—but, done anyway due to "the mentality of the Jewish shpilman and his audience," it creates processes of change eventually allowing the form's adaptation to internally Jewish (i.e., biblical) materials invested with the force of chivalric epic.[26] Whether or not Fuks' argument is historically true, it accords with Baumgarten's suggestion, at the end of his discussion of the *Shmuel-bukh*, that "the text demonstrates no strict division between the Christian and the Jewish culture, between scholarly and popular texts, but rather embodies the cultural exchange, reciprocal influence, and a dynamic circulation between the two"[27] and that "this capacity for integration of alien materials without at the same time breaking with the foundations of the Jewish tradition remains one of the constants of Old Yiddish literature."[28] This emphasis on porosity and union is vital with respect to the *production* of these literary texts;[29] such considerations can be further developed and questioned with respect to their *reception*, asking, in our analysis of these chivalric texts, how the texts themselves address these questions of cultural influence, and how readers' positioning (morally, ideologically, and informationally) might affect writers' decisions in these regards.

For example, these authors are clearly aware of popular sensibilities potentially different from their own with respect to tolerable levels of Christian imagery and reference; otherwise processes of "Judaization" might well have been unnecessary. To conceptualize Judaization, however, as catering to presumed popular sensibilities is perhaps indicative of "real" levels of communal (in)tolerance, much as contemporary creators and disseminators of popular culture know well that what is transmitted over the public airwaves is often tamer than what they or much of their audience would tolerate in the privacy of their own thoughts, sensibilities, or, for that matter, bedrooms. Instead, the presence of cultural and communal gatekeepers (taking rabbinical or other form) may have served as goads to self-censorship.[30]

Nonetheless, analyzing certain aspects of texts may inform us about the differences between those writers who were, by virtue of their adapting culturally foreign epics, "cultural transmitters," and those readers who by at least one definition (i.e., their inability to read the chivalric works in their original languages) were less able to participate in cultural interchange. More, it provides information as to how the writers perceived (and, perhaps more daringly, even constituted) the audience's perspectives on cultural adaptation; what it means, in other words, to read a culturally porous and adaptive text, and how one thinks about the world that text generates. We will do this through close textual analyses of a literary work taking its model (at least in its motifs)[31] from the chivalric sphere, the *Mayse Briyo ve-Zimro*, illustrating its attempt to strike a precarious and questioning balance between convention and variation and Jewish and non-Jewish form and content.

The "Tale of Briyo and Zimro": History and Summary

The question of the precise textual history, authorship, and provenance of the "Tale of Briyo and Zimro" is complex.[32] Frakes dates the earliest extant version, a manuscript copy of the text copied by Isaac b. Judah Reutlingen and now in Munich's Bayerische Staatsbibliothek, to either 1580 or 1585 (the discrepancy stems from an idiosyncrasy in the colophon);[33] he suggests, however, that the manuscript is itself based on an earlier, printed version. The first extant print version is a 1597 abridgement claiming to be from Giovanni da Gara's Venetian printing house and, according to Zfatman, is the last *mayse-bikhl* printed in Italy, illuminating the drastic decline of Yiddish printing in Italy by the end of the sixteenth century.[34] Later editions appear in mid-seventeenth-century Prague,[35] which themselves may stem from an earlier source expanded upon by Reutlingen.[36]

A brief plot summary will assist those unfamiliar with the story: Zimro is a wise and handsome young man who by dint of his wisdom and erudition has been granted a high position at the (Jewish) royal court and, along with his father, Tuvas, has been appointed judge over the people. After a brief episode demonstrating Zimro's wisdom—he rules on whether a two-headed individual deserves a double inheritance—the story begins in earnest. Zimro sees Briyo, the high priest Feygin's daughter, through a window; they profess their feelings to one another, and Zimro discovers his love is requited—and more—by Briyo. When Tuvas attempts to arrange the marriage, however, Feygin refuses to grant his daughter's hand; even royal intervention fails, in the face of Feygin's objections to Zimro's lower social status and the resulting scandalous mésalliance. Feygin's objections notwithstanding, the two swear love and fidelity to one another, kissing each other repeatedly. After some further setbacks, an opportunity presents itself: the pope has issued a decree forbidding circumcision and immersion in the ritual bath, adding that any Jew appearing before the pope (to, among other things, presumably appeal the decree) would be killed. The king wishes to send Zimro to attempt to annul the decree; Zimro agrees to undertake the mission if Feygin lets him marry Briyo; Feygin agrees, assuming the pope will dispatch the troublesome suitor; Briyo worries Zimro will die and she will therefore be unable to keep her oath; Zimro reassures her.

Arriving in Rome, Zimro essentially bribes the sentries in order to enter the papal court. He convinces the pope to listen to him, and uses the argument that ritual immersion and circumcision weaken the Jews, the pope's enemies, to persuade him to rescind the decree. Feygin, naturally discomfited by Zimro's success, retracts his promise; the two star-crossed lovers kiss once more, and Briyo dies of grief. Zimro mourns, and then, ostensibly traveling to a feast celebrating the passage of royal power from king to prince, enters a strange, symbolically charged world, eventually revealed to be a purgatorial world of the dead. There, he encounters Elijah the prophet and Briyo; the latter warns him not to touch anything, especially her, or he will die. However, seeing Briyo caressed by another man—despite Briyo's warning that this is Satan's attempt to tempt him—he decides to kiss her, allowing them a reunion in death. Zimro returns home, led by Elijah, and dies three days later; he is then taken to paradise by the angels Michael and Gabriel, where he and Briyo have a miraculous wedding. The narrator ends with a few choice remarks about love.

The text clearly exemplifies Baumgarten's more general assessment that "[a]lthough one observes both the genuine influence of the forms characteristic of Italian literature of the period and an opening up of Jewish society to extra-Judaic culture, the texts printed at the time, particularly the

Yiddish books, bear witness to the desire to root oneself firmly in the Jewish tradition and to invent a national literature that could counterbalance the influences of the surrounding culture."[37] Yet a closer analysis of the story, which deserves further modern critical attention in its own right, may usefully complement our understanding of authorial choices relating to cultural synthesis and differentiation. That analysis may show how an author's approach to the topics of sexuality (including masculinity and femininity), Judaization, the incorporation and employment of both Jewish and non-Jewish master narratives, and the interplay between "realism," historical consciousness, and the "supernatural" allows us to differentiate between shared thematic concerns, ways of thinking about those concerns, and possibilities for constructing and asserting audience reaction to those concerns.

Briyo and Zimro: Making a Jewish Hero, Beginning a Jewish Romance

What, in this author's view, constitutes a Jewish chivalric hero? How might the author create a particular character, and what can we learn from his strategies of doing so about both the specific story and its metonymic function of attempting to bridge two coterritorial literary worlds?

Zimro is idealized from the story's opening, extremely attractive both physically and intellectually: he "was very handsome and he was also very wise and learned in the holy text" (*eyn groyser khokhem un eyn lerner*, 82). Notably, though, the story first explicitly accentuates Zimro's intellectual virtues, in the puzzling preface where the young Zimro solves a case stumping his father, Tuvas, and the royal court. The narrator's brief coda to the preface—"The king and the entire royal court laughed happily about Zimro's wisdom and judgment" (83)—hints only at this first, narrative function; a closer look at the case's details and Zimro's solution, however, provides interpretive keys to the narrative as a whole, as a good preface should.[38]

The case was briefly summarized above: on Rosh Hashanah, a woman enters the royal court with two sons quarreling over their father's inheritance; one of the sons, with two heads, believes he deserves a double share. Zimro hits upon an intriguing solution to the conundrum:

> Zimro asked for a vessel filled with hot water. They brought him the hot water, and he poured it on one head of the two-headed man,

> whereupon the other head shrieked. Zimro said, "Why are you shrieking? I haven't done anything to you. I can see that you only have one body. So you should get only one portion of the inheritance." (82–83)

The narrator's summation is of course well-taken. First, the narrative generates an image resonant of the young Solomon in his later midrashic incarnation, who, while still at his father's court, displays a mastery of the subtleties of human psychology and behavior;[39] in doing so, it creates literary continuity with authorized narratives from a Jewish monarchic setting, helpful to preserving greater Jewish sensibility while establishing a chivalric tone. Secondly, it demonstrates strong structural links to the biblical ur-story of Solomon's wisdom. In both cases, a mother brings two children before a wise figure, who strives to achieve a certain ontological clarity;[40] both stories have the wise figure expressing his decision by advocating an extreme action, though in Solomon's case, unlike here, that extreme action is not taken;[41] and most clearly, each story treats the consequences of doubling, though here too the story transcends its biblical master narrative: Solomon has only one binary set to consider, while Zimro has two (the sons' two bodies, and the two heads on one of the sons' bodies). Transcendence of master narratives accomplished by shifting from contemplation to action (or actualization) will pervade the story as a whole.[42]

The doubling or pairing the story suggests expands in several directions: the test itself, determining inheritance and solved by the son Zimro, not the father Tuvas, profoundly addresses the paternal-filial relationship, significant not only within this episode and the master David-Solomon paradigm, but in *Briyo and Zimro* as a whole.[43] Such relationships, in chivalric stories, go beyond the personal to the political: generational inheritance relies not only on genetic, but virtue-based or heroic factors—a later instance of narrative doubling, when we discover the king also has a son who is Zimro's close friend, is illustrative. The center of the action and yet not the royal inheritor, at court and not precisely of it, Zimro is simultaneously the central figure and the alienated double: befitting, as will become clear, a narrative both centrally attuned to and alienated from a Jewish tradition that can smoothly marry monarchic centrality and contemporary diasporic Jewish reality.

The father-son relationship also, however, allows for the inclusion of discussions of masculinity and sexuality, reminding us in turn that any question of two beings' union in a single entity is generally framed as a *romantic* question. Regardless of the author's familiarity with the Aristophanic myth, first articulated in Plato's *Symposium*, that all lovers are two separated halves of a single whole searching for one another, comparable resonances are available to the Jewish writer and audience in the passage from Genesis suggesting a man and wife "cleave to each other and become one flesh."[44] Zimro's conclusion, as exemplified by his extreme experiment, that two heads are actually part of a single body, serves as a metaphorical introduction to and apotheosis of love's centrality in the text, demonstrating the propensity of fantastic narrative to actualize the generally metaphorical.

Before discussing the *story's* romantic and sexual elements, however, our analysis of the preface must address one final puzzling detail: the case's arrival before the court on Rosh Hashanah, presumably a time when Jewish courts would not normally be in session.[45] Perhaps the author is simply engaging in subtle wordplay: what day is more fitting for this case than one whose literal name means "Head of the Year?" Certainly there are plenty of heads present here. But arguably, such a dating, given Rosh Hashanah's identity as the Day of Judgment, is an invitation to interpret the story on multiple levels. Just as Rosh Hashanah's judgments partake of multiple spheres of meaning, from the personal to the communal to the universal—the narrative emphasis that "the king is sitting on his throne" during the judging period (82) reaccentuates the image of the King of Kings sitting in judgment, an allegorical dimension that will be developed throughout the analysis—so too Zimro's judgment may be seen to address a wider sphere of narrative and thematic issues. The question of inheritance before him is not limited to property, but relates to Jewish intellectual, philosophical, and historical trends and their comprehension and manipulation by creative figures.

Zimro, as his name suggests, has metaphorically musical tendencies: he harmonizes within his own body the varied rabbinic, royal, and priestly strands of Jewish identity. Though as mentioned, his main task seems intellectual and rabbinic, the text notably suggests that the king gives him a "house in Jerusalem *near the castle and near the houses of the priests*" (82, emphasis mine).[46] If Zimro's own body is presented as potentially harmonious and harmonizing, the prefatory judgment provides him opportunity to harmoniously integrate the Jewish body as well, represented in his accentuation of the unity of the split-but-unified body that stands in judgment before him. Such integration (though extreme means) of body-mind and rabbinism-royalty suggests the opportunity for a synthetic type of Jewish existence: one might even suggest, given the story's generic and conventional concerns, that the synthesis in question extends to that of external tropes and legends with internal Jewish literary trends. In creating the two-headed story that is *Briyo and Zimro*, and, finally, a synthesis of the present and the past, an effort is made to create a story "accurately" representing past ways of thinking about history and political crises while reflecting contemporaneous issues.

All these approaches will be further discussed throughout our analysis; returning, for now, to the story's sexual and romantic dimension, we may contrast Zimro's apparent (at least early) representation of harmony with Briyo's actions destabilizing a synthetic or equalizing impulse. One of her first statements to Zimro concerns her disproportionate love for him compared to his for her; later, her plan to see Zimro consciously puts the lovers on unequal fronts, both literally (she stands at a window, inside and presumably above ground, while he rides along) and metaphorically (she controls visual access and, unlike him, can determine if the two see each other). Later, overhearing Feygin's plan, she begs Zimro not to go on the mission, saving his life, but keeping them apart.

Indeed, Briyo, whose name, at least phonologically, suggests an earthy sensuality contrasting with the ethereal musicality of Zimro's,[47] seems, early on, even divided against *herself*: unlike, for example, the *Bovo-bukh*'s Druzeyne, who at first seems a purely lustful and desirous creature, Briyo's passion is matched by her early descriptions by the narrator in idealized terms of Jewish womanhood, "very modest and pious" (*demutik un gor frum*, 83). Perhaps the contrast stems at least partially from her embodiment of the paradoxical combination of traditionally Jewish feminine ideals and the conventional functions or role of chivalric heroine. Given this modesty, her erotic appeal unsurprisingly comes largely from passive display rather than activity, in a somewhat unusual instantiation of male objectification with roots in both internal and external literary traditions.[48] Zimro is invited to a banquet at Feygin's house; after the guests' compliments about his lovely silverware and dishes, Feygin brags, "These aren't so lovely. I have a far more beautiful possession" (*khefetz*, 83) and takes them to "a small room [where] he had locked in his beautiful daughter." Describing her, he asks, "Do you see my treasure? Do you like it?" (83).

Zimro's resulting erotic attraction—he "couldn't tear his eyes away" (83) and turns pale and mute—illustrates our author's comfort with the convention of the attraction of opposites. Indeed, both parties' source of attraction stems from the complement to their own "essential" state: Zimro falls in love with Briyo because of the objectified display of her physical charms; previously, Zimro had spotted her through a window, and "liked her instantly," and Briyo, conversely, seems attracted to Zimro for his nonphysical qualities: "the maiden cared for him too, for she had heard that he was very scholarly and pious" (*eyn talmid khokhem un frum*, 83). The difficulties in acting on such mutual attraction—an attraction attempting to harmonize not only physicality and intellectualized abstraction, but harmony and antiharmony itself—may serve as a thematic reminder of the difficulties of uniting Jewish content with non-Jewish form. The two lovers' first conversation is indicative; there, attention to appropriate decorum overpowers erotic attraction, despite Zimro's risking death (to his own mind, at least)[49] in approaching her in her room:

> When he opened the door, and she saw him,[50] she stood up and welcomed him, charming and beautiful. And he thanked her *modestly*. She took him by the hand, and they sat down together. He began: "There's something I'd like to discuss *with all due honor and respect. And please don't take it amiss.*" She said: "Dear Zimro, say anything you like. *I won't take it amiss.*" He said: "The instant I saw you, I fell hopelessly in love with you. I've lost my peace of mind. I beg you: if you promise to marry me, I'll get my father to proceed. He'll speak to your father and obtain his consent. *I'll make sure that it happens in an honorable fashion* (*mit groyser eren tsu geyt*)." She said: "Dear lord Zimro, I love you a lot more than you love me. I can't possibly describe how deeply I love you. *If God grants it, then we will bring it about.*" (83, emphasis mine)

This exchange displays throughout a constant subversion of its type-scene, the typical lovers' declaration, by its repeated caveats, verbal stutters, and called attention to the artificiality of its discourse, subversion stemming from the authorial juxtaposition of essentially antiromantic Jewish marriage conventions (Zimro the ardent lover talks about the procedures for obtaining parental consent in the throes of his proposal), with the conventional non-Jewish romances and chivalric stories, with their emphasis on *amor vincit omnia*. Crucial in that light is that objections are posed to the relationship as it is currently conducted from the couple themselves, not just their parents or other external forces. This is far different from the couples in, say, Boccaccio's

Decameron, an extremely educated and sophisticated author's vernacular work and a seminal influence on early modern Italian culture, and thus an important comparative text for consideration here.

Similarities to—and marked divergences from—the *Decameron* are apparent in the employment of another familiar trope: a woman's scheme to unite the lovers, an idea which, as we have seen, relates to general discourse about women's sexuality. Boccaccio fills his tales with schemes and witty stratagems to allow love predicated on erotic attraction to flourish between unevenly socially situated individuals. While Briyo takes on the role of a Boccaccian woman—or even of the figure of romance more generally—in arranging a towel as signal for when it is safe for Zimro to secretly visit her,[51] in this Judaized case the signal is arranged and further rendezvous made possible *only* once the two have plighted their troth, rendering them (in some sense) married.[52]

This is not to say that all non-Jewish lovers' tales are conducted without any attention to decorum; emphasis on virtue or parental objections is present in non-Jewish literature as well.[53] However, befitting the careful anatomization of Jewish life within the story and the differentiation between diverse strands of internal Jewish tradition, the two parents' manufactured objections are also meaningfully differentiated. Briyo's father Feygin, the priest representing Jewish bodily life, has a thematically appropriate objection: the potential groom's bloodline is insufficiently distinguished.[54] By contrast, Zimro's father, Tuvas, representing the Jewish mind, objects on no apparent grounds other than a simply recognized "fact" of insufficiency.[55] Such an objection, stemming from cognized self-assessment, may be dangerous on its own terms; Tuvas' suggestion that Zimro forget about marrying Briyo even before asking Feygin may characterize the intellectual's propensity to manufacture objections before they actually arise. Tuvas even inserts an intellectual's rationalizing preface: "I surely do not deceive myself [when I say]," or, in other words, "If I'm not mistaken" (*Ikh bin mikh nit toye*, not present in Neugroschel).

This said, Tuvas correctly predicts Feygin's refusal of Zimro's suit, even after the king's later intervention. Feygin's own reasoning, finally articulated concretely in response to the king—"Do you advise me to let my daughter marry into a clan that's lower than mine? All Jews will make fun of me" (85)—is certainly possible to read as a simple championing of *yikhes*. But perhaps, given Zimro's fairly elevated social position as royal judge and an intimate of the royal court, Feygin's objection may actually reveal another political theme of the text: Tuvas and Zimro's lack of status—even in Tuvas' own eyes—lies *precisely* in their proximity to the king.

Their insufficiency, in other words, stems from their subordination (in practice, if not in theory) of God's autonomy to man's. This hierarchization would be particularly offensive to the high priest, the lead representative of the opposing political-theocratic force, and possibly explain his willingness to kill his daughter rather than to marry her off. His willingness would, in a sense, constitute for him a blasphemous sacrifice to the powers of secularity and syncretism (a harmonic theme represented by Zimro, as we have said), rather than saving her for God's sole authority and autonomy by marrying her to a priest, for example, or even leaving her perfect in her unmarried state.[56]

Such a claim would of course be unthinkable for Feygin to express before the king himself, a reminder of the uneasy balance Jewish autonomists had to strike in a state ruled by others. As here, terror would characterize the encounters between the temporal and divine powers; gentle lies and discreet misdirections would be the order of the day. This opposition will reach its narrative and symbolic apotheosis later in the story, where the young, brash prince frames the priest's objection to his royal desire to have the marriage go forward in stark terms, invoking the classic Jewish terminology of treason with his use of the word *mored* (rebellion). Feygin nonetheless refuses to accommodate; and the crown ultimately refuses to assert its royal prerogatives. In the end, as we will see, only literature, not politics—romance and its consequences—lead Feygin to regret his decision.

This interpretation rests, of course, on the observation that though the king in this narrative is Jewish, he is rarely referred to in an explicit Jewish context, in contrast to the text's other politically inscribed figures, allowing the audience to read the story as both representing and resonating with internal Jewish traditions about monarchy and providing advice about negotiating with non-Jewish authority in a contemporary context, where Jewish political autonomy is absent.[57] Presenting the text this way not only allows another opportunity to reconceptualize audiences' capacities to explore differentiated textual levels of reality and metaphor, but shows how Feygin's violent objection to the marriage adumbrates central questions of potential synthesis between external forces, both political and literary, and internalizing, isolationist forces. The possibility of triumphing over Feygin and uniting Briyo and Zimro is, in turn, the possibility of not only incorporating

Briyo's literary and actual sensuality into a Jewish existence, but uniting secular and religious authority, temporal and ultimate potency.

Zimro's Quest: Politics, History, and Narrative

Zimro's opportunity to win Briyo's hand—his quest to attempt to annul the pope's decree—illustrates the narrative's further development of questions concerning Jewish literary and generic "domestication" of non-Jewish content, in part via the emergence of competing master narratives from internal and external sources, as well as contemporary political considerations. Zimro's quest, notably for our purposes, features the domestication of potentially fantastic elements to potentially realistic ones: its dangers stem not from mythic monsters but prosaic anti-Semitic sentiment, and the monster at its heart is the pope (*afifyor*),[58] whose sight, almost like a mythical creature, means certain death (at least to any Jew that appears before him). As in conventional chivalric literature, successful navigation of such a quest necessitates the display of wisdom and of virtue—but, in this subversive tale, which problematizes the juxtaposition of these Jewish and non-Jewish spheres, the wisdom displayed is knowing how to (ostensibly nonchivalrously) accommodate or placate the non-Jewish authority, and the questionable virtue is knowing how to deceive and bribe, and how to misrepresent oneself and one's people.

Seeing Zimro's particular quest as synthesizing Jewish and non-Jewish tropes is developed further in recognizing its thematic and literary parallels to the actions of Jacob, another figure often understood to symbolize the Jewish people. Besides his struggle with Esau, understood by Jews to be the ancestor of their contemporary Christian neighbors,[59] Jacob is well known as a scholar, who embarked on a quest of sorts to win his love. (The quest in Genesis—his labors to win Rachel—occurs essentially in time rather than space, but the fact that the father of the beloved, Laban, is a trickster and goes back on his word, like Feygin, seems significant.) Jacob's cleverness in handling "non-Jewish" authorities—Laban and Esau alike—with his combination of flattery, bribery, and appeal to his opponents' self-interest can be invoked not only to understand Zimro's behavior, but as paradigmatic behavior for readers in their own current political struggles.[60]

The story's political dimensions, then, are equally complexly structured between different worlds, or, more precisely, from different pasts. While the story ostensibly occurs in the past, presumably during the Hellenistic period—the naming of the viceroy Hyrcanos evokes Israel's Hellenistic rulers, and the story clearly occurs while the (Second) Temple existed, as Jews are still making pilgrimage and offering burnt sacrifice (82)[61]—and certainly with an implication of some form of Jewish autonomy, the papacy's mention confuses things. No historical overlap even vaguely exists between the Temple and the papacy, yet our narrative clearly incorporates both.[62] Additionally, the edicts, reminiscent of those promulgated by Antiochus and recorded in the book of Maccabees, and the prohibition on appearing before the pope, reminiscent of Ahasuerus' restrictions in the book of Esther, evoke, more than historical fact, a Jewish mythic time predating the lived Jewish-Christian encounters contemporaneous to the author.[63]

Any explanation for these varying materials' inclusion relying solely on sloppiness or a total lack of historical or historiographical consciousness seems unlikely here,[64] as this element is clearly and decisively demarcated from other narrative subsections; this overlap may instead reflect a studied attempt to read the lessons of the Temple and, allusively, biblical periods (the times of Jacob, Esther, and Judah Maccabee, which serve as Jewish master narratives) onto contemporary Jewish-Christian relationships.[65] As the exegetical principle has it, tales of the fathers are signs for the children; a resonant lesson for a narrative strongly featuring parents and children.[66] Befitting the contemporary context, the pope in this narrative is more powerful than the (Jewish) king; when the decree (*gzeyre*) is announced, the king goes unmentioned; the Jews hearing of the decree write the high priest Feygin to pray for the decree's annulment—which sparks his plan to send Zimro as a sacrificial lamb to the pope.

The king's notable absence here may be seen as testament to the increasing allegorical importance within the narrative of the absence of contemporary political Jewish power.[67] Such absence—whether reading the monarch as a stand-in for Jewish political power and autonomy or rather, if we continue to read the king as the King of Kings, the ability to achieve efficacious Divine intervention—provides the opportunity to display the consequences of this power's abdication to human representatives, first apparent when the king refuses to force Feygin into agreeing to the marriage. Whether the story reflects the political or theological corollaries and consequences of free will, the apparent fact is that the king's favorites, the Jews, cannot be saved from torment or punishment except through human action; Zimro may be sent, but the king is powerless to intervene, his hands tied by history and theology (in both cases, the narrative necessity to conform sufficiently to lived experience for its allegorical lessons to be meaningful).

Such a reading is seemingly clarified by a major Talmudic text featuring the figure of Hyrcanos, relevant here as another master narrative:[68]

> Our rabbis taught: when the kings of the Hasmonean House fought one another, Hyrcanus was outside and Aristobulus was inside. Each day they lowered denars in a basket, and raised up [animals for] the continual offerings. An old man was there, who was learned in Greek wisdom. He spoke to them with Greek wisdom saying, "As long as they carry on the Temple service, you will never capture them." The next day they lowered denars in a basket, and they raised up a pig. When it reached halfway up the wall, it stuck its claws into the wall, and the land if Israel was shaken four hundred parasangs in either direction. At that time they said, "Cursed be a man who raises pigs and cursed be a man who teaches his son Greek wisdom." (BT Sotah 49b)

A slightly different version of the story in the Yerushalmi (YT Berakhot 4:1 [7b]) reads as follows:[69]

> R. Simon in the name of R. Yehoshua ben Levi: "In the days of the Greek kingdom they would lower down two baskets of gold and would raise up two lambs. One time they lowered down two baskets of gold and were raising up two goats. At that time the holy One Blessed be He enlightened their eyes and they found two unblemished lambs in the [Temple] store of lambs." Said R. Levi, "Also in the days of the wicked kingdom [Rome] they would lower down two baskets of gold, and would raise up two lambs. Finally they lowered down two baskets of gold and raised up two pigs. They had reached less than halfway up the wall when a pig became stuck and jumped forty parasangs of the land of Israel. At that time, sins caused the daily sacrifice to be suspended and the Temple to be destroyed."

Given the particulars of our narrative, the prevalence of doublings here is noteworthy: the doubled story, in the two Talmuds, and two versions of the same story in the Yerushalmi, to say nothing of the fact that the Yerushalmi itself doubles the amount of material traded (in the Bavli, one basket is traded for another, while in the Yerushalmi two baskets are going in either direction).

And the names of the rabbis relating the stories in the Yerushalmi suggest a father-son relationship previously discussed as important to our text.[70]

But the most important theme adumbrated in master narrative is the opposition sketched between wisdom and piety, wisdom that (in the Babylonian Talmud, at least) is explicitly connected to the Greeks and leads to the Temple service's direct suspension or desecration, service the high priest nominally heads. Add to this the image of a besieged beautiful object (here, Jerusalem and the Temple), and the lesson that employing secular wisdom to possess the beautiful object—by playing on its own piety, no less—leads only to moral and political destruction. This master text helps clarify Feygin's objections to Hyrcanos' followers, even as those followers are paradoxically and integrally linked to David and Solomon in the tale's preface: Zimro (and Tuvas) can now be seen (in metaphoric and historiographic terms) as either Temple builders or Temple destroyers, and our narrative's ultimate question is which side of these two-sided images will they more fully represent.

The resulting debate over the value of internalizing external ideas, perceptions, and gazes is directly expressed in Zimro's behavior in "contemporary Rome." His easy success in entering the pope's chamber bespeaks his internalization of a non-Jewish tradition, Boccaccian among others:

> Zimro ... had brought a lot of money, so he went to a money exchange and obtained groschens for ten guldens. Next, he went to the pope's castle and dropped a lot of these coins. The sentries let him pass when they picked up the money. As he entered the court, many Christian counts and noblemen came toward him to ask him who he was. But he dropped some money, and they picked up the coins and let him pass. Finally, he reached the pope's chamber. (88)

Ironic reversal is the order of the day here: the money changer, the essential symbol for Christian charges of Jewish usuriousness and moral degeneracy, a basis of their perceptions of Jews, becomes the means to illustrate Christian cupidity inveighed against by reformists of many stripes, including Boccaccio. One story told on the *Decameron*'s first day concerns a Jewish merchant pressured to convert by his Christian friend.[71] Concerned about his future religion's quality, the Jew travels to Rome to assure himself of its sterling traits; his Christian friend, however, is dejected, knowing the church is corrupt and avaricious to the core, and nowhere more so than Rome. Boccaccio's humor comes from the tale's unexpected twist: upon the Jew's return, he informs his friend of his decision to convert, not because of his blindness to Christianity's faults, but the opposite. If a religion can so flourish despite its most eminent practitioners' immoral behavior, it must truly be the best goods available—and so should be eagerly adopted.

As my language above suggests, a mercantilic undertone to Boccaccio's satiric story is apparent that transcends the pervasive antiecclesiastical satire in the *Decameron*. Certainly it allows him to link religious tales to the doings of the secular middle class, a valuable strategy in the shift to vernacular literature, but it also allows him to cast his antireligious net widely to include Judaism, specifying the charge to the religion. Though on the surface the tale certainly disparages Christians more than Jews (the Jew is portrayed positively and virtuously, and most Christians are held up to opprobrium), read more deeply the tale holds *Christianity* in a higher light than *Judaism*. Its message, after all, is that Christianity's "religious essence" is the most valuable theological commodity, despite its corruption by current practitioners; conversely, Jews are presented as reified, stereotypical unprincipled businessmen, shopping for the best possible bargain. Boccaccio's Jew seemingly does not care about Christian dogma—he never raises the issue—instead grounding his decision on soteriological sales figures: how many served.

Our Jewish author's model of a Jewish-Christian encounter in Rome, however, takes a markedly different turn. Like in Boccaccio's story, Rome's Christians are victims to their own greed, and the Jew recognizes that essential weakness. Zimro's encounter with the pope develops this dynamic; his victory is achieved in his shrewd determination that the Christian leader's undoubted avarice is not for mere money, but rather for power[72] and the fulfillment of his earthly desires (to kill Jews). In the Jewish version of this master external narrative, however, the heroic Jew's confrontation at this heart of darkness with the monster at the end of the quest, and thus also with his self—resolves into questions concerning not his mercantile nature, but rather his religious, and, more subtly, his intellectual nature. In doing so, we will see how externalized projections of Jewish nature are—and are not—internalized.

Zimro's shrewd determination and approach is thematized not merely by reference to external sources, but internal ones as well, specifically the aforementioned book of Esther. Though as also mentioned, the evil decree's specifics belong more to Hasmoneans than to Persians, the former's narratives lack an appropriate description of the interaction between the homicidal king and supplicative figure. This relationship is only reinforced by Zimro's language in his papal appearance: the strangely doubled language of "I would like to ask your honorable grace for two things and may your grace not take it amiss" seemingly alludes to the strangely doubled use of "king" in Esther's appearance before Ahasuerus in Esther 7:3. This doubling, interpretively speaking, also has thematic resonances: the rabbis famously interpret the doubled language to suggest Esther alluded not only to King Ahasuerus, but to the King of Kings. This both develops our allegorical structure and arguably allows for a doubled level of narratological sophistication, perhaps suggesting that Zimro himself, familiar with the book of Esther and its rhetorical and practical lessons for dealing with non-Jewish authorities, has simply taken a page from the book. (Alternatively, the author merely places these words within the unconscious Zimro's mouth, providing interest and thematic, allusive resonance to the reader but not providing information regarding Zimro's own character, still interesting for our general purposes).

While Zimro's opening language may evoke the book of Esther, his continued discussion has entirely different resonances:

> The pope said: "Ask whatever you like, but nothing in regard to the Jews." Zimro said: "I want to ask a question about the Jews, which will be to your advantage." The pope said: "Then ask it." Zimro said: "Dear lord! If you had enemies, would you rather they were weak or strong?" The pope laughed and said: "That is an odd question! If I had enemies, wouldn't I rather they were weak than strong? Now my dear Jew, what are you aiming at, and why do you ask such a foolish question?" Zimro said: "Since you want to know, let me tell you, for I have come here for your sake. You are right, but your counselors have given you bad advice. The Jews may be your enemies, but there is no weaker or feebler nation on earth than the Jews. They are circumcised on the eighth day of their lives, and the loss of blood makes them weak. If a Jew were uncircumcised, he could kill ten Christians. Yet you have outlawed circumcision! Ten years from now on this country will be full of Jews." The pope said: "That is true. Now what is your other question?" Zimro said: "Dear lord! If you had enemies, would you rather they were few or many?" The pope laughed and said, "I would rather they were few than many. Tell me: what are you aiming at?" Zimro said: "I will tell you. You have issued an order prohibiting Jewish women from going to

> the bathhouse. So now, four times as many Jews are being born. You see, Jewish women are so shocked by the cold water that they do not conceive. Furthermore they are not allowed to lie with their husbands. But if they do not bathe in the cold water, then they will certainly lie with their husbands, and the Jews will become as numerous as the sands by the sea and they will multiply and go to war against you." (88–89)

The allusions to the Exodus story, with the asserted threat of Jewish multiplication and animalistic fecundity, and the clever midwives' rhetorical strategies to circumvent Pharaoh's decree, are clear. There, too, the midwives rely on animalistically stereotyping Jews in order to save them, suggesting that Jews give birth like animals in the field before the midwives' arrival, therefore frustrating Pharaoh's plan for the latter to kill the male children as they arrive on the birthing stool. Zimro's description ends with almost the precisely identical language Pharaoh's advisers employ in their attempts to develop legislation circumscribing Jewish activity: "they will multiply and go to war against you and kill you" (89).[73]

This intriguing passage yields several noteworthy points and problems catalyzing further analysis. First, the entire conversation is conducted on a "realistic," realpolitik level, reminiscent of both Exodus and (generally speaking) Esther: Zimro is under no illusions as to his ability to transform the pope from an anti-Semite to a philo-Semite, instead merely presenting his approach as the most plausible strategy for attaining the pope's own goal. Perhaps here the author's (and Zimro's) approach first seems to be at its weakest: why should anyone believe a representative of a weak and dominated people would actively suggest actions yielding their own further domination or destruction? One might argue the pope's blinding anti-Semitism could lead him to overlook a logical flaw; still, this seems a slight hope on which to fix the Jews' chances. This question emerges more clearly in comparison with the Exodus master narrative (and its midrashic expansion): there, Shifra and Puah merely revert to a passive role in suggesting their actions' uselessness, allowing Pharaoh to reaccept the "normal" Egyptian Jews' birth rate. Here, by contrast, the Jews' salvific protagonist goes much further, suggesting the monarch's actions are actually strengthening the Jews, and supporting *his* plan will weaken them.

Such an observation has a second point as its corollary: Zimro's argument presents Jewish law and custom itself as definitionally weakening the Jewish body. Were it not for circumcision, the Jew "could kill ten Christians," and would be more fecund to boot ("ten years from now the country will be full of Jews"), and the *mikve*'s cold water seems to have an analogous effect on the women. Why would Jews as an entity possibly engage in such behavior? Again, a comparison with the Exodus master narrative may be instructive: there, the Jewish image Shifra and Puah provide is less civilized, but animalistic, vital.[74] In the existence Zimro posits, by contrast, this vitality is actively snuffed, in a proto-Nietzschean fashion, by Jewish traditional culture's slave morality.

Finally, Zimro arguably, plays fast and loose with Jewish tradition in at least one of his own arguments. While few Jewish traditions or laws suggest circumcision to actually be a source of strength, except morally or in terms of covenant,[75] Jewish law would certainly contradict the statement that *mikve* attendance leads Jewish women to refrain from marital sexual activity. It is precisely the opposite: immersion permits the menstruant Jewish woman to her husband; and while sustained abandonment of the *mikve* cycle might eventually cause women to more frequently sleep with their husbands, yielding greater fecundity, the immediate repercussion, speaking legalistically, would simply be that Jewish men and women would refrain from sexual contact entirely—yielding the opposite of the desired result.

A potential solution to these problems lies in the constitution of the Jewish body and psyche (and/or the perception of same) as not merely different than, but reversed from, the non-Jewish body. Zimro's presentation inverts the master narrative, which asserts that reversal as from weak to strong, to present the Jews here as moving from strength to weakness. Such presentation is compelling to the pope quite simply because it accords with his current ideas, as representative of the Catholic Church, about Judaism's role in the contemporary world. For the pope, after all, Jews constitute an uncanny blend of strength and weakness: as both the covenant's former and primary possessors and the witnesses to its failure, they have both the power to emerge victorious over the church (through their genuine acceptance of Christ) and the bad faith never to take advantage of that power. This explains the pope's acceptance of Zimro's traitorous suggestions weakening his own community: *of course* a Jew will act self-destructively, against his own best interests; they have done so, individually and communally, ever since they spurned their opportunity to gain salvation by failing to accept Christ. This similarly explains Zimro's presentation of the Jews as empowered by nature and disempowered by law: it is the natural expansion of their unwillingness to release the old law and subscribe to the Pauline doctrine that has resulted in their weakness and defeat among the Christians. Failure to allow their continuance in their mistaken, law-based "Jewish" ways will necessarily result in the abrogation of the weakened role Christianity assigns them, allowing them to challenge the Holy Empire.

Such an argument also explains Zimro's misrepresentation of the rules of *mikve:* according to the symbolic structural order he has established, proper observance of Jewish law by definition cannot lead to the expression of potency—and what stronger symbol of potency exists than sexual intercourse? Conversely, his presentation of *mikve*, where usage leads to sexual impotence and sterility, serves as a lovely metaphor for the sterile impotence of Jewish law in Christian eyes. These arguments are therefore extensions of the previously posed political questions about effective negotiation—individual and communal—to survive and gain power in a non-Jewish world. As Shifra and Puah did in an Egyptian environment; Esther did in a Persian environment; the Hellenists did in a Greek environment; and now Zimro in a Catholic or Christian environment, one must turn the contemporary ruler's suppositions against him, as Zimro certainly does here.

This approach can even explain the pope's subsequent behavior, which seems ostensibly puzzling in light of its accordance with master narratives (though reversed) of Jewish and Christian behavior. After hearing Zimro out, and deciding to rescind his edict, the pope gives Zimro "a great deal of money and jewels" (89). Perhaps this detail is included purely for reasons of structure or to maintain folkloric resonances—in the former case, it parallels the money Zimro spends to gain access to the pope, thus producing a textual pyramidal structure (money-pope-money);[76] in the latter, it allows inclusion of a typical quest submotif—the hero's enriched return from his quest. Neither approach seems thematically or narratively sufficient, though, particularly since this love story has not particularly thematized wealth, Zimro having refused it on several occasions. Rather, the pope's action may be seen as a continued reification of Zimro to the "Jewish" paradigm within Christian perception: a paradigm that involves him receiving his thirty pieces of silver for betraying his people. Though not a precise match to the New Testamental master narrative (Jesus was hardly the one to pay Judas), these divergences allow the paradigm to resonate even more powerfully from the pope's perspective: despite history's radical changes, the Jews have remained exactly as they were.

Such an interpretation reveals the powerful schism at the heart of Zimro's first journey. Though successful in both straightforwardly narrative terms (the edict was indeed cancelled) and metagenerically (illustrating the possibilities of self- and refashioning the Jew into the successful, questing hero), he has done so at a price. He has undercut his personal virtue (by engaging in deceit, even instrumentally, predicated on slandering his people), his masculinity (by championing a kind of desexualized weakness for himself and his people), and his representative ability to Judaize the chivalric story (since his quest's success is attained by transforming the Jews into their Christian image, thus domesticating them into the Christian chivalric narrative, rather than accentuating independence). This essential metaphorical and thematic failure is actualized in the story's next section, illustrating the failure of Zimro's apparent success. In fact, Zimro's ultimate "success" is only achieved by an act whose very nature illustrates its own impossibility. To understand this more fully, we must first investigate another textual aspect: the narrator's role and his engagement with questions of morality and "reality."

Narrating, Moralizing, Promising: Between Words and Deeds

The narrator's functions in the *Tale of Briyo and Zimro*, as in other works of early modern Yiddish literature like the *Bovo-bukh*, are quite varied. Baumgarten observes, for example, that the *Bovo-bukh* contains "many formulae addressed to the audience designed to retain their attention or reinvigorate the plot, numerous classic traditional comments characteristic of minstrel performance to introduce changes of scene, and finally direct interventions by the poet who, as it were, accosts the audience" (*OYL* 179–180). In our text, the narrator occasionally mentions his inability to describe certain aspects of the narrative; concerning Briyo, he writes: "Her beauty was indescribable, so I won't try to describe it" (*ir sheynheyt is nit tsu shraybn / darum mus ikhs losn blaybn*, 83). Such comments remind us of the narrator's control over the narrative, the difficulties of mimetic description, and the corollary tension with authorial claims of (limited) authenticity: "this is the story that happened (*mayse is geshen*) with a girl named Briyo and a boy named Zimro" (82). Emphasizing indescribability elevates the narrative to mythic or allegorical levels, while simultaneously alerting readers to its own constructed (or at least mediated) nature.

A particularly intriguing example of narratorial accentuation of the text's constructed nature appears after Zimro's triumphant return, and Feygin's subsequent refusal to allow the marriage. The narrator says that "he kissed her, and she kissed him, and their kisses were so wonderful that if she hadn't already been beautiful, then she would have become beautiful now" (90). Ostensibly a straightforward rendering of the subjective, psychological increased attractiveness during intense erotic activity, the narrator's language is unusual: he does not assert Briyo would *look* more beautiful to Zimro, but that she would *become* more beautiful. More than just metaphor in a text permeated with shifts from metaphor to actualization, this narrative magic illuminates the author's role in an ostensibly "true" story in refashioning descriptions, characters, and narrative elements to fit his own aesthetic or literary judgments. Unsurprisingly, in light of analyses in previous chapters, these narratorial (and here arguably authorial) judgments may be moral ones; befitting a story about romance in both the word's senses, and the blurred lines between metaphor and reality, those moral judgments relate to both eros and the concept connecting word and deed—promises.

Immediately before the lovers kiss, Briyo says: "Dear Zimro, God help us! I know that I'm going to die of grief!" And indeed she does, soon after Zimro's departure: the narrator then interjects, "That is why you should never kiss anyone when you leave him!" (90) Most straightforwardly, the narrator's interjection seemingly illustrates the forcible imposition of exotic Jewish moral codes[77] on the generically asserted chivalric ones: Briyo has attempted to escape the Jewish maiden's role with its ideal of chastity for that of secular literature's romantic heroine, whose ideal is erotic engagement. For the narrator, or, at least, for the ostensibly pious mask he dons here, no such escape is possible in this Judaized domestication of that foreign genre: eros is clearly linked to death.

It is not merely the narrator's moral stance that attracts interest, but his confidence, his certainty of the ineluctable connection between Briyo's erotic engagement, symbolized by her kisses, and her subsequent death. This confidence may offer space for an explicit narratorial role: not merely an impotent judge of the events he chronicles, but, taken together with the earlier intimations of narratorial power that invested Briyo with beauty, the sense that *he* is implicated in arranging Briyo's death. The resulting dynamic, analogous to the king's behavior earlier in the story, allows us the rudimentary awareness that the narrator *can* change the story (an awareness granted us by the narrator himself), but, like God, will not "intervene in history," essentially allowing his characters to make their own mistakes, which result in inevitable punishment. Such comparison illustrates a certain compensatory power in a story thematizing Jewish impotence (a word used intentionally, given Zimro's desexualizing strategy) in the face of non-Jewish authority and non-Jewish narrative.

Narratorial control is matched by the certainty of Tuvas and the four Jews he asks to serve as intermediaries that, respectively, Feygin will "certain[ly]" disagree to the marriage and that they will "bring about the marriage for sure." Such contradictory asseverations of certainty and promise raise narrative questions: how does the story uphold or betray these statements? More importantly, though, this thematization of certainty may display metanarrative purpose: to call into question the "certain" secular literary and historical conventions as they encounter Jewish ahistorical conceptualizations and particularistic literary modes.

The consequences of this encounter are apparent at the text's highest levels, implicating the king himself, who tells Zimro to "forget about your desire. Nothing is going to happen—no matter what you do" (85). The king's suggestion would have Zimro passively submit to entrenched historical and social categories, accepting royal dictum of the unchangeable world order. Indeed, the paradoxical manifestation of the king's will in doing nothing—when Feygin theoretically acquiesces to the king's ultimate power with regard to Briyo's marriage, saying, "May your royal majesty do as you wish," the king merely responds, "I won't force you" (85)—allegorically signifies the uneasy line God (the King of Kings) straddles between free will and predestination.[78] The story thus seemingly aligns the decision to simply tolerate this unjust state of affairs with traditionally approved acceptance of history's moral component. Zimro's rebellion against it, then, is not merely a lover's rebellion against social barriers and hierarchies, but marks a religious and historiographical opposition. We will have to see how the rebellion's results reflect on its possibilities.

This emphasis on certainty is also thematized in the narrative centrality of oaths.[79] Erik notes that the Venice version's introduction explicitly stresses the importance of keeping promises as well as proper erotic conduct;[80] both messages are thematically, narratively, and narratorially connected. More generally, oaths function both as statements of implied certainty and of creative control, since in connecting word and deed they shape an ostensibly certain and immutable course of future behavior, though in practice, as the story makes plain, such a course is subject to contingency, creative interpretation, and malicious behavior.

Several statements in this story are quite clearly stated as oaths, words, decrees, or edicts. To give just a few examples:

1. Briyo and Zimro's mutual promises: "He said, 'Please don't take any husband but me, and I promise not to take any other wife but you.' She said, 'I promise.' And so they swore their troth."
2. The pope's edict that any Jew appearing before him will be killed.[81]
3. The high priest's oath taken "in front of witnesses" (88) that Zimro will be granted his daughter's hand if his mission is successful.
4. The new king's (formerly prince's) guarantee to Zimro that, in the event of his death, Zimro will inherit the throne (90).
5. Briyo's statement that "I know well I'm going to die of grief" (*ikh veys voyl dos ikh muz shtorbn far leyd*, 90).

Though promises pervade the story, they are taken most seriously by Briyo: speaking to Zimro before he departs on his quest, she says: "Don't let [Feygin] talk you into going to the pope, otherwise you'll die and I won't be able to keep my promise to you!" (87) She seems to either not grasp or disregard the disjunction between word and deed, the mutability of an immutably phrased statement or oath: aware of the pope's edict, she seemingly considers Zimro essentially dead from the moment he agrees to the mission. After another statement of certainty by Feygin following Zimro's departure ("We've gotten rid of Zimro, he won't come back alive," 88), she "wept and wailed and loudly lamented when Zimro was gone, and she fasted three days and three nights every week during his absence" (88), never considering he might not go to the pope, or survive the encounter.

Briyo's position on the inextricable connection between word and deed is, of course, contradicted by readers' experiential reality and their narrative context—within Zimro's adventures, the pope himself breaks two promises (that any Jew appearing before him will be killed, and the implied permanent state of the prohibitions expressed in his edict).[82] And Feygin, despite Zimro's triumphant homecoming, refuses to keep his word: "Zimro then said to the high priest: 'Please keep your promise.' But the high priest went back on his word and refused to give Zimro his daughter's hand—'even if I lose my life!' " (89) More subtly, even Zimro may be portrayed as breaking an implied promise to present the Jewish people truthfully and positively: certainly his strategy relies on implied promises to the pope about eventualities that will never occur.

While characters presented as intellectual in one way or another—the pope, Feygin, and even Zimro—display that intellectuality through their ability to dissociate word and action, Briyo, the physical creature who cannot differentiate between the two, dies in fulfillment of her own words. The narrator's comment, "That is why you should never kiss someone when you leave him!" (90), then, can be read not merely as a snide or didactic explanation of the chaste Jewish maiden's punishment for eschewing properly decorous behavior, but rather as the acknowledgment of some characterological types' essential continuity between action and emotion. As such, Briyo, too good for this world, represents the obverse approach to the elevated king's chosen path: wisely knowing that ontologically binding someone to his (or His) word could yield extreme results, the king consciously refrains from doing so; Briyo makes rash statements and, in her limited (or purely simple) morality, lives up to them with catastrophic consequences to herself.

Zimro, by contrast, represents intellectual compromise and abstraction from simple deed, aware of the (important) artificiality of convention. Zimro's eventual reaction to Briyo's death, with a number of puzzling details added by the author to the narrative, is indicative.

> *One day Zimro appeared before the king and the prince, who received him warmly. Upon leaving the castle, Zimro ran into his father, who said: "Dear son, I'd like to ask you something. Can you keep from being terrified (der shrekn)?" Zimro said: "I won't be terrified!"* "You felt very wretched because the high priest refused to give you his daughter's hand. Now you'll feel even more wretched because she has died of sorrow. *Don't be terrified!" Zimro said, "Why should I be terrified?* What the good Lord does is properly done." *But everyone can imagine what was in his heart (kan eyn itlekher voyl gedenken)!* Upon arriving home and going to his room, he wailed loudly and was so grief-stricken that he tore out his hair. *His sorrow was indescribable (itzt nit tsu shraybn).* After lamenting, he left his room and wiped his eyes *so that no one would notice. And he did that for an entire week.* (90, emphasis mine)

Questions abound. Why are we first told that Zimro didn't hear of Briyo's death, if the immediately subsequent episode relates his discovery of that death? His ignorance seemingly plays no narrative role whatsoever. Why does the text stress Zimro's apparently narratively extraneous visit to the king and prince? Why is Tuvas so worried about his son becoming terrified (or "distraught") that he repeats it? And most importantly, what explains Zimro's strangely private mourning? Given the entire community's knowledge of his feelings for Briyo—from the quest he took to win her—why hide his melancholy, a Hamlet in reverse?

The answers to all these questions seem linked to narrative efforts to present Zimro as divorced from surrounding circumstances, perhaps directly by virtue of his intellectual, rather than emotional, symbolic cast. Zimro would fail the test he himself administers the two persons in one at the tale's preface: his emotional and psychic linkage to Briyo is insufficient to somehow intuit her death. Similarly, the text specifies Zimro's odd mourning behavior precisely for its illustration of his ability to separate private emotion from public performance. Such ability, demonstrably absent in Briyo, is the subject of Tuvas' intensive questioning: does his harmonizing son unite thought and emotion and, by extension, do as his beloved did? If so, he may troublingly meet the same end.

Zimro's "success" at separation—which, simultaneously, is his failure at harmony—allows the development of the David-Solomon master paradigm in this father-son encounter. David, of course, was the king unable to separate passion and politics: his problematic behavior with Bathsheba, Uriah, and Absalom are cases in point. Solomon, in the sensus litteralis of the text, as the avatar of intellectualization is able to separate his thousand wives from his temple building and military campaigns. Accordingly, the narrative notes Zimro's visit to the king and prince to accentuate again the allegory's political dimensions as well as the problematized disjunction of politics and eros. That is, the very same ability to separate emotion from action that makes Zimro a highly successful politician and emissary and allows him to be so warmly received in the royal chambers of the king sheds concern on his romantic abilities, accounting for his "not hearing" about Briyo's death. Zimro's oaths and certainties are final cases in point: he also expressed his desire to die if he could not marry Briyo on several occasions (see, for example, 84). His failure to do so at this point in the narrative itself testifies to his "failure" to unify word and deed, to naturally and organically fulfill his promise as Briyo does.

Zimro's next actions attempt to overcome this recognized disjunction; to return to his desired state of internal and external harmony, expressed as ultimate union with Briyo. These efforts are neatly structured to additionally unify within him two slightly differentiated aspects of his Solomonic paradigm. If the biblical Solomon is (essentially) portrayed as the rational master politician, the midrashic Solomon is both driven by eros and constantly associated with fantastic adventures; he is perhaps most famously connected to a fantastic quest, where his search for the Shamir worm leads to his capture of, then capture by, the demon king Ashmedai, who then impersonates him.[83] Zimro's second quest—the fantastic double of his first—thus unifies not only the various portrayals of Solomonic behavior, the rational and nonrational, the biblical and midrashic, but also his own, in its final effort to unify emotion and action and his role as Jewish and chivalric hero. Investigating this final quest and the story's final outcome allows some final comments about the text's balance between external and internal traditions and "reality" and fantasy, and the narrator's complex role in negotiating that balance.

The Final Quest: Between This World and the Other

As briefly mentioned above, the narrative seems to discretely shift between "realistic" and "fantastic" modes; the wondrous and marvelous are marginalized either narratively (the two-headed man, for example, appears in the preface, before the love story begins) or spatially (in Zimro's fantastic quest to the land of the dead).[84] Zimro's trip marks a final, conscious shift from total engagement in the political sphere: though Briyo's death has offered him, in his de-harmonized, dissociated state, the opportunity to rise to third in line to the throne, after the prince (90), the temporal and spatial obstacles present—his impatience and ultimate failure to wait for the prince and to reach the castle, almost unreachably located on a high mountain, can be seen, possibly, to underscore the impossibility of ever truly achieving empowerment in a contemporary Christian world.[85] Indeed, to attempt to hurry political acculturation or emancipation by independently moving ahead, not waiting for the philo-Semitic "prince," will result only in rendering the goal that much harder to attain.

Zimro's political emphasis, which ignores Briyo and romance, is clearly mistaken: failing to recognize his own lesson from the story's beginning—that it is union, linkage, that obtains—he risks losing everything. Even Zimro's reaction to the horse he sees as he stops walking towards the castle suggests his current inclination to head in the wrong direction, towards singularity, not harmony: "All at once, he saw a beautiful horse galloping in front of him and wearing armor more beautiful than Zimro had ever seen. The horse seemed to be galloping down the mountain. Zimro thought to himself: 'If I could catch it, I'd ride up the mountain' " (91). Though Zimro's efforts to catch the horse seem successful, "the instant Zimro mounted the horse, it took off, dashing over hill and dale *as if it were the Devil*" (91, emphasis mine), leading Zimro, who has no control over it, to the mythic locale, which will culminate in the realm of the dead.[86]

The horse and Zimro are at cross-purposes: one attempts to ascend the mountain, and reach the elevated Solomonic exercise of political power without emotion; the armored horse, symbolic of knightly romance[87] and thus emotion, literature, and external forces, attempts to descend with him in the opposite direction. Zimro's assumption that he could control the horse's direction is shown to be overweening fantasy: but the narrator's demonic characterization of its chosen path has ominous resonance, as it is also the path to union with Briyo.

The demonization and problematization of the extrusively coded path becomes evident in the description of Zimro's early travels: he finds himself in a forest, a well-known symbol of doubt, mystery, and alienation, and then "a meadow, where there were many roots" (91), and where the horse disappears: "He yelled and felt wretched beyond description. He kept shouting: 'Sorrow upon sorrow! Misery, how closely you've surrounded me! I have no idea what to do. *I'm so far away from my father and my friends, and I don't see or hear a human being or a house or a town!* Where am I and what has happened to me?' " (91) This emphasis on solitude and alienation is classically linked to a purgatorial or limbo-like state in a master narrative of Italian vernacular culture: real similarities exist here with the first canto of Dante's *Inferno*; there, the protagonist also wanders through a wood, confronts a hill, and encounters a wild animal "guarding" the hill, preventing simple passage, potentially suggesting a second great vernacular non-Jewish writer's domestication for Jewish literary purpose.

Significant differences exist, naturally: while by the first canto Dante, the pilgrim of faith, is assured he is not alone in his journey by receiving Virgil as his guide, Zimro is essentially alone.[88] Such a distinction evokes the first external master narrative, the tale of the Jew in Boccaccio's *Decameron:* both cases offer Christian comfort in the active display of supernatural support, either (in Boccaccio) in the Church's remarkable survival and flourishing despite its manifold flaws, or (in Dante) the heavenly support in his navigation of the infernal (and purgatorial and paradisiacal) sphere. Our story, shouldering questions of Jewish political, romantic, and literary isolation, with its theological and national corollaries, requires the Jewish Everyman to reenact this sense of abandonment. For a medieval Christian, convinced of the power of the Christians' God as manifested in ecclesiastical representatives' omnipresent power, Inferno is where sinners receive their just punishment. For the Jew, by contrast, bedeviled by thoughts of divine abandonment, hell is a place of God's utter absence—the actualization of Christian charges that God has now passed them over.

Were this a conventional romantic tale where the author is not problematizing those conventions and their possibilities, this physical abandonment and isolation might be seen as the metaphorical complement of the lover's emotional loneliness and alienation suffered upon the beloved's death. The unlikeliness of that here—given Zimro's failure to act the lover throughout much of this episode, not mentioning Briyo's name or even the idea of love during his plaint, may be taken as possible support for this approach. True, Zimro's romantic sufferings are presumably the subject of his oblique "sorrow upon sorrow," but the obliqueness is the point: what *clearly* disturbs Zimro (and therefore the narrator and the reader) is his alienation from both Jewish community and non-Jewish civilization. That is, this episode can be read as Zimro's realization that his attempts to abandon his Jewish identity in seeking an unattainable political and, indeed, ontological status, have led him metaphorically and literally nowhere.[89]

Such realization, expressed through Zimro's utter despair, leads to a process of return—but a return with a questionable destination. Zimro's alienating sin, it has been argued, is exemplified by his turn towards intellectualization and his artificial separation of emotion and reason—belying the romantic and harmonic promise of his name—apotheosized by his abstract practice of politics predicated on the dissemination of false perceptions and artificial identities. The result has been a turn away from the physical, earthy Briyo—who, complexly, bears within herself a different, arguably unstable union: of Jewish and chivalric, romantic and feminine ideals. The resulting tension and inability to achieve a sustainable union within herself has yielded her destructive, overcompensating conflation of word and deed, leading to her death. Analogously and by extension, Zimro's desired union with her, perceived as an attempt to generate an authentic mixture of the external and internal, chivalric and Jewish worlds, exists only in the world of the dead, in the world of fantasy or myth. An ambivalent lesson, certainly.

This ambivalence is articulated in the complex symbolic and emotive structure of the fantastic world Zimro encounters. Zimro's ability to continue on his journey by gaining strength from eating roots (*vortzleyn*) and drinking water metaphorically suggests his reengagement with authentic Jewish tradition (water, famously a traditional metaphor for the Torah). Further, in a shift familiar to us, the water then transforms from metaphor to (fantastic) actualization. The narrative moves directly from the "little water" he drinks to water firmly associated with paradise, the Torah-water, filled with precious gems of divine wisdom: "Eventually he came to a beautiful brook and he stepped into it for it wasn't deep. There he found a lot of precious stones, which he picked up, slipping many of them into his shirt. The brook, which was filled with jewels, flowed from paradise. Zimro took off his shoes and walked through the water: it was harsh and strong" (91). Zimro has reversed his previous intellectual behavior: in the past he instrumentally mined the Jewish canon for nuggets usable for temporal political purposes, such as defeating the pope; he can now study the Torah for its own sake, internalizing its treasures by placing them close to his heart.[90] This movement of Zimro's "with the current," directly and consciously contrasts his movement with the horse: engaging in symbolically Jewish pursuits, results in a simple, flowing path to paradise.

However, obstacles remain to be overcome: "Upon leaving the brook, he came to a beautiful road, where he found a large rock with an inserted sword. The rock also had a wheel which kept turning and that prevented Zimro from walking any further, for the wheel guarded the road to paradise (*gan eden*). But Zimro said a prayer, and the wheel stopped and let him pass" (91). The author's choice of symbols here at first seems slightly unusual for a traditional perspective, given the Bible's explicit provision of an image of Eden's barriers: true, a sword is involved, but a flaming and turning sword, possibly in the hands of angels guarding the entrance.[91] The author's divergence from these traditional motifs for conventional chivalric and external ones, including the Arthurian sword in the stone,[92] and the turning wheel symbolizing Fortune, demonstrates how Zimro's navigation of these obstacles in his entrance to paradise—by reciting a prayer (*tfile*), no less—reflects the realized necessity to vanquish both literary and theological Gentile influences in the name of a more traditionalist Judaism, doctrinally and literarily speaking. The ultimately deconstructive and conscious irony here—one central to the text as a whole, and our discussion more generally—is that to display this defeat one must employ, and thus perpetuate, the generic forms and symbols of the problematized literature. Take, for example, the turning wheel; the concept of *fortuna* directly conflicts with a principle of Jewish belief, already discussed earlier in the book: that the Jews are not subject to fortune's force.[93] Zimro's prayer to God—reflecting the Jews' special, covenantal relationship with the divine—reaccentuates their special position vis-à-vis fortune, and so the wheel unsurprisingly stops. Yet its function as a symbol of blockage once more reinforces for the reader its precise centrality as a meaningful oppositional force; full credence of it prevents entrance to paradise.

The problematic necessity of narratively incorporating these materials—even as obstacles to be overcome—is corporealized through a purgatorial sphere's presence in paradise, seemingly modeled more on Dante's travels than on traditional internal accounts of paradise.[94] Entering a small cottage, Zimro sees many people eating. After greeting him with "shalom," indicating their Jewishness:[95]

> Zimro wanted to wash his hands and eat. But they cried, "Don't wash your hands, and make sure you touch nothing!" He asked: "Why?" They answered: "We are all dead, and we are neither well off nor badly off. We have to wait here for an entire year until we have redeemed our sins. Dear Zimro, pray for us! We know what you're doing here. We heard yesterday that the horse would be sent to you." He asked them a lot of questions but they refused to say anything. So he left. (91–92)

Certainly the idea that Jewish souls lacking the requisite righteousness to immediately enter paradise must wait a year for their elevation, most explicitly accomplished through the recitation of kaddish, stems from internal sources.[96] But the group's insistence that Zimro eat and touch nothing, later echoed by Briyo's warning against Zimro touching her, evokes external traditions, expressed most notably in Persephone's story, that consumption of anything in the dead world, no matter how small, means eternal death—a tradition largely absent from Jewish canonical material.[97] Metonymically, the trope thus embodies ambivalent and complex sentiment about the consumption of classical mythologies and ideas, building on the earlier employment of the sword and wheel motifs to warn again about adoption of a given culture through its own symbolic structure.

Briyo's subsequent appearance therefore similarly serves as both warning and promise; when Zimro sees her, she says:

> "Dear Zimro, I never committed any sin on earth except letting you kiss me." He went over to her and wanted to kiss her. But she said: "Guard your life and don't touch me, or you'll die!" He then said: "I don't know where I am or what's happened to me or where I should go. I want to kiss you—so I'll die and stay here with you." She said: "No, not on your life (*neyn bay daynem leybe*)! Leave me and go across the heath. That way you'll get back home." He went away from her in deep sorrow, weeping and wailing. (92)

Problematized consumption of the external is now linked to problematized eros: touching food and touching Briyo have identical, fatal results, in the violation of ideal Jewish sexual and cultural porosity. Zimro's own previously problematized skills at separating word and deed, symbol from reality, life from literature, have been overthrown; but the wrong kind of union, it turns out, may be as dangerous as the artificial separation. By accepting Briyo's unifying perspective on such matters, the deed of his kiss will connect to the words of her promise of his fatality.[98] The subtle charms of erotic love (and, by extension, the charms of its literature) have succeeded where the pope's edict failed: Zimro has become so ungrounded (explicitly saying, "I don't know where I am or what's happened to me or where I should go," 92) that he flirts with self-destruction for the sake of a lost cause. The former case, at least, resulted in the communal survival and the reestablishment of Jewish tradition, if through problematic means; the latter, in individual destruction (if only temporarily).

Briyo, by contrast, has learned the lesson of chivalric love's dangers in an essentially Jewish setting, and thus can issue the antierotic warning, returning Zimro on his journey with the virtuous request to pray for her.[99] Her effort, significantly, fails; after a meeting with Elijah the Prophet, discussed below:

> Zimro forgot that he hadn't prayed for Briyo. When he reentered the cottage, he thought he saw a person standing with her (*do dukht in vi eyner bay ir var*) and holding both her breasts in his hands. Zimro said, "Dear Briyo, who's embracing you?" She said: "Dear Zimro, don't be afraid! Satan (*sotn*) is trying to lure you." Zimro went over to his Briyo, and she said, "Be careful, don't touch me until I've

> finished speaking." He said: "Then please speak!" She said: "Dear Zimro, do you want to sit on this chair or do you want to wait some more?" He said: "I don't want to wait any more." She said: "Then go home and tell your father and my father: for better or for worse, you want to have me. My father refused to give you my hand while I was alive, so he has to suffer because you will have me in the afterlife (*yener velt*) without silver or money. Go and pray and cleanse yourself (*gey tvile*) and say good-bye to your friends. You will die on the third day. I assure you: if you touch me, you will definitely die on the third day." He said: "I want to touch you even if it costs me my life." And he threw his arms around her and kissed her and then she went away. (92–93)

Zimro, overcome by his erotic desire and internalization of the romantic perspective Briyo represents to him, reshapes the fantastic, creative, and created world in which she finds herself. His problematic approach is apotheosized in spiritual *and* romantic bankruptcy (his failure to pray and his disobedience of her command);[100] the result is a vision (or reality) of her metaphorical (or literal) hijacking by demonic erotic forces. The language of "he *thought* he saw" and Briyo's insistence that this is only Satan's temptation suggests Briyo may merely be a ghost Briyo, an imagined construct whose sexual conquest is a reflection of Zimro's losing battle between erotic temptation and chaste piety. His acceptance of the vision's truth, of the powers of the (literary) imagination concretized in his approach to the *sexualized* Briyo, consigns him to death. Zimro's impatience and immaturity, his desire for erotic, romantic, literary consumption, sign his death warrant. Notably, the story never asserts that the figure touching Briyo's breasts has vanished as Zimro embraces her; we may thus visualize (at least metaphorically) Zimro simultaneously embracing both Briyo and the satanic individual, undoubtedly generating a certain moral ambiguity.

The passage's language further suggests the inversion of traditional topoi: the linkage of touching and death, a period of prayer and cleansing, and a three-day waiting period recalls not only the papal episode earlier in the story or the book of Esther, but, most powerfully, the Sinaitic revelation, where the Jews were forced to wait for three days of prayer, purification, and total sexual separation, unable to touch the mountain on pain of death, before achieving an unparalleled union with the divine, compared, traditionally, to a wedding.[101]

That metaphor, however, is clearly de-eroticizing, elevating the wedding image through its conjunction to the Sinaitic miracles; here, inversely, the story performs its own dangers by eroticizing paradise and Sinai in providing its variation on a traditional love story. It is only by reading the couple's death—and union only in death, *pace* Romeo and Juliet—as failure, rather than success, that these allusions, and the narrative dynamics, become fully comprehensible. This inverted Sinaitic image recalls not the revelation of Torah, but a second worshipping of the Golden Calf, obeisance at the altar of desire and romance. Zimro's return from the other world, then, is not a personal victory, but a personal defeat that heralds communal victory in its upholding of communal standards. His death proves submission to eros must be so punished; his actions lead to the *only* place these lovers can meet, in death, for Jewish life prohibits otherwise.

The magnitude of these actions is illustrated by Zimro's two encounters with the text's only Virgilian figure. Zimro is guided back to his world (the "real" world) by "an old gray-haired man with a long beard" previously identified as the prophet Elijah (92).[102] Upon first meeting Zimro, the prophet, asked by Zimro what he has done to deserve his fate (here, *mikro*), answers, "You've committed no sin that cost Beria her life. You should go home again."[103] However, when Zimro asks him for a blessing, Elijah refuses, saying he "will not bless you now, [since] I know that you have to go home again." After Zimro's second encounter with Briyo,

> the old graybeard came back and he said to Zimro: "Come here, dear Zimro. I want to lead you back home and prepare you for your wedding." And he blessed Zimro. And now Zimro prayed for his dear Briyo to redeem her from her place under the stairs in the cottage. His prayer was answered, and she entered Paradise. And even if you don't believe me, you're still a Jew (*vers nit gleyb der iz oykh eyn yud*). (93)

To understand this passage, the plot's final details must be rehearsed. Zimro returns home, tells the king, Tuvas, and Feygin about his upcoming death, and makes one odd request: not to bury him postmortem, but simply to leave his body in the graveyard. Zimro prays, cleanses himself, and bids farewell to all, who mourn loudly and communally; even Feygin does so, "for he now regretted (*hot groys kharote*) losing his daughter" (93). Zimro dies after the third day, and his friends, as he wished, leave him uninterred. Subsequently:

> the angels Michael and Gabriel came and took him and carried him, as was only just, for Zimro had never committed any sin (*den er hot nokh ni keyn zund geton*), and they brought him to Paradise, to his dearest Briyo, and they gave the couple a beautiful wedding. God Himself gave the blessing, and the angels were the jesters (*leytsonim*). Moses and Aaron escorted the bride and groom to the canopy. After that they all ate and drank and danced, and King Solomon recited the Seven Blessings. A more wonderful wedding had never been celebrated in any Jewish community. (93–94)

The narrator then finishes with an ostensibly straightforward traditionalist ending:[104]

> And now you've read in this book, dear friend / About what great love brings / And so everyone should deeply consider / About what may come of all that. / There are many lovely and pious people in this world / Who might come to choose that / which promises luck and salvation (*hot er anderst dos gluck un heil*). / And with this I will end. / May God also send us the old gray friend / And with him the messiah here. / Amen—may it happen this year. (94)

The most pressing question the text raises, of course, is the seeming contradiction between Zimro's apparently negative or sinful actions and the text's peculiar characterization that he has committed no sin, to say nothing of those actions' apparent reward by everyone, including heaven itself. Secondary puzzles include: Zimro's peculiar insistence on his remaining unburied, the text's inclusion of Zimro's meeting with Elijah, and the apparent dependence of his blessing on Zimro's return home (a condition, incidentally, seemingly contradicted by his later decision to bestow the blessing even after Zimro's return, and the narrator's final, guarded language asking for the audience's deep consideration, and the odd employment of language suggesting many Jews *would* choose great love, which *promises* luck and salvation, but seemingly not insisting they *should* do so.

Taken together, these authorial choices seem key to understanding the text's ultimate message, one deeply concerned about secular erotic or romantic literature while entirely convinced of its power and seductiveness. So convinced is the author, in fact, that he presents its power even entering—and conquering—heaven itself. The text's ending, at least at first blush, seems to illustrate the romance's victorious subversion of Jewish tropes and characters, rather than its domestication within a Jewish framework. Though the text clearly implies Zimro has indeed sinned, in purgatory if not on earth, the secular literary convention of lovers' reunion—in heaven if not on earth—is so forcible that heaven goes along with it and so seductive that God himself smiles on it.[105]

In this reading, Elijah's appearance accordingly functions in two ways: first, the movement from nonblessing to blessing analogously illustrates the domestication of the structure of Jewish sainthood, Elijah's transformation into a supporter of romance even—and especially—after the romantic hero's fall. But it also serves, by contrast, to show the real Elijah to be Zimro himself, who is not merely an earthly messenger illustrating the love story's wisdom and power (he makes everyone regret their failure to submit to romance, after all), but a heavenly one, heralding the love story's universal future. Zimro's request to remain unburied can thus be understood as his attempt to resemble, as much as possible, his paradigmatic predecessor, who ascended bodily to heaven.

This reading's portrayal of Zimro's acceptance may be illuminated by a slightly earlier narratorial intervention: after Zimro's prayer for Briyo towards the fantastic interlude's end, the narrator writes, "His prayer was answered, and she entered Paradise. And even if you don't believe me, you're still a Jew" (93). Its conventional nature notwithstanding,[106] the particularities of the narrator's statement and its unusual placement nonetheless provide grist for the analytic mill. Of all the credulity-stretching, skepticism-generating occurrences throughout the narrative, why emphasize this particular event, whose claim—that praying for an individual can help him or her to enter paradise—is, far from unbelievable, a normative pillar of Jewish belief?

It may be that the narratorial response is less about the particularities of the truth-claim than how the narrative action accords harmoniously or otherwise with thematic and characterological development. Zimro's moral ambiguity and his immediately previous engagement in an erotic act sufficiently problematic (and arguably sinful) to be fatal should generate skepticism on the part of the traditionally positioned reader (and certainly of the narrator) as to the efficacy of his prayer. The narrator's answer—"if you don't believe me, you're still a Jew"—once more poses the ambivalence of the entire text itself about the hierarchy of traditional morality and romantic impulse.[107] This ambivalence—and its comfortable embrace of a broad spectrum of belief—suggests the liberal stratum beneath its overly traditionalist focus. In this reading, Zimro can therefore be simultaneously a sinner punished for his deeds and a romantic hero, allowing the text to entertain (albeit uneasily) *both* of these as authentic truths, reflecting a new kind of synthesis for the synthesizing Zimro. To accept this version of the story, however, nonetheless demands a certain surprising—and thus, perhaps, problematic—transvaluation of the moral structure.

Such a transvaluation, metaphorically expressed in the text by sin's becoming mitzvah and death becoming life, not only raises concerns on the moral level, as we will see, but may be seen as anagogical to the Jewish communal body's historiographic or self-understood political behavior.[108] It may be a cruel reflection (conscious or not) of medieval and early modern Jewish political consciousness that a postmortem reunion can be seen as victory rather than defeat. If this story does indeed treat Jewish political power and identity in addition to morality and literature, the definitive retreat to the world of death may be read as victorious only and precisely in the literary—that is, fantastic—realm. Were we to regard the authorial position as reflecting the unqualified triumph of Jewish literature in its morally unproblematic domestication of non-Jewish genres, that victory, preaching submission and defeatism in life for ecstatic union in death, can noticeably and meaningfully occur only on the page. Briyo and Zimro may be reunited in death, true; but in a text that is also so centrally concerned with this-worldly political behavior, what does it say at the end merely to hope for paradise?

Indeed, the final union's location and the narrator's open-ended, ambiguous conclusion suggests the much darker view that this tale is not simply a romance, but a warning about romances; a *muser*-story about those who fully subscribe to it, by essence (Briyo) or by choice (Zimro). The narrator, aware of this literature's power and its meaning—having consciously, problematically, employed it himself—subtly expresses his concern that some will choose romance, take the heavenly celebration at face value, and hail Zimro, the herald of the erotic messiah, not the true one. The narrator thus ends with his plea for "the old gray friend," the true messiah's real herald. He may be neither flashy nor young, but he faithfully reflects traditionalist literary spirit.

Daniel Boyarin has written of traditional Jewish culture's "alternative civilities, *edelkayt*, and alternative paradigms of manliness," defining *edelkeyt* as "nobility," a "counter-ideal to many of the markers of the noble in romantic culture, in that its primary determinants within the culture were delicacy and gentleness, not bravery and courtliness."[109] Boyarin further argues that traditional Jewish culture rejects what he calls *goyim naches* ("violent physical activity, such as hunting, dueling, or wars—all of which Jews traditionally despised, for which in turn they were despised—and . . . the association of violence with male attractiveness and with sex itself"),[110] ultimately defining the term as "the contemptuous Jewish term for those characteristics that in European culture have defined a man as manly: physical strength, martial activity and aggressiveness, and contempt for and fear of the female body."[111] Boyarin specifically targets courtly love, writing that "courtly love with its conventions (honored in the breach, perhaps?) of chaste adultery would have seemed silly and immoral to Jews like Rashi" and that Jews did not recognize courtly love's values.[112]

Boyarin may well be correct about "Jews like Rashi," the traditional elites; his claim of Jewish rejection of chivalric values may even ultimately apply to broader Jewish audiences and communal spheres as well. The texts examined and analyses developed in these chapters, though, may illustrate that within at least the Yiddish, vernacular, popular sphere—a field largely unaddressed in Boyarin's important work, and thus complementary to his study—where composing elites attempt to generate popular appeal, decisions about the display of Jewish masculinity are predicated on a complex and ambivalent negotiation of attitudes about popular and elite acceptance—and employment—of external values.[113] Simple dismissiveness is hardly the order of the day; rather, regardless of our ultimate decision about the valence placed on Briyo and Zimro's final fate, authorial decisions about accepting or rejecting such value and the literature that articulates them are highly fraught.

The text, then, while somehow reveling in the opportunities created by cultural and literary porosity,[114] simultaneously expresses genuine doubt about the possibility of generating genuinely internalized examples of this literature and genuine concern about the incorporated genres' moral valences. Perhaps this can be expressed by ending our discussion with a return to our general questions about reality and the fantastic. Despite its significantly more mythic setting and its manifold fantastic elements, the tale of Briyo and Zimro, in grappling with contemporary themes of politics, power, erotic morality, and literature, seems ultimately to touch deeply on reality. Did the readers—schooled in allegory, displaying some familiarity with historiographical consciousness, attentive to symbolism, aware of the complexities and conventions of the narrator's role—take these texts' lessons to heart? An ultimately unknowable answer; all we can do is to speculate, one hopes fruitfully, about the subtle possibilities the authors, presumably aware of their readers' capabilities, gave them.

Coda

Looking Back: Concluding Considerations

Towards the end of her memoirs, the woman now generally known as Glikl of Hameln "cannot refrain from mentioning" a remarkable incident that occurred in her Metz synagogue on June 5, 1715, on the second day of Shavuot, a Saturday. As the cantor was engaged in prayer, "many people heard the sound as of something breaking, and there was a great noise. The women in the upper gallery thought the arch of the roof would fall in on them ... The fear was very great," and in the ensuing chaos and crush of attempted escape "six women were killed and thirty injured, some subsequently dying."[1] Subsequent observation revealed no damage of any sort, and Glikl writes the community "do[es] not know whence the evil fortune (*siba ra*) came";[2] Glikl ends that she "would not have written of this in my book, only it was an occurrence that had never happened before and, I hope, never will again."[3]

Glikl's vivid description of the event is in the main a sterling example of masterfully rendered, astutely characterized observation of the horrific consequences of mass panic. While, like a number of the authors in this book, she gestures at narratorial insufficiency, writing that "the terror of what happened can neither be told nor written (*nit tsu zogn oder tsu shraybn*),"[4] her memoirs belie her modesty. A more accurate assessment of Glikl's attitude, perhaps, is that, to her mind, the event posed difficulties not in description, but in *explanation*—both in general moral terms, and, in one specifically puzzling subepisode, in its specific, quasi-supernatural details.

Glikl's response to this horrific occurrence, metonymic for all the tragic events she has chronicled in the preceding six books and therefore for the questions of theodicy that have necessarily emerged, is to cast the occurrence, as did the chronicler of our dybbuk tale, as congruent with her conservative, pious worldview[5] and with the aims of the moralistic genre in which she composes.[6] Her conclusions that "[w]e can only put [the event] down to our sins"[7] and that "[n]ow it rests with each of us to examine his sins according to his deeds"[8] fit the event into an established moral framework (albeit one potentially unclear in its specific permutations) and serve as a blueprint for her readers' response to future chaotic disruptions, trials, and tribulations. Indeed, those of us accepting the assessment that we are reading "a supremely controlled narrative in which the author is fully conscious of how to manipulate the telling of her own tale"[9] may be tempted to see Glikl's description of a synagogue's apparent collapse, which, though causing human chaos and trauma, is ultimately revealed as illusion, as a neatly crafted metaphorical stand-in for the frailties, chaos, and incomprehension attendant on the human condition in comparison to the eternal, unchanging, and undamaged Synagoga.

And yet this straightforward model of belief is complicated by the undercurrent of skepticism and doubt attendant on a particular detail of its telling: Glikl's description and characterization of an apparently uncanny event occurring during the chaos. She writes:

> Much has been already said about this misfortune, but who can write or believe everything? Yet I, Mother, will write what Esther, wife of Jacob our present teacher told me. This mother and her child, a boy of five, sat on the highest step of the women's gallery, when all this began. She saw six very tall women with short head-veils; they pushed her down the steps. She shouted, "Do you want to kill me and my child?" They set the child in a corner and went on their way. It was at this very moment that the noise and confusion began and the women came rushing down from the top gallery. But she and her child were saved. ... I, Mother, have just spoken with this woman. She swore to me that it happened just as she related. Her husband and parents confirmed all that she said. Many distinguished people and scholars called on her and she told them this on oath. She, her husband, and parents are honest folk of whom no one has heard falsehood or any evil. Further, one night shortly before all this happened, the wife of the rich Jacob Krumbach, whose house is close by the synagogue, heard a great noise (*eyn godel mehume*) in the synagogue as though thieves had broken in, and were taking

> everything out, and the candelabra were falling down. . . . They sent for the beadle, who unlocked the synagogue, but there was 'no voice and no answer.' Not a single object was moved from its place. No one knows whence this misfortune came.[10]

Given our discussion about primary and secondary skepticism, implicit and explicit, throughout the book, we may now be prepared to note how elegantly Glikl navigates the shoals of general belief and local skepticism, on her own and her future readers' behalf. Earlier in her memoirs, she has often attempted to distance herself from the truth-claims of remarkable stories she has read in books and heard from other sources, perhaps apotheosized in her characterization of a story about Alexander the Great as a "heathenish fable (*heydisher fabl*)" and not written "as truth (*far ayn emes*)"[11]—a strategy of distancing we have seen in our discussion of the *Seyfer Mesholim*, for example, and one Glikl most explicitly does *not* use when, for example, she refers to biblical characters and events.[12]

Glikl, then, demonstrates the capacity for both belief and skepticism; the question is solely how she balances them in her judgment of this account of an uncanny event (as Glikl has not herself witnessed it, the account is, in its own way, analogous to the textual reports we have seen elsewhere). As her statements clearly illustrate, Glikl refuses to take the account at face value; instead, potential subordination to her belief structure requires that she subject it to a rationalized investigative procedure, a procedure that includes establishing the witnesses' bona fides and trustworthiness at great length, both to her own satisfaction and hopefully to her readers'. She insists on an oath, not merely taken before authorities with presumed wisdom and deterrent power against perjury, but in her own presence, refusing to accept even those authorities' sanction given the possibility of personal evaluation of Esther's probity. And all this notwithstanding, she frames the account with a distancing rhetorical flourish—"who can write or believe everything?"—inviting her readers to disbelieve the particular account, if they so choose.

Given this assessment of Glikl's complex epistemological approach to this episode, it may be unsurprising to note how few wondrous or marvelous episodes appear in her *Zikhroynes*, and how those few that do appear are generally in the context of dreams or potentially explicable encounters or coincidence.[13] This skepticism, it should be said, befits Glikl's own skeptical nature: in her report, life has been sufficiently full of deceptions, lies, misrepresentations, and disappointments—most notably that of her second marriage—that the extension of her skeptical bent to accounts of the miraculous seems only natural. But this is secondary skepticism, not primary; and her choice to end her work with what is clearly characterized as a moment of revelation, where an unnamed woman sees the night turned into day, accentuates the possibility of faith and hope.[14]

While this book's conclusion is less eventful (and, perhaps, less revelatory) than Glikl's, I hope Glikl's example may illustrate several points accentuated throughout the book in addition to her ability to serve as an example of the complex negotiations of belief and skepticism in early modern Jewry—points that may also indicate directions for future research. From the first, comparative study of *Macbeth* and *Doctor Faustus*, our analysis illustrates the utility of investigating such patterns of belief and skepticism with regard to specific texts through a combination of close textual analysis, grounded in an attention to seemingly extraneous, puzzling, or even ostensibly erroneous details that can, when viewed through different lenses, be seen as parts of a coherent, complex whole; and an analysis of general (and generically inflected) discourse and its effect on, not only the contours of the text itself, but readerly comprehension of the text.

Macbeth's belief and skepticism, and Faustus', are related to, but distinctly different from, *Macbeth*'s and *Faustus*', which in turn are different from audiences' perspectives on both. Such perspectives may be roughly concentric, but are also overlapping: as we have seen, certain moments in the two plays can be best understood by recognizing audiences' recognition of these moments as precisely artificial ones—the artificiality read back into the "real" world of the play. Such complex operations by the audience—operations that serve as exempla for the patterns of epistemological, theological, ideological, and literary skepticism that are offered in all of the book's subsequent chapters—suggest new and future opportunities to redefine or reconceptualize the various audiences for the works as sophisticated readers. This is particularly the case when, as the introduction has attempted to show, we decouple traditional markers such as linguistic knowledge and textual awareness from necessary definitions of readerly sophistication.

One specific way in which such sophistication may be particularly apparent is with regard to audience apprehension of genre and convention. Many of the book's chapters attempt to balance the economical power of explanations predicated on generic convention with the desire to acknowledge authorial ability to make, and readerly ability to comprehend, unconventional choices. Regression to the conventional mean, interpretively speaking, does the recognition of authorial quality few favors; and recent rehabilitations of Glikl's literary ability may serve as an encouraging sign for similar efforts about other contemporary Yiddish works.[15] But, even more importantly, authors' relationship with readers—a relationship fraught, particularly in the message-laden texts studied here, with anxiety predicated precisely on readerly sophistication and ability to derive alternative or oppositional messages from their texts—yields a trove of fascinating textual moments; when taken together, those moments provide major clues for understanding these texts' meaning, function, and reception in early modern Jewish society, and, most importantly, reveal them to *be* complex texts, with nuance and sophistication demanding concomitant interpretation.

The *Seyfer Mesholim*, for example, transcends basic questions of primary belief and skepticism—generically knowledgeable, audiences are well aware that the fables are "unreal"—to attempt to provide potentially controversial lessons about the nature of life itself. An animal fable, predicated on the continuity of characterological essence (an eagle will always be proud, a raven can never have a sweet voice) and symbolic continuity (to understand fables, communal consensus about ravens' and eagles' qualities must obtain), leads, perhaps inherently, to a message of conservatism, to stability of hierarchies. Only Fortune can intervene to change states; otherwise, the order of the day is acceptance of the world as it is. Such stability, counseled by the author, is concretized through the insistence on shrinking the narrative polysemy of the fable to the single interpretation of the moral. The *Seyfer Mesholim*, though, is shot through with interpretive instability, and anxiety about that instability; readers will, the author suspects, insist on putting their own interpretations on the material, inspired as they are by their own experiences and ideas. The tension ripples through the text, allowing it to serve as a site for the varying fissures and conflicts in early modern Jewish society.

One of the most important such conflicts—which receives intriguing and powerful treatment in the *Seyfer Mesholim* and the *Mayse fun Vorms* particularly—is that of class. The complex ideology of essentialism preached in the fables is not primarily political, but socioeconomic; invested with moral and theological force, it counsels quietism, not revolution or class warfare. Similarly, the tale of the marriage of a man and a she-demon—a tale of the supernatural we may think with to investigate borders and anxieties of early modern society—reveals itself, through close investigation of early modern discourse and puzzling textual elements, to be less about sex than about class. (By comparison, a later she-demon text appearing in the *Kav ha-yoshor*, from a different discursive framework, illustrates how generic convention can be reshaped to reflect the differing theme of demonized sexuality.)

The message the Worms tale subtly propagates—a message best understood through a recognition of audiences' allusive awareness—is the literal demonization of wealth acquired for its own sake, a message sure to play well with its general vernacular audience, along with simultaneous counseling of modesty, passivity, and acceptance of the socioeconomic status quo. The resulting apparent paradox is neatly solved in the story's fairy-tale ending, suggesting that audiences' internalization of such an approach can indeed lead to fortune and fecundity—but only through the operations of miracle and fortune contingent on socially appropriate behavior. Perhaps, given the orientation of earlier Yiddish critics like Max Erik,[16] such focus should have been less surprising; nonetheless, future analyses, less concerned with the vicissitudes of the modern class struggle, might focus on the anxieties, dreams, and concerns of the period under discussion equally intensely but from different perspectives. Again, Glikl, as writer and as subject, points the way: the reader hardly needs reminding how pervasive economic matters are to her life, and her *Life*.

The doubled images of women apparent in the story of the "Tale of Worms"—the demonic, homicidal visitant and the poor pious, bride—reflect another central occupation of this book: the way these stories, and genres, shed light on questions of gender and sexuality in early modern Jewish culture, a topic that has of course been of great interest to those studying Glikl's life and work. As the introduction makes clear, the study of gender and readership has been a crucial aspect of early modern Yiddish literary history since its composition; the works' prefaces and title pages, to say nothing of their content, reveal women to be a central audience and a central preoccupation of the works' authors. The bifurcation of perspectives on women as exempla of both virtue and vice appears, in different ways, throughout the book, from their complex and frequently misogynist depiction in the *Seyfer Mesholim*, to their varied and thus polyphonic presentation in the *Mayse fun Vorms*, to their construction as readers in the introduction. But they never appear more complexly and multiply than in the "Tale of the Evil Spirit of Koretz," the story of dybbuk possession.

Again, the discursive and comparative framework assists, as looking at scholarship on witchcraft trials and gender allows us to more easily view the tale as one of social control and domestication of "unruly" gendered activity; it also allows us once more to summon a model of complex primary and secondary skepticism to see how the author negotiates allegory and history to create a compelling and meaningful tale. Doing so necessitates once more reconceptualizing the audience as skilled and allusive readers, following the example of the possessed Mindl, who speaks in a man's textually allusive voice. When she does so, she poses the skeptical audience's challenge of theodicy in the wake of communal trauma; the text's answer, accentuating the value of community and belief, once more acts to put women in their place and readers firmly into traditional structures of theology. However, just as the dybbuk tale itself is disruptive and liminal—acting to prove the metaphysical order, it does so through an illustration of that order's failure to function correctly—we are left wondering, in our investigation of the tale, whether it is Mindl's empowered, tragic voice that dominates; whether, as in many of our other works, the stories transcend their author's attempts to domesticate them.

Perhaps the most complex attempt at domestication—one of nothing less than literature itself—comes in the book's final chapter, where an analysis of the "Tale of Briyo and Zimro" affords the opportunity to reflect most explicitly on the relationship between genres of Jewish and non-Jewish literature. Briyo and Zimro's story, read closely and with an eye to narrative complexities and fissures, becomes itself a story about the possibilities of romance, as a concept and a genre, within the Jewish cultural and literary tradition; Briyo and Zimro's attempt at harmony, achieved only and ultimately in the land of the dead, can be seen as one author's concern about the possibilities of creating a vibrant syncretic tradition that lives as a Jewish genre.

Romance is a genre that practically by its very definition invites analysis of gender, and the "Tale of Briyo and Zimro" is highly valuable in that regard insofar as it allows the critic to go beyond the equation of the study of gender and the study of women's issues and to explore questions of masculinity. The construction of masculinity in the story itself provides another perspective on the adaptation of coterritorial chivalric norms into a Jewish context; Zimro's behavior, in his relationship with Briyo and particularly in his arguments to the pope while attempting to save his Jewish community, illuminates the frustrating and paradoxical construction of heroism based on championing problematic, and at times even impotent, presentations of the

Jewish body, and may allow for further studies complicating previous models of Jewish masculinity in the medieval and early modern period.

Such reflections on bodily power lead smoothly into the story's concern with questions of politics. The uneasy mixture of coterritorial entities is not only *literarily* problematic for the work's author, and the story accordingly offers numerous reflections on strategies for Jewish political survival in a non-Jewish world. These "real world" considerations are, it should be said, presented against a panchronic, mythic, and romantic backdrop. While such features allow the critic to speculate fruitfully on readerly perspectives on historiography, particularly in a vernacular rather than elite context, they may also remind us that belief and skepticism narrowly defined may not be the only concern—or at least not the primary one—that readers have in decoding their texts. Truth may be, as it turns out, read meaningfully between the lines.

These studies reflect just some of the early modern Yiddish literary genres and subgenres, and are, of course, only individual representatives of those genres. Few of the genres, much less their exemplary (or, more accurately, transexemplary) works, have received their deserved treatment; hopefully, more literary analyses will be forthcoming, building on the work by Frakes, Baumgarten, Starck, Turniansky, Zfatman, and many others. Some of these analyses will certainly take a more localized and historicized approach than this book's, as studies of Glikl have focused on illuminating historical and social detail;[17] the choice of the supernatural or fantastic mode, broadly defined, and remarkable texts to redefine them, resulted in wide geographical and temporal variety. A comparative study set within a specific time and place (works only from sixteenth-century Italy, for example) would yield highly valuable dividends, as would one tracing the literary and thematic peregrinations of genres or subgenres as they "followed" the Yiddish-speaking population from western to central and eastern Europe, along with the concomitant changes in linguistic development.[18] These tales are the ancestors of the later efflorescence of Yiddish writing, whose authors looked back eagerly and consciously to them: whether it was I. L. Peretz and Isaac Bashevis Singer with their demonic tempters and temptresses, Nachman of Bratslav's adaptation of the exploits of kings and princesses to weave his stories of cosmic struggle and universal redemption, or Itzik Manger's cheerfully anachronistic Bible poems. Linkages can, and should, be investigated, viewing the golden chain of Yiddish literature in its fullest and most magnificent perspective.

In the end, however, Glikl is, and will always remain, a mystery to her modern readers, as puzzling and elusive a sight as the six tall women she herself writes about. As with her detective work in that instance, ours can only go so far; as interpreters and critics, we investigate as best we can, apply our own intelligence, rational capabilities, worldviews, and beliefs—and then we sit back and acknowledge there is much we will never truly know. Humility is Glikl's watchword, and should be our own as well; but Glikl's humility, of course, is carefully framed within her confident attitude, the firm conviction she has something worthwhile to say. Hopefully a similar dynamic obtains for us as well, as we read, cherish, speculate on, and attempt to interpret these centuries-old works of literature.

Notes

CHAPTER 1. THE STUDY OF EARLY MODERN YIDDISH LITERATURE

1. See, for example, Max Weinreich, who makes this argument among others. *Bilder fun der yidisher literature-geshikhte* (Vilna: Tomor, 1928).
2. The book, when necessary, will of course also treat Jewish canonical texts, Hebrew and otherwise, that serve as conscious or unconscious complements to the Yiddish texts which are its primary focus.
3. Compare Wolfgang Iser, *The Range of Interpretation* (New York: Columbia University Press, 2000), 45–52.
4. For one recent assessment of the medieval field's general lack of awareness of contemporary Jewish texts' historical and theoretical utility, see Sheila Delany, " 'Turn It Again': Jewish Medieval Studies and Literary Theory," *Exemplaria* 12:1 (2000), 1–5; compare also William Chester Jordan, "Jewish Studies and the Medieval Historian," *Exemplaria* 12:1 (2000), 7–20.
5. Paris: Éditions du Cerf, 1993.
6. Jean Baumgarten, *Introduction to Old Yiddish Literature*, ed. and trans. Jerold C. Frakes (Oxford: Oxford University Press, 2005, henceforth *OYL*). This is hardly to imply that Baumgarten's was the first survey of the field: it is, however, the first broad-ranging survey since before the Second World War. Earlier surveys include Elias Shulman, *Sfas yehudis ashkenozis usifruso* (Riga: Levin, 1913); Max Weinreich, *Shtaplen: fir etudyn tsu der yidisher shprakhvisnshaft un literature-geshikhte* (Berlin: Vostok, 1923); idem., *Bilder fun der yidisher literatur-geshikhte* (Vilna: Tomor, 1928); Max Erik, *Vegn altyidishn roman un novele: fernster-zekhnster yorhundert* (Warsaw: Der veg tsum visn, 1926); idem., *Di geshikhte fun der yidisher literatur fun di eltste tsaytn biz der haskole-tkufe* (Warsaw: Kultur-lige, 1928); Yisroel Zinberg, *Di geshikhte fun der literatur bay yidn*, Vol. 6 (Vilna: Tomor, 1929–1937). See also the studies in Chone Shmeruk, *Sifrut yidish: perakim letoldoteha*

(Tel Aviv: Porter Institute, 1978), and *Prokim fun der yidisher literature-geshikhte* (Jerusalem: Hebrew University, 1988).

7. Albany: State University of New York Press, 1989. For other surveys of previous scholarship, compare Sara Zfatman-Biller, "Hasiporet beyidish mereshita ad 'shivkhei habesht' " (PhD thesis, Hebrew University, 1983), 2 vols. (hereafter Zfatman, "S"), 1:16–22.
8. Oxford: Oxford University Press, 2004.
9. An excellent popular overview of the period, in addition to the earlier sources, can be found in Dovid Katz, *Words on Fire: The Unfinished Story of Yiddish* (New York: Basic Books, 2004), 11–154.
10. See *OYL* 72–81, esp. 75; Weinreich *History* 45–174.
11. The Codex will be dicussed in more detail at the beginning of chapter 6.
12. Weinreich's *linguistic* division includes Earliest Yiddish (–1250); no Yiddish literature exists from this period, however. See Max Weinreich, *History of the Yiddish Language* (Chicago: University of Chicago Press, 1980), 9, 719–722, for a complex valuation of the relevance of written (and writerly) language for linguistic periodization. See also Dov-Ber Kerler, *The Origins of Modern Literary Yiddish* (Oxford: Clarendon Press, 1999), 15–16.
13. Kerler's close attention to Yiddish texts as they are reprinted (in constantly changing and adapting form) in emergent eastern European Yiddish markets is a sterling example of such analysis. See Kerler, passim, esp. 23–24.
14. If definition is necessary, then following Weinreich's reference to the general period as "Middle Yiddish" (*Bilder* 20) will do; on the ambiguity of any such demarcations, compare Andrew Lloyd Sunshine, "Opening the Mail: Interpersonal Aspects of Discourse and Grammar in Middle Yiddish Letters" (PhD dissertation, Columbia University, 1991), 37–39. I will instead generally use the phrases "premodern" or "early modern" to refer to the contemporary period's language and literature, following Sunshine's definition of the former in "Mail" 23 "as a catch-all for Yiddish prior to +/-1700; unless otherwise specified, it usually refers to Old and especially Middle Yiddish."
15. A far more detailed discussion of the scholarly history and landscape (up to its time of publication in 1989) can be found in Jerold C. Frakes, *The Politics of Interpretation: Alterity and Ideology in Old Yiddish Studies* (Albany: State University of New York Press, 1989), esp. 165–189.
16. The scholarly agenda and ideology of each constituency naturally differed; see, for discussion, Jerold C. Frakes, *The Cultural Study of Yiddish in Early Modern Europe* (New York: Palgrave Macmillan, 2007), esp. 11–81, and

Dovid Katz, "On Yiddish, in Yiddish, and for Yiddish: 500 Years of Yiddish Scholarship," in Mark Gelber, ed., *Identity and Ethos: A Festschrift for Sol Liptzin on the Occasion of His Eighty-fifth Birthday* (New York: Peter Lang, 1986), 23–36.

17. The work on Jewish multilingualism is vast. For just a few examples, see Max Weinreich, "*Yidishkayt* and Yiddish: On the Impact of Religion on Language in Ashkenazic Jewry," in Joshua A. Fishman, ed., *Readings in the Sociology of Language* (The Hague: Mouton, 1968), 410–412; Weinreich *History* 247–280; Bal-Makshoves (I. Eliashiv), "Tsvey shprakhn—eyn eyntsike literatur," in *Geklibene verk* (New York: Congress for Jewish Culture, 1953), 112–123; and *OYL* 72–81.
18. Compare Frakes *Politics*, passim.
19. Moritz Steinschneider, *Jüdisch-deutsche Literatur (Serapeum, Leipzig 1848–1849)* (repr. Jerusalem: Hebrew University, 1961); on literary criticism, see the sources cited in n. 6.
20. See David E. Fishman, *The Rise of Modern Yiddish Culture* (Pittsburgh: University of Pittsburgh Press, 2005), 139–153.
21. The linguistic considerations here, at least, are relevant to work being done in the Netherlands as well; the two areas will be discussed jointly.
22. See, for example, L. Fuks, *The Oldest Known Literary Documents of Yiddish Literature (c. 1382)*. (Leiden: E. J. Brill, 1952, 2 vols). Fuks' work there is dedicated largely to presentation, transcription, and philological investigation, rather than literary analysis; see Fuks 1:xxx–xxxiii.
23. Perhaps most famous in this respect is the work on the *Dukus Hornt*, a Yiddish adaptation of a Germanic epic of which the German original is no longer extant. The critical literature on the work is vast: compare *OYL* 133–136; Frakes *Politics*, passim, esp. 74–88 and the sources cited there. P. F. Ganz, F. Norman, and W. Schwarz's edition of *Dukus Horant* (Tübingen: Max Niemayer Verlag, 1964), now unsurprisingly, possesses both linguistic and its literary introductions, where the former is given pride of place; in the second introduction, much of the critical attention is devoted to possible complementary texts or questions of provenance within German epic literature. Even more recent studies take a comparative approach, stressing its intermediating role between Jewish and Christian cultures: see, for example, Gabriele L. Strauch, *Dukus Horant: Wanderer zwischen zwei Welten* (Rodopi: Amsterdam, 1990), esp. 41–54. For other examples of the comparative dimension, see John A. Howard, ed., *Wunderparlich und seltsame Historien Til Eulen Spiegels* (Würzburg: Königshausen und Neumann, 1983).

24. See, for example, Erika Timm, "Jiddische Sprachmaterialen aus dem Jahre 1290: Die Glossen des Berner kleine Aruch. Edition un Kommentar," in Hermann-Josef Müller and Walter Röll, eds., *Fragen des älteren Jiddisch* (Trier: Universität Trier, 1977), 16–34; Walter Röll, "Das älteste datierte jüdisch-deutsche Sprachdenkmal: Ein Verspaar im Wormser Machsor von 1272–1273," *Zeitschrift für Mundartforschung* 33 (1966), 127–138.
25. Germany is one of the rare places where new generations of scholars are being actively trained in the field of Old Yiddish; much of the exciting forthcoming work in the field will be produced by students of Timm, Marion Aptroot, and others.
26. Compare Erika Timm, *Graphische und phonische Struktur des Westjiddischen unter besonderer Berücksichtigung der Zeit um 1600* (Tübingen: Niemeyer, 1987); Walter Röll and Simon Neuberg, eds., *Jiddische Philologie: Festschrift für Erika Timm* (Tübingen: Niemeyer, 1999); many of the essays in Astrid Starck, ed., *Westjiddisch* (Aarau: Verlag Sauerländer, 1994); and, most recently, Erika Timm and Gustav Adolf Beckmann, *Etymologische Studien zum Jiddischen* (Hamburg: Helmut Buske Verlag, 2006).
27. See, as just one example, Wulf-Otto Dreeßen and Hermann-Josef Müller, eds., *Doniel: das altjiddische Danielbuch nach dem Basler Druck von 1557* (Göppingen: Küpperle, 1978).
28. Chone Shmeruk, *Research Collections on Microfiche: Jewish Studies, Yiddish Books* (Leiden: Zug: Inter Documentation Company, 1976).
29. Sara Zfatman, *Hasiporet beyidish: mereshita ad 'shivkhei habesht' (1504–1814): bibliografiya mueret* (Jerusalem: Hebrew University, 1985).
30. Chone Shmeruk, "Defusei yidish beitaliyah," *Italia* 3 (1982), 112–175; *Sifrut yidish bepolin* (Jerusalem: Magnes, 1981), 75–116.
31. Chone Shmeruk, "Di mizrekh-eyropeyishe nuskhoes fun der *Tsene-rene* (1786–1850)," *For Max Weinreich on His Seventieth Birthday* (The Hague: Mouton, 1964), 195–211 (Yiddish section); Chava Turniansky, "Iberzetsungen un baarbetungen fun der 'Tsene rene,' " in Shmuel Werses et al., *Sefer Dov Sadan* (Tel Aviv: Kibbutz hameyukhad, 1977), 165–190. Non-Israelis have also treated these topics, of course: compare, for example, Kerler *Origins* 55–139.
32. See, for example, Chava Turniansky, "Vegn di literatur-mekoyrim in Glikl Hamels zikhroynes," in Israel Bartal et al., eds., *Keminhag ashkenaz upolin* (Jerusalem: Zalman Shazar, 1993), 153–178, and Sara Zfatman, *Beyn ashkenaz lisefarad: letoldot hasipur hayehudi bimey-habeynayim* (Jerusalem: Magnes Press, 1993).

33. For some attempts to provide an overview in this area, see Dovid Katz, "Origins of Yiddish Dialectology," in Dovid Katz, ed., *Dialects of the Yiddish Language* (Oxford: Pergamon Press, 1988), 39–55, and the sources cited there.
34. Another notable French(-language) scholar who should not be omitted is Astrid Starck, whose recent facsimile edition of the *Mayse-bukh*'s *editio princeps*, accompanied by a monograph-length introductory essay, is a necessity for any study of early modern Yiddish literature; see Starck, *Un beau livre d'histoires* (Basel: Schwabe, 2004), 2 vols.
35. Baumgarten's survey is (roughly) organized according to generic categories; for another example of his genre-based approach, compare his *Récits hagiographiques juifs* (Paris: Éditions du Cerf, 2001).
36. See, for example, Eli Katz, "Six Germano-Jewish Poems from the Cairo Genizah," PhD dissertation, UCLA, 1963.
37. See Natalie Zemon Davis, *Women on the Margins: Three Seventeenth-Century Lives* (Cambridge, MA: Harvard University Press, 1995), 5–62; Marcus Moseley, *Being for Myself Alone: Origins of Jewish Autobiography* (Stanford: Stanford University Press, 2006), 155–175; and Michael Stanislawski, *Autobiographical Jews: Essays in Self-Fashioning* (Seattle: University of Washington Press, 2004), 32–53.
38. Other qualifications are also necessary: to name just two, that the interpretations advanced here are necessarily shaped by the modern interpreter's personal bias, and that varying levels of interpretive explication necessarily only hold for certain strata of the intended audience, sometimes at the more elite end.
39. We will return to this vital temporal distinction shortly. Attempting to recover the reading and reception dynamics of an accordingly believing society means treating much of the discussion in the subfield of "philosophy of fiction," which relies on a strong understanding of the fictionality of the discussed texts, with care. Compare Kendall L. Walton, "Appreciating Fiction: Suspending Disbelief or Pretending Belief?" *Dispositio* 5.13–14 (1980), 1–18, and Felix Martinez-Bonati, "Representation and Fiction," *Dispositio* 5.13–14 (1980), 19–33.
40. A highly nuanced discussion of the murky boundaries between belief and skepticism can be found in Paul Veyne, *Did the Greeks Believe Their Myths?: An Essay on the Constitutive Imagination* (Chicago: University of Chicago Press, 1988). The approach here is not identical to Veyne's, but is indebted to it; on this point, compare Veyne 42–43, 48–49. For examples of the blurred boundaries in Jewish life, compare Shulvass' discussion of Renaissance

Italy's Jewish elites and their "supernatural" beliefs (328–332); Trachtenberg's nuanced comments in *Magic* 23–24; Elisheva Carlebach's discussion of converts' dismissal of tropes of popular messianism such as the return of the Ten Lost Tribes and the Sambatyon river in "Jews, Christians, and the Endtime in Early Modern Germany," *Jewish History* 14 (2000), 332–333; and Mordechai Breuer's discussion of David Gans' "high susceptibility" in "Modernism and Traditionalism in Sixteenth-Century Jewish Historiography: A Study of David Gans' *Tzemah David*," in Bernard Dov Cooperman, ed., *Jewish Thought in the Sixteenth Century* (Cambridge, MA: Harvard University Press, 1983), 56–59, 63–64.

41. See the very general comments about audiences' "half-belief" in Weinreich *Bilder* 51.

42. Such differentiation between what I will term "primary" and "secondary" skepticism accounts for the general inapplicability of the scholarly category of the "fantastic" as conventionally defined (predicated on the intrusion of an uncanny element into an essentially if not entirely skeptical world) to our current discussion (though naturally what constitutes an uncanny element in the real or literary world can be subject to shift and redefinition). A review of the enormous corpus of theoretical literature on the fantastic is beyond our scope here; a few illuminating overviews or perspectives include Eric S. Rabkin, *The Fantastic in Literature* (Princeton: Princeton University Press, 1976), 3–5, 8–10, 28–29, 41; and José B. Monléon, *A Specter is Haunting Europe: A Sociohistorical Approach to the Fantastic* (Princeton: Princeton University Press, 1990), esp. 3–20.

43. See chapter 2 and the sources cited there, as well as William Nelson, *Fact or Fiction: The Dilemma of the Renaissance Storyteller* (Cambridge: Harvard University Press, 1973), 7, 36–37, 52; *OYL* 31; Diane Purkiss, *At the Bottom of the Garden: A Dark History of Fairies, Hobgoblins, and Other Troublesome Things* (New York: New York University Press, 2001); Keith Thomas, *Religion and the Decline of Magic* (New York: Charles Scribner's Sons, 1971), esp. 166–173; Lucien Febvre, *The Problem of Unbelief in the Sixteenth Century: The Religion of Rabelais* (Cambridge: Harvard University Press, 1982), esp. 6–16, 410–418, 438–464. For a specific Jewish context, see Joseph Davis, "The *Ten Questions* of Eliezer Eilburg and the Problem of Jewish Unbelief in the Sixteenth Century," *JQR* 91:3–4 (2001), 294, 313–314, 320–322; more generally, compare Gavin I. Langmuir, *Toward a Definition of Antisemitism* (Berkeley: University of California Press, 1990), esp. 13–14, 100–133. Langmuir's analysis of empiricism's role in creating doubt resonates here too.

44. For some discussion, often of the taxonomizing sort, compare Caroline Walker Bynum, *Metamorphosis and Identity* (New York: Zone Books, 2001), 54–55; Thomas 641–642; and Stuart Clark, introduction to Stuart Clark, ed., *Languages of Witchcraft: Narrative, Ideology, and Meaning in Early Modern Culture* (New York: St. Martin's Press, 2001), 2–3, 6.
45. Compare Veyne's comments on "the time of the pagans" on 17–18; Rabkin 181–182; and Thomas G. Pavel, *Fictional Worlds* (Cambridge, MA: Harvard University Press, 1986), 40–41. David Stern, in his characterization of "an analogous 'aggadic time and space' " to Veyne's, has made important conceptual steps in this regard. See his "The Character(s) of God in Rabbinic Literature," *Prooftexts* 12:2 (1992), 169–171.
46. Any detailed treatment of the broader issues relating to the philosophy of knowledge suggested by this line of thinking are far beyond the scope of this book (and its author). For some investigation, compare Riffaterre *Fictional*, passim; Timo Airakinsen, "Five Types of Knowledge," *American Philosophical Quarterly* 15:4 (1978), 263–274; and the essays in the still valuable *Knowledge and Belief*, ed. A. Phillips Griffiths (Oxford: Oxford University Press, 1967).
47. Natalie Zemon Davis' words are worth recalling: "it is especially important to realize that people do not necessarily agree with the values and ideas in the books they read." *Society and Culture in Early Modern France* (Stanford: Stanford University Press, 1975), 191–192. Compare also her *Fiction in the Archives* (Stanford: Stanford University Press, 1987), esp. 3–5, 16–19, 47–48.
48. Compare Nancy K. Miller's conception of the "constraints of likeliness" in her "Emphasis Added: Plots and Plausibilities in Women's Fiction," in Elaine Showalter, ed., *The New Feminist Criticism: Essays on Women, Literature, and Theory* (New York: Pantheon Books, 1985), 339–340; Gabrielle M. Spiegel's characterization of texts' "social logic" in "History, Historicism, and the Social Logic of the Text in the Middle Ages," *Speculum* 65 (1990), 77–78; and the discussion in Peter L. Berger and Thomas Luckmann, *The Social Construction of Reality: A Treatise in the Sociology of Knowledge* (New York: Irvington Publishers, 1966), esp. 21–25.
49. See Veyne 36, 47; James L. Kugel, *The Bible As It Was* (Cambridge, MA: Belknap, 1997), 17–23; and David B. Ruderman, "Unicorns, Great Beasts, and the Marvelous Variety of Things in Nature in the Thought of Abraham B. Hananiah Yagel," in Isadore Twersky and Bernard Septimus, eds., *Jewish Thought in the Seventeenth Century* (Cambridge, MA: Harvard University Press, 1987), 346–352. For a rigorous treatment of the last condition more

generally, see Richard Foley, "Justified Inconsistent Beliefs," *American Philosophical Quarterly* 16:4 (1979), 247–257; compare also Tamar Yacoby, "Fictional Reliability as a Communications Problem," *Poetics Today* 2:2 (1981), 113–126, and P. G. Maxwell-Stuart, *Witchcraft in Europe and the New World, 1400–1800* (New York: Palgrave, 2001), 15.

50. Compare Veyne 12, 84–85 and Nelson 19–23, 26–28.

51. See Nelson 28–29. Our schematic model focusing on ideal types here assumes the writer's engagement in an act of fictional creation: he is producing a story he knows to be untrue, as he created it entirely de novo; it simply did not exist before he began to write. It must be noted that in practice much of early modern Yiddish literature consisted of the vernacularization, adaptation, synthesization, and/or republication of older materials, which complicates at least the authorial (and to a certain extent, readerly) side. The works discussed in this book, however, are more evenly split between "original" and "repackaged" materials than the literature more generally. For a fuller exploration of this perspective of the "repackager," compare Veyne 95–102.

52. Such attempts at positioning may recall the efforts of the new historicist scholarship; for the potential relevance of new historicist materials and methodologies to these cases, see my discussion in *Antonio's Devils*, chapter 2.

53. These transitions occurred in every realm of Jewish textual life; see Fram *Daughter* 8–11, 15–21; and Hanoch Avenary, "Orale Judendeutsche Volkspoesie in der Interaktion mit Literarischer Überlieferung," *LBI Bulletin* 87 (1990), 5–8.

54. The general scholarly literature is enormous; valuable sources include Elizabeth L. Eisenstein, *The Printing Press as an Agent of Change* (Cambridge: Cambridge University Press, 1979, 2 vols.), esp. 1:3–43; Lucien Febvre, *The Coming of the Book: The Impact of Printing 1450–1800* (London: NLB, 1976), passim; Henri-Jean Martin, *The History and Power of Writing* (Chicago: University of Chicago Press, 1994), esp. 182–295, 324–365; Walter J. Ong, *Orality and Literacy: The Technologizing of the Word* (New York: Methuen, 1982), esp. 10–12, 37–57; and Roger Chartier, *The Order of Books* (Stanford: Stanford University Press, 1994), esp. 8–9, 18–21. On the Jewish context, compare Zeev Gries, *The Book in the Jewish World, 1700–1900* (Oxford: Littman Library of Jewish Civilization, 2007), esp. 3–4, 14–16.

55. Recent scholarship has stressed models of continuity, rather than disruption, between script and print, oral and textual cultures. Some examples include the essays in Alexandra Walsham and Julia Crick, eds., *The Uses of*

Script and Print, 1300–1700 (Cambridge: Cambridge University Press, 2004), especially the editors' introductory essay; Matei Calinescu, "Orality in Literacy: Some Historical Paradoxes in Reading," *Yale Journal of Criticism* 6:2 (1993), esp. 177–179; and John Miles Foley, *Immanent Art: From Structure to Meaning in Traditional Oral Epic* (Bloomington: Indiana University Press, 1991), esp. 55, 193. For earlier treatments of the subject of the relations between author and reader and the transition between orality and literacy, compare Robert Scholes and Robert Kellogg, "The Problem of Reality: Illustration and Representation," in Philip Steivick, ed., *The Theory of the Novel* (New York: The Free Press, 1967), 371–384; Ruth Finnegan, "Literacy Versus Non-literacy: The Great Divide?" in Robin Horton and Ruth Finnegan, eds., *Modes of Thought: Essays on Thinking in Western and Non-Western Societies* (London: Faber and Faber, 1973), 112–144; Finnegan, *Literacy and Orality: Studies in the Technology of Communication* (Oxford: Basil Blackwell, 1988), esp. 61–69, 140–146; and Burke O. Long, "Recent Field Studies in Oral Literature and the Question of *Sitz im Leben*," *Semeia* 5 (1976), esp. 36–37.

56. See, for example, Franz Bauml, "Medieval Texts and the Two Theories of Oral-Formulaic Composition," *New Literary History* 16:1 (Autumn 1984), esp. 39–40.
57. See discussion in chapter 6.
58. Compare Albert B. Lord, *The Singer of Tales* (Cambridge: Harvard University Press, 1960), esp. 13–67; John Miles Foley, *The Singer of Tales in Performance* (Bloomington: University of Indiana Press, 1995), 3–7, 47–49. See also Alberto Manguel, *A History of Reading* (New York: Viking, 1996), 47, 116–122.
59. See Donald K. Fry, "The Memory of Cadmon," in John Miles Foley, ed., *Oral Traditional Literature: A Festschrift for Albert Bates Lord* (Columbus, OH; Slavica Publishers, 1981), 282–293.
60. See Lord *Singer* 49–50, 78–79, 94–96. This should not imply that the oral formulae preserved within written texts, or even the written texts themselves, are faithful models to contemporary oral speech. See Sunshine "Mail" 14–16.
61. See Chartier *Forms* 93–95 and Fram *Daughter* 17–19. Even the rare partial exceptions to this general lacuna are illustrative, however: see Erika Timm's examination of the genizah at Veitshöchheim, which contained Yiddish printed books from the sixteenth to the nineteenth century and is "of substantial interest for the reception and sociology of Yiddish literature of the

'middle' period," affording a glimpse "into the literary taste of a west-Yiddish reading public during the eighteenth century." *Yiddish Literature in a Franconian Genizah* (Jerusalem: Akademon Press, 1988), 11; see esp. 18–47, 51–55. On elite attitudes, see Elchanan Reiner, "The Ashkenazi Elite at the Beginning of the Modern Era: Manuscript versus Printed Book," *Polin* 10 (1997), 85–98.

62. See Zinberg 6:29–30; Abrahams *Jewish Life* 26; and Fram *Daughter* 65; for a broader examination of the possibilities of prayer in Yiddish, particularly before the dissemination of printed texts, see David E. Fishman, "Mikoyekh davenen af yidish: a bintl metodologishe bamerkungen un naye mekoyrim," *YIVO Bleter* (n.s.) 1 (1991), 69–92.

63. Compare Pollack (7–8), who focuses on elite readers; Abrahams *Jewish Life* 344; and, more recently, Ivan G. Marcus, "Mothers, Martyrs, and Moneymakers: Some Jewish Women in Medieval Europe," *Conservative Judaism* 38:3 (Spring 1986), esp. 36–37. A good new general source for home life from a slightly earlier period is Elisheva Baumgarten, *Mothers and Children: Jewish Family Life in Medieval Europe* (Princeton: Princeton University Press, 2004). On the specific question of children's reading habits, particularly girls', see Chava Turniansky, "Meydlekh in der alt-yidish literatur," in Walter Röll and Simon Neuberg, eds., *Jiddische Philologie: Festschrift für Erika Timm* (Tübingen: Niemeyer, 1999), 7*-20*; Ephraim Karnafogel, *Jewish Education and Society in the High Middle Ages* (Detroit: Wayne State University Press, 1992), esp. 15–39; Gries 93–95; and Zfatman "S" 1:82–83.

64. Compare, mutatis mutandis, the discussions about "collaborative literacy" in Sunshine 162–164. See also Chartier *Cultural* 7; Foley *Singer* 42–44; and Eric A. Havelock, *The Muse Learns to Write: Reflections on Orality and Literacy from Antiquity to the Present* (New Haven: Yale University Press, 1986), 44–98, esp. 72–73; Alain Renoir, "Oral-Formulaic Rhetoric and the Interpretation of Written Texts," in John Miles Foley, ed., *Oral Tradition in Literature: Interpretation in Context* (Columbia, MO: University of Missouri Press, 1986), 103–135; and Walter J. Ong, "Text as Interpretation: Mark and After," in *Oral Tradition* 148–149, 152–153.

65. Compare the discussion in Wendy Harding, "Body into Text: *The Book of Margery Kempe*," in Linda Lomperis and Sarah Stanbury, eds., *Feminist Approaches to the Body in Medieval Literature* (Philadephia: University of Pennsylvania Press, 1993), 168–187, esp. 172.

66. One may also comment here on the potentially fruitful application of the discussion over "intensive" reading (where readers "faced a narrow and

finite body of texts, which were read and reread, memorized and recited, heard and known by heart, transmitted from generation to generation") and "extensive" reading (where readers "consum[e] numerous and diverse print texts, reading them with rapidity and avidity and exercis[e] a critical activity over them that spares no domain from methodical doubt"). See Chartier *Forms* 17 and Fram *Daughter* xvii.

67. Compare Mendele Mocher Seforim (=S. Y. Abramovitch), "Of Bygone Days," in Ruth Wisse, ed., *A Shtetl and Other Novellas* (Detroit: Wayne State University Press, 1986).

68. The theoretical literature on the subject is of course vast; see Jeremy Dauber, *Antonio's Devils: Writers of the Jewish Enlightenment and the Birth of Modern Hebrew and Yiddish Literature* (Stanford: Stanford University Press, 2004), esp. chapter 2 and the sources cited there for some discussion, as well as *OYL* 39–40, 57–71 and the seminal essays in Susan R. Suleiman and Inge Crosman, eds., *The Reader in the Text: Essays on Audience and Interpretation* (Princeton: Princeton University Press, 1980).

69. Compare Baumgarten's similar conclusion in *OYL* 67.

70. For the fullest exploration of this aspect of Yiddish literature, see Shlomo Berger, "An Invitation to Buy and Read: Paratexts of Yiddish Books in Amsterdam, 1650–1800," *Book History* 7 (2004), 38–42.

71. Compare Shmuel Niger, "Di yidishe literatur un di lezerin," in Niger, *Bleter-geshikhte fun der yidisher literatur* (New York: Alveltlekhn yidishn kultur-kongres, 1959), 37–107. See Naomi Seidman's discussion of Niger's approach in Naomi Seidman, *A Marriage Made in Heaven: The Sexual Politics of Hebrew and Yiddish* (Berkeley: University of California Press, 1997), 3–5.

72. Compare Seidman, passim and Berger 50–51. On women's roles in the production and composition of premodern Yiddish literature, see *OYL* 61–62.

73. See *OYL* 69–70; Chava Weissler, "For Women and for Men Who Are Like Women: The Construction of Gender in Yiddish Devotional Literature," *Journal of Feminist Studies* 5 (1989), 7–24, esp. 11–12; and, more recently, compare Edward Fram, *My Dear Daughter: Rabbi Benjamin Slonik and the Education of Jewish Women in Sixteenth-Century Poland* (Cincinnati: Hebrew Union College Press, 2007), 6–7. For an earlier, subtle disagreement with Niger's position, compare Weinreich (*History* 274–277), who insists on "scholarship" as a determinant criterion.

74. See Weinreich "*Yidishkayt*," esp. 389, and Zfatman "S" 1:79–86.

75. Precisely defining this functional literacy is itself of course complex. Sunshine writes that there is "no way of finding out with any precision who could read

and/or write in Yiddish and who could not in the middle Yiddish period" ("Mail" 35–36). We will attempt to investigate further throughout the chapter.

76. Efforts were clearly made to assist in broad comprehension, including but not limited to the appending of glossaries and the calculated effort to "universalize" the Yiddish employed. Compare Kerler, passim.

77. The scholarship on nonelite Jewish education is enormous, and its survey is beyond our scope here; see, inter alia, Herman Pollack, *Jewish Folkways in Germanic Lands (1648–1806): Studies in Aspects of Daily Life* (Cambridge: MIT Press, 1971), 50–84 (whose generally elite-oriented approach nonetheless betrays much of other groups' education, esp. 63–64); Israel Abrahams, *Jewish Life in the Middle Ages* (New York: Athenaeum, 1969 [1896]), 340–372; Robert Bonfil, *Jewish Life in Renaissance Italy* (Berkeley: University of California Press, 1994), 125–135; and Moses A. Shulvass, *The Jews in the World of the Renaissance* (Leiden: E. J. Brill, 1973), 168–172.

78. For readability's sake, I will omit quotation marks around "educated" and "uneducated" in future usage, proceeding with the understanding that I have problematized the terms sufficiently and will use them in the sense in which they have been employed here.

79. Translation taken from *OYL* 69.

80. See my *Antonio's Devils*, passim, and the sources cited there; compare also Michael Riffaterre's model of "hypogrammatic" reading and decoding in his *Semiotics of Poetry* (Bloomington: Indiana University Press, 1978), esp. 4–6, 23, 109–110, 164–165, and his *Text Production* (New York: Columbia University Press, 1983), 9–12, 24–25, 87–100.

81. This is Yehoyesh's (modern) translation: *Khumesh neviyim kesuvim* (New York: Tog, 1937), 1:14.

82. Comprehension of biblical texts in general, however, even among elites, is also scattered along a continuum: the simpler narrative sentences of Genesis, for example, may have been fully available to more Hebrew readers than the gnomic aphorisms of Proverbs. Such greater levels of nuance should be theoretically kept in mind.

83. I have addressed this aspect of allusion in detail in *Antonio's Devils*. Excluded here are allusions definable as parts of what Sunshine terms "phatic formulae," a type of speech where exchanges of words whose meanings are almost entirely irrelevant create communicative ties between individuals; for comments on contemporary Yiddish phatic formulae, see Sunshine 207–210.

84. See Gen. 6:9 and Rashi ad loc.

85. Compare Linda Hutcheon, *A Theory of Parody* (New York: Methuen, 1985), esp. 43–44.
86. See *OYL* 68; Weinreich *Bilder* 33; Jacob Katz, *Tradition and Crisis: Jewish Society at the End of the Middle Ages* (New York: Schocken Books, 1961), 145–146; and Abrahams *Jewish Life* 20–22.
87. Weinreich, for example (*Bilder* 33–34), does not mention such a category; Zfatman ("S" 1:85) acknowledges elite readers of Yiddish texts but differs in her approach to them.
88. Such an approach echoes Roger Chartier's emphasis on "fluid circulations" and "blurred distinctions" in varying groups' consumption of popular culture in early modern France; see his *The Cultural Uses of Print in Early Modern France* (Princeton: Princeton, NJ, 1987), 3–5, quote 3, and Chartier, *Forms and Meanings: Texts, Performances, and Audiences from Codex to Computer* (Philadelphia: University of Pennsylvania Press, 1995), 88–90.
89. This continuum is of course applicable within a monolinguistic system as well, since multiple levels of discourse exist within a single language. Examples range from abstruse or jargon-laden material (an English-language article in a scientific journal, for example) to broader definitions of "elite" (even the most gifted child, an elite in some sense, has difficulties with Dostoevsky).
90. Given the nature of the Jewish linguistic polysystem, and the potential availability of these texts in several languages, this process can be more fruitfully thought of at times as a series of choices.
91. See *OYL* 70. Putting aside the latter point for the moment, this refined model of knowledge acquisition among elites may yield changes in our model of their strategies, upon their transformation into authors of vernacular texts, of *knowledge reference* or *citation*. Contemporary (and modern) elites may well have learned a particular narrative, idea, or concept originating in an elite source from a nonelite, non-Hebrew, or even nontextual source, and conceptualized it in that form for a significant period of time before either (a) learning the elite source, then substituting it (or overlaying it on) their earlier referential marker, or (b) learning how to refer to or access the elite source without having directly encountered it; when the necessity arises to cite their source—in writing, lecturing, or otherwise—current ideological biases or anxieties stemming from elite membership militate against citing the nonelite source; they therefore seek out the elite, original source to cite instead.
92. On parody as a mode, compare Hutcheon, esp. 30–49; Robert L. Mack, *The Genius of Parody: Imitation and Originality in Seventeenth- and*

Eighteenth-Century English Literature (New York: Palgrave Macmillan, 2007), 16–23 and Bond Johnson, *The Mode of Parody: An Essay at Definition and Six Studies* (Frankfurt a.M.: Peter Lang, 2000), 13–14.

93. This is particularly the case given the construction of some ancient forms of parody as a simple string of quotations; see Margaret A. Rose, *Parody: Ancient, Modern, and Post-Modern* (Cambridge: Cambridge University Press, 1993), 16–17, 179–186, and Hutcheon 19–24.

94. Quote Rose 31. The problematized definition of parody as the "imitation of form with a change to content" (Rose 15) could underlie this process; see also the treatment of "simulation" in 29–30 and Johnson 18.

95. While, of course, remaining mindful of their theoretical distinctions; see Rose 54–99 and David Kiremidjian, *A Study of Modern Parody* (New York: Garland, 1985), 39–57.

96. Compare Rose 32, 41–42.

97. Compare Rose 37–45 and Joseph A. Dane, *Parody: Critical Concepts Versus Literary Practices, Aristophanes to Sterne* (Norman, OK: University of Oklahoma Press, 1988), 21.

98. Such considerations are naturally related to the reader's generically shaped horizon of expectations; compare Rose 25–26, 33–39, 170–177, Hutcheon 42–43, 87–88, 94–95, and Dane 92–93.

99. The intended nature of this gradual awareness, it seems to me, marks a distinction between this sort of parody and satire; compare Rose 82–86 and Dane 10–13.

100. Compare this to the discussion of the literary hoax in Rose 69–71.

101. The historical claims, for example, that certain nineteenth-century anti-Hasidic parodies were originally accepted as genuine Hasidic writings by the movement reminds us that the evaluation of such claims necessitates consideration of ideology's role in historiography, a necessary speculation when dealing with material from sufficient temporal distance to be able to rely only on accounts of their reception.

102. Formal considerations obtain here as much—or more—than in the former category; for example, no one watching the 1980s British parody program "Spitting Image," whose signature identifying feature was its employment of highly detailed puppet versions of leading political and cultural figures, ever mistook it for an actual Tory broadcast. On caricature in a parodic context, see Kiremidjian 50–52.

103. Such definitions and approaches to particular texts by readers can change over time, as "definitions of information change sufficiently" to make that

information more apparently parodic: see the treatment of this phenomenon with regard to the traveler's tale in Dane 67–118, esp. 68–69, 71–72.

104. Compare *Antonio's Devils*, passim, and John Gardner, *On Moral Fiction* (New York: Basic Books, 1978), 108.

105. Compare the discussion on rhetoric in Gary Wihl, preface, in Gary Wihl and David Williams, eds., *Literature and Ethics: Essays Presented to A. E. Malloch* (Kingston: McGill-Queens University Press, 1988), vii–xii, esp. viii.

106. With very few exceptions, these texts' *writers* are male; I will use the male pronoun accordingly, except in certain cases (such as Glikl of Hameln's memoirs) where clear or very strong evidence exists of the author's possible or potential femininity. On the rare phenomenon of contemporary female authorship, compare the sources on Glikl of Hameln supra; M. Kayserling, *Die jüdischen Frauen in der Geshichte, Literatur, und Kunst* (Leipzig: F. M. Broadhaus, 1879), 150–156; and A. Korman, *Yidishe dikhterins: antologye* (Chicago: L. M. Stein, 1928), xxvii–xxxi, 5–17.

107. I use "narrative polemic" here to refer to works like fable and exempla literature, rather than the moral treatises common in the early modern period.

108. Compare Irving Massey, *Find You the Virtue: Ethics, Image, and Desire in Literature* (Lanham, MD: George Mason University Press, 1987), 58–59, and Frank Palmer, *Literature and Moral Understanding* (Oxford: Clarendon Press, 1992), 124–125.

109. Compare Palmer 106–110.

110. See the discussion, with reference to modern literature, in Massey 53–57. Massey's insistence that "in a fable, it is perfectly clear on whose side we are supposed to be, and sentimental identification with the fool or wrong-doer is never open for consideration" (57) may be complicated by the longer fabular works we will discuss in the next chapter.

111. See Palmer 195 on the writer's consciousness of his literary achievement.

112. Compare Gardner 14–15.

113. Compare Palmer 184–186.

114. On allegory as mode, compare Gay Clifford, *The Transformations of Allegory* (London: Routledge, 1974), 5.

115. On this "allegorical spectacle," see Carolynn Van Dyke, *The Fiction of Truth: Structures of Meaning in Narrative and Dramatic Allegory* (Ithaca: Cornell University Press, 1985), 106–155, esp. 127–128.

116. Compare Jon Whitman, *Allegory: The Dynamics of an Ancient and Medieval Technique* (Cambridge: Harvard University Press, 1987), 3–8; Clifford

10–13; and Stephen A. Barney, *Allegories of History, Allegories of Love* (Hamden, CT: Archon Books, 1979), 16–17, 25–26.

117. See Philip Rollinson, *Classical Theories of Allegory and Christian Culture* (Pittsburgh: Duquesne University Press, 1981), 26. Compare Clifford 47.

118. Compare Rollinson 20–24 and Clifford 53.

119. See Rollinson xii, 50, 63–64 and the discussion of typological allegory in Barney 32–33. Another permutation is of course possible: that an audience can read a text as allegorical when the author lacked any such intent. See Zhang Longxi, *Allegoresis: Reading Canonical Literature East and West* (Ithaca: Cornell University Press, 2005), 101–102. Such processes can be particularly achieved when a work that seems prima facie abstract is "identified with a historical figure and related to a historical situation," thus "radically redefin[ing] ... the reader's basic horizon of expectations" (109).

120. See Longxi 63 and passim on the possibility of translating "the concept of the allegorical ... across linguistic and cultural boundaries."

121. The identification and characterization of such gaps in a narrative context is essentially the basis of reading reception theory: compare Hans Robert Jauss, *Towards an Aesthetic of Reception* (Minneapolis: University of Minnesota Press, 1982); Wolfgang Iser, *The Act of Reading: A Theory of Aesthetic Response* (Baltimore: Johns Hopkins University Press, 1978); and Joseph Michael Pucci, *The Full-Knowing Reader: Allusion and the Power of the Reader in the Western Literary Tradition* (New Haven: Yale University Press, 1998).

122. See also Dorrit Cohn, *Transparent Minds: Narrative Modes for Presenting Consciousness in Fiction* (Princeton, NJ: Princeton University Press, 1978); the series of works by Gérard Genette: *Narrative Discourse: An Essay in Method*, trans. Jane E. Lewin. (Ithaca, NY: Cornell University Press, 1980), esp. 23–27, 94–112; *Figures of Literary Discourse*, trans. Alan Sheridan (New York: Columbia University Press, 1982), 16–21, 269–273; *Narrative Discourse Revisited*, trans. Jane E. Lewin. (Ithaca, NY: Cornell University Press, 1988), esp. 45–67, 136–150; *Fiction and Diction*, trans. Catherine Porter. (Ithaca: NY, Cornell University Press, 1993), esp. 6–7, 24, 54–57; and *Mimologics*, trans. Thaïs E. Morgan (Lincoln, NE: University of Nebraska Press, 1995); the essays in W. J. T. Mitchell, ed., *On Narrative* (Chicago: University of Chicago Press, 1981), especially those by Hayden White, Barbara Herrnstein Smith, and Louis O. Mink; the essays in Hayden White, *Tropics of Discourse: Essays in Cultural Criticism* (Baltimore: Johns Hopkins University Press, 1978); and Michael Riffaterre, *Fictional Truth* (Baltimore: Johns Hopkins University Press, 1990), esp. 5–7.

123. Compare, for an expression of similar sentiments in a more general context, Janice A. Radway, "The Aesthetic in Mass Culture: Reading the 'Popular' Literary Text," in P. Steiner, M. Cervenka, and R. Vroon, eds., *The Structure of the Literary Process* (Philadelphia: John Benjamins, 1982), 399–400.

124. On the relation of modes and genres, compare Gérard Genette, *The Architext: An Introduction* (Berkeley: University of California Press, 1992), esp. 58–61, 72–74.

125. For a nuanced discussion of this topic, see Tzvetan Todorov, *Genres in Discourse* (Cambridge: Cambridge University Press, 1990), esp. 8–10. Two extremely helpful general overviews of the topic and theoretical literature are Heather Dubrow, *Genre* (London: Methuen, 1982) and John Frow, *Genre* (London: Routledge, 2006).

126. See Dubrow 2–3, 31–34, 85; Frow 9–10; Todorov *Genres* 18–19; Pavel 115–138; Jonathan Culler, *The Pursuit of Signs: Semiotics, Literature, Deconstruction* (Ithaca: Cornell University Press, 1981), 11–12; and Charles Eric Reeves, "Convention and Behavior," in P. Steiner, M. Cervenka, and R. Vroon, eds., *The Structure of the Literary Process* (Philadelphia: John Benjamins, 1982), 431–454, esp. 438–440, 444–449. Classic approaches to the topic are still highly useful: compare Northrop Frye, *Anatomy of Criticism: Four Essays* (Princeton: Princeton University Press, 1957), 246–337; Wayne Booth, *The Rhetoric of Fiction* (Chicago: University of Chicago Press, 1961), esp. 37; and Harry Levin, *The Gates of Horn* (New York: Oxford University Press, 1963), 18–22.

127. Compare Todorov *Genres* 14–15 and Dubrow 24–25, 37.

128. See Genette *Architext*, passim; Dubrow 46–104; and Frow 51–71. The concept of "context" itself can be fruitfully complicated and interrogated: compare Frow 14, 124–125, 128–139; Jonathan Culler, *Framing the Sign: Criticism and Its Institutions* (Norman: University of Oklahoma Press, 1988), esp. xiii–xiv; Culler *Pursuit* 51–52, 54; Adena Rosmarin, *The Power of Genre* (Minneapolis: University of Minnesota Press, 1985), esp. 14–15; and, for a more charged view, Thomas O. Beebee, *The Ideology of Genre: A Comparative Study of Generic Instability* (University Park, PA: Pennsylvania State University Press, 1994), esp. 7–9, 12–19, 249–250, 253–258.

129. Genre definition is always to some extent speaking of ideal types; specific works often combine various genres. Subgenres exist within the genres as well, with their own definitions and dynamics of change; compare Genette *Architext* 64–66, Dubrow 5–6, Frow 24–26, and Susan Einbinder's analysis of women's representation of women as idealized figures and its change

from subgenre to subgenre of martyrological materials (lists of names, prose chronicles, piyyutim, and laments), though arguably all are located within a particular more broadly defined genre (martyrdom chronicles). Susan Einbinder, "Jewish Women Martyrs: Changing Models of Representation," *Exemplaria* 12:1 (2000), 105–127. The hermeneutic circle must again be employed, examining contemporary evidence of textual production to prevent the imposition of modern categories on the contemporary literary corpus.

130. Compare Frow 81–82, 101–103 and Culler *Pursuit* 58–59.
131. Confirmation of such competency and/or sophistication, in the absence of external independent data, is definitionally an act of speculative historicized reconstruction; such reconstruction may be aided in broader studies by tracking "family similarities" within a group of texts ostensibly generically related. Such a study is beyond our scope here. Compare Todorov *Genres* 21–24; Femke Kramer, "Rigid Readings of Flexible Texts: The Case of Sixteenth-Century Comic Drama," in Bert Roest and Herman Vanstiphout, eds., *Aspects of Genre and Type in Pre-modern Literary Cultures* (Groningen: Styx, 1999), 37–41; and especially Beebee 249–259.
132. Compare the very different discussion in Rabkin 117–118, 133, 136–138.
133. Compare Dubrow 106–107.
134. This need not universally be the case, particularly if one adopts an expansive definition of "hegemony"; the role of parodic or carnivalesque texts which operate in a subversive fashion to uphold the hegemonic order (as in the extent carnivalesque Purim literature) is a case in point.
135. For a more modern analysis of the tendency to "resist genre," compare Rosmarin 8–10.
136. Compare, in a different context, Dubrow 9–10 and Rosmarin 34–36.
137. Nelson 39. See also Genette *Architext* 31–33.
138. Again, such generic divisions are evident not primarily by previous critical traditions of generic taxonomy, nor even by the authors' own description of the works as members of specific genres, though the latter serves as a meaningful marker for the readership, but rather by the "family resemblance" that associates texts in readers' minds defined by their conceptual, conventional, and formal similarities; see Rosmarin 41–42. Compare Genette *Architext* 44–46, 67–69 and Kramer 33–36.
139. See, for example, Zfatman "S" 1:2–3, 11–12, 2:11–12, 54–60; Sunshine 26–28; Fuks 1:xiv–xv; Leo Landau, *Arthurian Legends, or, the Hebrew-German Rhymed Version of the Legend of King Arthur* (Leipzig, 1912), 13; Weinreich

"*Yidishkayt*" 391–394; Salo Baron, *A Social and Religious History of the Jews* (New York: Columbia University Press, 1952–1993, hereafter *SRH*), 11:118–120 and esp. 182–183; and Jean Baumgarten, "Les manuscrits Yidich de la Bibliothèque Nationale de Paris," in David Goldberg, ed., *The Field of Yiddish, Fifth Collection: Studies in Language, Folklore, and Literature* (Evanston, IL: Northwestern University Press, 1993), 121–151.

140. See R. Po-chia Hsia, *Trent 1475: Stories of a Ritual Murder Trial* (New Haven: Yale University Press, 1992), 24; Pollack 12–14; and Robert Bonfil, *Jewish Life in Renaissance Italy* (Berkeley: University of California Press, 1994), ix–xi, 5–6, 101–116. On medieval and early modern eastern Europe, compare Ivan G. Marcus, *Rituals of Childhood: Jewish Acculturation in Medieval Europe* (New Haven: Yale University Press, 1996), 8–13, 25–34, 53–69; Edward Fram, *Ideals Face Reality: Jewish Law and Life in Poland, 1550–1655* (Cincinnati: Hebrew Union College Press, 1997), 29–32; Katz *Tradition* 17–30.

141. One of the genres most prominently considered in a comparative context is the early modern Yiddish drama, in the form of the Purim-shpil. Though space considerations prohibit its treatment here, see, for some of its comparands, Eckerhard Catholy, *Das deutsche Lustspiel* (Stuttgart: W. Kohlhammer Verlag, 1969), esp. 15–81; Catholy, *Fastnachtspiel* (Stuttgart: J. B. Metzlersche Verlagsbuchhandlung, 1966), esp. 5–8, 18–20, 26–47; Catholy, *Das Fastnachtspiel des Spätmittelalters: Gestalt und Funktion* (Tübingen: Max Niemayer Verlag, 1961), esp. 276–329; Davis, *Early Modern France*, 97–123 (with special attention to the political aspects of misrule more generally); on the Purim-shpil itself, see Zinberg 6:270–307 and now Evi Bützer, *Die Anfänge der jiddischen purim shpiln in ihrem literarischen und kulturgeschichtlichen Kontext* (Hamburg: Helmut Buske Verlag, 2003).

142. For one example of such an intellectual biography, derived inductively from the author's work itself, see Jacob Meitlis' introduction to *Midrash lepirkei avot beyidish kamait leanshel levi* (Jerusalem: Israel Academy of Sciences and Humanities, 1978), esp. 19–23. For more general comments, compare Zfatman "S" 1:56–62.

143. Compare Todorov *Genres* 6.

144. Compare Nils H. Roemer, *Jewish Scholarship and Culture in Nineteenth-Century Germany: Between History and Faith* (Madison: University of Wisconsin Press, 2005), 67–70, 117–123.

145. Compare Frakes *Politics*, passim, esp. xii, 1–6.

146. However, for a strong and considered statement of the limits to a historicist approach, compare René Wellek, "Literary Theory, Criticism, and History,"

in Wellek, *Concepts of Criticism* (New Haven: Yale University Press, 1963), 1–20, and his comments in "Comparative Literature," 293–294.

147. For similar considerations, compare Chartier *Order* 16–17.

148. See Yosef Hayim Yerushalmi, *Zakhor: Jewish History and Jewish Memory* (Seattle: University of Washington Press, 1982), and Michael Stanislawski, "The Yiddish Shevet Yehudah: A Study in the 'Ashkenization' of a Sephardic Classic," in Elisheva Carlebach, John M. Efron, and David Myers, eds., *Jewish History and Jewish Memory: Essays in Honor of Yosef Hayim Yerushalmi* (University Press of New England, 1998), 134–149, esp. 135–137.

149. The songs commemorated joyous or tragic events such as fires and expulsions. See Chava Turniansky, "Yiddish 'Historical' Songs as Sources for the History of the Jews in Pre-Partition Poland," *Polin* 4 (1989), 42–52.

150. See sources cited in note 35 above.

151. Compare, by contrast, the discussion of rabbinic texts in Miriam B. Peskowitz, *Spinning Fantasies: Rabbis, Gender, and History* (Berkeley: University of California Press, 1997), 90–92, 132–133, and their role in inscribing certain conceptualizations of gender into frameworks of social control.

152. See, for example, the works by Chava Weissler, Naomi Seidman, and Natalie Zemon Davis cited elsewhere in the chapter, as well as Weissler, *Traditional Yiddish Literature: A Source for the Study of Women's Religious Lives* (Cambridge, MA: Harvard College Library, 1988), esp. 2–5, 18–19.

153. See Alice A. Jardine, *Gynesis: Configurations of Woman and Modernity.* (Ithaca: Cornell University Press, 1985), esp. 48, 60, 118–119; Teresa de Laurentis, "The Technology of Gender," in *Technologies of Gender* (Bloomington: Indiana UP, 1987), 1–30; Judith Butler, *Gender Trouble: Feminism and the Subversion of Identity* (New York: Routledge, 1990), esp. 13–18; Luce Irigaray, *This Sex Which Is Not One* (Ithaca: Cornell University Press, 1985); Luce Irigaray, *Speculum of the Other Woman* (Ithaca: Cornell University Press, 1985); Nina Baym, "Melodramas of Beset Manhood: How Theories of American Fiction Exclude Women Authors," in Elaine Showalter, ed., *The New Feminist Criticism: Essays on Women, Literature, and Theory* (New York: Pantheon Books, 1985), 64–65; Jane P. Tompkins, "Sentimental Power: *Uncle Tom's Cabin* and the Politics of Literary History," in Showalter, *The New Feminist Criticism*, 83–85.

154. See, for example, Tracy Guren Klirs, *The Merit of Our Mothers: A Bilingual Anthology of Jewish Women's Prayers* (Cincinnati: Hebrew Union College Press, 1992), 5–6; Chava Weissler, *Voices of the Matriarchs: Listening to the*

Prayers of Early Modern Jewish Women (Boston: Beacon Press, 1998), passim, esp. 8–9, 45–50, 74–75, 173, 177–179. An earlier perspective can be found in Solomon B. Freehof, "Devotional Literature in the Vernacular: Judeo-German Prior to the Reform Movement," *Central Conference of American Rabbis Yearbook* 33 (1923), 375–415, esp. 377–379.

155. For an overview, see Thelma Fenster, "Preface: Why Men?," in Clare A. Lees, ed., *Medieval Masculinities: Reading Men in the Middle Ages* (Minneapolis: University of Minnesota Press, 1994), ix–xiii, and Clare A. Lees, introduction to *Medieval Masculinities*, xv–xxv. See also Stanley Chojnacki, "Subaltern Patriarchs: Patrician Bachelors in Renaissance Venice," in Lees *Medieval Masculinities*, 73–90, esp. 74.

156. See, for example, Jo Ann McNamara, "The *Herrenfrage:* The Restructuring of the Gender System, 1050–1150," in Lees *Medieval Masculinities*, 3–29, and Susan Mosher Stuard, "Burdens of Matrimony: Husbanding and Gender in Medieval Italy," in Lees *Medieval Masculinities* 61–71, quote from 61.

157. Compare Louise Mirrer, "Representing 'Other' Men: Muslims, Jews, and Masculine Ideals in Medieval Castilian Epic and Ballad," in Lees *Medieval Masculinities* 169, 172–173, 179–181, and the discussion of Daniel Boyarin's work in the final chapter.

158. See Barbara Kirshenblatt-Gimblett, "The Corporeal Turn," *JQR* 95:3 (Summer 2005), 447–461, and the sources cited there; note particularly Eli Yassif, "The Body Never Lies: The Body in Medieval Jewish Folk Narratives," in Howard Eilberg-Schwartz, ed., *People of the Body: Jews and Judaism from an Embodied Perspective* (Albany: SUNY, 1992), 206–207, and Naomi Seidman, "Carnal Knowledge: Sex and the Body in Jewish Studies," *Jewish Social Studies* (n.s.) 1:1 (Fall 1994), 115–143.

159. Compare Seth L. Wolitz and Joseph Sherman, "Bashevis Singer as a Regionalist of Lublin Province: A Note," in Seth L. Wolitz, ed., *The Hidden Isaac Bashevis Singer* (Austin: University of Texas Press, 2001), 219–224.

160. Take, for example, the way the printing press was used to spread anti-Semitic representations of the Jew: see R. Po-chia Hsia, *Trent 1475: Stories of a Ritual Murder Trial* (New Haven: Yale University Press, 1992), esp. 56, and idem, *The Myth of Ritual Murder* (New Haven: Yale University Press, 1988), 46–61. For other comparative examples of this approach, focusing on the business of printing and ideological trends and drawn from a vast critical literature, compare Natalie Zemon Davis, *Society and Culture in Early Modern France* (Stanford: Stanford University Press, 1975), 1–16, 189–226; Henri-Jean Martin, *The French Book: Religion, Absolutism, and Readership,*

1585–1715 (Baltimore: Johns Hopkins University Press, 1996), esp. chapter 1; Martin, *Print, Power, and People in Seventeenth-Century France* (Metuchen, NJ: Scarecrow Press, 1993), esp. 1–123; Chartier *Order* 28–29; Chartier *Cultural* 145–264. On the Jewish context, compare Agnes Romer-Segal, "Sifrut yidish ukehal koreha bemeah hat"z: yetsirot beyidish bireshimot 'hazikuk' mimantova 1595," *Kiryat Sefer* 53 (1978), 779–790; and, for a specific recent example, see Stephen G. Burnett, "German Jewish Printing in the Reformation Era (1530–1633)," in Phillip Dean Bell and Stephen G. Burnett, *Jews, Judaism, and the Reformation in Sixteenth-Century Germany* (Leiden: Brill, 2006), 503–527.

161. A job for the linguists, for example, is to determine precisely the dynamics of how printing resulted in a "supradialectal variety of Yiddish" (Sunshine "Mail" 24–25); see also Kerler, *Origins*, passim.
162. Compare Shmeruk's full study of the comparative versions of the *Tsene-rene* (n. 31 supra) and the comments in Weinreich *Bilder* 50.
163. Compare Zfatman "S" 1:63–69.
164. See, for example, Herbert C. Zafren, "Variety in the Typography of Yiddish, 1535–1635," *Hebrew Union College Annual* 53 (1983), 137–163; and Zafren, "Early Yiddish Typography," *Jewish Book Annual* 44 (1986), 106–119. For comparative discussion, compare Martin *The French Book* 77–86.
165. See, for example, Diane Wolfthal, *Picturing Yiddish: Gender, Identity, and Memory in the Illustrated Yiddish Books of Renaissance Italy* (Leiden: Brill, 2004); note, however, the comments made by Jerold C. Frakes in his review in *Shofar* 24:3 (2006), 156–159.
166. For one example of this process in the Yiddish context, see Chone Shmeruk, "Haiyurim min haminhagim beyidish, venezia shn'g/1593, behadpasot khozrot bidefusei prag bemeah ha-17," *Studies in Bibliography and Booklore* 15 (1984), 31–52.

CHAPTER 2. "ARE YE FANTASTICAL, OR THAT INDEED WHICH OUTWARDLY YE SHOW?"

1. The precise dates of composition and first performance of *Doctor Faustus* are uncertain, but scholars generally assume 1588–1589 for the former, the winter of 1592–1593 for the latter; Alleyn certainly performed the role in a September 1594 production. See David Wootton, "Appendix One: The Date of the *English Faust Book* and of *Doctor Faustus*," in Christopher Marlowe, *Doctor Faustus*, ed. David Wootton (Indianapolis: Hackett Publishing Co., 2005), xxiv–xxvii, xxvii, and Sylvan Barnet, "Marlowe's

Doctor Faustus on the Stage," in Christopher Marlowe, *Doctor Faustus*, ed. Sylvan Barnet (New York: Signet Classics, 2001), 199.

2. Marlowe's play is heavily based on the *English Faust Book*, a 1588–1589 translation of the 1587 German prose volume *Historia von D. Iohan Fausten*. See Wootton xxvi–xxvii for an overview of the issues surrounding the *English Faust Book*'s chronology.
3. See, for just one example, T. McAlindon, *Doctor Faustus: Divine in Show* (New York: Twayne Publishers, 1994).
4. The words "supernatural" and "fictional" demand further analysis, of course; such analysis will be undertaken later in the chapter.
5. Frances Yates, *The Occult Philosophy in the Elizabethan Age* (London: Routledge & Kegan Paul, 1979), 119.
6. Yates *Occult* 115–116.
7. Barnet 200.
8. Cited in John Russell Brown, "*Doctor Faustus* at Stratford-upon-Avon, 1968," in *Faustus*, ed. Barnet, 184–185. Brown adds (186) that "two versions of this story say that the actors themselves fell to prayer and piety."
9. On the aspersion of the theater as a site of demonic activity by its opponents, see Stuart Clark, *Thinking with Demons: The Idea of Witchcraft in Early Modern Europe* (Oxford: Clarendon Press, 1997), 20–23. Note also Armando Maggi, *Satan's Rhetoric: A Study of Renaissance Demonology* (Chicago: University of Chicago Press, 2001), 90–91, which discusses a contemporary's view: "In this sense, it is not inappropriate to state that Satan may be the indirect addressee of a theatrical production ... the play, the stage, the actors, and the audience [may] participate in a performative act that aims to summon the Enemy's presence in the world." It is then uniquely unsurprising that the performance of *Doctor Faustus* would be the performative act nonpareil.
10. Compare Yates 75.
11. Compare Clark *Thinking*, passim.
12. See *OED*, s.v. "visible" and "apparition," which suggests these definitions of becoming apprehensible.
13. On the history of the Wandering Jew in legend and discourse, see R. Edelmann, "Ahasuerus, The Wandering Jew: Origin and Background," in Galit Hasan-Rokem and Alan Dundes, ed., *The Wandering Jew: Essays in the Interpretation of a Christian Legend* (Bloomington: Indiana University Press, 1986), 1–10, 6; *SRH* 11:177–182; and most importantly, the exhaustive survey of traditions and legends in George K. Anderson, *The Legend of the Wandering Jew* (Providence: Brown University Press, 1965), esp. 11–70.

14. See Anderson 106–127, esp. 106 and 113.
15. Anderson 40. The Wandering Jew was not the only "Jewish" "charlatan" to bedevil Christian communities. Elisheva Carlebach, speaking of Jewish converts to Christianity, notes that "[w]hile most were sincere, some were charlatans who became beggars, wandering about pretending to be candidates for conversion from Judaism. After collecting whatever money and gifts were reserved for converts, they would leave town to replay the scam in another locale." *Divided Souls: Converts from Judaism in Germany, 1500–1750* (New Haven: Yale University Press, 2001), 37; see also 43–44.
16. Compare Lorraine Daston and Katharine Park, *Wonders and the Order of Nature, 1150–1750* (New York: Zone Books, 1998), esp. 13–14; see also Bynum *Metamorphosis* 37–75, on a slightly earlier period, esp. 40–42. On "marvels," see particularly Jacques Le Goff, *The Medieval Imagination* (Chicago: University of Chicago Press, 1988), 27–44.
17. See Maggi 77; compare McAlindon 68–69 and Clark *Thinking* 166–167.
18. See the discussion on Faustus and legerdemain below.
19. The heritable markers of things such as "second sight" differ substantially from one cultural context to the next. For the Jewish analogue, see Joshua Trachtenberg, *Jewish Magic and Superstition* (New York: Athenaeum, 1984 [1939]), 134.
20. See the discussion of *Doctor Faustus* below.
21. For an overview of the issues, see Nicholas Brooke, introduction, William Shakespeare, *The Tragedy of Macbeth* (Oxford: Clarendon Press, 1990), 59–64.
22. See Stephen Orgel, "*Macbeth* and the Antic Round," *Shakespeare Survey* 52 (1999), 143–153, repr. in Robert S. Miola, ed., *Macbeth: A Norton Critical Edition* (New York: W. W. Norton, 2004), 345, and Yates *Occult* 148–149, 154–155. Other elements of the play also speak to the supernatural and thus to our theme here—perhaps most notably the critics' characterization of Lady Macbeth's behavior as "a lightly rationalized version of demonic possession." A. R. Braunmuller, introduction to Braunmuller, ed., *Macbeth* (Cambridge: Cambridge University Press, 1997), 20, 33; see also W. Moelwyn Merchant, "'His Fiend-Like Queen,'" in Kenneth Muir and Philip Edwards, ed., *Aspects of Macbeth* (Cambridge: Cambridge University Press, 1977), 51–52. But a full treatment of the supernatural in the play is beyond our scope here.
23. On Holinshed, the only history that we know Shakespeare to have definitely been familiar with, see Brooke introduction 67–71, esp. 69; and Carroll, 118,

124. It is the Holinshed account, in contrast to other historical accounts, which "develops the full-blown account of the three Weird Sisters who confront Macbeth ... with their prophecies"; for the account, see below. By contrast, compare George Buchanan's account of the events in his 1582 *History of Scotland*, where the "three women, whose beauty was more august and surprising than bare women's useth to be" appear only in "a dream which [Macbeth] had." Indeed, Buchanan's entire account imbues the whole story with a note of skepticism: "Some of our writers do here record many fables, which are like Milesian tales, and fitter for the stage, than an history; and therefore I omit them." Buchanan quotes from William C. Carroll, ed., *Macbeth: Texts and Contexts* (Boston: Bedford/St. Martin's, 1999), 130, 133–134 and Braunmuller, 13–15.

24. Samuel Taylor Coleridge perceptively noted that the Weird Sisters "are wholly different from any representation of witches in the contemporary writers and yet presented a sufficient external resemblance to the creatures of vulgar prejudice to act immediately on the audience." (Coleridge, *On Macbeth*, 1808–1819, cited in Miola 219). For a more detailed look at contemporary images of witches, and Shakespeare's conflation of those images, see M. C. Bradbrook, "The Sources of *Macbeth*," in Muir and Edwards, 18–21.

25. See Braunmuller 29–30. Brooke importantly writes that "there is no evidence at all that Shakespeare made use of any of these works," and that these texts should rather be used to "illustrate common beliefs, not to suggest verbal borrowings" (79).

26. On Scot and his writing, see David Wootton, "Reginald Scot / Abraham Fleming / The Family of Love," in Stuart Clark, ed., *Languages of Witchcraft: Narrative, Ideology, and Meaning in Early Modern Culture* (New York: St. Martin's Press, 2001), 119–138, and Carroll 302.

27. Reginald Scot, *The Discoverie of Witchcraft* (London, 1584), Book 1, Chapter 3. I rely here on the excerpt, with modernized punctuation and spelling, by Miola 131–138, quote 136.

28. Scot 1:3; Miola 133.

29. Scot 1:1, cited in Carroll 310.

30. Scot 1:1; Miola 131; also see the excerpt in Carroll 307–310.

31. Scot 1:5; Miola 137; P. G. Maxwell-Stuart, *Witchcraft in Europe and the New World, 1400–1800* (New York: Palgrave, 2001), 101–103, quote 103. See also Wootton, "Reginald Scot," 120–124. On the bounded skepticism of other noted witchcraft skeptics like Johann Weyer (or Wier) and Johann Brenz,

see Maxwell-Stuart *Witchcraft* 100–101 and H. C. Midelfort, *Witch Hunting in Southwestern Germany 1562–1684: The Social and Intellectual Foundations* (Stanford: Stanford University Press, 1972), 36–40.

32. See *News From Scotland* (London: 1592), cited in Miola 138–144; quotes 138, 143.
33. See the selections in Carroll 325–328, quote 325.
34. James I, *Daemonologie* (Edinburgh: 1597), cited in Carroll 328–330. On James' own exposure to, and experience with, witchcraft and witchcraft literature, see Maxwell-Stuart *Witchcraft* 47–51; on the 1604 act, see Robin Briggs, *Witches and Neighbours: The Social and Cultural Context of European Witchcraft*. (London: HarperCollins, 1996), 28–29.
35. Compare, by contrast, James' "reluctant use of his supposed healing powers" over the "King's Evil," or scrofula; compare Kenneth Muir, "Image and Symbol in *Macbeth*," *Shakspeare Survey* 19 (1966), 45–54, repr. Miola, 258; and Carroll 222–226.
36. See *Daemonologie* cited in Miola 144–148, esp. 144. Quote from Maxwell-Stuart *Witchcraft* 50–51.
37. Johnson, *Miscellaneous Observations on the Tragedy of Macbeth*, cited in Miola, 206–207.
38. Cited in Miola 207.
39. Carroll 301.
40. Carroll 306.
41. Orgel 345. Worth noting, too, is that witches, no matter what they represented or stood for, apparently made for crackerjack entertainment and were employed as such; this said, though, contemporary allusions and references suggest that *Macbeth* may have been a fairly unpopular play. See Orgel 348–349.
42. Brooke introduction 1; see also 34–35 on Shakespeare's company's move from a light to a dark theater.
43. Brooke introduction 23.
44. Sight is not the only sense Shakespeare calls attention to in *Macbeth;* Brooke (introduction 35–36) rightly notes sound's importance. Nonetheless, sight is the primary sense activated in the text; comparing the number of appearances of "see" and its respective cognates in *Macbeth* to "sound," "hear" and *their* respective cognates, the ratio is approximately five to one. See *Macbeth: A Concordance to the Text of the First Folio* (Oxford: Clarendon Press, 1971), 96, 183–184, 197. On sound in the contemporary theater and its apperception, compare Julie Stone Peters, *Theatre of the Book, 1480–1880: Print, Text, and Performance in Europe* (Oxford: Oxford University Press, 2000), 159–165.

45. Technically, Macbeth may not actually see the last sight himself, possibly relying on the Messenger's account in 5:5; however, the conversation still revolves around sight (Messenger: "within this three mile may you see it coming"; Macbeth: "If this which he avouches does appear"). If preferable, this "strange sight" may be replaced by Macbeth's vision of "a man not of woman born" in the form of his nemesis Macduff; as we will see, both partake of the same category of perception. Finally, the famously problematic Hecate-related material must be taken into account; for the purposes of our discussion, we will follow the critical tradition treating the material as interpolated. For a full discussion, see Brooke introduction 51–55.
46. A similar taxonomy (though a different analysis) can be found in Brooke introduction 2–6. On perception and the senses in contemporary theater more generally, compare Peters, passim, esp. 148–155.
47. Brooke introduction 23.
48. *Macbeth* may also be the perfect choice for discussion practically as well as thematically, as some critics believe its comparative brevity suggests significant proximity to the performed version. See, for example, Brooke introduction 56 and Orgel 344–345.
49. On the stage direction's "disappointingly vague" nature, and for suggestions as to the possible staging, see Brooke's commentary ad loc, and introduction 4. All line numbers follow Brooke's text, based on the Folio of 1623 with modernized spellings; see his comments on lineation in Brooke, Appendix A, 213–217; for more textual concerns, see Braunmuller 95–96.
50. See Brooke ad loc.
51. Such an explanation may have been particularly plausible to contemporary audiences given *Macbeth*'s setting in Scotland, which was then conceived as a distant land where wonders unavailable to the English public were regularly on display. Compare Holinshed's catalog of Scottish "strange sights" in *The First and Second Volumes of Chronicles* (London, 1587), vol. 2 folios 150–152, 168–176, as cited in Miola 98–113. See also Carroll 276 and Daston and Park 25–27.
52. Compare Holinshed's account: "there met them three women in strange and wild apparel, resembling creatures of elder world ... Herewith the foresaid women vanished immediately out of their sight. *This was reputed at the first but some vain fantastical illusion by Macbeth and Banquo* ... But afterwards the common opinion as, that these women were either the Weird Sisters, that is (as ye would say) the goddesses of destiny, or else some nymphs or fairies, indued [sic] with knowledge of prophecy by their necromantical

science, because everything came to pass as they had spoken." Carroll, 141–142, emphasis mine.

53. That most of this intellectualization is Banquo's, not Macbeth's, is hardly accidental: critical discussion has raged around A. C. Bradley's famed characterization of Macbeth as "an exceptionally imaginative man" (cited in Miola 245–246), some rejecting it (see Brooke introduction 10). Imaginative or no, Macbeth's catalysts are certainly more emotional, less intellectual.
54. Or perhaps they don't: one of the play's many tragedies is that Macbeth already understands, at least in part, the nature of these beings—his ambiguous reference to the witches as "imperfect speakers" at the very beginning strongly implies it—and it is his choice to ignore this construction of their speech that returns to haunt him in the play's end.
55. James I *Daemonologie* (*Works* 1616, 98), cited in Brooke ad loc.
56. See Brooke commentary ad loc.
57. Compare 's Brooke commentary ad loc. This is particularly important given, as Marina Favila points out, that aural hallucinations and perceptions also occur in the play, most famously in the case of the voice Macbeth hears crying that "Macbeth does murder sleep" (2.2.33). See Marina Favila, " 'Mortal Thoughts' and Magical Thinking in Macbeth," *Modern Philology* 99:1 (2001), 14–15.
58. Compare Brooke introduction 4.
59. See Brooke commentary ad loc in 3.4.37. In addition, Simon Forman seems to have seen an actor playing the Ghost at the Globe in 1610–1611; for the account, quoted in full, see Brooke 4, 36, and 234–236. This evidence, as well as a seeming parodic allusion to this scene in Francis Beaumont's *Knight of the Burning Pestle*, written almost immediately after *Macbeth*'s production, where an apprentice enters pretending to be his own ghost (5.1.18–28; see Braunmuller 59–60 and Carroll 151), all add up to fairly convincing proof that an actor played the Ghost. It was only "when Kemble reopened Drury Lane on 21 April 1794 [... that he] omitted a visible Ghost of Banquo and thus initiated a long theatrical and critical debate." Braunmuller 67.
60. That it was the tradition not to use a real dagger *seems* clear from the very beginning, but is made explicit in Thomas Davies' eighteenth-century description of David Garrick's impromptu performance of the scene before the Duke of Parma; see the account in Miola 216. A pamphlet possibly written by Garrick in 1744, *An Essay on Acting*, clarifies further, saying that the actor playing Macbeth "should not rivet his Eyes to an *imaginary* Object, as if it *really* was there, but should shew an *unsettled Motion* in his Eye, like one

not quite awak'd from some disordering Dream ..." which certainly implies the dagger's imaginariness. Cited in Braunmuller 62.

61. Compare Brooke introduction 4.
62. On this prophecy's essentially visual nature, see Maurice Hunt, "Reformation / Counter-Reformation Macbeth," *English Studies* 86:5 (October 2005), 388.
63. See Hunt 388. Unlike the dagger and Banquo's ghost, the apparitions all speak, and speak equivocally. Equivocation played a large role in contemporary political and theological discourse; particularly important here is its relationship to religious fraud and the skepticism it generates. Hunt refers, for example, to the phenomenon of concealed priests speaking prophetically through tubes connected to the mouth of fraudulent icons (see 390).
64. They "look not like th' inhabitants o'th' earth / And yet are on't" (1.3.41–42), they "should be women" but they have beards (45–47).
65. Many critics have noted the specific importance of doubling to *Macbeth:* see, for example, Favila 9–10.
66. For a discussion employing the term in Jewish literary study, see T. A. Perry, "Cain's Sin in Genesis 4:1–7: Oracular Ambiguity and How to Avoid It," *Prooftexts* 25:3 (2005), 258–275. On signs and their ambiguity in a particularly demonological context, see Maggi *Satan* 82–83.
67. Q.v. *OED*, "strange," definitions 8 and 10, for contemporary usages of this word in similar contexts.
68. Robert S. Miola, introduction to Robert S. Miola, ed., *Macbeth: A Norton Critical Edition* (New York: W. W. Norton, 2004), vii–xxi, x.
69. Miola introduction xi.
70. McAlindon 70–72.
71. For some brief background, see Yates *Occult* 119–121.
72. Marlowe may have known Scot's work; see McAlindon 33.
73. This said, Marlowe's mastery of the playwright's structural craft is evident in observing these and other developments throughout the play's action. Compare G. K. Hunter, "Five-Act Structure in *Doctor Faustus*," in Harold Bloom, ed., *Christopher Marlowe's Doctor Faustus: Modern Critical Interpretations* (New York: Chelsea House, 1988), 13–25.
74. Here, I follow Wootton's suggestion (see 34n96) identifying the two figures.
75. On theatricality in *Faustus*, see McAlindon 62–80.
76. On limitations of the devil's knowledge and power within the natural world, see Clark *Thinking* 161–164.
77. The former sense of the word was also in use at Marlowe's time, see *OED* "hot" adj., def. 6c.

78. And even a third option exists: that, like a diabolic version of Schrödinger's cat, the entity's existential (demonological) status exists in an essential state of uncertainty until clarified by the resulting conversation: the resulting toleration of uncertainty (and indeed undecidability) in definition by the audience will play a role in our subsequent discussion of allegory in this and other texts.
79. For another example of Faustus' spectatorship, compare his magical travel from Trier to Rome and his response to the sights Mephastophilis shows him: see 3.1.849–866.
80. Barbara Howard Traister writes that "simple dramatic considerations of what would play to an Elizabethan audience must have been responsible for some of Marlowe's decisions about what sort of magic to show onstage." "*Doctor Faustus:* Master of Self-Delusion," in Harold Bloom, ed., *Christopher Marlowe's Doctor Faustus: Modern Critical Interpretations* (New York: Chelsea House, 1988), 77–92, 91. Much of this chapter is dedicated to exploring—from the textual evidence left behind—how the vagueries in this eminently true observation can be methodologically explicated by a combined application of contextual information and internal analysis.
81. See 4.1.1081–1090. For more on the limits to Faustus' magical powers, see Traister 89–90.
82. See 2.1.453–460; compare the discussion of psychomachia in McAlindon 99–100 and Traister 86.
83. A similar phenomenon may occur with the "old man" appearing in 5.1.1377–1380.
84. On comic elements in *Doctor Faustus* in general, compare McAlindon (86–95), who notes they are "studiously integrated into the play's pattern of meaning" (87).
85. Compare Walter Stephens' perceptive comment that "Bodies, particularly the ones assumed by Mephastophilis and Helen, have been the medium of proof throughout the play." Walter Stephens, *Demon Lovers: Witchcraft, Sex, and the Crisis of Belief* (Chicago: University of Chicago Press, 2002), 353.
86. In the original text, Helen is spelled "Hellen," allowing a visual pun (for readers of the text) and strongly suggesting an aural one, a reading encouraged by the inclusion of the phrase "heavenly Hellen"; see McAlindon 48. In a thematically similar context (about the doubled sense of the word "erring"), McAlindon notes that "conceits and similitudes of this kind were well established in theological discourse and *would presumably have been easily picked up by Marlowe's audience.*" McAlindon 54, emphasis mine.

87. See Wootton 65n59.
88. See Wootton's note, 63n48.
89. Compare Traister 84–85.
90. See Wootton introduction xx.
91. Maxwell-Stuart *Witchcraft* 5.
92. In 3.2. Rafe, a comic figure, comically precedes and prefigures Faustus' actions with respect to both legerdemain and conjuration.
93. Mephastophilis suggests in his first appearance that human control over his appearances is less pronounced than generally believed: see 1.3.291–296.
94. On (in a different context) the "rhetoric of paradox" in *Doctor Faustus*, compare Johannes H. Birringer, "Faustus's Rhetoric of Aspiration," in Harold Bloom, ed., *Christopher Marlowe's Doctor Faustus: Modern Critical Interpretations* (New York: Chelsea House, 1988), 102.
95. Compare on this note Faustus' and Mephastophilis' discussion in 2.3, where Mephastophilis delightedly discourses at length on scientific knowledge related to planetary motion, seemingly representing the contemporary state of Elizabethan knowledge and which would presumably have been so conceptualized by the audience. But when the discussion turns to matters verging on the metaphysical—"Tell me, who made the world?" (2.3.694)—Mephastophilis refuses to answer. The devil, it seems, will only talk science.
96. Compare Wilbur Sanders, "Doctor Faustus's Sin," in Harold Bloom, ed., *Christopher Marlowe's Doctor Faustus: Modern Critical Interpretations* (New York: Chelsea House, 1988), 39. Sanders writes that Faustus' "particular form of skepticism is accompanied by, perhaps derived from, a profound emotional involvement with the ideas he rejects; and if his atheism is superficial, it is superficial because his theism is ineradicable."
97. On the more specific case of Jews in Elizabethan England, see most notably James Shapiro, *Shakespeare and the Jews* (New York: Columbia University Press, 1996), passim; *SRH* 15:132–135; and Yates *Occult* 109–114.
98. Braunmuller 67.
99. McAlindon 38–39.

CHAPTER 3. THE SEYFER MESHOLIM

Epigraphs: Cited in Nelson, 1; *The Gates of Horn* (New York: Oxford University Press, 1963), 26.

1. See Aron Freimann's facsimile edition *Die Fabeln des Kuhbuchs* (Berlin: 1926), viii. The date on the title page, 1687, is an error, as the approbation

makes clear. See also Eli Katz's notes in Moshe Wallich, *Book of Fables: The Yiddish Fable Collection of Reb Moshe Wallich, Frankfurt am Main, 1697*, trans. and ed. Eli Katz (Detroit: Wayne State University Press, 1994), 272.

2. Eli Katz, introduction to Wallich, 9–11; see also Moritz Steinschneider, *Jüdisch-deutsche Literatur (Serapeum, Leipzig 1848–1849)* (Jerusalem: Hebrew University, 1961), 55n212; Zinberg 6:236–240, and Katz, "Das 'Kuhbukh' und das 'Seyfer Mešolim': Die Überlieferung eines mitteljiddischen Textes," *Beiträge zur Geschichte der deutschen Sprache und Literatur* 112 (1990), 81–95. For recent discussion of the dating of the *Ku-bukh* (proposing a possible earlier 1555 date), compare Jerold C. Frakes, ed., *Early Yiddish Texts, 1100–1750* (Oxford: Oxford University Press, 2004, henceforth *EYT*), 415; and Jean Baumgarten, *Introduction to Old Yiddish Literature* (Oxford: Oxford University Press, 2005, henceforth *OYL*), 320–326, esp. 321n94. References here refer to Katz's facsimile edition's pagination and line numbering; translations are generally Katz's, but have frequently been altered to accentuate certain themes or features that necessitate a more literal and less artful translation.
3. A critical edition of the work has appeared; see Moshe N. Rosenfeld, *The Book of Cows: A Facsimile Edition of the Famed Kuhbuch* (London: Hebraica Books, 1984). On the book's provenance and authorship, see Rosenfeld's introduction there (n.p.).
4. See Katz introduction 10–11 and Zfatman "S" 1:98; 2:62n142.
5. The changes suggest that Wallich may have also consulted an even earlier, no longer extant, version of the *Ku-bukh*. Compare Katz introduction 13 and "Überlieferung" 85.
6. See Katz "Überlieferung" 86–95 and introduction 11–12, 19–23, as well as his appendices and critical apparatus (259–302) for substantially more detailed discussion.
7. See Katz introduction 20–22.
8. On authorial approaches to title pages more generally, compare Erik *Roman* 25.
9. A brief reference to the *Ku-bukh* appears (in bold letters) in one of the prefaces (3a.39; see Katz introduction 9); it is in bold letters, so Wallich cannot be charged with *complete* duplicity. Still, one must look deep inside the book to find any evidence of his acknowledgment of the earlier text.
10. On ibn Sahula's *Meshal Ha-kadmoni* and its relation to Eastern fabular literature, see Raphael Loewe, introduction to Isaac ibn Sahula, *Meshal Haqadmoni: Fables From the Distant Past*, ed. and trans. Loewe (Oxford: Littman Library of

Jewish Civilization, 2004), xv–cxxxi, esp. l–lix; Katz introduction 16–17. The work appeared in Yiddish translation several years before the *Seyfer Mesholim*'s publication (Frankfurt a.M. 1693); see A. M. Haberman, "Di yidishe oysgabes fun 'moshel hakadmoyni,'" *Yivo-bleter* 13 (1938), 95–101 and Baumgarten *OYL* 322. The *Meshal Ha-kadmoni* is (at least a) source for fables 26 through 33; for more details, see discussion of the individual fables, though this chapter lacks the space to engage in individual studies of influence.

11. On the *Mishlei Shualim* and its relation to the Aesopian tradition of fable, see Moses Hadas' introduction to his translation: *Fables of a Jewish Aesop* (New York: Columbia University Press, 1967) and, crucially, Haim Schwarzbaum, *The Mishlei Shu'alim (Fox Fables) of Rabbi Berechiah Ha-Nakdan: A Study in Comparative Folklore and Fable Lore* (Tel Aviv: Institute for Jewish and Arab Folklore Research, 1979), esp. xviii–xxx. The *Mishlei Shualim* was translated into Yiddish; see Baumgarten *OYL* 322; Erika Timm, "Zur jiddischen Fabelliteratur des 16. Jahrhunderts," *Proceedings of the Eighth World Congress of Jewish Studies* (1981), C159; and now, for a modern edition and detailed introduction to the Freiburg 1583 edition, Jutta Schumacher, ed., *Sefer Mišle Šu'olim (=Buch der Fuchsfabeln) von Jakob Koppelmann* (Hamburg: Helmut Buske Verlag, 2006), esp. xi–xiii.

12. See Katz introduction 10 and Erika Timm, "Die 'Fabel vom alten Löwen' in jiddisticher und komparatisticher Sicht," *Zeitschrift für deutsche Philologie* 100 (1981), 109–170, 158–164. For each tale's particular source, see introduction 16.

13. Compare Katz introduction 13, 16.

14. For biographical information on Wallich (d. 1739), see Freimann, vii–viii and, more recently, Daniel J. Cohen, "An Autographic Letter by Moshe Wallich, Author of the KUH-BUCH: The Key to his Biography and Family Connections in Worms, Frankfort, and Hamburg," *Studies in Bibliography and Booklore* 14 (1982), 4–16. Wallich's father was a rabbi and the director of almsgiving in Worms, and there were connections to the Luria family through his mother's side; it would be surprising were he not to have had significant Jewish education.

15. See Katz introduction 15, 17; Eli Katz, "Dos ku-bukh: mekoyrim un baarbetung," *Yidishe kultur* 5/44 (1982), 7; and Febvre (254), who notes that fifteen German editions of Aesop's fables alone were printed in Germany before 1500.

16. On the typographical errors in the books' titles—examples of errors in typography of Hebraisms in contemporary Yiddish books more generally—see Katz 272.

17. On this last point, see Katz "Ku-bukh" 6.
18. Katz introduction 22; R. Joseph Samuel (d. 1703) served as rabbi of Cracow, then subsequently (during the time of publication) as rabbi of Frankfurt am Main. See Katz 272 for more details. On monopolies and restrictions on publication in the early modern world more generally, see Febvre 159–163, 239–244.
19. See L. Fuks, "*Dos ku-bukh*," *Di Goldene keyt* 118 (1985), 181; Haberman, "Oysgabes," 95; Timm, "Fabelliteratur"; Schwarzbaum, i–iv. A detailed comparison of the *Seyfer Mesholim* and the Yiddish versions of the two Jewish sources is beyond our scope here.
20. The *Seyfer Mesholim* actually contains two works titled *Hakdome* (conventionally translated "Introduction"); the first (2a–3a) is an address to the reading audience, and the second (3b) an invocation to God for success in the book's writing and sales. To avoid confusion, I refer to the former as "introduction" and the latter as "invocation" throughout the chapter.
21. *Akyr* (for amen, ken yehi rotzon), 1a.15.
22. As with many acrostics, the first letters' bolded typography helps illuminate the feature, but still necessitates some understanding of the form's conventions. Compare Katz's comments on 272–273 on both this acrostic's conventional nature and the resulting changes from the *Ku-bukh*'s preface which, in Katz's words, "often involve reordering of lines and replacing the first word in a line with a substitute bearing the desired initial letter, *frequently result[ing] in obscuring the meaning*" (272–273, emphasis mine).
23. Note that the mathematical calculations are improperly done. See Katz 272.
24. *EYT* 751.
25. Allusions and Hebraisms are not the only kinds of textual quotations that allow us into that reading community's canon of knowledge: the moralist occasionally uses a proverb (*shprikh vort*), presumably a contemporary one, to illustrate his point, possible evidence for the dissemination of that particular proverb; see, for example, 16a.140–141. For a discussion of proverb in fable, compare Pack Carnes, ed., *Proverbia in Fabula: Essays on the Relationship of the Proverb and the Fable* (New York: Peter Lang, 1988).
26. This knowledge may be surprisingly expressed and bounded, though; as we have seen, the seeming misspelling of some Hebraisms may indicate unfamiliarity with Hebrew writing, at least on the printer's part. See n. 16 above, and note the misprints of *metsie* (6b.21) and *azus ponim* (39b.189–190).
27. Katz introduction 15.
28. The introduction has a notably different (and more challenging) rhyme scheme containing internal rhyme, which can be rendered aaab/cccd/eeed/fffb.

29. See, for example, the description of the fabliau as possessing a "secondary orality" in Mary Jane Schenck, "Orality, Literacy, and the Law," *Reinardus* 8 (1995), 65. Compare Ruth Webber, "The *Cantar de mio cid:* Problems of Interpretation," in John Miles Foley, ed., *Oral Tradition in Literature: Interpretation in Context* (Columbia, MO: University of Missouri Press, 1986), 65–88, esp. 69–72, and Christopher Hutton, "Early Yiddish Texts and Western Yiddish Dialectology," in Dovid Katz, ed., *Dialects of the Yiddish Language* (Oxford: Pergamon Press, 1988), 23.
30. Indeed, some stories' and dialogues' length (like that of the city mouse and the country mouse in 13a.70–140) seems intended primarily to illustrate authorial virtuosity; but displays of virtuosity are only meaningful if they are communally and contextually so understood.
31. If not perceived as a conventional pose, the invocation may be viewed as a remnant of the oral versions of such stories, since any oral performer, even had the story been completed and told many times before, could reasonably invoke God's assistance in this particular telling.
32. This trope also occurs at the beginning of several other fables; see 17b.1–2; 24b.1–2; 33b.1; 35a.1; 42b.1.
33. 6b.34–35, reading (as Katz does) "Abonai" as a version of God's name to prevent its being taken in vain; see also Katz 277.
34. The terminology of authorship is particularly difficult to apply to a text where one could (and perhaps, optimally, should) differentiate between, at a minimum, the author of the fables, the author of the morals attached to those original fables, the hand (if different) that stitched these together into a particular printed text, the *Ku-bukh*, and Wallich's reshaping hand. Interpretive agendas and ideological or textual viewpoints may apply to some, not all, of these levels differently at different points. For some clarification, I use "moralist" in referring only to the writer of the epimyth, whose texts must be considered differently than those of the "narrator" or "fabulist," referring to the teller of, or author of, the fable section of the text. "Wallich" is only used to refer to materials specific to (or the specific versions of earlier materials in) the *Seyfer Mesholim*. "Author" and its various forms is a looser, more catch-all term employed when the point potentially or actually transcends several of these entities.
35. For a more preliminary discussion of ideology in the fable, focusing on readerly acceptance rather than interpretation and skepticism, compare Susan Suleiman, *Authoritarian Fictions* (New York: Columbia University Press, 1983), 45–54.

36. Compare Frakes (*EYT* 415–416), who notes that the *Ku-bukh* has eighty-three woodcuts in sixty-seven folios. On woodcuts more generally, see Febvre 45–49, 90–93.
37. See Katz 272. Katz has also noted (13) that the "woodcuts of [*Seyfer Mesholim*] were actually traced from [the *Ku-bukh*] and reproduced in reverse (left to right) as dictated by the limited technology then available." In other contemporary illustrated texts, the process of reprinting or reproduction often introduces a change in image placement which generates aesthetic dissonance; see, for example, the discussion of the woodcuts in the 1526 edition of the Prague Haggadah in Lazarus Goldschmidt, *The Earliest Illustrated Haggadah* (London: Bamerlea Book Sales, 1940), 33–36. Our discussion of the images here will focus primarily on the final product as readers encountered it and as the author released it, and the potential effect on those readers and their author.
38. See Booth *Rhetoric* 101.
39. Famously, Jewish historic attitudes towards the visual arts are far more complex than the rejectionist attitude often suggested. See Steven Nadler, *Rembrandt's Jews* (Chicago: University of Chicago Press, 2003), 73–76; Kalman Bland, *The Artless Jew* (Princeton: Princeton University Press, 2000), esp. 74–76, 141–153; Elliott Horowitz, "The People of the Image," *The New Republic*, Sept. 25, 2000, 41–49; and Abrahams *Jewish Life* 146–147.
40. The word *bayshpil* could also profitably be translated as "exemplum" or "example," but given the work's generic nature, I have chosen, following Katz, to maintain the translation of "fable."
41. See Frances Yates, *The Art of Memory* (Chicago: University of Chicago, 1966), 82–104.
42. Both possibilities beg the question of articulating criteria by which the artist/author/editor determined the particular scenes within a narrative to be illustrated. Compare Beatrix Zumbült, "Approaching the Medieval Illustration Cycles of the Fox-Epic as an Art Historian: Problems and Perspectives," *Reinardus* 15 (2002), 191–204; and Chartier, "General Introduction: Print Culture," in Chartier, ed., *The Culture of Print: Power and the Uses of Print in Early Modern Europe* (Princeton: Princeton University Press, 1987), 5–7.
43. Cited in Manguel 101. For more on convention's role in artistic representation and interpretation, compare E. H. Gombrich, *Art and Illusion: A Study in the Psychology of Pictorial Representation* (London: Phaidon, 1977 [5th ed.]), 21, 53–59, 162–163, 199–200.

44. Compare Manguel's discussion of the fifteenth-century *Bibliae Pauperum* in *History of Reading* 103. Manguel also discusses preachers' embroidery on, and retelling of, textually narrated material, as well as readers' multiple hearings (and presumably reinterpretations of) the material over their lifetimes.
45. On this phenomenon, compare Peters 183–185, 194–196.
46. Compare, for example, the two images of the dog scrutinizing his reflection on 6a and 6b.
47. On captions' role more generally, see Gombrich 60–61.
48. Additionally, the captions also occasionally omit what some readers might consider the essential active detail of the picture; at the beginning of the eighteenth fable, the woodcut depicts a wolf on a throne stretching out his staff, and the staff goes unmentioned in the caption (21b). Such "omission" may of course suggest a reorientation of our current perspective about what seems central and tangential; as a result, our awareness of the dissonance of the choices on which we base our interpretation must always keep in mind the historically contextualized position of our judgments of that dissonance.
49. On size in medieval art, see Gombrich 248.
50. Irksomeness may be beyond the artist's capacities, but he can at times rely on other visual features to aid interpretation: take, for example, the almost (though not quite) identical expressions on the lazy servant and good servant's faces (54b–55a); what instead informs readers of their emotions and their identity is their conventional, stylized body language according with the narrative facts (the lazy servant is apparently kneeling, hands clasped together beseechingly; the righteous servant is standing, bowing, and clasping the king's hand). The artist seems more skilled at depicting stasis than action, setting than figural posture.
51. On Jewish clothing and differentiation in a slightly earlier period, compare Abrahams *Jewish Life* 291–306 and Diane Owen Hughes, "Distinguishing Signs: Ear-Rings, Jews and Franciscan Rhetoric in the Italian Renaissance City," *Past and Present* 112 (Aug. 1986), 16ff.
52. On Jewish familiarity with the trope of cuckold's horns as early as the thirteenth century, see Davidson *Parody* 14.
53. Examples are widely varied, but include types of food eaten, such as kreplekh and almond rice (4b.43–44); mentions of places, such as Florence (9b.47), the Po River (30b.1), and Venice (30b.12); specific punishments of the time, such as hanging and cutting of the ear (9b.48–49, see also 28b.135–137); methods for storing food (12b.47), catching mice (13a.118–120),

and hunting (20b.70–82); and even details concerning contemporary pet ownership (29b:37–38).

54. This reminds us, in a different context, of the argument over the "ethos of the fabliau": do fabliaux, for example, "demonstrate the insufficiency of language as representation," or are they "evidence for the history of medieval sensibility"? See Mary Jane Schenck, "The Fabliau Ethos: Recent Views on its Origins," *Reinardus* 1 (1988), 121.
55. See also Baumgarten *OYL* 326.
56. Compare Katz introduction 18.
57. See Erika Timm, *Yiddish Literature in a Franconian Genizah* (Jerusalem: Akademon Press, 1988), 38.
58. Katz introduction 16–17.
59. On the genre, its form, and its conventions more generally, compare B. E. Perry, "Fable," in Pack Carnes, ed., *Proverbia in Fabula* (New York: Peter Lang, 1988), 65–116, esp. 74–75, 99–100; for an interpretive approach to fables inflected by reader-response theory, compare Sandra K. Dolby-Stahl, "Sour Grapes: Fable, Proverb, Unripe Fruit," in Carnes *Proverbia* 295–309, esp. 296–297, 300–302.
60. Compare, for example, 49b.137, where a man is referred to as "ravenous as a dog."
61. Compare 39a.149.
62. One example is his transformation of the lion's fear of the mouse into a perfectly legitimate phenomenon: the lion's fear in the narrative results from his startled wakening by the mouse scampering over his body.
63. The moralist, however, is less definitive about viewing this as simply a matter of human agency, suggesting perhaps God has brought this about; see 29a.162–165.
64. Compare Bynum *Metamorphosis*, esp. 18–21, 25–28, for a brilliant overview of the issues in a slightly earlier period.
65. For the *Meshal Ha-kadmoni*'s version, see III:415–580.
66. In the words of one critic, "From its beginnings [the genre of the fable] has been almost exclusively a masculine one—a means of transmitting patriarchal wisdom and culture." Harriet Spiegel, "The Male Animal in the Fables of Marie de France," in Clare A. Lees, ed., *Medieval Masculinities: Reading Men in the Middle Ages* (Minneapolis: University of Minnesota Press, 1994), 111.
67. See Katz introduction 18.
68. Significant scholarship exists on medieval Jewish misogyny and its relation to women's simultaneous definition as paragons of virtue and piety. For

some discussion on this in the Spanish Sephardic context, see Tova Cohen, "Sexual Politics in a Medieval Hebrew Marriage Debate," *Exemplaria* 12:1 (2000), 157–184, esp. 162.

69. The story itself appears as early as Petronius' *Satyricon*, in the form of the Matron of Ephesus; compare Baumgarten *OYL* 325 and Schwarzbaum 394–417. On this charge in medieval and early modern society generally, particularly as attributed to older women and widows whose sexual appetite has already been awakened by their husbands, see Anne Llewellyn Barstow, *Witchcraze: A New History of the European Witch Hunts* (San Francisco: Pandora, 1994), 137, and Joan Ferrante, *Woman as Image in Medieval Literature* (New York: Columbia University Press, 1975), 6–7.

70. This discussion of sexuality necessitates some brief comments on that sexuality's presentation, that is to say, on vulgarity. Critics have noted that the genre of *fabliau* in Old French literature "holds the distinction of focusing repeatedly, even obsessively, on the body ... fabliau tales of conjugal unrest speak openly, often crudely, about human genitalia and their various functions in the sex act." E. Jane Burns, "This Prick Which is Not One: How Women Talk Back in Old French Fabliaux," in Linda Lomperis and Sarah Stanbury, eds., *Feminist Approaches to the Body in Medieval Literature* (Philadephia: University of Pennsylvania Press, 1993), 188. Cultural porosity operates in this context as well: explicit sexual reference to sexual and bodily functions are hardly unknown in pre- and early modern Jewish writing, perhaps most notably the ninth- or tenth-century *Alphabet of Ben Sira*, which was "translated and published in a number of shortened Yiddish versions" from 1610 on (Daniel Boyarin, *Unheroic Conduct: The Rise of Heterosexuality and the Invention of the Jewish Man* [Berkeley: University of California Press, 1997], 98). The *Alphabet*'s fables of ravens inseminating their mates through the mouth and nonkosher animals having sex with other animals' parents and wives "conceal fantasies of oral sex and forbidden unions by displacing them onto unclean animals ... The audience is permitted an outlet for its erotic imagination, but the outlet is safe since the stories contain the appropriate normative criticisms of deviant practices" (David Biale, *Eros and the Jews: From Biblical Israel to Contemporary America* [Berkeley: University of California Press, 1997], 84). In the *Seyfer Mesholim*, though, the potentially pagan, sexual, and animalistic promise of the author's introduction—which swears to the book's uniqueness by asserting that "Nothing like it, I swear to you by a goat's head, beard, and knee / Ever came before your eyes" (3a.36)—yields to a far tamer set of sexual

references than in some of its medieval Jewish and non-Jewish predecessors, including even the *Ku-bukh* (see Frakes *EYT* 750). A number of references to tails or tail feathers (for which the word employed is *shvantz*), their length, and their forcible removal leads to potential phallic puns (see, for example, 8b.39, 11b.66, 25a.58, 36a.100), and occasionally there are mentions of scatologically inappropriate words like "shit" (*bashisn*, 34a.88) or "piss" (*bazaykhn*, 34b.121). Even the more explicit depictions of sexual activity are comparatively demure: the adulterous pair is depicted in bed together with covers over their bodies (43a), and the text's description of their activity—"they lay together all night. A bit longer and they would have made a baby" (42b.39–40)—titillates without being vulgar. Such demureness more easily allows the material's presentation as a pietistic text.

71. In fact, the story states that as a result everyone "excuses" her for her behavior! Cf. 24b.78–79.
72. The wife, in her boasts to her lover that it is precisely her husband's virtue and piety that permit her sinful behavior (his long hours at prayer allow opportunities for rendezvous), mentions his pious refusal to look at women, certainly implying a lack of sexual fulfillment on her part (42b.34–36). Matters only worsen as the man's pious behavior increases: his frequent absences for the penitential prayers surrounding the high holidays (46b.375) simply allow greater opportunities for adulterous behavior.
73. Compare the discussion on cynicism and worldly wisdom between the ram and the goat after the fable's presentation in the *Meshal Ha-kadmoni* (II:138–491, esp. 407–453, 477–491).
74. Compare Pack Carnes' important comments about the fable's polysemous nature in "How Phaedrus' Fables 'Mean': Notes on Aesop in a Contextual Model," *Reinardus* 13 (2000), 49–53.
75. Cited in Katz introduction 10.
76. Katz introduction 24n30.
77. The fables in the *Seyfer Mesholim* are not given titles in the work, though they are always prefaced by captioned woodcuts; for convenience's sake, I generally use Katz's titles for reference. On other versions of this fable, compare Schwarzbaum 269–272.
78. Notably, the language of repayment, often repeated in the book (see 5a. 101–102) is, in Yiddish as in English, evocative of actual commodity and commercial transaction (*fargeltn*), again according with the economic mindset we have identified. See also 4b.50, where *tsoln* is used in the sense of "repaying you for your meal," which has overtones of both commerce and vengeance.

79. This is not to imply, however, that such concepts were not internalized into the Jewish culture. Shame, for example, has its own chapter in an important contemporary moral text, *Orkhot Zaddikim*; see Seymour Cohen, ed. and trans. *The Ways of the Righteous* (New York: Ktav, 1982) esp. 77. For another example of shame's featured role in the text, see fable 26, the fable of the peasant and the scribe, where the scribe's appeal to the peasant to change his behavior is predicated on displaying shame; see 31a.145–155, 32b.258, 262.
80. Compare this to earlier versions of the fable, where the pursuing animal is a leopard; see Schwarzbaum 502–504.
81. Cf. Deut. 22:3.
82. As Katz points out (Critical Apparatus 279), the sixth fable lacks an explicit epimyth, appending only a statement that "this fable is similar to the preceding one which you have read before" (8b.53), presumably referring to the fable of the raven and the fox (second in our version, not fifth). This provides internal evidence, before the *Ku-bukh*'s rediscovery, of Wallich's reordering the tales from an earlier source. It also proves the original editor's sense of internal consistency and characterization—and that Wallich, in his reordering (incomplete as it sometimes was; he failed to change this epimyth, after all), chose to ignore these structures. Our attempt here is to suggest other ordering structures Wallich may have found more compelling, suggesting issues crucial to him and his assumed and intended reading community.
83. Economic issues are hardly limited to the Jewish context: for a (very different) treatment of the role of money in the fabliaux, see An Smets, "De la maille à la livre et de l'amour au commerce: le rôle de l'argent dans les fabliaux," *Reinardus* 12 (1999), 173–188.
84. For a possible historical source for such eventuality in the fable's earlier Spanish context, see Loewe introduction xcvi–xcvii.
85. To take just one example: immediately after the *melamed* concludes his long speech to the peasant about his duties, we learn the peasant has been paying it almost no heed, choosing instead to attend to his donkey (31b.126–127).
86. Lack of space here, for example, prohibits a full investigation of how hypocrisy in general, and in the form of religious observance more specifically, accords with our schema of essential natures and their temporary masking of or deception of same; wit and trickery's role in leading to those essential natures' revelation; and the conceptual prominence of reward/repayment (*lon*, 42a.462–463) and public shame (which catalyzes the old man's decision to hang himself after the ruin of his public reputation). Similarly, compare

also the fable of the greedy innkeeper (31), where the hypocrisy is portrayed as a dynamic process: the innkeeper's seeming honesty allows him to lure customers regularly to his inn, where he pads their bill outrageously. The bill's presentation leads to the disappointing reminder of humanity's deceitful aspect: but, paradoxically—and key to the narrative structure of deception-related fable—such deception is only useful for knowledge upon its revelation, when it ceases to become deceitful by definition.

87. The resulting readerly positioning as a woman can be fruitfully compared to our previous discussion of reading reception and gender.

88. Note in this vein the telling comparison of the lion to a figure that has "lost his way" (9a.7).

89. For extensive studies of the more famous earlier version, see Hans Peter Althaus, *Die Cambridger Löwenfabel von 1382* (Berlin: Walter de Gruyter, 1971), esp. 33–45, and Timm " 'Fabel,' " esp. 152–164. Compare Fuks' comments: his analysis of the fable's unusual features suggests to him that the composition's inspiration lies in a particular incident in Egypt; see xxiv–xxv. Leo Fuks, *The Oldest Known Literary Documents of Yiddish Literature (c. 1382)* (Leiden: E. J. Brill, 1952, 2 vols), 1:xxiv. Compare also Schwarzbaum 1–4.

90. The identical lesson—reliance on the divine—is given by the moralist after the next (twelfth) fable, that of the donkey held in partnership, and a similar fable and lesson occurs later: the seventeenth fable, the fable of the lion and the mouse.

91. For some different considerations on the classic Jewish fable and politics more generally, compare Schwarzbaum vii–xi.

92. On international versions of the fable and its political relevance, compare Paul Franklin Baum, "The Fable of Belling the Cat," in Pack Carnes, ed., *Proverbia in Fabula* (New York: Peter Lang, 1988), 37–46.

93. Such a reading depends on an interpretation of the fable where the squabbling mice are various poor folk, unable to unite in coherent strategies of opposition against a wealthy and powerful figure: alternatively (or complementarily) the fable can be viewed as rich and poor squabbling with one another, unable to achieve unanimity in the face of an external threat.

94. On the "celebration of quick-wittedness" in this and related genres, with the concomitant recognition of its occasional result in moral problems, compare Schenck "Fabliau" 127–128.

95. Note the usage of *shpotn*, for example, in 18a.96. Other stories also have examples of the trickster tricked, or mockery redounded onto one's own head: take, for example, the story of the murdered Jew and the partridge,

where the servant's clever use of doubled language, such as his statement to the king about the murdered Jew that "he has already gone to his resting place" (cf. 27b.71–74) shows a deceptiveness in turn deceived later in the narrative. Compare 28b.122, 125.

96. See esp. 19a.50–52 (page misnumbered as 16 in original edition); but also 19a.40 and 19b.72, 76, 79.

97. On the importance of oaths in early modern culture, compare Peter Rushton, "Texts of Authority: Witchcraft Accusations and the Demonstration of Truth in Early Modern England," in Stuart Clark, ed., *Languages of Witchcraft: Narrative, Ideology, and Meaning in Early Modern Culture* (New York: St. Martin's Press, 2001), 24.

98. See Katz Critical Apparatus 301.

99. Compare, for example, the New Testament's parable of the talents (Matthew 25:14–30).

100. See, for just one of many examples, BT Sanhedrin 91a.

CHAPTER 4. THINKING WITH SHEDIM

1. Stuart Clark, *Thinking with Demons: The Idea of Witchcraft in Early Modern Europe* (Oxford: Clarendon Press, 1997), 10.

2. Walter Stephens, *Demon Lovers: Witchcraft, Sex, and the Crisis of Belief* (Chicago: University of Chicago Press, 2002), 29.

3. See Zfatman *Bibliografiya*, item 3c (manuscript). This story (MS 12.45 Trinity College Cambridge fols. 2y4r–31r) also appears in transliteration in Sara Zfatman, *Nisuei adam vesheda: gilgulav shel motiv besiporet haamamit shel yehudei ashkenaz bemeot ha16–19* (Jerusalem: Akademon, 1987), 119–127 (modern transcription), 149–163 (facsimile of manuscript), and is translated in Joachim Neugroschel, *The Dybbuk and the Yiddish Imagination: A Haunted Reader* (Syracuse, NY: Syracuse University Press, 2000), 118–123. Translations are Neugroschel's, very occasionally altered to bring out certain literal aspects of the work for analytic purposes. On the work in general, see Zfatman *Nisuei* 19–65, on the manuscript and its dating, see 19–22.

4. In Yiddish, *zoyne*; in the Hebrew, simply *isha*.

5. See n. 87 *infra* for bibliographic information. The *Kav ha-yoshor*'s first edition was solely in Hebrew; the second and most subsequent editions were bilingual. I have employed Neugroschel's translations, changing certain details to reflect literal features important for analysis. Neugroschel's

translations are from the Yiddish; I have also, at times, reflected meanings that are gleaned from a complementary analysis of both versions.

6. On Christian concerns linking masturbation with demonic copulation as early as the fifteenth century, see Stephens *Demon* 69–70.
7. Neugroschel 115.
8. This is not to say, of course, that there were no concerns in the medieval and early modern period—from both sides—about what Salo Baron referred to as "mixed mating." See *SRH* 11:77–87, esp. 80–81.
9. See Norman Cohn, *Europe's Inner Demons: The Demonization of Christians in Medieval Christendom* (Chicago: University of Chicago Press, 1993 rev. ed.), 16–19; citation from 17; for a full discussion of the earlier history of demonic copulation and corporeality, see Stephens, passim, esp. 58ff.
10. On the notion of female roaming as demonic from earliest times, see Tikva Frymer-Kensky, *In the Wake of the Goddesses: Women, Culture, and the Biblical Transformation of Pagan Myth* (New York: The Free Press, 1992), 28, 67–68. See also Jacob Lassner, *Demonizing the Queen of Sheba: Boundaries of Gender and Culture in Postbiblical Judaism and Medieval Islam* (Chicago: University of Chicago Press, 1993), 27, 32.
11. The fullest discussion of the role of demons in the Talmudic and post-Talmudic era remains Joshua Trachtenberg, *Jewish Magic and Superstition* (New York: Athenaeum, 1984), esp. 25–60. Compare BT Khulin 105b (where the discussion is framed in economic terms); BT Temurah 14b; and a story of demon visitation in BT Meilah 17b, also related to possession (the Tosafists refer to the demon here as a *lantukh*).
12. See Cohn 24–26 and Trachtenberg *Magic* 30–31.
13. Cohn 31.
14. Stories about incubi begin to proliferate in the twelfth century, though mentions exist as early as the ninth century. See Cohn 31–34 and Stephens *Demon* 23.
15. See, among many other sources, H. C. Midelfort, *Witch Hunting in Southwestern Germany 1562–1684: The Social and Intellectual Foundations* (Stanford: Stanford University Press, 1972), 182–184. Compare also Clark *Thinking* 130–131 and Anne Llewellyn Barstow, *Witchcraze: A New History of the European Witch Hunts* (San Francisco: Pandora, 1994), 138–139.
16. See chapters 1, 2, and 5 for a more detailed discussion of this topic. On skepticism about the existence of demons in the fourteenth century and beyond, see Stephens *Demon* 74–75 and Midelfort, esp. 14–27.
17. See Stephens *Demon* 7.

18. Compare Vern L. Bullough, "On Being a Man in the Middle Ages," in Clare A. Lees, ed., *Medieval Masculinities: Reading Men in the Middle Ages* (Minneapolis: University of Minnesota Press, 1994), 31–45, esp. 41.
19. See Cohn (113 and esp. 211), who cites accounts as early as the tenth century connecting a man's impotence with a new sexual partner to bewitchment from the previous one. Compare also Bullough 42.
20. See Daniel Boyarin, *Carnal Israel: Reading Sex in Talmudic Culture* (Berkeley: University of California Press, 1993), 95–96 for this and other discussion of midrashic demons. On Lilith, see also Theodor H. Gaster, *The Holy and the Profane* (New York: William Sloane, 1955), 18–28; Trachtenberg *Magic* 36–37; Lassner 4, 33; and, for a more cross-cultural perspective, Diane Purkiss, *At the Bottom of the Garden: A Dark History of Fairies, Hobgoblins, and Other Troublesome Things* (New York: New York University Press, 2001), 33–34.
21. Compare Pollack 18; David Biale, *Eros and the Jews: From Biblical Israel to Contemporary America* (Berkeley: University of California Press, 1997), 84; Joseph Dan, "Samael, Lilith, and the Concept of Evil in Early Kabbalah," *AJSReview* 5 (1980), esp. 23–25, 39; and a fuller discussion of the medieval context (though drawn primarily from the Sephardic sphere) in Tova Rosen, *Unveiling Eve: Reading Gender in Medieval Hebrew Literature* (Philadelphia: University of Pennsylvania Press, 2003), 12–13, 181–182. The most developed general treatment of these issues is still Erich Neumann, *The Great Mother: An Analysis of the Archetype* (New York: Pantheon, 1963, 2nd ed.); see his discussion of the goddess as either the Great Mother or the Terrible Mother on 38, 148.
22. See Robin Briggs, *Witches and Neighbours: The Social and Cultural Context of European Witchcraft* (London: HarperCollins, 1996), quote 31, and Clark *Thinking* 71–73, 84–87, quote 71. With regard to the maternal aspects particularly, see Briggs 243 and Karen Newman, *Fashioning Femininity: Femininity and English Renaissance Drama* (Chicago: University of Chicago Press, 1991), 58.
23. The most thorough study of this Christian phenomenon remains Trachtenberg, *The Devil and the Jews* (see, e.g., xv, 6, 11–31); see also Cohn 20 and Trachtenberg *Magic* 1–2, 9–10. On the demonic image of the Jew as well as other anti-Semitic tropes in the Polish commonwealth period, see Janusz Tazbir, "Images of the Jew in the Polish Commonwealth," *Polin* 4 (1989), 18–30, esp. 18–20. One can imagine that this constant identification of Jews and devils on the part of the Christians led to a self-identification (in an ironic

or parodic way) with the demonic side of things. This may, however, be primarily a phenomenon of the modern period.

24. For general details and sources, see Zfatman *Nisuei* 11.
25. See his discussion in *Hasipur haivri biyemei habeinayim* (Jerusalem: Keter, 1974), 95–99. "The Tale of the Jerusalemite" can be found in David Stern and Mark J. Mirsky, eds., *Rabbinic Fantasies: Imaginative Narratives from Classical Hebrew Literature* (New Haven: Yale University Press, 1990), 123–142. For discussion of the tale and some of its contemporary parallels, see Tamar Alexander, "Theme and Genre: Relationships Between Man and She-Demon in Jewish Folklore," *Jewish Folklore and Ethnology Review* 14 (1992), 58 and Zfatman *Nisuei* 12–13.
26. Dan's discussion of the unique Judaic elements (*Hasipur* 98) does not precisely focus on these issues of inversion or mimesis, nor does the discussion in Zfatman *Nisuei* 35.
27. Compare Dan *Hasipur* 97–98. On later demonological texts—particularly in the work of the *Hasidei Ashkenaz*—see 170–176 and Dan, "Sipurim demonologiyim me-kitve R. Yehuda Hasid," *Tarbiz* 30 (1961), 273–289, esp. 277.
28. See Zfatman "S" 1:108–109, 119.
29. See Zfatman's discussion in "S" 1:94.
30. J. H. Chajes, *Between Worlds: Dybbuks, Exorcists, and Early Modern Judaism* (Philadelphia: University of Pennsylvania Press, 2003), 3. Compare Pollack 16.
31. In fact, the period (mostly the second half of the sixteenth century) saw the rise of the "devil book" as a genre; these works either showed how a particular human vice was devilish, or gave analyses of the devil's or his servants' power. See Midelfort 69–70, quote 69.
32. Compare Zfatman "S" 1:94 and her extensive discussion in Zfatman *Nisuei* 13, 32–40.
33. For the fullest discussion of the sources of the tale, Jewish and non-Jewish alike, and their development within the story, see Zfatman *Nisuei* 41–65; compare Zinberg 6:164, which attests to the tale's popularity on "the Jewish street." The tale may also be a variant of Jean d'Arras' extraordinarily popular 1393 *Mélusine de Lusignan*, which itself is a variation on the story of Amor and Psyche. In *Mélusine*, the woman tells the husband never to seek her company on Saturdays, or to learn where she goes then. For a full discussion, see Williams *Dominion* 23–44.
34. Historically, this might relate to anxieties provoked over the intrusion of Sephardic conceptualizations of the limitations of Rabbenu Gershom's ban

making their way into Ashkenazic territory in the preceding decades; for a discussion of the general phenomenon in more detail, see Elimelech Westreich, "The Ban on Polygamy in Polish Rabbinic Thought," *Polin* 10 (1997), 66–84, esp. 66–68.

35. By referring to the town in these terms, the text refers to the well-known legend, appearing in the *Mayse Nisim*, that the city of Worms was actually founded by King David. But the learned reader may also remember the midrashic story concerning Jesse: namely, that he was one of the four individuals that did not sin. In this sense, then, the narrator, with a few well-chosen words, is already combining the mythic past with the sense of a moral golden age. On the later printed history of the *Mayse Nisim*, see L. Fuks and R. G. Fuks-Mansfeld, *Hebrew Typography in the Northern Netherlands* 1585–1815 (Leiden: E. J. Brill, 1987), 2:398–399. See also Erik *Geshikhte* 58–59 and Zfatman "S" 1:35–36, 146–149.

36. Compare Zfatman *Nisuei* 62–63. This said, if Zfatman's assumptions about the story's provenance are correct, that it was written in northern Italy for, presumably a northern Italian audience, it may have been that few of the individuals actually addressed were aware of the geographical details of Worms. On the real—rather than the imagined—Jewish Worms more generally, see Fritz Reuter, *Warmaisa: 1000 Jahre Juden in Worms* (Frankfurt a.M.: Athenäum, 1987). It is interesting in this light that later, the rabbi's son makes a match with the daughter of a community leader of Speyer, another of the three great medieval German Jewish towns, along with Mayence; as is well known, the three towns entered not only into historical record, but mythopoesis as well, signs of a golden age of Jewish history and learning, complete with martyrological endpoints. As such, what seems to be historical authenticity is perhaps better portrayed as an appeal to collective memory of Jewish sanctuarial idealism under threat from some outside force—though what exactly that force may be remains to be determined. Additionally, such narratorial fidelity depends in actuality on not only shared knowledge about geography and history, but also shared psychological presuppositions about the way in which individuals behave, presuppositions which yield the groundwork for the extension into the realm of the fantastic.

37. On the attraction in medieval folklore to liminal states, compare Purkiss *Garden* 60.

38. The Talmudic origins of the holiday, which refer to the stoppage of the plague that killed tens of thousands of the students of Rabbi Akiva, are also testament to this view of the day.

39. For discussion of the practice of Lag Ba'omer as a pastoral day, see Julian Morgenstern, "Lag Ba'Omer—Its Origins and Import," *Hebrew Union College Annual* 39 (1968), 81–90. Such a presentation of nature in this fashion may remind us of the idea, common in Renaissance demonology, that the devil is much more connected than angels are with nature, and much more capable of understanding and reading nature's signs (and then hopes to annihilate them); see Armando Maggi, *Satan's Rhetoric: A Study of Renaissance Demonology* (Chicago: University of Chicago Press, 2001), 41–42.
40. Such embodiment might remind us that the demon itself is a liminal being, on the borders between angel and human, bound to human laws of "sex, sustenance and death"; unbound to conventional rules of law. See Alexander "Theme" 56. For this reading's similarities to folkloric structures more generally, compare V. Propp, *Morphology of the Folktale* (Bloomington, IN: Indiana University Research Center in Anthropology, Folklore, and Linguistics, 1958), esp. 24–32.
41. One might add another convention of the horror story: it was well known in the Jewish community that the occasion of marriage (as, indeed, any joyful life cycle occasion), left individuals particularly vulnerable to demonic attack. On this phenomenon, see Trachtenberg *Magic* 47–48 and Jacob Z. Lauterbach, "The Ceremony of Breaking a Glass at Weddings," *HUCA* 2 (1925), 351–380, esp. 355–361. On Worms wedding customs relating to marriage and death (including the groom's donning a mourner's hood the Sabbath before the wedding), see Pollack 35–38.
42. Though the text clearly characterizes it as a prank, the decision of the rabbi's son to play this specific prank obviously calls out for analysis. The expression of incipient homoerotic tendencies in the son's desire to marry Anshel, even in jest—one of the few decisions the son actively makes in the entire narrative—throws a certain light on the difficulties that the son will have later in consummating and maintaining his marriages: in such a reading, the she-demon who he marries may also be symbolic of what was, to the contemporary Jewish community, a kind of aberrant sexuality that interposed between the schoolboy and his absorption into the norms of the traditional heterosexual community. Compare Chanita Goodblatt, "Women, Demons, and the Rabbi's Son: Narratology and 'A Story from Worms,'" *Exemplaria* 12:1 (2000), 241–242. Goodblatt notes the homosexual element but interprets it very differently.
43. Goodblatt deemphasizes the son's passivity in her presentation of the rabbi's son as another somewhat active fairytale hero (though she acknowledges

that he falls into the paradigm of the passive husband); see 239–240. In doing so, however, and accentuating that parts of her reading depends on actions that "do not explicitly appear in the story" (239), she creates a different image of the audience: while both Goodblatt and I acknowledge the importance of defining the audience by their ability to fill in "gaps of information" (241), Goodblatt's sophisticated audience attempts to smooth over puzzles and narrative cruxes by abstracting them to the general convention. Conversely, I choose to focus here on the act of interpretation of the story as it exists, which features divergence from the convention as extrusive, noticeable, and puzzling, and fill in the gaps by treating those extrusive details as significant—in much the same way that audiences would have been familiar with the midrashic hermeneutic (regardless of if they could read midrash in its original form), which bestows great interpretive significance on material that diverges from the norm.

44. Of course, there is no way she could have known the *reason* for their deaths, but this is not what she says.

45. The word used here, *meyn vushen*, is somewhat unclear; Goodblatt, translating it as "my shame," explains in a note that this also alludes "to the importance in Orthodox Judaism till today, of covering a married woman's hair. In addition, the use of the word shame in an expansion of its sexual connotations can also refer to pubic hair" (n.18). For earlier connections between female hair, sin, and the otherworld in rabbinic literature, see Saul Lieberman, "Sins and Their Punishment," in idem, *Texts and Studies* (New York: Ktav, 1974), 43. Neugroschel's translation of the phrase as "my feet," while tempting, given the long-standing tradition, among Jews and non-Jews alike, to assign the ineffaceable sign of demons' essence to their feet—a point which, as we will see, attains significant thematic importance in this reading—seems unfortunately a less likely reading. On demonic feet and their connection to Jews, compare Sander L. Gilman, *The Jew's Body* (New York: Routledge, 1991), 39; more generally, see Stephens *Demon* 95 and Purkiss *Garden* 36–37.

46. Goodblatt, passim; her article also includes a translation of the story (247–253). While I share many of Goodblatt's approaches, our readings and conclusions highlight different aspects of the stories, and thus reach certain different conclusions.

47. See Zfatman *Nisuei* 39; her conclusion is juxtaposed to the explicit moral ending of the "Tale of the Jerusalemite" and seems also based on her perspective that the "crimes" here—if there are any—must be related to the son's "transgressive" act.

48. See Pollack 29–32; Katz *Tradition* 116–122; and Goodblatt 256.

49. This is not to say, of course, that the rabbis were unmindful of the nexus of desire, marriage, and social control. The question is simply whether we may see this *in this particular case* as the primary, or a complementary, discourse within the tale and its reading as a whole. On complementary or multiple morals within the folk or fairy tale structure, compare Maria Tatar, *The Annotated Classic Fairy Tales* (New York: W. W. Norton, 2002), xiv–xv.

50. For a significant discussion of this and parallel stories as manifesting concern over "frivolous marriages" (*kiddushei hitul*), see Biale 66–67. On the topic, see also Zfatman 62n2; Goodblatt 232; Dan (*Hasipur* 96), who cites the earlier, non-Jewish tale of Caesarius of Heisterbach, and on Jewish betrothal more generally, Gaster *Holy* 64, 81–89, 127–128.

51. This is not to say that such passivity is impossible to account for at all in a reading focusing on the erotic nature of the text: it might simply focus, for example, on the self-abnegating masochistic nature of the individual with problematic affect towards patriarchal structures. Compare the discussion in Daniel Boyarin, *Unheroic Conduct: The Rise of Heterosexuality and the Invention of the Jewish Man* (Berkeley: University of California Press, 1997), 83.

52. It may be a significant sign of the parents' selfishness, reflecting outward into the norms of the text in general, that the son himself is never named: he is merely an outgrowth of the parents, an extension of their ego.

53. The forgetting of the ring, however, and metonymically of the first uncanny encounter, may allow us some considerations as to the text's horizon of expectations, as well as to answer another minor narrative concern. Such considerations are themselves dependent on the ambiguity surrounding who precisely is doing the forgetting (the text itself is in the passive voice, and refers only to the ring itself, not to the events surrounding the forgetting of the ring). The parents' forgetting of the ring may be more natural, given that they may have never been informed of the full nature of the encounter (we do not know what the rabbi has been told; compare Goodblatt 243); and so they rightly face the story's uncanny later circumstances—the brides' deaths—with a certain confusion. The son's amnesia, however, given the circumstances, seems less explicable. Three complementary suggestions may be advanced. First, a naturalistic, psychologized explanation that revolves around the suppression of traumatic or disturbing experiences. Such an explanation would accord with the son's general passivity, mentioned above. The second possibility is that the child assumed that this

occurrence was not uncanny at all, but had a perfectly natural explanation, and only realized later (if at all) the true nature of the encounter. This second point, however, depends on the shared assumption of storyteller and readers alike that (either "objectively" or within the conventions of this genre) it is *not* reasonable to encounter a she-demon in the woods. This gives rise to the third explanation: that encounters with supernatural forces are sufficiently unremarkable that they require no comment whatsoever, and, indeed, can be forgotten like anything else. This is not to suggest that it is wise to forget them, and indeed, as we see, the forgetfulness redounds to the detriment of the family and of the rabbi's son. But given that this is a fantastic world in which they live, it may be possible to suggest that one can regard this as merely a normal encounter within the sphere of normal encounters. I mean to suggest that these interpretations do not exist independently of one another, but the amorphous qualities of knowledge and ignorance, of memory of the primal uncanny situation and forgetting it, come together to create another kind of liminal space, the one that was at hand in all of the "fantastic" older Yiddish literature: one that teetered on the cognitive boundary between accepting the supernatural and one that rejected it.

When I use the phrase "supernatural," incidentally, I am also suggesting a blurry, cognitive distinction between types of folk and popular superstition that had common European roots (belief in which was shared by the local non-Jewish populace) and internal Jewish traditions of supernatural entities. For example, it seems fair to suggest at least the theoretical possibility that the Jews had a different affect towards, say, local sprites, naiads, and dryads (i.e., to make the point clearer in relation to this story, tree-spirits) than they do towards the archangels Gabriel and Michael or Elijah the Prophet. This is not to say that they didn't believe in the former; clearly, the preponderance of evidence (of which this story provides no little part) seems to suggest that they did. I only suggest that the ambivalences within this story seem to reflect a kind of cognitive differentiation, inchoate though it may be, between these two strata of fantastic or uncanny materials. If so, we may have a complex system of binary oppositions where the she-demon represents not only aberrant sexuality, women's empowerment, the dangers of wealth, and the fantastic in general, but a specific kind of fantastic or magical power.

54. It is noteworthy how the ebbs and flows of this part of the story so startlingly resemble the ebbs and flows of fortunes, and of capital: after the

bride's burial, rumors spread that the groom killed the bride, and so the rabbi's son remained unmarried for three years, "for no father wanted to risk his daughter's life." Eventually, a rich community leader related to the family allows his daughter to marry the rabbi's son, but she too dies at the she-demon's hands on the wedding night, and subsequently, "for some ten years the groom stayed put, unable to find another bride." (120) Were the rabbi's family a company, one could practically chart its stock price: starting off sky-high, then a sudden fall through a crisis in investor confidence (based, incidentally, on faulty analysis or false rumor), a slow climb back to a relative high, then another sudden drop, which subsequently plateaus.

55. On Jewish sumptuary legislation and the moral problematization of rich clothing, compare Pollack 86–88.
56. Luce Irigaray has developed a sustained examination of the connections between the commodified woman, aggressive sexual and economic jealousy, and monetary anxiety: compare Luce Irigaray, *This Sex Which Is Not One* (Ithaca: Cornell University Press, 1985), 32.
57. For a tradition connecting demons with trees within Judaism, see Trachtenberg *Magic* 34; compare also Neumann 241–253.
58. Strangulation is not limited to Jewish tales of demonic copulation: in one story from 1628, a female demon who has had sex with Johannes Junius turns into a goat after copulation, which then " 'bleated' that it would break Johannes' neck unless he renounced God." Stephens *Demon* 5.
59. It is not insignificant that the two murdered brides come from wealthy families; as such, they are implicated in the critique broadly as well as narrowly.
60. Cited in Trachtenberg *Magic* 155–156.
61. On issues of the stratification of Jewish society and the free choice that existed in theory against the lack of upward mobility in practice, see Biale 63; Abrahams *Jewish Life* 43–44, 321–323; Katz *Out of the Ghetto* 21–22; and Katz *Tradition* 36–42, 173–179; with specific reference to Worms, see Stow *Alienated* 165–166.
62. The choice of language here is significant, as the wife—whose plan this was in the first place—may, in her own way, be more monstrous than the she-demon. In fact, one might argue that the she-demon serves as a kind of demonic doubling of the mother, the nightmare side of Jewish society's images of women. For a treatment of woman's doubling in later Jewish literature, see Nechama Aschkenazy, "Women and the Double in Modern Hebrew Literature," *Prooftexts* 8:1 (1988), 113–128, esp. 113–115. See also Frye *Secular* 117.

63. A standard version of this standard phrase is *beavonoteinu harabim*, "because of our great sins." In this case—and the manuscript writer takes great pains to vowelize this text—it says *beavonot harabim*, "as a result of great sins." This may be another standard variant, but it may also illustrate the mother's inability to take moral responsibility for her actions.
64. We have no details on the cause of the poor family's poverty in the text; we are told, however, that they are highly moral and from a good family, and though these words come from the highly unreliable rich *rebbetsin*, their actions hardly seem to contradict these statements.
65. Zfatman does not call attention to the text; Goodblatt does (236) but cites it only in the form of its original Talmudic dictum, and does not employ it—or these specific strategies of allusion—as part of her interpretive schema. However, its operation within the world of midrashic narrative is by far the most compelling.
66. See Rashi to Genesis 29:11.
67. See especially Genesis 33:1–4. For a very different discussion of the typological meanings of the passage, see Amos Funkenstein, *Perceptions of Jewish History* (Berkeley: University of California Press, 1993), 110–111.
68. Certainly, both Jacob and Esau understand it in this fashion; regardless of whether Esau subsequently believes that he received a good deal in selling his birthright for a mess of pottage, the text clearly indicates his acquiescence to the concept that the birthright can be sold.
69. Certainly, this is the understanding that Jacob has of the affair in Genesis 32:14ff, when he hears that Esau is coming to meet him with four hundred men. His response is not merely to pray to God for salvation, but to send a significant financial gift to Esau. (It may also be noteworthy that in this paradigmatic story, Jacob is also concerned about Esau as a sexual predator as well, hiding Dinah in an ark so that she not be seen by him. (See Rashi to Gen. 32:22.) This continuation of the connection between commodification and sexualization of the Jacob/Esau encounter is obviously present in our tale, where the she-demon is a wife as well as golden.) Parenthetically, such a reading, where the she-demon is Esau and the wife is Jacob, puts the husband into the allegorical place of the birthright. This not only makes sense in terms of the role he seems to represent as the unwritten future of the Jewish people, but also explains his somewhat puzzling silence and sleeping throughout the text; as a symbol of a symbol, an allegory even within this allegorical work, he doesn't get to talk.
70. This satisfaction, expressed only after Jacob's offer, may stem from the same psychological understanding that we have ascribed to the she-demon:

once he knows of the possibility of his control, he doesn't need to get more money.

71. See Rashi to Gen. 33:4 and Bereshit Rabbah ad loc. This motif of the "homicidal kiss," besides this midrashic source, also importantly figures in the "Tale of the Jerusalemite," where the she-demon, claiming she wishes to kiss her husband, instead kills him. For a discussion of the latter (which does not mention Jacob and Esau), see Dan *Hasipur* 99.

72. In this sense, our heroine reminds us of the empowered figures in later women's fiction who, as Nancy Miller writes, "transcend the perils of plot with a self-exalting dignity"; see "Emphasis Added: Plots and Plausibilities in Women's Fiction," in Elaine Showalter, ed., *The New Feminist Criticism: Essays on Women, Literature, and Theory* (New York: Pantheon Books, 1985), 346–347.

73. While one could argue that the story itself self-consciously illustrates the seductive power of its own critique by falling prey to the norms it hopes to abjure—that is, the decision to valorize the wealth of the girl, to make the happy ending a variation on the "rags to riches" approach, shows how seductive the wealth lure can be—a more detailed approach can be advanced. Compare Zfatman (*Nisuei* 39), who considers the ending simply as a literary flourish, as a result of her recognition of the difficulty of drawing a moral example from the poor girl's behavior.

74. On this category of the "rise tale" within folk and fairy tale literature—as opposed to the "restoration tale," which "revolve[s] around social position lost through misfortune and restored by goodness, perseverance, courage, or magic," see Ruth B. Bottigheimer, *Fairy Godfather: Straparola, Venice, and the Fairy Tale Tradition* (Philadelphia: University of Pennsylvania Press, 2002), 1–2, 5, 13–17, 27–32, quote 1. Bottigheimer traces the development of the "rise plot" to mid-sixteenth-century Italy, almost precisely the time and place of our tale's composition, and her linkage of the tales to the economic aspirations of a "passive and powerless sixteenth-century urban apprentice and artisan readership" may have intriguing comparative resonances for our work, which also features a "magic-mediated marriage as an imaginary escape from the all-too-real miseries of poverty" (17). On Joseph Campbell's intriguing characterization of the "tyrant-monster" as "avid for the greedy rights of 'my and mine' " and conversely the hero as "the man of self-achieved submission," see his *Hero with a Thousand Faces* (New York: Pantheon, 1949), 15–16.

75. Sexual imagery abounds in the passage as well: "*Noting where he had left his keys, she took them and unlocked the door.* But her husband wasn't in the

chamber. She searched every nook and cranny. At last, under the bed she found a large rock. *As she spotted it, the rock moved from its place. She now saw a large hole with a ladder descending inside it.* The wife thought to herself, 'Dear God, should I go down? I'm sure my husband is down there.' *After pondering for a long time, she finally climbed down the ladder*" (122, emphasis mine). The phallic symbolism of the key and the lock and the fact that the passage to this other, demonic world is reached through the bedroom, under the bed, passing through a large hole, speak for themselves: note, however, that the woman, as the penetrator, is acting in (reversed) male terms here. Compare also Neumann 158–159, Propp 46, and, on the dreamlike nature of this and similar journeys to the lower world, Northrop Frye, *The Secular Scripture* (Cambridge, MA: Harvard University Press, 1976), 99. On the complex spatialization of the demonic otherworld in rabbinic literature, compare Saul Lieberman, "Some Aspects of After Life in Early Rabbinic Literature," in Saul Lieberman, *Texts and Studies* (New York: Ktav, 1974), 237–238.

76. Similarly, her reward is characterized not only by excellence in wealth but by excellence in that most essentialist of women's traits—in the sense that it definitionally only applies to women—maternity (explaining, at almost precisely the same moment as the statement about curiosity, the seemingly parenthetical statement that the woman had three sons).
77. On Cinderella stories, see Tatar 28–43.
78. One might also speculate on the voyeuristic or erotic pleasure taken here in subservience and simply observing the couple together, a pleasure certainly frowned on by traditional authorities; on the Talmudic prohibition against having anyone else watch an act of sexual intercourse, see BT Niddah 16b–17a and Boyarin *Carnal Israel* 125–126. Compare also a case from the responsa literature discussed in Fram *Ideals* 53.
79. See BT Kiddushin 49b.
80. The idea that the transformation is accomplished through the supernatural medium is a common motif, although often through positive or at least ambiguously positive supernatural figures. Compare Purkiss *Garden* 114, 221.
81. Compare Katz's discussion of the nuanced contemporary Jewish attitudes towards wealth and poverty in *Tradition* 58–60.
82. On Bluebeard and his unfortunate wife more generally, compare Tatar xiii, 145–157; particularly its moral that "Curiosity, with its many charms, can stir up serious regrets" (156), and the location of the forbidden space in a lower spatial area (here, the ground floor, 151).

83. On *structural* repetition in the work more generally, of which there is a great deal, see Goodblatt 235; and compare Zfatman (*Nisuei* 27–29), who deals with the work's separate (and interlocking) motifs.

84. Goodblatt has importantly made a distinction between sophisticated and naïve readers of the tale (see 234–235) and one can see how that distinction, in light of our understanding of the tale, can be developed even further. Her statement, "it is the naïve reader, following the closely delineated path of the narrative, who accepts the conventional norms of Jewish piety, while it is the sophisticated reader, whose interpretive powers are shifted onto the larger context, who challenges the explicit moral lesson stated at the story's end," may lead to the conclusion that the differentiation between naïve and sophisticated readership is contingent on the recognition of ironic and subversive moves within the tale. Such recognition is inherently difficult to quantify from the audience's side, and possibly dependent on a previous assessment of these readers as subversive from a pietistic viewpoint, which threatens a certain circularity. And, given that her apparent reason for the author's ironic move is largely a general ludic sense of subversiveness, it seems hard to transform a generalized perception of the author's view of his audience into a more concrete set of criteria.

85. This is a literal translation, with the intent of bringing out certain analytic points.

86. See Rashi ad loc.

87. The story appears in *Seyfer Kav ha-yoshor* 2:69 (Frankfurt a.M.: 1706), and is briefly treated in Trachtenberg *Magic* 52–54. Facsimile and modern transliteration are found in Zfatman *Nisuei* 168–171 (facsimile), 131–137 (transliteration); a translation can be found in Neugroschel, 115–117. On the *Kav ha-yoshor*, see Frakes *EYT* 848–849; Baumgarten *OYL* 236–246; Baumgarten, "Between Translation and Commentary: The Bilingual Editions of the *Kav hayosher* by Tsvi Hirsh Kaidanover," *Journal of Modern Jewish Studies* 3 (2004), 269–287, esp. 272–273, 278–279; Joseph Dan, *Sifrut hamusar vehaderush* (Jerusalem: Keter, 1975), 243; and Y. Soses, "Tsu der sotsialer geshikhte fun yidn in lite un vaysrusland," *Tsaytshrift* 1 (1926), 1–24, esp. 15–23. On the book's actual, original authorship and its sources, compare A. Tcherikover, "Di geshikhte fun a literarishn plagiat," *YIVO Bleter* 4 (1932), 159–167. For discussion of the particular story, see Zfatman *Nisuei* 82–102.

88. This detail appears only in the Yiddish version.

89. In the Yiddish: *on zera kayma*. The reference to "seed" is important, given the warning against masturbation in the moral (*motsi zera levatole*).

90. On the long-standing trope of demonic infestation of houses in Jewish demonology, compare Trachtenberg *Magic* 33.

91. Within contemporary Jewish culture, though, this type of demonic activity would have been more closely characterized of that as a *lantukh:* on this creature, see the discussion in Zfatman *Nisuei* 87n3.

92. Compare Zfatman *Nisuei* 100.

93. Literally, "that her husband was not behaving with her as a man does with his wife." On women's requirements in the Talmud for receiving sexual satisfaction, see Biale *Eros* 54 and Boyarin *Carnal Israel* 143–146; compare BT Ketubot 61b ff and BT BM 84a.

94. A long-standing debate existed in contemporary witchcraft theory about whether a succubus could, indeed, become impregnated. Such a debate seems not to have been as prominent, if indeed it appeared at all, in Jewish sources. Compare P. G. Maxwell-Stuart, *Witchcraft in Europe and the New World, 1400–1800* (New York: Palgrave, 2001), 33–34.

95. Compare Alexander "Theme" 59.

96. Some critics have wished to suggest that the she-demon stands for non-Jewish erotic appeal, and thus the tale also warns against intermarriage. Though intermarriage goes unmentioned in the moral, the demons' ultimate dismissal with the phrase "you are half-demons *and not part of the people of Israel*" suggests that it is possible in this story to present the she-demon mother in a more alienating light than in the *Mayse fun Vorms*, where the question of children and identity—a question which powerfully revolves around questions of intermarriage—is at best significantly muted.

97. On historical references in the story, compare Zfatman (*Nisuei* 96–99), who marshals evidence to assert the perceived authenticity and wide dissemination of the story in contemporary times. It might be added that later generations of readers—even ones within the same general structure of belief—could treat these various factors differently than contemporary ones who had outside authenticating forces of the type Zfatman cites.

98. See the discussion in Baumgarten *OYL* 237–248. The book's "original" author, Yosef of Dubno, was apparently known as a distinguished kabbalist, particularly interested in Lurianic kabbalah. See Tcherikover "Plagiat" 164.

99. The phrase is Scholem's. See Gershom Scholem, *On the Kabbalah and Its Symbolism* (New York: Schocken, 1965), esp. 99. See also Frakes *EYT* 849.

100. Biale 110. See also Alexander "Theme" 57. For more on the treatment of demons in the Lurianic period, compare Mijal Oron, "Sobre el Carácter de

Samael (Del Mite al Símbol)," in Ron Barkai, ed., *Curs la cabala* (Barcelona: Fundació Caixa de Pensions, 1989), 75–83.

101. See Zfatman *Nisuei* 94. Zfatman's suggestion that the author may have had theological and mystical reasons for refusing to change details of the text, or that, considering the text authentic at the time, he didn't wish to change it because this would have engendered skepticism (101–102), could certainly be taken into account as well.

102. Compare Zfatman *Nisuei* 88; on the role of inheritance and its connections to witchcraft accusations, see Briggs *Witches* 245–246. For the Jewish population of contemporary Poznan, see Fram *Ideals* 21–22 and the sources cited there.

103. Compare Trachtenberg *Magic* 52–54.

104. Cited in Baumgarten *OYL* 236–237. Soses' largely economic discussion of the *Kav ha-yoshor*, almost to the exclusion of all other elements, can be traced at least in part to the time and place of the article's publication in an early Soviet journal; compare Soses, passim.

105. The tale is printed in Zfatman *Nisuei* 128–130 (modern transcription), 164–166 (facsimile). For discussion, see 69–81.

106. See Zfatman *Nisuei* 72–73.

CHAPTER 5. THE ALLEGORICAL SPIRIT

1. For a more developed sketch of this theoretical structure with reference to literature of the later Jewish Enlightenment—a literature which nonetheless shares certain features with older Yiddish literature—see Jeremy Dauber, *Antonio's Devils: Writers of the Jewish Enlightenment and the Birth of Modern Hebrew and Yiddish Literature* (Stanford: Stanford University Press, 2004), chapter 2.
2. For an English translation, see "The Dybbuk, or Between Two Worlds: A Dramatic Legend in Four Acts," in S. An-sky, *The Dybbuk and Other Writings* (New Haven: Yale University Press, 2002 [1992]), ed. David Roskies, 1–49.
3. See, recently, the essays in Matt Goldish, ed. *Spirit Possession in Judaism: Cases and Contexts from the Middle Ages to the Present* (Detroit: Wayne State University Press, 2003), and J. H. Chajes, *Between Worlds: Dybbuks, Exorcists, and Early Modern Judaism* (Philadelphia: University of Pennsylvania Press, 2003), esp. 57–96.
4. See Matt Goldish, preface, in Goldish *Spirit Possession* 11–19; quote 11–12.
5. Compare Chajes *Between* 58–65. On the development of exorcisms and "prescriptive texts that invoke a variety of significant deities and powers to

expel spirits," see Jonathan Seidel, "Possession and Exorcism in the Magical Texts of the Cairo Geniza," in Goldish *Spirit Possession* 73–95, esp. 74–75.

6. A clear distinction between *dybbuk* and *ibbur* appears in Tamar Alexander, "Love and Death in a Contemporary Dybbuk Story: Personal Narrative and the Female Voice" in *Spirit Possession* 310–311. On *ibbur*, its role in thirteenth-century mysticism, and its relation to the rapidly increasing acceptance of reincarnation, particularly as a punishment, see Chajes *Between* 15.
7. On the *maggid* or angelic mentor, compare Lawrence Fine, "Purifying the Body in the Name of the Soul: The Problem of the Body in Sixteenth-Century Kabbalah," in Howard Eilberg-Schwartz, ed., *People of the Body: Jews and Judaism from an Embodied Perspective* (Albany: SUNY, 1992), 124–127, and Chajes (*Between* 28–29), who describes it as "a regularized, positive form of spirit possession with clear Iberian roots" (29). On other types of spirit possession among Jews, such as the Moroccan *aslai* or the Ethiopian *zar*, compare Bilu, "Dybbuk, Aslai, Zar" passim.
8. I will use the term *dybbuk* through this chapter, though, as Joseph Dan notes, the term only gains popularity after its use as the title of An-sky's famous play; the relevant contemporary term was *ruach*, as evident from our main work's title. Joseph Dan, introduction to *Spirit Possession* 27–28. On the meaning of *dybbuk* as cleaving or sticking, see Yoram Bilu, "The Taming of the Deviants and Beyond: An Analysis of *Dybbuk* Possession and Exorcism in Judaism," in *Spirit Possession* 69.
9. On the exception seemingly proving the rule—an eleventh-century account of spirit possession in the *Megilat Ahimaaz* which itself parallels BT Meilah 17b—see Chajes *Between* 3n12; compare more generally Chajes *Between* 11–13.
10. Dan introduction 28–30, 32–36, quote 28. For a more detailed discussion, compare Menachem Kallus, "Pneumatic Mystical Possession and the Eschatology of the Soul in Lurianic Kabbalah," in *Spirit Possession* 159–185, esp. 160–167.
11. Dan introduction 29. See also Bilu "Taming" 42–43 and Chajes *Between* 16.
12. See Dan introduction 35; Matt Goldish, "Vision and Possession: Nathan of Gaza's Earliest Prophesies in Historical Context," in *Spirit Possession* 226; and Fine "Purifying" 127–136.
13. See Dan introduction 35; Roni Weinstein, "Kabbalah and Jewish Exorcism in Seventeenth-Century Italian Jewish Communities: The Case of Rabbi Moses Zacuto," in *Spirit Possession* 239–240, 242–251; and Chajes *Between* 1–2; quote from Chajes *Between* 4. On the Islamic context, compare Dan

introduction 35 and Chajes (*Between* 6–7), who locates Safed's transformation into a "proverbial melting pot" in light of the Ottoman conquest of 1517. For more on the relationship between dybbuk accounts and witchcraft narratives, see below.

14. We should, however, keep in mind Weinstein's dictum that in reality—rather than representation and imagination—the "entrance of alien spirits into the body remained a numerically insignificant phenomenon." Weinstein "Kabbalah" 252.
15. On Safed in the sixteenth century and its role as a center of kabbalistic learning, see Fine, "Purifying" 122–136; J. H. Chajes, "City of the Dead: Spirit Possession in Sixteenth-Century Safed," in *Spirit Possession* 124–158 passim; Biale, *Eros and the Jews*, 114–118; and Lawrence Fine, "Benevolent Possession in Sixteenth-Century Safed," in *Spirit Possession*, 101–123, quote 102.
16. Fine, "Benevolent" passim; see esp. 117, and Bracha Sack, "Some Remarks on Prayer in the Kabbalah of Sixteenth-Century Safed," in Roland Goetschel, ed., *Prière, Mystique, et Judaïsme* (Paris: Presses Universitaires de France, 1987), 179–186 passim.
17. Chajes "City" 126. Dan's conclusion (introduction 35), that the phenomenon may be seen "as a particularly vivid case of cultural hybridity borne of the confluence of Christian, Islamic, and ancient Jewish traditions" seems apt; in our discussion in this chapter of a later, eastern European tale composed in the eastern European Jewish vernacular, we may have cause to privilege more prominently and justifiably the European aspects than the undoubted other components of this hybrid phenomenon. On hybridity with respect to the supernatural more generally, compare Bynum *Metamorphosis* 30–31, 126–127, 151–161.
18. Cited in Chajes "City" 125.
19. Chajes "City" 124.
20. Chajes *Between* 28. See also Biale 114–117.
21. See discussion in Chajes *Between* 17–21.
22. Cited in Chajes *Between* 22.
23. Cited in Chajes *Between* 13–14.
24. On Vital's exorcisms more generally, see Chajes *Between* 101–115; see also Zfatman "S" 1:34–35.
25. Chajes *Between* 84.
26. See Chajes *Between* 13–14, 71–85, quote 84.
27. See Goldish "Vision" 221–222, 228.
28. Chajes *Between* 90 and "City" 132. On the Christian context, see Stephens *Demon* 323. Chajes ("City" 130–131) walks a careful line between authenticity

and dissonance in cases of such "speech automatism," citing H. C. E. Midelfort's famous analysis of the 1605 demonic possession of a Silesian girl as an example. He writes: "On the one hand, possession accounts were written by learned writers and were crafted accordingly ... the theologically learned arguments that the devil pursued ... were so complex that 'any reader is bound to conclude that Seiler was composing not only his own lines but the Devil's, too.' On the other hand, threats to defecate in the pastor's throat until he became hoarse 'have the ring of spontaneous reporting.' "

29. Chajes "City" 136; for discussion, see 136–144; Chajes *Between* 45–55; and Morris Faierstein, "*Maggidim*, Spirits, and Women in Rabbi Hayim Vital's Book of Visions," in Goldish *Spirit Possession* 186–196 passim.
30. On hagiographic literature in this context, see Dan introduction 30–32; Bilu 63; and Alexander 317.
31. See Gedalyah Nigal, *Sipurei dibuk besifrut yisrael* (Jerusalem: 1994 [2nd ed.]) passim; idem, "Hadibuk bemistika yehudit," *Daat* 4 (Winter 1980), 77–78; Chajes "City" 127–128; Chajes *Between* 25–27, 35; and Faierstein "Maggidim" 187.
32. See Faierstein "Maggidim" 193. For a list of seventeenth-century dybbuk tales in Yiddish, see Zfatman "S" 1:186.
33. See Chajes "City" 129 and *Between* 37–44.
34. Chajes *Between* 36, 118. For more on Menasseh ben Israel and his collection, see Chajes *Between* 120–138 and the sources cited there.
35. See Alexander Altmann, "Eternality of Punishment: A Theological Controversy within the Amsterdam Rabbinate in the Thirties of the Seventeenth Century," *Proceedings of the American Academy for Jewish Research* 40 (1973), 1–88. Nadler connects the debate to the noted heretic Uriel da Costa, whose first *cherem* was issued against him in 1618 by virtue of, inter alia, his denial of the soul's immortality (*Rembrandt* 104–115, 191–197).
36. See Joseph Dan, "Manasseh ben Israel's *Nishmat Hayyim* and the Concept of Evil in Seventeenth-Century Jewish Thought," in Isadore Twersky and Bernard Septimus, eds. *Jewish Thought in the Seventeenth Century* (Cambridge, MA: Harvard University Press, 1987), esp. 69–72, and Chajes *Between* 127–129, 133–136, quote 136.
37. Chajes *Between* 127–129.
38. See Dan "Nishmat" 66 and Chajes *Between* 133–135, quote 135.
39. Chajes *Between* 123, 125.
40. The best and most detailed account of the Lurianic mystical texts, 'ideas,' and tropes' translation and popularization into Yiddish and their circulation within

the eastern European context remains Jean Baumgarten, "Textes mystiques en langue yiddish (xviie–xixe siècles): Les traductions des *Shivhei Hayyim Vital* et *Shivhei ha-Ari*," *Kabbalah: Journal for the Study of Mystical Texts* 2 (1997), 65–103. On the particular popularization of Lurianic stories of possession and transmigration, see esp. 76–77, 80–84, 96–97, and esp. 85, where Baumgarten discusses versions of Lurianic legends appearing in Prague around 1665, at almost precisely the time and place of our story's composition.

41. Chajes "City" 128, esp. nn.35–36, 135–136, *Between* 36; Zfatman "S" 1:186–190. For more on the Mayse-bukh, see: Astrid Starck, "Erzählstrukturen in der frühen jiddischen Prosa," in *Jiddische Philologie*, eds. Walter Röll and Simon Neuberg (Max Niemeyer Verlag: Tubingen, 1999), 157–174; Jakob Meitlis, *Das Ma'asehbuch: Seine Enstehung und Quellengeschichte* (Berlin: 1933); Bernard Heller, "Beiträge zur Stoff-und Quellengeschichte des Mas'asehbuchs," in *Occident and Orient: Festschrift M. Gaster* (London: 1936), 234–243; Erika Timm, "Zur Frühgeschichte der jiddischen Erzählprosa: Eine neuaufgefundene Maíse-Handschrift," *Beiträge zur Geschichte der deutschen Sprache und Literatur* 117 (1995), 243–280; Sara Zfatman, *Hasiporet beyidish mereshita ad shivkhei habesht*, 1504–1814 (Jerusalem: Hebrew University, 1985), and Zfatman, "Mayse-Bukh: kavim lidemuto shel zhanr besifrut yidish hayeshena," *Hasifrut* 28 (1979), 126–152.

42. See Chajes (*Between* 44–45), who notes the rarity of a spirit possession account where a male possesses a male.

43. Chajes ("City" 135) notes that the spirit's "death by drowning thus fulfilled the requirement that one guilty of adultery die by choking, a neat fact that may bespeak the learned construction of the entire account" (135).

44. On the linkage in the non-Jewish context between devil possession, witchcraft, and sodomy accusations, see Stephens *Demon* 332–333 and the discussion there.

45. Besides the story discussed in this chapter and the dybbuk story in the *Mayse-bukh*, several other seventeenth-century Yiddish dybbuk stories exist. For some preliminary discussion, compare Zfatman "S" 1:xvi–xvii, 34–35, 114–115, and 2:29n69, 2:67–68n28–29.

46. See Matt Goldish, "Vision and Possession: Nathan of Gaza's Earliest Prophesies in Historical Context," in *Spirit Possession* 217–236; Zvi Mark, "Dybbuk and Devekut in the Shivhe ha-Besht: Toward a Phenomenology of Madness in Early Hasidism," in *Spirit Possession* 270–276; and Chajes *Between* 87–92.

47. For analysis, see Chajes *Between* 85–87; quote from 87.

48. This distinction is the basis of a famed disagreement between Gershom Scholem and Moshe Idel; for an overview of the discussion, see Goldish "Vision" 225 and Weinstein "Kabbalah" 245.
49. See Bilu "Taming" 43 and Goldish preface 18–19.
50. See Zfatman *Bibliografiya* item 34 (print) and Sara Zfatman-Biller, " 'Maase shel ruakh bk'k koretz'—shlav khadash behitpatkhuto shel zhanr amami," *Mekhkerei yerushalayim befolklor yehudi* 2 (1982), 17–65 (hereafter "Zfatman-Biller"), for an analysis as well as a critical edition of the work; on the work's dating, see 18. This length of 16 pages is long for a contemporary *mayse-bikhl* (most were 4–16 pages) and therefore somewhat unusual. See Zfatman "S" 1:8–9, 2:8nn37, 39.
51. Zfatman "S" viii.
52. See Zfatman-Biller 18n7.
53. See Zfatman-Biller 19 and Max Weinreich, *Bilder fun der yiddisher literature-geshikhte* (Vilna 1928), 254–259.
54. Goldish preface 14; Chajes "City" 127.
55. Weinreich *Bilder* 259; see also Zfatman-Biller 26n24 for her position on the event's "historicity."
56. Compare his characterization of the work as almost journalistic in nature in *Bilder* 254.
57. This strategy is hardly limited to our text, and appears in other, earlier works of the genre. Though this specificity usually applies to the *baalei shem* (given the connections of the genre to hagiographical literature), we also have, as in this case, rarer examples of identification of the spirit and the victim. See Zfatman-Biller 26 and "S" 1:196.
58. See Zfatman-Biller 27 for list and identification; compare also Zfatman "S" 1:59–60. This was another common strategy among contemporary dybbuk accounts; see Bilu "Taming" 41.
59. This strategy also appears in many previous possession texts, usually by identifying the general time of the possession or exorcism event, or occasionally informing the reader of the time of another narrative event. See Zfatman-Biller 28–29.
60. On eyewitnessing in the Safedian possession narratives, see Chajes "City" 130 and *Between* 38; compare also Alexander 309 for modern treatments. On the figure of the "reporter-witness" more generally in these texts, see Zfatman-Biller 23–24, "S" 1:196–198.
61. As mentioned earlier, the narrator asserts he was present for later events in the narrative, but this fact is unmentioned in the proem. References here are

to Joachim Neugroschel's translation in his *The Dybbuk and the Yiddish Imagination* (Syracuse: Syracuse University Press, 2000), 61–80; all future page references will be given within the body of the article.

62. For some analogous comments in a non-Jewish context, see Roger Chartier, "The Hanged Woman Miraculously Saved: An *occasionel*," in Chartier, ed., *The Culture of Print: Power and the Uses of Print in Early Modern Europe* (Princeton: Princeton University Press, 1987), 59–91, esp. 67–68.
63. See Zfatman-Biller 30–31 for discussion, particularly how the work straddles the categories of *agada* and *maasiya*, legend and folktale.
64. See Zfatman-Biller 31.
65. Other stories of dybbuk possession, differently structured and omitting or reaccentuating varying authenticating (or skepticism-producing) elements may of course produce different epistemological effects on the audience's behalf. For one comparative example, see Zfatman-Biller's treatment of a slightly earlier spirit possession account from Prague—one whose "characters" may have been well known to certain contemporary audiences—in "Geirush rukhot biprag bemeah ha-17: Lisheilat meheimnuto hahistorit shel gen'r amami," *Mekhkerei yerushalayim befolklor yehudi* 3 (1983), 7–33, esp. 15–19.
66. See Zfatman-Biller 18n5.
67. See Zfatman "S" 1:155; see also her comments about rhyme and authenticity with respect to this story in 1:199.
68. Analogously (though she refers to a modern, nonrhymed context), compare Tamar Alexander's attempt to reprivilege orality over textuality in dybbuk accounts: "Love and Death in a Contemporary Dybbuk Story: Personal Narrative and the Female Voice," in *Spirit Possession* 307–345, esp. 308.
69. My thanks to Sheila Jelen for her comments on this point.
70. See Zfatman-Biller 20 and "S" 1:196–197; and compare Zfatman-Biller "Geirush" 9n15.
71. See, for example, Erich Auerbach, *Mimesis: The Representation of Reality in Western Literature* (Princeton, NJ: Princeton University Press, 1953), passim.
72. This historical question has linguistic overtones that render it irrelevant to almost any other extant contemporary dybbuk tales. Most are composed in Hebrew, and so the assumptions of veracity stemming from a Yiddish text are necessarily absent from the start; the other Yiddish text—from the *Mayse-bukh*—is in prose, and no similarly complex literary speech is present.

73. More complexly, the narrator refuses to describe the evil spirit's celebration when a fire strikes Lubar, stymieing efforts to expel him, and writes that the celebration "defied all description and narration." (68) Such defiance is not merely the result of literary limitation; the narrator has no problem describing the dybbuk suffering, shouting, and arguing. Instead, we may ascribe his difficulty to friction generated through his importation of nuanced ideological positions into the conventional generic narrative form; a possible inability (or unwillingness) to give credence to a position that "accepts" the wicked's rejoicing in innocent suffering by devoting descriptive space and energy to it as it "really happened." Instead, the narrator uses indirection and allegoresis in the larger sense, studding his dybbuk account with so many questions, contradictions, and odd citations and intertexts, as this analysis will show, that he forces us to examine it in more detail.
74. See Thucydides, *History of the Peloponnesian War*, Book One. Compare Auerbach *Mimesis* 39, 87 and Veyne's remarks on "history as tradition or vulgate" (6–7, quote 6) and on invention of detail (103–105). On the rejection of this attitude by historians in the decades leading up to the dybbuk narrative in the "historical revolution," compare Nelson 40–41.
75. Compare Amos Funkenstein, *Perceptions of Jewish History* (Berkeley: University of California Press, 1993), 23–35, 40–41.
76. Zfatman-Biller 31.
77. See Zfatman-Biller 32–33, esp n.39. This common Jewish trope of the exorcism's failure is most emphatically absent in Catholic exorcism literature; see Chajes *Between* 43–44.
78. See Zfatman-Biller 33–34.
79. On the conjunction of spirit possession events and messianic events in Safedian circles, particularly around Hayyim Vital, compare Harris Lenowitz, "A Spirit Possession Tale as an Account of the Equivocal Insertion of Rabbi Hayyim Vital into the Role of Messiah," in *Spirit Possession* 197–212.
80. Perhaps the penitential resonances attributed to the dybbuk's wandering bear similarities to the *gerushin*, or the wandering among Safed's gravesites "in self-conscious imitation of the exiled Shekhinah" practiced by Moses Cordovero and Solomon Alkabetz. See Fine "Purifying" 123–124, quote 123; on *gerushin* as a preparation rite for benevolent possession, see Fine "Benevolent" 105–106, and compare Chajes *Between* 19–20.
81. Compare Zfatman-Biller 27n27 and Zfatman "S" 1:xvi, where she writes that "there is no effort [...] to give the story any 'authentic' documentary credibility." See also Zfatman "S" 1:190.

82. Compare this account to "the spasms described in the *vita* of Lukardis of Oberweimar, in which her spine was arched and her legs and head drawn back so tightly that her body nearly formed a circle, [which] are a recognized form of hysterical behavior known as *opisthotonos*." Caroline Walker Bynum, *Holy Feast and Holy Fast: The Religious Significance of Food to Medieval Women* (Berkeley: University of California Press, 1987), 203. See also Boyarin *Unheroic Conduct* 193 and Gilman 63.
83. Compare Bilu "Taming" 45–51.
84. Though male victims of possession are not rare, the majority of the possessed are certainly female, and the vast majority of possessing spirits are male, findings which seem to obtain cross-culturally. See Bilu 46 and the materials cited there, as well as Bilu, "Dybbuk, Aslai, Zar," passim. Compare, however, Faierstein's revisionist study ("Maggidim" 188ff).
85. See Bilu 47–48. Compare also Teresa de Laurentis, "The Violence of Rhetoric: Considerations on Representation and Gender," in de Laurentis, *Technologies of Gender* (Bloomington: Indiana University Press, 1987), 36–37, and, in a Jewish context, the prevalent descriptions of women "as passive and as victims of sexual violence" within martyrological literature composed earlier but contemporarily known. See Susan Einbinder, "Jewish Women Martyrs: Changing Models of Representation," *Exemplaria* 12:1 (2000), 108, 112–113, 116–117.
86. Underwear not having been invented then (see Chajes "City" 152n61); compare the woman's immodest exposure in the Falcon case (Chajes "City" 132–133), which, adding the detail of her writhing, seemingly mimics sexual intercourse. See also Weinstein ("Kabbalah" 243), who notes how this long confinement to bed, exposed to strange masculine gaze, would have been "unthinkable in normal life" in both Jewish and Christian contexts.
87. See, for example, the oath taken by Eliezer to Abraham in Gen. 24:2 and Rashi ad loc.
88. On the use of sulfur in the exorcisms described by Elijah Falcon in 1571 and the controversial fumigation technique in exorcism more generally, see Chajes *Between* 69–70.
89. See Genesis 34:1 and Genesis 38, passim.
90. Compare Chajes "City" 140–141 and Bilu 46, 49.
91. See Zfatman-Biller 18–19 and "S" 1:195. For a powerful sense of the regional fear and devastation, both physical and psychic, during the late 1650s, see Meir Balaban, *Yidn in poyln* (Vilna: Kletzkin Farlag, 1930), 151–168, esp. 155; on the war, see Mordechai Nadav, *The Jews of Pinsk, 1506 to 1880* (Stanford:

Stanford University Press, 2007), 163–180; the still valuable S. M. Dubnow, *History of the Jews in Russia and Poland from the Earliest Times until the Present Day* (Philadelphia: JPS, 1916), 153–158; and Fram *Ideals* 32–34.

92. See Neugroschel 61 and Weinreich *Bilder* 260; for other literary responses in Yiddish, compare Khone Shmeruk, "Yidishe literatur un kolektiver zikoren: di chmelnitzki-gzeyres," *Oksforder yidish* 1 (1990), 357–382, esp. 358, 362, 366, 369; Weinreich *Bilder* 192–218; and Erik *Geshikhte* 379–380. More generally, see Dubnow 144–153, 199–202.
93. Compare Einbinder "Jewish Women" 121. On the allegorized female body in premodern times more generally, compare Helen Solterer, "At the Bottom of Mirage, A Woman's Body: *Le roman de la rose* of Jean Renart," in Linda Lomperis and Sarah Stanbury, eds. *Feminist Approaches to the Body in Medieval Literature* (Philadephia: University of Pennsylvania Press, 1993), 215, 230.
94. Much later in the text we learn that Mindl is a survivor of a sort: she is one of a pair of sisters, the other one also attacked by a dybbuk but who failed to survive the attack (73). We may thus add survivor guilt to the list of Mindl's agonies and also note how our author has added another level of doubling to the constant binary divisions that attend all dybbuk stories.
95. On the constitution of the Jewish community in this period more generally, compare Fram *Ideals* 38–47.
96. Bilu 60 and Goldish preface 14.
97. An interesting avenue for further analysis would be an extensive comparison of the prayers with contemporary *tkhines*, women's devotional prayers, to compare this ostensible male possession with the ostensibly unmediated female voice. For the usage of the *tkhines* in a slightly later period to reconfigure the relationship between the living and the dead to a "more complex and reciprocal one, see especially Chava Weissler, " 'For the Human Soul is the Lamp of the Lord': The *Tkhine* for 'Laying Wicks' by Sarah bas Tovim," *Polin* 10 (1997): 40–65, esp. 61–63; more generally, see Chava Weissler, *Voices of the Matriarchs: Listening to the Prayers of Early Modern Jewish Women* (Boston: Beacon Press, 1998).
98. On theodicy in Jewish medieval and early modern literature, see Funkenstein *Perceptions* 203–206.
99. See Weissler "Mitzvot" 107–108 for discussion of a similar dynamic within eighteenth-century *tkhines*.
100. See Exodus 34:7.
101. See the reference in Tana debei Eliyahu Zuta 17, understood as a commentary to BT Sanhedrin 104a. See also, however, BT Sanhedrin 17a and n.113

infra. On the kaddish, compare Raphael Posner, Uri Kaploun, and Shalom Cohen, eds. *Jewish Liturgy: Prayer and Synagogue Service through the Ages* (Jerusalem: Keter, 1975), 112–115.

102. The particular reference in the Yiddish text, to Ps. 145:9, is from the *Ashrei*, recited three times a day by traditional Jews, whose recitation guarantees life in the world to come according to the Talmud (see BT Berakhot 4b). Its location in a tale about life after death may not be coincidental.
103. See BT Rosh Hashanah 17b.
104. I use the word in the descriptive sense; this is not, however, considered by traditional authorities as one of the Thirteen Divine Attributes.
105. The verse is also one of the Bible's most noted contradictions; Deuteronomy 24:16 states precisely the opposite, that children should not die for their fathers' sins. The rabbis, well aware of these problems, essentially reinterpret our verse to reverse its plain meaning; they claim that children are only punished for their parents' sins if they continue in their ways—thus deserving some punishment (though perhaps not to such degree); see BT Sanhedrin 27b. Mindl also avoids this question of contradiction.
106. The classic example is probably the book of Esther; other examples abound, however, often in the hagiographic genre.
107. Possibly punished wandering souls or dybbuks are subject to separate rules than those in Gehenna; I have yet to find a source that clearly makes such a distinction, however. More to the point, the force of Mindl's prayer seems dependent on the fact that such distinctions are at best blurry and presumably nonexistent.
108. For more on the Akedah's centrality, see Shalom Spiegel, *The Last Trial* (New York: Pantheon Books, 1963), esp. xii, xvi, 20; and Yael S. Feldman, "Isaac or Oedipus? Jewish Tradition and the Israeli Aqedah," in J. Cheryl Exum and Stephen D. Moore, eds., *Biblical Studies/Cultural Studies* (Sheffield: Sheffield Academic Press, 1998), 159–189, esp. 161–162.
109. Compare, for example, Genesis 23:2 and Rashi *ad loc*; Leviticus Rabbah *ad loc*; Midrash Pirkei de-Rabbi Eliezer 31.
110. Arguably, Mindl rather intends the audience to learn from the *dybbuk*'s punishment. However, given her characterization of the experience in terms of her own testing and suffering, this seems unlikely; even if so, her accentuation of her own problems make any such solution highly unsatisfactory to readers now predisposed to read the story as more than simply a conventional dybbuk tale.
111. The christological aspects of this position have not gone unnoted.

112. Compare Bilu "Taming" 44.
113. See BT Rosh Hashanah 16a. For a comparative cultural perspective on the New Year as a time for expulsion and exorcism, as well as a moment for the return of dead souls, compare Mircea Eliade, *The Myth of the Eternal Return or, Cosmos and History* (London: Arkana, 1954), 51–54.
114. On excommunication as a tool of spirit exorcism by Joseph Karo, see Chajes *Between* 68–69. One technique used—the recitation of "Aleinu" [It is on us] backwards and forwards—indicates by its very name the significantly communal aspect of the exorcism. Compare, more generally, Abrahams *Jewish Life* 52–53.
115. For a brief discussion of other magical means of exorcism attempted here—excommunication, prayer, cursing, the blowing of seven shofars and the holding of seven Torah scrolls—see Zfatman-Biller 22. A full discussion of the employment of these techniques in our narrative must await a fuller treatment; see, for now, Alexander 312 and Bilu 56–58.
116. See BT Megillah 23b; the notion of God's presence appearing in a quorum is also based on a conventional understanding of Proverbs 14:28, "In the multitude of people is the king's glory."
117. Compare Zfatman-Biller 22.
118. Perhaps it is this nomenclatural representativeness that causes the dybbuk to greet him so respectfully, asking the rabbi if he may bless the holy man (69). However, the fact that *kat* more precisely means "sect"—a word with specifically antinomian resonances in Hebrew—may remind us of the contemporaneous Sabbatean currents highly relevant to this area, as mentioned above, and even possibly suggest this as a crypto-Sabbatean work. Full investigation of such possibilities is beyond the scope of the chapter, but for a more general connection of the work to the Sabbatean atmosphere, see Weinreich *Bilder* 260–261.
119. On whether "fate" (*mazel*) is applicable to Israel, see BT Nedarim 32a, Shabbat 156a, Isaiah M. Gafni, *The Jews in the Talmudic Era: A Social and Cultural History* (Jerusalem, 1990), 166n84, and the discussion in Funkenstein *Perceptions* 293.
120. On the shofar's role in repelling demons in rabbinic literature, see Chajes *Between* 82–83.
121. The term is Chajes'; see Chajes *Between* 70. For other conventional features, compare Zfatman-Biller 32–34; a highly significant feature, mentioned only briefly here, is the emphasis on discovering the dybbuk's name and thus identity. In our case, the dybbuk's revealed name, Yakov, is

symptomatic both of the Jewish people's essential nature and of the paradigmatic deceiver who disguises his own essence, and is itself highly significant in its paradoxical implications.

122. Bilu "Taming" 61.
123. Compare Chajes *Between* 81. This is not the only such circumstance; it was possible, for example, to see visions of the deceased. All of these—both in "reality" and its literary representation—are of course subject to varying degrees of skepticism on the part of their experiencing, hearing, or reading audience.
124. Compare Zfatman-Biller 21.
125. Compare Chajes *Between* 22, 27 on the spirit's painful treatment. On the idea that sin and punishment are worked out on the body, compare the popular medieval stories of Rabbi Akiva and the wandering soul discussed in Yassif "The Body" 208.
126. See also Zfatman-Biller 21n12 for comparative transmigrations in other contemporary dybbuk tales.
127. See Lieberman "Some Aspects" 242–244 for discussion.
128. Compare Numbers 19 passim. Indeed, the waters in which the ashes are diluted are called *mei khatat* ("waters of sin").
129. Compare Bamidbar Rabbah 19.
130. For an extensive reading of the sotah through the lens of gender, see Bonna Devora Haberman, "The Suspected Adulteress: A Study in Textual Embodiment," *Prooftexts* 20:1+2 (2000): 12–42. For a further discussion of *sotah* in its rabbinic context, see Peskowitz *Spinning* 131ff, esp. 135, where she claims that "tractate Sotah presents this fantasy of the bound and controlled female body," which again is relevant to the sadomasochistic trends present in our text.
131. In light of the shifting nature of the test, it is notable that according to the Talmud certain women who were barren actually tried to get their husbands to submit them to the *sotah* water so that they would become pregnant; see BT Sotah 26a.
132. This ending also highlights the seeming mutual exclusivity between sexualized spiritual possession and the husband's sexual act; see Bilu ("Taming" 52), who also notes that in ancient Greece marriage was considered a cure for hysteria, "which was allegedly caused by disordered sexuality—the product of a 'wandering womb.' "
133. Yakov met a woman with whom he had committed adultery; the two entered into the bodies of Mindl and her sister; the latter died immediately.

On "the zoharic tendency to regard reincarnation as an opportunity to rectify sexual transgressions," see Chajes *Between* 16.

134. Compare also Bilu 50–52 and Chajes *Between* 28.
135. See Boyarin *Carnal Israel* 188–189.
136. Boyarin *Carnal Israel* 191.
137. Boyarin *Unheroic Conduct* 179. Boyarin importantly distinguishes between Talmud study and other kinds of Jewish textual study and information available to women.
138. Chajes has attempted to relate spirit possession to "broader notions of women's religiosity, as perceived and experienced by women as well as by the male religious elite" (*Between* 97). See Chajes *Between* 97–98, 115–117.
139. On legal and regulative control of women's sexually disruptive presence more generally, see Carol Smart, "Disruptive Bodies and Unruly Sex," in Smart, ed., *Regulating Womanhood: Historical Essays on Marriage, Motherhood, and Sexuality* (London: Routledge, 1992), 7–32, esp. 7–11; with respect to literature, Alice Jardine's perceptive comments are worth noting: "If the 'author' is male, one finds that the female destiny (at least in the novel) rarely deviates from one or two seemingly irreversible, dualistic teleologies: monster and/or angel, she is condemned to death (or sexual mutilation or disappearance) or to happy-ever-after marriage." *Gynesis: Configurations of Woman and Modernity*. (Ithaca: Cornell University Press, 1985), 52. See also Annette Kolodny's "Dancing through the Minefield: Some Observations on the Theory, Practice, and Politics of a Feminist Literary Criticism," in Elaine Showalter, ed., *The New Feminist Criticism: Essays on Women, Literature, and Theory* (New York: Pantheon Books, 1985), 147. Kolodny notes that "what is important about a fiction is not whether it ends in death or a marriage, but what the symbolic demands of that particular conventional ending imply about the values and beliefs of the world that engendered it."
140. Bilu 54. In the Falcon case, the possessing spirit (though not the victim) has asserted that "all religions are the same" (Chajes *Between* 40).
141. Chajes "City" 143; compare also Yassif, who connects the psychotic development of disbelief in society's basic tenets to the possession's somatic effects ("The Body" 212–213).
142. For perhaps the most famous contemporary literary example, see *Hamlet*, Act I.
143. The relevant blessing is "Blessed be you, Adonai, our God, ruler of the world, who has given the rooster the intelligence to distinguish between day and night."

144. I use this term in distinction from "literal"; see the discussion in *Antonio's Devils*.

145. The connection between *kapparot* and the Akedah has already been noted by Spiegel in a very different context; see *Trial* 65.

146. A classic convention of the dybbuk story is that the victim speaks in the possessor's physical voice. Though our narrative seemingly omits this detail, it is eminently possible that this was assumed to be the case by the reader; either way, the dybbuk certainly crows through her.

147. Chajes *Between* 5, 119–120. For discussion of demonic possession in a non-Jewish context, see Anne Llewellyn Barstow, *Witchcraze: A New History of the European Witch Hunts* (San Francisco: Pandora, 1994), 71–72, 80, 112; Chajes 13; Cohn 22, 26–27, 42; Clark *Thinking* 84; Briggs *Witches* 131–132; Behringer 166, citing the contemporary "widespread view that possession was caused by witches, who induced a demon to enter the body of their enemy"; and particularly Maggi, 10–12, 100–102, 111–112, 122. Of particular relevance here is the Christian exorcist's insistence on determining the possessing devil's name and biography, the exorcism's theatricality, and, most intriguingly, Maggi's conceptualization of the exorcist's view of the entire matter as partaking of both reality and metaphor simultaneously. That the possessing spirit is a devil, and not a human soul, is a tremendous difference between Jewish and Christian perspectives on the phenomenon. Briggs (*Witches* 131–132) reminds us of the existence of skepticism as well as belief with regard to Christian possession.

148. On Jewish views of witchcraft, compare H. C. Erik Midelfort, "Social History and Biblical Exegesis: Community, Family, and Witchcraft in Sixteenth-Century Germany," in David C. Steinmetz, ed., *The Bible in the Sixteenth Century* (Durham: Duke University Press, 1990), 12–13, and Trachtenberg *Magic* 11–16.

149. See Briggs, *Witches and Neighbours*, passim; and Alison Rowlands, *Witchcraft Narratives in Germany: Rothenburg, 1561–1652* (Manchester: Manchester University Press, 2003), 1–8.

150. Compare Midelfort 27; P. G. Maxwell-Stuart, *Witchcraft in Europe and the New World, 1400–1800* (New York: Palgrave, 2001), 13; and Behringer 87.

151. Williams *Dominion* 100.

152. See, for example, Peter Rushton, "Texts of Authority: Witchcraft Accusations and the Demonstration of Truth in Early Modern England," in Stuart Clark, ed., *Languages of Witchcraft: Narrative, Ideology, and Meaning in Early Modern Culture* (New York: St. Martin's Press, 2001), 21–39, esp.

28–29, 34 and Marion Gibson, "Understanding Witchcraft? Accusers' Stories in Print in Early Modern England," in *Languages of Witchcraft* 42. Gibson differentiates between what we might term subgenres in witchcraft narratives, those that use "almost exclusively legal documentary sources" and "basically third-person narratives of witchcraft," whose reliability she feels is compromised; she then analyzes these genres' importance as a means of organizing experience. Compare also Stephens *Demon* 237–238.

153. See Peter Elmer, "Towards a Politics of Witchcraft in Early Modern England," in *Languages of Witchcraft* 104–105. In literary terms, there is certainly no reason a polyphonic text—and a dybbuk is nothing if not polyphonic—cannot simultaneously hint at both functions. See also Clark *Thinking* 28, 134–135, 144.
154. Barstow, 1–2, quote from xiv.
155. For an excellent overview of this approach, see Briggs (*Witches* 259–263), who concludes that many men were tried as witches, the critical literature, contemporary rhetoric, and (arguably) contemporary mentality more generally notwithstanding. Compare also Cohn 227 and, intriguingly, Midelfort (184–186), who connects the period's rising marriage age, the increasing proportion of women, women's resulting melancholy and isolation, and the increase in witchcraft accusations.
156. Rowlands 169.
157. Rowlands 135; compare Rowlands 135–179 more generally, and Cohn, *Europe's Inner Demons*, 143–233.
158. This inversion in Christian perspective and its relevance to Jewish supernatural literature has been discussed in the previous chapter; see here Clark *Thinking* 9; Cohn *Europe's Inner Demons* 147, and Briggs *Witches* 99.
159. The careful understanding of patterns of thinking *about* inversion as well as inversion itself receives its best treatment in Clark, *Thinking*. Clark's similar discussion of structures of complementarity within early modern thought, where "opposites were said to require each other ... [as they were] believed to be in conformity to a world order based on the unity of contrasting elements" (*Thinking* 40–41), is even more useful in our regard.
160. See Rowlands 68–75.
161. On this point, see Barstow 28–29 and Midelfort 182–183. Such a perspective is itself part and parcel of a general misogynist discourse; on the text generally and centrally marshaled in support of this point, the *Malleus Maleficarum*, which referred to witchcraft not only as "treason against God" but as "female rebellion," see Barstow 61–63, cites 62 and Midelfort 5.

Compare also Gerhild Scholz Williams, *Defining Dominion: The Discourses of Magic and Witchcraft in Early Modern France and Germany* (Ann Arbor: University of Michigan Press, 1995), 1–2.

162. Compare Barstow 153 and Midelfort 73–74.

163. See Barstow 3–13, esp. 9, 12, and 129–145. Compare also Newman (*Fashioning* 26), who speaks of "public shaming and spectacle" as a means of managing "woman's voracious sexuality."

164. See Rowlands 180–200, esp. 183–185; see also Diane Purkiss, "Sounds of Silence: Fairies and Incest in Scottish Witchcraft Stories," in *Languages of Witchcraft* 81–98, 81.

165. Compare Briggs' comments on countermagics in *Witches* 182–183.

166. See here esp. Barstow 149–155 and Rowlands 25, 29–33, 40–41. According to Behringer (41) some witches' punishment was to be burned alive, the punishment for heresy—the same punishment with which Mindl is threatened by the non-Jewish ruler, perhaps helping explain this bizarre, parenthetical textual moment.

167. Barstow 85.

168. See Barstow 63 and Midelfort 189, quote Midelfort.

169. Midelfort 76–77, quote 77. On the rare prosecution of Jewish witches, see *SRH* 11:143; Trachtenberg *Devil* 80–81, 86–87; and Stow *Alienated* 235.

170. Compare Richard Kieckhefer, *Repression of Heresy in Medieval Germany* (Philadelphia: University of Pennsylvania Press, 1979), 6, 30, 41–42, 69, 76, 110; Stephens *Demon* 5; and Williams *Dominion* 121–145, esp. 124–126.

171. Compare, more generally, Clark *Thinking* 152.

172. Williams *Dominion* 9. As Newman argues in substantial detail, these developments interact with other social, economic, and gender processes as well. In the English context, for example, "between 1580 and 1640 ... enormous economic and demographic as well as political changes ... were figured variously in the social fabric as acute anxiety about conventional hierarchies ... [including] female rebellion." Newman *Fashioning* xvii–xviii. She subsequently notes that witchcraft accusations reach their peak in this period (xviii).

173. See, for example, Rowlands 198. On the "ravages" to the Jewish community during the Thirty Years' War, compare *SRH* 14:261–271.

174. Rowlands 200. For an alternative perspective on this "turmoil of war" view, compare Wolfgang Behringer, *Witchcraft Persecutions in Bavaria* (Cambridge: Cambridge University Press, 1997), esp. 4–5, 104. Behringer speaks (104) about a contemporary "radical shift in mentalities" more generally, due

to population surge, great poverty, the agrarian crises, and strong and forceful political centralization. Compare also Briggs *Witches* 7, 308.

175. Midelfort 82–83, quote 83. See also Behringer 327–331.

176. For a closer study of this region, see Rowlands, passim, esp. 105–134 for the period of the Thirty Years' War; a more general treatment of the area is H. C. Midelfort's *Witch Hunting in Southwestern Germany 1562–1684: The Social and Intellectual Foundations* (Stanford: Stanford University Press, 1972). On regionalism and regional politics, compare Behringer 7, 9–11. On Poland, which "was more open to the transmission of demonological theory from Germany" and whose most active period of witch trials come later than its Western counterpart (around 1675 to 1700), see Maxwell-Stuart *Witchcraft* 77.

177. See Barstow 61–63.

178. Compare Rowlands 22–43 and Briggs 8. Quote from Rowlands 60.

179. Behringer 187, 200. Compare also Stuart Clark, introduction to *Languages of Witchcraft* 4; Rushton "Witchcraft" 22, 26; and Thomas Robisheaux, "Witchcraft and Forensic Medicine in Seventeenth-Century Germany," in *Languages of Witchcraft* 197–215, esp. 198. Robisheaux, referring to suspicious deaths and their relation to witchcraft accusations and trials, writes, "common folk and public authorities were quite skilled and experienced in reading the signs surrounding odd, unexpected or distressing misfortunes, and could call upon a wide variety of explanations. Witchcraft was actually a comparatively rare explanation, especially in the late seventeenth century." See also Robisheaux 212 and Briggs *Witches* 69–72 on the complex combinations of medicine, cunning, folk, natural, and magical healing, home work, natural philosophy, and theological belief in explication for misfortune involved in diagnosing witchcraft.

180. Compare Rowlands 56–60.

181. Briggs *Witches* 320–321.

182. Rowlands 40; see also Clark *Thinking* 146–147, 176.

183. Compare Newman *Fashioning* 6. On the specific linkage between female literacy and women's increasing freedom for theological speculation (and the inevitable and concomitant male anxiety), compare Natalie Zemon Davis, *Society and Culture in Early Modern France* (Stanford: Stanford University Press, 1975), 76.

184. See Rowlands 11–12, 52–55; Midelfort 10, 24–25.

185. Compare, for example, Newman *Fashioning* 17–18. To the best of my knowledge, even quasi-statist contemporary Jewish European institutions

like the *kahal* or the *va'ad* are rarely mentioned in dybbuk tales, which instead focus either on communal structures in the most abstract fashion or provide hagiographic accounts of individual figures.

186. Perhaps most notable are the contemporary debates over purgatory's existence, which like our spirit possession narratives are inextricably related to questions of the soul's disposition. Compare Stephen Greenblatt, who discusses the Jewish contrast. See his *Hamlet in Purgatory* (Princeton: Princeton University Press, 2001), especially 7–8, 41, 61ff, 102.

187. Goldish preface 15.

188. Bilu 44, 54, 59. See also Zfatman-Biller "Geirush" 26–28.

189. The witchcraft trials' and executions' intense and simultaneously displaced violence, for example, may provide a paradigm for considering how violence against women, and against these possessed women in particular, may have operated within a Jewish sphere.

190. Recall once more that the mid-seventeenth century was an age of new skepticism; see Chajes *Between* 119–120.

191. It is parenthetically worth noting that some Jewish critics, reading medieval Jewish treatments of allegory, have considered the form as gendered and in its own way possessed. Compare Rosen's sketch of Maimonidean views of allegory in *Eve* 81. On types of allegory more generally, compare Northrop Frye, *Anatomy of Criticism: Four Essays* (Princeton: Princeton University Press, 1957), 90–91.

192. Compare Hayden White, "The Value of Narrativity in the Representation of Reality," in W. J. T. Mitchell, ed., *On Narrative* (Chicago: University of Chicago Press, 1981), 19–21, and Pavel 77–78.

193. Such discussion is not limited to contemporary Jewish ways of reading, of course: for significant discussion in a very different context, compare Frank Kermode's incisive remarks in *The Sense of an Ending: Studies in the Theory of Fiction* (Oxford: Oxford University Press [1967] 2000), esp. 16–18.

194. See Zfatman-Biller 18n4; "S" 1:31–33; and *Bibliografiya*, passim, esp. items 16, 31, 32, 43–44 (print). The first of these will be the subject of the subsequent chapter.

195. See Goldish preface 15; for more on Jews, medieval medicine, and contemporary folk medicine, see Pollack 113–145; Helmut Dinse, *Die Entwicklung des jiddischen Schrifttums im deutschen Sprachgebiet* (Stuttgart: J. B. Metzlerche Verlagsbuchhandlung, 1974), 101–105; Joseph Shatzmiller, *Jews, Medicine, and Medieval Society* (Berkeley: University of California, 1994), esp. 10–14, 86, 120–123 (the last on connections between Jewish

medical belief and skepticism); Trachtenberg *Magic* 193–207; and David Ruderman, *Jewish Thought and Scientific Discovery in Early Modern Europe* (New Haven: Yale University Press, 1995), esp. 20–21, though Ruderman focuses more on elite traditions.

196. Isaac Luria compared the kabbalist to the good doctor (see Fine "Purifying" 131–132); on how " 'falling' or epileptic seizures" were "commonly viewed as an ailment reflecting or accompanying possession," see Chajes *Between* 75, 89 (quote 75). See also Pollack 114–117 and Trachtenberg *Magic* 199–202.

197. Compare, for example, the discussion in Mordechai Bernstein, "Two Remedy Books in Yiddish From 1474 and 1508," in Raphael Patai, ed., *Studies in Biblical and Jewish Folklore* (Bloomington: Indiana University Press, 1960), 289–305; in the remedy books, cures for fever and cancer occur side by side with remedies for avoiding witchcraft (292–293). Such remedies could also refer to non-Jewish tropes, implicitly including transubstantiation and baptism. See, for an example in Judeo-French, Menahem Banitt, "Une formule d'exorcisme en ancien français," in John Fisher and Paul A. Gaeng, eds. *Studies in Honor of Mario A. Pei* (Chapel Hill: University of North Carolina Press, 1972), 37–48, esp. 45. Compare also Chajes *Between* 93–94, 223n169; Jean Baumgarten, "Textes médicaux en langue yiddish (XIVe–XVIIe siècles)," in Gabrielle Sed-Rajna, ed., *Rashi 1040–1990* (Paris: Éditions du Cerf, 1993), 723–740, esp. 727–728, 736; and Israel Abrahams, *Jewish Life in the Middle Ages* (New York: Athenaeum, 1969 [1896]), xx. On the evil eye specifically, see Regina Lilienthal, "Eyn hore," *Yidishe filologiye* 1 (1924), 245–271, esp. 256–262.

198. In a letter written by Moses Zacuto to his disciples discussing how to treat a possessed woman, for example, he explicitly differentiates between "spirit possession" and "a case of madness." Cited in Weinstein "Kabbalah" 244; Weinstein also notes (246) that "this distinction is shared by both physicians and churchmen practicing exorcism" in seventeenth-century Italy. For a comparative approach, compare Midelfort (83–84), who mentions the courts' recognition of medical illnesses (here, feeblemindedness) as opposed to witchcraft. Even what we would term mental illness may fall explicitly under medical professionals' purview: compare Pollack 138–141 and Zfatman-Biller "Geirush" 9–10.

199. Diane Purkiss, *The Witch in History*, 78, cited in Chajes *Between* 8–9.

CHAPTER 6. THE "TALE OF BRIYO AND ZIMRO"

Epigraph: Northrop Frye, *The Secular Scripture* (Cambridge, MA: Harvard UP, 1976), 23.

1. The phrase is Fuks'; see Fuks, *Oldest Literary Documents*.
2. See, for an invaluable history of the topic, Baumgarten *OYL* 128–206, to which the historical aspects of this chapter are heavily indebted.
3. The fable of the sick lion, discussed in its later iteration(s) in chapter 3.
4. *OYL* 132–133; see also Shmeruk *Prokim* 33–36, 46–49. On the *Dukus Hornt*, an adaptation of the Kudrun cycle lacking any extant analogue in German and thus of great interest to German scholars, see *OYL* 134–136 and the sources cited there. Particularly notable are the discussions surrounding the text's "Yiddishness"; on these discussions' ideological resonances, and indeed those behind much of old Yiddish studies, see Frakes *Politics*.
5. *OYL* 131. See also Zfatman "S" 1:4; Walter Röll, "Zu den ersten drei Texten der Cambridger Handschrift von 1382/1383," *Zeitschrift für deutsches Altertum* 104 (1975), 54–68; Chava Turniansky, "On Old-Yiddish Biblical Epics," *International Folklore Review* 8 (1991), 26–33; and Wulf-Otto Dreeßen, "Die altjiddischen Estherdichtungen: Überlegungen zur Rekonstruktion der Geschichte der älteren jiddischen Literatur," *Daphnis* 6 (1977), 27–39, for further analysis.
6. See *OYL* 131, 140–155. On the *Shmuel-bukh*'s authorship, see L. Fuks, ed., *Das Schemuelbuch des Mosche Esrim Wearba* (Assen: Van Gorcum, 1961), esp. 4–6; *OYL* 149–151 and Zinberg 6:103–110; see also Jean Baumgarten, "Une chanson de geste en yidich ancien: Le *Shmuel bukh*," *Revue de la Bibliothèque Nationale* 13 (1984), 24–38, and Nechemiah Allony, "Mekorot khadashim le-'Shmuel bukh' vele-'Melokhim bukh,' " *Beer-Sheva* 1 (1973), 90–113; and Bettina Simon, *Jiddische Sprachgeschichte* (Frankfurt: Athenäum, 1988), 65–130, esp. 65–68, 118–130. On the *Melokhim-bukh*, see L. Fuks, ed., *Das Altjiddische Epos Melokim-Buk* (Assen: Van Gorcum, 1965, 2 vols.), 1:21–26, 42–51; Meyer Wolf, "Mekom khiburo shel ha-'melokhim bukh,' " *Tarbiz* 51 (1992), 131–134; and Zinberg 6:110–111.
7. See Fuks *Schemuelbuch* 10–13.
8. In the *Melokhim-bukh*, despite its title's implications, moral and ethical elements dominate over the "chivalric aspect and references to the style and rhetoric of heroic poetry." See *OYL* 152 and Fuks *Melokhim* 1:24–25, 42–43.
9. *OYL* 143, 147, cite 147.
10. See discussion in *OYL* 155–162.
11. Leo Landau, *Arthurian Legends, or, the Hebrew-German Rhymed Version of the Legend of King Arthur* = Teutonia 21 (Leipzig, 1912); see esp. 32–41, 65–84; see

also Zinberg 6:54–66; Erik *Roman* 105–112; Curt Leviant, trans. and ed., *King Artus: A Hebrew Arthurian Romance of 1279* (New York: Ktav, 1969); Wulf-Otto Dreeßen, "Zur Rezeption deutscher epischer Literatur im altjiddischen," in Wolfgang Harms and L. Peter Johnson, *Deutsche Literatur des späten Mittelalters* (Berlin: Erich Schmidt Verlag, 1975), 116–128; for a more recent treatment, see Robert G. Warnock, "The Arthurian Tradition in Hebrew and Yiddish," in Valerie M. Lagorio and Mildred Leake Day, *King Arthur through the Ages* (New York: Garland, 1990), 189–208. For a later Yiddish treatment (from the late seventeenth century), see M. Bassin, *Antologye: Finf hundert yor idishe poezye* (New York: Literarishe Farlag, 1917), 1:51–61.

12. Landau 21. See also Leviant 56–57.
13. Landau 31–32.
14. For an extensive list with references, see *OYL* 159. For more on *Ditrikh von bern* and similar works, as well as analysis of their integration into Jewish culture, compare Erik *Geshikhte* 102–103; N. Shtif, "Ditrikh von bern: yidishkeyt un veltlekhkeyt in der alter yidisher literature," *Yidishe filologiye* 1 (January–February 1924), 1–11, 112–122; and Theresia Friderichs-Müller, ed., *Die 'Historie von dem Kaiser Octaviano'* (Hamburg: Helmut Buske Verlag, 1981–1990, 3 vols.), 1:9–11, 3:9–13.
15. The historical literature on this topic is vast. See the general discussion in Jerry Christopher Smith, *Elia Levita Bachur's Bovo-Buch: A Translation of the Old Yiddish Edition of 1541 with Introduction and Notes* (Tucson, AZ: Fenestra Books, 2003), xv–xviii, which mentions inter alia German Jews' spectatorship at "various Christian festivals and public amusements, e.g., tournaments, dances, and town fairs" (xv), their participation (as musicians) at non-Jewish weddings, and public sermons to attempt to convert the Jews which "familiariz[ed them] with Christian beliefs, superstitions, and folklore" (xvi). On at least some Italian Jews' familiarity with Italian literature (though generally not the more recent German immigrants), see Smith *Bovo-buch* xviii and idem., "Elia Levita's *Bovo-Buch*: A Yiddish Romance of the Early Sixteenth Century." (PhD diss., Cornell University, 1968), 12–14.
16. See *OYL* 155–157; Zinberg 6:115–116; and Erik *Roman* 15–16. On *Ditrikh*, which has an extant Yiddish version, see *OYL* 157–158.
17. See *OYL* 157; Zinberg 6:42; and Fuks 1:xvi. Compare also Reb Zelmeleyn's early- to mid-fifteenth-century *Shabbes-lid*, sung to the same melody, printed in Bassin 1:8–9.
18. *OYL* 140. For comparative considerations, see Edward R. Haymes, "Oral Composition in Middle High German Epic Poetry," in John Miles Foley,

ed., *Oral Traditional Literature: A Festschrift for Albert Bates Lord* (Columbus, OH; Slavica Publishers, 1981), 341–346, esp. 341–342.

19. *OYL* 129.
20. *OYL* 141.
21. Fuks xvi–xvii. On the *shpilman*'s existence, see, for example, Landau's argument for their existence on 24–27; Zinberg 6:32–33, 54; and Erik *Roman* 16–17 and *Geshikhte* 67–129; compare, however, Shmeruk's sentiment in his "Tsi ken der kembridger manuscript shtisn di shpilman-teorie in der yidisher literatur?" *Di goldene keyt* 100 (1979), 251–271. For more general overviews of the discussion, see Smith "Elia" 60–64 and, more recently, *OYL* 141–142.
22. Fuks 1:xiv–xv.
23. *OYL* 141.
24. Fuks 1:xvii.
25. See Zinberg 6:52; Shmeruk *Prokim* 37–38; Zfatman "S" 1:12; Leviant 61ff; Arnold Paucker, "Yiddish Versions of Early German Prose Novels," *Journal of Jewish Studies* 10 (1959), 151–167, 155–161; and *OYL* 160–161 for examples.
26. Fuks 1:xvii–xviii.
27. *OYL* 148–149.
28. *OYL* 162.
29. On the porosity between Jews and non-Jews in contemporary Italy—porosity leading to actual conversion but also to a kind of "conversion" of text and mind—compare Elisheva Carlebach, *Divided Souls: Converts from Judaism in Germany, 1500–1750* (New Haven: Yale University Press, 2001), 7–9.
30. Compare Erik's comments in *Roman* 52–53.
31. Shtif ("Yidishkeyt" 120) considers this an "original composition"; however, later research has focused on some of the text's foreign sources, particularly versions of the Persian epic *Leylā and Mejnun*; see Erika Timm, "Zwischen Orient und Okzident: Zur Vorgeschichte von 'Beria und Zimro,' " *Literaturwissenschaftliches Jahrbuch* 27 (1986), 297–307. See also Frakes' description in *EYT* 355–356, which offers a neat round-up of some of the external motifs.
32. For bibliographic details and critical editions of the three main textual versions (transliterated into the Latin alphabet), see Erika Timm, "Beria und Simra: Eine jiddische Erzählung des 16. Jahrhunderts," *Literaturwissenschaftliches Jahrbuch* 14 (1973), 1–44; for the original Yiddish text of the 1580/85 version, on which this analysis is based, see Frakes *EYT* 357–367. See also Zfatman *Bibliografiya* items 6b (manuscript) and 15, 25, 26 (print),

and Max Erik, "Vegn mayse briyo vezimro," *Shriftn fun yidishn visenshaftlekhn institut* 1 (*filologishe seriye*) (1926), 153–154, 161–162, and Erik, *Vegn alt-yidishn roman un novele* (1926), passim. Translations here are generally taken from Neugroschel, *Dybbuk*, 82–94; I have occasionally altered his translation both to bring out certain analytic elements which necessitate a more literal rendering, and because Neugroschel has incorporated aspects of the different textual variants into a blended translation. (I will occasionally address certain later variant aspects, but will note them explicitly as such; some of the emergent themes can benefit from a complementary analysis.)

33. See Frakes *EYT* 356.
34. See Zfatman "S" 1:24, 2:22n3. On da Gara's Yiddish printing, see Baumgarten *OYL* 44. On Italian history during the late medieval and Renaissance period, more generally, compare *SRH* 11:249–262; the still valuable Shulvass, passim; Bonfil *Renaissance*, passim, esp. 19–20; and David B. Ruderman, introduction to Ruderman, ed., *Essential Papers on Jewish Culture in Renaissance and Baroque Italy* (New York: New York University Press, 1992), 1–39, esp. 6–9. On Yiddish printing in Italy more generally, see Zfatman "S" 1:25–30; *OYL* 164–165; Shmeruk *Prokim* 122–127; Shulvass 38–43, 146–147, 257–267, and, in greater detail, Ch. [Chayim] Friedberg, *Toldot hadefus haivri beitalya* (Tel Aviv: M. A. Bar-Juda, 1956), 9–90; Franz Delitzch, *Zur Geschichte der jüdischen Poësie* (Leipzig: Karl Tauchnitz, 1836), 69–75; Claudia Rosensweig, "La letteratura yiddish in Italia: L'esempio del *Bovo de-Antona* di Elye Bokher," *Acme* 50:3 (1997), 159–189, esp. 160–163; and Erika Timm, "Wie Elia Levita sein Bovobuch für den Druck überarbeitete," *Germanisch-Romanische Monatsschrift* 72 (1991), 61–63.
35. On the Venetian version's (substantial) differences, see Erik "Mayse" 157–158. Frakes places this version's actual publication in Prague (see Frakes *EYT* 356; Erik *Geshikhte* 348–349; and Zfatman 2:9–10n42 [n. 15, 25, 26, 119], and 18n100 on the different texts and later Prague versions); this does not mean that a no longer extant, earlier printed version could not have actually been printed in Venice.
36. See Erik "Mayse" 162. Erik also considers the possibility of Reutlingen's authorship, not merely scribal function, though he (like most later scholars) considers this unlikely.
37. *OYL* 166.
38. Erik suggests that the source of the two-headed man story is a 1551 Hebrew chapbook published in Venice, "Khibur hamaasiyot vehamidrashot vehaagadot"; see Erik "Mayse" 156 and Timm "Beria" 55–56. For a contemporary Yiddish

analogue found in manuscript which connects the story to underworld motifs perhaps relevant to our tale's larger focus, see J. J. Maitlis, "Some Extant Folktales in Yiddish Mss.," *Fabula* 12 (1971), 214–216.

39. Examples of such tales appear in the nearly contemporaneous *Mayse-bukh*. On the "great jungle of the pseudo-Solomonic writings" in the Middle Ages, see Cohn 104–105, Timm "Beria" 55, and Trachtenberg *Devil* 25, 63–64; and for other Yiddish contemporary works involving Solomon, see Zfatman *Bibliografiya*, item 2d (manuscript) and 64 (print).

40. See 1 Kings 3:16–28. There, that clarity is formulated in the answer to the question "Which of these is my son?," while here it might be phrased as "Is this my son, or my sons?"

41. See Jerold Frakes, "Registers of Legal Discourse in Early Yiddish Epic," unpublished paper presented at a conference on German-Yiddish Encounter, Columbia University, 2004, 18. It seems reasonable to suggest Zimro could have employed a less painful or extreme method of detection; perhaps his extreme behavior here is predictive of his later extreme behavior as a lover.

42. In fact, Solomon is the final figure mentioned in the narrative, having, in some sense, "the last word," as he recites the *sheva brokhes* at Briyo and Zimro's heavenly wedding.

43. Timm makes a similar point in "Beria" 56. We will return later to a final aspect of the father-son relationship relevant here: the role that this has in inviting the reader to engage in questions of historical and historiographic consciousness.

44. Genesis 2:24.

45. See BT Beitzah 36b and Rashi ad loc. This methodological approach of posing narrative questions by applying traditional Jewish law to early modern Yiddish narrative literature, particularly (though not solely) literary works derived in some or large part from external contexts, owes a debt to Jerold Frakes' formulation: "traditional texts from early Ashkenazic culture ... assume the underlying determinative function of the rabbinical tradition with respect to the constituent principles of law ... Nonetheless, with the growing interchange of Jewish and coterritorial non-Jewish cultures ... the multiple legal discourses at least indirectly represented in Christian literary texts that were translated and adapted into Yiddish were not consistently jettisoned by Jewish adapters and simply replaced by traditional Jewish discourse ... reflect[ing] the complex mode of reception found generally in the genre of early Yiddish literature" (Frakes "Legal" 1–2). I hope to build on

Frakes' important observations by suggesting that choices made concerning the maintenance, manipulation, and development of the interaction between the various legal discourses (as well as other discursive strands) can be literarily analyzed with regard to the work's thematic structures, balanced with an understanding of those discourses' comprehension—and their narrative and thematic challenge—by the reading audience. On the relationship of the law of the land and the law of God more generally, compare Salo Baron, *A Social and Religious History of the Jews* (New York: Columbia University Press, 1952–1993), 11:20; Stow *Alienated* 159, 178–179, 192; and, with specific relation to contemporary Italy, see Robert Bonfil, *Rabbis and Jewish Communities in Renaissance Italy* (Oxford: Littman Library of Jewish Civilization, 1990), 200–251, esp. 246–251.

46. Note that the fact that Hyrcanos is presented as "near" the king (although this is complex; see Timm "Beria" 47–49 and Zinberg 6:168) suggests an allusion to the proxy structures of the late Hasmonean dynasty, where a Jew stands in for the non-Jewish ruler; however, given the king's active role in judgments in the preface, and his location in Jerusalem, we are presumably meant to understand him as a Jewish presence. Obviously, the anachronistic nature of the text prevents definitive answers.
47. The similarity seems only phonological, as the manuscript edition spells her name differently than that of the Hebrew or Yiddish word for "creature," *briye*.
48. Compare Herodotus and the book of Esther, the latter especially in light of the emphasis on the lovely dishes (*fil hipshe kelim*).
49. This is the first textual indication that this love may lead to death, and the concomitant suggestion of containing or reconciling opposites—eros and thanatos—is also in line with the work's themes. The continued linkage of love and death throughout the story also recapitulates a particular dynamic familiar to contemporary Jewish and non-Jewish literature and already discussed above: the shift from metaphor to actualization. Zimro's plaint to his father that "If I don't marry the beautiful daughter, I'll die of grief" (85) is a case in point.
50. This is the first explicit indication in the text that Briyo actually sees Zimro. Perhaps she has seen him when her father displays her in the tower, but the text is unclear: it may be, for example, that he shows her off through another window or a peephole. Certainly the previous scene's emphasis is on Briyo as a passive observed object, not the reverse. A possible argument for this as the first sighting is the later scene, which offers its thematic reversal

mentioned above, when Briyo creates a situation where "I can see you. But you won't see me" (86). The structural parallelism here is too pleasing to ignore.

51. In a text about the juxtaposition of Jewish and non-Jewish worlds, this particular moment may allow a subtle allusion to one of the Bible's more intriguing *non*-Jewish figures. Rahab, mentioned in the book of Joshua, also employs the device of hanging something from her window to get her Jewish captor-suitors' attention, and, in Talmudic writings, is presented as particularly beautiful, just like Briyo: connecting Rahab to a particularly earthly, sensual beauty, the rabbis link speaking her name to involuntary seminal emission. (See Joshua 4 and BT Megillah 15a.) Moving from narrative to thematic similarities, Rahab's symbolic representation of erotic and secular elements' intrusion into a holy mission is highly relevant here; we may once more suggest that this is an attempt to sublimate the narrative's non-Jewish norms or subversive forces (here, the eruption of a specifically non-Jewish trope, the Boccaccian feminine usage of wit to achieve specifically sexual purposes) into traditional Jewish structures.

52. Particularly given the substantive and complex role a formal promise (analogous to engagement) had in Italian Jewish society; see Bonfil *Renaissance* 260–261.

53. On marriage in the face of parental opposition more generally in Jewish Renaissance Italy, see Moses A. Shulvass, *The Jews in the World of the Renaissance* (Leiden: E. J. Brill, 1973), 163–164.

54. On family lineage's importance to contemporary Italian Jewish marriage arrangements, compare Bonfil *Renaissance* 255–256.

55. A later, anonymous Prague edition provides a specific reason for Tuvas' assumption that the marriage will never occur: his and his family's insufficient piety (or general belief that such is the case). See Timm "Beria" 13. (Neugroschel adopts this reason in his translation.) Though the impulse to add a specific reason is certainly narratively and psychologically understandable, this particular choice is problematic, since (a) no evidence exists within the text that Tuvas and Zimro are impious; we know them to be learned, and Briyo has heard that Zimro is not only scholarly, but also "pious" (83), and (b) more importantly, Tuvas is wrong about Feygin's grounds for objection, which are, as we have suggested, a matter of *yikhes*; indeed, Feygin's own admission—"I know very well Zimro is the handsomest and most intelligent boy in this land" (84), while not directly indicating his disagreement with Tuvas' assessment, certainly suggests he has no problems with Zimro's *personal* qualities.

56. See Timm ("Beria" 56–60), who discusses Zimro's and the priest's struggle in terms of a similar master paradigm of Pharisee or Sadducee.
57. On the confusion as to the precise nature of the king's identity, see Erik *Roman* 148.
58. In the Venice edition, this is a "Kaiser"; see Timm "Beria" 50–55 for discussion of both terms.
59. See, on this, Elliott Horowitz, *Reckless Rites: Purim and the Legacy of Jewish Violence* (Princeton: Princeton University Press, 2006), 125–129.
60. Such a connection is made explicitly in one of the most popular contemporary Yiddish texts, the *Tsene-rene* (on Gen. 32:8–9). See discussion in Joseph P. Schultz, "The 'Ze-enah U-Re'enah': Torah for the Folk," *Judaism* 36:1 (1987), 93–94. On another early modern Yiddish text's very different approach to these tactical questions, compare Jean Baumgarten, "Seigneurs et clercs dans les exempla en yiddish du xviie siècle," *Pardès* 7 (1988), 95–104.
61. For much more detailed discussion and attempts to locate the text historically (at least in part), see Timm "Beria" 45–49.
62. This said, the reference to Rome in the pope's description ("Sometime later in Rome the pope, a very wicked man ...") reminds us of the traditional Jewish understanding of the linkage between Hyrcanos and Rome. Nachmanides writes, regarding Jacob's sending messengers to the land of Seir, "And in my opinion this hints that we initiated our downfall through the hand of Edom. For the kings of the second temple [i.e., the Hasmoneans] entered into a treaty with Rome and some of them came to Rome and it was the cause of their falling into their hands; and this is mentioned in the sayings of our sages and noted in books." See the discussion of this passage in Funkenstein *Perceptions* 111, esp. n. 74, where some confusion exists about the precise identity of the event Nachmanides refers to; nonetheless, those events as *understood* might well find their parallel in Zimro's travels.
63. This said, numerous historical and literary precedents exist for decrees forbidding circumcision; see Erik "Mayse" 157 and Timm "Beria" 50 for discussion. On a contemporary (1555) anti-Semitic papal bull and its propagator and reiterator, Paul IV and Pius V, which may have served as authorial inspiration, see David Philipson, *Old European Jewries* (Philadelphia: Jewish Publication Society, 1894), 122–124, 128–130.
64. Compare Timm "Beria," passim. This is not to suggest, however, that contemporary audiences were, necessarily, *deeply* conscious of these historiographical divisions, and certainly not narrow, fine-grained shifts in historical periodization. On contemporary audiences' tendency to engage in

a kind of "panchronism," a "way of thinking [which] abolishes the distance of time between the present and antiquity, and highlights atemporal patterns of behavior and thought which permit a Jew to identify with the past," see Sunshine "Mail" 93–94; Frakes "Legal" 14; Robert Chazan, "Representation of Events in the Middle Ages," in Ada Rapaport-Albert, ed., *Essays in Jewish Historiography* (Atlanta: Scholars Press, 1988), 40–55, esp. 46–47, 50–55; and Chazan, "The Timebound and the Timeless: Medieval Jewish Narration of Events," *History and Memory* 6 (1994), 14, 20–21.

65. See Timm "Beria" 54–55 for potentially resonant contemporary historical events.
66. See Funkenstein *Perceptions* 98–121, esp. 110–117, on the relationship between Christian typology and prefiguration and (particularly Nachmanides') sense of *maase avot siman lebanim*. On this "historical patterning," compare also Chazan, esp. 42–43, and Marc Saperstein, "Jewish Typological Exegesis After Nachmanides," *Jewish Studies Quarterly* 1 (1993/1994), 158–170, esp. 162–163.
67. The Venice edition mentions the king, but simply to insist that he and his courtiers "didn't know what to do; they were terrified" (87). On this theme, compare the complementary approach taken by Frakes ("Legal" 15–16).
68. On Hyrcanos and the consequences of Greek wisdom, see BT Sotah 49b. This topic is discussed, in a very different fashion, in Yonah Fraenkel, *Darkhei haagada vehamidrash* (Givatayim: Yad Latalmud, 1991), 236ff, and Richard Kalmin's review essay of same in *Prooftexts* 14:3 (1994), 194–195.
69. For analytic purposes, the two texts will be read complementarily, though our argument suggests the author follows the Babylonian Talmud's primacy, in accordance with general European Jewish hierarchies (indeed, it is only there that Hyrcanos is mentioned by name).
70. I do not mean to claim that R. Levi is *actually* R. Yehoshua ben Levi's father; simply that the nomenclatural similarities constitute an important textual moment regardless of historical truth.
71. *Decameron*, Day One, Story Two.
72. An example of his lust for power is his anger at seeing it abrogated: when Zimro reveals himself as a Jew, the pope decrees the sentries who allowed him in will be killed. (88)
73. See Exodus 1:18–20, and the discussions of the topic in BT Sotah 11b and Exodus Rabbah 1:16. The 1580/85 manuscript (*pace* Frakes and Timm) seemingly reads *ken yirbe* ("may they multiply") here; the original Exodus text reads *pen yirbe* ("lest they multiply")—both readings are (with a little

ingenuity) possible in this context, but the source—and thus the textual allusion—is clear.

74. The biblical language indicating the Jews' "swarming" in Egypt is a case in point. See Exodus 1:7.

75. Narratives in Genesis (when Simeon and Levi kill the people of Shechem) and midrashic commentaries (surrounding the account of Abraham's circumcision) strongly suggest circumcision, particularly adult circumcision, is physiologically enervating.

76. Though space precludes a full structural analysis of "Briyo and Zimro," the fairly simple bipyramidal structure of the tale can be briefly noted, where the encounters with the pope and the deceased Briyo are its twin apexes. On the work's structure more generally, see Timm "Beria" 87.

77. On traditional punishment for sexual offenses, and the kiss's role within the Jewish context as a sexual offense, see Timm "Beria" 61–62. Warnock ("Proverbs" 183) notes the phrase's possible proverbial origin.

78. The classic adumbration of this paradoxical balance, "All is foreseen, and free will is granted," is found in BT Avot 3:15.

79. On oaths' centrality in Ashkenazic culture, see Kenneth R. Stow, *Alienated Minority: The Jews of Medieval Latin Europe* (Cambridge, MA: Harvard University Press, 1992), 91.

80. See Erik "Mayse" 159 and Zfatman "S" 1:93–94.

81. Death does, uncoincidentally, result from Zimro's papal meeting—just not his own: the sentries are killed, as mentioned above, and Feygin almost dies, in his reaction to Zimro's return: "When [Zimro] arrived [home], everyone was delighted, especially his beloved Briyo. But the high priest was so dumbfounded *that he nearly gave up the ghost: he had been certain that Zimro would be killed.*" (89, emphasis mine)

82. Compare this to one of the master narratives to fully appreciate the inherent tensions here: as we have said, this moment relies heavily on the book of Esther, and much of the action in the last third of the book of Esther is dependent on the fact that the king's word cannot be overturned, even by the king himself.

83. Perhaps of relevance, this impersonation results in a doubled Solomon; the real Solomon, according to tradition, wanders the world as Kohelet (Ecclesiastes). See BT Gittin 68a–b.

84. This reveals another thematic pyramidal structuring: including the preface and this final quest, a fantastic-realistic-fantastic structure is apparent; contrast Zinberg's characterization of the split between realism and fantasy

as binaristic (6:169; he omits the court case in his summary of the tale). On Zimro's fantastic quest more generally, see Timm "Beria" 65–76; for general comments on a hero's venture "from the world of common day into a region of supernatural wonder," compare Campbell *Hero* 30, 36–37, 217.

85. In this reading, attaining the castle reads the monarchy as representing non-Jewish authority, an idealized triumph unavailable to the lived Jew embodied in Zimro.
86. For earlier appearances of this motif in chivalric and Jewish literature, see Erik "Mayse" 157 and Timm "Beria" 66–68.
87. A similar episode appears in the chivalric *Ditrikh von Bern*; see Erik *Roman* 149.
88. Arguably, the horse provides an equine analogue to Virgil, given the decedents' later comment in purgatory that they heard in advance the horse would be sent to Zimro (92), suggesting (parodic?) annunciation or assignment akin to Beatrice's of Virgil, the obvious enormous differences between the two, such as the horse's abandonment of Zimro rather than accompanying him, notwithstanding. Similarly, Zimro's encounter with Elijah later in the narrative is almost too late to provide him any insight or character development.
89. This almost inherent lack of spatial and geographical specificity within Zimro's fantastic journey can be contrasted to the significantly greater spatial and temporal specification of the earthly paradise and Eden in contemporary Christian text, particularly though not solely cartographic text. Compare Alessandro Scafi, *Mapping Paradise: A History of Heaven on Earth* (Chicago: University of Chicago Press, 2006), 6, 19, 27, 37, 55–56, 129, 193, 288–289, especially his attention to the allegorical and theological dimensions invested in textual and graphic "concept-representations."
90. The midrashic tradition cited by Timm in this regard ("Beria" 68–71) also connects this motif to traditional rabbinic concerns.
91. See Genesis 3:24 and commentaries ad loc.
92. Erik ("Mayse" 157, *Roman* 149) notes the parallels to both Genesis and the Arthurian legends but does not comment further; see also Timm "Beria" 71–72; Zinberg 6:170; and Warnock "Proverbs" 184.
93. Though the Talmudic statement of *ein mazel leyisroel* refers most explicitly to astrological speculation, over time *mazel* developed to include a much broader rubric, and I use it here in that sense.
94. Though the highly complex history of Jewish purgatorial states is beyond our scope here, I have seen no evidence for a traditional location of a purgatorial state within Eden's spatial limits. The Venice text, perhaps in

part to deal with this concern, relocates Briyo to Gehenna; see Timm "Beria" 38, and, for discussion, 72–74.

95. The narrative clarifies that after their greeting, Zimro is happy to discover they are Jewish, so presumably "shalom" is intended as a specific Jewish greeting, not just a general salutation.
96. See the discussion in chapter 5; this also explains their request that the living Zimro pray for them.
97. See Timm "Beria" 75–76.
98. Compare Erik's approach in *Roman* 151 and *Geshikhte* 350–351.
99. One might even suggest Briyo functions as a second, Jewish Beatrice. The names are not dissimilar, and both figures die too young and serve as symbolic guiding lights for an unrequited lover. Such a comparison illuminates even more clearly the author's Jewish diminution and pietistic subversion: while Dante places Beatrice in the heavenly firmament, at the Virgin Mary's right hand, Briyo, at least at first, is located under the stairs like a scullery maid.
100. Another discrepancy between the Divine Beatrice and the somewhat sexualized Briyo: Dante's total obedience to Beatrice in the *Commedia* can be juxtaposed to the disobedience here.
101. See Exodus 19–20 and *Mekhilta* ad loc; see also BT Shabbat 88b.
102. In the original text, we only discover the figure's Jewishness (much less his identity as Elijah) at the first encounter's end; the Prague edition has them greeting each other with *sholem aleykhem*. In the Venice text, Elijah is replaced by the angel Dumah; see Timm "Beria" 38, 74–75 and Erik "Mayse" 158. The choice of Elijah is particularly fitting in establishing analogues to Dante, as his status as a living man in the land of the dead, having ascended to heaven alive, is analogous (though not identical) to Virgil's positioning; compare Timm "Beria" 66 and 94.
103. Parenthetically, this suggests a narrative double standard: after all, Zimro has kissed Briyo as much as Briyo has kissed Zimro. Perhaps the disparate perspective in punishment stems from Briyo's imbalanced passion for Zimro and her activist plotting of their rendezvous; perhaps it is simply a matter of chauvinism.
104. Both the text and Neugroschel's translation here rhyme; I have removed the rhyme in altering the translation for the sake of greater accuracy. On the ending's traditionalist moral valence, see Zfatman "S" 1:94.
105. Zinberg's identification of the wedding scene as a Judaization of the heavenly marriage that closes the tale of Amor and Psyche (6:170–171), not an original motif, is a case in point. Compare also David Biale's discussion

of this story as proof of the existence of "countervailing fantasies" to "official norms" of the "normative marital system," simultaneously affirming those norms and undermining them by "offering a fictional alternative" (*Eros and the Jews*, 66) and Y. Shiper, "A yidisher libe-roman fun mitl-elter," *YIVO Bleter* 13 (1938), 237–238 on the "Tristan and Isolde" motif in the work. On the tradition of the wedding in heaven, see Timm "Beria" 80–82.

106. On the saying's history, see Robert G. Warnock, "Proverbs and Sayings in Early Yiddish Literature," in Walter Röll and Simon Neuberg, eds. *Jiddische Philologie: Festschrift für Erika Timm* (Tübingen: Niemeyer, 1999), 176–178.

107. Erik's characterization of the story in halves, as half-cautious, half-supportive of romance, seems on the mark, though his imputation of irony and *khutzpe* to the narrator and the text may result in inattention to some of its complexities. Compare Erik "Mayse" 159–160.

108. Such inversion also occurs in the wedding account: it may be ironic that Solomon, a man whose marital troubles were legion, recites the wedding blessings. Conversely, as alluded to above, it neatly evokes and structurally completes the earlier master paradigm: the man who administered the original case where division was prevented now presides over a union.

109. Daniel Boyarin, *Unheroic Conduct: The Rise of Heterosexuality and the Invention of the Jewish Man* (Berkeley: University of California Press, 1997), 36. See also 143–144.

110. Boyarin *Unheroic Conduct* 42.

111. Boyarin *Unheroic Conduct* 78. Compare also 210–211.

112. Boyarin *Unheroic Conduct* 43–44, quote 43. Compare Sol Liptzin's comments: "knightly adventures ... had no basis in Jewish reality ... they could not speak to the inmost feelings of [authors'] Jewish listeners ... exploits of the biceps or the deft handling of a lance were not as highly regarded by the Jews as were wisdom, moral courage, and the sanctification of God's name through martyrdom." *A History of Yiddish Literature* (Middle Village, NY: J. David, 1972), 8.

113. Compare, for example, Boyarin's discussion of Haggadahs (*Unheroic Conduct* 51–53), and his analysis there of "the oppositions between the knight and the sage as respectively abjected and valued stereotypes of maleness"; Bovo and Zimro certainly at least complicate the presentation of such ideal types. On this approach more generally, compare Christoph Daxelmüller, "Jewish Popular Culture Since the Middle Ages," in R. Po-Chia Hsia and Hartmut Lehmann, eds. *In and Out of the Ghetto* (Cambridge: Cambridge University Press, 1995),

29–48, esp. 35–37; on the "surprisingly high" Jewish interest in matters military, compare Shulvass 352–353 and Weinreich's comments in *Bilder* 56.

114. Compare Baumgarten *OYL* 131.

CODA

1. Translations from Glikl's memoirs are taken from Beth-Zion Abrahams, *The Life of Glückel of Hameln* (New York: Thomas Yoseloff, 1963, hereafter "Abrahams"). I have occasionally altered the translation either for the sake of greater accuracy or, by employing more literal but less felicitous wording, to evoke certain aspects of the work for analytic purposes. References to Glikl's original version are taken from Chava Turniansky's critical edition, with Hebrew translations and annotations: *Glikl: Zikhronot 1691–1719* (Jerusalem: Zalman Shazar, 2006, hereafter *Zikhronot*). For this episode, see Abrahams 178–182, *Zikhronot* 586–602; quote Abrahams 178, *Zikhronot* 586–588; for other contemporary, critical, and historical accounts of the event, see *Zikhronot* 587n188.
2. Abrahams 180; *Zikhronot* 594; see n.*238 there on *siba ra*.
3. Abrahams 182; *Zikhronot* 602.
4. Abrahams 178; *Zikhronot* 590.
5. Michael Stanislawski has correctly noted that Glikl was, in this sense, a typical member of her community, "deeply committed to [her] faith, never for once doubting its eternal veracity and its requirements that [she] live entirely bounded and defined by its norms, laws, and strictures" (*Autobiographical* 35). See also Turniansky's introduction, 28–29.
6. See Moseley 159, and 170–171, where he notes that in her "life-account proper ... she is constantly aware of and kept in line by the conventions of the 'Ethical Will.' " On Glikl and her work more generally, see the sources cited in chapter 2, as well as Turniansky's introduction to *Zikhronot* and the works cited there.
7. Abrahams 180; *Zikhronot* 594.
8. Abrahams 180; *Zikhronot* 596.
9. Stanislawski *Autobiographical* 52.
10. Abrahams 180–181; *Zikhronot* 598–600.
11. Abrahams 11; *Zikhronot* 40. See also Stanislawski *Autobiographical* 45 and Moseley 160.
12. Take, as one example, her discussion of David's reaction to Absalom's death (Abrahams 167, *Zikhronot* 552); there, she refers to David as *alav*

hashalom, a formula only employed for real, not fictional individuals. I cite this hardly to suggest that it is surprising that Glikl believed David to be a historical figure; rather to indicate its value in comparison to its absence in other contexts.

13. Compare, for example, Glikl's accounts of mysterious noises, both cited above, and immediately preceding her father's death (Abrahams 91, *Zikhronot* 308), or the dream of the woman buried without her shroud (Abrahams 20, *Zikhronot* 74). In each of these cases, Glikl's consciously vague descriptions (she uses the word "something" (*etvas*), for example, to describe the force doing the knocking in the episode of her father's death) allow for the possibility of dream, external natural factors, or psychological disturbance, while still holding open the possibility of supernatural intervention.
14. Abrahams 182; *Zikhronot* 604. Though even here Glikl's pessimistic side gets its innings in: the last full sentence of the book stresses the sign's ambiguous nature through Glikl's prayer that "this is a sign for good"—implying, of course, that the converse is a possibility as well.
15. See, for example, Stanislawski, passim.
16. See Erik *Geshikhte*, passim.
17. See, as just one example, the essays in Monika Richarz, ed., *Die Hamburger Kauffrau Glikl: Jüdische Existenz in der Frühen Neuzeit* (Hamburg: Christians, 2001).
18. For two discussions of this process, see Zinberg 6:46–47 and Zfatman "S" 1:24. This could be, in other words, the literary analogue to the linguistic study undertaken by Kerler; see *Origins*, passim, esp. 258–261.

Bibliography

Abrahams, Beth-Zion. *The Life of Glückel of Hameln*. New York: Thomas Yoseloff, 1963.

Abrahams, Israel. *Jewish Life in the Middle Ages*. New York: Athenaeum, 1969 (1896).

Abramovitch, S. Y. (=Mendele Mocher Seforim). "Of Bygone Days." In Ruth Wisse, ed. *A Shtetl and Other Novellas*. Detroit: Wayne State University Press, 1986.

Airakinsen, Timo. "Five Types of Knowledge." *American Philosophical Quarterly* 15:4 (1978), 263–274.

Alexander, Tamar. "Theme and Genre: Relationships between Man and She-Demon in Jewish Folklore." *Jewish Folklore and Ethnology Review* 14 (1992), 56–61.

Alexander, Tamar. "Love and Death in a Contemporary Dybbuk Story: Personal Narrative and the Female Voice." In Matt Goldish, ed. *Spirit Possession in Judaism: Cases and Contexts from the Middle Ages to the Present*. Detroit: Wayne State University Press, 2003, 307–345.

Allony, Nechemiah. "Mekorot khadashim le-'Shmuel bukh' vele-'Melokhim bukh.' " *Beer-Sheva* 1 (1973), 90–113.

Althaus, Hans Peter. *Die Cambridger Löwenfabel von 1382*. Berlin: Walter de Gruyter, 1971.

Anderson, George K. *The Legend of the Wandering Jew*. Providence: Brown University Press, 1965.

Anonymous. *News from Scotland*. London, 1592. Cited in Miola, 138–144.

Auerbach, Erich. *Mimesis: The Representation of Reality in Western Literature*. Princeton, NJ: Princeton University Press, 1953.

Avenary, Hanoch. "Orale Judendeutsche Volkspoesie in der Interaktion mit Literarischer Überlieferung." *LBI Bulletin* 87 (1990), 5–17.

Bal-Makshoves (I. Eliashiv). "Tsvey shprakhn—eyn eyntsike literatur." In Bal-Makhshoves, *Geklibene verk.* New York: Congress for Jewish Culture, 1953, 112–123.

Banitt, Menahem. "Une formule d'exorcisme en ancien français." In John Fisher and Paul A. Gaeng, eds. *Studies in Honor of Mario A. Pei.* Chapel Hill: University of North Carolina Press, 1972, 37–48.

Barkai, Ron, ed. *Curs la cabala.* Barcelona: Fundació Caixa de Pensions, 1989.

Barnet, Sylvan. "Marlowe's *Doctor Faustus* on the Stage." In Christopher Marlowe, *Doctor Faustus.* Ed. Sylvan Barnet. New York: Signet Classics, 2001.

Barney, Stephen A. *Allegories of History, Allegories of Love.* Hamden, CT: Archon Books, 1979.

Baron, Salo. *A Social and Religious History of the Jews.* New York: Columbia University Press, 1952–1993. 20 vols.

Barstow, Anne Llewellyn. *Witchcraze: A New History of the European Witch Hunts.* San Francisco: Pandora, 1994.

Bartal, Israel, et al., eds. *Keminhag ashkenaz upolin.* Jerusalem: Zalman Shazar, 1993.

Baskin, Judith. "Rabbinic Judaism and the Creation of Woman." In Miriam Peskowitz and Laura Levitt, eds. *Judaism Since Gender.* New York: Routledge, 1997, 125–130.

Bassin, M. *Antologye: Finf hundert yor idishe poezye.* New York: Literarishe Farlag, 1917.

Baum, Paul Franklin. "The Fable of Belling the Cat." In Pack Carnes, ed. *Proverbia in Fabula.* New York: Peter Lang, 1988, 37–46.

Baumgarten, Elisheva. *Mothers and Children: Jewish Family Life in Medieval Europe.* Princeton: Princeton University Press, 2004.

Baumgarten, Jean. "Une chanson de geste en yidich ancien: Le *Shmuel bukh.*" *Revue de la Bibliothèque nationale* 13 (1984), 24–38.

Baumgarten, Jean. "Les traductions de la bible en yidich (xvie–xviie siècles) et le *zeenah ureenah* (Bâle, 1622) de yaakov ishaq achkenazi de janow." *Revue des Études juives* 144:1–3 (Jan.–Sept. 1985), 305–310.

Baumgarten, Jean. "Seigneurs et clercs dans les exempla en yiddish du xviie siècle." *Pardès* 7 (1988), 95–104.s.

Baumgarten, Jean. *Introduction à la littérature yiddish ancienne.* Paris: Éditions du Cerf, 1993.

Baumgarten, Jean. "Les manuscrits Yidich de la Bibliothèque Nationale de Paris." In David Goldberg, ed. *The Field of Yiddish, Fifth Collection: Studies in Language, Folklore, and Literature.* Evanston, IL: Northwestern University Press, 1993, 121–151.

Baumgarten, Jean. "Textes médicaux en langue yiddish (XIVe–XVIIe siècles)." In Gabrielle Sed-Rajna, ed. *Rashi 1040–1990.*. Paris: Éditions du Cerf, 1993, 723–740.

Baumgarten, Jean, ed. *Le yiddish: Langue, culture, société.* Paris: CNRS, 1999.

Baumgarten, Jean. "Textes mystiques en langue yiddish (xviie–xixe siècles): Les traductions des *Shivhei Hayyim Vital* et *Shivhei ha-Ari.*" *Kabbalah: Journal for the Study of Mystical Texts* 2 (1997), 65–103.

Baumgarten, Jean. *Récits hagiographiques juifs.* Paris: Éditions du Cerf, 2001.

Baumgarten, Jean. "Between Translation and Commentary: The Bilingual Editions of the *Kav hayosher* by Tsvi Hirsh Kaidanover." *Journal of Modern Jewish Studies* 3 (2004), 269–287.

Baumgarten, Jean. *Introduction to Old Yiddish Literature.* Ed. and trans. Jerold C. Frakes. Oxford: Oxford University Press, 2005.

Bauml, Franz. "Medieval Texts and the Two Theories of Oral-Formulaic Composition." *New Literary History* 16:1 (Autumn 1984), 31–49.

Baym, Nina. "Melodramas of Beset Manhood: How Theories of American Fiction Exclude Women Authors." In Elaine Showalter, ed. *The New Feminist Criticism: Essays on Women, Literature, and Theory.* New York: Pantheon Books, 1985, 63–80.

Beebee, Thomas O. *The Ideology of Genre: A Comparative Study of Generic Instability.* University Park, PA: Pennsylvania State University Press, 1994.

Behringer, Wolfgang. *Witchcraft Persecutions in Bavaria.* Cambridge: Cambridge University Press, 1997.

Bell, Dean Phillip, and Stephen G. Burnett. *Jews, Judaism, and the Reformation in Sixteenth-Century Germany.* Leiden: Brill, 2006.

Berger, Peter L., and Thomas Luckmann. *The Social Construction of Reality: A Treatise in the Sociology of Knowledge.* New York: Irvington Publishers, 1966.

Berger, Shlomo. "An Invitation to Buy and Read: Paratexts of Yiddish Books in Amsterdam, 1650–1800." *Book History* 7 (2004), 31–61.

Bernstein, Mordechai. "Two Remedy Books in Yiddish from 1474 and 1508." In Raphael Patai, ed. *Studies in Biblical and Jewish Folklore.* Bloomington: Indiana University Press, 1960, 289–305.

Biale, David. *Eros and the Jews: From Biblical Israel to Contemporary America.* Berkeley: University of California Press, 1997.

Bilik, Dorothy. "Jewish Women and Yiddish Literature: *Glückel of Hameln.*" *Studies on Voltaire and the Eighteenth Century* 265 (1989), 1217–1220.

Bilik, Dorothy. "*The Memoirs of Glikl of Hameln:* The Archaeology of the Text." *Yiddish* 8 (1992), 5–22.

Bilik, Dorothy. "Tsene-rene: A Yiddish Literary Success." *Jewish Book Annual* 51 (1993–1994), 96–111.

Bilu, Yoram. "Dybbuk, Aslai, Zar: The Cultural Distinctiveness and Historical Situatedness of Possession Illness In Three Jewish Milieus," in Matt Goldish, ed. *Spirit Possession in Judaism: Cases and Contexts from the Middle Ages to the Present.* Detroit: Wayne State University Press, 2003, 346–365.

Bilu, Yoram. "The Taming of the Deviants and Beyond: An Analysis of *Dybbuk* Possession and Exorcism in Judaism," in Matt Goldish, ed. *Spirit Possession in Judaism: Cases and Contexts from the Middle Ages to the Present.* Detroit: Wayne State University Press, 2003, 41–72.

Birringer, Johannes H. "Faustus's Rhetoric of Aspiration." In Harold Bloom, ed. *Christopher Marlowe's Doctor Faustus: Modern Critical Interpretations.* New York: Chelsea House, 1988, 93–103.

Bloom, Harold, ed. *Christopher Marlowe's Doctor Faustus: Modern Critical Interpretations.* New York: Chelsea House, 1988.

Bonfil, Robert. *Rabbis and Jewish Communities in Renaissance Italy.* Oxford: Littman Library of Jewish Civilization, 1990.

Bonfil, Robert. *Jewish Life in Renaissance Italy.* Berkeley: University of California Press, 1994.

Booth, Wayne. *The Rhetoric of Fiction.* Chicago: University of Chicago Press, 1961.

Bottigheimer, Ruth B. *Fairy Godfather: Straparola, Venice, and the Fairy Tale Tradition.* Philadelphia: University of Pennsylvania Press, 2002.

Boyarin, Daniel. *Carnal Israel: Reading Sex in Talmudic Culture.* Berkeley: University of California Press, 1993.

Boyarin, Daniel. *Unheroic Conduct: The Rise of Heterosexuality and the Invention of the Jewish Man.* Berkeley: University of California Press, 1997.

Bradbrook, M. C. "The Sources of *Macbeth.*" In Kenneth Muir and Philip Edwards, eds. *Aspects of Macbeth.* Cambridge: Cambridge University Press, 1977, 12–25.

Braunmuller, A. R., ed. *Macbeth.* Cambridge: Cambridge University Press, 1997.

Breuer, Mordechai. "Modernism and Traditionalism in Sixteenth-Century Jewish Historiography: A Study of David Gans' *Tzemah David.*" In Bernard Dov Cooperman, ed. *Jewish Thought in the Sixteenth Century.* Cambridge, MA: Harvard University Press, 1983, 49–88.

Briggs, Robin. *Witches and Neighbours: The Social and Cultural Context of European Witchcraft.* London: HarperCollins, 1996.

Brooke, Nicholas. Introduction. In William Shakespeare, *The Tragedy of Macbeth*. Oxford: Clarendon Press, 1990.

Bullough, Vern L. "On Being a Man in the Middle Ages." In Clare A. Lees, ed. *Medieval Masculinities: Reading Men in the Middle Ages*. Minneapolis: University of Minnesota Press, 1994, 31–45.

Burnett, Stephen G. "German Jewish Printing in the Reformation Era (1530–1633)." In Phillip Dean Bell and Stephen G. Burnett. *Jews, Judaism, and the Reformation in Sixteenth-Century Germany*. Leiden: Brill, 2006, 503–527.

Burns, E. Jane. "This Prick Which is Not One: How Women Talk Back in Old French Fabliaux." In Linda Lomperis and Sarah Stanbury, eds. *Feminist Approaches to the Body in Medieval Literature*. Philadephia: University of Pennsylvania Press, 1993, 188–212.

Butler, Judith. *Gender Trouble: Feminism and the Subversion of Identity*. New York: Routledge, 1990.

Bützer, Evi. *Die Anfänge der jiddischen purim shpiln in ihrem literarischen und kulturgeschichtlichen Kontext*. Hamburg: Helmut Buske Verlag, 2003.

Bynum, Caroline Walker. *Holy Feast and Holy Fast: The Religious Significance of Food to Medieval Women*. Berkeley: University of California Press, 1987.

Bynum, Caroline Walker. *Metamorphosis and Identity*. New York: Zone Books, 2001.

Calinescu, Matei. "Orality in Literacy: Some Historical Paradoxes in Reading." *Yale Journal of Criticism* 6:2 (1993), 175–190.

Campbell, Joseph. *The Hero with a Thousand Faces*. New York: Pantheon, 1949.

Carlebach, Elisheva, John M. Efron, and David Myers, eds. *Jewish History and Jewish Memory: Essays in Honor of Yosef Hayim Yerushalmi*. University Press of New England, 1998.

Carlebach, Elisheva. "Jews, Christians, and the Endtime in Early Modern Germany." *Jewish History* 14 (2000), 331–344.

Carlebach, Elisheva. *Divided Souls: Converts from Judaism in Germany, 1500–1750*. New Haven: Yale University Press, 2001.

Carnes, Pack, ed. *Proverbia in Fabula: Essays on the Relationship of the Proverb and the Fable*. New York: Peter Lang, 1988.

Carnes, Pack. "How Phaedrus' Fables 'Mean': Notes on Aesop in a Contextual Model." *Reinardus* 13 (2000), 49–65.

Carroll, William C., ed. *Macbeth: Texts and Contexts*. Boston: Bedford / St. Martin's, 1999.

Catholy, Eckerhard. *Fastnachtspiel.* Stuttgart: J. B. Metzlersche Verlagsbuchhandlung, 1966.

Catholy, Eckerhard. *Das deutsche Lustspiel.* Stuttgart: W. Kohlhammer Verlag, 1969.

Chajes, J. H. *Between Worlds: Dybbuks, Exorcists, and Early Modern Judaism.* Philadelphia: University of Pennsylvania Press, 2003.

Chajes, J. H. "City of the Dead: Spirit Possession in Sixteenth-Century Safed." In Matt Goldish, ed. *Spirit Possession in Judaism: Cases and Contexts from the Middle Ages to the Present.* Detroit: Wayne State University Press, 2003, 124–158.

Chartier, Roger. *The Cultural Uses of Print in Early Modern France.* Princeton, NJ: Princeton University Press, 1987.

Chartier, Roger, ed. *The Culture of Print: Power and the Uses of Print in Early Modern Europe.* Princeton, NJ: Princeton University Press, 1987.

Chartier, Roger. "The Hanged Woman Miraculously Saved: An *occasionel.*" In Roger Chartier, ed. *The Culture of Print: Power and the Uses of Print in Early Modern Europe.* Princeton, NJ: Princeton University Press, 1987, 59–91.

Chartier, Roger. *The Order of Books.* Stanford: Stanford University Press, 1994.

Chartier, Roger. *Forms and Meanings: Texts, Performances, and Audiences from Codex to Computer.* Philadelphia: University of Pennsylvania Press, 1995.

Chazan, Robert. "Representation of Events in the Middle Ages." In Ada Rapaport-Albert, ed. *Essays in Jewish Historiography.* Atlanta: Scholars Press, 1988, 40–55.

Chazan, Robert. "The Timebound and the Timeless: Medieval Jewish Narration of Events." *History and Memory* 6 (1994), 5–34.

Chojnacki, Stanley. "Subaltern Patriarchs: Patrician Bachelors in Renaissance Venice." In Clare A. Lees, ed. *Medieval Masculinities: Reading Men in the Middle Ages.* Minneapolis: University of Minnesota Press, 1994, 73–90.

Clark, Stuart. *Thinking with Demons: The Idea of Witchcraft in Early Modern Europe.* Oxford: Clarendon Press, 1997.

Clark, Stuart, ed. *Languages of Witchcraft: Narrative, Ideology, and Meaning in Early Modern Culture.* New York: St. Martin's Press, 2001.

Clifford, Gay. *The Transformations of Allegory.* London: Routledge, 1974.

Cohen, Daniel J. "An Autographic Letter by Moshe Wallich, Author of the KUH-BUCH: The Key to his Biography and Family Connections in Worms,

Frankfort, and Hamburg." *Studies in Bibliography and Booklore* 14 (1982), 4–16.

Cohen, Tova. "Sexual Politics in a Medieval Hebrew Marriage Debate." *Exemplaria* 12:1 (2000), 157–184.

Cohn, Dorrit. *Transparent Minds: Narrative Modes for Presenting Consciousness in Fiction*. Princeton, NJ: Princeton University Press, 1978.

Cohn, Norman. *Europe's Inner Demons: The Demonization of Christians in Medieval Christendom*. Chicago: University of Chicago Press, 1993 rev. ed.

Cooperman, Bernard Dov, ed. *Jewish Thought in the Sixteenth Century*. Cambridge, MA: Harvard University Press, 1983.

Culler, Jonathan. *The Pursuit of Signs: Semiotics, Literature, Deconstruction*. Ithaca: Cornell University Press, 1981.

Culler, Jonathan. *Framing the Sign: Criticism and Its Institutions*. Norman: University of Oklahoma Press, 1988.

Dan, Joseph. "Sipurim demonologiyim me-kitve R. Yehuda Hasid." *Tarbiz* 30 (1961), 273–289.

Dan, Joseph. *Hasipur haivri biyemei habeinayim*. Jerusalem: Keter, 1974.

Dan, Joseph. *Sifrut hamusar vehaderush*. Jerusalem: Keter, 1975.

Dan, Joseph. "Samael, Lilith, and the Concept of Evil in Early Kabbalah." *AJSReview* 5 (1980), 17–40.

Dan, Joseph. "Manasseh ben Israel's *Nishmat Hayyim* and the Concept of Evil in Seventeenth-Century Jewish Thought." In Isadore Twersky and Bernard Septimus, eds. *Jewish Thought in the Seventeenth Century*. Cambridge, MA: Harvard University Press, 1987, 63–75.

Dan, Joseph. Introduction. In Matt Goldish, ed. *Spirit Possession in Judaism: Cases and Contexts from the Middle Ages to the Present*. Detroit: Wayne State University Press, 2003.

Daston, Lorraine, and Katharine Park. *Wonders and the Order of Nature, 1150–1750*. New York: Zone Books, 1998.

Dauber, Jeremy. *Antonio's Devils: Writers of the Jewish Enlightenment and the Birth of Modern Hebrew and Yiddish Literature*. Stanford: Stanford University Press, 2004.

Davis, Joseph. "The *Ten Questions* of Eliezer Eilburg and the Problem of Jewish Unbelief in the Sixteenth Century." *JQR* 91:3–4 (2001), 293–336.

Davis, Natalie Zemon. *Society and Culture in Early Modern France*. Stanford: Stanford University Press, 1975.

Davis, Natalie Zemon. *Fiction in the Archives*. Stanford: Stanford University Press, 1987.

Davis, Natalie Zemon. *Women on the Margins: Three Seventeenth-Century Lives.* Cambridge, MA: Harvard University Press, 1995.

Daxelmüller, Christoph. "Jewish Popular Culture Since the Middle Ages." In R. Po-Chia Hsia and Harmut Lehmann, eds. *In and Out of the Ghetto.* Cambridge: Cambridge University Press, 1995, 29–48.

De Laurentis, Teresa. *Technologies of Gender.* Bloomington: Indiana University Press, 1987.

De Laurentis, Teresa. "The Technology of Gender." In Teresa de Laurentis, *Technologies of Gender.* Bloomington: Indiana University Press, 1987, 1–30.

De Laurentis, Teresa. "The Violence of Rhetoric: Considerations on Representation and Gender." in Teresa de Laurentis, *Technologies of Gender.* Bloomington: Indiana University Press, 1987, 31–50.

Delany, Sheila. " 'Turn It Again': Jewish Medieval Studies and Literary Theory." *Exemplaria* 12:1 (2000), 1–5.

Delitzch, Franz. *Zur Geschichte der jüdischen Poësie.* Leipzig: Karl Tauchnitz, 1836.

Dinse, Helmut. *Die Entwicklung des jiddischen Schrifttums im deutschen Sprachgebiet.* Stuttgart: J. B. Metzlerche Verlagsbuchhandlung, 1974.

Dolby-Stahl, Sandra K. "Sour Grapes: Fable, Proverb, Unripe Fruit." In Pack Carnes, ed. *Proverbia in Fabula.* New York: Peter Lang, 1988, 295–309.

Dreeßen, Wulf-Otto. "Zur Rezeption deutscher epischer Literatur im altjiddischen." In Wolfgang Harms and L. Peter Johnson, *Deutsche Literatur des späten Mittelalters.* Berlin: Erich Schmidt Verlag, 1975, 116–128.

Dreeßen, Wulf-Otto. "Die altjiddischen Estherdichtungen: Überlegungen zur Rekonstruktion der Geschichte der älteren jiddischen Literatur." *Daphnis* 6 (1977), 27–39.

Dubrow, Heather. *Genre.* London: Methuen, 1982.

Edelmann, R. "Ahasuerus, The Wandering Jew: Origin and Background." In Galit Hasan-Rokem and Alan Dundes, eds. *The Wandering Jew: Essays in the Interpretation of a Christian Legend.* Bloomington: Indiana University Press, 1986.

Eilberg-Schwartz, Howard, ed. *People of the Body: Jews and Judaism from an Embodied Perspective.* Albany: SUNY, 1992.

Einbinder, Susan. "Jewish Women Martyrs: Changing Models of Representation." *Exemplaria* 12:1 (2000), 105–127.

Eisenstein, Elizabeth L. *The Printing Press as an Agent of Change.* Cambridge: Cambridge University Press, 1979, 2 vols.

Eliade, Mircea. *The Myth of the Eternal Return or, Cosmos and History.* London: Arkana, 1954.

Elmer, Peter. "Towards a Politics of Witchcraft in Early Modern England." In Stuart Clark, ed. *Languages of Witchcraft: Narrative, Ideology, and Meaning in Early Modern Culture*. New York: St. Martin's Press, 2001, 101–118.

Erik, Max. "Vegn mayse briyo vezimro." *Shriftn fun yidishn visenshaftlekhn institut* 1 (*filologishe seriye*) (1926), 153–162.

Erik, Max. *Vegn altyidishn roman un novele: fernster-zekhnster yorhundert*. Warsaw: Der veg tsum visn, 1926.

Erik, Max. *Di geshikhte fun der yidisher literatur fun di eltste tsaytn biz der haskole-tkufe*. Warsaw: Kultur-lige, 1928.

Exum, J. Cheryl, and Stephen D. Moore, eds. *Biblical Studies / Cultural Studies*. Sheffield: Sheffield Academic Press, 1998.

Faierstein, Morris. "*Maggidim,* Spirits, and Women in Rabbi Hayim Vital's Book of Visions." In Matt Goldish, ed. *Spirit Possession in Judaism: Cases and Contexts from the Middle Ages to the Present*. Detroit: Wayne State University Press, 2003, 186–196.

Febvre, Lucien. *The Coming of the Book: The Impact of Printing 1450–1800*. London: NLB, 1976.

Febvre, Lucien. *The Problem of Unbelief in the Sixteenth Century: The Religion of Rabelais*. Cambridge: Harvard University Press, 1982.

Feldman, Yael S. "Isaac or Oedipus? Jewish Tradition and the Israeli Aqedah." In J. Cheryl Exum and Stephen D. Moore, eds. *Biblical Studies / Cultural Studies*. Sheffield: Sheffield Academic Press, 1998, 159–189.

Ferrante, Joan. *Woman as Image in Medieval Literature*. New York: Columbia University Press, 1975.

Fine, Lawrence. "Purifying the Body in the Name of the Soul: The Problem of the Body in Sixteenth-Century Kabbalah." In Howard Eilberg-Schwartz, ed. *People of the Body: Jews and Judaism from an Embodied Perspective*. Albany: SUNY, 1992, 117–142.

Fine, Lawrence. "Benevolent Possession in Sixteenth-Century Safed." In Matt Goldish, ed. *Spirit Possession in Judaism: Cases and Contexts from the Middle Ages to the Present*. Detroit: Wayne State University Press, 2003, 101–123.

Finnegan, Ruth. "Literacy Versus Non-literacy: The Great Divide?" In Robin Horton and Ruth Finnegan, eds. *Modes of Thought: Essays on Thinking in Western and Non-Western Societies*. London: Faber and Faber, 1973, 112–144.

Finnegan, Ruth. *Literacy and Orality: Studies in the Technology of Communication*. Oxford: Basil Blackwell, 1988.

Fisher, John, and Paul A. Gaeng. *Studies in Honor of Mario A. Pei*. Chapel Hill: University of North Carolina Press, 1972.

Fishman, David E. "Mikoyekh davenen af yidish: a bintl metodologishe bamerkungen un naye mekoyrim." *YIVO Bleter* (n.s.) 1 (1991), 69–92.

Fishman, David E. *The Rise of Modern Yiddish Culture*. Pittsburgh: University of Pittsburgh Press, 2005.

Fishman, Joshua A., ed. *Readings in the Sociology of Language*. The Hague: Mouton, 1968.

Foley, John Miles, ed. *Oral Traditional Literature: A Festschrift for Albert Bates Lord*. Columbus, OH; Slavica Publishers, 1981.

Foley, John Miles, ed. *Oral Tradition in Literature: Interpretation in Context*. Columbia, MO: University of Missouri Press, 1986.

Foley, John Miles. *Immanent Art: From Structure to Meaning in Traditional Oral Epic*. Bloomington: Indiana University Press, 1991.

Foley, John Miles. *The Singer of Tales in Performance*. Bloomington: Indiana University Press, 1995.

Foley, Richard. "Justified Inconsistent Beliefs." *American Philosophical Quarterly* 16:4 (1979), 247–257.

Frakes, Jerold C. *The Politics of Interpretation: Alterity and Ideology in Old Yiddish Studies*. Albany: State University of New York Press, 1989.

Frakes, Jerold, C. ed. *Early Yiddish Texts, 1100–1750*. Oxford: Oxford University Press, 2004.

Frakes, Jerold C. "Registers of Legal Discourse in Early Yiddish Epic." Unpublished paper presented at conference on German-Yiddish Encounter, Columbia University, 2004.

Frakes, Jerold C. *The Cultural Study of Yiddish in Early Modern Europe*. New York: Palgrave Macmillan, 2007.

Fram, Edward. *Ideals Face Reality: Jewish Law and Life in Poland, 1550–1655*. Cincinnati: Hebrew Union College Press, 1997.

Fram, Edward. *My Dear Daughter: Rabbi Benjamin Slonik and the Education of Jewish Women in Sixteenth-Century Poland*. Cincinnati: Hebrew Union College Press, 2007.

Freehof, Solomon B. "Devotional Literature in the Vernacular: Judeo-German Prior to the Reform Movement." *Central Conference of American Rabbis Yearbook* 33 (1923), 375–415.

Freimann, Aron, ed. and trans. Moshe Wallich's *Die Fabeln des Kuhbuchs*. Berlin: 1926.

Friderichs-Müller, Theresia, ed. *Die 'Historie von dem Kaiser Octaviano.'* Hamburg: Helmut Buske Verlag, 1981–1990, 3 vols.

Friedberg, Ch. [–Chayim]. *Toldot hadefus haivri beitalya.* Tel Aviv: M. A. Bar-Juda, 1956.

Frow, John. *Genre.* London: Routledge, 2006.

Fry, Donald K. "The Memory of Cadmon." In John Miles Foley, ed. *Oral Traditional Literature: A Festschrift for Albert Bates Lord.* Columbus, OH; Slavica Publishers, 1981, 282–293.

Frye, Northrop. *Anatomy of Criticism: Four Essays.* Princeton: Princeton University Press, 1957.

Frye, Northrop. *The Secular Scripture.* Cambridge, MA: Harvard University Press, 1976.

Frymer-Kensky, Tikva. *In the Wake of the Goddesses: Women, Culture, and the Biblical Transformation of Pagan Myth.* New York: The Free Press, 1992.

Fuks, L. *The Oldest Known Literary Documents of Yiddish Literature (c. 1382).* Leiden: E. J. Brill, 1952, 2 vols.

Fuks, L., ed. *Das Schemuelbuch des Mosche Esrim Wearba.* Assen: Van Gorcum, 1961.

Fuks, L., ed. *Das Altjiddische Epos Melokim-Buk.* Assen: Van Gorcum, 1965, 2 vols.

Fuks, L. "*Dos ku-bukh.*" *Di Goldene keyt* 118 (1985), 181–183.

Fuks, L. and R. G. Fuks-Mansfeld. *Hebrew Typography in the Northern Netherlands 1585–1815.* Leiden: E. J. Brill, 1987.

Ganz, P. F., F. Norman, and W. Schwarz, eds. *Dukus Horant.* Tübingen: Max Niemayer Verlag, 1964.

Gardner, John. *On Moral Fiction.* New York: Basic Books, 1978.

Gaster, Theodor H. *The Holy and the Profane.* New York: William Sloane, 1955.

Gelber, Mark, ed. *Identity and Ethos: A Festschrift for Sol Liptzin on the Occasion of His Eighty-fifth Birthday.* New York: Peter Lang, 1986.

Genette, Gérard. *Narrative Discourse: An Essay in Method.* Trans. Jane E. Lewin. Ithaca, NY: Cornell University Press, 1980.

Genette, Gérard. *Figures of Literary Discourse.* Trans. Alan Sheridan. New York: Columbia University Press, 1982.

Genette, Gérard. *The Architext: An Introduction.* Berkeley: University of California Press, 1992.

Genette, Gérard. *Narrative Discourse Revisited.* Trans. Jane E. Lewin. Ithaca, NY: Cornell University Press, 1988.

Genette, Gérard. *Fiction & Diction*. Trans. Catherine Porter. Ithaca: NY, Cornell University Press, 1993.

Gibson, Marion. "Understanding Witchcraft? Accusers' Stories in Print in Early Modern England." In Stuart Clark, ed. *Languages of Witchcraft: Narrative, Ideology, and Meaning in Early Modern Culture*. New York: St. Martin's Press, 2001, 41–54.

Gilbert, Sandra M. "What Do Feminist Critics Want? A Postcard from the Volcano." In Elaine Showalter, ed. *The New Feminist Criticism: Essays on Women, Literature, and Theory*. New York: Pantheon Books, 1985, 29–45.

Gilman, Sander L. *The Jew's Body*. New York: Routledge, 1991.

Goetschel, Roland, ed. *Prière, Mystique, et Judaïsme*. Paris: Presses Universitaires de France, 1987.

Goldish, Matt, ed. *Spirit Possession in Judaism: Cases and Contexts from the Middle Ages to the Present*. Detroit: Wayne State University Press, 2003.

Goldish, Matt. "Vision and Possession: Nathan of Gaza's Earliest Prophesies in Historical Context." In Matt Goldish, ed. *Spirit Possession in Judaism: Cases and Contexts from the Middle Ages to the Present*. Detroit: Wayne State University Press, 2003, 217–236.

Goldschmidt, Lazarus. *The Earliest Illustrated Haggadah*. London: Bamerlea Book Sales, 1940.

Gombrich, E. H. *Art and Illusion: A Study in the Psychology of Pictorial Representation*. London: Phaidon, 1977 (5th ed.).

Greenblatt, Stephen. *Hamlet in Purgatory*. Princeton: Princeton University Press, 2001.

Gries, Zeev. *The Book in the Jewish World, 1700–1900*. Oxford: Littman Library of Jewish Civilization, 2007.

Griffiths, A. Phillips, ed. *Knowledge and Belief*. Oxford: Oxford University Press, 1967.

Haberman, A. M. "Di yidishe oysgabes fun 'moshel hakadmoyni.' " *Yivo-bleter* 13 (1938), 95–101.

Haberman, Bonna Devora. "The Suspected Adulteress: A Study in Textual Embodiment." *Prooftexts* 20:1+2 (2000): 12–42.

Hadas, Moses. *Fables of a Jewish Aesop*. New York: Columbia University Press, 1967.

Harding, Wendy. "Body into Text: *The Book of Margery Kempe*." In Linda Lomperis and Sarah Stanbury, eds. *Feminist Approaches to the Body in Medieval Literature*. Philadephia: University of Pennsylvania Press, 1993, 168–187.

Harms, Wolfgang, and L. Peter Johnson. *Deutsche Literatur des späten Mittelalters*. Berlin: Erich Schmidt Verlag, 1975.

Hasan-Rokem, Galit, and Alan Dundes, ed. *The Wandering Jew: Essays in the Interpretation of a Christian Legend*. Bloomington: Indiana University Press, 1986.

Havelock, Eric A. *The Muse Learns to Write: Reflections on Orality and Literacy from Antiquity to the Present*. New Haven: Yale University Press, 1986.

Haymes, Edward R. "Oral Composition in Middle High German Epic Poetry." In John Miles Foley, ed. *Oral Traditional Literature: A Festschrift for Albert Bates Lord*. Columbus, OH; Slavica Publishers, 1981, 341–346.

Holinshed, Raphael. *The First and Second Volumes of Chronicles* (London, 1587), vol. 2, folios 150–152, 168–176, as cited in Miola, 98–113.

Horowitz, Elliott. "The People of the Image." *The New Republic*, Sept. 25, 2000, 41–49.

Horowitz, Elliott. *Reckless Rites: Purim and the Legacy of Jewish Violence*. Princeton: Princeton University Press, 2006.

Horton, Robin and Ruth Finnegan, eds. *Modes of Thought: Essays on Thinking in Western and Non-Western Societies*. London: Faber and Faber, 1973.

Howard, John A., ed. *Wunderparlich und seltsame Historien Til Eulen Spiegels*. Würzburg: Königshausen und Neumann, 1983.

Hsia, R. Po-chia. *The Myth of Ritual Murder*. New Haven: Yale University Press, 1988.

Hsia, R. Po-chia. *Trent 1475: Stories of a Ritual Murder Trial*. New Haven: Yale University Press, 1992.

Hsia, R. Po-Chia, and Harmut Lehmann, eds. *In and Out of the Ghetto*. Cambridge: Cambridge University Press, 1995.

Hughes, Diane Owen. "Distinguishing Signs: Ear-Rings, Jews and Franciscan Rhetoric in the Italian Renaissance City." *Past and Present* 112 (Aug. 1986), 3–59.

Hunter, G. K. "Five-Act Structure in *Doctor Faustus*." In Bloom, Harold, ed. *Christopher Marlowe's Doctor Faustus: Modern Critical Interpretations*. New York: Chelsea House, 1988, 13–25.

Hutcheon, Linda. *A Theory of Parody*. New York: Methuen, 1985.

Hutton, Christopher. "Early Yiddish Texts and Western Yiddish Dialectology." In Dovid Katz, ed. *Dialects of the Yiddish Language*. Oxford: Pergamon Press, 1988, 21–26.

ibn Sahula, Isaac. *Meshal Haqadmoni: Fables from the Distant Past*. Ed. and trans. Raphael Loewe. Oxford: Littman Library of Jewish Civilization, 2004.

Irigaray, Luce. *This Sex Which Is Not One*. Trans. Catherine Porter. Ithaca: Cornell University Press, 1985.

Irigaray, Luce. *Speculum of the Other Woman.* Trans. Gillian C. Gill. Ithaca: Cornell University Press, 1985.

Iser, Wolfgang. *The Act of Reading: A Theory of Aesthetic Response.* Baltimore: Johns Hopkins University Press, 1978.

Iser, Wolfgang. *The Range of Interpretation.* New York: Columbia University Press, 2000.

James I. *Daemonologie.* Edinburgh: 1597. Cited in Miola, 144–148.

Jardine, Alice A. *Gynesis: Configurations of Woman and Modernity.* Ithaca: Cornell University Press, 1985.

Jauss, Hans Robert. *Towards an Aesthetic of Reception.* Minneapolis: University of Minnesota Press, 1982.

Johnson, Bond. *The Mode of Parody: An Essay at Definition and Six Studies.* Frankfurt a.M.: Peter Lang, 2000.

Jones, Ann Rosalind. "Writing the Body: Toward an Understanding of l'Écriture Féminine." In Elaine Showalter, ed. *The New Feminist Criticism: Essays on Women, Literature, and Theory.* New York: Pantheon Books, 1985, 361–377.

Jordan, William Chester. "Jewish Studies and the Medieval Historian." *Exemplaria* 12:1 (2000), 7–20.

Kallus, Menachem. "Pneumatic Mystical Possession and the Eschatology of the Soul in Lurianic Kabbalah." In Matt Goldish, ed. *Spirit Possession in Judaism: Cases and Contexts from the Middle Ages to the Present.* Detroit: Wayne State University Press, 2003, 159–185.

Karnafogel, Ephraim. *Jewish Education and Society in the High Middle Ages.* Detroit: Wayne State University Press, 1992.

Katz, Dovid. "On Yiddish, in Yiddish, and for Yiddish: 500 Years of Yiddish Scholarship." In Mark Gelber, ed. *Identity and Ethos: A Festschrift for Sol Liptzin on the Occasion of His Eighty-fifth Birthday.* New York: Peter Lang, 1986, 23–36.

Katz, Dovid, ed. *Dialects of the Yiddish Language.* Oxford: Pergamon Press, 1988.

Katz, Dovid. "Origins of Yiddish Dialectology." In Dovid Katz, ed. *Dialects of the Yiddish Language.* Oxford: Pergamon Press, 1988, 39–55.

Katz, Dovid. *Words on Fire: The Unfinished Story of Yiddish.* New York: Basic Books, 2004.

Katz, Eli. "Six Germano-Jewish Poems from the Cairo Genizah." PhD diss., UCLA, 1963.

Katz, Eli. "Dos ku-bukh: mekoyrim un baarbetung." *Yidishe kultur* 5/44 (1982), 6–10.

Katz, Eli. "Das 'Kuhbukh' und das 'Sefer Mešolim': Die Überlieferung eines mitteljiddischen Textes," *Beiträge zur Geschichte der deutschen Sprache und Literatur* 112 (1990), 81–95.

Katz, Eli. Introduction. In Moshe Wallich. *Book of Fables: The Yiddish Fable Collection of Reb Moshe Wallich, Frankfurt am Main, 1697.* Trans. and ed. Eli Katz. Detroit: Wayne State University Press, 1994.

Katz, Jacob. *Tradition and Crisis: Jewish Society at the End of the Middle Ages.* New York: Schocken Books, 1961.

Kerler, Dov-Ber. *The Origins of Modern Literary Yiddish.* Oxford: Clarendon Press, 1999.

Kermode, Frank. *The Sense of an Ending: Studies in the Theory of Fiction.* Oxford: Oxford University Press (1967) 2000.

Kieckhefer, Richard. *Repression of Heresy in Medieval Germany.* Philadelphia: University of Pennsylvania Press, 1979.

Kirshenblatt-Gimblett, Barbara. "The Corporeal Turn." *JQR* 95:3 (Summer 2005), 447–461.

Klirs, Tracy Guren. *The Merit of Our Mothers: A Bilingual Anthology of Jewish Women's Prayers.* Cincinnati: Hebrew Union College Press, 1992.

Kolodny, Annette. "A Map for Rereading: Gender and the Interpretation of Literary Texts." In Elaine Showalter, ed. *The New Feminist Criticism: Essays on Women, Literature, and Theory.* New York: Pantheon Books, 1985, 46–62.

Kolodny, Annette. "Dancing through the Minefield: Some Observations on the Theory, Practice, and Politics of a Feminist Literary Criticism." In Elaine Showalter, ed. *The New Feminist Criticism: Essays on Women, Literature, and Theory.* New York: Pantheon Books, 1985, 144–167.

Korman, A. *Yidishe dikhterins: antologye.* Chicago: L. M. Stein, 1928.

Kramer, Femke. "Rigid Readings of Flexible Texts: The Case of Sixteenth-Century Comic Drama." In Bert Roest and Herman Vanstiphout, eds. *Aspects of Genre and Type in Pre-modern Literary Cultures.* Groningen: Styx, 1999, 33–46.

Kugel, James L. *The Bible As It Was.* Cambridge, MA: Belknap / Harvard, 1997.

Landau, Leo. *Arthurian Legends, or, the Hebrew-German Rhymed Version of the Legend of King Arthur* = Teutonia 21. Leipzig, 1912.

Lassner, Jacob. *Demonizing the Queen of Sheba: Boundaries of Gender and Culture in Postbiblical Judaism and Medieval Islam.* Chicago: University of Chicago Press, 1993.

Lauterbach, Jacob Z. "The Ceremony of Breaking a Glass at Weddings." *HUCA* 2 (1925), 351–380.

Le Goff, Jacques. *The Medieval Imagination*. Chicago: University of Chicago Press, 1988.

Lees, Clare A., ed. *Medieval Masculinities: Reading Men in the Middle Ages*. Minneapolis: University of Minnesota Press, 1994.

Lenowitz, Harris. "A Spirit Possession Tale as an Account of the Equivocal Insertion of Rabbi Hayyim Vital into the Role of Messiah." In Matt Goldish, ed. *Spirit Possession in Judaism: Cases and Contexts from the Middle Ages to the Present*. Detroit: Wayne State University Press, 2003, 197–212.

Leviant, Curt, ed. and trans. *King Artus: A Hebrew Arthurian Romance of 1279*. Assen: Van Gorcum and New York: Ktav, 1969.

Levin, Harry. *The Gates of Horn*. New York: Oxford University Press, 1963.

Lieberman, Saul. "Sins and Their Punishment." In Saul Lieberman, *Texts and Studies*. New York: Ktav, 1974, 29–56.

Lieberman, Saul. "Some Aspects of After Life in Early Rabbinic Literature." In Saul Lieberman, *Texts and Studies*. New York: Ktav, 1974, 235–270.

Lieberman, Saul. *Texts and Studies*. New York: Ktav, 1974.

Lilienthal, Regina. "Eyn hore." *Yidishe filologiye* 1 (1924), 245–271.

Liptzin, Sol. *A History of Yiddish Literature*. Middle Village, NY: J. David, 1972.

Loewe, Raphael. Introduction. In Isaac ibn Sahula, *Meshal Haqadmoni: Fables from the Distant Past*. Ed. and trans. Raphael Loewe. Oxford: Littman Library of Jewish Civilization, 2004.

Lomperis, Linda, and Sarah Stanbury, eds. *Feminist Approaches to the Body in Medieval Literature*. Philadephia: University of Pennsylvania Press, 1993.

Long, Burke O. "Recent Field Studies in Oral Literature and the Question of *Sitz im Leben*." *Semeia* 5 (1976), 35–49.

Longxi, Zhang. *Allegoresis: Reading Canonical Literature East and West*. Ithaca: Cornell University Press, 2005.

Lord, Albert B. *The Singer of Tales*. Cambridge, MA: Harvard University Press, 1960.

Lukács, Georg. *The Historical Novel*. London: Merlin Press, 1962.

Macbeth: A Concordance to the Text of the First Folio. Oxford: Clarendon Press, 1971.

Mack, Robert L. *The Genius of Parody: Imitation and Originality in Seventeenth- and Eighteenth-Century English Literature*. New York: Palgrave Macmillan, 2007.

Maggi, Armando. *Satan's Rhetoric: A Study of Renaissance Demonology*. Chicago: University of Chicago Press, 2001.

Manguel, Alberto. *A History of Reading*. New York: Viking, 1996.

Marcus, Ivan G. "Mothers, Martyrs, and Moneymakers: Some Jewish Women in Medieval Europe." *Conservative Judaism* 38:3 (Spring 1986), 34–45.

Marcus, Ivan G. *Rituals of Childhood: Jewish Acculturation in Medieval Europe*. New Haven: Yale University Press, 1996.

Mark, Zvi. "Dybbuk and Devekut in the Shivhe ha-Besht: Toward a Phenomenology of Madness in Early Hasidism." In Matt Goldish, ed. *Spirit Possession in Judaism: Cases and Contexts from the Middle Ages to the Present*. Detroit: Wayne State University Press, 2003, 257–301.

Martin, Henri-Jean. *Print, Power, and People in Seventeenth-Century France*. Metuchen, NJ: Scarecrow Press, 1993.

Martin, Henri-Jean. *The History and Power of Writing*. Chicago: University of Chicago Press, 1994.

Martin, Henri-Jean. *The French Book: Religion, Absolutism, and Readership, 1585–1715*. Baltimore: Johns Hopkins University Press, 1996.

Martinez-Bonati, Felix. "Representation and Fiction." *Dispositio* 5.13–14 (1980), 19–33.

Massey, Irving. *Find You the Virtue: Ethics, Image, and Desire in Literature*. Lanham, MD: George Mason University Press, 1987.

Maxwell-Stuart, P. G. *Witchcraft in Europe and the New World, 1400–1800*. New York: Palgrave, 2001.

McCracken, Peggy. "The Body Politic and the Queen's Adulterous Body in French Romance." In Linda Lomperis and Sarah Stanbury, eds. *Feminist Approaches to the Body in Medieval Literature*. Philadephia: University of Pennsylvania Press, 1993, 38–64.

McNamara, Jo Ann. "The *Herrenfrage:* The Restructuring of the Gender System, 1050–1150." In Clare A. Lees, ed. *Medieval Masculinities: Reading Men in the Middle Ages*. Minneapolis: University of Minnesota Press, 1994, 3–29.

Meitlis, Jacob, ed. *Midrash lepirkei avot beyidish kamait leanshel levi*. Jerusalem: Israel Academy of Sciences and Humanities, 1978.

Merchant, W. Moelwyn. " 'His Fiend-Like Queen.' " In Kenneth Muir and Philip Edwards, eds. *Aspects of Macbeth*. Cambridge: Cambridge University Press, 1977, 46–52.

Midelfort, H. C. *Witch Hunting in Southwestern Germany 1562–1684: The Social and Intellectual Foundations*. Stanford: Stanford University Press, 1972.

Midelfort, H. C. Erik. "Social History and Biblical Exegesis: Community, Family, and Witchcraft in Sixteenth-Century Germany." In David C. Steinmetz, ed. *The Bible in the Sixteenth Century*. Durham: Duke University Press, 1990, 7–20.

Miller, Nancy K. "Emphasis Added: Plots and Plausibilities in Women's Fiction." In Elaine Showalter, ed. *The New Feminist Criticism: Essays on Women, Literature, and Theory*. New York: Pantheon Books, 1985, 339–360.

Miola, Robert S., ed. *Macbeth: A Norton Critical Edition*. New York: W. W. Norton, 2004.

Mirrer, Louise. "Representing 'Other' Men: Muslims, Jews, and Masculine Ideals in Medieval Castilian Epic and Ballad." In Clare A. Lees, ed. *Medieval Masculinities: Reading Men in the Middle Ages*. Minneapolis: University of Minnesota Press, 1994, 169–186.

Mitchell, W. J. T., ed. *On Narrative*. Chicago: University of Chicago Press, 1981.

Monléon, José B. *A Specter is Haunting Europe: A Sociohistorical Approach to the Fantastic*. Princeton: Princeton University Press, 1990.

Moseley, Marcus. *Being for Myself Alone: Origins of Jewish Autobiography*. Stanford: Stanford University Press, 2006.

Muir, Kenneth. "Image and Symbol in *Macbeth*." *Shakspeare Survey* 19 (1966), 45–54. Reptd. Miola, 254–266.

Muir, Kenneth, and Philip Edwards, eds. *Aspects of Macbeth*. Cambridge: Cambridge University Press, 1977.

Müller, Hermann-Josef, and Walter Röll, eds. *Fragen des älteren Jiddisch*. Trier: Universität Trier, 1977.

Nadav, Mordechai. *The Jews of Pinsk, 1506 to 1880*. Stanford: Stanford University Press, 2007.

Nadler, Steven. *Rembrandt's Jews*. Chicago: University of Chicago Press, 2003.

Nelson, William. *Fact or Fiction: The Dilemma of the Renaissance Storyteller*. Cambridge: Harvard University Press, 1973.

Neugroschel, Joachim. *The Dybbuk and the Yiddish Imagination: A Haunted Reader*. Syracuse, NY: Syracuse University Press, 2000.

Neumann, Erich. *The Great Mother: An Analysis of the Archetype*. New York: Pantheon, 1963 (2nd ed.).

Newman, Karen. *Fashioning Femininity: Femininity and English Renaissance Drama*. Chicago: University of Chicago Press, 1991.

Nigal, Gedaliya. "Hadibuk bemistika yehudit." *Daat* 4 (Winter 1980), 75–101.

Niger, Shmuel. "Di yidishe literatur un di lezerin." In Niger, *Bleter-geshikhte fun der yidisher literatur*. New York: Alveltlekhn yidishn kultur-kongres, 1959, 37–107.

Nora, Pierre. "Between Memory and History: *Les lieux de mémoire*." *Representations* 26 (1989), 7–25.

Ong, Walter J. *Orality and Literacy: The Technologizing of the Word*. New York: Methuen, 1982.

Ong, Walter J. "Text as Interpretation: Mark and After." In John Miles Foley, ed. *Oral Tradition in Literature: Interpretation in Context*. Columbia, MO: University of Missouri Press, 1986, 147–169.

Orgel, Stephen. "*Macbeth* and the Antic Round." *Shakespeare Survey* 52 (1999), 143–153. Reptd. Miola, 342–356.

Oron, Mijal. "Sobre el Carácter de Samael (Del Mite al Símbol)." In Ron Barkai, ed. *Curs la cabala*. Barcelona: Fundació Caixa de Pensions, 1989, 75–83.

Palmer, Frank. *Literature and Moral Understanding*. Oxford: Clarendon Press, 1992.

Patai, Raphael, ed. *Studies in Biblical and Jewish Folklore*. Bloomington: Indiana University Press, 1960.

Paucker, Arnold. "Yiddish Versions of Early German Prose Novels." *Journal of Jewish Studies* 10 (1959), 151–167.

Pavel, Thomas G. *Fictional Worlds*. Cambridge, MA: Harvard University Press, 1986.

Perry, B. E. "Fable." In Pack Carnes, ed. *Proverbia in Fabula*. New York: Peter Lang, 1988, 65–116.

Perry, T. A. "Cain's Sin in Genesis 4:1–7: Oracular Ambiguity and How to Avoid It." *Prooftexts* 25:3 (2005), 258–275.

Peskowitz, Miriam. "Engendering Jewish Religious History." In Miriam Peskowitz and Laura Levitt, eds. *Judaism Since Gender*. New York: Routledge, 1997, 17–39.

Peskowitz, Miriam B. *Spinning Fantasies: Rabbis, Gender, and History*. Berkeley: University of Califonia Press, 1997.

Peskowitz, Miriam, and Laura Levitt, eds. *Judaism Since Gender*. New York: Routledge, 1997.

Peters, Julie Stone. *Theatre of the Book, 1480–1880: Print, Text, and Performance in Europe*. Oxford: Oxford University Press, 2000.

Philipson, David. *Old European Jewries*. Philadelphia: Jewish Publication Society, 1894.

Pollack, Herman. *Jewish Folkways in Germanic Lands (1648–1806): Studies in Aspects of Daily Life*. Cambridge: MIT Press, 1971.

Posner, Raphael, Uri Kaploun, and Shalom Cohen, eds. *Jewish Liturgy: Prayer and Synagogue Service through the Ages*. Jerusalem: Keter, 1975.

Propp, V. *Morphology of the Folktale*. Bloomington, IN: Indiana University Research Center in Anthropology, Folklore, and Linguistics, 1958.

Pucci, Joseph Michael. *The Full-Knowing Reader: Allusion and the Power of the Reader in the Western Literary Tradition*. New Haven: Yale University Press, 1998.

Purkiss, Diane. *At the Bottom of the Garden: A Dark History of Fairies, Hobgoblins, and Other Troublesome Things*. New York: New York University Press, 2001.

Purkiss, Diane. "Sounds of Silence: Fairies and Incest in Scottish Witchcraft Stories." In Stuart Clark, ed. *Languages of Witchcraft: Narrative, Ideology, and Meaning in Early Modern Culture*. New York: St. Martin's Press, 2001, 81–98.

Rabkin, Eric S. *The Fantastic in Literature*. Princeton: Princeton University Press, 1976.

Radway, Janice A. "The Aesthetic in Mass Culture: Reading the 'Popular' Literary Text." In P. Steiner, M. Cervenka, and R. Vroon, eds. *The Structure of the Literary Process*. Philadelphia: John Benjamins, 1982, 397–430.

Rapaport-Albert, Ada, ed. *Essays in Jewish Historiography*. Atlanta: Scholars Press, 1988.

Reeves, Charles Eric. "Convention and Behavior." In P. Steiner, M. Cervenka, and R. Vroon, eds. *The Structure of the Literary Process*. Philadelphia: John Benjamins, 1982, 431–454.

Reiner, Elchanan. "The Ashkenazi Elite at the Beginning of the Modern Era: Manuscript versus Printed Book." *Polin* 10 (1997), 85–98.

Renoir, Alain. "Oral-Formulaic Rhetoric and the Interpretation of Written Texts." In John Miles Foley, ed. *Oral Tradition in Literature: Interpretation in Context*. Columbia, MO: University of Missouri Press, 1986, 103–135.

Reuter, Fritz. *Warmaisa: 1000 Jahre Juden in Worms*. Frankfurt a.M.: Athenäum, 1987.

Richarz, Monika, ed. *Die Hamburger Kauffrau Glikl: Jüdische Existenz in der Frühen Neuzeit*. Hamburg: Christians, 2001.

Riffaterre, Michael. *Semiotics of Poetry*. Bloomington: Indiana University Press, 1978.

Riffaterre, Michael. *Fictional Truth*. Baltimore: Johns Hopkins University Press, 1990.

Robisheaux, Thomas. "Witchcraft and Forensic Medicine in Seventeenth-Century Germany." In Stuart Clark, ed. *Languages of Witchcraft: Narrative, Ideology, and Meaning in Early Modern Culture*. New York: St. Martin's Press, 2001, 197–215.

Roemer, Nils H. *Jewish Scholarship and Culture in Nineteenth-Century Germany: Between History and Faith*. Madison: University of Wisconsin Press, 2005.

Roest, Bert, and Herman Vanstiphout, eds. *Aspects of Genre and Type in Pre-modern Literary Cultures*. Groningen: Styx, 1999.

Röll, Walter. "Das älteste datierte jüdisch-deutsche Sprachdenkmal: Ein Verspaar im Wormser Machsor von 1272–1273." *Zeitschrift für Mundartforschung* 33 (1966), 127–138.

Röll, Walter. "Zu den ersten drei Texten der Cambridger Handschrift von 1382/1383." *Zeitschrift für deutsches Altertum* 104 (1975), 54–68.

Röll, Walter, and Simon Neuberg, eds. *Jiddische Philologie: Festschrift für Erika Timm*. Tübingen: Niemeyer, 1999.

Rollinson, Philip. *Classical Theories of Allegory and Christian Culture*. Pittsburgh: Duquesne University Press, 1981.

Romer-Segal, Agnes. "Sifrut yidish ukehal koreha bemeah hat"z: yetsirot beyidish bireshimot 'hazikuk' mimantova 1595." *Kiryat Sefer* 53 (1978), 779–790.

Rose, Margaret A. *Parody: Ancient, Modern, and Post-Modern*. Cambridge: Cambridge University Press, 1993.

Rosen, Tova. *Unveiling Eve: Reading Gender in Medieval Hebrew Literature*. Philadelphia: University of Pennsylvania Press, 2003.

Rosenfeld, Moshe N. *The Book of Cows: A Facsimile Edition of the Famed Kuhbuch*. London: Hebraica Books, 1984.

Rosensweig, Claudia. "La letteratura yiddish in Italia: L'esempio el *Bovo de-Antona di Elye Bokher*," *Acme* 50:3 (1997), 159–189.

Rosmarin, Adena. *The Power of Genre*. Minneapolis: University of Minnesota Press, 1985.

Rowlands, Alison. *Witchcraft Narratives in Germany: Rothenburg, 1561–1652*. Manchester: Manchester University Press, 2003.

Ruderman, David B. "Unicorns, Great Beasts, and the Marvelous Variety of Things in Nature in the Thought of Abraham B. Hananiah Yagel." In Isadore Twersky and Bernard Septimus, eds. *Jewish Thought in the Seventeenth Century*. Cambridge, MA: Harvard University Press, 1987, 343–364.

Ruderman, David B., ed. *Essential Papers on Jewish Culture in Renaissance and Baroque Italy*. New York: New York University Press, 1992.

Rushton, Peter. "Texts of Authority: Witchcraft Accusations and the Demonstration of Truth in Early Modern England." In Stuart Clark, ed. *Languages of Witchcraft: Narrative, Ideology, and Meaning in Early Modern Culture*. New York: St. Martin's Press, 2001, 21–39.

Sack, Bracha. "Some Remarks on Prayer in the Kabbalah of Sixteenth-Century Safed." In Roland Goetschel, ed. *Prière, Mystique, et Judaïsme*. Paris: Presses Universitaires de France, 1987, 179–186.

Sanders, Wilbur. "Doctor Faustus's Sin." In Harold Bloom, ed. *Christopher Marlowe's Doctor Faustus: Modern Critical Interpretations.* New York: Chelsea House, 1988, 27–45.

Saperstein, Marc. "Jewish Typological Exegesis After Nachmanides." *Jewish Studies Quarterly* 1 (1993/1994), 158–170.

Scafi, Alessandro. *Mapping Paradise: A History of Heaven on Earth.* Chicago: University of Chicago Press, 2006.

Schenck, Mary Jane. "The Fabliau Ethos: Recent Views on its Origins." *Reinardus* 1 (1988), 121–129.

Schenck, Mary Jane. "Orality, Literacy, and the Law." *Reinardus* 8 (1995), 63–75.

Scholes, Robert, and Robert Kellogg. "The Problem of Reality: Illustration and Representation." In Philip Steivick, ed. *The Theory of the Novel.* New York: The Free Press, 1967, 371–384.

Schultz, Joseph P. "The 'Ze-enah U-Re'enah': Torah for the Folk." *Judaism* 36:1 (1987), 84–96.

Schumacher, Jutta, ed. *Sefer Mišle Šu'olim (=Buch der Fuchsfabeln) von Jakob Koppelmann.* Hamburg: Helmut Buske Verlag, 2006.

Schwarzbaum, Haim. *The Mishlei Shu'alim (Fox Fables) of Rabbi Berechiah Ha-Nakdan: A Study in Comparative Folklore and Fable Lore.* Tel Aviv: Institute for Jewish and Arab Folklore Research, 1979.

Scot, Reginald. *The Discoverie of Witchcraft.* London, 1584.

Sed-Rajna, Gabrielle, ed. *Rashi 1040–1990.* Paris: Éditions du Cerf, 1993.

Seidel, Jonathan. "Possession and Exorcism in the Magical Texts of the Cairo Geniza." In Matt Goldish, ed. *Spirit Possession in Judaism: Cases and Contexts from the Middle Ages to the Present.* Detroit: Wayne State University Press, 2003, 73–95.

Seidman, Naomi. "Carnal Knowledge: Sex and the Body in Jewish Studies." *Jewish Social Studies* (n.s.) 1:1 (Fall 1994), 115–143.

Seidman, Naomi. *A Marriage Made in Heaven: The Sexual Politics of Hebrew and Yiddish.* Berkeley: University of California Press, 1997.

Shakespeare, William. *The Tragedy of Macbeth.* Oxford: Clarendon Press, 1990.

Shapiro, James. *Shakespeare and the Jews.* New York: Columbia University Press, 1996.

Shatzmiller, Joseph. *Jews, Medicine, and Medieval Society.* Berkeley: University of California, 1994.

Shiper, Y. "A yidisher libe-roman fun mitl-elter." *YIVO Bleter* 13 (1938), 232–245.

Shmeruk, Chone. "Di mizrekh-eyropeyishe nuskhoes fun der *Tsene-rene* (1786–1850)." *For Max Weinreich on His Seventieth Birthday.* The Hague: Mouton, 1964, 195–211 (Yiddish section).

Shmeruk, Chone. *Research Collections on Microfiche: Jewish Studies, Yiddish Books*. Leiden: Zug: Inter Documentation Company, 1976.

Shmeruk, Chone. *Sifrut yidish: perakim letoldoteha*. Tel Aviv: Porter Institute, 1978.

Shmeruk, Chone. "Tsi ken der kembridger manuscript shtisn di shpilman-teorie in der yidisher literatur?" *Di goldene keyt* 100 (1979), 251–271.

Shmeruk, Chone. *Sifrut yidish be-polin*. Jerusalem: Magnes Press, 1981.

Shmeruk, Chone. "Defusei yidish beitaliyah." *Italia* 3 (1982), 112–175.

Shmeruk, Chone. "Haiyurim min haminhagim beyidish, venezia shn'g/1593, behadpasot khozrot bidefusei prag bemeah ha-17." *Studies in Bibliography and Booklore* 15 (1984), 31–52.

Shmeruk, Chone. *Prokim fun der yidisher literature-geshikhte*. Jerusalem: Hebrew University, 1988.

Shmeruk, Chone. "Yidishe literatur un kolektiver zikoren: di chmelnitzki-gzeyres." *Oksforder yidish* 1 (1990), 357–382.

Showalter, Elaine, ed. *The New Feminist Criticism: Essays on Women, Literature, and Theory*. New York: Pantheon Books, 1985.

Shtif, N[okhem]. "Ditrikh von bern: yidishkeyt un veltlekhkeyt in der alter yidisher literatur." *Yidishe filologiye* 1 (Jan–Feb. 1924), 1–11, 112–122.

Shulman, Elias. *Sfas yehudis ashkenozis usifruso*. Riga: Levin, 1913.

Shulvas, Moshe. "Hayedia behistoriya vehasifrut hahistorit bitekhum hatarbut shel hayahadut haashkenazit biyemei habenayim." In *Sefer Hayovel Lerabi khanokh albeck*. Jerusalem: Rav Kook, 1963, 465–495.

Shulvass, Moses A. *The Jews in the World of the Renaissance*. Leiden: E. J. Brill, 1973.

Simon, Bettina. *Jiddische Sprachgeschichte*. Frankfurt: Athenäum, 1988.

Smart, Carol. "Disruptive Bodies and Unruly Sex." In Carol Smart, ed. *Regulating Womanhood: Historical Essays on Marriage, Motherhood, and Sexuality*. London: Routledge, 1992, 7–32.

Smart, Carol, ed. *Regulating Womanhood: Historical Essays on Marriage, Motherhood, and Sexuality*. London: Routledge, 1992.

Smets, An. "De la maille à la livre et de l'amour au commerce: le rôle de l'argent dans les fabliaux." *Reinardus* 12 (1999), 173–188.

Smith, Jerry Christopher. "Elia Levita's *Bovo-Buch*: A Yiddish Romance of the Early Sixteenth Century." PhD diss., Cornell University, 1968.

Smith, Jerry Christopher. *Elia Levita Bachur's Bovo-Buch: A Translation of the Old Yiddish Edition of 1541 with Introduction and Notes*. Tucson, AZ: Fenestra Books, 2003.

Solterer, Helen. "At the Bottom of Mirage, A Woman's Body: *Le roman de la rose* of Jean Renart." In Linda Lomperis and Sarah Stanbury, eds. *Feminist Approaches to the Body in Medieval Literature.* Philadephia: University of Pennsylvania Press, 1993, 213–233.

Spiegel, Gabrielle M. "History, Historicism, and the Social Logic of the Text in the Middle Ages." *Speculum* 65 (1990), 59–86.

Spiegel, Harriet. "The Male Animal in the Fables of Marie de France." In Clare A. Lees, ed. *Medieval Masculinities: Reading Men in the Middle Ages.* Minneapolis: University of Minnesota Press, 1994, 111–126.

Spiegel, Shalom. *The Last Trial.* New York: Pantheon Books, 1963.

Stanislawski, Michael. "The Yiddish Shevet Yehudah: A Study in the 'Ashkenization' of a Sephardic Classic." In Elisheva Carlebach, John M. Efron, and David Myers, eds. *Jewish History and Jewish Memory: Essays in Honor of Yosef Hayim Yerushalmi.* University Press of New England, 1998, 134–149.

Stanislawski, Michael. *Autobiographical Jews: Essays in Self-Fashioning.* Seattle: University of Washington Press, 2004.

Starck, Astrid, ed. *Westjiddisch.* Aarau: Verlag Sauerländer, 1994.

Starck, Astrid. *Un beau livre d'histoires.* Basel: Schwabe, 2004, 2 vols.

Steinmetz, David C., ed. *The Bible in the Sixteenth Century.* Durham: Duke University Press, 1990.

Steinschneider, Moritz. *Jüdisch-deutsche Literatur (Serapeum, Leipzig 1848–1849).* Jerusalem: Hebrew University, 1961.

Steivick, Philip, ed. *The Theory of the Novel.* New York: The Free Press, 1967.

Stephens, Walter. *Demon Lovers: Witchcraft, Sex, and the Crisis of Belief.* Chicago: University of Chicago Press, 2002.

Stern, David. "The Character(s) of God in Rabbinic Literature." *Prooftexts* 12:2 (1992), 151–174.

Stern, David, and Mark J. Mirsky, ed. *Rabbinic Fantasies: Imaginative Narratives from Classical Hebrew Literature.* New Haven: Yale University Press, 1990.

Stow, Kenneth R. *Alienated Minority: The Jews of Medieval Latin Europe.* Cambridge, MA: Harvard University Press, 1992.

Strauch, Gabriele L. *Dukus Horant: Wanderer zwischen zwei Welten.* Rodopi: Amsterdam, 1990.

Stuard, Susan Mosher. "Burdens of Matrimony: Husbanding and Gender in Medieval Italy." In Clare A. Lees, ed. *Medieval Masculinities: Reading Men in the Middle Ages.* Minneapolis: University of Minnesota Press, 1994, 61–71.

Suleiman, Susan R., and Inge Crosman, eds. *The Reader in the Text: Essays on Audience and Interpretation.* Princeton: Princeton University Press, 1980.

Suleiman, Susan. *Authoritarian Fictions.* New York: Columbia University Press, 1983.

Sunshine, Andrew Lloyd. "Opening the Mail: Interpersonal Aspects of Discourse and Grammar in Middle Yiddish Letters." (PhD diss., Columbia University, 1991).

Tatar, Maria. *The Annotated Classic Fairy Tales.* New York: W. W. Norton, 2002.

Tazbir, Janusz. "Images of the Jew in the Polish Commonwealth." *Polin* 4 (1989), 18–30.

Tcherikover, A. "Di geshikhte fun a literarishn plagiat." *YIVO Bleter* 4 (1932), 159–167.

Thomas, Keith. *Religion and the Decline of Magic.* New York: Charles Scribner's Sons, 1971.

Timm, Erika. "Jiddische Sprachmaterialen aus dem Jahre 1290: Die Glossen des Berner kleine Aruch. Edition un Kommentar." In Hermann-Josef Müller and Walter Röll, eds. *Fragen des älteren Jiddisch.* Trier: Universität Trier, 1977, 16–34.

Timm, Erika. "Beria und Simra: Eine jiddische Erzählung des 16. Jahrhunderts." *Literaturwissenschaftliches Jahrbuch* 14 (1973), 1–94.

Timm, Erika. "Die 'Fabel vom alten Löwen' in jiddisticher und komparatisticher Sicht." *Zeitschrift für deutsche Philologie* 100 (1981), 109–170.

Timm, Erika. "Zur jiddischen Fabelliteratur des 16. Jahrhunderts." *Proceedings of the Eighth World Congress of Jewish Studies* (1981), C159–164.

Timm, Erika. "Zwischen Orient und Okzident: Zur Vorgeschichte von 'Beria und Zimra.' " *Literaturwissenschaftliches Jahrbuch* 27 (1986), 297–307.

Timm, Erika. *Graphische und phonische Struktur des Westjiddischen unter besonderer Berücksichtigung der Zeit um 1600.* Tübingen: Niemeyer, 1987.

Timm, Erika. *Yiddish Literature in a Franconian Genizah.* Jerusalem: Akademon Press, 1988.

Timm, Erika. "Wie Elia Levita sein Bovobuch für den Druck überarbeitete." *Germanisch-Romanische Monatsschrift* 72 (1991), 61–81.

Timm, Erika, and Gustav Adolf Beckmann. *Etymologische Studien zum Jiddischen.* Hamburg: Helmut Buske Verlag, 2006.

Todorov, Tzvetan. *Genres in Discourse.* Cambridge: Cambridge University Press, 1990.

Tompkins, Jane P. "Sentimental Power: *Uncle Tom's Cabin* and the Politics of Literary History." In Elaine Showalter, ed. *The New Feminist Criticism: Essays on Women, Literature, and Theory.* New York: Pantheon Books, 1985, 81–104.

Trachtenberg, Joshua. *The Devil and the Jews.* Philadelphia: JPS, 1983 (1943).

Trachtenberg, Joshua. *Jewish Magic and Superstition.* New York: Athenaeum, 1984 (1939).

Traister, Barbara Howard. "*Doctor Faustus:* Master of Self-Delusion." In Harold Bloom, ed. *Christopher Marlowe's Doctor Faustus: Modern Critical Interpretations.* New York: Chelsea House, 1988, 77–92.

Turniansky, Chava. "Iberzetsungen un baarbetungen fun der 'Tsene rene.' " In Shmuel Werses et al., eds. *Sefer Dov Sadan.* Tel Aviv: Kibbutz hameyukhad, 1977, 165–190.

Turniansky, Chava. "On Old-Yiddish Biblical Epics." *International Folklore Review* 8 (1991), 26–33.

Turniansky, Chava. "Yiddish 'Historical' Songs as Sources for the History of the Jews in Pre-Partition Poland." *Polin* 4 (1989), 42–52.

Turniansky, Chava. "Vegn di literature-mekoyrim in Glikl Hamels zikhroynes." In Israel Bartal et al., eds. *Keminhag ashkenaz upolin.* Jerusalem: Zalman Shazar, 1993, 153–178.

Turniansky, Chava. "Meydlekh in der alt-yidish literatur." In Walter Röll and Simon Neuberg, eds. *Jiddische Philologie: Festschrift für Erika Timm.* Tübingen: Niemeyer, 1999, 7*–20*.

Turniansky, Chava. *Glikl: Zikhronot 1691–1719.* Jerusalem: Zalman Shazar, 2006.

Twersky, Isadore, and Bernard Septimus, eds. *Jewish Thought in the Seventeenth Century.* Cambridge, MA: Harvard University Press, 1987.

Veyne, Paul. *Did the Greeks Believe Their Myths?: An Essay on the Constitutive Imagination.* Chicago: University of Chicago Press, 1988.

Wallich, Moshe. *Book of Fables: The Yiddish Fable Collection of Reb Moshe Wallich, Frankfurt am Main, 1697.* Trans. and ed. Eli Katz. Detroit: Wayne State University Press, 1994.

Walton, Kendall L. "Appreciating Fiction: Suspending Disbelief or Pretending Belief?" *Dispositio* 5.13–14 (1980), 1–18.

Walsham, Alexandra, and Julia Crick, eds. *The Uses of Script and Print, 1300–1700.* Cambridge: Cambridge University Press, 2004.

Warnock, Robert G. "The Arthurian Tradition in Hebrew and Yiddish." In Valerie M. Lagorio and Mildred Leake Day, eds. *King Arthur through the Ages.* New York: Garland, 1990, 189–208.

Warnock, Robert G. "Proverbs and Sayings in Early Yiddish Literature." In Walter Röll and Simon Neuberg, eds. *Jiddische Philologie: Festschrift für Erika Timm.* Tübingen: Niemeyer, 1999, 175–196.

Webber, Ruth. "The *Cantar de mio cid:* Problems of Interpretation." In John Miles Foley, ed. *Oral Tradition in Literature: Interpretation in Context.* Columbia, MO: University of Missouri Press, 1986, 65–88.

Weinreich, Max. *Shtaplen: fir etudyn tsu der yidisher shprakhvisnshaft un literature-geshikhte*. Berlin: Vostok, 1923.

Weinreich, Max. *Bilder fun der yidisher literature-geshikhte*. Vilna: Tomer, 1928.

Weinreich, Max. "*Yidishkayt* and Yiddish: On the Impact of Religion on Language in Ashkenazic Jewry." In Joshua A. Fishman, ed. *Readings in the Sociology of Language*. The Hague: Mouton, 1968, 382–413.

Weinreich, Max. *History of the Yiddish Language*. Chicago: University of Chicago Press, 1980.

Weinstein, Roni. "Kabbalah and Jewish Exorcism in Seventeenth-Century Italian Jewish Communities: The Case of Rabbi Moses Zacuto." In Matt Goldish, ed. *Spirit Possession in Judaism: Cases and Contexts from the Middle Ages to the Present*. Detroit: Wayne State University Press, 2003, 237–256.

Weissler, Chava. *Traditional Yiddish Literature: A Source for the Study of Women's Religious Lives*. Cambridge, MA: Harvard College Library, 1988.

Weissler, Chava. "For Women and for Men Who Are Like Women: The Construction of Gender in Yiddish Devotional Literature." *Journal of Feminist Studies* 5 (1989), 7–24.

Weissler, Chava. "Mitzvot Built into the Body: Tkhines for Niddah, Pregnancy, and Childbirth." In Howard Eilberg-Schwartz, ed. *People of the Body: Jews and Judaism from an Embodied Perspective*. Albany: SUNY, 1992, 101–115.

Weissler, Chava. " 'For the Human Soul is the Lamp of the Lord': The *Tkhine* for 'Laying Wicks' by Sarah bas Tovim." *Polin* 10 (1997), 40–65.

Weissler, Chava, and Jacob Katz. "On Law, Spirituality, and Society in Judaism: An Exchange between Jacob Katz and Chava Weissler." *Jewish Social Studies* 2:2 (1996), 87.

Weissler, Chava. *Voices of the Matriarchs: Listening to the Prayers of Early Modern Jewish Women*. Boston: Beacon Press, 1998.

Wellek, René. "The Crisis of Comparative Literature." In René Wellek. *Concepts of Criticism*. New Haven: Yale University Press, 1963, 282–295.

Wellek, René. "Literary Theory, Criticism, and History." In René Wellek. *Concepts of Criticism*. New Haven: Yale University Press, 1963, 1–20.

Werses, Shmuel, et al. *Sefer Dov Sadan*. Tel Aviv: Kibbutz hameyukhad, 1977.

Westreich, Elimelech. "The Ban on Polygamy in Polish Rabbinic Thought." *Polin* 10 (1997), 66–84.

White, Hayden. *Tropics of Discourse: Essays in Cultural Criticism*. Baltimore: Johns Hopkins University Press, 1978.

White, Hayden. "The Value of Narrativity in the Representation of Reality." In W. J. T. Mitchell, ed. *On Narrative*. Chicago: University of Chicago Press, 1981, 1–23.

Whitman, Jon. *Allegory: The Dynamics of an Ancient and Medieval Technique.* Cambridge: Harvard University Press, 1987.

Wihl, Gary. Preface. In Gary Wihl and David Williams, eds. *Literature and Ethics: Essays Presented to A. E. Malloch.* Kingston: McGill-Queens University Press, 1988.

Williams, Gerhild Scholz. *Defining Dominion: The Discourses of Magic and Witchcraft in Early Modern France and Germany.* Ann Arbor: University of Michigan Press, 1995.

Wisse, Ruth, ed. *A Shtetl and Other Novellas.* Detroit: Wayne State University Press, 1986.

Wolf, Meyer. "Mekom khiburo shel ha-'melokhim bukh.' " *Tarbiz* 51 (1992), 131–134.

Wolfthal, Diane. *Picturing Yiddish: Gender, Identity, and Memory in the Illustrated Yiddish Books of Renaissance Italy.* Leiden: Brill, 2004.

Wolitz, Seth L., and Joseph Sherman. "Bashevis Singer as a Regionalist of Lublin Province: A Note." In Seth L. Wolitz, ed. *The Hidden Isaac Bashevis Singer.* Austin: University of Texas Press, 2001, 219–224.

Wolitz, Seth L., ed. *The Hidden Isaac Bashevis Singer.* Austin: University of Texas Press, 2001.

Wootton, David. "Reginald Scot / Abraham Fleming / The Family of Love." In Stuart Clark, ed. *Languages of Witchcraft: Narrative, Ideology, and Meaning in Early Modern Culture.* New York: St. Martin's Press, 2001, 119–138.

Wootton, David. "Appendix One: The Date of the *English Faust Book* and of *Doctor Faustus.*" In Christopher Marlowe, *Doctor Faustus.* Ed. David Wootton. Indianapolis: Hackett Publishing Co., 2005.

Yacoby, Tamar. "Fictional Reliability as a Communications Problem." *Poetics Today* 2:2 (1981), 113–126.

Yassif, Eli. "The Body Never Lies: The Body in Medieval Jewish Folk Narratives." In Howard Eilberg-Schwartz, ed. *People of the Body: Jews and Judaism from an Embodied Perspective.* Albany: SUNY, 1992, 203–221.

Yates, Frances. *The Art of Memory.* Chicago: University of Chicago, 1966.

Yates, Frances. *The Occult Philosophy in the Elizabethan Age.* London: Routledge & Kegan Paul, 1979.

Yehoyesh (=Bloomgarden, Solomon). *Khumesh neviyim kesuvim.* New York: Tog, 1937.

Yerushalmi, Yosef Hayim. *Zakhor: Jewish History and Jewish Memory.* Seattle: University of Washington Press, 1982.

Zfatman, Sara. "Mayse-Bukh: kavim lidemuto shel zhanr besifrut yidish hayeshena." *Hasifrut* 28 (1979), 126–152.

Zfatman-Biller, Sara. " 'Maase shel ruakh bk'k koretz'—shlav khadash behitpatkhuto shel zhanr amami." *Mekhkerei yerushalayim befolklor yehudi* 2 (1982), 17–65.

Zfatman-Biller, Sara. "Geirush rukhot biprag bemeah ha-17: Lisheilat meheimnuto hahistorit shel gen'r amami." *Mekhkerei yerushalayim befolklor yehudi* 3 (1983), 7–33.

Zfatman-Biller, Sara. "Hasiporet beyidish mereshita ad 'shivkhei habesht.' " PhD thesis, Hebrew University. 1983. 2 vols.

Zfatman, Sara. *Hasiporet beyidish: mereshita ad 'shivkhei habesht' (1504–1814): bibliografiya mueret*. Jerusalem: Hebrew University, 1985.

Zfatman, Sara. *Beyn ashkenaz lisefarad: letoldot hasipur hayehudi bimeyhabeynayim*. Jerusalem: Magnes Press, 1993.

Zinberg, Yisroel. *Di geshikhte fun der literatur bay yidn*. Vol. 6. Vilna: Tomor, 1929–1937.

Zumbült, Beatrix. "Approaching the Medieval Illustration Cycles of the Fox-Epic as an Art Historian: Problems and Perspectives." *Reinardus* 15 (2002), 191–204.

Index

Abramovitch, S. Y., 17
adultery: adulterous wife in *Seyfer Mesholim*, 107, 108, 113, 114–15; deceived husbands, 106–8, 114–15, 148–51, 304n72; financial consequences of, 170; *sotah*, 200–201, 334n130, 334n131; as transgression of Yakov (dybbuk), 201, 334n133
Ahasuerus, 228, 232
Akedah (binding of Isaac), 192–93
Alexander, Tamar, 148, 328n68
allegory: allegorical mode, 26; gendering of, 340n191; historical reality read as, 28; political allegories, 134–35; reading audience comprehension of, 27–28, 280n119; realistic perspectives, 134–35
Alleyn, Edward, 50, 51, 52, 67, 84, 286n1
allusions, 19–23, 94, 233, 298n25
Alphabet of Ben Sira, 145, 303n70
Alsheikh, Moshe, 175
Amor and Psyche (tale), 353–54n105
anachronism, tolerance of, 39–40, 45–46
animals in fables: donkeys, 102, 103, 109, 113, 114, 127–28, 134, 136–37; foxes, 101–2, 104, 120–22, 133; hens, symbolism of, 203–4; human characteristics of, 32–33, 94, 101–2, 104, 108–10, 126; mortality and death, 119–20; ravens, 94, 104, 122, 123, 125, 126–27, 303n70; talking animals, 32–33, 109. See also *Seyfer Mesholim*
Aristobulus, 229
Aristophanic myth, 222
Artus-Hof, 215
authenticity: eyewitness accounts as, 177–78, 181–82, 194; fictiveness of saga, 181–82; of historical references, 28, 31–32, 167, 170–71, 321n97; knowledge of geography as marker of, 46, 149, 181, 311n35; of narrative, 236–37; proem as generating reader anxiety about, 181–82; slippage between authenticity and inauthenticity, 185–86; of spirit possession accounts, 181
authors: chivalric heroism defined by, 220–21; commercial interests of, 90–91, 182, 187; fictional creation by, 13, 272n51; identity of, 33–34, 36, 299n34; moral teachings (see *Seyfer Mesholim*); as narrators, 97–98, 299n31
Ayn hipshe mayse fun drey vayberin, 210

ba'al shem, 166, 167–68, 180. *See also* "The Tale of the Spirit of the Holy Community of Koretz During the Chaos of War"
Bachrach, Naftali, 174, 177, 188
Banquo (in *Macbeth*), 63–65, 66, 67, 68, 292n59
Barstow, Anne Llewellyn, 206
Bass, Shabbatai, 116–18
Baumgarten, Jean, 5, 18–19, 214, 217, 219, 220, 236
Beatrice (in *Divine Comedy*), 352n88, 353n99, 353n100
Beaumont, Francis, 292n59
Behringer, Wolfgang, 207, 336n147, 338n166, 339n176

belief: context as important to, 53–54; in demonic appearances, 51–53, 56–58, 59, 287n9, 288–89n23; eyewitness accounts as authentication strategies, 181–82; in *Macbeth*, 59, 288–89n23; proof of perceptions, 57–58, 63–70, 292n53, 292n54; skepticism compared with, 11, 51–52, 54, 269–70n40; theodicy, 197, 256, 261; Wandering Jew (legend), 53–54, 288n15; witchcraft, 206–7, 211; witches, 59–60. *See also* supernatural
betrothals, 146, 147, 152, 153, 313n53
Biale, David, 303n70, 353–54n105
biblical figures: Adam, 93, 145; David, 221, 241; Dinah, 188; Eliphaz (Esau's son), 155, 156, 163; Esau, 155–56, 163, 317n69; Esther, 133–34, 231, 232, 257; Isaac, 192–93; Jacob, 156, 227, 349n62; Jesse, 149, 311n35; Jewish and non-Jewish tropes, 227; Jonah, 197; Puah, 233, 234; Rahab, 348n52; Samson, 93; Sarah, 192–93; Shifra, 233, 234; Solomon, 220–21, 230, 241, 346n42, 352n83, 354n108; Tamar, 188
Bilu, Yoram, 189, 196, 202
Bluebeard's wife, 161, 319n82
Boccaccio, Giovanni, 225, 230–31, 243, 348n51
Boner, Ulrich, 89
book production, 43–44, 45–46, 285n160
Booth, Wayne, 99
Borekh Kat, 180, 181, 186, 195, 196, 333n118
Bottigheimer, Ruth B., 318n74
Bovo-bukh, 2, 223, 236
Boyarin, Daniel, 201–2, 252–53, 354n112, 354–55n113
Bradley, A. C., 292n53
Brantshpigl, 19
Breuer, Mordechai, 270n40
Briggs, Robin, 207, 336n147, 337n155, 339n179
Briyo ("Tale of Briyo and Zimro"): attraction to Zimro, 224–25; as Beatrice, 353n99; beauty of, 237; danger of chivalric love, 247–48; death of, 237, 240–41; disassociation of word and action, 239–40; eroticism, 223, 348n51; ideal of chastity, 237; Jacob as historical precedent for, 227, 349n62; narrator's description of, 236; traditional Jewish feminine ideals, 223
Brooke, Nicholas, 62, 289n25
Buchanan, George, 289n23
Cambridge Codex (1382), 6, 132, 213, 214
Campbell, Joseph, 318n74
Carlebach, Elisheva, 270n40
Carnes, Pack, 302n59, 304n74
Carroll, William C., 62
Chajes, J. H., 177, 178, 180, 202, 204, 333–34n121, 336n147
chapbooks, 48, 53, 55, 65; *mayse bikhl*, 179, 180, 183; Wandering Jew (legend), 53–54, 288n15. *See also* "The Tale of the Spirit of the Holy Community of Koretz During the Chaos of War"
Chartier, Roger, 277n88
chivalric literature, 37, 213; doubling or pairing the story, 221; Solomonic motifs in, 220–21, 346n42; tension between Jewish content and non-Jewish form in, 223–26; traditional Jewish paradigms of masculinity compared with, 41–42, 252–53, 354n112; value structures, 135. *See also* "Tale of Briyo and Zimro"
Christian Hebraists, 7, 178
Christianity: conversion to, 230–31; demonology of, 144, 145–46, 204, 205, 206, 336n147, 337n159; Esau identified with, 227; exorcism in, 204, 336n147; intermarriage, 143, 148, 156, 321n96; Jewish adaptation of Christian religious material, 217; Jewish paradigms within, 217, 235–36; Jewish stereotypes in, 206, 230–31, 232–33, 235, 350–51n73; legal discourse represented in Christian literary texts, 346n45; Wandering Jew (legend), 53–54, 288n15; xenoglossia as evidence of possession in, 176, 190. *See also* "Tale of Briyo and Zimro"
Chronicles (Holinshed), 59, 288–89n23, 291n52
circumcision, 219, 232, 234, 242, 349n63
Clark, Stuart, 141–42, 154, 337n159
Cohn, Dorrit, 337n155
Coleridge, Samuel Taylor, 71, 289n24
Cooperman, Bernard Dov, 270n40
Cordovero, Moses, 175
courtly love, Jewish views on, 253, 354n112, 354–55n113
cultural porosity: in biblical epic poems, 214–15, 342n8; of chivalric epics, 214–17, 342n8; in chivalric literature, 215, 343n15; concepts of shame, 121, 305n79; German

influence on Jewish fabular literature, 89; historiographical consciousness, 37–39; Judaization of non-Jewish material, 94–95, 105–6, 217–18; and literary transmission, 33–37, 214; non-Jewish moral concepts, 121, 305n79; origins of genre and, 33–34; psychological motivations from non-Jewish cultures, 121; vulgarity in fables, 303n70

Daemonologie (James I), 59, 60, 61, 64
dagger in *Macbeth*, 62, 65–66, 67–68, 292n60
Dan, Joseph, 146, 160, 174, 323n8, 324n17
Dante, 243, 246, 353n99, 353n102
David (biblical figure), 210, 221, 241
David-Solomon paradigm, 221, 241
Davis, Natalie Zemon, 37
death, 175, 191–92, 237, 240–41, 246, 247–48, 351n81
Decameron (Boccaccio), 225, 230–31, 243, 348n51
Delmedigo, Joseph, 177
demonology. *See* witchcraft
demons (*shedim*): in Christianity, 144, 145–46, 204, 205, 206, 336n147, 337n159; corporealization by, 144; demidemons, 165, 166, 167, 168; experiences of demonic activity, 51–53, 56–57, 287n9; invasion of homes by, 164–65; invisibility of, 168; liminality of, 149–50, 312n40; Lucifer, 72, 77, 83; Mephastophilis (*Doctor Faustus*), 72–73, 74, 75, 80–81; *ruah ra'ah* compared with, 175–76; vulnerability at time of marriage, 312n41
Ditrikh von Bern, 215–16, 352n87
Divine Comedy (Dante), 243, 352n88, 353n99, 353n100
Divrei Yosef (Sambari), 177, 178
Doctor Faustus: angels in, 76–77; comedy in, 77–78; diabolical pact in, 72–73, 74, 75, 77; Helen, conjuration of, 79–80, 294n86; hell described in, 84; illusion in, 51–53, 71, 74–75, 81–83; Mephastophilis, 72–73, 74, 75, 80–81; William Prynne on, 51, 52–53, 65; theater audience reaction to, 50–51, 74
Dukus Hornt, 214, 267n23, 342n4
dybbuk and dybbuk possession: Akedah compared with, 193; authentication strategies in works of, 182–83; *ba'al shem* as healers of, 166, 167–68, 180; diagnoses of, 175–76, 211; impact on community, 189, 192–95, 197; in kabbalah, 174–76; *Mayse-bukh* narrative, 178; Safed, 174–78, 324n17; sexual assault in dybbuk tales, 188, 330n84, 330n86, 339n85; symptoms of, 180, 187–88, 330n82; terms for, 173–74, 175, 323n7, 323n8; voice of, 336n146; witchcraft accounts compared with dybbuk narratives, 208; xenoglossia, 176, 190. *See also* Mindl (possession victim); spirit possession; "The Tale of the Spirit of the Holy Community of Koretz During the Chaos of War"; witchcraft; Yakov (dybbuk)

economic tropes: anxieties about money in "Queen of Sheba" tale, 170; commodification of marriage, 146, 152, 153, 313n53; in *Decameron* (Boccaccio), 225, 230–31, 243, 348n51; Fortune, 124–30, 136–37, 259, 315–16n54; marriage, 148, 152–54, 155, 156, 157–58; moral activity, 187; of possession saga author, 182; witchcraft craze, 208. *See also* wealth
Edelstein, Der (Boner), 89
Einbinder, Susan, 281–82n129
Elijah (biblical figure), 247–48, 249, 250, 352n88, 353n102
Eliphaz (biblical figure), 155, 156, 163
elite readers: allusion understood by, 22–23; knowledge acquisition of, 16–17, 22–23, 277n91; of nonelite texts, 17, 22–23, 277n88, 277n91; slumming elites, 17, 22–23; transmission of knowledge to elites, 16; transmission of knowledge to nonelites, 16
Elizabethan audiences: balance between belief and skepticism, 51–52, 61–62; perceptual strategies of, 62–63, 68, 69, 71; on supernatural forces, 51, 52
Emek Hamelekh (Bachrach), 174, 177, 188
Envy (Seven Deadly Sins), 83, 130–31
Erik, Max, 238, 260, 345n36, 345n38
eroticism: bending backward as sign of rebelliousness, 188; death, 237; homoeroticism, 147, 150, 312n42; images of, 318–19n75; kisses, 237, 247; Rahab as representation of, 348n52; secular literature's romantic heroine, 237; traditional Jewish feminine ideals, 223

Esau (biblical figure), 155–56, 163, 227, 317n69
essentialism, 114, 121–22, 124, 154, 155, 159, 259
Esther (biblical figure), 133–34, 231, 232, 257, 351n82
Ethics of the Fathers, 163
Everyman, 27, 28
exorcism: attempts at, 194–95; Borekh Kat, 180, 181, 186, 195, 196, 333n118; children's role in, 195; Christian exorcism, 204, 336n147; communal role in, 192, 194, 195, 197; dybbuk's account of, 196–98; excommunication as tool of, 333n114; fumigation in, 188, 330n88; in kabbalah, 174–76; of *mashkhisim*, 165–66, 168; during Sabbatean period, 179; theatrical elements of, 179; violence, 199; Yiddish as language of exorcism tales, 183, 184, 329n72

fables: allegory/allegorical mode in, 26; authoritarian voice in, 98; displays of virtuosity in, 95–96, 299n30; elixirs of life and death, 111; essentialism of, 122–25; humor in, 94; illusion in, 122, 123–24; language of repayment in, 120–21, 131, 132, 133, 304n78; moral teachings in, 98, 116–20, 299n31, 303n70; narratorial intrusions in, 97, 299n31; as oral performance, 299n31; psychological aspects of, 111, 121, 146, 153, 314–15n53; pyramidal structures in, 235, 351n76, 351n84; rhymed texts in, 93, 95–96, 103, 105, 181, 183, 184, 185; use of proverbs in, 298n25; vulgarity in, 106, 303n70. *See also* animals in fables; illustrations; sexuality; *Seyfer Mesholim*
Falcon, Elijah, 177, 330n84
Faustus (in *Doctor Faustus*): contract with Mephastophilis, 72–73, 74, 75, 80–81; diabolical pact in, 72–73, 74, 75, 77; fictionalization by, 80–81; legerdemain of, 81–82; psychological instability of, 75, 79; recognition of angels, 76–77; recognition of the devil, 72; use of body and spirit by, 78–79
Favila, Marina, 292n57
Foley, John Miles, 15
forgetfulness, 147, 153, 156, 314–15n53
Forman, Simon, 292n59
Fortune, 124–30, 136–37, 259, 315–16n54
foxes, in fables, 101–2, 104, 120–22, 133
Frakes, Jerold C., 8, 35–36, 93, 218, 346n45
Frank, Jacob, 7
Fuks, Leo, 91–92, 217, 267n22

galkhes bikher/galkhes seforim, 215
Galya Raza, 174
Gans, David, 270n40
Gehenna/Gehinnom, 175, 179, 194, 332n107
gender: allegory, 340n191; of author, 335n139; homoeroticism, 147, 150, 312n42; in *kapparot* liturgy, 203–4; misogyny, 113–15, 118–19, 145, 159, 205–6, 337n161; perceptions of, in *Doctor Faustus*, 74; in possession narratives, 48, 188, 200–207, 330n84; power structures and, 201–2, 205; premodern Yiddish readership, 18–19; voice of prayer, 190–91; witch trials, 205, 337n155, 340n189; Yiddish literature, 40. *See also* masculinity; sexuality; women
genre: consciousness of, 33, 282n138; definition of, 29–30, 281–82n129; historical contexts in, 31–32; narrative irrelevancy, 39; reader reception of text, 30–31; skepticism and genre identification, 31–33, 282n138; theory of, 30–35, 281–82n129, 282n138; in witchcraft narratives, 337n152
geography: authentication strategies in dybbuk possession narratives, 182–83; language in Yiddish publications, 46; of *Mayse fun Vorms*, 149, 311n35; in spirit possession accounts, 181
Germany: development of Yiddish language in, 5–8, 9, 266n12; *Dukus Hornt*, 214, 267n23, 342n4; fable collections, 89; premodern Yiddish literature, 9, 267n23; *Shmuel-bukh*, 14, 214–15, 217. See also *Mayse fun Vorms*
Gibson, Marion, 337n152
gilgul, 174, 198
Glikl of Hameln, 10, 40, 255, 260; humility of, 263; as narrator of disaster, 255–57; skepticism of, 256–57, 355n12
God: and belief in the supernatural, 61; fables of servants and masters reflecting Jews' relationship with, 135–36; mercy of, 190,

191, 192, 332n105; reward and punishment in fables, 137; theodicy, 48, 189, 190–91, 192–94, 197, 256, 261; Thirteen Attributes of Mercy, 190, 191, 332n105
Goldish, Matt, 173, 180, 189
Goodblatt, Chanita, 152, 312n42, 312–13n43, 313n45, 317n65, 320n84
Great Event in Safed, The (Falcon), 177, 330n84
greed, 98, 103, 104, 112, 122, 123, 231, 305–6n86
Greek mythology, 269n40

hair, 106, 148, 159, 170, 313n45
Hallewa, Judah, 176
Hamlet, 62
Ha-nakdan, Berachiah, 89
Hasidism, 168, 278n101
haskome (rabbinic approbation), 90, 92–93
Hebraisms, 90, 92, 93, 94, 95, 298n25, 298n26
Hebrew language: acrostics, 92, 298n22; allusions in, 19–21, 30–31; Christian Hebraists, 7, 178; Jewish vernaculars, 5; popular recognition of, 90; reader comprehension of, 90, 92–96, 298n25; valorization of, 90
Helen (in *Doctor Faustus*), 79–80, 294n86
"Herzog Ernst," 216
Hildebrand, 215
historiography and historical texts: audience reading of, 28, 280n119; Greece in, 228, 229; Hyrcanos, 228, 229, 349n62; ideology's role in, 278n101
Holinshed, Raphael, 59, 288–89n23, 291n52
homoeroticism, 147, 150, 177, 312n42
horns, symbolism of, 106, 108, 196, 301n52
Horowitz, Isaiah, 174
horror stories, 312n41; deception in, 148, 151; nature in, 149–50, 312n39, 314n53–54; social class, 147–48, 151, 154–58; transgression of borders in, 141, 148–50, 151–52. *See also* demons (*shedim*); male demons (incubi); *Mayse fun Vorms;* she-demons (succubi); supernatural
horse imagery, 242, 243, 245, 246, 352n88
Hunt, Maurice, 293n63
Hyrcanos, 228, 229, 349n62
hysteria, 187–88, 330n82, 334n132

ibbur/ibburim, 174, 175, 323n6
ibn Sahula, Isaac, 89, 93
illustrations: captions for, 101–3, 104, 106, 301n48; interpretive power of, 45–46, 100–101, 103–5, 301n48; Jews identified in, 106; moral authority of, 99–101; in textual interpretation, 45–46, 99–102; visual puns, 294n86; woodcuts in *Seyfer Mesholim*, 99–104, 106, 108, 300n37, 301n48, 301n50, 301n52
inheritance, 109, 166, 169, 220, 221, 222
intellectuals, compromises and abstractions of, 220, 225, 234, 240–41, 244
intermarriage, 143, 148, 156, 321n96
Irigaray, Luce, 40, 316n56
itinerant preachers (*maggidim*), 15, 16

Jacob (biblical figure), 156, 227, 349n62
James I (king), 59, 60, 61, 64
Jardine, Alice A., 40, 335n139
Jewish holidays: Lag Ba'omer, 147, 149, 311n38, 312n39; Passover, 166, 170, 195; Purim, 39, 133–34, 228, 231, 232, 257, 283n141; Rosh Hashanah, 194, 220, 222, 333n113; Yom Kippur, 203–4
Jewish identity: abandonment of, 243–44; engagement with authentic Jewish tradition, 245; prayer, 245–46; refashioning of, 232–36; stereotypes of, 206, 219, 230–31, 232–33, 234, 235, 242, 349n63, 350–51n73; traditional Jewish paradigms of masculinity, 41–42, 252–53, 354n112; in visual images, 105–6
Johnson, Samuel, 61, 62
Joseph Samuel of Cracow, Rabbi, 90
Jubilees, book of, 144
Judaism: abandonment of, 243–44; conversion to Christianity, 230–31; engagement with authentic Jewish tradition, 245; non-Jewish tropes, 159–60; paradigms of masculinity in, 252–53, 354n112, 354–55n113; sexual relationships between men and she-demons, 145
Judaization: of chivalric epics, 216–18; of fables, 94–95; Hebraisms, 90, 92, 93, 94, 95, 298n25, 298n26; of text, 105–6; of Yiddish literature, 94–95

kabbalah/kabbalists: Joseph Dan on, 146, 160, 323n8, 324n17; encounters with Yiddish, 7; esoteric kabbalah, 170. *See also* Lurianic kabbalah
kaddish, 190, 246
Kaidanover, Tzvi Hirsh. See *Kav ha-yoshor* (Tale of Poznan)
kapparot, 203–4
Karo, Joseph, 175
Kat, Borekh, 180, 181, 186, 195, 196, 333n118
Katz, Eli, 88, 91, 108, 113, 298n22, 300n37. See also *Seyfer Mesholim*
Kav ha-yoshor (Tale of Poznan): admonition against sexual relationships between men and she-demons, 142–43, 164–66, 321n94; exorcism in, 167; historical references in, 167, 170–71, 321n97; *mashkhisim* in, 165–66, 167, 168; Passover as setting for, 166, 170. *See also* she-demons (succubi)
Kerler, Dov-Ber, 266n13
Kirshenblatt-Gimblett, Barbara, 42
kisses, 78, 79, 237, 247, 318n71
Kolodny, Annette, 335n139
Koretz (community). *See* "The Tale of the Spirit of the Holy Community of Koretz During the Chaos of War"
Ku-bukh, 88, 116–17, 119, 120, 298n22, 300n37

Lag Ba'omer, 147, 149, 311n38, 312n39
Landau, Leo, 215
Langmuir, Gavin I., 270n43
Liptzin, Sol, 354n112
Lord, Albert B., 15
Lurianic kabbalah: dissemination of, 174; *para aduma* (red heifer), 198–99; popularity in eastern Europe, 179; representations of the supernatural and, 167–68; speculation about the soul, 174; spirit possessions in, 179; *tikkun*, 168, 197, 198

Maase shel ruakh bk'k koretz bishaat haraash milkhama. See "The Tale of the Spirit of the Holy Community of Koretz During the Chaos of War"
Macbeth (character): changing psychological state of, 67–68; proof of perceptions, 65–68, 292n53, 292n54; prophecies, 70–71; psychological instability of, 67–68, 79–80, 294n86; strange sights seen by, 62–63, 291n45; transformation of the dagger, 65–66, 67–68, 292n60; witches perceived by, 69–70, 292n54
Macbeth (play): Banquo, 63–65, 66, 67, 68, 292n59; dagger used in, 62, 65–66, 67–68, 292n60; illusions in, 62–63; ocular experience in, 66, 67–68, 292n60; oracular ambiguity in, 70–71; sense of sight in, 62–63, 290n44; Weird Sisters, 59, 61, 63–66, 69–70, 288–89n23, 289n24, 291n52, 292n53, 292n54. *See also* supernatural; witchcraft
Maggi, Armando, 336n147
maggid (spirit), 174, 323n7
maggidim (itinerant preachers), 15, 16
magic, 57–58, 61–62, 81–82, 206–7
male demons (incubi), 144–45
maleficia. See witchcraft
Marlowe, Christopher. See *Doctor Faustus*
marriage: anti-romantic Jewish conventions, 224–25; betrothals, 146, 147, 152, 153, 313n53; brides, 147, 148, 153, 154; commodification of, 146, 152, 153–54, 313n53; consummation of, 312n42; demons in wedding customs, 312n41; economic considerations in, 148, 152–54, 155, 156, 157–58; Hebraisms related to, 94; of a man and a she-demon (see *Mayse fun Vorms*); parental objections to, 225–26, 348n54, 348n55; parents' roles in, 225–26, 348n55; piety as qualification for, 348n55; polygamy, 148, 150, 310n34; procreation, 153; sexuality of strong women in, 145; social class and, 154–55, 219; and stages of life, 163; as transaction, 152
masculinity: compromises to, 231–35; deceived husbands, 106–8, 114–15, 148–51, 304n72; of dybbuks, 48; father-son relationship, 221–22, 241; homoeroticism, 147, 150, 312n42; impotence, 109, 131–32, 145, 163, 235; marital relations, 114–15, 304n72; in *Seyfer Mesholim*, 106, 108, 301n52; traditional Jewish paradigms of, 41–42, 49, 252–53, 354n112. *See also* she-demons (succubi)
mashkhisim, 165–66, 167, 168
Massey, Irving, 279n110
masturbation, 145, 166, 167, 168, 320n89
Maxwell-Stuart, P. G., 81

Mayse Beit Dovid bimei malkhut peras, 210
mayse bikhl, 179, 180, 183. *See also* "Tale of Briyo and Zimro"; "The Tale of the Spirit of the Holy Community of Koretz During the Chaos of War"
Mayse Briyo ve-Zimro. *See* "Tale of Briyo and Zimro"
Mayse-bukh, 37, 178, 187, 196, 201
Mayse fun ludvig un aleksandr, 210
Mayse fun Vorms: antecedents to, 147, 149, 310n33, 311n35; appearance of hand in, 147, 150; chronology of, 163–64; class conflict in, 259–60; demonization of wealth in, 260; geographic boundaries of, 149, 311n35; Lag Ba'omer, 147, 149, 311n38, 312n39; moral ambiguity, 156–57; psychological aspects of, 146, 153; quietism in, 259–60; reading audience for, 162, 164, 320n84; sexual imagery, 159–60, 318–19n75; summary of, 147–48, 310n33; "Tale of the Jerusalemite," 146, 147, 313n47; transgression of borders in, 147, 148, 149, 151, 311n38, 312n39. *See also* rabbi's son (in *Mayse fun Vorms*)
Mayse Nisim, 169–70, 311n35
McAlindon, Thomas, 294n86
medical texts in Yiddish, 210–11, 341n197
meeting of Jacob and Esau, 155–56, 317n69
Melokhim-bukh, 14, 214, 342n8
Mélusine de Lusignan, 310n33
Menasseh ben Israel, 177–78, 181, 194
Mephastophilis (*Doctor Faustus*), 72–73, 74, 75, 80–81, 84, 295n95
Meshal Ha-kadmoni (ibn Sahula), 89, 90, 93, 108
Meshivat Nafesh (Zemah), 177
messianism, 7, 100, 178, 187, 200, 270n40, 329n79
Midelfort, H. C. Erik, 206, 337n155, 341n198
mikve, 219, 234
Miller, Nancy, 318n72
mimesis, 95–96, 146, 185, 236
Mindl (possession victim): on the Akedah, 192–93; bending backward as sign of rebelliousness, 187–88, 330n82; children punished for parents' sins, 191, 332n105; medical treatments for, 211; prayers of, 184, 186, 189–92; reader identification with, 210; sexual assault of, 188, 189, 200–201, 202; as survivor of possession, 331n94; symptoms of possession, 187–88; testing of, by dybbuk possession, 193, 332n110; theodicy discussed by, 192–93, 261; voice of, 189–90, 331n97
Minkhat Eliyahu, 188
Miola, Robert, 71
Mishlei Shualim (Fox Fables), 89, 121
misogyny, 113–15, 118–19, 145, 159, 205–6, 337n161
morality and moral teachings: of capital accumulation, 118–20; contentment, 124; on deception, 74, 84, 97, 106–7, 111, 113–15, 123–26, 134, 148, 151, 157, 303n69, 303–4n70, 304n72, 305n86, 306n95; in dybbuk possession narratives, 178–79; of foxes, 101–2, 104, 120–22; illustrations as interpretations of, 101–2, 103–4, 301n48, 301n50; language of repayment in, 120–21, 131, 132, 133, 304n78; of narrational judgments, 237; reader competency in analyzing moral polemic, 26–27, 97–98; shame, 121, 136–37, 148, 151, 159, 305n79, 313n45; skepticism about, 108; vulgarity in fables, 303n70. See also *Seyfer Mesholim;* wealth
Moseley, Marcus, 37
muser haskel: consequences of deceit, 120, 121; contentment in, 124; as generic indicator, 186; omnipresence of falsehood, 134; political aspects of, 132; reader comprehension of, 98; on relations with she-demons, 142–43; self-deception in, 123–24; on vanity, 122

narrator: authenticity of tale established by, 149, 311n36; control over narrative, 185–86, 236, 237–38, 255–56, 329n73; eyewitness accounts as authentication strategies, 181–82; manipulation of dialogue by, 185–86, 329n73; as moralist, 98–99; narratology, 28–29, 96–97; shifts from metaphor to actualization, 236–37
naturalistic explanations of the supernatural, 55, 56–58, 69–71, 73, 176
Nelson, William, 32
Neugroschel, Joachim, 143, 164–65, 307n5, 313n45
Newman, Karen, 338n172

News from Scotland (Scot), 61
Nishmat Khayyim (Israel), 177–78
nonelite readers: *Mayse fun Vorms*, 162, 320n84; oral reception and transmission of information, 16, 17–18; reaction to stratification of Jewish society, 152, 154–55, 157–58, 316n61; reading habits of, 15, 17, 273n61

oaths, 135, 146, 238–40, 241, 256, 257
Orgel, Stephen, 62

para aduma (red heifer), 198–99
paradise, 245–46, 246n89, 250
parody, 23–27, 278n101, 278n102
Passover, 166, 170, 195
Persephone, 246
Peskowitz, Miriam B., 284n151
Poland, demonology in, 207, 339n176
pope: breaking of oaths by, 239; circumcision prohibited by, 219, 232–33, 234, 242, 349n63; as evil, 349n62; Exodus story used by Zimro, 232–33; Jewish paradigms within Christianity, 235–36; Zimro's encounters with, 219, 227, 230, 232–36, 242, 349n63
poverty, 154–60, 161, 316n61, 318–19n75
Poznan (community). See *Kav ha-yoshor* (Tale of Poznan)
praestigia, 81
prayer: *Ashrei*, 190, 332n102; gender roles in, 203–4; kaddish, recitation of, 190, 246; morning blessings, 202–3, 335n143; in "Tale of Briyo and Zimro," 245–46; Thirteen Attributes of Mercy, 190, 191, 332n105; women and, 1–2, 15, 17, 18, 184, 189–91, 331n97
procreation, 153, 166, 233, 319n76, 321n94
promiscuity, 114–15, 143, 304n72
prostitution, 114, 143, 166–67
Prynne, William, 51, 52–53, 65
Psalms, book of, 92, 190, 192, 332n102
psychological instability: of Faustus (*Doctor Faustus*), 75, 79–80; of Macbeth (character), 67–68, 79–80, 294n86
psychomachia, 76, 77
purgatory, 246
Purim: Ahasuerus, 228, 232; Esther, 133–34, 231, 232, 257; plays, 39, 42, 283n141
purity, 219, 234, 248

"Queen of Sheba" (tale), 169–70

rabbi's son (in *Mayse fun Vorms*): homoeroticism, 147, 150, 312n42; loss of golden ring, 146, 152, 153, 313n53; passivity of, 150, 153, 154, 312–13n43, 314–15n53; relations with parents, 147–48, 152, 153
rape, 188, 200–201, 330n85
reader-response theory, 29, 38–39
reading audience: access to non-Jewish materials, 89; allegory understood by, 27–28, 280n119; allusions recognized by, 19–20, 93–94, 163–64; anachronism tolerated by, 39–40; authentication strategies in spirit possession accounts, 181; author's relations with, 19, 34, 92; Bible knowledge of, 93–94; captions of illustrations used by, 101–3, 104, 106, 301n48; Christian readers of *Nishmat Khayyim* (Israel), 178; as conscious of historiographical divisions, 227–28, 349–50n64; engagement with fables, 101, 107, 110; expectations of the supernatural, 12, 72, 111; experience with oaths in narrative, 239; generic norms recognized by, 34–35; Hebrew language comprehension of, 92–96, 298n25; historical reality, 38; illustrations used by, 45–46, 99–103, 301n43; interpretive skill of, 26–27, 100–101; linguistic abilities of, 178; literacy of, 15, 17, 18, 19, 92, 178, 275–76n75; oral performances of text, 14–17, 161, 273n61, 274–75n66; parodic texts recognized by, 24; polemics understood by, 25–27; political consciousness of, 37–39; rabbinic approbation understood by, 92; reality recognized by, 108–10; recognition of historical conditions, 38; skepticism of possession tales, 182–85; social mores recognized by, 114–15; sophistication of, 19–20, 93–94, 97–98, 101, 106, 275n75, 298n25; "time zero" (transmission of knowledge), 8, 16, 17, 36, 44, 46; tolerance of Christian imagery in chivalric epics, 217–18; truth claims of author-narrator, 24, 97–98, 299n31. *See also* elite readers; nonelite readers
red heifer, 198–99
repayment, language of, 120–21, 131, 132, 133, 304n78
Reutlingen, Isaac b. Judah, 218, 345n36

rhymed texts: critical readership of, 96; in *mayse bikhlekh*, 181, 183; questionable authenticity of tale, 181, 183, 184, 185; *Seyfer Mesholim*, 93, 95–96, 103, 105, 298n28
rings in betrothals, 146, 152, 153, 313n53
rise tale, 318n74
Robisheaux, Thomas, 339n179
romantic literature: biblical adaptations in, 214–15, 342n8; *Decameron* (Boccaccio), 225, 230–31, 243, 348n51; *Dukus Hornt*, 214, 342n4; Jewish familiarity with, 215–16, 343n15; melodies for, 215, 216; rabbinic opposition to, 216, 218. *See also* "Tale of Briyo and Zimro"
Rome, 230, 231, 349n62
Ronu le-Yaakov (Zemah), 176–77
rooster, crowing of, 202–3, 204, 335n143
Rosen, Tova, 340n191
Rosh Hashanah, 194, 220, 222, 333n113
Rowlands, Alison, 205, 207, 208
ruach, 174, 175, 323n8

Sabbatai Zevi, 7, 178, 179, 333n118
Safed, 174–78, 324n17
Sambari, Joseph, 177, 178
Sanders, Wilbur, 295n96
Satan, 247, 248
Schwäbisch Hall witchcraft case, 206
Scot, Reginald, 59–60, 60–61
secular wisdom, 228–30
seduction, 145, 148, 164–65
Sefer Hahezyonot (Vital), 176
Seven Deadly Sins, 83, 130–31
Seventh Church Council of Nicaea, 101
sexuality: bending backward as sign of rebelliousness, 187–88, 330n82; deception, 106–7, 113–15, 303n69, 303–4n70, 304n72; and moral decline, 165–67; purity, 219, 234, 248; sexual assault, 188, 330n84, 330n86, 339n85; in *Seyfer Mesholim*, 106, 108; shame, 121, 136–37, 148, 151, 159, 305n79, 313n45; vulgarity, 303n70. *See also* women's sexuality
Seyfer Mesholim
—audience for, 91–92, 259
—audience knowledge of religious practices, 110
—class conflict in, 259–60
—fables: adulterous wife, 107, 108, 113, 114–15; ape, 109; ass and lapdog, 109; ass in lion's skin, 127–28; belling of cat, 109, 132; clever doves, 133; diligent and lazy servants, 135–36; dog and cow, 94, 130–31; dog's reflection, 123; donkey and lap dog, 103; donkey as inheritance, 109; donkey held in partnership, 102; faithful watchdog, 107, 109; false guardian, 93, 103, 106, 129–30; father, son, and donkey, 102, 134; flayed donkey, 113, 114; fox and chicks, 133; fox and raven, 94, 122, 305n82; fox and stork, 97, 101–2, 104, 120–22; fox, raven, and cheese, 104, 123; greedy innkeeper, 98, 103, 104, 112, 305–6n86; horse and donkey, 136–37; ill lion, 133; lady mocking chivalric swain, 126–27, 305n82; lion with thorn in his paw, 109, 131–32; *melamed*, 93, 107, 128–29; miller and his ass/donkey, 127–28; monkey children, 124–25; murdered Jew and partridge, 110–11, 135, 306–7n95; peasant and scribe, 128–29; prostitution in, 114; raven and eagle, 125–26; raven and its borrowed plumage, 126–27; religious hypocrite, 93; rooster and hen, 109; shepherd and lion's paw, 107, 109, 110; sick and dying lion, 132; widow and young guard, 113–14; wolf as evil advisor, 133–34; wolf as judge, 134
—Hebrew used in, 90, 92, 95
—introduction (*hakdome*) of, 92, 99, 100, 116–20, 298n20, 298n28
—*Ku-bukh*, 88–89, 119, 120, 298n22, 300n37
—material goods, 107, 301n53
—*Meshal Ha-kadmoni* (ibn Sahula), 89, 90, 93, 108
—*Mishlei Shualim* (Fox Fables), 89, 121
—misogyny in, 113–15, 118–19
—moral lessons in, 26, 106, 107, 116–20
—narrative voice in, 97–99, 299n31
—publication of, 44, 88, 90–91, 99
—rabbinic approbations for, 90, 92–93
—reliance on the divine in, 132, 306n90
—rhymed texts in, 93, 95–96, 103, 105
—skepticism of religious beliefs in, 108
—sources of, 89, 90, 93, 121
—vulgarity in, 304n70
—wealth criticized in, 119–20

—woodcuts in, 99–104, 106, 108, 300n37, 301n48, 301n50, 301n52. *See also* illustrations
Shakespeare, William. See *Macbeth* (play)
shame, 121, 136–37, 148, 151, 159, 305n79, 313n45
she-demons (succubi): in Christianity, 145; dangers of intermarriage, 143, 148, 156, 321n96; erotic desire, 153–54, 164–67; Esau in role of, 1, 156, 317n69; Lilith, 143, 145; Makhles, 143, 164–65; marriage tales (see *Kav ha-yoshor* [Tale of Poznan]; *Mayse fun Vorms*); as mother, 145, 166, 321n94; offspring of, 165–66; reaction to poor girl, 158; seduction by, 148, 165–66; sexual intercourse with human males, 165–66, 318–19n75, 321n94, 321n96; shame, 136–37, 148, 151, 159, 313n45; wives' encounters with, 147–48, 151, 318–19n75. *See also* adultery; demons (*shedim*); *Kav ha-yoshor* (Tale of Poznan); *Mayse fun Vorms*
shedim. *See* demons (*shedim*)
Shmeruk, Chone, 9
Shmuel-bukh, 14, 214–15, 217
Shnei Lukhot Habrit (Horowitz), 174
shpilman/shpilmener, 14–15, 216, 343n21
Shtif, Nokhem, 218n31
Shulvas, Elias, 269–70n40
sight, sense of: characters' visibility, 75, 77–78, 291n45; dagger, perceptions of, 62, 65–66, 67–68, 292n60; *Mayse fun Vorms*, 147, 149, 150, 310n33, 311n35; supernatural sights in *Doctor Faustus*, 82–83
Sinaitic revelation, 248, 249
skepticism: accuracy of recorded dialogue, 185–86; authentication strategies, 180–81; of author's moral virtue, 118–19; autobiographical elements in *Seyfer Mesholim*, 97–98, 299n31; belief compared with, 11–13, 51–52, 269–70n40, 270n42; defeating the dybbuk, 209; of disaster, 256–57; in Elizabethan theater, 51, 52, 59, 288–89n23; existence of the soul, 177–78; eyewitness accounts as authentication strategies, 181–82; and genre identification, 31–33, 282n138; historicity of "The Tale of the Spirit of the Holy Community of Koretz During the Chaos of War," 180–81; illustrations in Yiddish printed materials, 45–46; perceptual skepticism, 55, 56, 58, 63–71, 73, 292n53, 292n54; of possession accounts, 204, 336n147; proof of perceptions, 57–58, 63–70, 292n53, 292n54; of reading audience comprehension of themes in *Seyfer Mesholim*, 108; of reading audience of possession tales, 182–85; realism in fables, 107–10; of religious beliefs, 108; sensational credulity, 62; theatrical performances, 57, 58; of truth-claims in literature, 31–32, 54; unusual narrative representations of visual scenes and activities, 185; witchcraft, 59–61, 204, 206–8, 211, 288–89n23, 337n152; about witches' existence in *Macbeth* (play), 63–64, 291n45; writers' fictional creation, 13, 272n51. *See also* supernatural
social class: and belief in witchcraft, 59–60; class strife in fables, 127–28, 132–33, 306n93; economic hierarchies of, 127–28, 130–31, 153, 154, 157–58, 169, 316n61; economic submission, 148, 154, 155, 156, 157–58; literacy and, 15–17, 22–23, 274–75n66; marriage and, 153, 219, 314n53; poverty, 154–60, 161, 316n61, 318–19n75; servants, 135–36, 138; in supernatural horror story, 147–48, 151, 154–58; of women, 154–60, 318–19n75
Sodom, destruction of, 193–94
Solomon (biblical figure), 220–21, 230, 241, 346n42, 352n83, 354n108
sotah, 200–201, 334n130, 334n131
soul and soul possession: Christian sources on, 178; controversies in Amsterdam Jewish community, 177; kaddish, recitation of, 190, 246; reincarnation, 174; Safed, 177–78, 324n17; suffering of, after death, 191–92; theodicy in, 189, 190–91, 192–94, 197, 256, 261; transmigration of, 198
spirit possession, 31; allegory/allegorical mode, 26; authentication strategies in narratives, 180, 181; bending backward as sign of rebelliousness, 187–88, 330n82; portrayal of victims in narratives, 184; *psychomachia*, 76, 77; during Sabbatean period, 179; Safedian narratives of, 177–78, 324n17; sexual assault in, 188, 330n84, 330n86, 339n85; theatrical elements of, 179

Stanislawski, Michael, 37, 355n5
Starck, Astrid, 269n34
Stephens, Walter, 142, 145, 151
Stern, David, 271n45
strangulation, 154, 316n58
succubi. *See* she-demons (succubi)
Sunshine, Andrew, 275–76n75, 276n83
supernatural: contractual forms in relationship with, 73; credible occurrences of, 56–58; defined, 314–15n53; devil, 51–53, 56–57, 287n9, 336n147; divine intervention in, 61; in *Doctor Faustus*, 51–52, 76–77; fable readers' expectation of, 111; gifted perceptions of, 57–58; in Jewish tradition, 315n53; literary representations of, 55; magic, 57–58, 61–62, 81–82; manifestations of, 147, 150; naturalistic explanations of, 55, 56, 58, 70–71, 73; oracular ambiguity, 70–71; proof of perceptions, 63–70, 292n53, 292n54; reality as clarified by, 111; secular perspectives on, 55–56; sensational credulity, 62; viewer as witness to, 55–56. *See also* demons (*shedim*); male demons (incubi); *Mayse fun Vorms;* she-demons (succubi); witchcraft; witches

Taalumot Hokhmah (Delmedigo), 177
"Tale of Briyo and Zimro": ambivalence in, 251–52; anti-romantic Jewish conventions in marriage, 224–25; death in, 237, 240–42, 248–50, 347n49, 351n81; disassociation of word and action, 239–40; doubling language in, 219, 220–23, 229, 232; Elijah in, 247–48, 249, 250, 352n88, 353n102; erotic desire in, 223–24, 247–48; father-son relationship in, 221–22, 241; historical context of, 228, 349n64; Jewish monarchy in, 220, 226, 228–29; juxtaposition of Jewish and non-Jewish worlds in, 223–26, 228, 229, 243, 244–47, 347n46, 348n51, 352n85; language of Sinaitic revelation in, 248; monarchy in, 226; narrator's function in, 236–41; oaths in, 238–40; paradise, 245–46, 250, 352n89; plot summary, 218–19; political dimensions of, 227–32; Rosh Hashanah as motif in, 222; Solomonic motifs in, 220–21; two-headed man story, 219, 220–21, 223, 345–46n38
"Tale of Poznan" (*Kav ha-yoshor*): admonition against sexual relationships between men and she-demons, 142–43, 165–66, 321n94; historical references in, 167, 170–71, 321n97; *mashkhisim* in, 165–66, 167, 168; Passover as setting for, 166, 170. *See also* she-demons (succubi)
"Tale of the Jerusalemite," 146, 147, 160, 313n47, 318n71
"The Tale of the Spirit of the Holy Community of Koretz During the Chaos of War": author's strategies of authentication in, 181; community suffering in, 189; historicity of, 180–81; Borekh Kat, 180, 181, 186, 195, 196, 333n118; as medical text, 210–11, 341n197; origins of, 179–80, 182–85, 186; reading of, 209; rhymed texts in 183–184; theodicy in, 189, 190–91, 192–94, 197, 256, 261; war identified in, 189. *See also* Mindl (possession victim); Yakov (dybbuk)
Talmud, 22, 144, 163, 201, 202, 229, 230
Temple service, 228, 230
Testament of the Twelve Prophets, 144
theater audience: character visibility, 75, 77–78, 291n45; demonic appearances, 51–53, 56–57, 287n9; expectations of the supernatural, 51, 52, 56–58; reaction to *Doctor Faustus*, 50–51, 74; Shakespearean-era belief in witchcraft, 61–62
theodicy, 48, 189, 190–91, 192–94, 197, 256, 261
Thirteen Attributes of Mercy, 190, 191, 332n105
Thirty Years' War, 206–7
tikkun, 168, 197, 198
"time zero" (transmission of knowledge), 8, 16, 17, 36, 44, 46
Timm, Erika, 273n61
tkhines, 15, 40, 41, 331n97
Traister, Barbara Howard, 294n80
Tsene-rene, 1–2, 17, 18
Turniansky, Chava, 9, 37
turning wheel motif (*fortuna*), 245, 246
two-headed man story ("Tale of Briyo and Zimro"), 219, 220–21, 223, 345–46n38

vanity, 118–19, 126–27
Veyne, Paul, 269n40, 271n45
Virgil (*Divine Comedy*), 352n88
Vital, Hayyim, 175, 176, 202
Vital, Samuel, 179

Wallich, Moses b. Eliezer: acrostics used by, 92, 119, 298n22; commercial interests of, 44, 88, 90–91, 99; fables reordered by, 120, 122, 126, 298n22, 305n82; Hebrew used by, 89–90, 94–95; misogyny of, 113–14, 118–19; mortality and death discussed by, 119–20; rabbinic approbations for, 90, 91. See also *Seyfer Mesholim*
Wandering Jew (legend), 53–54, 288n15
wealth: in children-parent relationships, 146, 153; demonic world associated with, 160; economic mobility, 158, 166, 169, 318n74; goldsmith as symbolic of, 165; hero's enriched return from his quest, 235; inheritance, 109, 166, 169, 220, 221, 222; seduction of, 160, 170, 318n73; in story of Jacob and Esau, 155–56, 317n69; valorization of, 158, 161
weddings, 15, 147, 148, 153, 154, 248, 249–50, 354n108
Weinreich, Max, 5, 7–8, 180–81, 266n12, 266n14
Weinstein, Roni, 324n14, 330n86, 341n198
Weissler, Chava, 18
Williams, Gerhild Scholz, 206
witchcraft, 12; and changing social norms, 206–7; *Daemonologie* (James I), 59, 60, 61, 64; European witchcraze, 204; intellectual foundations of, 60; Jews' involvement in witchcraft, 206; in *Macbeth* (play), 59, 288–89n23; misogyny, 145; sensational credulity, 62; skepticism about, 59–61, 204, 206–8, 211, 288–89n23, 337n152
witches: in *Macbeth* (play), 59, 61, 63–66, 69–70, 288–89n23, 289n24, 291n52, 292n53, 292n54; sabbat, 207
wives: brides, 147, 148, 153, 154; commodification of, 152; curiosity of, 148, 160, 161, 170; deception of, 148, 151; demonic doubling of, 316n62; devil as, in *Doctor Faustus*, 73, 74; Jacob in role of, 317n69; sexual behavior of, 150–51, 152
women: as audiences for performance of medieval works, 216; bending backward as sign of rebelliousness, 187–88, 330n82; as deceptive, 106–7, 113–15, 148, 151, 303n69, 303–4n70, 304n72; Glikl of Hameln, 10, 40, 255–57, 256–57, 260, 263, 355n12; in the Hebrew Bible, 93, 133–34, 188, 192–93, 231–34, 257, 348n52; misogyny, 113–15, 118–19, 145, 159, 205–6, 337n161; piety of, 72, 113–15, 154, 158, 219, 234; poverty, 154–60, 161, 318–19n75; prayer, 1–2, 15, 17, 18, 184, 189–91, 331n97; as readers, 17, 18, 19, 92; and satanic magic, 206–7; in *Seyfer Mesholim*, 113, 118–19, 303n69. *See also* Mindl (possession victim); she-demons (succubi); witchcraft
women's bodies: genitalia, 159, 166, 188, 303n70, 330n86; hair, 106, 148, 159, 170, 313n45; sexual assault of, 188, 189, 200–201, 202, 330n84, 330n86, 339n85
women's sexuality: demonic copulation, 144–45; eroticism, 164–67, 223, 348n51; in fables, 113–14; juxtaposed with Torah study, 201–2; promiscuity, 106, 107, 113–14, 304n72; prostitution, 114, 143, 166–67; scheme to unite lovers, 224–25; sexuality of strong women in Judaism, 145; *sotah*, 200–201, 334n130, 334n131; women as sexually disruptive presence, 201, 335n139. *See also* she-demons (succubi); wives
woodcuts in *Seyfer Mesholim*, 99–104, 106, 108, 300n37, 301n48, 301n50, 301n52
Worms, Germany, 149, 311n35. See also *Mayse fun Vorms*
Wust, Johannes, 88

xenoglossia, 176, 190

Yakov (dybbuk): adultery as transgression of, 201, 334n133; Borekh Kat greeted by, 196, 333n118; monologue of, 196–97, 334n125; on possession of Mindl, 199–200; reader identification with, 210; relations with the community, 199, 202–3; rooster in morning blessings, 202–3, 335n143; significance of name, 333n121; suffering of, 197–98, 334n125
Yehuda Ben Tema, 163
Yerushalmi, Yosef, 37
Yiddish language: Cambridge Codex (1382), 6, 132, 213, 214; development of, 5–8, 266n12, 266n14; in Germany, 5–8, 9, 14, 89, 214–15, 217, 266n12, 267n23, 342n4; *loshn-koydesh*, 46, 90
Yom Kippur, 203–4

Zacuto, Moses, 341n198
Zafnat Paaneah (Hallewa), 176
Zemah, Jacob, 176–77
Zfatman, Sara: on anxieties about wealth, 170, 318n73; on authentication strategies in spirit possession accounts, 181, 183; historical references in *Kav ha-yoshor* (Tale of Poznan), 321n97; on midrashic narrative, 317n65; on Mindl's marriage, 201; moral components of *Mayse fun Vorms*, 146, 152, 165–67, 318n73; on origins of "The Tale of the Spirit of the Holy Community of Koretz During the Chaos of War," 179–80, 182–85, 186; printing of "Tale of Briyo and Zimro," 9, 146; on provenance of *Mayse fun Vorms*, 160, 311n35
Zimro ("Tale of Briyo and Zimro"): attributes of, 219, 220–21, 222, 223, 248, 348n55; erotic desire of, 223–24, 247–48; familiarity with Esther (biblical figure), 231, 232, 351n82; fantastic quest of, 242–43, 351–52n84; meetings with Elijah (biblical figure), 247–48, 249, 250, 352n88, 353n102; moral ambiguity of, 219, 223–24, 227, 232–36, 242–45, 247–50, 349n63; oaths broken by, 239–40; papal audience with, 219, 231–36, 242, 349n63; rebellion against social and religious mores, 238; separation of public and private spheres by, 240–41, 242, 247; use of the Exodus story by, 232–33; vision of a horse seen by, 242–43, 352n88
Zinberg, Yisroel, 351–52n84, 353–54n105